I Tatti Research Series

4

ARIOSTO AND THE ARABS

Contexts for the *Orlando Furioso*

edited by
Mario Casari, Monica Preti, *and* Michael Wyatt

I TATTI

I TATTI

I Tatti – The Harvard University Center
for Italian Renaissance Studies
Via di Vincigliata, 26
50135 Florence – Italy
itatti.harvard.edu

Project coordinator: Thomas Gruber

Published and distributed in Italy by

OFFICINA LIBRARIA

Officina Libraria
Via dei Villini, 10
00161 Rome – Italy
officinalibraria.net

Publisher and project coordinator: Marco Jellinek
Art director: Paola Gallerani
Layout: Elisabetta Mancini
Editorial assistant: Matilde Fracchiolla
Copyediting: Wendy Keebler
Index: Simone Sirocchi
Color separation: Premani srl, Pantigliate (Milano)
Printed and bound by Esperia, Lavis (Trento)

Publication of this volume has been made possible by

The Myron and Sheila Gilmore Publication Fund at I Tatti
The Robert Lehman Endowment Fund
The Jean-François Malle Scholarly Programs and Publications Fund
The Andrew W. Mellon Foundation Fund for Scholarly Programs and Publications
The Barbara and Craig Smyth Fund for Scholarly Programs and Publications
The Lila Wallace-Reader's Digest Endowment Fund
The Malcolm Wiener Fund for Scholarly Programs and Publications

Worldwide distribution by Harvard University Press

Italian distribution by Officina Libraria

ISBN 978-06-7427-879-0 (Harvard University Press)
ISBN 978-88-3367-152-9 (Officina Libraria)

CONTENTS

ACKNOWLEDGMENTS

The volume presented here is the culmination of a long process of reflection, research, and discussion carried on over a number of years between its three editors, Mario Casari, Monica Preti, and Michael Wyatt; Lino Pertile and Alina Payne, the prior and current directors of I Tatti, the Harvard University Center for Italian Renaissance Studies in Florence; and a diverse group of internationally prominent scholars working across disparate disciplines.

We are particulary grateful to Lino Pertile for having enthusiastically welcomed our initial proposal for the project and generously seeing it through its infancy. Our profound thanks are due to Alina Payne for the manifold ways in which she has helped us to refine the parameters of the project and for the support she has unflaggingly provided throughout its elaboration.

Among the participants and guests of the exploratory seminar held at I Tatti in February 2016, we wish to thank Marzia Faietti, Mahnaz Yousefzadeh, and Gabriele Pedullà, whose contributions to a day of stimulating *conversatio* have proven to be fundamental in defining the scope and specific topics of both the international conference hosted at I Tatti in October 2017 and this volume. We are grateful to Karla Mallette for the provocative keynote address with which the conference proceedings opened, and to the session chairs—Lina Bolzoni, Joseph Luzzi, Marzia Faietti, and Julie Cummings—as well as to all who contributed, whether through prepared talks or questions and comments, for so richly informing the colloquium and initially articulating many of the ideas developed in these pages.

The performative dimensions of the chivalric and literary traditions that gave rise to the *Orlando furioso* and followed from it have been central to our considerations from the start. So it was with enormous pleasure that we were able to welcome the Figli d'Arte Cuticchio (Palermo)—the most distinguished of the current practitioners of the *opera dei pupi* (Sicilian puppet theater)—to the Limonaia at I Tatti for a thrilling performance of *La pazzia di Orlando, ovvero il meraviglioso viaggio di Astolfo sulla luna* (The madness of Orlando, including the marvelous journey of Astolfo to the moon) which concluded the conference on a very high note indeed. A unique moment in the long history of performance at I Tatti, this was an experience shared not only by conference presenters and participants but also by members of their families and those of the extended Tatti community.

We owe a huge debt to the dedicated administrative, academic, house, and security staff at I Tatti, without whom complex initiatives such as ours would be impossible to realize there. Our greatest thanks in this regard go to Susan Bates, Jonathan Nelson, and Ingrid Greenfield. Thomas Gruber has been an indispensable collaborator on the project, and particulary this volume, reading everything carefully, managing its peer review, and serving as intermediary between Alina Payne, the editors, and Officina Libraria.

For their uncompromising professionalism and expertise in the production of this book, we express our sincere gratitude to Marco Jellinek and his collaborators at Officina Libraria: Paola Gallerani (art director), Elisabetta Mancini (layout), and Wendy Keebler, who has been an excellent copyeditor of the completed manuscript, skillfully negotiating among much else a dense thicket of terms in Arabic, Turkish, Hebrew, and Byzantine Greek. Simone Sirocchi created the Index and ably handled the final proof-reading, saving us from a number of mistakes that had previously gone unnoticed. Elizabeth Brooks provided invaluable assistance with her careful initial editing of those contributions written by authors whose principal language is not English. Mario Casari undertook the final editing of all of the terminology transliterated from non-Latin languages. Michael Wyatt translated the chapters of Massimo Rossi, Vincenzo Farinella, and Monica Preti from Italian and was responsible for the final English-language editing of the entire volume.

Generous financial resources were made available to support the exploratory seminar, the conference, and this publication through the Lila Wallace–Reader's Digest Endowment Fund and the Scholarly Programs and Publications Funds in the names of Malcolm Hewitt Wiener, Craig and Barbara Smyth, Jean-François Malle, the Andrew W. Mellon Foundation, the Robert Lehman Foundation, and the Myron and Sheila Gilmore Publication Fund.

EDITORIAL NOTE

Unless otherwise indicated, quotations from *Orlando furioso* are from the third edition of 1532, the final version prepared and authorized by Ariosto and the one today most commonly in use. The critical edition cited throughout is Ludovico Ariosto, *Orlando furioso,* introduction and commentary by Emilio Bigi, ed. Cristina Zampese (Milan: Rizzoli, 2012 [1982]), which reproduces the text established by Cesare Segre (Milan: Mondadori, 1976).

Citations from *Orlando furioso* (*Fur.*) are styled as follows: cantos in uppercase Roman numerals, octaves in Arabic numerals, without a comma: *Fur.,* XXXV 25–27. For citations within a single octave, verses are indicated in Arabic numerals preceded by a comma: *Fur.,* XIX 2, 1–6. When cited, the two earlier editions of the *Furioso,* 1516 and 1521, are indicated within parentheses as A and B, respectively (sometimes together as AB), followed by canto, octave, and verse: *Fur.* (A XXVII 40–42; 45, 3–8; 47), while 1532 is occasionally referred to as C. References to Bigi's commentary are given in the notes as Ariosto (2012), followed by page number: Ariosto (2012): 967–968.

English prose translations of Ariosto's verse—which, for ease of reading, we place immediately following citations of the Italian text—are from Ludovico Ariosto, *Orlando Furioso,* trans. Guido Waldman (Oxford: Oxford University Press, 2008 [1972]), which has occasionally been corrected to better conform to the sense of Ariosto's text.

The poem of Matteo Maria Boiardo—earlier known as *Orlando innamorato,* following the *rifacimento* of Francesco Berni first published in 1541—is cited, unless otherwise noted, as *L'inamoramento de Orlando* (*Inam.*), eds. Antonia Tissoni Benvenuti and Cristina Montagnani (Milan: Ricciardi, 1999); its books are indicated in uppercase Roman numerals, cantos in lowercase Roman numerals, octaves in Arabic numerals, without commas, and verse(s) within an octave, when given, in Arabic numerals preceded by a comma: *Inam.,* III ii 40, 1–4.

English translations of Boiardo are from *Orlando innamorato,* trans. Charles Stanley Ross (Berkeley: University of California Press, 1989), adjusted where necessary to follow the 1999 critical edition of the poem.

For languages written in alphabets other than Latin, transliteration in Latin characters is employed systematically, in accordance with scholarly protocols for each language. Arabic, Persian, and Ottoman Turkish names and words have been transliterated according to the table set for the current *Encyclopaedia of Islam Three*, unless they have an established spelling in the English language.

In a volume centered on the chivalric tradition revolving around the *Orlando furioso*, and inspired by Borges's poem "Ariosto y los Arabes," the terms "Arab" and "Turk" are sometimes used with reference to their pre- and early modern literary value as synonyms of "Saracen," as the opponents of Christian knights were usually labeled in that tradition; in such cases, the context makes clear how these terms are used. Otherwise, all ethnonyms (Arab, Turk, Persian, Jew, Greek, Italian, French, Spaniard, and so on) are used with reference to precise ethnic or linguistic characteristics. According to linguistic usage, religious terms may refer to a specific faith and its followers as well as to aspects of the cultures and institutions expressed by people of that faith, for which a religious connection is relevant (e.g., Christian rites and Christian art; Jewish families and Jewish lore; Muslim population and Islamic philosophy; and so on). When used throughout the volume, expressions such as "Christian world" and "Christian sphere" or "Islamic world" and "Islamic sphere" should be understood as the web of societies in which Christianity or Islam was recognized as politically and socially dominant, although substantial minorities lived and operated within them.

Introduction: Investigating Landscapes around "Ariosto and the Arabs"

Mario Casari, Monica Preti, Michael Wyatt

Quién sabe si de Persia o del Parnaso
Vino aquel sueño del corcel alado
Que por el aire el hechicero armado
Urge y que se hunde en el desierto ocaso.

Como desde el corcel del hechicero,
Ariosto vio los reinos de la tierra
Surcada por las fiestas de la guerra
Y del joven amor aventurero.

[From Persia, or perhaps Parnassus, there
Emerged another dream, of a wing-borne courser
Driven across the sky by the armored sorcerer
And down to where the desert sun repairs.

As from the vantage of that conjurer,
Ariosto saw the earthly kingdoms, scored
With the celebrations of a land bewarred
And the young love of an adventurer.]
—Borges, "Ariosto y los Árabes," pp. 122-123[1]

The idea for this project took its inspiration from a poem by Jorge Luis Borges, "Ariosto y los Arabes," originally published in the collection *El hacedor* (1960). Borges positions the *Orlando furioso* in relation to its European literary avatars, past and future—the *Chanson de Roland*, Arthurian romance, the *Nibelunglied*, and *Paradise Lost*—to then see reflected in the love between Ludovico Ariosto's Asian princess Angelica and the Muslim common soldier Medoro intimations of *One Thousand and One Nights*, with the Italian poet flying "from Persia, or perhaps Parnassus" astride "a wing-borne courser/ . . . [as he] saw the earthly kingdoms, scored / With the celebrations of a land bewarred / And the young love of an adventurer." The dense cluster of elements employed by Borges—scattered in time and place but unified in the poetic imaginary—offers opportunities for probing the relations and interconnections that emerge from the *Furioso* and from the themes that it both touches upon and incarnates.

Situated at the apex of one of the foundational European literary traditions—the *chansons de geste* that found their bearings in the rout of Charlemagne's troops at Roncesvalles, subsequently grafted onto Crusade narratives and embedded in the "histories" of the European conflict with the Ottoman Empire—Ariosto's poem presents itself as a prism through which to examine various links in the chain of cultural interactions that characterized the Mediterranean landscape from late antiquity through the medieval period, into early modernity, and beyond.

As Borges notes, Ariosto traveled "los caminos de Ferrara / Y al mismo tiempo andaba por la luna" (Ferrara's streets / And upon the moon's unearthly dust)[2], underlining the translation from the local to the universal that is central to the *Furioso*'s cultural and spatial teleology. The social and linguistic *mise-en-scène* of Ariosto's poem is multifaceted, drawing on a huge cache of classical and medieval sources originally written in Latin, Old and Middle French, and Romance as well as other "localized" European languages but "contaminated" by the literatures of a considerably more extended pre-modern world. Its first edition in 1516, conceived in an Italian strongly marked by the dialect of the eastern Po Valley, for a court that utilized a number of languages (various forms of Italian, French, and Latin), patronized artists whose influences were pan-European and Mediterranean, and did a lively business with the same interconnected world.

Between the end of the fifteenth and the beginning of the sixteenth century, the Italian states were at the center of a Mediterranean region undergoing deep transformation. Far from marking a rigid dividing line between Christian and Muslim polities, the Mediterranean world of this period was a political, religious, ethnic, and linguistic melting pot, in which relations between dominant regimes and minorities were in constant flux. With the fall of the Nasrid Emirate of Granada in 1492, the endgame of the Iberian Reconquista led to an exodus of Jews and Muslims to North Africa and the eastern Mediterranean but also to the forced Christian conversion of a great many Muslims who, nevertheless, secretly maintained strong bonds with their religious, linguistic, and cultural traditions. The Berber kingdoms of the Maghreb, the result of the disintegration of Almohad domination, were in regular diplomatic commerce with various state entities of the northern Mediterranean that entailed trade agreements, the establishment of merchant colonies, the negotiation of peace treaties in order to rectify minor conflicts and efforts to deal with piracy. In the final century before its conquest by the Ottomans in 1517, Mamluk Egypt was a crucial center of trade and a meeting place for Catalan, French, Venetian, Genoese, and other embassies. After the capture of Constantinople in 1453, the Ottoman Empire consolidated its power on the Balkan Peninsula, while the center of Greek Byzantine culture moved to Venice and its colonies. But while Venice maintained a studied balance between formal fidelity to the defense of Christianity and the preservation of privileged ties with the Turks, many Italian states projected their hopes of an anti-Ottoman alliance onto Persia, first through contacts with the Aq Qoyunlu sovereign Ūzūn Ḥasan and then with the originally Kurdish, subsequently Turkicized, Safawid dynasty that had converted the entire country to the Shiite branch of Islam, about which a Greek ambassador in a 1502 report for the Venetian Senate wrote that it was "a Catholic religion in its own way." From the Republic of Venice to that of Genoa, the Duchy of Urbino to the Republic of Florence, and the Papal States to the Kingdoms of Naples and Sicily, Italian territories were traversed by merchants, ambassadors, intellectuals, artists, performers, exiles, and prisoners who constituted small human aggregates representative of the Mediterranean ecumene.

Focusing on the role of the Muslim as the essential Other in Ariosto's text and on Islam in vicinity to the poet's world, our objective has been to investigate the relational systems of the various landscapes that might be reconstructed around the *Furioso* from the vantage point of its anteriority (where and what it came from), its contemporaneity (the text in its own historical context), and its posterity (aspects of its reception and influence through to our own day). Investigating landscapes does not mean for us coercing philology into establishing direct textual relationships with exotic literary traditions that would be quite difficult to demonstrate and which in the long sixteenth century existed at best tangentially. Instead, the attempt has been to situate the *Furioso* within a wider relational perspective than the one in which Romance studies have usually tended to examine the poem. We owe a considerable debt, in this regard, to the work of several scholars: Sanjay Subrahmanyin's notion of "connected histories," developed in a series of influential essays and books from the late 1980s onward; Benoît Grévin's *Le parchemin des cieux: Essai sur le Moyen Âge du langage* (2012), especially its concept of "paysages sonores" ("soundscapes") that characterized the tricontinental geographical context centered around the Mediterranean Sea from the Middle Ages to the dawn of the early modern period; the volume *A Sea of Languages: Rethinking the Arabic Role in Medieval*

Literary History (2013), edited by Suzanne Conklin Akbari and Karla Mallette, a collection of essays inspired by the seminal work of María Rosa Menocal in expanding the geographical, linguistic, and cultural scope of Romance studies; and Lina Bolzoni, whose digital project at the Scuola Normale Superiore in Pisa, "Galassia Ariosto: L'archivio digitale dei poemi narrativi illustrati tra Cinque e Seicento," provides an extensive series of visual tools to explore the enormous extratextual impact of the *Furioso* in the century after the publication of its definitive 1532 edition, a crucial factor in the canonization of the poem.[3]

The effort to offer a comprehensive picture of this network of landscapes has involved various levels of inquiry. First of all, of course, are contexts related to language production, not only textual relations, both written and oral, and both internal and external to the literary tradition in which the *Furioso* is inscribed, but also linguistic ecology, the broader soundscapes that encompassed the period of the poem's production, together with the question of the degree of awareness of this complexity within Ariosto's own milieu or on the part of the poet himself. At the same time, the issues addressed by the text of the poem have long posed fundamental questions about the relationship of the *Furioso* to the political framework of the contemporary Mediterranean, marked by the intricate system of relations outlined above. Attempting to both demystify and substantiate the narrative of historical dynamics of the time has meant probing the multihued image of the Other that the figure of the Saracen assumes in the poem, challenging any rigid demarcation line between the Christian and Muslim worlds. Such strict divisions can only partially account for the circumstances of the Italian environment at the time, and even within the *Furioso*, they are often intertwined with religious and philosophical concerns of a more nuanced and multivalent nature. But the remarkable dynamism of the medieval and early modern Mediterranean has called for several further threads of research. One of these is the rapidly growing body of knowledge associated with geographical exploration that in so many respects defined these centuries; another is the recognition of ambient residua resulting from the (never interrupted) circulation of material cultures. These elements also constitute encompassing landscapes that in specific moments came to permeate—even physically—the times and places of the poem's production. At least two other additional spaces for which the *Furioso* has for centuries represented a referential epicenter are the visual arts and performance. Long the subject of significant studies, here, too, is a landscape of interconnections whose horizon expands outward from Ariosto's *immaginario*, both geographically and temporally and at times in unexpected and dizzying ways.

We aimed, therefore, both to define the conceptual areas of our research —textual/linguistic, historical-political/religious, scientific/material culture, and figurative/performative arts—and to identify the topographical and cultural cornerstones that we assumed would serve as hinge for, and occasionally limit to, the scope of our circumnavigation of the topic "Ariosto and the Arabs." Our pursuit of connections, reflections, or gaps between the numerous threads of the dense fabric of the *Furioso* and the cultural world of Arabic linguistic expression—the fulcrum of the whole project—therefore had to be grounded by incursions into at least three areas that played a fundamental role of either mediation or circumscription in relations between Christian Western Europe and the Arab-Islamic sphere, with a particular eye to the epic-chivalric literature at the center of our study: Jewish culture, the Byzantine world, and the Iberian Peninsula (in both its Muslim and Christian phases). Matters of time at the conference and space in this volume have inevitably imposed limits on the lengths to which it has been possible to pursue this plan, just as we have been constrained to leave aside—at least for the time being—other potential areas of research in various directions that we had originally proposed. We believe, however, that we have delineated a useful framework for developing an innovative method with which to further contextualize and explore not only the *Furioso* and Ariosto's other literary work but also the manifold Mediterranean cultural traditions that contributed to making Italian chivalric narrative poetry what it is.

Central themes and motifs of this investigation reverberate between one contribution and another throughout the volume, at times with a proximity that might have suggested a different material arrangement of the chapters from the one adopted here. We nevertheless preferred to maintain the structure used for the conference, which seems to us to most clearly trace a trajectory of spatial and conceptual movement starting from the center of our attention, the *Furioso*, and moving outward from there toward the discovery and definition of increasingly broader perspectives around it.

Within this framework, we therefore directed our concerns first of all to looking inside the text itself, in part I of the volume, "Textual Contexts: Inside the *Furioso*." In the first chapter, serving as a prologue and an orientational map for our project, Mario Casari discusses the evidence of a centuries-old trail of unaccomplished contiguity between the *Furioso* and the Arabic language, by looking at the presence of traces of this language inside the poem, in Ariosto's lived experience and personal environment, and in terms of the reception of the text on the part of an Arabophone audience. Through this investigation, Casari summarizes some of the issues concerning the positioning of Ariosto's work within a Mediterranean matrix, which most of the contributions to the volume address from different vantage points. Continuing with the theme of language, Jacopo Gesiot in the second chapter explores the highly relevant motif of plurilingualism as it is enacted in Italian chivalric literature. Through the presentation of the evolution of this motif in the Franco-Italian and subsequent Italian literary traditions, Gesiot focuses on the pathway leading toward Ariosto's more wide-open approach to the question, one that within the frame of a humanistic reflection on the link between *ratio* and *oratio* concedes a wider space and respect for the language of the Other. The portrayal of the Other in the *Furioso* is the topic of the third chapter, in which Maria Pavlova discusses the role that the more than 130 Saracen characters play in the poem's intricate, interlaced plots, asking several key questions: Is this representation the result of an established literary tradition? Is it a reaction to the *Furioso*'s contemporary historical context, and if so, in what direction? And is it rigidly polemical or symbolically ambiguous? Challenging established scholarship concerning the role of religion in defining the poem's characters, Pavlova shows that the chivalric universe Ariosto creates is one of bewildering complexity, where characters and events are often open to different interpretations. The theme of religion is the central concern of the fourth chapter, in which Stefano Jossa explores relevant passages in the poem in which issues of faith, ideology, and affiliation are raised. Jossa tackles the much-debated topic of Ariosto's religious engagement from the standpoints of epic/romance dialectic and the invention of the enemy, and in drawing attention to Ariosto's interest in the heterodox intra-Christian debates of the early sixteenth century he challenges the notion of a Christian/Muslim divide within the *Orlando furioso* as part of a broader philosophical framework that can no longer be ignored.

Part II of the volume, "Textual Contexts: Around the *Furioso*," extends our examination of the textual field, here moving in the direction of literary traditions external to the poem that provide points of either contact or specularity via the literary genealogy and reception of the *Furioso*. Inevitably, our inquiry into "Ariosto and the Arabs" needed to engage directly with the literary patrimony that the Saracen Other—the Arab—had produced and was continuing to produce elsewhere in the Mediterranean and in parallel with the birth of the *Furioso*. We have inevitably had to pose an elusive question regarding the possibilities and modalities of the transmission of literary subjects through proximity across a variety of genres in this region, a question that specifically addresses audience, readership, and authorship within the context of both the southeastern and western shores of the Mediterranean. Thus, notwithstanding the difficulty of tracing lines of direct literary exchange, via either oral or written communications, in the fifth chapter Thomas Bauer delineates the landscape that pertained to the forms of literary creation, reception, and circulation in Egypt and Syria precisely at the time of the formation and production of Ariosto's text, highlighting the parallels and differences with the contemporary intellectual life of Italian courts and cities. Touching upon the question of the possible interpenetration of narrative themes and concepts in the epic and chivalric traditions on the two shores of the Mediterranean, Bauer also hints at the Arabic side of this mountain of potential correspondences—often embodied in the *sīra* genre—which is also dealt with in the earlier contribution by Mario Casari and particularly in Dwight Reynolds's chapter in part IV, which primarily explores the performative aspects of this literary production. The question of possible textual relationships between the *Furioso* and works of Arabic literature has, however, long been part of the critical reading of Ariosto's work, and in the sixth chapter, Claudia Ott provides a new look into the long-debated matter of the relationship between the infamous story of Astolfo and Iocondo in the *Furioso* and the Arabic tradition of the *Arabian Nights* narrative cycle. By presenting various stages in the transmission of this tale and by proposing a relevant etymological tie for a debated toponym from Ariosto's poem, Ott shows that this connection should be situated, rather than in *One Thousand and One Nights*, around the considerably less well-known *One Hundred and One Nights*, a conclusion also due to the geographical location of the latter's production, in the western part of the Arab world, between al-Andalus and the Maghreb. The crucial issue of intermediation thus enters the picture, and as mentioned above, it has become more and more clear to us that effective contextualization of the *Furioso* could not be undertaken—either in terms of thematic appropriation or mirroring, or with regard to circulation and reception—without taking into consideration two fundamental vehicles of cultural mediation in the Mediterranean area: Jewish and Iberian. Both traditions made significant contributions within and around Ariosto's poem that can hardly be overstated, beginning with the significant presence of a polyglot Jewish community in Ferrara and extending to the profound impact of the poem in Spain, Portugal, and their colonies. In the seventh chapter, Fabrizio Lelli first recalls the traces of the significant role played by Ariosto's poem in Jewish literary education of the late Renaissance. Then, in grounding his analysis in both the *Furioso* and Ariosto's comedy *Il negromante*, Lelli explores another side of Ariosto's approach toward the Other through assessing the extent of Ariosto's actual knowledge of Jews and Judaism. In the eighth chapter, the last of part II,

Vincent Barletta draws our attention to the widespread impact of Ariosto's poem on the Iberian Peninsula throughout the sixteenth century. Although it was ultimately banned in Portugal, Barletta examines the way Luís de Camões had used the *Furioso* to give form to his own epic, *Os Lusíadas* (1572), highlighting in particular the role that the union between Angelica and Medoro could play as a model for similar (albeit more culturally and historically differentiated) intercultural "marriages."

The historical-political framework in which the production of the *Furioso* is located is touched upon, explicitly or implicitly, by almost all the contributions to the volume, but part III, "Geographical and Visual Contexts," opens with a series of reflections that address in particular the varied, rich, and composite world of Ferrarese culture, in which ideas and currents with very different origins mingled. Despite its subsidiary position on the power grid of early modern Italy, Ferrara was extraordinarily attentive to what was happening in the mutable world beyond its confines: epistolary, chronicles, and the *Furioso* itself testify to an extraordinary curiosity toward news that arrived from all ends of the earth, including the far side of the Mediterranean, whether regarding the Europeans' "discovery" of America or the threat of the Turks. In the ninth chapter, Giovanni Ricci consequently examines the poem initially in search of impressions of the ongoing conflict with the "Moors" as well as evidence of the religious and political dynamics that shook the balance of power in the Mediterranean region of Ariosto's time. But Ricci also seeks to account for Islamic traces in Ferrara—where Ariosto lived the better part of his life and wrote his poem—through the documented presence of domestic and public slaves, material objects displayed in public spaces (carpets, arms, etc.), and more generally vis-à-vis the weight that the threat of the "infidels," actual ones or their phantasms, imposed on artistic production as well as on social and political life even in a "backwater" city such as Ferrara. This intercultural dimension of Ariosto's environment is further explored in the two following contributions. In the tenth chapter, Massimo Rossi investigates a classic topos of Ariostan historiography: the poet's geographical interests and cartographic knowledge. The Ptolemaic culture onto which the narrative texture of the poem is grafted, updated thanks to contemporary maritime culture, demonstrates the admixture of ancient and contemporary cartographic sources (nautical charts, hybrid *mappae mundi*, nautical atlases) used by Ariosto. Rossi underlines the contribution of the *Furioso* to the renewal of the concept of *ventura* and in the creation of a reinvigorated, more objective geographical culture conforming more accurately to the reality of the early modern Mediterranean and Asian worlds. In the eleventh chapter, Anna

Contadini outlines a detailed panorama of evidence related to visual and material culture that in Ariosto's immediate world suggested a tangible connection with the Middle East. Contadini shows how Ariosto's visual and tactile environment contained, in addition to their representations in paintings, numerous artifacts—from carpets to ceramics to metalwork, as well as bookbindings and other objects—of Middle Eastern origin or inspiration, and she notes the growing humanist engagement with Arabic book production. Contadini highlights the incessant dynamism of a Mediterranean trade network and the presence of Islamic culture as a consistent background to the imagery within which Ariosto's literary achievements were conceived. But as is well known, in addition to its potential connections to the aforementioned visual and material legacy, the *Furioso* is at the origin of an explosion of the visual arts, to whose intercultural implications the last two contributions of part III are dedicated. In the twelfth chapter, Vincenzo Farinella discusses the representation of Rodomonte in the figurative tradition, arguing that Ariosto in the first edition of the *Furioso* was alluding in this central Saracen character of the poem to a specific historic actor, Selim I (1515–1520), famous for his brutality according to the widespread stereotypes that then circulated about the Ottoman sultan. As Ariosto's Saracen was progressively more humanized in later versions of the poem, in presenting the *Furioso*'s visual afterlife, Farinella outlines the evolution of Rodomonte's image as more and more subtly ambiguous, the cruel and arrogant "infidel" reinterpreted and translated with a discernibly growing degree of sympathy by painters, engravers, and other figurative artists. In the thirteenth chapter, Monica Preti further elaborates on the theme of the iconographic fortune of the *Furioso*, highlighting European connections attributable precisely to those elements of the poem that several of its most notable exegetes have linked to textual transmission involving Arab mediation. The figurative thread unfolded by Preti starts from two little-known plates engraved in the early-seventeenth-century Netherlands and reaches as far as the India of the Mughal emperors of the time.

In a study of the landscapes, possible exchanges, or more straightforward parallels that encircle the *Furioso* and the Franco-Italian epic-chivalric tradition of which it is in many respects the culmination, an investigation into performative-theatrical representation was essential to our project. The "performative" here exemplifies another mode of the fruition and circulation of literary texts in the Mediterranean world from antiquity to the present day, uniting different but connected cultural and linguistic areas in the Arabic, Byzantine Greek, and Romance traditions. These three distinct fields are addressed, respectively, by the contributions included in part IV of the volume, "Performative

Contexts." In the fourteenth chapter, Dwight Reynolds presents the genre of Arabic epic-chivalric narrative, which mirrors in many ways the parallel evolution of the same genre in the European tradition. Presenting the status of the *sīra* genre with respect to the Arabic literary canon, Reynolds deals with the intersection of improvisation and recitation—popular and elite forms—in the performance of Arabic heroic epic beginning in the eleventh century and their relationship to the written texts that emerged from this dynamic exchange. In the fifteenth chapter, Adam Goldwyn and Przemysław Marciniak present a survey of the performance context of Byzantine romance, a corpus of imaginative fiction composed between the tenth and sixteenth centuries from the Arab/Greek borderlands in the east to Venetian-occupied Crete in the west. Examining the meaning of literary performance within the context of a Byzantine culture that was constitutively performative and yet never developed specifically designated performing spaces, Goldwyn and Marciniak highlight the growing influence of the Franco-Italian and Italian traditions, up to the absorption as a model of the *Furioso* itself. Finally, Michael Wyatt's sixteenth chapter, also serving as an epilogue to the volume, proposes another centuries-long journey of connections that both anticipate and emerge from the performative core of the *Furioso*. Wyatt reflects upon performed articulations of the epic-chivalric tradition and its generically hybrid oral and textual sources that arose out of the real and imagined (or reimagined) relations between Muslims and Christians in the medieval Mediterranean world. Following from the birth of troubadour lyric between al-Andalus and Provence in the eleventh and twelfth centuries to the practices of both Matteo Maria Boiardo and Ariosto writing from within a decidedly performative ecology in Ferrara and reciting their works in progress for their Este patrons, the conjunction of orality and materiality is explored through the Sicilian traditions of *cuntastorie* (oral recitation) and the puppets of the *opera dei pupi*.

In his poem, Borges laments the gradual eclipse of the centuries-long enthusiasm of the European public for the *Orlando furioso*, supplanted, at the dawn of the "Orientalist era," by the overwhelming success of *One Thousand and One Nights*, "de ese enorme diamante . . . / [en que] Europa se perdió" (That enormous diamond . . . / [in which] Europe was lost), an Arabic text that "soñó la sarracena gente / Que sigue las banderas de Agramante" (was the dreaming of a dispossessed, / Devoted people, Saracens who hailed / The flags of Agramante).[4] Reduced to the status of a "classic,"

Y el Orlando es ahora una risueña
Región que alarga inhabitadas millas
De indolentes y ociosas maravillas
Que son un sueño que ya nadie sueña.

Por islámicas artes reducido
A simple erudición, a mera historia,
Está solo, soñándose.

[Orlando has become an unesteemed,
Unpeopled region, silently enlarging
Its nameless miles, of languid and lethargic
Monuments, and of a dream undreamed.

Reduced by Islamic arts to trivia—
Mere erudition and a simple story—
It is left alone to dream itself.]
—"Ariosto y los Árabes," pp. 126-127

The tables have thus been turned on the *Furioso*'s own dream of subduing its Saracen protagonists, its enchantments that had mapped a shared cultural patrimony among the world of Charlemagne's "Franks" now transformed into the stuff of fairy tales and fodder for scholars. But the reception history alluded to by Borges naturally also concerns the differing fortunes of elite and popular literatures. If it is true, as noted above and reiterated in several of the essays in this collection, that Ariosto's poem and the *Arabian Nights* have also crossed paths at times, the present volume can be considered an attempt to reflect on the possibility of resituating them, together with a number of other kindred texts and cultural objects discussed here, within a system of connected histories that explores them anew, with due care and determination, in relation to one another and from the vantage point of a broadly intercultural gaze. We are keenly aware that addressing a text as complex as the *Furioso*, already so widely studied, from this novel perspective has meant posing many more questions than we have been able to answer. Utilizing a diverse array of methodologies, we have sought to relocate within a more expansive framework issues that Ariosto criticism has richly probed in various other ways over the five hundred years that the poem has been in the hands of its readers. In shifting the parameters of inquiry, we have aimed to formulate new questions. We also knew that positioning the *Orlando furioso* at the center of a space as expansive as the Mediterranean and its contiguous territories would in some instances have risked displacing the locus of our investigation in such a way that the relationship with Ariosto's text might at times appear to be tenuous, if not imperceptible. But it seemed to us that this was a gamble worth taking, and we believe that it has led to a wider—yet still, of course, partial—understanding of the polyvalent prospects that Ariosto's book continues to offer. Through its confirmation of various initial intuitions and hypotheses, making several surprising discoveries, and pointing the way to subsequent research, we hope that this volume might find its place alongside the earlier Ariosto scholarship that made it possible and at the same time open up possibilities for even newer approaches to Ariosto's great poem as well as providing stimuli for new directions in the comparative study of the past.

Notes

1. These and subsequent citations of the original poem and its English translation by Eric McHenry are from Jorge Luis Borges, "Ariosto y los Árabes" / "Ariosto and the Arabs," in *Selected Poems*, edited by Alexander Coleman, pp. 122-127. New York: Viking, 1999.

2. "Ariosto y los Árabes," pp. 124-125.

3. Sanjay Subrahmanyam, especially "Connected Histories: Notes towards a Reconfiguration of Early Modern Eurasia," *Modern Asian Studies* 31, no. 3 (1997): pp. 735–762, and *Courtly Encounters: Translating Courtliness and Violence in Early Modern Eurasia* (Cambridge, MA: Harvard University Press, 2012); Benoît Grévin, *Le parchemin des cieux: Essai sur le Moyen Âge du langage* (Paris: Seuil, 2012); Suzanna Conklin Akbari and Carla Mallette, eds., *A Sea of Languages: Rethinking the Arabic Role in Medieval Literary History* (Toronto: University of Toronto Press, 2013); and Lina Bolzoni, ed., "Galassia Ariosto: L'archivio digitale dei poemi narrativi illustrati tra Cinque e Seicento," http://www.galassiaariosto.sns.it/.

4. "Ariosto y los Árabes," pp. 124-127.

PART I

Textual Contexts: Inside the *Furioso*

Ariosto and Arabic: Notes on an Unaccomplished Contiguity—A Prologue

Mario Casari

One of the main objectives of this volume is to outline a series of landscapes that—concentrically and with different degrees of contact, nearness, or distance—precede, surround, and follow the production of Ludovico Ariosto's *Orlando furioso* and its relation with the worlds of the "Saracen" adversary that lie at the center of the narration. As demonstrated by the essays in this collection, these landscapes may be investigated through a number of different variables. From this perspective, and particularly with a work of literature at the center of our attention, the linguistic sphere bears a significant and specific weight in these considerations. In his magisterial study *Le parchemin des cieux*, Benoît Grévin emphasizes the importance of more accurately redescribing the *paysages sonores* (soundscapes) that characterized the tricontinental geographic context centered around the Mediterranean Sea from the Middle Ages to the dawn of the early modern period. The area was characterized by the presence of two great linguistic cultures—Latin and Arabic—and by a congeries of other related languages and linguistic registers in such continuous evolution that rigid geographic boundaries would be impossible to define around them.[1] At the beginning of the sixteenth century, Italy presented an extremely complex linguistic panorama in which the humanist tension between Latin and vernaculars coexisted with the languages of numerous occupying powers or allies of the various Italian states; the languages of slaves, traders, and ambassadors of different origins; those of intellectuals, travelers, or correspondents; and the mute but widespread languages of epigraphic artifacts or artistic objects and growing collections of manuscripts.

In this panorama, there was also a place—and a less marginal one than is often believed—for Arabic. Within the framework of a reflection on "Ariosto and the Arabs," it thus seems worthwhile to take stock of what we know and might assume about the contiguity between Ariosto and the *Orlando furioso* with the Arabic language (or, better, the many Arabic languages), both *per se* and as a medium for the literary and cultural content that it conveyed. Ariosto did not know Arabic, but the very subject of his poem inevitably evokes its existence and included stratified traces of it, albeit through the mediation of the chivalric tradition in literary fiction. Indeed, Arabic was present in Italy at the time, at different levels of society and with different functions, including in spheres that were relatively close to the Ferrarese poet. Moreover, it was one of the principal languages of the fictitious enemy, the so-called Saracens, Muslim adversaries of the Christian paladins of Charlemagne: thus it belonged to a cultural world that also possessed a rich epic and chivalric tradition and would have had many reasons to ponder this substantial and sophisticated poem that addressed the conflict and confrontation that (in different forms and with different names) had characterized Mediterranean history for so many centuries. These were various levels of contact, especially indirect ones, that can be investigated through different time frames (anteriority, contemporaneity, posteriority) and that also imply different modes of intersection and relation (particularly absorption, awareness, and reception).

1. Anteriority: Absorption

The vast circulation of narrative texts on the Eurasian continent, both in oral and written form, between late antiquity and the Middle Ages led not only to the transmission of themes, literary motifs, or short narratives, but also to the transferal of isolated terms that were detached from their original texts and repositioned in new ones, often with transformed meanings. Today those who observe the expansion of this course of literary intercommunication between Europe, Asia, and Africa are struck by the sheer dimension and complexity of the transmission of at least five great texts—or, better, textual convoys—conceived to convey knowledge and wisdom. These works, which had already been partially encoded and transmitted between the third and eighth centuries, were restored to new life in the Arabic and Persian mediation that transformed them into the literary pillars of the entire Middle Ages and propelled them well beyond the period of the Renaissance in Europe and the Mongol-Timurid era in Asia. The *Alexander Romance, Kalila and Dimna*, the *Book of Sinbad, Barlaam and Josaphat*, and the *One Thousand and One Nights* are narrative cycles that are firmly rooted in the areas of the greatest cultural production of late antiquity—Greece, India, Persia, Central Asia—but also branched out into a multitude of languages, from Greek, Sanskrit, and Middle Persian into Armenian, Georgian, Syriac, Hebrew, Arabic, Persian, Latin, and the Romance and Germanic vernaculars. These works shared a series of characteristics that promoted their fragmentation, intersection, recomposition and continuous re-encoding, shifting through the literary modes, languages, and cultural environments of their new editors or authors.[2] The most evident factor is certainly the compositional structure of these works: macrotexts that host a range of independent stories and sequences held together by a unifying framework. The frame story of these master texts is based on the dichotomy between princes/kings, the direct addressees of the knowledge conveyed by these stories, and the figure of the sage—a wise hermit, a court philosopher, or a shrewd minister, wife, or handmaiden—and often more than one of these, in juxtaposed and complementary roles. The narrative trajectory plays out in a more or less linear manner within the often dramatic meetings/clashes that constitute the literary representation of the central ancient dilemmas concerning the relationship between power and knowledge. The fictional sovereign who is portrayed in these narratives is the literary transfiguration of the patron or addressee of the work. These works, therefore, circulated widely both in the West and the East on account of their nature as "mirrors for princes." The universal issue of managing the power of monarchs extended beyond religious and linguistic confines to address the legitimacy, ethics, strategies, glory, degeneration, and downfall of rulers.[3]

Positioned around this central bookshelf in our imaginary Eurasian library, there are other shelves with literary works that are rooted in relatively more circumscribed linguistic and geographic domains, including the many epic cycles, amorous literature, hagiographic traditions, and so on. Even in these cases, we can find traces of intersection and contamination, often as "fossils:" fragments or terms that have been decontextualized and that cannot be traced back to their source of origin. Indeed, a bold proposal has recently been advanced, with reference to the Arthurian cycle, for the still unknown origin of the term referring to the sword of excellence in medieval Christianity, *Escalibor* (this is the preferred form, in which *Es-* represents an emphatic pseudo-prefix from Old French), which is often unconvincingly traced back to purported Celtic roots. A hypothetical Persian etymology from **qalʿībur/qalībor*, with the value of (sword) "swordcutter" is based on the association of the eponymous knight present in the Arthurian saga, "Escalibor le Mesconneü, quêteur du Graal," with a comrade or close family member, the knight Sephar, another "mescongnu," sometimes with the variant name Separ (in Rustichello da Pisa's Arthurian romance, ca. 1270–1274). In Persian, *separ* means "shield." The two foreign knights—the "sword" and the "shield"—sat at places XXVII and XXVIII at the Round Table.[4]

Ariosto's *Orlando furioso* belongs on a specific shelf of the epic-chivalric literature of Mediterranean Christian Europe. It sits at the apex of one of the founding literary traditions of its identity, the *chansons de geste* that arose from the episode of the battle at the Pass of Roncesvalles and then became intertwined with Crusade accounts and interwoven into the ideological and narrative framework of the clash with the Ottoman Empire. In the past, several attempts were made to correlate this literary tradition with the parallel tradition of popular Arabic epic, embodied by the *sīra* and pseudo-*maghāzī* genres. In addition to identifying numerous aspects of folkloric coloration in settings, devices, and certain events, this effort at establishing correspondences addressed the very nature of the relationship and system of values of the hero-protagonists of various narrative works: the *chévalerie* of medieval Christian Europe and the previous and contemporary *muruwwa* and *futuwwa* of the Muslim Arabic world.[5] In particular, the *Sīrat ʿAntar* has been compared to the *Chanson de Roland* and its related literary tradition. This Arabic popular romance, which was probably first written out in the eleventh or twelfth century, is the culmination of the confluence of various legends surrounding the celebrated pre-Islamic poet ʿAntara ibn Shaddād, known as one of the Arabic "crows" on account of his African origin and black skin.[6] While the fight against the Saracens provides the framework and central core of the narrative in the European tradition concerning the adventures of the Paladins, in the *Sīrat ʿAntar*, as well as in some other *siyar* (e.g., the *Sīrat Baybars* about the Mamluk sultan al-Malik al Ẓāhir Baybars, a fierce foe of the Crusaders and governor of Egypt and Syria between 1260 and 1277), only a few sections are dedicated to the clash against the Christian European enemy.[7] Nonetheless, the two traditions mirror the peculiar lexical journey that provided a term identifying the enemy through synecdoche. On the one side, there still is a lively debate about the etymology of the term "Saracen" used in European languages in its different forms; it is certainly related to an ethnonym that several classical sources attribute to a population of Arabia Petraea (the northern part of the Sinai Peninsula), distinct from the Arabs, which may have then been juxtaposed with later Arabic words such as *sharqiyyūn* (Orientals), *sāriqūn* (thieves), or others.[8] On the other side, there are two Arabic terms that alternate and are sometimes present together. Depending on literary genres and texts, the word *Rūm* (adjective *Rūmī*) may refer to the ancient history of Greece (sometimes indicated more precisely as *Yūnān*, adjective *Yūnānī*), to Byzantium and the territory that it gradually lost to the Turkish invasions, or to Western Rome (and its state entities) in the heart of the Mediterranean, over a lengthy chronology. From a general point of view, this term often refers to an alterity as opposed to the entities of the Islamic caliphates, sultanates, and emirates: a political power located in the western area of Eurasia that would assume the mantle of Christianity. The other common term is *Ifranj*, the "Franks," who were an entity recognized by the Arabs from the time of the presumed ambassadorial exchanges between Charlemagne and Hārūn al-Rashīd, as well as the Christian opponents in Syria and Palestine during the Crusades. As for their original homeland, sometimes the *Ifranj* were located in the north of Europe, but already in the tenth century this term could generally indicate the Christian population of Western Europe. Masʿūdī (Arab geographer and historian, d. 955) declared: "Rome is the greatest seat of the Franks' kingdom in ancient as well as modern times."[9]

When this Arabic popular epic tradition began to appear in Europe, during the nineteenth century, some readers and experts emphasized the possibility that these Arabic texts had strongly influenced the nature and form of European chivalric cycles. These issues were discussed at length, and today most scholars agree that any structural and thematic resemblance between the two epic traditions is due to coincidence or, more likely, to the common narrative heritage of Mediterranean storytellers, one based on conflict and revenge, horses and journeys, weapons and magic, unrequited love and happy reunions. This natural narrative reservoir was supplemented, on both sides, by the Crusades, with issues related to the perception of others, religious conflicts, abuse and appeasement, and possible conversions. Indeed, even if we have no explicit reports or traces of such transmission, it is difficult to imagine that portions of these narratives did not reach Christian ears in the polyglot milieus of Muslim Andalus; at the courts of the Sicilian kingdoms of Roger II (1130–1154), Frederick II (1198–1250), or Manfredi (1258–1266, who welcomed an embassy sent by Mamluk Sultan Baybars, who eventually became the protagonist of a popular *sīra*); or in the cities and fortifications occupied by Frankish crusaders in Palestine and Syria during the twelfth and thirteenth centuries. It has been pointed out that certain similarities increased toward the end of the medieval period (on the Arabic side, for example, with the most recent parts of the *Sīrat ʿAntar* and much of the *Sīrat Sayf ibn Dhī Yazan*), and this raises the question of a possibly corresponding wider oral circulation of stories, thanks to the stabilization of trade routes and the journeys of storytellers of various nationalities and languages all along the coasts of the Mediterranean.[10]

Whatever the case, it is interesting to note that the tradition of the *chansons de geste* inevitably includes specific terms that are of Arabic origin, even in unexpected places. The *Chanson de Roland* refers to a divine triad venerated by the Saracens: Mahom, Tervagan, and Apollin (who, transformed through the Italian tradition, appear only as Macon[e] and Trivigante in the *Orlando furioso,* paired in XII 59; XXXVIII 18). While the derivation of the first from an incorrect reading or pronunciation of Muḥammad/Moḥammad has always been evident, possible etymologies for the second and third names were long based on the classical tradition. In fact, concrete hypotheses regarding the Arabic etymologies of these names were not formulated until the latter half of the twentieth century, when it was suggested that (T)ervagan could be a corruption of a Koranic epithet (*al-Furqān,* the Criterion) or of a term usually attributed to Satan (*al-rajīm,* the stoned). Similarly, Apollin was traced back to the epithet *Abū'l-laʿīn* (father of the accursed one) or *Ibn al-laʿīn* (son of the accursed one). These names, therefore, were Arabic epithets for Muḥammad that had been articulated in Christian environments with a derogative intent.[11] According to a more recent hypothesis, founded for the most part on plausibly incorrect interpretations of defective Arabic writing, these two names could be corruptions of the names of two of the Prophet's companions, his successors at the helm of the Islamic community as the first and third caliph: Abū Bakr and (ʿUthmān) bin ʿAffān.[12] This clue also points to further, even more surprising hypotheses that attribute an Arabic origin to some of the names of important swords in the *chanson* tradition (the sword of Roland, Durendal, Durindana in the *Furioso,* from the Arabic term *dhū'l-jandal,* master of stone; the sword of Turpin, Almace, from the Arabic term *al-māḍī,* cutter, sharp; the sword of Ganelon, Murglies, from the Arabic term *māriq ʾalyas,* valiant, piercer), Roland's horse (Veillantif, from the Arabic term *dhayl kathīf,* thick tail), and even the mythical horn that Roland failed to sound at Roncesvalles until it was too late, the Oliphant, whose usual association with the elephant (it is made of ivory) has been challenged by a hypothetical derivation from the Arabic term *al-bīqān,* plural of *al-būq* (trumpet, horn). According to a narrative variant in the *Chanson d'Aspremont* (twelfth century), Roland had obtained a sword, horse, and horn as spoils from the Saracen king Aymes, whom he had defeated to help Charlemagne.[13]

In addition to these terms of (possible) Arabic origin that belong to the heritage of the *chanson de geste* and were partially incorporated into Ariosto's *Orlando furioso,* and some clearly Arabic proper names (such as Norandino from Nūr al-Dīn), there are several further terms of Arabic etymology that were assimilated by Ariosto into the poetic texture of his work. These were perceived as issuing from a semi-specialized vocabulary used to refer to characters of the Islamic world, a conventional lexicon inherited from the chivalric tradition.[14]

Therefore, the absorption of Arabic linguistic traces into the chivalric texts of the period appears to have been indirect and heavily mediated. This is also true for the narrative fragments of possibly Arabic origin (or that underwent an intermediate Arabic phase) inserted into the *Orlando furioso*, independent of the epic-chivalric tradition. The two famous episodes of "Astolfo and Iocondo" and "Isabella and Rodomonte" reveal two opposite trajectories that are both typical of the transmission of Arabic material toward the European vernacular literatures of the early modern period. As illustrated by Claudia Ott in this volume, we should assume that the first of these *novelle*, narrated to Rodomonte by an innkeeper as a reflection on the malice of women (*Fur.*, XXVIII 4–74), is principally based on the Arabic text of the *One Hundred and One Nights* that was produced in the Islamic West (between al-Andalus and the Maghreb) and probably transmitted through Iberian vernaculars to other Romance languages, as witnessed, in a variant, by a famous novella by Giovanni Sercambi.[15] As for the second *novella*, Pio Rajna had traced Isabella's heroic deceit of Rodomonte concerning her chastity back to an episode narrated in the *De re uxoria* by the Venetian humanist Francesco Barbaro (1390–1454). Subsequent studies by Enrico Cerulli and Giorgio Levi della Vida, however, situated its origin in a Greek story about the Persian conquest of Jerusalem in 614, in which the trick of the invulnerability-inducing drug was used by a pious virgin to avoid the violence of the conquerors. The story would have reached Giovanni da Ravenna, Francesco Barbaro's teacher, through the indispensable mediation of Byzantine and Arabic (both Christian and Muslim) sources, absorbing especially from the latter passage a typically Muslim tone.[16] Despite this notably indirect relationship, it must nevertheless be emphasized that certain details, such as the use of the term Albracca/*al-barqā* presented by Ott, once again underscore the value of "fossils," if not to fully retrace a textual journey, at least to indicate a possible directionality. Indeed, the complex onomastics of the *Orlando furioso*, which include terms of still uncertain etymology, may well provide further promising clues of assimilation.

2. Contemporaneity: Awareness

Moving from the literary tradition to the living reality surrounding the production of the *Orlando furioso*, it bears emphasizing that the life and intellectual work of Ariosto belong to a particular historical context—and a "soundscape"—in which the presence of the Arabic language was, even if marginal, not a negligible fact.

First of all, however, we must define what we mean by "Arabic language." Today we normally use the term "Classical Arabic" to refer to the literary language that took shape between the fourth and seventh centuries on the Arabian Peninsula, possibly as a *koinè* of various Bedouin dialects, through the production of a body of poetry known as of the *jāhiliyya* (lit. "ignorance," a term that indicates the pre-Islamic era) and in the revelation of the Koran, the sacred book of Islam. Starting in the seventh to eighth centuries, this language was progressively codified by Arabic grammarians and philologists, leading to the production of an immense corpus of texts in all literary genres over a number of centuries and a vast geographical area: all of northern Africa and into Spain, to the west, and reaching Syria and the border of the Iranian plateau, in the east. As the language spread, partially in connection with the transmission of the Islamic religion, Classical Arabic (known as *fuṣḥa*, "eloquent") gradually crystallized and then maintained a substantial homogeneity on account of the respect due to its sacred status as the language of the Koran. This, however, concerns its nature as a language used for literature and elevated communication. In terms of the spoken language, it is still unclear what language was actually used by the first Arabs and how different it was from the Koranic codification. But the process of differentiation certainly established itself over the centuries, giving rise to a permanent state of diglossia between the literary and spoken languages, following a complex and regionally distinct course that is difficult to trace, notwithstanding the presence of documents in numerous variants of so-called Middle Arabic, texts in which the literary language is colored, to various degrees, with dialectal features. We can thus affirm that between the eleventh and sixteenth centuries, the Arabic world was substantially characterized by the situation described above: a diglossia similar to the current one in which a prestigious literary language, sacred by statute, was accompanied by "Arabic dialects" that were used for daily conversation at all social levels. These dialects varied widely from region to region and were sometimes recorded in written documents within the context of Middle Arabic. Moreover, many people living in areas that had been conquered by Arab armies continued for centuries to use their original languages, such as Berber, Coptic, Aramaic, Persian, Hebrew, and so on. These languages survived in different degrees alongside the diffusion of Arabic.[17]

In medieval and early modern Christian Europe, the study of this language (or languages) had different protagonists and fortunes, especially starting from the eleventh century. The differing attitudes of the scholars and beneficiaries of this knowledge, and the disparate levels of linguistic competence acquired, gave rise to different levels of interaction with native speakers and the range of knowledge that could be accessed through various linguistic registers. If, on the one hand, literary Arabic was the main route of access to the classical scientific and philolosophical heritage that the Arabs had preserved in translation (particularly from Greek and Syriac), reworked and updated in an original manner, on the other hand, it also served as a tool to understand the Islamic religious heritage (mainly the Koran and its commentaries)—often, at first, in a polemical spirit. Furthermore, the need to politically counter the Muslim adversary and preach the Gospel for the purpose of conversion also implied the need to acquire an oral level of fluency, considerably distinct from reading ability, correlated to the various regions where evangelization was attempted. The first missionary orders, the Franciscans and especially the Dominicans, opened language schools that addressed both registers of Arabic with the help of native language teachers. In terms of the religious debate, however, Arabic was not only the language of Islam but also that of large communities of the Eastern Christian churches, a division that had continued to represent a painful issue for many of the Roman popes from the Schism of 1054 onward. Arabic Christian versions of the Scriptures would represent an important field of study and debate all through the era of the Protestant Reformation. Forms of spoken Arabic and a multitude of documents in Middle Arabic were also a significant part of the network of trade communications along the coasts of the Mediterranean, which was also responsible for the arrival of slaves—some of whom were highly educated and worked as important tutors and writers—in Italian families and courts. Another important category of Arabic teachers and conveyers of forms of Arabic knowledge on Italian soil was that of a significant, partially Arabic-speaking, minority population: Jewish communities, especially those in Sicily, which had maintained within their range of linguistic skills a high level of Judeo-Arabic, Arabic written in Hebrew script and rich in Hebrew overlaying. It was particularly thanks to the mediation of several of these teachers that Arabic caught the attention of a select number of humanists, who were often isolated from one another but united by the firm belief that this language was an essential tool of access to the patrimony of ancient wisdom. The traditional wisdom of the *Arabes* was considered as virtually independent from the Islamic identity that characterized the Arabic-speaking world of the time. Between the fifteenth and sixteenth centuries, Arabic had become one of the pivots of a five-language system, which included Latin, Greek, Hebrew, and Chaldaic (Aramaic or Syriac, depending on the case), that was considered a fundamental pillar of humanist education.[18]

The degree to which these immediate realities actually touched the life and work of Ariosto is difficult to ascertain as we have no significant evidence of such influence. In this reflection on landscapes, nevertheless, it is worthwhile shedding light on certain aspects of the question. While Arabic speakers—slaves, merchants, and ambassadors—circulated in Ferrara in Ariosto's day, he probably had only minimal contact with these figures;[19] indeed, the poet's greater opportunity for proximity to the Arabic language was tied to his humanist interests and his participation in intellectual circles whose foci were not always strictly orthodox.

A significant role in the intellectual life of Ariosto was played by his friend Alberto Pio (1475–1531), the last prince of Carpi. Pio was the nephew of Giovanni Pico della Mirandola, who in many ways was paradigmatic of the humanist interest in Arabic as the language of ancient wisdom. Pico's Hebrew and Arabic teacher had been Shemu'el ben rabbi Nissim Abū'l-Faraj, a Jew from Caltabellotta who converted to Catholicism as Guglielmo Raimondo Moncada and later became known by his humanist nickname, Flavius Mithridates (ca. 1450–post 1491). Pico's *Oration on the Dignity of Man*, one of the most representative texts of Renaissance humanism, opens its fundamental declaration on the supremacy of humankind over other worldly creatures with a quotation from an Arabic text attributed to a still uncertainly identified "Abdalla Saracenus." In a paragraph of the *Oration* that was partially erased by Pico's nephew Gianfrancesco, editor of the text, but that can be read in the extant manuscript Palatino 885, Pico reported that for the sake of his deep *philosophiae studium*, "it was necessary to know not only the Greek and Latin languages, but also the Hebrew and Chaldean languages, and the Arabic language as well, with which I have just begun to labor under the guidance of William Mithridates, an expert on all these languages."[20] According to the existing inventories, Pico's personal library included, besides various Hebrew and Chaldean codices, a list of several Arabic books: two copies of the *Psalterium*, one copy of the four Gospels, one copy of Saint Paul's Epistles, two copies of the Koran (one in Hebrew script), Avicenna's *Canon of Medicine*, the *Secretum Secretorum*, Ptolemy's *Almagest*, a historiographical text, two unidentified books, and an alphabet.[21] Pico's enthusiasm for his own small steps in reading the Koran is demonstrated in his correspondence with Marsilio Ficino.[22] One should also add the various originally Arabic works whose Latin translations had become a significant section of the humanist library, such as those by Avicenna and Averroes. Pico's familiarity with the Dominican environment, and in particular with Girolamo Savonarola, should not induce us to view his interest in Arabic within the confines of the missionary engagement that the Ferrarese friar promoted so strongly after being elected prior of the Florentine Convent of San Marco in 1491. Instead, both Pico's reflections and the foundational declarations concerning the language school that Savonarola established at San Marco, confirmed the role of the five languages: "In our religion there are three perfect languages, that is, Latin, Greek, and Hebrew; and then we also have the Moorish and the Chaldean; and believe that God did not send them to us without a reason. Thus, come to learn; come, and do not worry that the place is narrow, since God will provide. Come soon, because you shall need to have learned these languages when the sword will arrive."[23] As a youth, Ariosto must have been aware of many of the issues addressed by the sermons of Savonarola. Two of Savonarola's works were, in fact, printed by the publisher of the *Orlando furioso*, Giovanni Mazzocchi del Bondeno, in 1513 and 1516.[24]

On Giovanni Pico's recommendation, the humanist and publisher Aldo Manuzio stayed in Carpi from 1479 to 1480, working as the preceptor of Giovanni's nephews Alberto and Lionello Pio, the sons of Caterina Pico. Subsequently, Alberto Pio was called to Ferrara, where Giovanni Pico was studying, and beginning in 1494, Alberto and Ariosto were instructed for several years (together with the sons of Rinaldo d'Este, brother of Duke Ercole I) by the Augustinian monk Gregorio da Spoleto. Alberto Pio was certainly in Ferrara until 1500, but there also is proof of his living there in 1504–1506. Ariosto dedicated a *carmen* in Latin to the death of Alberto Pio's mother. The bond between the two grew weaker when Alberto embarked upon his diplomatic activities, first for the king of France and then as ambassador in Rome for the Emperor Maximilian. In 1510, Alberto and Ariosto were both in Rome and frequented the same intellectual circles, although in November of that year they fell out over the clash between Alberto and the House of Este over the control of Carpi.[25] Alberto had been the favorite pupil and protector of Manuzio, who, in the dedication of his edition of Aristotle's *Organon* (1495), praised him as an equal of his uncle Giovanni and as a scholar of the Latin, Greek, and Hebrew linguistic triad: "You lack nothing: not intelligence, which you possess in abundance; nor eloquence, with which you are well endowed; not books of Latin, Greek, or even Hebrew learning, which you seek with the greatest love and commitment; nor very learned tutors, whom you have procured at great expense."[26] Manuzio, however, overlooked Pio's interest in the other two languages of the "quintet," including Arabic. Interestingly enough, Manuzio would subsequently be the publisher of the first European printed book containing an engraved Arabic inscription: the celebrated *Hypnerotomachia Poliphili* (1499).[27]

At the beginning of the sixteenth century, Alberto Pio spent 800 Italian scudos to purchase the library of Giorgio Valla, a friend and correspondent of Giovanni Pico, which included a group of Arabic codices in Hebrew script, mostly about medicine. Alberto Pio's library expanded around this nucleus. A comparison between the *Inventario* of 1564—which constitutes the most comprehensive documentation of this library following its many moves—and the codices that are currently in the Estense Library in Modena provides a list of at least thirteen volumes that can be identified as Arabic, Judeo-Arabic, or Syro-Arabic. These can be divided into three homogeneous groups: six books on medicine and two on philosophy in Hebrew script that may have possibly belonged to Valla; a five-volume collection of Muslim traditions, including various sections from the *al-Musnad al-Ṣaḥīḥ*, "The Correct Support," by al-Bukhārī (810–870), a fundamental collection of the *ḥadīth* ("facts and sayings" about the Islamic Prophet Muḥammad), composed of ninety-seven books; and four books of Christian Scriptures that were commissioned by Alberto Pio or collected by him during his period in Rome.[28] Alberto's "Orientalist" activity, which included interest in Syriac texts, was conducted in preparation for the Fifth Lateran Council (1512–1517), called by Pope Julius II and concluded under the papacy of Leo X, and which aimed at the reunion of the Roman and Eastern churches. Three humanists, whose scholarly pursuits also included Arabic studies, participated in the council: Egidio da Viterbo, Alberto Pio da Carpi, as ambassador of Emperor Maximilian, and Agostino Giustiniani, the bishop of Nebbio. It appears that Alberto Pio was interested in adding Eastern-language versions to the Greek text of the New Testament. As is evident from the colophon, an Arabic version of the Letters of Saint Paul, now preserved in the Estense Library in Modena, was transcribed for Alberto Pio in 1521 by Yuḥannā al-Asad al-Gharnaṭī al-Fāsī, in Rome, Campo Marzio, for the palatial library (*khizāna*) of Count Alberto Pio.[29] This was the Arabic version of the name acquired after converting to Catholicism by Ḥasan ibn Muḥammad al-Wazzān al-Fāsī, a Muslim merchant and ambassador from Granada, and then Fez. Ḥasan al-Wazzān was captured by Sicilian pirates, presented to Pope Leo X, baptized, and freed with the Latin name of Iohannes Leo Granatinus. Commonly known as Leo Africanus, he became the Arabic teacher of Cardinal Egidio da Viterbo and a collaborator of Alberto Pio. He also was the author of the celebrated geographical and bibliographical text entitled *Della descrittione dell'Africa et delle cose notabili che ivi sono* (1550), an Arabic-Hebrew-Latin medical vocabulary, and an Arabic grammar, the last two works surviving only in fragments.[30]

It is difficult to assess how much Ariosto and Alberto Pio might have shared about this activity conducted by the prince of Carpi, due to the weakening of their friendship and personal contacts during this period. In any case, the potential intersections with Giovanni Pico and Savonarola, and their linguistic theoretical legacies, and the important friendship with Alberto Pio likely represent Ariosto's nearest points of direct contact with the Arabic language (either evoked or written) in his own personal milieu. Considering these circumstances, it is also legitimate to ask whether Ariosto was ever informed —perhaps by Alberto Pio himself—of the work surrrounding a new translation and commentary of the Koran that was being carried out (albeit piecemeal) between the fifteenth and sixteenth centuries in Spain and Italy thanks to a growing interest within environments close to the Roman curia and the involvement of figures such as Juan de Segovia, Guglielmo Raimondo Moncada, Giovanni Pico della Mirandola, Federico da Montefeltro, Leo Africanus, Egidio da Viterbo, and others.[31] Indeed, even if, outside the literary fiction, we can assume that a certain knowledge of the basics of Islam was part of Ariosto's cultural baggage—as seems certain regarding Boiardo—the representation of the religion of the Saracens in the *Orlando furioso* is in line with the literary tradition that ascribes to them belief in pagan gods, although there are some hints at the presence of a supreme entity on a couple of occasions.[32] Given the figures and circumstances that could have acted as potential mediating factors, however, Ariosto's proximity to Arabic, if any, would seem to have been oriented not toward its standing as the language of Islam and the "Saracens" but rather around its quality as a language of science and philosophy as well as its role as one of the languages of the Eastern churches, in accordance with the interest in hermetic philosophical themes and heterodox religious debates that characterized some aspects of Ariosto's intellectual world and that would have been common currency in the early sixteenth century.[33]

The fact remains that no unarguable trace of this proximity seems to have found its way into the *Furioso* or other writings of Ariosto, and we are thus inclined to acknowledge that his awareness of the presence and value of the Arabic language may have remained marginal and ephemeral. In the final version of the *Orlando furioso* (1532), however, Ariosto added to the list of figures awaiting him at the shore upon his return from the "sea voyage" of his narrative poem both the illustrious friend of his youth, Alberto Pio, and his cousin Gianfrancesco Pico, the other famous nephew of Giovanni Pico della Mirandola:

> Veggo sublimi e soprumani ingegni
> di sangue e d'amor giunti, il Pico e il Pio.
> —*Fur.*, XLVI 17, 1–2
> [I can see Pico and Pio, sublime, godlike geniuses connected by ties of affection and of blood.]

One final suggestive element, entirely in line with the preceding chivalric literary tradition, merits attention. The only explicit mention made of Arabic ("arabico") in the *Orlando furioso* is related to the knowledge of this language not by a Saracen but by a true *Ifranj*, a Frank, Count Orlando, the eponymous hero of the poem. Praise is heaped upon him for his knowledge of the language that had served him so well in his forays against the enemy. But the eventual suffering that this knowledge also imparts is lamented by the poet when Orlando discovers, reads, and understands the graffito etched by Medoro in the cave where he and Angelica had first consummated their love.[34] In a certain sense, we may say that Orlando's linguistic skills, explicitely revealed at the exact center of the poem, at the end of canto XXIII, function as the trigger of the madness that constitutes the pivotal crux of the poem's plot and provides its title:[35]

> Era scritto in arabico, che 'l conte
> intendea così ben come latino:
> fra molte lingue e molte ch'avea pronte,
> prontissima avea quella il paladino;
> e gli schivò più volte e danni ed onte,
> che si trovò tra il popul saracino:
> ma non si vanti, se già n'ebbe frutto;
> ch'un danno or n'ha, che può scontargli il tutto.
> —*Fur.*, XXIII 110
>
> [It was written in Arabic, which the count knew as well as he knew Latin. He knew many and many a tongue, but Arabic is one with which he was most familiar: his grasp of it had saved him on more than one occasion from injury and insult when he was among the Saracens. But he was not to boast if formerly his knowledge had helped him—the pain it now brought him quite discounted every former advantage.]

3. Posteriority: Reception

There remains one final aspect to examine regarding the potential contiguity between the *Orlando furioso* (and Ariosto's literary activity in general) and the Arabic language. It concerns the possible interest in Ariosto's poem, and hence its possible forms of reception, within Arabophone and Arabographic contexts, for the *Furioso* is a work that belongs to a markedly identitarian European epic tradition and provides an explicit representation—filtered albeit by the stylistic features of literary fiction—of "Arabs" in the abstract form of "Saracens," a term used to refer to various rival powers throughout a stratification of historical periods.

The Arabic-Islamic world's apparent lack of interest in the languages, history, and literary forms of Christian Europe has been the object of extensive academic debate that has not been immune to ideological connotations. Bernard Lewis was one of the first to address this issue. He proposed that the Muslim populations of the Middle Ages and the pre-modern period exhibited arrogance, ignorance, and a lack of curiosity toward the cultural manifestations of Christian Europe, because they fundamentally believed in the superiority of their religion and civilization—at least until they began to be crushed by European imperialism after the Industrial Revolution, starting in the nineteenth century. In Lewis's view, this attitude could explain the different approach to languages and the textual products of the European Christian world within the Arabic-Islamic sphere, as opposed to the great interest demonstrated by Christian Europe in Arabic, other Islamic languages, and their cultural production. Lewis's harsh perspective has been criticized and challenged, especially on account of its essentialism, and recent studies have shed light on a far more complex interaction of the Arabic-Islamic world with the languages and linguistic production of the European Christian world. In particular, Jocelyn Dakhlia's studies of the prevalently oral approach of Muslims to the cultures of European Christian society between the Middle Ages and the pre-modern period, and the elucidations made by Daniel König concerning the differing importance ascribed by Muslim intellectuals to texts of the Greek and Syriac traditions as opposed to those of Latin (with several significant exceptions) and, to a certain extent, Romance ones, provide a much more in-depth description of the interests, cultural content, occasions, obstacles, and geographic variables that characterized the attitude of Muslim intellectuals, from different areas, toward the literary heritage of the "European" tradition, initially that of classical antiquity and then primarily of Christianity.[36]

Even within this renewed historiographical framework, there is little evidence of a two-way exchange for the ramifications of the epic-chivalric genres, as observed above. In terms of Arabic reception, already during the Abbasid epoch it appears to be the case that few narrative works drew upon Greek and Latin literature, and this was due to a number of reasons: the selectivity that had already been performed by Syriac-Christian filtering; the scarce diffusion of the necessary linguistic and cultural tools as compared to the Syriac or Persian spheres; and religious scruples. The Arabs, for instance, in eviscerating Aristotle had translated and commented his *Poetics* but had no direct knowledge of the Greek tragedies to which a large part of that work had been dedicated. Concerning epic, we know of a partial (lost) Syriac version of the *Iliad* produced by the court astrologer of the Abbasid caliph al-Mahdī (775–785), Thawāfil ibn Tūma (Theophilus of Edessa, d. 785), but knowledge of the narrative texture of this work never extended beyond the elite of the time. Both a vague image of the Greek poet and fragments of Homeric verse (often misattributed) appear in Arabic and Persian literary and philosophical works, where they were usually selected for their gnomic value, in segments of wisdom literature, while at the same time features of the Greek heroic tradition entered the Islamic world through the complex transmission of the *Alexander Romance*.[37] For the Latin world, interest was oriented, especially in Andalusia, principally toward historiographic literature, as in the important case of the *Kitāb Hurūshiyūsh* (tenth century), an Arabic translation of the *Historiae adversus paganos* by Orosius, integrated with extracts from other Latin texts.[38] With regard to chivalric traditions closer to those of the *Orlando furioso*, the discovery of fragments from a *chanson de geste* dedicated to the Saracen knight Fierabras (end of the twelfth century) and of other ones from the *Enfances Godefroi* (a late-twefth-century *chanson* belonging to the Crusade Cycle) in the deposit of the *Qubbat al-khazna* (Treasure Cupola) of the Great Mosque of Damascus, together with other texts in various languages (Arabic, Greek, Armenian, Coptic, Hebrew, Aramaic, Georgian, Latin, and Old French), may bear witness to the existence of plurilingual communities in medieval urban society in the Middle East, but could also simply represent war spoils, and their effective circulation beyond a small nucleus of Christian colonies would be difficult to establish. The recent discovery of another chivalric fragment (from Chrétien de Troyes's poem *Yvain ou le Chevalier au lion*), now preserved in Vienna, provides new elements for reflection, since it appears to have been produced in Egypt on typical Arabic paper around the mid-thirteenth century; however, this should also probably be related to the ephemeral presence in Egypt of French soldiers at the orders of Louis IX, during the seventh crusade, which shattered against the solid resistance of the Mamluk general and future sultan Baybars.[39] Compared to other literary genres whose transmission was more consistently entrusted to the written text, it is most likely that if ever epic and chivalric narratives crossed linguistic and religious barriers between the Latin-Christian and the Arabic-Islamic worlds, this probably occurred for the most part through oral transmission, leaving faint traces, isolated "fossils"—as we have seen above—not easily identifiable. We have already noted the improbability of locating specific reciprocal influences by comparing texts from the different epic-chivalric traditions. But it is also difficult to hypothesize that texts of the Christian chivalric tradition could have been received, even if only in oral form, at the courts or in the squares of the Ayyubid and Mamluk dominions, notwithstanding the fervid literary activities of those Mediterranean regions at the time.[40]

Undoubtedly, the environment that could present the greatest opportunity for the transmission of texts and motifs was Andalusia, where the different chivalric traditions came into contact for a longer time than elsewhere. We know that the epic-chivalric stories of the *Sīrat 'Antar* and the *Sīrat Baybars* found interested audiences in Granada and Seville, where at the same time, chivalric themes and Arthurian motifs may have penetrated so far as to be illustrated among the ceiling paintings of the Hall of Justice in the Alhambra (*al-ḥamrā'*, "the Red One").[41] A further relevant matter is represented by the Andalusian production of Arabic literary texts with content related to the Crusades, developed particularly in the final period of the Reconquista, such as the Andalusī chivalric romance dedicated to the adventures of Ziyād ibn 'Āmir al-Kinānī.[42] Especially significant within this context is what appears to be a direct translation: the Aljamiado version of the romance *Historia de los amores de París y Viana*. Structured as a classic tale of almost defeated love, this widely traveled chivalric narrative revolves around the figure of a Christian hero, Paris, who, in order to help the Crusaders in their fight against Islam, learns Arabic, grows a beard, and dresses as a Moor to travel behind enemy lines incognito. The romance is based on an original French version and at least one Castilian and one Catalan version were produced for the Iberian world.[43] The Aljamiado iteration probably dates to around 1560, suggesting that this story was potentially appealing to a Moorish Muslim audience, as they, too—in the period following the end of the Christian Reconquista—lived in a perpetual state of concealment.[44]

Although the case of the *Historia de los amores de París y Viana* (a chivalric Christian work that crossed the cultural frontier toward a Muslim audience in written form) seems practically unique, it is precisely within the Iberian context that we must first imagine the potential resituating of a work such as the *Furioso* for a possibly Arabic-speaking audience. The main conduit would seem to have been the Jewish communities there, which showed considerable interest in the work of Ariosto and the *Orlando furioso* in particular.[45] The existence of a nearly complete Judeo-Castilian translation of the poem (the first thirty-six cantos) from the latter half of the sixteenth century demonstrates its reception in non-Christian Iberian contexts.[46] We have no evidence, however, not even a fragment, that this linguistic demarcation line was ever crossed in the direction of Arabic (or even in Aljamiado).

Notwithstanding the absence of concrete proof and the unlikelihood that any such translation was ever made—also taking into account the difficulties imposed by the sophisticated poetic form as opposed to simpler popular narratives in prose—the hypothesis of an Arabic version of the *Orlando furioso* started to circulate at a very early date. In 1584, Camillo Pellegrino asserted in his dialogue *Il Carrafa, o vero dell'epica poesia*: "This seems to me a great thing: that Ariosto is a man of great fame, not only in Italy, but practically throughout the whole world, since his Orlando has been translated into so many languages, that not only Spanish, French, and German, but also other languages, even Arabic (if what they say is true), have been keen to sing and discuss it."[47] As already emphasized by Pio Rajna,[48] this idea may have been encouraged by the Ferrarese humanist Giovan Battista Pigna, who in his commentary to Ariosto's work exalted its potential for diffusion in other languages: "With all this, the Furioso was translated from his and our language into French; and into Spanish; and in rhyme as it is, and in prose; and into Greek verse; and into German writing. And it is the hope that if outside Europe composition ever becomes custom, the Arabs and the Turks will make it theirs, before they set themselves to doing anything else."[49] While Pigna may also have seen the possibility of such a translation in view of the respectful attitude that Ariosto exhibited toward the Saracens of his poem, bucking much of the literary tradition on this issue, as has been suggested,[50] Pellegrino's proposition has a more polemical basis: the affirmation of the superiority of Torquato Tasso's poetic masterpiece, *Gerusalemme liberata*, which had just been published. The diatribe provoked by this hostile critique drove other advocates of an Arabic translation, but the news seems to have faded by the end of the sixteenth century, buried in the absence of voices or clues that could otherwise testify to its plausibility.[51]

This silence persisted, in fact, even when Italian literature began to be taken into serious consideration by Arab intellectuals, at first especially Egyptians, in the context of the *nahḍa*, the "Arab Renaissance" in the nineteenth to twentieth centuries, following the conflictual yet fertile encounter with European powers initiated by Napoleon's invasion of Egypt in 1798. Although attracting significantly less interest than French and English literature, a select number of Italian texts were soon at the center of focused and growing attention in this period.[52] This wave of interest involved—at times more in the form of rewritten works rather than actual translations—classic works such as Niccolò Machiavelli's *Il principe* (ca. 1823, a second edition in 1912, and a third in 2004, all published in Egypt), Giovanni Boccaccio's *Decameron* (1929 and 1933, 1956, 1994, 1997, all in Egypt, and 2006, in Syria, the only unabridged version), and

Dante Alighieri's *Divina commedia* (in Libya 1930–1933, in Egypt 1959–1969, in Syria 2002, and in Lebanon, albeit for a UNESCO series by an Iraqi scholar living in France, also in 2002). The absence of the *Orlando furioso* here is all the more striking if compared to the abundant presence of the *Divina commedia* in Arabic (in some cases also in excellent, commented translations, like the one published between 1959 and 1969 in three volumes by the Egyptian Italianist Ḥasan ʿUthmān), a text that presents various issues for a Muslim readership, in particular due to the terrible fate that befalls the prophet of Islam Muḥammad and his son-in-law ʿAlī in canto XXVIII of the *Inferno* (though the Libyan and Syrian translations were produced by Christian translators). Particular interest in the *Divina commedia* had been prompted in the Arabic-speaking world through the debate aroused by the famous essay of Miguel Asín Palacios on the possible influence of the Muslim eschatological literary tradition on both the structure and numerous details of Dante's poem.[53] It is, in fact, again in relation to the possible influence of an Arabic source that we find what may be considered the first reference in Arabic to Ariosto's work, at least to date. In October 1934, the Egyptian Italianist Ṭāhā Fawzī—a scholar of Dante and translator from Italian, including the first novel to appear in Arabic, *Terra di Cleopatra* by Annie Vivanti (1927), followed by *Cuore* of Edmondo de Amicis, Alessandro Manzoni's *I promessi sposi*, and various others—published a short article on Ariosto in the journal *al-Muqtaṭaf*, in which he raises the issue of the possible influence of the *One Thousand and One Nights* on the *Orlando furioso*. Preceding a general presentation of Ariosto and his work, Fawzī notes the question concerning the *novella* of "Astolfo and Iocondo"—the terms of which he had acquired from contemporary Italian literary criticism and a conference held in Cairo by Luigi Rinaldi—without, however, expressing a personal judgment, but concluding with open praise for the Ferrarese poet: "even admitting that this influence were true, this would not diminish the value of Ariosto's stories which would lose nothing of their beauty, flow, or magnificence, for they are a masterpiece of Italian poetry that has resisted time and will remain eternal."[54]

As far as can be determined, Fawzī's praise has still not led to a translation of the poem into Arabic. To some extent, this is undoubtedly due to the subject of the poem, which would clearly be challenging for a Muslim Arabic audience, but it must also owe something to the enormous structural and linguistic complexity of the work, which apparently has also discouraged Christian translators within the Arabic world who might otherwise have exercised a defiant posture in presenting the work in Arabic, as had been the case with several of the translations of the *Divina commedia*. Presentations of Ariosto's works are, however, beginning to appear in Italian studies programs in various universities throughout the Arabic world, and at least one PhD dissertation that focuses on the relationship between reality and poetic invention in the *Orlando furioso* (and which included the translation of short excerpts into Arabic) was defended at the Ain Shams University in Cairo in 2004.[55] These are still nothing more than first steps, but they may well allow the completion of a journey toward an actual—and not just potential—future contiguity.

4. Conclusions: An Unaccomplished Contiguity

So far—this is the result of this first partial investigation—any contiguity between the *Orlando furioso* and the Arabic language remains unaccomplished, notwithstanding the fact that scattered indications provide opportunities for reflection on the positioning of Ariosto's poem within a wider framework. Probing the temporal period anterior to the composition of the *Orlando furioso* reveals that the movement of themes, narrative fragments, and possibly even individual terms between the Arabic epic-chivalric tradition (or other parallel genres) and that of the *chansons de geste* belongs to a preceding age, especially the eleventh to thirteenth centuries. What we find absorbed into the narrative and linguistic texture of the *Orlando furioso* certainly appears to have been mediated by earlier texts and the progressive formation of a specialized area of the Italian language that included terms derived from Arabic to refer to cultural aspects of the Arabic-Islamic world. New hypotheses regarding the etymology of certain terms, however, especially with reference to onomastics, suggest that these routes of contact should be further pursued in various directions. Exploring Ariosto's own historical moment and his intellectual development, we have seen that there was a certain awareness and knowledge of Arabic language and culture in the circles frequented by the Ferrarese poet and among several of his closest acquaintances, but also that the "degrees of separation" were perhaps sufficient to weaken their force and proximity within Ariosto's own system of cultural references. The suggestive fact remains, nevertheless, that Count Orlando's knowledge of "arabico" (a term that is mentioned only once in the long course of the poem) elicits the poet's admiration in a stanza at the heart of the work that also establishes—specifically through this linguistic mastery—Orlando made "Furioso." Finally, studying the issue of a possible reception of the *Orlando furioso* in Arabic (or, at any rate, in any of the possible contexts of the Arabic-Islamic sphere) reveals that, notwithstanding a few spurious declarations in the Italian debate at the end of the sixteenth century and some slight hints by Arab scholars of the *nahḍa* period, Ariosto's poem has received very little attention in Arabic. Once again, however, recent signals promise that more substantive action may soon be taken.

As suggested by the American Sanskritist Sheldon Pollock in a recent reflection on the renewed mission of philology in the twenty-first century, the profound meaning of a text—and, we might add, perhaps its most complete function—is represented by the sum of three levels of textual reconstruction, reading, and contextualization: that which concerns the genesis of the text itself, that which deals with the interpretation or interpretations of its first readers (and also those of subsequent readers, all the more relevant for texts with complex histories of transmission and reception), and, finally, the level of interpretation by current readers and scholars who question what that text may still represent.[56] This is thus a long-term perspective, over which the assembled evidence documents a slow but patient journey through the continuous evolution of "soundscapes" over a vast geographic area. Given this volume's reflections on the relationship between Ariosto, his masterpiece, the *Orlando furioso*, and Arabic language and culture, a complete translation of the poem into Arabic, whenever it may be accomplished, would allow for the direct and unmediated confirmation of its natural collocation within the literature of the "Mediterranean".[57]

Notes

1. See Grévin 2012. Grévin borrows the expression "paysages sonores" from Fritz 2000.

2. Each of these textual cycles has been the subject of a vast scholarly bibliography, exploring their origins, development, transmission, structure, themes, and motifs. For a general overview, see, e.g., Piemontese 1999b; Casari 2003; Cupane and Krönung 2016, with related bibliographies.

3. Casari 2003, pp. 469–480. The powerful path of these textual cycles intersects in a natural way with the production of related texts of medieval European literature, such as Giovanni Boccaccio's *Decameron* or Geoffrey Chaucer's *Canterbury Tales*. The role of Arab mediation in the formation of other areas of European literature has been emphasized by a significant historiographical thread in the last fifty years; see, e.g., the provocative study Menocal 1987 and its updated reconsideration, Akbari and Mallette 2013.

4. Piemontese 2002b. The sword was latinized as *Caliburnus* in Geoffrey of Monmouth's *Historia regum Britanniae* (early twelfth century), the first author to name the sword in a language different from Welsh.

5. For a general overview of these efforts, see Heller 1931; Grégoire 1942–1943; Heath 1984; Norris 1989; Lyons 1995.

6. On the Arab epic tradition, in addition to the texts mentioned in the previous note, see Heath 1996; Lyons 2001; Herzog 2006; Reynolds 2010. See also the observations offered in the contributions by Thomas Bauer and Dwight Reynolds in this volume.

7. A concise survey of this aspect is in Lyons 2001.

8. See Taylor 1932; Christides 1972; O'Connor 1986.

9. Masʿūdī 1894, p. 182. See also Khalil Samir 1984; Lewis 1986; Di Branco 2009, pp. 107–142; Hermes 2012.

10. See in particular the notes in Norris 1989. See also the other references given here in notes 5–7 above. On the arrival of manuscripts of the *Sīrat ʿAntar* in Europe, see also van den Boogert 2007.

11. See Casanova 1909; Viré 1958; Pellat 1964.

12. Bellamy 1987.

13. Bellamy 1987. On the Oliphant and the question of its origin and etymology, see Shalem 2004, esp. pp. 8–14.

14. See the contribution by Jacopo Gesiot in this volume; see also Pavlova 2020, pp. 43–44.

15. See the outline of the first hypotheses in Rajna 1975, pp. 436–455. See then Marzolph and Chraïbi 2012; Ott 2012; Ott and Benigni 2017; and in particular Ott's contribution in this volume.

16. Rajna 1975, pp. 456–471; Cerulli 1946; Cerulli 1947; Levi della Vida 1959.

17. For an overview of these issues, see Versteegh 2014; Zack and Schippers 2012. See also Grévin 2012.

18. On various aspects of these observations, see the recent specialist and synthetic work (including their bibliographies) of Bresc 2001; Piemontese 2002a; Speer and Wegener 2006; Burman 2007; Pizzorusso 2009; Grévin 2010; Griffith 2013; Grévin and Mandalà 2013; Tommasino 2013; Grévin 2015; Piemontese 2016; Loop, Hamilton, and Burnett 2017; Casari 2018a; Grévin 2019.

19. See Ricci 2002, and Ricci's considerations in his contribution to the present volume; Pavlova 2020, pp. 14–15, 58–65, and Pavlova's notes on this matter in her contribution to this volume.

20. Pico della Mirandola 2012, pp. 109, 201n215. See Piemontese 2012; Piemontese 2016.

21. Piemontese 2016, pp. 39–42, with related bibliography. For an updated assessment of Pico's library, see Murano 2018. See also Murano 2020.

22. Pico della Mirandola 2018, pp. 113–114; see also Piemontese 1996.

23. "Nella nostra religione ci è tre lingue in perfettione, cioè Latina, Greca, Hebraica: et dipoi la Moresca et Caldea anche habbiamo: et credi che non sanza cagione Idio ce l'ha mandate. Sicché vieni adunque ad imparare: vieni et non guardare che il luogo sia strecto, che idio provederà lui. Vieni presto, perché bisognia che tu habbia imparato queste lingue quando sarà venuta la spada": Savonarola 1972, p. 358. See also Piemontese 2002a.

24. Jossa 2019.

25. For a picture of Alberto Pio's life and activities, see Morselli 1931; Ori and Saetti 2015.

26. "Nihil enim tibi deest: non ingenium, quo valde abundans; non eloquentia, qua tu praeditus; non libri nec Latinae nec Grecae neque Hebraicae disciplinae, quos tibi summo studio curaque perquiris; non doctissimi praeceptores, quos tu conductus habes multa pecunia"; see Manuzio 1975, Vol. 2, p. 317.

27. See Piemontese 1999a.

28. See Cavedoni 1854; Di Pietro Lombardi 2004. On Alberto Pio's Roman period, see Minarelli 2015. I wish to thank Stefano Minarelli for the extensive information and bibliography he has given me regarding Alberto Pio.

29. Levi della Vida 1939, pp. 103–108.

30. See Zemon Davis 2006; Pouillon 2009.

31. See Piemontese 2016.

32. See Pavlova 2020, pp. 19–33, with related bibliography.

33. On Ariosto's philosophical and religious interests, see Jossa 2019 and Jossa's contribution to this volume.

34. In another case, the language known by Orlando is called "africano" (*Fur.*, IX 5), a term from the chivalric tradition that along with other expressions such as "saracino," "moresco," and "Soriano" is not present in the *Furioso*. The copresence of these terms could also mirror a stratified perception of the variety of dialects relevant to different geographical origins. On the topic of plurilingual competence and in particular of the knowledge of Arabic by Christian knights in the Italian epic-chivalric tradition and in the *Furioso*, see Jacopo Gesiot's contribution to this volume.

35. On this central episode of the *Furioso*, see Ascoli 1987, pp. 304–331; Shapiro 1988, pp. 123–151.

36. See Lewis 1982; Dakhlia 2008; König 2015; König 2016. For a comparison of similarities and differences between the textual cultures of Latin Europe and medieval Islam, and for an examination of the as yet little studied entangling between Latin and Arabic, see also König 2019, especially part I, with contributions by Grévin and König.

37. See Kraemer 1956; Pormann 2007; Graziosi 2015, pp. 28–36; Cupane and Krönung 2016; Casari 2018b.

38. Penelas 2001.

39. See Minervini 2015; Ammirati 2018; Giannini and Minervini 2020.

40. See Bauer's contribution in this volume.

41. See Robinson 2008 and the entire special issue of *Medieval Encounters* (14, no. 2, 2008) devoted to the paintings in the Alhambra Hall of Justice.

42. See Wacks 2019, esp. pp. 39–58.

43. It also provided the narrative framework for the late Byzantine romance *Erotokritos*, which additionally drew on elements of the *Orlando furioso*; see Goldwyn and Marciniak in this volume. See Lelli in this volume on a Yiddish translation from an Italian version of the text, *Paris e Vienna*.

44. See Galmés de Fuentes 1970.

45. On this topic, see Fabrizio Lelli's contribution in this volume, with related bibliography.

46. Minervini 1993.

47. "Questo a me par gran cosa: che l'Ariosto è pur huomo di tanta fama, non solo in Italia, ma quasi nel mondo tutto, poi che il suo Orlando è stato tradotto in tante lingue, che non solo la Spagnuola, la Francese, e la Tedesca, ma altre, insino all'Arabica (se vero è quel che si dice) è stata vaga di cantarlo, o di ragionarlo": Pellegrino 1584, p. x.

48. Rajna 1975, p. 439 n 2.

49. "Con tutto ciò è stato il Furioso dal suo e nostro parlare nel Francese tradotto: e nello Spagnuolo: et in rima come sta: et in prosa: et in verso Greco: et in iscrittura Tedesca. Et è speranza che se fuor dell'Europa il comporre ha mai da venire in usanza, che gli Arabi anchora et i Turchi se l'habbiano a far famigliare, prima che a cosa altra si pongano": Pigna 1554, p. 69.

50. Pavlova 2014, p. 478.

51. See, e.g., Accademia della Crusca 1584, p. 11v; Oddi 1587, p. 46.

52. See a concise outline in Borruso 2002.

53. See Benigni 2011.

54. Fawzī 1934.

55. Ḥasan 2004.

56. Pollock 2016.

57. See the many suggestions provided in Akbari and Mallette 2013.

Bibliography

Accademia della Crusca 1584

Degli Accademici della Crusca difesa dell'Orlando Furioso dell'Ariosto, contra il Dialogo dell'epica poesia di Camillo Pellegrino: Stacciata prima. Florence: Domenico Manzani Stampator della Crusca, 1584.

Akbari and Mallette 2013

Akbari, Suzanne C., and Karla Mallette, eds. *A Sea of Languages: Rethinking the Arabic Role in Medieval Literary History*. Toronto: University of Toronto Press, 2013.

Ammirati 2018

Ammirati, Serena. "Chrétien de Troyes tra le sabbie d'Egitto: P.Vindob. L 114 (P.Capasso 1)." In Πολυμάθεια. *Studi classici offerti a Mario Capasso*, edited by Paola Davoli and Natascia Pellé, pp. 9–14. Lecce: Pensa MultiMedia, 2018.

Ascoli 1987

Ascoli, Albert R. *Ariosto's Bitter Harmony. Crisis and Evasion in the Italian Renaissance*. Princeton, NJ: Princeton University Press, 1987.

Bellamy 1987

Bellamy, James A. "Arabic Names in the *Chanson de Roland*: Saracen Gods, Frankish Swords, Roland's Horse, and the Olifant." *Journal of the American Oriental Society* 107, no. 2 (1987): pp. 267–277.

Benigni 2011

Benigni, Elisabetta. "La Divina *Commedia* nel mondo arabo: Orientamenti critici e traduzioni." *Critica del Testo* 14, 3 (2011): pp. 391-413.

Borruso 2002
Borruso, Andrea. "La letteratura italiana nei paesi arabi." In Andrea Borruso, *Arabeschi: Saggi di letteratura araba*, pp. 144–158. Milan: Franco Angeli, 2002.
Bresc 2001
Bresc, Henri. *Arabes de langue, juifs de religion: L'évolution du judaïsme sicilien dans l'environnement latin, XIIe–XVe siècles*. Saint-Denis: Bouchène, 2001.
Burman 2007
Burman, Thomas E. *Reading the Qur'ān in Latin Christendom 1140–1560*. Philadelphia: University of Pennsylvania Press, 2007.
Casanova 1909
Casanova, Paul. "Mahom, Jupin, Apollon, Tervagant, dieux des Arabes." In *Mélanges Hartwig Derenbourg (1844–1908)*, pp. 391–395. Paris: Leroux, 1909.
Casari 2003
Casari, Mario. "Percorsi tematici nel viaggio euro-asiatico dei testi." In *Lo spazio letterario del Medioevo 3: Le culture circostanti*, Vol. 2, *La cultura arabo-islamica*, edited by Franco Cardini and Biancamaria Scarcia Amoretti, pp. 459–498. Rome: Salerno, 2003.
Casari 2018a
Casari, Mario. "'This Language Is More Universal Than Any Other': Values of Arabic in Early Modern Italy." In *City, Court, Academy: Language Choice in Early Modern Italy*, edited by Andrea Rizzi and Eva Del Soldato, pp. 173–198. Oxford: Routledge, 2018.
Casari 2018b
Casari, Mario. "Alessandro in area islamica: problemi e prospettive di ricerca." *Rivista degli Studi Orientali* N.S. 91 (2018): pp. 74–99.
Cavedoni 1854
Cavedoni, Celestino. "Notizia letteraria di alcuni codici orientali e greci della R. Biblioteca Estense che già furono di Alberto Pio Principe di Carpi." *Memorie di religione, di morale e di letteratura* 17 (1854): pp. 212–230.
Cerulli 1946
Cerulli, Enrico. "'La conquista persiana di Gerusalemme' ed altre fonti orientali cristiane di un episodio dell'*Orlando Furioso*." *Orientalia* n.s. 15 (1946): pp. 439–481.
Cerulli 1947
Cerulli, Enrico. "Nuovi testi sulla 'conquista persiana di Gerusalemme' come fonte di un episodio dell'*Orlando Furioso*." *Orientalia* n.s. 16 (1947): pp. 377–390.
Christides 1972
Christides, Vassilios. "The Name ΑΡΑΒΕΣ, ΣΑΡΑΚΗΝΟΙ, etc., and Their False Byzantine Etymologies." *Byzantinische Zeitschrift* 65 (1972): pp. 329–333.
Cupane and Krönung 2016
Cupane, Carolina, and Bettina Krönung, eds. *Fictional Storytelling in the Medieval Eastern Mediterranean and Beyond*. Leiden: Brill, 2016.
Dakhlia 2008
Dakhlia, Jocelyne. *Lingua franca: Histoire d'une langue métisse en Méditerranée*. Arles: Actes Sud, 2008.
Di Branco 2009
Di Branco, Marco. *Storie arabe di Greci e di Romani: La Grecia e Roma nella storiografia arabo-islamica medievale*. Pisa: Pisa University Press, 2009.
Di Pietro Lombardi 2004
Di Pietro Lombardi, Paola. "I codici greci e orientali di Alberto III Pio." In *Alberto III e Rodolfo Pio da Carpi collezionisti e mecenati*, edited by Manuela Rossi, pp. 215–227. Udine: Arti Grafiche Friulane, 2004.
Fawzī 1934
Fawzī, Ṭāhā. "Lūdufīk Āryūstū—shāʿir īṭālī ta'aththara bi-*alf Layla wa-layla*." *Al-Muqtaṭaf* 85, no. 2 (October 1934): pp. 223–228.
Fritz 2000
Fritz, Jean-Marie. *Paysages sonores du Moyen Âge: Le versant épistémologique*. Paris: Champion, 2000.
Galmés de Fuentes 1970
Galmés de Fuentes, Alvaro, ed. *Historia de los amores de París y Viana*. Madrid: Gredos, 1970.

Giannini and Minervini 2020
Giannini, Gabriele, and Laura Minervini. "The Old French texts of the Damascus Qubba." In *The Damascus Fragments. Towards a History of the Qubbat al-khazna Corpus of Manuscripts and Documents*, edited by Arianna D'Ottone Rambach, Konrad Hirschler and Ronny Vollandt, pp. 331–361. Beirut: Ergon Verlag, 2020.

Graziosi 2015
Graziosi, Barbara. "On Seeing the Poet: Arabic, Italian and Byzantine Portraits of Homer." *Scandinavian Journal of Byzantine and Modern Greek Studies* 1 (2015): pp. 25–47.

Grégoire 1942–1943
Grégoire, Henri. "The Historical Element in Western and Eastern Epics: Digenis—Sayyid-Battal—Dat-El-Hemma—Antar—'Chanson de Roland.'" *Byzantion* 16, no. 2 (1942–1943): pp. 527–544.

Grévin 2010
Grévin, Benoît. "Connaissance et enseignement de l'Arabe dans l'Italie du XVe siècle: Quelques jalons." In *Maghreb-Italie: des passeurs médiévaux à l'orientalisme moderne (XIIIe-milieu XXe siècle)*, edited by Benoît Grévin, pp. 103–138. Rome: École française de Rome, 2010.

Grévin 2012
Grévin, Benoît. *Le parchemin des cieux: Essai sur le Moyen Âge du langage*. Paris: Seuil, 2012.

Grévin 2015
Grévin, Benoît. "De Damas à Urbino: Les savoirs linguistiques arabes dans l'Italie renaissante (1370–1520)." *Annales: Histoire, Sciences Sociales* 70 (2015): pp. 607–635.

Grévin 2019
Grévin, Benoît. "Between Arabic and Latin in Late Medieval and Renaissance Italy." In *Latin and Arabic: Entangled Histories*, edited by Daniel G. König, pp. 145–177. Heidelberg: Heidelberg University Publishing, 2019.

Grévin and Mandalà 2013
Grévin, Benoît, and Giuseppe Mandalà. "Le rôle des communautés juives siciliennes dans la transmission des savoirs arabes en Italie, XIIIe–XVe siècle." In *La frontière méditerranéenne du XVe au XVIe siècle: Échanges, circulations et affrontements*, edited by Albrecht Fuess and Bernard Heyberger, pp. 283–299. Turnhout: Brepols, 2013.

Griffith 2013
Griffith, Sidney H. *The Bible in Arabic: The Scriptures of the "People of the Book" in the Language of Islam*. Princeton, NJ: Princeton University Press, 2013.

Ḥasan 2004
Ḥasan, ʿAbd al-Fattāḥ. "Malḥama shiʿriyya lil-shāʿir al-īṭālī Aryūstū." PhD diss., Ain Shams University, Cairo, 2004.

Heath 1984
Heath, Peter. "A Critical Review of Modern Scholarship on *Sīrat ʿAntar Ibn Shaddād* and the Popular *Sīra*." *Journal of Arabic Literature* 15 (1984): pp. 19–44.

Heath 1996
Heath, Peter. *The Thirsty Sword: Sirat ʿAntar and the Arabic Popular Epic*. Salt Lake City: University of Utah Press, 1996.

Heller 1931
Heller, Bernhard. *Die Bedeutung des arabischen ʿAntar-Romans für die vergleichende Literaturkunde*. Leipzig: H. Eichblatt, 1931.

Hermes 2012
Hermes, Nizar F. *The [European] Other in Medieval Arabic Literature and Culture: Ninth–Twelfth Century AD*. New York: Palgrave Macmillan, 2012.

Herzog 2006
Herzog, Thomas. *Geschichte und Imaginaire: Entstehung, Überlieferung und Bedeutung der Sirat Baibars in ihrem sozio-politischen Kontext*. Wiesbaden: Harrassowitz, 2006.

Jossa 2019
Jossa, Stefano. "L'*Orlando Furioso* nel suo contesto editoriale." In *"Dreaming Again on Things Already Dreamed": 500 Years of Orlando Furioso (1516–2016)*, edited by Marco Dorigatti and Maria Pavlova, pp. 147–172. Oxford: Peter Lang, 2019.

Khalil Samir 1984
Khalil Samir, Samir. "Quelques notes sur les termes Rūm et Rūmī dans la tradition arabe: Étude de sémantique historique." In *La nozione di "romano" tra cittadinanza e universalità*, pp. 461–478. Naples: Edizioni Scientifiche Italiane, 1984.
König 2015
König, Daniel. *Arabic-Islamic Views of the Latin West*. Oxford: Oxford University Press, 2015.
König 2016
König, Daniel G. "The Unkempt Heritage: On the Role of Latin in the Arabic-Islamic Sphere." *Arabica* 63 (2016): pp. 419–493.
König 2019
König, Daniel G., ed. *Latin and Arabic. Entangled Histories*. Heidelberg: Heidelberg University Publishing, 2019.
Kraemer 1956
Kraemer, Jörg. "Arabische Homerverse." *Zeitschrift der Deutschen Morgenländischen Gesellschaft* 106 (1956): pp. 259–316.
Levi della Vida 1939
Levi della Vida, Giorgio. *Ricerche sulla formazione del più antico fondo di manoscritti orientali della Biblioteca Vaticana*. Vatican City: Biblioteca Apostolica Vaticana, 1939.
Levi della Vida 1959
Levi della Vida, Giorgio. "Fonti orientali dell'Isabella ariostesca." In Giorgio Levi della Vida, *Aneddoti e svaghi arabi e non arabi*, pp. 170–190. Milan: Ricciardi, 1959.
Lewis 1982
Bernard Lewis, *The Muslim Discovery of Europe*. New York: Norton, 1982.
Lewis 1986
Lewis, Bernard. "Ifrandj." In *The Encyclopedia of Islam, New Edition*, edited by Bernard Lewis, Victor Louis Ménage, Charles Pellat, and Joseph Schacht, Vol. 3, pp. 1044–1046. Leiden: Brill, 1986.
Loop, Hamilton, and Burnett 2017
Loop, Jan, Alastair Hamilton, and Charles Burnett, eds. *The Teaching and Learning of Arabic in Early Modern Europe*. Leiden: Brill, 2017.
Lyons 1995
Lyons, Malcolm C. *The Arabian Epic*. 3 vols. Cambridge: Cambridge University Press, 1995.
Lyons 2001
Lyons, Malcolm C. "The Land of War: Europe in the Arab Hero Cycles." In *The Crusades from the Perspective of Byzantium and the Muslim World*, edited by Angeliki E. Laiou and Roy Parviz Mottahedeh, pp. 41–51. Washington, D.C.: Dumbarton Oaks Research Library and Collection, 2001.
Manuzio 1975
Aldo Manuzio Editore: Dediche, prefazioni, note ai testi: Testo latino con traduzione e note, edited by G. Orlandi. 2 vols. Milan: Il Polifilo, 1975.
Marzolph and Chraïbi 2012
Marzolph, Ulrich, and Aboubakr Chraïbi. "The Hundred and One Nights: A Recently Discovered Old Manuscript." *Zeitschrift der Deutschen Morgenländischen Gesellschaft* 162, no. 2 (2012): pp. 299–316.
Masʿūdī 1894
Masʿūdī, Abū al-Ḥasan ʿAlī b. al-Ḥusayn b. ʿAlī, al-. *Kitāb al-tanbīh wa-l-ishrāf*, edited by Michael Jan de Goeje. Leiden: Brill, 1894.
Menocal 1987
Menocal, María Rosa. *The Arabic Role in Medieval Literary History: A Forgotten Heritage*. Philadelphia: University of Pennsylvania Press, 1987.
Minarelli 2015
Minarelli, Stefano. "Alberto III Pio Civis Romanus." In *Alberto Pio da Carpi e l'arte della diplomazia: Le "lettere americane" e altri inediti*, edited by Anna Maria Ori and Luciana Saetti, pp. 257–286. Modena: MC Offset, 2015.
Minervini 1993
Minervini, Laura. "Una versione giudeospagnola dell'*Orlando Furioso*." *Annali di Ca' Foscari* 32, no. 3 (1993): pp. 35–45.

Minervini 2015
Minervini, Laura. "Sui frammenti epici della moschea di Damasco (Fierabras, lasse 106–108, 117–118)." In *Codici, testi, interpretazioni: Studi sull'epica romanza medievale*, edited by Paolo Di Luca and Doriana Piacentino, pp. 93–103. Naples: University Press, 2015.
Morselli 1931
Morselli, A. "Notizie e documenti sulla vita di Alberto Pio." *Memorie storiche e documenti sulla città e sull'antico principato di Carpi* 11 (1931): pp. 51–204.
Murano 2018
Murano, Giovanna. "La biblioteca di Giovanni Pico della Mirandola: Un primo censimento." *Scriptorium* 72 (2018): pp. 213–250.
Murano 2020
Murano, Giovanna. "La collezione arabo-ebraica di Giovanni Pico della Mirandola." *Materia giudaica* 25 (2020): pp. 291–301
Norris 1989
Norris, Harry T. "Arabic Folk Epic and Western *Chanson de Geste*." *Oral Tradition* 4, nos. 1–2 (1989): pp. 125–150.
O'Connor 1986
O'Connor, Michael P. "The Etymology of Saracen in Aramaic and pre-Islamic Contexts." In *The Defence of the Roman and Byzantine East*, edited by Philip Freeman and D. Kennedy, Vol. 2, pp. 603–632. Oxford: BAR, 1986.
Oddi 1587
Oddi, Niccolò degli. *Dialogo di don Nicolo de gli Oddi padouano in difesa di Camillo Pellegrini, contra gli Academici della Crusca*. Venice: Fratelli Guerra, 1587.
Ori and Saetti 2015
Ori, Anna Maria, and Luciana Saetti, eds. *Alberto Pio da Carpi e l'arte della diplomazia: Le "lettere americane" e altri inediti*. Modena: MC Offset, 2015.
Ott 2012
101 Nacht, translated into German, with commentary, by Claudia Ott. Zurich: Manesse, 2012.
Ott and Benigni 2017
Ott, Claudia, and Elisabetta Benigni, eds. *Cento e una notte*, translated by Isabella Amico di Meane. Turin: Einaudi, 2017.
Pavlova 2014
Pavlova, Maria. "Ludovico Ariosto." In *Christian-Muslim Relations: A Bibliographical History*, Vol. 6, *Western Europe, 1500–1600*, edited by David Thomas and John Chesworth, pp. 469–483. Leiden: Brill, 2014.
Pavlova 2020
Pavlova, Maria. *Saracens and Their World in Boiardo and Ariosto*. Cambridge: Legenda, 2020.
Pellat 1964
Pellat, Charles. "Mahom, Tervagan, Apollin." In *Primer Congreso de Estudios Árabes e Islámicos*, pp. 265–269. Madrid: Comité Permanente del Congreso de Estudios Árabes e Islámicos, 1964.
Pellegrino 1584
Pellegrino, Camillo. *Il Carrafa, o vero della epica poesia: Dialogo di Camillo Pellegrino all'illustrissimo Signor Marco Antonio Carrafa*. Florence: Stamperia del Sermartelli, 1584.
Penelas 2001
Penelas, Mayte, ed. *Kitāb Hurūšiyūš (traducción árabe de las historiae adversus paganos de Orosio)*. Madrid: CSIC, 2001.
Pico della Mirandola 2012
Pico della Mirandola, Giovanni. *Oration on the Dignity of Man: A New Translation and Commentary*, translated and with commentary by Francesco Borghesi, Michael Papiro, and Massimo Riva. Cambridge: Cambridge University Press, 2012.
Pico della Mirandola 2018
Pico della Mirandola, Giovanni. *Lettere*, edited by Francesco Borghesi. Florence: Olschki, 2018.
Piemontese 1996
Piemontese, Angelo Michele. "Il corano latino di Ficino e i corani arabi di Pico e Monchates." *Rinascimento*, 2nd series, 36 (1996): pp. 227–273.

Piemontese 1999a

Piemontese, Angelo Michele. "Le iscrizioni arabe nella *Poliphili Hypnerotomachia*." In *Islam and the Italian Renaissance*, edited by Charles Burnett and Anna Contadini, pp. 199–220. London: Warburg Institute, 1999.

Piemontese 1999b

Piemontese, Angelo Michele. "Narrativa medioevale persiana e percorsi librari internazionali." In *Medioevo romanzo e orientale: Il viaggio dei testi*, edited by Antonio Pioletti and Francesca Rizzo Nervo, pp. 1–17. Soveria Mannelli: Rubbettino, 1999.

Piemontese 2002a

Piemontese, Angelo Michele. "Lo studio delle cinque Lingue presso Savonarola e Pico." In *Europa e Islam tra i secoli XIV e XVI: Europe and Islam between 14th and 16th centuries*, edited by Michele Bernardini, Clara Borrelli, Anna Cerbo, and Encarnació Sánchez García, Vol. 1, pp. 179–202. Naples: Istituto Universitario Orientale, 2002.

Piemontese 2002b

Piemontese, Angelo Michele. "Tracce del Romanzo di Artù in testi narrativi persiani." In *Medioevo Romanzo e Orientale: Macrotesti fra Oriente e Occidente*, edited by Antonio Pioletti, pp. 171–184. Soveria Mannelli: Rubbettino, 2002.

Piemontese 2012

Piemontese, Angelo Michele. "Pico, Moncada e Abdala Saracenus nella *Oratio de Hominis Dignitate*." In *Flavio Mitridate Mediatore fra culture nel contesto dell'Ebraismo siciliano del XV secolo*, edited by Mauro Perani and Giacomo Corazzol, pp. 151–171. Palermo: Officina di Studi Medievali, 2012.

Piemontese 2016

Piemontese, Angelo Michele. "Il Corano in Italia umanistica." In *Bibbia e Corano: Edizioni e ricezioni*, edited by Carmela Baffioni, Anna Passioni Dell'Acqua, Rosa Bianca Finazzi, and Emidio Vergani, pp. 31–66. Milan: Biblioteca Ambrosiana-Bulzoni, 2016.

Pigna 1554

Pigna, Giovan Battista. *I romanzi di M. Giovan Battista Pigna, al S. Donno Luigi da Este, vescovo di Ferrara, divisi in tre libri: Ne quali della poesia, e della vita dell'Ariosto con nuovo modo si tratta*. Venice: Bottega d'Erasmo, Vincenzo Valgrisi, 1554.

Pizzorusso 2009

Pizzorusso, Giovanni. "La preparazione linguistica e controversistica dei missionari per l'Oriente islamico: Scuole, testi, insegnanti a Roma e in Italia." In *L'Islam visto da Occidente: Cultura e religione del Seicento europeo di fronte all'Islam*, edited by Bernard Heyberger, Mercedes García-Arenal, Emanuele Colombo, and Paola Vismara, pp. 253–288. Genoa: Marietti, 2009.

Pollock 2016

Pollock, Sheldon. "Philology and Freedom." *Philological Encounters* 1 (2016): pp. 4–30.

Pormann 2007

Pormann, Peter E. "The Arabic Homer: An Untold Story." *Classical and Modern Literature* 27, no. 1 (2007): pp. 27–44.

Pouillon 2009

Pouillon, François, ed. *Léon l'Africain*. Paris: IISMM-Karthala, 2009.

Rajna 1975

Rajna, Pio. *Le fonti dell'*Orlando Furioso*: Ristampa della seconda edizione 1900 accresciuta d'inediti*, edited by Francesco Mazzoni. Florence: Sansoni, 1975.

Reynolds 2010

Reynolds, Dwight F. "Epic and History in the Arabic Tradition." In *Epic and History*, edited by David Konstan and Kurt A. Raaflaub, pp. 392–410. Chichester, UK: Wiley-Blackwell, 2010.

Ricci 2002

Ricci, Giovanni. *Ossessione turca: In una retrovia cristiana dell'Europa moderna*. Bologna: Il Mulino, 2002.

Robinson 2008

Robinson, Cynthia. "Arthur in the Alhambra? Narrative and Nasrid Courtly Self-Fashioning in the Hall of Justice Ceiling Paintings." *Medieval Encounters* 14, no. 2 (2008): pp. 164–198.

Savonarola 1972

Savonarola, Girolamo. *Prediche sopra Amos e Zaccaria, Vol. 3*, edited by Paolo Ghiglieri. Rome: Belardetti, 1972.

Shalem 2004
Shalem, Avinoam. *The Oliphant: Islamic Objects in Historical Context.* Leiden: Brill, 2004.
Shapiro 1988
Shapiro, Marianne. *The Poetics of Ariosto.* Detroit: Wayne State University Press, 1988.
Speer and Wegener 2006
Speer, Andreas, and Lydia Wegener, eds. *Wissen über Grenzen: Arabisches Wissen und lateinisches Mittelalter.* Berlin: De Gruyter, 2006.
Taylor 1932
Taylor, Walt. "The Etymology of 'Saracen.'" *Leeds Studies in English* 1 (1932): pp. 31–35.
Tommasino 2013
Tommasino, Pier Mattia. *L'Alcorano di Macometto: Storia di un libro del Cinquecento europeo.* Bologna: Il Mulino, 2013.
Van den Boogert 2007
Van den Boogert, Maurits H. "ʿAntar Overseas: Arabic Manuscripts in Europe in the Late 18th and Early 19th Century." In *O Ye Gentlemen: Arabic Studies on Science and Literary Culture, in Honour of Remke Kruk,* edited by Arnoud Vrolijk and Jan P. Hogendijk, pp. 339–352. Leiden: Brill, 2007.
Versteegh 2014
Versteegh, Kees. *The Arabic Language.* 2nd ed. Edinburgh: Edinburgh University Press, 2014.
Viré 1958
Viré, F. "A propos de Tervagan, idole des Sarrasins." *Les Cahiers de Tunis* 1, no. 2 (1953): pp. 141–152.
Wacks 2019
Wacks, David A. *Medieval Iberian Crusade Fiction and the Mediterranean World.* Toronto: University of Toronto Press, 2019.
Zack and Schippers 2012
Zack, Liesbeth, and Arie Schippers, eds. *Middle Arabic and Mixed Arabic: Diachrony and Synchrony.* Leiden: Brill, 2012.
Zemon Davis 2006
Zemon Davis, Natalie. *Trickster Travels: A Sixteenth Century Muslim between Worlds.* New York: Hill and Wang, 2006.

Chivalric Plurilingualism as a Motif in Italian Literature: From the Franco-Italian Tradition to Ariosto

Jacopo Gesiot

1. *In Suo Linguaggio*

The theme of mutual intelligibility with speakers of non-European languages emerges rather precociously in Italian chivalric literatures, dating at least as far back as the Franco-Italian tradition, which consists of works chiefly concerned with war and set at the time of Charlemagne, written between the fourteenth and the fifteenth centuries in a literary language that combines Padanian dialects and French. One need only skim through a few of the more notable artifacts of this tradition, including the *Entrée d'Espagne*, the *Geste Francor*, and the *Aquilon de Bavière*, to see how their authors dealt with multilingualism. Among the central polyglot figures of this tradition are its eponymous epic heroes: Roland and Alexander the Great. Roland knows well

> le langaje de Perse e l'Aufricaine,
> la Greçoise, la Hermine e . . . la Suriaine;[1]
> [the Persian and African languages,
> Greek, Armenian, and . . . Syrian;][2]

and Alexander

> entent sens autre latiner,
> qui de trestoz lengatges s'esteit faiz ensegner.[3]
> [(he) understands without an interpreter,
> (Alexander) who had been instructed in each and every language.]

In addition to these literary characters, there were also language professionals, such as the *latinier*—or "interpreter"—cited here,[4] but also spies, as in the case of Torlion, who, in Niccolò da Casola's *Attila*,

Le lengaç tartaresch savoit et çil d'Ongrie,
et de mant autres lengaçes fu . . . fornie.[5]
[Knew the Tartar language and that of Hungary,
And was of many other languages . . . equipped.]

Among the "pagans" of this tradition, linguistic expertise was more limited, but there were nevertheless efforts on the part of various "gentlemen," among them Anachin of Saligoç, *giantil home*, who *un pitit avoit impris le langaje* (had learned a smattering of the languages of the Europeans).[6] The theme of mutual comprehension was not, therefore, taken for granted, just as it had not been ignored in the French epic that coined a series of more general locutions such as *in sua lingua* (in his tongue) and *in suo Latino* (in his Latin), accompanied by a declarative verb;[7] this is evidence of a certain attention to verisimilitude and furnished the shared poetic repertory with a set of clauses found everywhere in both Franco-Italian literature—above all in the fourteenth-century *Entrée d'Espagne*—and the narrative stock of the *canterini*, popular storytellers whose lively performances in town squares were a feature of the High Middle Ages.[8]

It has long been recognized that the epic masterpieces of Luigi Pulci and Matteo Maria Boiardo were nurtured by French/Romance literary practices from the other side the Alps and in the Po Valley, significant traces of which can be found in the inventories of court libraries, particularly those in northern Italy, where the earliest evidence of the Italianized chivalric epic dates from the beginning of the fifteenth century.[9] But it is equally important to recall the influence of oral culture issuing from "below," a dynamic to which the two authors were relatively open, especially Pulci, who attributes the whole of *Morgante* to a significantly reflected popularism, which could not but have appropriated the customs of itinerant entertainers. It is not surprising, then, that expressions such as *in sua lingua* and *in suo linguaggio* (in his language) reappear in crystallized form in *Morgante* and *L'inamoramento de Orlando*,[10] exemplars of the late-fifteenth-century Italian chivalric tradition, composed under the patronage, respectively, of Lorenzo de' Medici and Ercole I d'Este.

Terms such as *africano* (African), *saracino* (Saracen), *moresco* (Moorish), and the *lingua soriana* (Syrian tongue)[11] are often employed in these works, but if the label *saracino* appears rather vague—so much so that here it is used to refer to the entire ethnolinguistic group of "infidels"—the adjectives *africano* and *moresco* usually refer, when they are not merely used for rhyming purposes, to Roman provinces inhabited by Berber peoples, specifically Africa Proconsularis and Mauretania. In other words, they refer to the geographic origins of the core component of Agramante's army.[12] We find even greater precision in *Mambriano*, an epic poem written by Francesco Cieco da Ferrara and published in 1509, where the *alessandrino* (Alexandrian) language is mentioned. Just as Rinaldo and the wizard Carandina are at the point of furtively penetrating the lair of the pirate Arpia, leader of a crew of brigands that infested the entire Aegean Sea and had its base in Chalcedon, the conjurer urges Rinaldo to dissemble:

> Disse a Rinaldo: Io vo' che tu saluti
> la prima guardia in lingua Alessandrina,
> e l'usato idioma alquanto muti,
> perché fra questa turba malandrina
> usano molti geniti, e nutriti
> in Alessandria dal soldan sbanditi.
> —*Mambriano*, XXIV 89, 3–8
> [She said to Rinaldo: I want you to greet the first guard in Alexandrine language, and to rather change the language that you usually use, because among this dishonest rabble many people live who were born and raised in Alexandria, who were banned by the Sultan.]

These verses might be referring to the expulsion from Alexandria in 827 of the followers of Abū Ḥafṣ ʿUmar ibn ʿIsā, Andalusian corsair and conqueror of Crete, by order of the Abbasid caliph al-Maʾmūn.[13] It seems noteworthy, then, that *Mambriano* may possibly be alluding to what was going on in the eastern Mediterranean at roughly the same time as the setting of the Carolingian cycle, but, conjecture aside, it is relevant—and consistent with the tradition—that the part of the interloper is once again played by a polyglot.

2. Multilingualism and Incomprehension

We should at this point take a step backward, to *Morgante* and to the theme of chivalric polyglossy. Its function in this poem appears to go beyond mere convention. In fact, the shift to a new language, when made explicit, rather than bringing about mutual intelligibility, is usually followed by incomprehension on the part of the auditor, which has a comedic effect. This sort of thing became very popular in the following century, particularly within the context of sixteenth-century multilingual comedy, which includes the use of Arabic, for instance, in Gigio Artemio Giancarli's *Zingana*.[14] The multilingualism of characters in sixteenth-century Italian comedy had no realistic objective, serving instead to distinguish the Other in a system of dramatis personae that already prefigured the typecasting of the commedia dell'arte.[15] It is thus hardly surprising that already in Pulci, when the provenance of a character is made explicit through the use of specific linguistic markers, this authorial choice contributes to the delineation of a one-dimensional figure, captive to his incommunicability. Generally, the comic effects of such incomprehension fall on those who represent the minority voice, the Other, as in the case of Gano di Maganza, who by order of Antea—daughter of the sultan—is beaten up by four guards of the princess:

> E fecegli imbottire il giubberello
> da quattro mamalucchi co' bastoni;
> né mai campana sonò sì a Martello
> quanto e' sonavan le percussïoni:
> Guicciardo ne godea, così il fratello.
> Poi che battuto fu, que' compagnoni
> lo rizzon su con ischerno e con beffe,
> dicendo tutti:—Nasserì bizeffe.—
>
> Non intendeva Gan questo linguaggio
> se non che la fanciulla gliel chiarì:
> —I mamalucchi voglion per vantaggio
> per ogni bastonata un nasserì.
> —*Morgante*, XVII 68–69, 1–4
>
> [So she gave orders to four mamelukes dearly to sound their clubs upon his back: never did alarm bell more clearly ring than all those echoing, down-falling blows. Guicciardo and his brother were in bliss; after he was well beaten up, those friends raised him up straight with many a scorning laugh, all saying to him, "*Nasserì bizeffe!*" Gan did not know the meaning of those words; Antea soon translated them for him: "These mameluks desire as their reward one *nasseri* for every blow they give.][16]

Gano's disorientation is made clear by the long succession of Arabic words —*nasserì, bizeffe, mamalucchi*[17]—chosen for their acoustic effect but also to highlight the interlocutors' mutual unintelligibility. Elsewhere in the poem, even the reader is excluded from understanding, in relation to which the narrator presents himself as, at best, an unreliable translator; this leads to a sort of mediated estrangement, as in the following two passages. In the first, Antea, commanding her troops, is again the protagonist of the situation as she elicits the admiration of the foreign knights in the land of Pagania:

E giunti appresso alla gentil pagana,
ognun la salutò con grande onore;
ella rispose in lingua soriana
cose che tutti infiammava nel core;
—*Morgante*, XVI 5, 1–4

[The gentle pagan maiden they approached, and greeted her with mighty reverence. She soon replied to them in Syrian, uttering words that melted all their hearts.][18]

In the second, the scene of action having returned to Europe, we witness the sack of the Muslim city of Saragozza, in Spain, by the troops of Charlemagne:

Eran saliti sopra certe torri,
gridando forte, alcun talacimanno,
come dicessi:—Accorri! Accorri! Accorri!
Aiuta il popol, Macon, mussurmanno!
Ma tutte alfine eran bucce di porri,
ch'ogni cosa n'andava a saccomanno
—*Morgante*, XXVII 242, 1–6

[Now from the top of certain minarets some old muezzins very loudly screamed as if to say, "Come quick! Come quick! Come quick! Help, god Mahound, your faithful Saracens!" But all their words were only wasted breath, for things were seen to fare from bad to worse.][19]

In the first passage, the reader is practically left in the dark, shielded from the seductive words of the *gentil pagana*; in the second extract, the desperation felt by the *talacimanno* (Pers. *dānešmand*)[20]—that is, the muezzin, the Muslim caller to prayer—is only partly translated, as the indefinite adjective *certe* (certain ones) and the term *come se* (as if) cast doubt on the narrator's reliability. As a result, linguistic otherness has the result of making "weak" characters appear ridiculous, all the more so when they are also humiliated, as is the *talacimanno* when his song is compared, elsewhere, to that of a *corbacchione* (crow) (*Morgante*, XIX 179, 4). Just as the unanswered prayers of the *talacimanni* are limited by their cultural auto-referentiality, in the same way, the Saracen princess Meridiana—even if described by the Christians in much more flattering terms—remains equally excluded from the possibility of communication, as demonstrated by the sexual ambitions of the knights who seek to take advantage of her linguistic alterity; at her appearance, in fact, Rinaldo anticipates *in sua lingua* an unscrupulous approach implied by the circumlocution *fare alla francese* (to do as the Frenchmen do):[21]

> Rinaldo, quando vide la donzella,
> tentato fu di farla alla franciosa;
> a Ulivieri in sua lingua favella:
> —Quant'io, non vidi mai più degna cosa!—
> Disse Ulivieri:—È non è in cielo stella
> che aspetto a lei non fusse tenebrosa—
> —*Morgante*, VI 9, 1–6
> [Rinaldo, when he saw the damsel there, wanted to kiss her as all Frenchmen do. He in that language said to Oliver, "Never such beauty have I seen before." And Oliver replied, "Compared to her, the sky's most shining star is dark as night."][22]

3. Levantine Babel and Chivalric Competence

By contrast, the Christian knight is usually capable of avoiding confusion, as we can see, for example, in *L'inamoramento de Orlando* and, ultimately, in *Orlando furioso*. From the examples cited below, it will become clear how at ease Europeans found themselves among the peoples of the Levant in this literature, be it Egypt, as for Grifone and Aquilante, or in the encampment of the invading army of Agramante, as in the case of Orlando:

> Ma Grifone e Aquilante altro camino
> presero insieme, perché eran germani,
> e, sapendo il linguaggio saracino
> securi andarno un tempo tra' Pagani
> —*Inam.*, III ii 40, 1–4
> [Grifon and Aquilant, the brothers, traveled another road together, and since they spoke in Saracen, they safely passed through pagan lands.]

> Tutto cercò l'esercito moresco:
> e ben lo potea far sicuramente,
> avendo indosso l'abito arabesco;
> et aiutollo in questo parimente,
> che sapeva altro idioma che francesco,
> e l'africano tanto avea espedito,
> che parea nato a Tripoli e nutrito.
> —*Fur.*, XIX 5, 2–8

> [He continued his search throughout the Moorish camp; this he could safely do, dressed as he was in Arab costume. He was also aided by the fact that French was not his only tongue: he spoke African with such fluency that he could have passed for a native of Tripoli.]

Leaving aside the fact that the phrase *nato e nutrito* (native) recalls its use, in a similar context, in *Mambriano* (XXIV 89), in both cases, the author highlights the ease with which the paladins walk *sicuri* and *sicuramente* (safely) among the "pagans." Indeed, the confident serenity of the Christians is further highlighted by its implicit comparison to the Eastern milieu of their "pagan" counterparts, itself described as a chaotic hodgepodge, a Babel. In the first case, it is again the warrior princess Antea who describes in hyperbolic terms the solidarity of her troops, while in the second, the census corresponds to the Homeric catalogue, here adapted to the army of Agramante:

> Io ho di tanti paesi e sì strani
> gente, che Anibal non ne menò tante
> quando e' venne alla guerra de' Romani:
> qui son linguaggi di tutto Levante
> sanza intender l'un l'altro, come i cani.
> —*Morgante*, XXIV 73, 1–5
> [So many men from diverse lands have I, not even Hannibal could count on such a number when he came to plunge on Rome: I hear around me every Eastern tongue, which make these men like dogs ignore each other.][23]

> Africa tutta e le sue nazione
> Intorno de Biserta son distese,
> Vari di lingue e stranii di fazone.
> Diversi de le veste e de lo arnese;
> Né se numererebbe a minor pena
> Le stelle in celo o nel lito l'arena.
> —*Inam.*, II xxii 28, 3–8
> [Now all the men of Africa were stretched around Biserta's walls, varied in language, strange of face, so different in their clothes and arms that one could sooner count the stars in heaven or the ocean sands.]

Unsurprisingly, this impression of multilingualism attributed to the "Orient" is firmly rooted in Homeric epic, where the Trojans—precursors, according to many humanists, of numerous different Levantine lineages[24]—are described in these terms in the *Iliad*: "so arose the clamor of the Trojans through the wide army; for they had not all like speech or one language, but their tongues were mixed, and they were men summoned from many lands."[25] Add to this the disgrace of mutual incomprehension among the Eastern peoples, a condition that is seen as making them animal-like (*Sanza intender l'un l'altro, come i cani*) and which, at least according to European medieval thought, the West evolved away from through the adoption of Latin, a language that was both bound by strict rules and unbound from geographic boundaries. Enemy forces, then, bear the mark of beastliness, in the same way that Cicero understood the term when he used it to refer to humanity's prelinguistic past in *De inventione*, a source widely cited between the medieval and Renaissance periods to refer to the inextricable link between *ratio* and *oratio*;[26] the same argument is valid for a famous passage of *De civitate Dei*, in which Augustine explains that "if two men, each ignorant of the other's language, meet and are compelled by some necessity not to pass on but to remain together, then it is easier for dumb animals, even of different kinds, to associate together than for them, though both are human beings."[27] The rather conventional attribution of canine traits to the barbarian and the infidel, a constant in humanist and Renaissance literary propaganda,[28] also depends on the translation of the traditional Homeric epithet into the domain of communication, a step already recognized as such within the context of classical Latin:[29] the *canina eloquentia*, understood in its aggressive sense, came to coincide in the medieval period with perceived barbarism, as demonstrated by the historian Landulphus Senior in his late-eleventh-century *Historia mediolanensis*, which defines the courtiers of the Germanic emperor as *canis palatini* (dogs of court) and then mocks them for their language akin to a *latrato saevissimo* (very wild bark).[30] As for the catalogue of the Moorish army, there is an effort to impose order in the Babel of the "pagans," even though Boiardo does not himself always manage to evade linguistic confusion, as his employment of the term *fazone* (feature)—normally used to describe the polymorphism of plants and animals—demonstrates both in *L'inamoramento* and in Latin texts translated into the vulgar tongue under the supervision of Boiardo.[31]

4. Ariosto's Subversion

Ariosto surrenders in part to the traditional vision of a zoomorphic "pagan" army, to the extent that—as had already been the case in earlier French epics[32]—information originating from within those troops reprises the communication typical of the animal world. Putting aside the case of Orlando, reduced in his madness to a feral state, the only warriors to emit cries, screams, and groans are those of Agramante, compared to a *setolosa frotta* (bristling herd).[33] The excitement of the "pagan" crowd in the face of the summary execution of Brunello authorized by Agramante is emblematic:

> Sopra tutti i rumor, strepiti e gridi,
> di che 'l campo era pien quasi ugualmente,
> Brunel, ch'ora pietade ora sussidi
> domandando venìa, così si sente,
> ch'al suono de' ramarichi e de' stridi
> si fa d'intorno accor tutta la gente.
> —*Fur.*, XXVII 90, 1–6
> [Above the confusion of cries and shouts which pervaded the camp from end to end Brunello could be heard so clearly yelling now for mercy, now for help, that at the sound of his wails and shrieks the whole assembly came running.]

But while apparently reaffirming the conventional tropes, Ariosto reaches beyond them, with altogether more modern results. First, however implicitly, he gives an "ethnographic" slant to canto XXXVIII, wherein he describes the Christian armies from the perspective of King Sobrino:

> Di questi fo più stima e più tema aggio,
> che d'ogni altro lor duca e cavalliero
> che di Lamagna o d'altro stran linguaggio
> sia contra noi per aiutar l'impero.
> —*Fur.*, XXXVIII 58, 3–5
> [I respect and fear them more than any other captain or knight arrived from Germany or other country of foreign speech to confront us in the Empire's cause.]

For the first time, then, we have a reference to polyglossy within Charlemagne's army, traditionally depicted as a cultural monolith. However, it is worth noting that what we see here is not a barbarian's discovery of Western diversity. Rather, as Michel de Montaigne, a great admirer of Ariosto, intuited not long after, we are witnessing the reflection of the European self in the gaze of the Other and its consequent discovery that it, too, is politically and culturally fragmented.[34] In a very short space of time, the land of "Lamagna" (corresponding to a region that is today divided between France, Germany,

Switzerland, and Austria), alongside the other central states, would become the cradle of modern Europe's first schism, which the poet himself actualized for the setting of his *Cinque canti*.[35] Exactly where the border between East and West was thinnest and the Turks' pressure most urgent, the Christian alliance appeared most chaotic. Ariosto had already foretold this when he wrote about Matthias Corvino's campaign to seize control of Bohemia's Hussite kingdom, saying that the *possente re* (powerful king) was waging war *o contra Turchi, o contra Alamanni* (against the Turks, or against the Germans; *Fur.*, XLVI 88, 5–6).

The reference to the Turks refocuses our attention on another factor already noted in Ariosto criticism but here finds further substantiation: that the Abrahamic religions are traditionally in agreement on the value of the revealed and transmitted word, a motif re-presented in reciprocal terms in canto CCCVIII of the *Furioso*, where both Charlemagne and Agramante swear on their respective sacred texts in order to certify their stipulated agreements:

> E similmente con parlar non basso,
> chiamando in testimonio il gran Maumette,
> sul libro ch'in man tiene il suo papasso,
> ciò che detto ha, tutto osservar promette.
> —*Fur.*, XXXVIII 86, 1–4
> [Similarly, calling Mahomet to witness in no uncertain voice, he promised on the book held by his Imam to observe all he had said.]

This gesture of the Muslim king is not a simple literary invention, derived from that of Charlemagne through symmetrical adaptation, but rather it replicates a royal convention also known in the West, as shown by a contemporary of Ariosto's, Marin Sanudo, who reports the oath that Meḥmed II made as part of the peace treaty negotiated with Venice in 1479: *Gram Signor et grande Amirà Soldam Mohammed Bey . . . zuro in Dio creator del cielo et dela terra, et in el gran propheta nostro Moameth et in li 7 musaphi quali tenimo et confessemo nui Musulmani* (Great Lord and Great Emir Soltan Muḥammad Bey . . . swore his faith in God creator of heaven and earth, and in the great prophet our Muḥammad and in the seven books that we Muslims hold and confess).[36] The seven *musaphi* are the seven accepted versions of the Koran (*muṣḥaf*), an element traditionally cited in other analogous formulas transcribed in contemporary Venetian documents.[37] The accreditation of a foreign speech as a universal motive of assurance, despite it being sacred only to the counterparty, is therefore doubly significant—insofar as it is replicated fictionally.

Second, as noted by other scholars, certain fundamental octaves in canto XXIII ironically question whether Orlando's ability to read the language of his rival (in love as in war) is truly an advantage.[38] The paladin stumbles upon a billet-doux written by Medoro, a Moorish foot soldier, inscribed at the entrance to the grotto that had welcomed him and Angelica in their lovemaking. The narrator, following the method of the Byzantine Manuel Chrysoloras, translates the text *ad sensum* (according to its sense)[39]—*Et era ne la nostra tale il senso* (in our [tongue] this is how it reads; *Fur.*, XXIII 107, 8)—and also because Orlando is by this point very close to being driven mad due to his disappointment in love:

> Era scritto in arabico, che 'l conte
> intendea così ben come latino:
> fra molte lingue e molte ch'avea pronte,
> prontissima avea quella il paladino;
> e gli schivò più volte e danni ed onte,
> che si trovò tra il popul saracino:
> ma non si vanti, se già n'ebbe frutto;
> ch'un danno or n'ha, che può scontargli il tutto.
> —*Fur.*, XXIII 110
>
> [It was written in Arabic, which the count knew as well as he knew Latin. He knew many and many a tongue, but Arabic is one with which he was most familiar: his grasp of it had saved him on more than one occasion from injury and insult when he was among the Saracens. But he was not to boast if formerly his knowledge had helped him—the pain it now brought him quite discounted every former advantage.]

Not only is Petrarch's "serene and unlimited" trust in the "transitive and transpositive potential of *eloquentia*" here overturned, but so is the trope of security and mastery that we looked at earlier.[40] For example, the hyperbolic insistence on the adjective *pronto* (ready), with *pronte*, then *prontissime*, recalls—with irony and only a slight semantic shift—a fixed expression, *lingua pronta*, which appears frequently in *Mambriano*, thus calling into question the entire chivalric tradition.[41] As Albert Russel Ascoli rightly notes, Orlando's madness is accompanied by the loss of the faculty of speech—*e ficca gli occhi al cielo e non fa motto* (and he gazed mutely up at the sky; *Fur.*, XXIII 132, 2)—a fundamental property of humanist anthropology.[42] The inversion in the scene is self-evident: while the narrator suggests the rhetorical merit of the Arab Medoro's text (the Petrarchan contamination of its style is now widely recognized),[43] the communicative skills of the Christian knight are reduced to the silence of animals. Through the theme of madness, the one-to-one correspondence of *ratio* and *oratio* is confirmed as an exclusive gift of Western self-representation, whose fragility is negatively demonstrated by the provocative swap with the alternative profile of the foreigner. Here again, the author critiques epic literature's obligatory absolutes; he expresses his skepticism that it is at all possible, in an ethical as well as an intellectual sense, to impose order on a universe that is chaotic and multiform and that is embodied, in this case, by both the Levantine world's otherness and its linguistic plurality.[44]

5. Foreign Words in the *Furioso*

The theme of the written word also encourages us to reflect on the correspondence between the narrator as fictional character and his fictional source, Turpino's chronicle.[45] The fact that the author/narrator is in every way enmeshed in the fictional process has long been firmly established by critics, so it is worth spending some time on a few samples from the poem, showing how Ariosto as hypothetical reader handled foreign words. As may be expected, *Orlando furioso* includes a varied range of manneristic exoticisms, including a series of "technical rhymes" widely attested in preceding chivalric poems, such as the following pairings: *giardino/assassino* (garden/assassin; *Fur.* VI 79, 3–5, Ar. *hashshāshīn*), *inante/amostante* (earlier/caliph; VIII 85, 7–8, Ar. *al-mustakhlaf*), *sbarra/scimitarra* (bar/scimitar; XXVII 58, 7–8, Pers. and Tur. *shamshīr*), *mano /Alcorano* (hand/Koran; XXXVIII 81, 4–6, Ar. *al-Qur'ān*), *basso/papasso* (low/imam; XXXVIII 86, 1–3, Tur. *papas*), *promette/Maumette* ([he] promises/Muḥammad; XXXVIII 86, 2–4), *padrone/giubbone* (master/coat; XLI 19, 1–3, Ar. *jubba*), and *Dite/meschite* (Dis/mosques; XL 33, 4–6, Ar. *masjid*), this last pairing derived from Dante Alighieri,[46] for which there is a variant in canto XVIII, *moschea* (mosque; 55, 4), selected in Italian through a different procedure and employed by Ariosto outside of the rhythmic context.[47] As in the case in question, where the word is alliterated with *Macon/morto* (Mohammed/dead; XVIII 55, 2–3), the reappearance of *talacimanno* (muezzin) is particularly indicative: by contrast with *Morgante* (XXVII 241, 2–4), Ariosto here avoids the facile rhyme *mussurmano* (Muslim) so that it is instead completely assimilated within the poem's phonic tapestry:

> Fur molti che temer che 'l fier Grifone
> sopra le mura avesse preso un salto.
> Non vi sarebbe più confusione,

> s'a Damasco il soldan desse l'assalto.
> Un muover d'arme, un correr di persone,
> e di talacimanni un gridar alto,
> e di tamburi un suon misto e di trombe
> il mondo assorda, e'l ciel par ne rimbombe.
> —*Fur.*, XVIII 7, 3–8
>
> [There were many who were afraid that fierce Grifon had leapt up onto the battlements. There could not have been greater disarray if Damascus were under attack from the Sultan: everywhere arms and men were mustering, muezzin were wailing, the whole place was deafened by the noise of drums and clarions which echoed to the high heavens.]

The word, then, in alliteration with *tamburi*, is also consonant with *salto* leap, *alto* (loud), and *misto* (mixed), as well as the previously discussed rhyming words, making up one single graphic-phonetic category, perhaps like the one identified by Corrado Bologna for rhymes ending in *-ella*.[48] Similar things could be said about *diodarro* (official in medieval Islamic states), from the Arabic-Persian *dawā[t]dār*,[49] which does not appear in the poems sung by the *canterini* but may instead be found, for example, in Leonardo da Vinci's literary writings, which happen to include fictional letters addressed to *Diodario di Soria, locotenente del sacro Soldano di Babilonia*" (Diodario of Syria, lieutenant of the sacred Sultan of Babylon):[50]

> Ne la lizza era entrato Salinterno,
> gran diodarro e maniscalco regio,
> e che di tutto 'l regno avea il governo,
> e di sua mano era guerriero egregio.
> —*Fur.*, XVII 97, 1–4
>
> [But Salintern had entered the lists. He was Lord Great Chamberlain and Master of the Horse to the king, and held sway over the whole kingdom. He was an outstanding champion.]

In this extract, the word *diodarro* is nested within a series of words combining vowels and alveolar trills—*Salinterno* (Salintern), *governo* (administration), and *guerriero* (warrior)—similar to the one the author uses at the poem's outset.[51] Impossible as it is to prove that the use of *diodarro* was a deliberate reference to Leonardo, besides the potential for a meticulously planned coup de théâtre, what matters is the nonchalance with which Ariosto handles foreign words.

Specifically, he does not use them to elicit disharmony with the poem's phonic tapestry, as is the case in *Morgante* or in *Ciriffo calvaneo*, nor are they deployed merely as accessories or superficialities; instead, they reflect the sound fabric of the surrounding verses and give new meaning to the entire octave, removing it from an Apollonian indeterminacy and giving it "diatopic" connotations.

The same attention is evident in the contextual use of other exoticisms: while the Christians are always housed in pavilions, the tents of the "infidels" are also described supposedly as *trabacche* (tents; VII 35, 4; XXXI 53, 8, Ar. *ṭabaqa*); the garments of Saracen warriors, made of cotton, are cruelly pierced by the *fatal Durindana* (fateful Durindana of Orlando; XII 79, 8; 80, 1, Ar. *quṭun*); Carmondo, who confronts Grifone in Damascus in canto XVII, is called *del mar grande almiraglio* (Lord High Admiral of the sea; 99, 4, Ar. *al-amīr*), with great precision and once again betraying the expected rhyme with respect to the traditional title of *amirante* (admiral; seventeen attestations between *Morgante* and *L'inamoramento* but only one within the body of the verse);[52] and finally, the fury of the king of Algiers, Rodomonte, is compared to the *garbino* (libeccio wind; XVIII 11, 3, Ar. *gharbī*), this time a term associated with *Saracino* (Saracen) and, as with the two preceding ones, a hapax in the poem.[53]

To conclude, this essay set out to note the continuity in the Renaissance Italian—and earlier Franco-Italian—literary context of a certain category of stereotypical forms derived from the French tradition and adapted to generically indicate the intrusion of different languages, a rarely balanced but often apposite copresence for marking an ethically oriented communicative inequality, also emphasized through an explicit comic function. The Christian, European part in this equation obviously prevailed in these exchanges, and given the growing impulse and influence of humanist thought, it sought to bring into alignment linguistic and rational propriety, this in contradistinction to the opposing troops, described instead in antithetical and subhuman terms. But Ariosto's perspective reveals itself to be both more open-ended and problematic: beyond the renewal of techniques and conventions that support the poetic enterprise, there emerges a specific critique of human discursive and rational faculties, so as to effect a more general rebalancing (downward) of communicative abilities. Accordingly, by virtue of this trend toward balance, the language of the hypothetical Ariostan narrator allows the voice of the Other to filter through more easily at the lexical level, the latter being chosen on the basis of a more neutral and modern criterion of purely aesthetic character.

Notes

1. Thomas 2007, vv. 11465–11466.

2. Translations are my own, unless otherwise indicated.

3. *Alexandre* 1937, vv. 2279–2280.

4. On the role of *latinier, latimier, latiner*, see Folena 1991, pp. 17–19.

5. Niccolò da Casola 1941, 16, vv. 5152–5153.

6. Raffaele da Verona 1982, 14, 96.

7. See Vörös 2015, p. 208.

8. For some examples, see Thomas 2007, vv. 896, 2930, 10427, 11588, 12949, 14929. In Italian, Andrea da Barberino 1882, p. 237; Gritti and Montagnani 2009, 5.35.6, 15.21.3, 17.9.2, 17.11.6, 17.31.5, 20.39.1; *Ancroia* 1479, 29.162.4, 29.365.6; Durante 1508, 9.56.8. On this recurring mark, see also Tuscano 1974, p. 117n4.

9. On a Mantuan lost translation of *Entrée d'Espagne*, see Dionisotti 1959, pp. 207–211. For library inventories, see Rajna 1873 and Braghirolli, Meyer, and Paris 1880.

10. Pulci 1955 (hereafter *Morgante*), VI 9, 3; XXVI 6, 7; *Inam.*, II xv 31, 6.

11. See, respectively, *Inam.*, II xiv 49, 1; III ii 40, 3; *Morgante*, XXII 4, 8; XVI 5, 3.

12. For this argument, see Cavallo 2013, pp. 85–94.

13. See Vassilios 1984, pp. 83–84; Tredgold 1988, p. 251.

14. See Tommasino 2006.

15. See Paccagnella 1983 and esp. Caniato 2004.

16. Pulci 1988, p. 327.

17. On Pulci's Arabic words, see Cardona 1969; Tavoni 1992, p. 112.

18. Pulci 1988, p. 291.

19. Pulci 1988, p. 721.

20. See GDLI 1961–2002, Vol. 20, p. 688, s.v. *talacimanno.*

21. See Schweickard 2002–2013, Vol. 2, p. 112.

22. Pulci 1988, p. 89.

23. Pulci 1988, p. 554.

24. For this argument, see Meserve 2008, pp. 22–64.

25. Homer 1999, 4.433–436.

26. "For there was a time when men wandered at large in the fields like animals and lived on wild fare." See Cicero 1949, p. 5. On trust in and the exaltation of *oratio* as fundamental to humanism, see Garin 1949, pp. 2–3.

27. Augustine 1957–1972, Vol. 6, p. 149. On Cicero and Augustine, see Rosier-Catach 2015.

28. See Hampton 1998.

29. See Masselli 2011, pp. 106–108, bearing in mind the observation of Donatus in *Eunuchus*, v. 803.

30. Landulphus Senior 1848, pp. 59–60; for commentary, see Cian 1923, Vol. 1, p. 61.

31. *De cocodrillo e in mille altre fazone* (*Inam.*, II x 46, 8) [a crocodile's (form) and thousands more]; *Era il destrier ch'io dico, granatino: / Altra volta descrissi sua fazone* (*Innam.*, II 16 56, 1–2) [The steed that I mean was from Granada: I described its form at another time]; *per poco spacio distanti erano rose di molte fazone* (Apuleius 1518, c. B6) [in closed space there were roses of many different forms].

32. See Vörös 2015, pp. 213–221.

33. *Con qual rumor la setolosa frotta / correr da monti suole o da campagne, / se 'l lupo uscito di nascosa grotta, / o l'orso sceso alle minor montagne, / un tener porco preso abbia talotta, / che con grugnito e gran stridor si lagne; / con tal lo stuol barbarico era mosso / verso il conte, gridando:—Adosso, adosso!—*" (*Fur.*, XII 77) [Imagine the racket made by a herd of pigs running down the hillside or across the fields if a wolf slinking out of a hidden cave, or a bear venturing down from the mountain heights, has just seized a young porker which is grunting and shrieking in terror; such was the noise made by this brutish horde as it surged towards the knight, shouting "Kill! Kill!"]; *Aspro concerto, orribile armonia / d'alte querele, d'ululi e di strida / de la misera gente che peria* (*Fur.*, XIV 134, 1–3) [A ghastly concert of high-pitched shrieks, bellows, and yells arose from the poor wretches perishing]; *L'alto rumor de le sonore trombe, / de' timpani e de' barbari stromenti, / . . . e quel di che più par che 'l ciel rimbombe, / gridi, tumulti, gemiti e lamenti* (*Fur.*, XVI 56, 21–26) [The shrill screech of the sonorous trumpets, the din of drums, and barbarous instruments . . . and the even higher pitched tumult of shrieks, groans, wails]; [Rodomonte and Sacripante] *Venner da le parole alle contese, / ai gridi, alle minaccie, alla battaglia* (*Fur.*, XXVII 78, 1–2) [From words they passed to growls, to shouts, to threats, to blows].

34. On the question of the Other in Montaigne, see Starobinski 1985, pp. 89–137. On Montaigne's "ariostisme," see Balsamo 2008.

35. See Villa 2011, pp. 18–19. On the assimilation of Ottomans to Lutherans, see Formica 2012, pp. 84–85.

36. Sanudo 1989, p. 139.

37. See Pedani 1996, pp. 18–19, esp. n. 45.

38. See, e.g., Sangirardi 2014.

39. For Chrysoloras's teaching, see, in brief, Vasoli 2002, pp. 74–75.

40. See Folena 1991, p. 57: "La fiducia del Petrarca nelle possibilità transitive e traspositive della 'eloquentia' sembra tranquilla e illimitata."

41. *Mambriano*, XVIII 2, 3; XXXV 49, 8; XLV 31, 6.

42. See Ascoli 1987, pp. 311–312.

43. First noted by Bigi 1954, pp. 47–76, then revisited and clarified by Cabani 1990, pp. 44–46.

44. Ariosto pursues "un'etica tendenzialmente flessibile, così come si andava delineando nel pensiero non ancora post-cristiano, ma certamente di forte crisi quanto a ortodossia cattolica, a causa delle sempre più forti spinte riformiste o laiche (come quella di Machiavelli o Guicciardini, oppure, a suo modo, quella di Castiglione)" [an essentially flexible ethics, as it was taking shape in not yet post-Christian thought, but certainly representing a serious crisis in Catholic orthodoxy, due to steadily increasing reformist or secular pressures (such as those of Machiavelli or Guicciardini, or, in its own way, that of Castiglione]; therefore, "vengono interpretate liberamente la tradizione letteraria nonché la morale stereotipata: un testo collocabile nel suo presente, come suggestiva riscrittura se non travestimento di un passato cavalleresco che per molti, alla corte estense, rappresentava ancora uno sfondo culturale praticabile" [literary tradition as well as stereotypical morality comes to be freely interpreted: a text that can be situated in its present moment, as a suggestive rewriting if not quite camouflaging of a chivalrous past that for many, at the Este court, still represented a viable cultural model.] See Casadei 2008, pp. 182–183, 190.

45. See Cabani 1988, pp. 135–136.

46. See, respectively, GDLI, Vol. 1, p. 750, s.v. *assassino*; Vol. 1, p. 430, s.v. *amostante*; Vol. 18, p. 40, s.v. *scimitarra*; Vol. 1, p. 296, s.v. *alcorano*; Vol. 12, p. 513, s.v. *papasso*; Vol. 6, p. 857, s.v. *giubba*; Vol. 10, p. 187, s.v. *meschita*.

47. If *meschita* filters through the Spanish *mezquita*, *moschea* comes from a superimposition of the Arabo-Hispanism with the root *mosc* or *muse* in the sense of *profumo* (fragrance) and *profumato* (fragrant). See GDLI, Vol. 10, p. 986, s.v. *moschea*.

48. See Bologna 1998, pp. 172–175.

49. See GDLI, Vol. 4, p. 500, s.v. *diodarro*.

50. Leonardo da Vinci 1974, pp. 194–199.

51. See Bologna 1998, pp. 155–157.

52. See, respectively, GDLI, Vol. 21, p. 98, s.v. *trabacca*; Vol. 3, p. 920, s.v. *cotone*; Vol. 1, p. 410, s.v. *ammiraglio*; Vol. 1, p. 393, s.v. *amirante*. For the opposition *ammiraglio/amirante*, see Pellegrini 1972, p. 94.

53. GDLI, Vol. 6, p. 587, s.v. *garbino*.

Bibliography

Alexandre 1937
The Medieval French Roman d'Alexandre: Text of the Arsenal and Venice Versions, with introduction and commentary by Milan S. La Du. Princeton, NJ: Princeton University Press, 1937.

Ancroia 1479
Libro della Regina Ancroia. Venice: Filippo di Pietro, 1479.

Andrea da Barberino 1882
Andrea da Barberino. *Storia di Ugone d'Avernia*, edited by Francesco Zambrini. Bologna: Romagnoli, 1882.

Apuleius 1518
Apuleius, Lucius. *Apulegio volgare: Traducto per il Magnifico Conte Mattheo Maria Boiardo*. Venice: Niccolò Zoppino/Vincenzo di Paolo, 1518.

Ascoli 1987
Albert Russel, Ascoli. *Ariosto's Bitter Harmony: Crisis and Evasion in the Italian Renaissance*. Princeton, NJ: Princeton University Press, 1987.

Augustine 1957–1972
Augustine. *The City of God against the Pagans*, translated by George E. McCracken. 7 vols. Cambridge, MA: Harvard University Press, 1957–1972.

Balsamo 2008
Balsamo, Jean. "'Qual l'alto Ægeo . . .': Montaigne et l'essai des poètes italiens." *Italique* 11 (2008): pp. 109–129.

Bigi 1954
Bigi, Emilio. *Dal Petrarca al Leopardi: Studi di stilistica storica*. Milan: Ricciardi, 1954.

Bologna 1998
Bologna, Corrado. *La macchina del "Furioso": Lettura dell'"Orlando" e delle "Satire."* Turin: Einaudi, 1998.

Braghirolli, Meyer, and Paris 1880
Braghirolli, Willelmo, Paul Meyer, and Gaston Paris. "Inventaire des manuscrits en langue française possédés par Francesco Gonzaga I, capitaine de Mantoue mort en 1407." *Romania* 36 (1880): pp. 497–514.

Brucurelli 1521
Brucurelli, Cassio. *La morte del Danese di Cassio da Narni*. Ferrara: Lorenzo Rossi, 1521.

Cabani 1988
Cabani, Maria Cristina. *Le forme del cantare epico-cavalleresco*. Lucca: Pacini Fazzi, 1988.

Cabani 1990
Cabani, Maria Cristina. *Fra omaggio e parodia: Petrarca e petrarchismo nel "Furioso."* Pisa: Nistri-Lischi, 1990.

Caniato 2004
Caniato, Manuela. "Lingua e dialetto come espressione dell'altro nella commedia del Cinquecento." In *Atti del XV Congresso Internazionale A.I.P.I.*, pp. 49–54. Florence: Cesati, 2004.

Cardona 1969
Cardona, Giorgio Raimondo. "L'elemento orientale nel *Morgante* e nel *Ciriffo*." *Lingua nostra* 30 (1969): pp. 95–101.

Casadei 2008
Casadei, Alberto. "Nuove prospettive su Ariosto e sul *Furioso*." *Italianistica* 37, no. 3 (2008): pp. 167–192.

Cavallo 2013
Cavallo, Jo Ann. *The World beyond Europe in the Romance Epics of Boiardo and Ariosto*. Toronto: University of Toronto Press, 2013.

Cian 1923
Cian, Vittorio. *La satira: Storia dei generi letterari italiani*. 2 vols. Milan: Vallardi, 1923.

Cicero 1949
Cicero, *De inventione; De optimo genere oratorum; Topica*, translated by H. B. Hubbell. Cambridge, MA: Harvard University Press, 1949.

Dionisotti 1959
Dionisotti, Carlo. "*Entrée d'Espagne, Spagna, Rotta di Roncisvalle*." In *Studi in onore di Angelo Monteverdi*,

pp. 207–241. Modena: Società Tipografica Editrice Modenese, 1959.
Durante 1508
Durante, Pietro. *Libro chiamato Leandra*. Venice: Penzio, 1508.
Folena 1991
Folena, Gianfranco. *Volgarizzare e tradurre*. Turin: Einaudi, 1991.
Formica 2012
Formica, Marina. *Lo specchio turco: Immagini dell'Altro e riflessi del Sé nella cultura italiana d'età moderna*. Rome: Donzelli Editore, 2012.
Francesco Cieco da Ferrara 1986
Francesco Cieco da Ferrara. *Libro d'arme e d'amore nomato "Mambriano,"* with introduction and notes by Giuseppe Rua. Turin: UTET, 1926.
Garin 1949
Garin, Eugenio. "Introduzione." In *L'educazione umanistica in Italia*, edited by Eugenio Garin. Bari: Laterza, 1949.
GDLI 1961–2002
Grande dizionario della lingua italiana, Salvatore Battaglia. 21 vols. Turin: UTET, 1961–2002.
Gritti and Montagnani 2009
Gritti, Valentina, and Cristina Montagnani, eds. *Spagna ferrarese*. Novara: Interlinea, 2009.
Hampton 1998
Hampton, Timothy. "'Cani Turchi': Rabelais, Erasmo e la retorica dell'alterità." In *La rappresentazione dell'altro nei testi del Rinascimento*, edited by Sergio Zatti, pp. 113–132. Lucca: Pacini Fazzi, 1998.
Homer 1999
Homer. *Iliad*, translated by Augustus T. Murray, revised by William F. Wyatt. 2 vols. Cambridge, MA: Harvard University Press, 1999.
Landulphus Senior 1848
Landulphus Senior. *Landulphi Senioris Historia Mediolanensis*, edited by Ludwig Conrad Bethmann and Wilhelm Wattenbach. In *Monumenta Germaniae Historica Scriptores*, Vol. 8, pp. 32–100. Hannover: Impensis Ro, 1848.
Leonardo da Vinci 1974
Leonardo da Vinci. *Scritti letterari*, edited by Augusto Marinoni. Milan: Rizzoli, 1974.
Masselli 2011
Masselli, Grazia Maria. "Caninam facundia exercere: Forme dell'invettiva nella cultura pagana." *Auctores Nostri* 9 (2011): pp. 105–129.
Meserve 2008
Meserve, Margaret. *Empires of Islam in Renaissance Historical Thought*. Cambridge, MA: Harvard University Press, 2008.
Niccolò da Casola 1941
Niccolò da Casola. *La guerra d'Attila: Poema franco-italiano pubblicato dall'unico manoscritto della R. Biblioteca Estense di Modena*, text, introduction, notes, and glossary by Guido Stendardo. 2 vols. Modena: Società Tipografica Modenese, 1941.
Paccagnella 1983
Paccagnella, Ivano. "Plurilinguismo letterario: Lingue, dialetti, linguaggi." In *Letteratura italiana*, Vol. 2, *Produzione e consumo*, edited by Alberto Asor Rosa, pp. 103–167. Turin: Einaudi, 1983.
Pedani 1996
Pedani, Maria Pia. *La dimora della pace: Considerazioni sulle capitolazioni tra i paesi islamici e l'Europa*. Venice: Cafoscarina, 1996.
Pellegrini 1972
Pellegrini, Giovan Battista. *Gli arabismi nelle lingue neolatine con speciale riguardo all'Italia*. 2 vols. Brescia: Paideia, 1972.
Pulci 1955
Pulci, Luigi. *Morgante*, edited by Franca Ageno. Milan: Ricciardi, 1955.
Pulci 1988
Pulci, Luigi. *Morgante: The Epic Adventures of Orlando and His Giant Friend Morgante*, translated by Joseph Tusiani. Bloomington: Indiana University Press, 1998.

Raffaele da Verona 1982
Raffaele da Verona. *Aquilon de Bavière: Roman franco-italien en prose (1379–1407)*. Edited and with introduction and commentary by Peter Wunderli. Tübingen: Niemeyer, 1982.
Rajna 1873
Rajna, Pio. "Ricordi di codici francesi posseduti dagli Estensi nel secolo XV." *Romania* 5 (1873): pp. 49–58.
Rinaldi 2007
Rinaldi, Rinaldo. "La rete imperfetta di Boiardo." In *Boiardo, Ariosto e i libri di battaglia*, edited by Andrea Canova and Paola Vecchi Galli, pp. 375–384. Novara: Interlinea, 2007.
Rosier-Catach 2015
Rosier-Catach, Irène. "Communauté politique et communauté linguistique." In *La légitimité implicite*, edited by Jean-Philippe Genet, pp. 225–243. Paris: Éditions de la Sorbonne, 2015.
Sangirardi 2014
Sangirardi, Giuseppe. "Trame e genealogie dell'ironia ariostesca." *Italian Studies* 69, no. 2 (2014): pp. 189–203.
Sanudo 1989
Sanudo, Marin il Giovane. *Le vite dei dogi (1474–1494)*, edited by Angela Caracciolo Aricò. 2 vols. Padua: Antenore, 1989.
Schweickard 2002–2013
Schweickard, Wolfgang. *Deonomasticon Italicum: Dizionario storico dei derivati da nomi geografici e da nomi di persona*. 4 vols. Tübingen: Niemeyer, 2002–2013.
Starobinski 1985
Starobinski, Jean. *Montaigne in Motion*, translated by Arthur Goldhammer. Chicago: University of Chicago Press, 1985.
Tavoni 1992
Tavoni, Mirko. *Storia della lingua italiana: Il Quattrocento*. Bologna: Il Mulino, 1992.
Thomas 2007
Thomas, Antoine, ed. *L'Entrée d'Espagne: Chanson de geste franco-italienne*. Anastatic reprint with introduction by Marco Infurna. Florence: Olschki, 2007.
Tommasino 2006
Tommasino, Pier Mattia. "Approfondimenti sull'arabo della *Zingana* di Gigio Artemio Giancarli." *Lingua e Stile* 41, no. 2 (December 2006): pp. 201–228.
Tredgold 1988
Tredgold, Warren. *The Byzantine Revival*. Stanford, CA: Stanford University Press, 1988.
Tuscano 1974
Tuscano, Pasquale, ed. *Cantari inediti umbri e altri testi*. Bergamo: Minerva Italica, 1974.
Vasoli 2002
Vasoli, Cesare. *Le filosofie del Rinascimento*, edited by Paolo Costantino Pissavino. Milan: Mondadori, 2002.
Vassilios 1984
Vassilios, Christides. *The Conquest of Crete by the Arabs (ca. 824), a Turning Point in the Struggle between Byzantium and Islam*. Athens: Akadimia Athinon, 1984.
Villa 2011
Villa, Alessandra. "Variazioni sull'idea di barbarie nell'*Orlando furioso*." *Chroniques italiennes* 19, no. 1 (2011): pp. 1–20.
Vörös 2015
Vörös, Zsófia. "La langue comme outil ou obstacle de communication entre Orient et Occident dans les chansons de geste." In *Byzance et l'Occident II: Tradition, transmission, traduction*, edited by Emese Egedi-Kovács, pp. 203–236. Budapest: Collège Eötvös József ELTE, 2015.

Orlando furioso: The Saracen Perspective

Maria Pavlova

1. The Este and Their Muslim Relatives: History and Fiction

In his *De Ferraria et Atestinis principibus commentariolum* (1556), Giovan Battista Giraldi Cinthio, a conspicuous figure on the literary scene of mid-sixteenth-century Italy and a great admirer of Ariosto,[1] praises Ercole II d'Este (1508–1559) for extending his hospitality to Muslim rulers and their envoys. Ercole, says Giraldi, courteously welcomed the Hafsid sultan Muḥammad Ḥasan, who had been dethroned and blinded by his own son, and, feeling sorry for his plight, "licet barbari, & à religione nostra penitus alieni" (although he was a barbarian and very distant from our religion), had him treated (albeit unsuccessfully) by the best doctors and showered him with gifts.[2] Word of this act of kindness and generosity reached the ears of the future Ottoman sultan Selīm II (who would ascend the throne in 1566, succeeding his father, Süleymān the Magnificent), prompting him to send

> Cassanum Chaus nobilem familiarem suum Corcyrae oriundum cum perhumanis ad eum literis Herculem usque Ferrariam salutatum . . ., cum amplissima praeclarissimae illius in eum voluntatis testificatione, quem nuntium, & large, & benignissime Hercules suscepit, & Regiis muneribus liberaliter ornatum ad Principem, qui eum miserat, remisit, cum summa suae erga illum voluntatis, testificatione.[3]
>
> [Hassan Cavus (from the Turkish word çavuş, meaning "messenger"), his noble servant born in Corfu, to Ferrara with his most affectionate letters to greet Ercole, with most ample proofs of his immense goodwill toward him. Ercole received this ambassador courteously and most kindly and, having generously given him regal gifts, sent him back to the prince who had sent him, with supreme proofs of his goodwill toward him.]

As we see from Giraldi Cinthio's account of these two visits, Italy's most important center of chivalric literature—the home of Boiardo, Ariosto, and

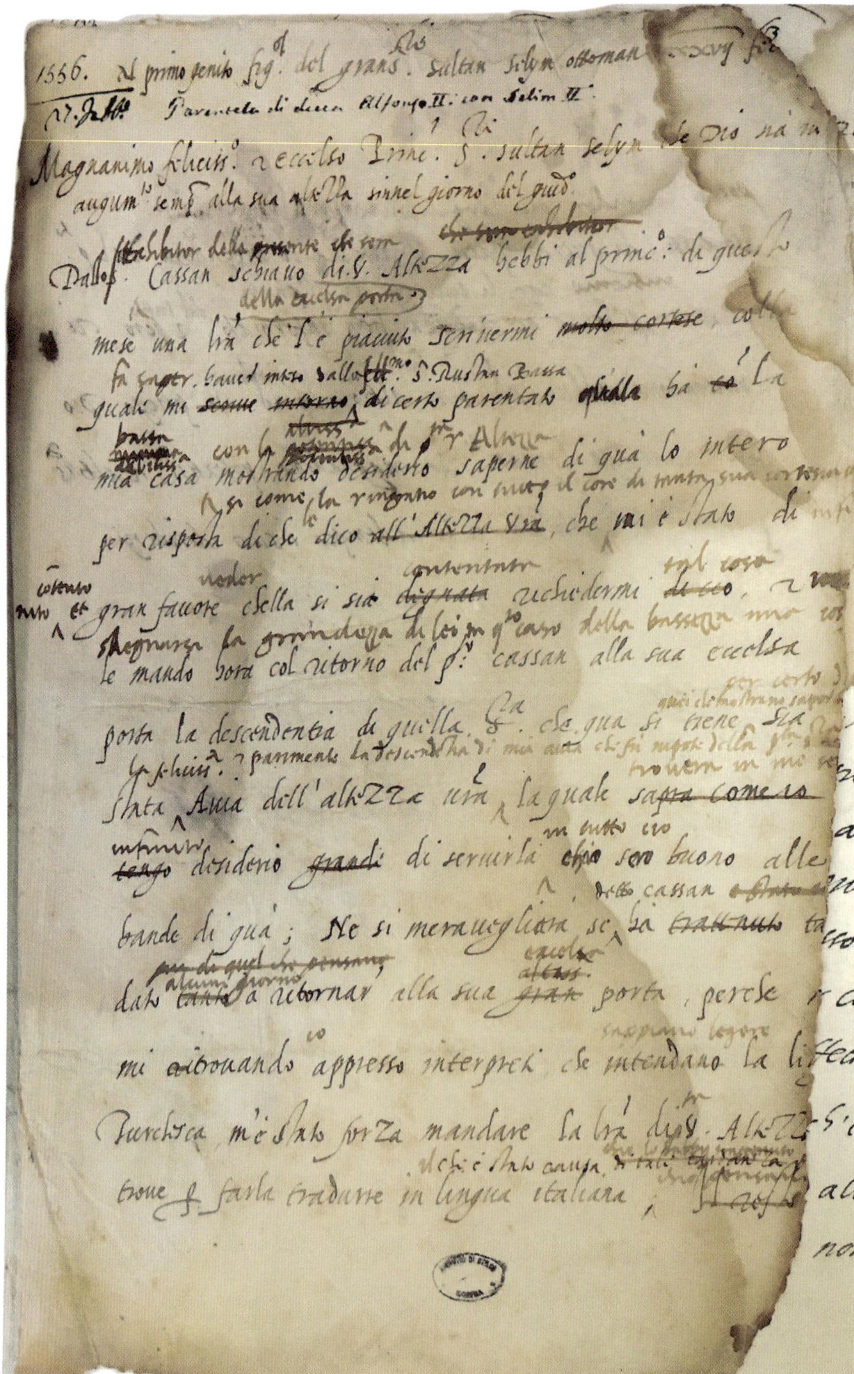

Fig. 1. A draft of Ercole II d'Este's letter to Selīm II, 1556. Modena, Archivio di Stato, Archivio Segreto Estense, Principi Esteri, folder 1644

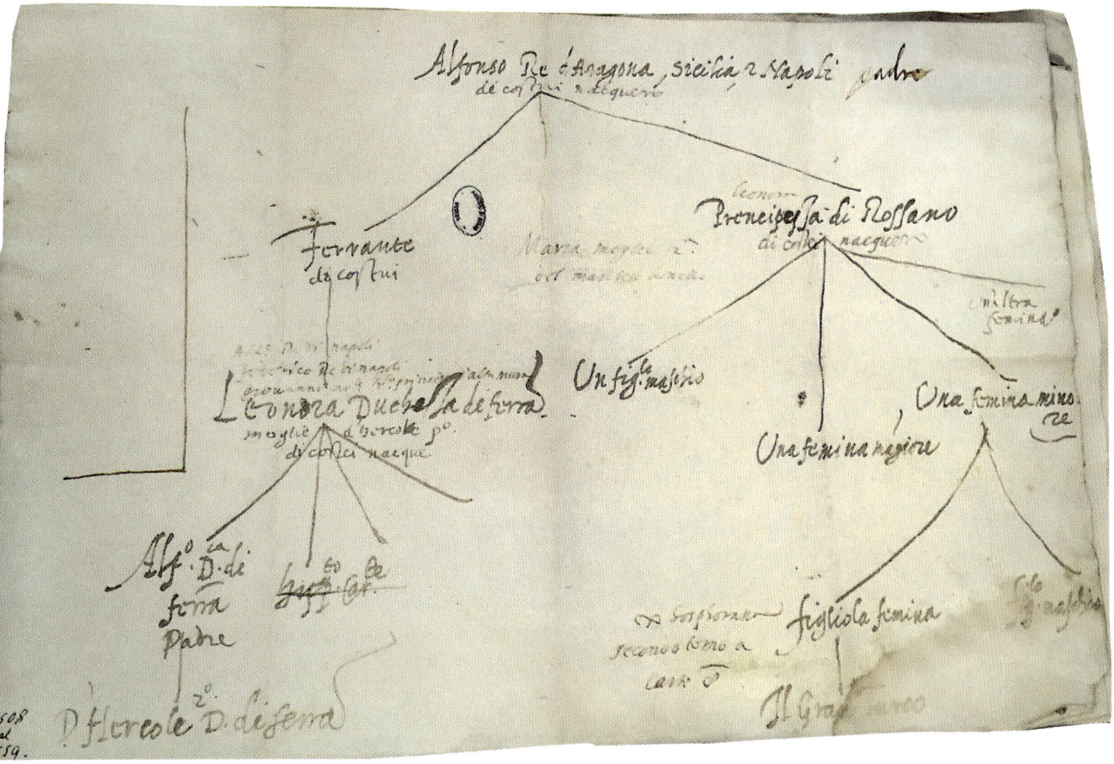

Fig. 2. A sketch of the Este genealogical tree, 1556. Modena, Archivio di Stato, Archivio Segreto Estense, Principi Esteri, folder 1612

later Tasso—opened its doors to Muslim guests, with the descendants of Borso, Ercole I, Cardinal Ippolito I, and Alfonso I d'Este living up to the chivalric ideal of *cortesia* (courtesy).[4] But while Muslim travelers were not a rare sight in Renaissance Italy (suffice it to consider Venice and its dynamic exchanges with the Islamic Mediterranean), the Ferrarese sojourn of Selīm's envoy deserves special attention. The Este Archive contains little-known letters that reveal that this was more than a mere courtesy visit. Having been told by Rüstem Pāşā Opuković (ca. 1500–1561), grand vizier to Sultan Süleymān the Magnificent, that he and the duke of Ferrara were blood relatives, Selīm was eager to find out if there was indeed a blood tie between him and the "Signior di signiori . . . de gran legniazo degnio di nostra parentella nostro Cl.mo Signor di Ferrara" (Lord of lords . . . of noble lineage worthy of our kinship our illustrious Lord of Ferrara).[5] For his part, Ercole II was happy to oblige his Turkish "relative." In his reply, he explained that "la mia bassa, e vilissima casa" (my low, and most humble house) and *la potentissima di Vra Altezza* (the most powerful [house] of your Highness) were related through Selīm's *avia* (grandmother) (fig. 1),[6] as can be gleaned from this sketch of the Este genealogical tree (fig. 2)—where Ariosto's patron Cardinal Ippolito appears next to the *Gran Turco*—and some explanatory comments now preserved therein, this *avia* was a noblewoman who descended from Alfonso I of Naples (the grandfather of Eleonora d'Aragona, wife of Ercole I d'Este, mother of Alfonso I d'Este, and grandmother of Ercole II). She was allegedly kidnapped by the Turks in Schiavonia and then, in a spectacular turn of fortune, became the wife of the Ottoman sultan Selīm I.[7]

This epistolary exchange between Selīm and Ercole II is all the more interesting, considering that the fictional genealogies of the Este family that we find in Boiardo's *Inamoramento de Orlando* and Ariosto's *Orlando furioso* both start with a Saracen ancestor . By the mid-1550s, Ariosto's poem had become a true best seller, with eight editions published in 1556 alone, of which the most influential one, the sumptuous Valgrisi edition, was dedicated to the future Alfonso II d'Este by its editor, Girolamo Ruscelli. Boiardo (who may have been drawing on the encomiastic poem *Borsias* composed by his maternal uncle Tito Vespasiano Strozzi) prophesied that the Saracen knight Rugiero would become the progenitor of the Este dynasty.[8] Ariosto fulfilled this prophecy: the *Furioso* ends with the marriage of Ruggiero (who by then has converted to Christianity) and his Christian bride, Bradamante, a union that would subsequently give rise to the House of Este. Although Ruggiero is not an entirely original character insofar as the topos of the noble Saracen convert to Christianity features rather prominently in preceding chivalric literature,[9] the fact that the dynastic protagonist has a strong Saracen identity is undoubtedly a bold and innovative move. Nor should we overlook the significance of the fact that through Ruggiero, the Este are related to the African king Agramante, Ruggiero's maternal cousin, who declares war on Charlemagne in Boiardo and pays for this with his life in Ariosto. The *Inamoramento* (whose three books contain more than 200 Saracen characters) and the *Furioso* (which features around 140 Saracens, 92 of whom are taken from Boiardo) are poems where Saracens play a central role, where the boundary between Christians and Saracens is remarkably fluid, and the latter's point of view is often foregrounded in original and thought-provoking ways.

In what follows, I give a (necessarily concise) overview of Ariosto's portrayal of his Saracen characters, paying special attention to his engagement with the Saracen world of the *Inamoramento*. My discussion will be divided into two parts, mirroring the opening of the 1532 *Furioso*: "Le donne, i cavalier, l'arme, gli amori" ([I sing] of ladies and knights, of arms and love). I start by considering some of the Saracens involved in the pivotal theme of war, while the second half of my essay is devoted to the Saracens' contribution to the no less important theme of love.[10]

2. Agramante's War

Boiardo's Agramante—a glory-seeking Saracen king introduced at the beginning of Book II, the writing of which in all probability began in the last months of Borso's reign—descends from Alexander the Great, the forebear of the North African dynasty in the *Aspramonte* stories, the Italian *rifacimenti* (remakings) of the twelfth-century *Chanson d'Aspremont*.[11] It has been argued that Boiardo portrays Alexander as a bad ruler whose boundless *aroganza* (*Inam.*, II i 5, 4) brought much suffering to the world.[12] But if calling someone "arrogant" is normally not a compliment, in chivalric works, this term is often free from negative connotations and best translated as "fierce courage."[13] In the context of chivalric romance, wherein warfare is usually romanticized, Alexander is not an aggressor but a chivalrous knight for whom war is an opportunity to show his valor and *cortesia* and who is compassionate to defeated enemies. The beautiful frescoes in Agramante's palace in Biserta that glorify Alexander's military campaigns—recalling a similar cycle of frescoes in the Castle of Noble in the fourteenth-century *Entrée d'Espagne* (vv. 10406–10434) but also the tapestries depicting scenes from Alexander's life that decorated the palaces of Renaissance noblemen, such as those in the great hall of Castel Nuovo in Naples or the magnificent tapestries owned by Cardinal Francesco Gonzaga—present his *guerre* (wars) as dazzling feats of arms, each of them *bela a rriguardare* (beautiful to see; *Inam.*, II i 28, 2). Such a positive portrayal of Alexander is not surprising, given his glowing image in the medieval romance tradition and, most important, the overlooked fact that he was among Borso's personal heroes. Several months after Boiardo had embarked upon the composition of Book II, Borso was buried in a magnificent tomb in the Certosa cemetery, which featured his portrait flanked by Latin epitaphs by Tito Vespasiano Strozzi, Rinaldo Cosa, and Battista Guarino il Vecchio. Cosa's epitaph reads as follows: *Caesar, Alexander, tumulo Traianus in isto / clauduntur, nec treis tenet Urna, sed unum* (Caesar, Alexander, and Trajan are buried / in this tomb, but the Urn contains one body, not three).[14]

Eager to prove himself as a military leader, Boiardo's Agramante launches a military expedition against the Christians. He is driven not by religious hatred but solely by the desire to emulate his legendary ancestor. While this behavior is reckless and, as his older advisers warn him, will lead to his downfall,

Agramante is a sympathetic character inasmuch as he possesses most of the knightly virtues—apart from the very rare quality of prudence—that are celebrated in the *Inamoramento de Orlando*. In light of Boiardo's highly idealized representation of warfare, Agramante's recklessness is, if not forgivable, at least understandable. He takes after his ancient forefather in fearlessness, in humanity, and in *cortesia*, which is not the superficial *cortesia* practiced by some of the Saracen protagonists of the *Aspramonte* but an earnest commitment to this ideal.[15]

Taking up the thread of Agramante's story, Ariosto adds new complexity to the portrayal of the character. His Agramante is no longer a starry-eyed youth who dreams of following in Alexander's footsteps. Ariosto's narrator never mentions the fact that Agramante has descended from Alexander, and Agramante himself does not refer to the Macedonian origins of his family. Moreover, Ariosto introduces the theme of revenge, which, while present in many fifteenth-century chivalric texts, is absent from Agramante's story in Boiardo. As we are told in the very first stanza of the *Furioso*, Agramante has sailed to Europe to avenge the death of his father, Troiano.[16] And yet Ariosto does not turn him into a revenge-craving villain. Nor does he—contrary to what some critics have argued—suppress Agramante's adventurous side.[17]

Ariosto's Agramante is a brave and intrepid warrior. He takes part in the battle of Paris, fearlessly flinging himself into the thick of the fighting, and his excellent martial skills impress Rinaldo, one of the *Furioso*'s most valiant knights:

> Il buon Rinaldo, il quale a porre in terra
> i più dannosi avea sempre riguardo,
> la spada contra il re Agramante afferra,
> che troppo gli parea fiero e gagliardo,
> (facea egli sol più che mille altri guerra);
> e se gli spinse adosso con Baiardo:
> lo fere a un tempo et urta di traverso,
> sì che lui col destrier manda riverso.
> —*Fur.*, XVI 84
> [Good Rinaldo made a point of laying low the most dangerous of the enemy, so he turned his sword against King Agramant, who seemed to him somewhat too fierce and bold: all alone he wrought more damage than a thousand, so the paladin rode at him on Bayard: and struck him a slanting blow which knocked him and his mount onto their backs.]

Undeterred by this fall, Agramante jumps back into the saddle and confronts Zerbino, more or less his equal in terms of physical strength (*Fur.*, XVIII 40, 1–4), which reminds us of the joust at the foot of Mount Carena in *Inam.*, II xvii, 27–29, where Agramante is unhorsed by Rugiero (whom he believes to be Brunello); upset by this defeat, Agramante nevertheless demonstrates the moral courage to praise the winner of the contest.[18] Such an attitude stands in stark contrast to the inability of Agramante's uncle Almonte to accept defeat. This Saracen (anti)hero of the *Aspramonte* stoops to treachery to conceal the fact that he is physically weaker than his Christian adversary Riccieri/Rugieri (the father of Boiardo's and Ariosto's Ru[g]giero).

In the *Furioso*, Agramante is portrayed as an excellent knight, but he is too young and inexperienced to be an effective military leader. To his credit, he values the advice of his African vassal Sobrino and his ally Marsilio, king of Spain—"i duo più antiqui e saggi" (the eldest and wisest; *Fur.*, XXXVIII 37, 8) in the Saracen army—even if he does not always follow through on it. Thus, on Sobrino's suggestion, he decides to put an end to the bloodshed by staging a duel between Ruggiero and a Christian knight chosen by Charlemagne; but alarmed at the half-hearted performance of Ruggiero against Rinaldo (brother of Bradamante and hence Ruggiero's future brother-in-law) and tricked by the sorceress Melissa, who conjures up an apparition of his comrade in arms Rodomonte, Agramante interrupts the duel, which then leads to a crushing defeat of his forces.[19] For Ariosto, Agramante's most reprehensible action is the fact that he orders the bridges over the Rhône to be cut when retreating into Arles after the final debacle, which leads to many of his soldiers being slaughtered by the enemy. Genuinely outraged, the poet condemns this order in no uncertain terms:

> . . . Ah sfortunata plebe,
> che dove del tiranno utile appare,
> sempre è in conto di pecore e di zebe!
> Chi s'affoga nel fiume e chi nel mare,
> chi sanguinose fa di sé le glebe.
> Molti perir, pochi restar prigioni;
> che pochi a farsi taglia erano buoni.
> —*Fur.*, XXXIX 71, 2–8
>
> [Alas, unfortunate populace, where the monarch's needs are at stake, you are always accounted as no better than sheep or goats! Some drown in the river, some in the sea; others stain the earth with their blood. Many were slain, few taken prisoner, few being worth a ransom.]

Ariosto's gaze falls on the anonymous mass of rank-and-file soldiers whose lives have almost no value in the eyes of kings and renowned knights. Lashing out against Agramante, however, Ariosto does not juxtapose his cruelty with the Christians' clemency but rather points out that Charlemagne's troops only spared those Saracens who were capable of paying a ransom.

On their way back home, Agramante's subjects call him *superbo* (arrogant), *crudele* (cruel), and *stolto* (ill advised; *Fur.*, XXXIX 75, 5–6). There is, nevertheless, a fair degree of exaggeration in these taunts, for Agramante is certainly not a bloodthirsty tyrant, and his shortcomings are quite insignificant compared to the cruelty of Saracen kings in other chivalric works.[20] An attentive reading of the closing chapter of Agramante's story reveals that rather than adopting a moralizing posture vis-à-vis the defeated African king, Ariosto celebrates his unflinching courage and his readiness to die for the chivalric ideal of glory that made him declare war on Charlemagne in Boiardo's poem.

It is interesting to compare Agramante's death in the *Furioso* and in Nicolò degli Agostini's *Quinto libro* (1514), an alternative sequel to Boiardo's *Inamoramento*. Both Agostini (who must have been a soldier by profession) and Ariosto register sympathy for the African monarch. In the *Quinto libro*, Agramante is portrayed as both the author of his own downfall and a noble knight who meets his death with the fortitude of a hero, rejecting Rugiero's advice to surrender (*Quinto libro*, VII 31–36).[21] He is a lonely figure thrown into tragic relief: Sobrino retreats to a forest to fight Grifone; Sacripante is killed; Rodomonte, whom Agramante believes to be dead, simply rides away together with Gradasso and Feraguto; and shortly afterward, Mandricardo leaves, too, as he feels no obligation to stay when everyone else has abandoned Agramante.[22] By contrast, Ariosto's Agramante is not alone in his hour of tribulation. Unbeknownst to him, Rodomonte—who had left the Saracen camp following Doralice's betrayal and Agramante's failure to protect his honor but still considers himself his king's *vero amico* (true friend; *Fur.*, XXVII 126)—has decided to wait until Agramante loses his kingdom, to then help him regain it, while Ruggiero has boarded a ship to Africa despite the fact that he had sworn to enter Charlemagne's service should Agramante interrupt his duel with Rinaldo: *Ruggiero ama Agramante, e se si parte / da lui per questo error non lieve stima* (Ruggiero loves Agramante, and if he deserts him over this [i.e., because of the violation of the pact], he deems it no trifling fault; *Fur.*, XL 65, 3–4).[23] When all seems to be lost, the faithful Sobrino stays by Agramante's side and prevents him from killing himself. Not a word of reproach escapes Sobrino's lips; he assumes a mask of optimism even if "dentro di sé Sobrino avverte l'inutilità di ogni iniziativa e l'inevitabilità della catastrofe" (deep down Sobrino acknowledges the pointlessness of any course of action and the inevitability of the catastrophe).[24] The two Saracens are then joined by the king of Sericana, Gradasso, whom Fortuna has brought to the island of Lipadusa (today's Lampedusa) and who is happy to see his ally and friend:

> l'un re con l'altro s'abbracciò all'asciutto;
> ch'erano amici, e poco inanzi furo
> compagni d'arme al Parigino muro.
> —*Fur.*, XL 46, 6–8
> [On dry land, the two kings embraced each other: they were friends, and shortly before this had been comrades in arms under the walls of Paris.]

Gradasso had earlier abandoned Agramante and the other Saracen forces in France after taking possession of Rinaldo's horse Baiardo (*Fur.*, XXXIII 95). The decision to sail home at a time when the Saracens were suffering heavy losses seems at odds with the character that Gradasso had previously displayed. One could say that he temporarily lost his adventurous spirit, forgetting that his quest for Baiardo was but a pretext for showing off his valor. But his willingness to help Agramante as the story is drawing to a close reassures the reader that he is neither a coward nor a traitor and, more important, that he still believes in the values that underpin the notion of chivalry in the *Inamoramento de Orlando*: readiness to embark on adventures, *cortesia*, friendship, and glory. Upon his return, Gradasso brings with him a fresh breeze of optimism, dispelling the clouds of gloom that have gathered around Agramante. His cheerfulness fills Agramante with hope—*ben so ch'in arme ritrovar compagno / di te miglior non si può in tutto il mondo* (I know that I can't find a better comrade in arms than you in the whole wide world; *Fur.*, XL 53, 3–4)—helping the reader to "recover" from the highly distressing description of the Christian conquest of Biserta.[25]

Jo Ann Cavallo has argued that "the systematic degradation of Saracen heroes and the progressive development of the plot towards a holy war narrative" point to Ariosto's complete break with Boiardo.[26] In fact, far from being degraded, Agramante, Gradasso, and Sobrino show great courage in the face of adversity, earning readers' respect and even admiration. On the eve of the battle of Lipadusa, Brandimarte tries to persuade Agramante to convert to Christianity, telling him that if he does so, Orlando will reinstate him as king of Africa, whereupon Agramante delivers one of the most moving speeches of the *Furioso*:

> Ch'io vinca o perda, o debba nel mio regno
> tornare antiquo o sempre starne in bando,
> in mente sua n'ha Dio fatto disegno,
> il qual né io, né tu, né vede Orlando.
> Sia quel che vuol, non potrà ad atto indegno
> di re inchinarmi mai timor nefando.
> S'io fossi certo di morir, vo' morto,
> prima restar, ch'al sangue mio far torto.
> —*Fur.*, XLI 44
>
> [Whether I am to win or lose, whether I am to recover my ancestral kingdom or be forever banished from it—the decision is known to God, whose thoughts neither I nor you nor Orlando can search. Come what may, base terror shall never reduce me to any act unworthy of a king. Were I certain to die, I should sooner die than disparage my own blood.]

Agramante's relationship with God is very different from that of the "conventional" Saracen who threatens and curses Machon in similar situations. In addition, as Vincent Cuccaro points out, "Agramante is not presumptuous as are many paladins, including the newly converted Brandimarte. In the recognition of man's limitations with respect to divine design he is indeed more human and more wise than his counterpart."[27] It is interesting to note that his reply to Brandimarte was applauded by sixteenth-century commentators such as Simon Fornari, Clemente Valvassore, and Lionardo Salviati. According to Fornari, for example,

> In Agramante, che non solamente non accetta la conditione offertagli da Brandimarte, ma contro al lui gravemente se ne accende, et con parole sdegnose, et irate il rimprovera, si dipinge la fortezza dell'animo, che i Re nell'aversa fortuna debbono saldamente mantenere, et più tosto andare alla morte certa, che cosa commettere indegna, et fuori del real decoro.[28]
>
> [In Agramante, who not only refuses to accept the condition offered to him by Brandimarte but lashes out at him, and with disdainful and angry words rebukes him, we see depicted the strength of mind that Kings should firmly maintain in adversity, and rather face a certain death than commit an ignoble action that undermines royal decorum.]

Agramante's final speech echoes the words with which his young cousin Dardinello accepts Rinaldo's challenge to a duel: "Sia quel che vuol, non potrà alcun biasmarme / che mai traligni alla progenie mia" (Whatever the outcome, no one shall ever be able to accuse me of being false to my ancestry; *Fur.*, XVIII 150, 4–5). Although Agramante and Dardinello are enemies of the Christians, they are also Ruggiero's blood relatives, and hence their *sangue* is the same that flows in the veins of Cardinal Ippolito, Alfonso I, and Isabella d'Este, which imparts a special significance to Ariosto's insistence on their familial loyalty. Agramante's conduct in the Lipadusa duel is impeccable: he fights until the bitter end, that is, until the invulnerable Orlando severs his head with the enchanted sword Balisarda, the first of a series of concluding episodes in which Saracens figure prominently that tinge the final cantos of the *Furioso* with melancholy.

3. Saracen Lovers

Saracens are protagonists of the numerous love stories woven into the rich fabric of the *Furioso*. Suffice it to think of the elusive femme fatale Angelica, whose story line is inextricably linked to those of many of the male characters of the poem, from the Christian Orlando to the Saracen Medoro. Saracen characters experience love in different ways and with varying degrees of intensity: Brandimarte, Fiordiligi, Isabella, Lucina, and Norandino are models of marital affection; the surprising union between Angelica and Medoro is open to different interpretations; Ferraù's passion for Angelica is not always convincing, and, if truth be told, neither is Ruggiero's for Bradamante; Sacripante is no longer the idealistic Platonic lover he was in Boiardo; Fiordispina's affair with Ricciardetto has comic overtones, while Fiammetta's story is worthy of Boccaccio; the opportunistic Doralice and Mandricardo inspire mixed feelings; the perfidious Horrigille and the vile Martano earn the readers' contempt. Ariosto uses these Saracen characters to explore the many facets of love and related passions, and he does the same with his Christian lovers. Unlike Boiardo, for whom *"Amor è quel che dà la gloria / e che fa l'homo degno et honorato"* (Love is the source of glory / and what brings worth and honor to a man; *Inam.*, II xviii 3, 1–2), Ariosto does not view love through rose-tinted glasses. He problematizes the relationship between love and chivalry, without, however, adopting a distinctly moralizing tone. If love can potentially lead to madness, some love-induced folly makes one's life more exciting. Like his contemporary Erasmus, Ariosto seems to believe that folly is intrinsic to the human condition and that, in small quantities, it can even be productive of happiness.

In the Old French *chansons de geste* as well as in Italian fifteenth-century chivalric texts, Saracen women usually prefer Christian knights to their coreligionists. Boiardo reverses this traditional pattern, as his Saracens are in general braver and more successful in love than their Christian counterparts. Like Francesco Cieco da Ferrara and Nicolò degli Agostini, Ariosto is much more sympathetic toward Christian male lovers than was Boiardo. Thus, his Isabella gives her heart to Zerbino, while Marsilio's daughter Fiordispina loses her virginity to Ricciardetto. Isabella, of course, has many "sisters" in the earlier chivalric tradition, as late-medieval chivalric romances abound in Saracen ladies who elope with handsome Christian knights, leaving behind their Saracen families. Similarly, Fiordispina's fling with Ricciardetto reminds us of "late Carolingian narratives in which lusty Saracen princesses desire paladins who pass through their land and sometimes have love affairs with them but do not establish lasting, legitimate ties."[29] These two stories of interfaith and cross-cultural love testify to the fact that Ariosto's chivalric models are not limited to the *Inamoramento de Orlando*. And yet Ariosto does not make it easy for Christian men to get the most beautiful Saracen ladies. Angelica, for one, rejects the best Christian champion and instead offers herself as well as her kingdom to an obscure African soldier. The fact that Medoro—*un vilissimo Barbaro* (a barbarian of the lowest sort; *Fur.*, XLII 39, 4) in the eyes of Malagigi and Rinaldo but, at the same time, a gifted poet whose unwavering loyalty to his lord Dardinello is virtually without parallel in the universe of the *Furioso*—weds the most coveted Saracen lady shows that Ariosto's treatment of the love theme is far from conventional. This unexpected twist of fate has puzzled many generations of readers and critics alike, starting with sixteenth-century continuators of the *Furioso*, some of whom were scandalized by such a denouement, not so much because of Medoro's Saracen faith as because of his low birth.[30] While a number of modern critics have seen this marriage as a disgraceful *mésaillance* and hence a punishment for the arrogant, narcissistic Angelica, others have argued that by falling in love with a man who was ready to sacrifice his life for his lord, Angelica gains a "new, more fully human status in desire" that "brings her pleasure when Medoro returns her love."[31] Indeed, Angelica and Medoro—a Saracen couple—are among the relatively few characters who are granted genuine happiness in Ariosto's poem, whose love is free from jealousy or fear. It is true that Angelica's exit from the *Furioso* is both dramatic and comic: she and Medoro briefly meet the mad Orlando on their way to Cathay, and in an attempt to escape from him, the invisible Angelica tumbles down from her horse, which Orlando then rides to death.[32] But it is equally true that Ariosto's irony does not preclude sympathy. Although her story ends on a near-farcical—even carnivalesque—note, Angelica does not suffer a serious humiliation. A fall from a horse is arguably a small price to pay for what promises to be a happy marriage. However one interprets her return to Cathay, there is no doubt that

Ariosto treats his main Saracen heroine with much greater sympathy than does Raffaele Valcieco, a rival continuator of Boiardo, whose Angelica is struck by lightning, buried in a ditch, and forgotten by her worshipers.[33]

Nor are the characters of Isabella and Fiordispina as conventional as they may appear at first glance. Unlike her counterparts in the *chansons de geste* and fifteenth-century chivalric texts, Fiordispina believes, or pretends to believe, that her beloved is a woman whose sex has been changed by virtue of magic water with the full consent of "Machon e . . . tutti i dèi" (Mahomet and all the gods; *Fur.*, XXV 44, 2). She is initially attracted to Bradamante's feminine beauty, and Fiordispina's story is often read, consequently, as an exploration of questions of sexuality and gender. According to Valentina Denzel, the fact that Fiordispina is a Saracen is not devoid of significance. Drawing a parallel between Fiordispina and the Ethiopian man who shamelessly asks Anselmo for sexual favors, Denzel concludes that in the *Furioso*, "le *péché muet* existe surtout dans les pays d'Afrique qui sont loin de l'Europe et dans le cas de Fleurdépine, de la civilisation chrétienne" (the silent sin exists above all in the African lands that are far away from Europe and, in Fiordespina's case, far from Christian civilization).[34] Unlike the ugly Ethiopian's, however, the lovelorn and despairing Fiordespina's impossible same-sex desire for Bradamante is not without precedent in classical and medieval literature. Boiardo's and Ariosto's sources include Ovid's *Metamorphoses* (the story of the love between Iphis and Ianthe in Book IX 666–697), Antonio Pucci's *Reina d'Oriente* (which narrates the marriage between the daughters of the queen of the Orient and the Roman emperor), and Piero da Siena's *Bella Camilla* (where the eponymous heroine ignites the fire of love in the heart of another woman, Cambragia, whom she eventually marries).[35] The "unnatural" yearnings of the female heroines in these texts do not turn them into monsters, and their authors are sympathetic toward them; in each of these stories, one of the two women is turned into a man, and what appears to be an insurmountable obstacle to the lovers' happiness is removed. Ariosto decides not to resort to a deus ex machina but instead to replace Bradamante with her twin, Ricciardetto, leaving the reader to wonder whether Fiordispina understood what had happened or whether she genuinely believed that her beloved had metamorphosed into a man.

Both sixteenth-century and modern critics have analyzed Fiordispina's passionate yet short-lived affair with Ricciardetto in light of the poem's fundamental conflict between Christians and Saracens. Orazio Ariosto suggests that one should not judge the Christian knight too harshly because "l'inganno . . . è fatto à Donna di diversa religione, e nimica, se ben Regina" (the victim of the deceit is a Lady of a different religion and an enemy, even if she is a Queen).[36] According to Cavallo, the fact that this romantic relationship does not lead to marriage means that "the poet seeks to reinforce socially correct national and religious identities."[37] But had Fiordispina converted to Christianity and married Ricciardetto, this would have had repercussions for the ongoing war. Her conversion would have been a severe blow to her father, Marsilio, and his ally, Agramante, who would have perceived such actions as a betrayal. Unwilling to merge the themes of love and war, Ariosto keeps religion and politics out of this episode. Instead, as Giudicetti puts it, the young lovers embody "poesia . . . individuale e divertita" (individualistic and amusing poetry), as they make the most of the opportunities that life throws at them.[38] A similar opinion was expressed by Salviati, who, unlike many other Counter-Reformation critics, did not find this story distasteful: "Era Ricciardetto in età che l'haver fatto altrimenti sarebbe nel poema apparito fallo di sconvenevolezza, sì come anche in Fiordispina, il non aver mostrato di credere à cantafavola sì incredibile . . . sarebbe da molti stata tenuta sciochezza" (Given Ricciardetto's age, had he acted differently, this would have seemed out of place in the poem, and the same is true of Fiordispina, as many would have deemed her stupid had she not pretended to believe such an obvious fabrication).[39]

Although the episode of Fiordispina and Ricciardetto does not have a happy ending, it does not end in tragedy, and the lighthearted tone with which Ricciardetto recounts his adventure prevents us from being too emotionally involved in it. By contrast, it is difficult not to be moved by the story of Isabella. She first notices Zerbino, a Christian knight, at a joust in Baiona, in Galicia. Having set her heart ablaze—*poi che far pruove in campo vidi / miracolose di cavalleria, / fui presa del suo amore* (having seen him perform in the field incredible feats of chivalry I fell in love with him; *Fur.*, XIII 7, 1–3)—Zerbino, too, falls in love with her. The fact that they worship different gods, however, is a serious problem for these star-crossed lovers:

> E perché vieta la diversa fede
> (essendo egli cristiano, io saracina)
> ch'al mio padre per moglie non mi chiede,
> per furto indi levarmi si destina.
> —*Fur.*, XIII 10, 1–4
> [As we are of different faiths (he a Christian, I a Saracen), he cannot ask my father for my hand, but has to resort to abducting me.]

Like many other Saracen ladies in earlier chivalric works, Isabella is smitten by the valor and gallantry of a Christian knight. What sets her apart is the strength of her love. It is not unusual for Saracen ladies to have a pragmatic attitude to love: if they cannot marry their first choice, they marry another Christian man. Not so Isabella. Having endured much suffering before being reunited with Zerbino (the ship on which she sails away from Baiona is caught in a terrible storm; Zerbino's trusted friend attempts to rape her; she is captured by brigands and spends months in a cave waiting to be sold into the sultan's harem), she is presented as a paragon of constancy and faithfulness. When Fortuna deals her the cruelest of all blows and her Zerbino is dying of his wounds before her eyes, she assures him that she is ready to follow him to the other world:

> —Non vi pensate già, mia vita,
> far senza me quest'ultima partita.
>
> Di ciò, cor mio, nessun timor vi tocchi;
> ch'io vo' seguirvi o in cielo o ne lo 'nferno.
> Convien che l'uno e l'altro spirto scocchi,
> insieme vada, insieme stia in eterno.
> —*Fur.*, XXIV 80, 7–8; 81, 1–4
>
> [Do not imagine, my love, that you shall make this last journey without me. / Do not fear, my heart, this will not happen: I mean to follow you, to heaven or to hell. Our two spirits must set forth together, and go together and stay together in eternity.]

Isabella does not kill herself with Zerbino's sword but only because a hermit intervenes and persuades her to turn her thoughts to the Christian God; yet religion does not fill the void that Zerbino's demise has left in her life, and her death is only postponed. It will not be long before she tricks Rodomonte into killing her, thereby rejoining her Christian beloved in the *terzo ciel* (third heaven; *Fur.*, XXIX 30, 3), despite the fact that she has effectively committed suicide and dies without having been baptized.[40] According to Cavallo, Ariosto "refashions the neophyte Isabella as a Christian martyr who prefers death to the violation of her chastity."[41] Yet it is not religion that prompts Isabella to devise a way to end her days but her promise of eternal fidelity to "quel cavallier ch'in braccio spento / l'avea crudele e dispietata sorte" (that knight whom harsh and pitiless fate had allowed to expire in her arms; *Fur.*, XXIX 11, 5–6). It is his name rather than that of Jesus Christ that she utters as her severed head hits the ground:

> Quel [capo] fe' tre balzi; e funne udita chiara
> voce, ch'uscendo nominò Zerbino,
> per cui seguire, ella trovò sì rara
> via di fuggir di man del Saracino.
> —*Fur.*, XXIX 26, 1–4
>
> [Her head bounced thrice: from it a voice could be clearly heard pronouncing the name of Zerbin, to follow whom she had found so novel a way to escape from the Saracen.]

Isabella thus follows Zerbino to the grave. Her death has provoked mixed reactions from critics and readers. While Giraldi Cinthio maintains that it is undeserved (because virtuous characters should not die) and "contra la religion christiana" (against the Christian religion), because Christ does not want such sacrifices from his faithful,[42] feminist critics see in it a "triumph for [her] husband . . ., whose honor remains intact and whose worth is immortalised."[43] Today we may find it difficult to understand the high value Isabella places on her chastity, but it is not surprising that many of Ariosto's first readers deemed her a supreme example of virtue, considering how popular the myth of the Roman Lucretia was throughout the sixteenth century. Ariosto's God is so impressed by the Saracen lady's heroic death as to decree that her name—"il nome inclito e degno" (the praiseworthy, illustrious name; *Fur.*, XXIX 29, 6)—be given to none but the most exceptional members of her sex. If Boiardo had decided that the Saracen Rugiero would be a fitting ancestor for the Este family, Ariosto here not only takes over the dynastic theme introduced by his predecessor, but he also weaves the story of the Saracen Isabella into the encomiastic thread of the *Furioso*, paying homage to Isabella d'Este, who was one of his first and most enthusiastic readers and whose interest in the myth of Lucretia is recorded by Matteo Bandello.[44]

Isabella is not the only Saracen lady who loses the will to live after the tragic loss of her beloved. Fiordiligi (Ariosto's spelling of Fiordelisa) does not long survive her husband, either. She wastes away soon after the death of Brandimarte, who drew his last breath with her name on his lips. Boiardo's Fiordelisa became a very devout Christian after her conversion, with the narrator gently poking fun at her newly acquired religious zeal which manifested itself in long prayers. Bringing her story to a close, Ariosto shows that faith is not enough to help her overcome her despair, pointing perhaps to God's silence within the universe of the *Furioso*. The deaths of Isabella, Fiordiligi, and their beloveds recall and foreshadow those of Orlando and Alda (who dies of a broken heart when she learns of Orlando's death on the battlefield, an episode narrated in the *Chanson de Roland* as well as in the Italian versions of the *Spagna*, which was certainly one of Ariosto's sources), the most famous couple in medieval Carolingian literature.[45] While in the preceding tradition, it is unusual for Saracens—especially Saracen women—to die from emotional pain, in the 1516 *Furioso*, the most powerful manifestations of love—love that overrides the instinct for self-preservation—are to be found in the Saracens Isabella and Fiordiligi. Ariosto's Christian lovers believe themselves to be capable of dying from grief. Ariodante tries to commit suicide by hurling himself from a rock into the sea (*Fur.*, V 57–59; VI 4–6); Bradamante descends into a pit of despair when she suspects that Ruggiero has left her for Marfisa (*Fur.*, XXXII 35–46), as does the knight from the chalice novella when his wife betrays and then rejects him (*Fur.*, XLII 97; XLIII 49), but in actual fact, none of them departs this life.[46] Christians on the whole are more resilient to Fortuna's blows, generally to be seen as a positive quality but one that means their commitment to the crucial ideal of *fides* is not as unwavering as that of some of their Saracen counterparts.[47]

There is much more to the *Furioso* than a celebration of the Christians' glorious victory over Saracen invaders. The chivalric universe Ariosto creates is one of bewildering complexity, wherein characters and events are multifaceted and open to widely varying interpretations. The author himself encourages us not to take anything at face value; as John the Evangelist famously tells Astolfo, "E se tu vuoi ch 'l ver non ti sia ascoso, / tutta al contrario l'istoria converti" (But if you want to know what really happened, invert the entire story; *Fur.*, XXXV 27, 5–6). Ariosto's Agramante is thus both an enemy and a blood relative of Ruggiero and the Este, an inexperienced *condottiero* whose mistakes cause his downfall, and a valiant knight with a noble heart. This ambivalence in the representation of Agramante and other Saracen warriors can perhaps be partly explained by the context of the Italian Wars in which alliances were easily formed and broken and political relationships were in a state of considerable flux. Suffice it to mention that Francesco II Gonzaga of Mantua, Isabella's husband and an admirer of Ariosto (who is praised in the *Furioso* and who had already in 1512 asked the poet to send him the manuscript of his work), was appointed Gonfaloniere of the Church and captain of the Venetian army in 1510, thus allying himself with the traditional enemies of Ferrara.

The *Furioso* is not a dogmatic or propagandistic work, underpinned by a sharp dichotomy between good and evil. Rather, it is at once an entertaining *comédie humaine* and a profound study of human nature, an experimental space in which chivalry and related concepts are explored and scrutinized within a perspective that collapses the temporal and political coordinates between what we consider "medieval" and "early modern." Ariosto uses his Saracen characters to provide multiple perspectives on issues such as honor, *fides* and love, as well as to probe a number of themes—among which are death, defeat, and betrayal—that are merely hinted at in Boiardo's *Inamoramento* but come to the fore in the last third of the *Furioso*. Boiardo romanticizes war and offers a remarkably positive portrayal of Saracen chivalry. Ariosto distances himself from his predecessor's romantic worldview without rejecting it completely. He neither idealizes his Saracens nor degrades them, and he episodically portrays them as more idealistic than their Christian counterparts. The deaths of many of the Saracen protagonists that punctuate the last cantos of the poem leave the reader with a deep sense of loss and grief.

Notes

1. Some of the arguments set forth in this essay are developed in greater detail in Pavlova 2020.

Giraldi's manuscript notes on the *Furioso* have been recently published by Marco Dorigatti and Carla Molinari; see Giraldi Cinthio 2018.

2. Giraldi Cinthio 1556, p. 77*r*. Lodovico Domenichi's Italian translation of Giraldi's *Commentariolum* was published in the same year. The English translations of passages from *Commentariolum* and other Latin and Italian texts are my own unless otherwise stated.

3. Giraldi Cinthio 1556, p. 77*r*.

4. On Muḥammad Ḥasan's stay in Ferrara in March 1548, see Ricci 2008, p. 156.

5. Selīm 1555. I am citing from an Italian translation of Selīm's letter completed on Ercole's request. The Turkish original was published in Vitelli 1994, pp. 333–334. I intend to return to these letters in a separate study.

6. Este 1556.

7. Ercole seems to be referring to Ḥafṣa Khātūn, wife of Selīm I and mother of Süleymān the Magnificent, whose origins are shrouded in mystery and who died in 1534. Some historians believe that she was a Christian convert to Islam.

8. In Books II, III, IV, and VII of Strozzi's *Borsias*, Borso is referred to as "Rugerius heros" or "Rugeria stirps," while in Book VI, 240–550, Strozzi gives an account of Ruggero's life that resembles Boiardo's story (Strozzi 1977). On Boiardo's possible dependence on Strozzi, see Tissoni Benvenuti 1996, pp. 75–82.

9. One of the better-known examples of such converts is Guidon Selvaggio, who, like Ruggiero, is born of a Christian father and a Saracen mother. This character features in the very popular fifteenth-century poem *Ancroia* (first printed in 1479) as well as in the *Innamoramento de Guidon Salvaggio* (whose first extant edition was published in 1516 but which may have been composed much earlier). Absent from the *Inamoramento de Orlando*, Guidone appears in its famous sequel.

10. Apart from my monograph, the only book-length study of Saracens in Boiardo and Ariosto is Cavallo 2013. For a list of articles and book chapters on (or touching upon) Ariosto's Saracens, see Pavlova 2014.

11. Written around 1190, on the eve of the Third Crusade, the *Chanson d'Aspremont* narrates the story of the African king Agoulant's and his son Eaumont's disastrous attempt to invade Christian Europe. This

chanson de geste gave rise to at least four Italian versions, including Andrea da Barberino's prose adaptation and the anonymous fifteenth-century poem in *ottava rima* whose first extant edition was published in Florence around 1490. On Boiardo's engagement with the *Aspramonte* tradition, see Franceschetti 1970; Tissoni Benvenuti 1992, p. 291; Tissoni Benvenuti 1996, pp. 69–72; and Pavlova 2018a, pp. 193–199. On the composition of the *Inamoramento de Orlando*, see Tissoni Benvenuti 1996; Zanato 2015, pp. 145–161.

12. Cavallo 2004, pp. 34–44; Cavallo 2013, pp. 87–88; Favaro 2017, pp. 34–36.

13. Chivalric authors, including Boiardo, use it in descriptions of battles or duels. Ranaldo, for example, attacks the Saracens *con molta arroganza* (very boldly; *Inam.*, I iv 45, 6), and Orlando, too, shows *molta arroganza* (much pluck; *Inam.*, I xxiv 56, 6) on the battlefield. Among many other examples of *arroganza* used in a positive sense, at the opening canto of the *Spagna ferrarese*, King Salamone enthusiastically supports Charlemagne's decision to declare war on the Spanish Saracens, saying that he will follow Orlando *con la mia gente. // Otto milia Breton soto mia insegnia, / giente ardita, piena d'arogança, / che di combatar nium no ne sdegnia* (with my people. // Eight thousand Bretons under my banner, / audacious people, full of boldness, / all of them most eager to fight; *Spagna ferrarese*, I 11, 8–12, 1–3).

14. Guarini 1621, p. 166.

15. Agramante is a much more tolerant and compassionate ruler than Xerxes in Herodotus's *Histories*, which Boiardo translated into Italian and which, as Michael Murrin (1994, pp. 57–68) and Jo Ann Cavallo (2013, p. 88) suggest, could have been one of the sources for Book II of the *Inamoramento*. Xerxes conforms to the Western stereotype of the Eastern despot: following the destruction in a violent storm of a bridge that he had commanded be built over the Hellespont, he has its engineers decapitated and imposes a whipping on the offending sea; and he has a young man sundered into two parts because the youth's father had asked him to exempt his son from military service (Herodotus, *Histories*, Book VII). By contrast, Agramante exercises his power with compassion and wants to be loved rather than feared by his subjects.

16. On Troiano's death, see Pavlova 2013, pp. 142–143. The theme of revenge that emerges in the opening stanza of the *Furioso* is later mirrored in Marfisa's oath to avenge the murder of her father, Ruggiero II of Risa, by killing Agramante, the son of the murderer (*Fur.*, XXXVI 76–78). Like Agramante, she fails to complete her quest for revenge.

17. According to Mario Santoro, for example, "la sua iniziativa viene spogliata di quella brama inesausta e inesauribile di gloria, di avventura e di guerra, e ancorata ad un motivo personale di vendetta" (his venture is stripped of that insatiable and inexhaustible thirst for glory, adventure, and war, and linked to a personal motive of revenge; Santoro 1989, p. 28).

18. Agramante's martial valor did not go unnoticed by sixteenth-century critics: in his *Argomento* (Argument) to canto XVI in the 1556 Valgrisi edition, Girolamo Ruscelli states: "In Carlo . . . et in Agramante s'ha un rarissimo essempio di due valorosissimi Re, l'uno in combattere, l'altro in valorosamente difendere una Città" (In Charlemagne and in Agramante we see an extremely rare example of two most valorous kings, one of them fighting and the other one valorously defending a city; Ariosto 1556, p. 159).

19. We should not be too quick to condemn Agramante, for he is not the only character to violate the chivalric code in this episode, as Giovanna Rizzarelli observes: "L'intervento della magia sovverte ogni logica interna allo scontro codificato e soprattutto rende difficile capire chi non abbia rispettato le regole, se realmente Agramante o i suoi avversari per i quali Melissa è intervenuta" (The action of magic subverts the internal logic of codified conflict and above all makes it difficult to understand who had not respected the rules, if it was indeed Agramante or rather his enemies on whose behalf Melissa intervened; Rizzarelli 2009, pp. 92–93).

20. On one occasion, Cieco's Mambriano has his own men impaled (*Mambriano*, XIV, 85–86), while crucifixion is practiced in the kingdom of Fierabraccia's father in the *Cantari di Fierabraccia e Ulivieri.*

21. On this episode, see Pavlova 2018b, pp. 37–39.

22. See Agostini, *Quinto libro*, IV 57–96; VII 28–41. Similarly, Cieco's Mambriano has no shoulder to lean on following his final catastrophic defeat. After the Christians have routed his troops and his Saracen friends have surrendered to the victors, Mambriano flees into a forest in a state of total despair: *E sospirando dicea: Poco avante / mi trovai signor di tanta gente, / . . . / e ora non ho meco un vil sargente / che m'accompagni, io non ho pur un fante, / io non ho un paggio, ahi misero dolente!* (And, sighing, he was saying: "Not long ago / I ruled over so many people, / and now I don't have a lowly menial / with me, I don't have a soldier, / I don't have a page, oh wretched me!"; *Mambriano*, XXIV 31, 1–6).

23. I have examined Rodomonte's and Ruggiero's stories in Pavlova 2013.

24. Dorigatti 2010, p. 411.

25. According to Girolamo Ruscelli's *Argomento* to canto LX in the already mentioned Valgrisi 1556 edition of the *Furioso*, "In Agramante s'ha l'essempio d'un continuatamente forte, saggio, et valoroso Signore. In Sobrino d'un sapientissimo et amorevolissimo consigliere. In Gradasso d'un sincerissimo amico, et fermo, et stabile in ogni fortuna" (In Agramante we see an example of a continually strong, wise and valiant Lord. In Sobrino we see the wisest and most affectionate adviser. In Gradasso a most sincere friend, reliable, and stable regardless of the situation; Ariosto 1556, p. 447).

26. Cavallo 2013, p. 204.

27. Cuccaro 1981, p. 146.

28. Fornari 1549, p. 666. See also Valvassori's allegory to this canto: "Nel rè Agramante, che non volle ritornare nel perduto stato, offertogli sotto conditione, laquale gli pareva essere contro l'honor suo, si mostra che gli animi forti sempre sono a se stessi simili, se bene si veggono caduti in estrema fortuna" (In King Agramante, who did not wish to return to the forlorn state, which had been offered to him with the condition that he deemed to be contrary to his honor, one sees that strong minds always remain true to themselves, even when they have fallen into extreme misfortune; Ariosto 1553, f. 200*r*); and Salviati's *Infarinato secondo*: "Puossi sentir parlar più magnanimo, più reale, più eroico, e più accompagnante il decoro della persona, che quel d'Agramante a Brandimarte" (One cannot find a more magnanimous, more regal, more heroic, and more decorous speech than Agramante's to Brandimarte; Salviati 1588, p. 188).

29. Cavallo 2013, p. 133.

30. Surveying sixteenth-century sequels to the *Furioso*, Riccardo Bruscagli shows that Ariosto's continuators found it hard to accept that Medoro did not have an illustrious family tree, and they either portrayed him negatively, as a vulgar parvenu, or made him discover his royal origins; see Bruscagli 2003, pp. 75-101.

31. Shemek 1989, p. 136. Similarly, Mario Santoro (1983, pp. 72–81) and Ita Mac Carthy (2007, pp. 63–69) argue that Medoro is worthy of Angelica's affections. For a contrasting interpretation, see Wiggins 1986, pp. 180–182; Finucci 1992, pp. 109–144.

32. Angelica's final encounter with Orlando appears to have inspired the first known pictorial representation of a scene from Ariosto' poem, by Dosso Dossi ca. 1516; see Dorigatti 2018, pp. 25–26.

33. On Valcieco's Angelica, see Carocci 2016, p. 6.

34. Denzel 2016, p. 219.

35. For a detailed analysis of Ariosto's sources, see Denzel 2016, pp. 167–257; Strologo 2019.

36. Ariosto 1585, f. O 5*r*–5*v*.

37. Cavallo 2013, p. 133.

38. Giudicetti 2010, p. 49.

39. Salviati 1585, f. C 8*r*–*v*.

40. Isabella is admitted to heaven—which, as Emilio Bigi points out in his note to the stanza in question, is strongly reminiscent of the Platonic heaven—even if she is formally a Saracen at the time of her death (Ariosto 2012, pp. 967-968). The fact that she dies unbaptized is often overlooked by modern critics, but this circumstance did not escape Giraldi Cinthio's attention (Giraldi Cinthio 2018, p. 61).

41. Cavallo 2013, p. 135.

42. Giraldi Cinthio 2018, pp. 60–61.

43. Mac Carthy 2007, p. 107.

44. One of Bandello's novellas (*Novelle*, II 21) is devoted to Lucretia's suicide, and the story's setting is Isabella d'Este's palace near Mantua. Isabella asks Bandello to read Livy's account of Tarquin's rape of Lucretia, which gives rise to a heated discussion among Isabella's courtiers as to whether Lucretia was virtuous or insane; Baldassare Castiglione then retells her story, explaining why she should be admired rather than criticized. An early draft of Castiglione's *Cortegiano* contained a story of a Christian girl who tricked her Turkish captor into chopping off her head by persuading him that she could prepare a potion that would make him invulnerable. According to Maria Cristina Cabani, this story (which does not feature in the published 1528 version of the text) may well be one of Ariosto's sources for the episode of Isabella's death; see Cabani 2016, p. 161.

45. See Monteverdi 1961, who, however, points out that Brandimarte dies with the name of his beloved on his lips, while "quando Orlando si sente morire . . . il ricordo di Alda nella sua memoria non torna" (when Orlando feels his death approaching . . . he does not remember Alda; p. 408).

46. In the 1532 *Furioso*, Isabella's and Fiordiligi's example is followed by the Christian Drusilla. However, Ariosto also adds the character of Olimpia, a Christian lady who survives the death of her family and the betrayal of her lover, Bireno (for whom she sacrificed everything she had), marrying another man and rebuilding her life.

47. In the preceding Italian chivalric tradition, there is no shortage of examples of Saracen ladies who remarry after the deaths of their husbands. In the *Altobello* (a poem probably composed in Venice in the 1460s, which was printed at least seven times by the end of the fifteenth century), Anzilella marries Otonelo after Altobello's death, and her new husband adopts her son, Persiano. In the *Persiano* (first printed in 1483), her second husband dies, and although she is saddened by the loss, she does not die with him. One notable exception is the Saracen princess Duxelina in the *Falconetto* (1483), who, like Alda learning of Roland's death in the *Chanson de Roland*, drops dead when she discovers that Rolando has killed her beloved.

Bibliography

Ariosto 1553

Ariosto, Ludovico. *Orlando furioso ornato di nove figure & allegorie in ciascun canto*. Venice: Giovanni Andrea Valvassore, 1553.

Ariosto 1556

Ariosto, Ludovico. *Orlando furioso, tutto ricorretto, et di nuove figure adornato*. Venice: Vincenzo Valgrisi, 1556.

Ariosto 1585

Ariosto, Orazio. *Difese dell'Orlando furioso dell'Ariosto*. In *Apologia del Sig. Torquato Tasso in difesa della sua Gierusalemme liberata*, ff. N 3*r*–P 2*v*. Ferrara: Giulio Cesare Cagnacini, 1585.

Ariosto 2012

Ariosto, Ludovico. *Orlando furioso*, with introduction and commentary by Emilio Bigi, edited by Cristina Zampese. Milan: Rizzoli, 2012.

Bruscagli 2003

Bruscagli, Riccardo. "Medoro riconosciuto." In Riccardo Bruscagli, *Studi cavallereschi*, pp. 75–101. Florence: Società Editrice Fiorentina, 2003.

Cabani 2016

Cabani, Maria Cristina. "Ariosto e Castiglione." In Maria Cristina Cabani, *Ariosto: I volgari e i latini suoi*, pp. 141–174. Lucca: Maria Pacini Fazzi, 2016.

Carocci 2016

Carocci, Anna. "Il destino di Angelica: Il destabilizzante femminile nei poemi di primo Cinquecento." In *I cantieri dell'italianistica: Ricerca, didattica e organizzazione agli inizi del XXI secolo, Atti del XVIII congresso dell'ADI*, edited by Guido Baldassari, Valeria Di Iasio, Giovanni Ferroni, and Ester Pietrobon, pp. 1–10. Rome: Adi Editore, 2016.

Cavallo 2004

Cavallo, Jo Ann. *The Romance Epics of Boiardo, Ariosto, and Tasso: From Public Duty to Private Pleasure*. Toronto: University of Toronto Press, 2004.

Cavallo 2013

Cavallo, Jo Ann. *The World beyond Europe in the Romance Epics of Boiardo and Ariosto*. Toronto: University of Toronto Press, 2013.

Cuccaro 1981

Cuccaro, Vincent. *The Humanism of Ludovico Ariosto: From the "Satire" to the "Furioso."* Ravenna: Longo, 1981.

Denzel 2016

Denzel, Valentina. *Les Mille et Un Visages de la virago: Marphise et Bradamante entre continuation et variation*. Paris: Classiques Garnier, 2016.

Dorigatti 2010
Dorigatti, Marco. "Sobrino ariostesco e misconosciuto." *Belfagor* 65, no. 4 (2010): pp. 401–414.
Dorigatti 2018
Dorigatti, Marco. "Il presente della poesia. L'*Orlando furioso* nel 1516." In *Nel "segno" del* Furioso*: L'incantato cosmo di Ludovico Ariosto e la cultura dei suoi tempi, Atti del Convegno internazionale, XIX Settimana di Alti Studi Rinascimentali (Ferrara, Palazzo Bonacossi, 13–15 ottobre 2016), Schifanoia* 54–55 (2018): pp. 13–26.
Este 1556
Este, Ercole II. Letter to Selīm II. Archivio di Stato di Modena, Archivio Segreto Estense, Principi Esteri, folder 1644.
Favaro 2017
Favaro, Maiko. "Tra 'aroganza' e 'inclyte vertute': Le ambiguità di Alessandro Magno nell'*Inamoramento de Orlando*." In *La "virtù eccellentissima": Eroe e antieroe nella letteratura italiana da Boccaccio a Tasso*, edited by Vincenzo Caputo, pp. 33–42. Milan: Franco Angeli, 2017.
Finucci 1992
Finucci, Valeria. "The Narcissistic Woman: Angelica and the Mystique of Femininity." In Valeria Finucci, *The Lady Vanishes: Subjectivity and Representation in Castiglione and Ariosto*, pp. 109–144. Stanford, CA: Stanford University Press, 1992.
Fornari 1549
Fornari, Simon. *La spositione sopra l'Orlando furioso di M. Ludovico Ariosto*. Florence: Lorenzo Torrentino, 1549.
Franceschetti 1970
Franceschetti, Antonio. "L'*Orlando innamorato* e la tradizione dell'*Aspremont*." *GSLI* 147 (1970): pp. 518–533.
Giraldi Cinthio 1556
Giraldi Cinthio, Giovan Battista. *Ab epistolis de Ferraria et Atestinis principibis commentariolum ex Lilii Gregorii Gyraldi epitome deductum*. Ferrara: Francescum Rubeum (Francesco de' Rossi), 1556.
Giraldi Cinthio 2018
Giraldi Cinthio, Giovan Battista. *Note critiche all'*Orlando furioso *(Classe I 377 e Classe I 406 della BCAFe)*, edited by Marco Dorigatti and Carla Molinari. Ferrara: Edisai, 2018.
Giudicetti 2010
Giudicetti, Gian Paolo. *Mandricardo e la melanconia: Discorsi diretti e sproloqui nell'*Orlando Furioso. Brussels: Peter Lang, 2010.
Guarini 1621
Guarini, Marcantonio. *Compendio historico dell'origine, accrescimento, e prerogative delle chiese, e luoghi pij della città, e diocesi di Ferrara*. Ferrara: Vittorio Baldini, 1621.
Mac Carthy 2007
Mac Carthy, Ita. "Angelica: Poetry and Desire." In Ita Mac Carthy, *Women and the Making of Poetry in Ariosto's Orlando Furioso*, pp. 45–71. Leicester, UK: Troubador, 2007.
Monteverdi 1961
Monteverdi, Angelo. "Lipadusa e Roncisvalle." *Lettere italiane* 13 (1961): pp. 401–409.
Murrin 1994
Murrin, Michael. *History and Warfare*. Chicago,: University of Chicago Press, 1994.
Pavlova 2013
Pavlova, Maria. "Rodomonte e Ruggiero: Una questione d'onore." *Rassegna europea di letteratura italiana* 42 (2013): pp. 135–177.
Pavlova 2014
Pavlova, Maria. "Ludovico Ariosto and Islam." In *Christian-Muslim Relations: A Bibliographical History (1500–1600)*, edited by David Thomas and John Chesworth, pp. 469–483. Leiden: Brill, 2014.
Pavlova 2018a
Pavlova, Maria. "L'Africa nell'*Orlando furioso*." *Schifanoia* 54–55 (2018): pp. 193–205.
Pavlova 2018b
Pavlova, Maria. "Sul finale del *Furioso* A." In *Il* Furioso *del 1516 tra rottura e continuità*, edited by Alessandra Villa and Delphine Montoliu-di Stefano, pp. 29–54. Toulouse: Presses de l'Université de Toulouse–Jean Jaurè, 2018.

Pavlova 2020
Pavlova, Maria. *Saracens and Their World in Boiardo and Ariosto*. Cambridge: Legenda, 2020.
Ricci 2008
Ricci, Giovanni. *I turchi alle porte*. Bologna: Il Mulino, 2008.
Rizzarelli 2009
Rizzarelli, Giovanna. "'Cominciar quivi una crudel battaglia': Duelli in ottave nell'*Orlando furioso*." In *Per violate forme: Rappresentazioni e linguaggi della violenza nella letteratura italiana*, edited by Fabrizio Bondi and Nicola Catelli, pp. 79–100. Lucca: Maria Pacini Fazzi, 2009.
Salviati 1585
Salviati, Lionardo. *Degli Accademici della Crusca difesa dell'Orlando Furioso dell'Ariosto contra 'l Dialogo dell'epica poesia di Cammillo Pellegrino*. In *Apologia del sig. Torquato Tasso*, ff. A 1*r*–G 8*v*. Ferrara: Giulio Cesare Cagnacini et Fratelli, 1585.
Salviati 1588
Salviati, Lionardo. *Lo 'nfarinato secondo ovvero dello 'nfarinato Accademico della Crusca*. Florence: Anton Padovani, 1588.
Santoro 1983
Santoro, Mario. "L'Angelica del *Furioso*: Fuga dalla storia." In Mario Santoro, *L'anello di Angelica: Nuovi saggi ariosteschi*, pp. 57–81. Naples: Federico & Ardia, 1983.
Santoro 1989
Santoro, Mario. *Ariosto e il Rinascimento*. Naples: Liguori, 1989.
Selīm 1555
Selīm II. Letter to Ercole II. Archivio di Stato di Modena, Archivio Segreto Estense, Principi Esteri, folder 1612.
Shemek 1989
Shemek, Deanna. "That Elusive Object of Desire: Angelica in the *Orlando Furioso*." *Annali d'italianistica* 7 (1989): pp. 116–141.
Spagna ferrarese 2009
Spagna ferrarese, edited by Valentina Gritti and Cristina Montagnani. Novara: Interlinea, 2009.
Strologo 2019
Strologo, Franca. "Trasgressione, travestimento e metamorfosi nel *Furioso*: Intorno alla storia di Ricciardetto e Fiordispina." In *"Dreaming Again on Things Already Dreamed": 500 Years of Orlando Furioso (1516–2016)*, edited by Marco Dorigatti and Maria Pavlova, pp. 173–198. Oxford: Peter Lang, 2019.
Strozzi 1977
Strozzi, Tito Vespasiano. *Die Borsias des Tito Strozzi: Ein lateinisches Epos der Renaissance*, edited and with commentary by Walther Ludwig. Munich: Fink, 1977.
Tissoni Benvenuti 1992
Tissoni Benvenuti, Antonia. "Note preliminari al commento dell'*Inamoramento de Orlando*." In *Il commento ai testi: Atti del seminario di Ascona*, edited by Ottavio Besomi and Carlo Caruso, pp. 277–309. Basel: Birkhäuser, 1992.
Tissoni Benvenuti 1996
Tissoni Benvenuti, Antonia. "Rugiero o la fabbrica dell'*Inamoramento de Orlando*." In *Per Cesare Bozzetti: Studi di letteratura e di filologia italiana*, edited by Simone Albonico et al., pp. 69–89. Milan: Mondadori, 1996.
Vitelli 1994
Vitelli, Assunta. "I documenti turchi dell'Archivio di Stato di Modena." *Annali dell'Università degli studi di Napoli "L'Orientale"* 53, no. 4 (1994): pp. 317–348.
Wiggins 1986
Wiggins, Peter DeSa. "Angelica." In Peter DeSa Wiggins, *Figures in Ariosto's Tapestry: Character and Design in the* Orlando Furioso. Baltimore: John Hopkins University Press, 1986.
Zanato 2015
Zanato, Tiziano. *Boiardo*. Rome: Salerno Editrice, 2015.

Ariosto's Religion

Stefano Jossa

1. The Unclean Turk

In canto XV of the first edition of the *Orlando furioso* in 1516—which would become XVII in the third and final 1532 edition—Ariosto the narrator takes center stage and admonishes Christians not to fight against one another but to go on a Crusade against the "renegades," that is, Muslims, identified with the metonymic expression *il Turco immondo* (the unclean Turk):[1]

> Se Cristianissimi esser voi volete,
> e voi altri Catolici nomati,
> perché di Cristo gli uomini uccidete?
> perché de' beni lor son dispogliati?
> Perché Ierusalem non riavete,
> che tolto è stato a voi da' rinegati?
> Perché Costantinopoli e del mondo
> la miglior parte occupa il Turco immondo?
> —*Fur.*, XVII 75
>
> [If you wish to be called Most Christian, if you wish to be called Catholic, why do you kill Christ's men? Why despoil them of their possessions? Why do you not retake Jerusalem, seized from you by renegades? Why is Constantinople and of the world the better part occupied by unclean Turks?]

Interestingly, Ariosto employs here the term *rinegati* (renegades), which has only one other occurrence in the poem as a proper technical term to define Christian converts to Islam (*Fur.*, XV 64, 2 [AB 13]). This usage implies that Ariosto would be following in the footsteps of the so-called Legend of Muḥammad, according to which the founder of Islam was considered nothing more than a schismatic Christian. Present in the highly influential *Roman de Mahomet* (The romance of Muḥammad, 1258) and other sources, and accepted by Dante, who placed Muḥammad in the ninth circle of Malebolge among the Sowers of

Religious Discord, the legend was more than likely still circulating in Ferrara at the opening of the sixteenth century.[2] Whether or not Ariosto was aware of it, his cultural memory and intellectual affiliation were certainly grounded in such a perception of the Islamic tradition.

In line with this, the narrator shows little doubt about the ecumenical mission of Christendom: to cultivate unity among themselves and fight against external enemies. Tobias Gregory has commented that "Ariosto employs the same line of exhortation used by Urban II in preaching the First Crusade: for God's sake, leaders of Christian nations, stop attacking each other and go attack the Muslim."[3] Yet the identification between Muslims and Turks evokes a "Turkish obsession" that Giovanni Ricci has convincingly reconstructed.[4] Ariosto would therefore be placing himself in the same mindset as that of many of his contemporaries, obsessed with the fear of Turks invading the Christian West, and Italy in particular.

Whether generically pro-Crusade or more specifically anti-Turk, the passage highlights the opposition between Christians and Others in such a way that it would be difficult to argue that Ariosto was indifferent to issues of identity, otherness, and religious warfare. Yet an immediate question is raised here: to what extent are Ariosto's Turks reflected in the poem's Saracens? After all, the words quoted above are spoken by the narrator, and therefore we as modern critical readers are invited to measure the extent to which Ariosto's own views are mirrored in his poem.

In this chapter, I will argue that Ariosto's engagement with contemporary cultural debates leads him to project more modern issues onto the "Christian/Muslim" divide in his poem, up to the point that religious conflict becomes an opportunity to discuss issues other than religious conflict itself. After a brief overview of the relevance of the subject and the reasons it has been overlooked in Ariosto criticism until very recently, I shall address a close reading of three key moments in defining the religious divide in the *Orlando furioso*, where the author seems to redirect his readers from the traditional contextual background of chivalry and lead them toward other, more urgent debates. These key moments are identified with three prayers: one Christian, Charlemagne's in canto XIV (AB XII); and two Saracen, Medoro's prayer to the moon in canto XVIII (AB XVI) and Fiordispina's prayer to Macon/Mohamed in canto XXV (AB XXIII).[5]

My claim will be that the closer Ariosto seems to be to issues of religious conflict, the more he pushes the boundaries of his religious engagement beyond the tradition of the chivalric genre. Ariosto would therefore be challenging his readers' horizon of expectations and moving from the religious divide of traditional chivalric epic to more contemporary religious interests. In the light of research on collective consciousness and memory as the shared set of knowledge and discussion of a social group that is significantly associated with its self-fashioning, I shall try to locate and assess Ariosto's participation in the broader framework of the religious debates of his time.

2. The Master Code of Early Modern Culture

At first sight, it would be tempting to connect Ariosto's sixteenth-century crusading spirit with the medieval epic framework of the poem, as the opening stanza of the *Orlando furioso* states:

> Le donne, i cavallier, l'arme, gli amori,
> le cortesie, l'audaci imprese io canto,
> che furo al tempo che passaro i Mori
> d'Africa il mare, e in Francia nocquer tanto,
> seguendo l'ire e i giovenil furori
> d'Agramante lor re, che si diè vanto
> di vendicar la morte di Troiano
> sopra re Carlo imperator romano.
> —*Fur.*, I 1
>
> [I sing of knights and ladies, of love and arms, of courtly chivalry, of courageous deeds—all from the time when the Moors crossed the sea from Africa and wrought havoc in France. I shall tell of the anger, the fiery rage of young Agramant their king, whose boast it was that he would avenge himself on Charles, Emperor of Rome, for King Trojan's death.]

The opening of the poem establishes its bellicose backdrop in terms of religious divisions, with the opposition between *i Mori* (the Muslims) and the Holy Roman Emperor (obviously Christian). Sixteenth-century readers, such as Simon Fornari, had little hesitation in acknowledging the military and religious partition between Agramante and Charlemagne as both the narrative driver and the ideological milieu of the poem.[6] Religion is, in fact, obviously related to the epic framework of the poem, where two opposing blocs fight against each other in terms of a crucial war between good and evil. Therefore, the Christian/Turk distinction of contemporary warfare could easily be associated with the Christian/Muslim conflict of the poem's historical setting.

Ariosto situates his poem within the framework of earlier religiously delineated romances that have at their narrative core the war between Saracens and Christians at the time of the Arab invasion of Western Europe and Charlemagne's defense of the Christian world (eighth to ninth centuries), as demonstrated by the fact that, of Boiardo's three war threads—the invasions of Gradasso, Mandricardo, and Agramante—"Ariosto privileges the campaign of Agramante, the most firmly Carolingian of Boiardo's three war themes" and therefore the most useful to ideologizing processes.[7]

The argument in favor of the thesis of Ariosto as a Christian poet (not only generically but militantly Christian) is supported by many points in the *Furioso*, including the epic framework of the poem, the representation of the principal Saracen knights as evil, and the need to convert Ruggiero in order to push the poem toward Christian outcomes.[8] Essentially, we can outline the following episodes to highlight Ariosto's attitude toward the Christian/Muslim divide: the battle in Paris, the battle of Lipadusa, the three episodes of conversion between cantos XLI and XLIII (attempted in the case of Agramante, XLI 37–45; successful in those of Ruggiero and Sobrino, XLI 47–67 and XLIII 193–194), and the duel between Ruggiero and Rodomonte.

Yet arguments in favor of a more nuanced representation of religious difference can also easily be made, up to the point that the question of whether Ariosto fully sides with the Christians remains an open one. Maria Pavlova, for instance, has argued that Ariosto's values are better embodied by Saracen knights than by Christians.[9] In fact, it looks as if Ariosto's interest in the matter, which is undeniable, leads him elsewhere, toward more urgent issues and arguments.

Critics as influential as Francesco De Sanctis and Benedetto Croce, however, denied that Ariosto had any religious motivation whatsoever. The former went so far as to claim that the world of *Orlando furioso* is "un mondo vuoto di motivi religiosi, patriottici e morali, un mondo puro dell'arte" (a world utterly wanting in any motive connected with religion, patriotism, or morality, a world purely and entirely of art);[10] the latter wrote that "[c]on disposizione, invece, affatto scherzevole egli guardava le credenze religiose, Dio, Cristo, il paradiso, gli angeli, i santi" (his was a distinctly facetious outlook regarding religious beliefs—God, Christ, Paradise, angels and saints).[11] More recently, Italo Calvino has maintained that "[l']'essere 'di fé diversi' non significa molto di più, nel *Furioso*, che il diverso colore dei pezzi in una scacchiera" (being "of two different faiths" does not mean, in the *Furioso*, much more than the different colour of pieces on a chessboard);[12] and Sergio Zatti has reiterated that "lo sfondo istituzionale della guerra di religione, con il sostanziale declino dei valori di contrapposizione collettiva, fornisce ad Ariosto non più che uno schema antagonistico dentro cui situare i conflitti del desiderio individuale" (the institutional background of the religious war, due to the substantial decline of collective opposing values, is for Ariosto nothing more than an adversarial framework within which he can locate the conflicts of subjective desire).[13]

It is mainly due to the efforts of Jo Ann Cavallo that the question of religion has come back into Ariosto criticism.[14] Taking into consideration the East/West divide as a geographical and ideological catalyst, Cavallo has promoted a reading of Ariosto's poem as far more religiously engaged than Boiardo's. Pia Schwartz Lausen, for her part, has peremptorily stated that "il *Furioso* esprime una valutazione negativa dei musulmani del suo tempo, gli Ottomani" (the *Furioso* expresses a negative view of contemporary Muslims, i.e., the Turks),[15] and Pavlova has argued that "the fact that modern scholarship is divided over the extent to which Ariosto's portrayal of the Saracen Other is positive and 'progressive' testifies to the complexity of the poem."[16] Prior to this, Marina Beer had already highlighted the relevance of biblical memory and providential design in Ariosto's tapestry,[17] while more recently, Davide Dalmas has remarked that Ariosto's poem is imbued with religious references and needs to be read against the historical circumstances of contemporary religious conflicts,[18] recalling yet again the words of one of Ariosto's earlier editors, Lodovico Dolce: "Ne si scordò l'Ariosto in piu parti della sua opera la religione; che se ben si ricordava esser Poeta; e cercava di abellirla con ogni ornamento, che a Heroica composizione appartenesse, ricordavasi anco di esser Christiano Poeta" (Nor did Ariosto in many parts of his poem forget religion; for even while he was certainly well aware of being a Poet and aimed to embellish his work with every ornament appropriate to Heroic poetry, he was also conscious of being a Christian Poet).[19]

The matter is therefore worth further investigation. For an author like Ariosto, who was deeply concerned with religious issues, as we shall see, the Christian/Muslim divide provided the opportunity to tackle theological matters at a time when issues of Church reform were increasingly debated among European intellectuals.[20] It will be useful, to this end, to acknowledge the notion of religion as the "master code" of early modern culture, as the Marxist critic Fredric Jameson has suggested:[21] a code within which all discourses must necessarily be inscribed in order to make them relate to the primacy of theology in the early modern episteme. This means that religion often offered a broader context within which writers could develop discourses other than strictly religious ones. As a consequence, we should avoid the mistake of projecting our modern notion of Orientalism onto works that were first and foremost interested in problematizing religious questions rather than ideologizing relationships and positions; in order to do so, we will first need to dismantle the alleged autonomy of religious discourse, taking into consideration wider issues, of both an ideological and a narrative nature, such as the invention of the enemy and the epic/romance disjunction.

3. The Invention of the Enemy

Two stanzas before the abovementioned passage inviting Christians to launch a Crusade,[22] Ariosto makes a point that clearly connects his outburst about the need for a new Crusade with the primary duty of Charlemagne's knights to fight against their Saracen enemies. In these lines, he calls the occupiers of Jerusalem, that is, the Muslims, *cani* (dogs):

> Soriani in quel tempo aveano usanza
> d'armarsi a questa guisa di Ponente.
> Forse ve gli inducea la vicinanza
> che de' Franceschi avean continuamente,
> che quivi allor reggean la sacra stanza
> dove in carne abitò Dio onnipotente;
> ch'ora i superbi e miseri cristiani,
> con biasmi lor, lasciano in man de' cani.
> —*Fur.*, XVII 73 (emphasis added)
>
> [In those days the Syrians were accustomed to wear armour after the Western fashion; perhaps this was due to the vicinity of the French settled there as rulers of the holy places where Almighty God dwelt in human flesh. Nowadays to their shame, Christians, the arrogant wretches, leave these places in the hands of dogs.]

Two cantos earlier, in his prayer to God before the decisive battle of Paris, Charlemagne had used exactly the same word to underline the need for the Christians to prevail:

> Difendi queste genti, che son quelle
> che 'l tuo sepulcro hanno purgato e mondo
> da' brutti cani, e la tua santa Chiesa
> con li vicari suoi spesso difesa.
> —*Fur.*, XIV 71, 5–8 (emphasis added)
>
> [Defend your faithful, then; they are the ones who have cleansed your sepul-

chre and purged it of brutish dogs; many a time have they defended your holy Church and her vicars.]

I will not enter here into the debate around Ariosto's historical mistake in attributing the "liberation" of Jerusalem to a time prior to the Arab invasion of Western Europe but wish rather to focus on the continuity between the language of the poem's characters and the language of the narrator, which leads to a commonality of values and views. Using the stereotypically derogatory language of the time, as explained by Timothy Hampton,[23] Ariosto equates contemporary anti-Turk sentiment with medieval anti-Arab convictions, in line with what Umberto Eco has named "the invention of the enemy." As suggested by Eco, "Having an enemy is important not only to define our identity but also to provide us with an obstacle against which to measure our system of values and, in seeking to overcome it, to demonstrate our own worth. So when there is no enemy, we have to invent one."[24]

It would be tempting to apply Eco's suggestion to Ariosto's poem. The world of the narrator would therefore be reflected in the world of the poem, creating a game of mirrors that is typical of Ariosto's play with reality and fiction, as well as past and present. Yet, when addressing the enemies as "dogs," be they either contemporary or historical Muslims, Ariosto seems to be paying tribute to a linguistic vogue rather than "inventing" the enemy and appears oriented more toward the warfare of his time than in developing an anti-Muslim position. While inviting Christians to undertake a new Crusade, Ariosto is, in fact, also hoping to divert them from their internecine conflicts, especially the scenario of the Italian wars:

Non hai tu, Spagna, l'Africa vicina,
che t'ha via più di questa Italia offesa?
E pur, per dar travaglio alla meschina,
lasci la prima tua sì bella impresa.
O d'ogni vizio fetida sentina,
dormi, Italia imbriaca, e non ti pesa
ch'ora di questa gente, ora di quella
che già serva ti fu, sei fatta ancella?

Se 'l dubbio di morir ne le tue tane,
Svizzer, di fame, in Lombardia ti guida,
e tra noi cerchi o chi ti dia del pane,

o, per uscir d'inopia, chi t'uccida;
le richezze del Turco hai non lontane:
caccial d'Europa, o almen di Grecia snida;
così potrai o del digiuno trarti,
o cader con più merto in quelle parti.

Quel ch'a te dico, io dico al tuo vicino
tedesco ancor; là le richezze sono,
che vi portò da Roma Costantino:
portonne il meglio, e fe' del resto dono.
Pattolo ed Ermo onde si tra' l'or fino,
Migdonia e Lidia, e quel paese buono
per tante laudi in tante istorie noto,
non è, s'andar vi vuoi, troppo remoto.

Tu, gran Leone, a cui premon le terga
de le chiavi del ciel le gravi some,
non lasciar che nel sonno si sommerga
Italia, se la man l'hai ne le chiome.
Tu sei Pastore; e Dio t'ha quella verga
data a portare, e scelto il fiero nome,
perché tu ruggi, e che le braccia stenda,
sì che dai lupi il grege tuo difenda.
—*Fur.*, XVII 76–79

[Spain, have you not Africa for neighbour—Africa, who has done far worse to you than Italy? And yet to bring suffering on our wretched country you abandon the fine enterprise you started so well. And you, besotted Italy, fetid sink of all iniquities, are you sleeping? Does it mean nothing to you that now of this people, once your servants, you now have been made theirs? You Swiss, if it is fear of starving to death in your lairs which tempts you down to Lombardy, and if you come among us looking for someone to give you bread or else release you from famine by slaying you: the riches of the Turk are not far to seek—drive them out of Europe, or at least dislodge them from Greece. Thus you shall be able to escape hunger or at any rate meet a more meritorious end in those regions.

What I say to you, I say also to your German neighbours: that is where the wealth is that Constantine brought from Rome—thither he took the best, giving away what remained: Pactolus and Hermus, rivers to be panned for pure gold, Mygdonia and Lydia, and all the country round, so widely praised for its virtues, extolled in so many histories—they are not too remote if you wish to travel there.

Great Leo, you shoulder the heavy burden of the keys of Heaven; if you hold Italy by the hair, do not leave her submerged in slumber. You are the shepherd: and if God gave you that staff to carry, and chose your proud name it was so that you should roar and stretch forth your hands to defend your flock from the wolves.]

The Turks are thus a means for other European powers to compensate for their loss of Italy.[25] Rather than being interpreted only with an eye to Christian/Muslim hostilities, the passage defining the Saracens in the poem as "dogs" is therefore also legible within the broader context of both Ariosto's discourse in the poem, a narrative tool, and the poet's own historical experience, a political strategy. No more ideological is the keyword "barbarian," which does not define a border between the Western and Eastern worlds but simply applies to indistinct multitudes and is primarily useful in interpreting contemporary warfare, as Alessandra Villa's analysis has demonstrated.[26] In discussing the following examples, I will argue that when dealing with such matters as the representation of the Saracen world and the religious wars within the narrative of the poem, Ariosto is engaging with his audience's horizon of expectations, that is, the reader's cultural knowledge of the world, rather than with the historical and religious divide between Christians and Muslims.[27] In other words, this opposition works as a tool to develop arguments beyond its apparent focus and opens up a horizon of change, inviting readers to shift their attention from the familiar expectations of the chivalric code to new interpretive possibilities.

4. Epic and Romance

In canto XIV (AB XII), the reader is presented with the first crucial episode for an understanding of the Christian/Islamic conflict in the poem.[28] Before the battle in Paris, Charlemagne prays to the Christian God in order to beseech his intervention in the epic:

Ed egli tra baroni e paladini,
principi ed oratori, al maggior tempio
con molta religione a quei divini

atti intervenne, e ne diè agli altri esempio.
Con le man giunte e gli occhi al ciel supini,
disse:—Signor, ben ch'io sia iniquo ed empio,
non voglia tua bontà, pel mio fallire,
che 'l tuo popul fedele abbia a patire.

E se gli è tuo voler ch'egli patisca,
e ch'abbia il nostro error degni supplìci,
almen la punizion si differisca
sì, che per man non sia de' tuoi nemici;
che quando lor d'uccider noi sortisca,
che nome avemo pur d'esser tuo' amici,
i pagani diran che nulla puoi,
che perir lasci i partigiani tuoi.
—*Fur.*, XIV 69–70

[With his barons and paladins, princes and prelates, he repaired to the cathedral and most devoutly participated in the sacred rites, setting an example to the rest. Joining his hands and raising his eyes to heaven, he prayed: "Lord, though I am wicked and sinful, in your goodness suffer not your faithful people to be afflicted on account of my faults.

"But if it is your will that they should suffer and that our waywardness be punished as it deserves, do but defer the retribution that it be not administered by the hand of your enemies: for if it fell to their lot to slay us, who are accounted your friends, the pagans will say that you are powerless, leaving your own followers to perish."]

Here it looks as if Charlemagne is asking for God's protection for political rather than religious reasons: if God wants the Christians to succeed in the fight for religious truth, he must help his representatives to win the epic battle. Interestingly, Gregory has commented that "Charles's accents are those of a client addressing a prince: self-abasement, a heavy dose of flattery, and an appeal to his lordship's own best interests."[29] For her part, Cavallo has compared this prayer to the challenge posed by Iarbus to Zeus in *Aeneid* 4.[30] But rather than practically seeming to blackmail God, Charlemagne is instead seeking God's collaboration in the exercise of political power, as if God had with the emperor the same rapport that he enjoys with his subjects. In so doing, on the one hand, Charlemagne establishes a special relationship between himself and

God, that of a vassal to his feudal lord; while on the other hand, he brings God down to the level of one of the parties in the epic struggle. The status of the prayer is controversial, however, if, in agreement with Ascoli, we accept that Ariosto is playing here with double entendre, in order to suggest additional meanings that convey a sense of suspension "between silence and speech, truth and fraud, madness and reason, Logos and Babel," as we shall see below, when discussing the outcome of Charlemagne's prayer.[31]

As a consequence, religion becomes part of the epic framework of the *Orlando furioso*. Like Torquato Tasso in his later *Gerusalemme liberata*, Ariosto would thus be using religion for the purposes of his epic. Unlike Tasso's poem, however, religion in the *Furioso* works as a means to construct a practical opposition between the two camps in order to foster the narrative, rather than as a strict ideological border between good and evil. In this light, rather than serving as the enemies of Christendom, the Saracens would be considered poetically dangerous, because they embody the potential to destroy narrative coherence. As David Quint has suggested: "Epic's losers, the enemies of empire, whom epic ideology assimilates with the East, woman, nature, irrationality, and chaos, consequently also embody a potential, indeed inevitable, collapse of the narrative."[32]

Indeed, if God were not to intervene, the epic order would be overcome by a succession of disordered individual adventures. Because Ariosto's employment of Christian/Muslim conflict is less ideologically driven than it is in Tasso, God's intervention, as we shall see, does not lead to Christian victory but to further complications in the elaboration of the plot, in which the poet seizes the opportunity to reflect on issues that were of interest among his fellow humanists rather than to further develop the conventional strategies of epic and romance.

The question consequently becomes: to what extent is Ariosto truly interested in Christian/Muslim difference rather than its role in the narrative construction of his poem? It looks as if the opposition between Christians and Muslims is needed to allow the narrative machine to function rather than to set up an ethical and ideological partition. More relevant to either the ideological or the narrative framework of the *Orlando furioso* than in and of itself, the religious divide moves toward other, external and possibly more forcefully relevant, issues.

Religious difference is therefore both reasserted, because it helps readers to recognize what they already know (i.e., the epic division between two opposing fields), and manipulated, because it helps the author to divert his readers' attention away from traditional epic and toward more contemporary subjects (by means of "hidden" references to other matters). In other words, Ariosto's religiosity is both traditional and subversive.

5. Reform, Savonarolism, and Justification by Faith Alone

So far, Charlemagne's prayer appears to be rather conventional, in that it asks for God's help, as was common in earlier romances, including Boiardo's *Inamoramento de Orlando.*[33] Yet it concludes on another note, one that opens onto completely different religious issues, namely, justification by faith alone and predestination, which soon after the first edition of the *Furioso* would become Martin Luther's core arguments against the Roman Church's lack of spiritual integrity:

> So che i meriti nostri atti non sono
> a satisfare al debito d'un'oncia;
> né devemo sperar da te perdono,
> se riguardiamo a nostra vita sconcia:
> ma se vi aggiugni di tua grazia il dono,
> nostra ragion fia ragguagliata e concia;
> né del tuo aiuto disperar possiamo,
> qualor di tua pietà ci ricordiamo.—
> —*Fur.*, XIV 72
>
> [I acknowledge that our merits are not capable of satisfying our debt to you by so much as an ounce nor can we hope for your pardon when we consider the depravity of our lives. But if you throw on the scale the gift of your grace, our tribute is made up to the full amount. We cannot despair of your assistance when we remember your mercy.]

As highlighted by Gigliola Fragnito in relation to Ariosto's cultural milieu, the debate over justification by faith alone was a hot topic among fourteenth- and fifteenth-century humanists well before Luther's invective against the Roman Church.[34] Ariosto mentions Luther only once in his writings, shortly after the second edition of the *Furioso,* at a time when Luther had already been excommunicated by Pope Leo X.[35] Ariosto's citation is broadly sympathetic, and it may accordingly be argued that the poet was not among the Italian anti-Lutherans. In Ariosto's presentation, Luther's mistake is no different from that of the Averroist humanist Nicoletto Vernia (ca. 1420–1499), an expert in natural philosophy and a teacher at the University of Padua of the Mantuan philosopher Pietro Pomponazzi (1462–1525), later suspected of heterodox thinking: both Vernia and Luther simply exaggerated, in Ariosto's view, due to their ambition to understand God's nature. Nevertheless, it must be noted that the theory of justification by faith alone was also part of the preaching of the Ferrarese Dominican friar Girolamo Savonarola (1452–1498)—up to the point where Luther himself later associated his own understanding of the question with Savonarola's. Excommunicated by Pope Alexander VI in 1497 and executed in 1498, Savonarola would definitely have been a risky reference point during the time Ariosto was writing his poem. But being Ferrarese himself, Ariosto would likely have met Savonarola or heard or been informed about Savonarola's preaching in the years of his youth. Furthermore, two of Savonarola's books were published by the same publisher as that of the *Orlando furioso*—Giovanni Mazzocchi del Bondeno—in 1513 and 1516, thus circumscribing the publication of Ariosto's poem within the publisher's catalogue.[36] Although publishing policies were somewhat random at the time, this coincidence should not be minimized, given the extent to which Savonarolism was widespread, and even partially rehabilitated, in Ferrara during the years of the composition of *Orlando furioso*, as Gabriella Zarri, Tamar Herzig, and Luigi Lazzerini have demonstrated.[37]

Passages on justification by faith alone are widespread in Savonarola's writings, but the following can be taken as representative of an ongoing discussion that Ariosto seems to share:

> Non è adunque vero che per l'opere e meriti nostri preesistenti, Iddio ci dia la grazia, e che siamo predestinati a vita eterna, quasi che l'opere e li meriti sieno causa della predestinazione, cum sit ch'e' sia tutto l'opposito, perché l'opere e li meriti sono effetti della predestinazione, e la volontà divina è causa della predestinazione, come di sopra abbiamo detto.[38]
> [Hence, it is not true that God gives us grace for our preexisting works and merits, and that we are predestined to eternal life, as if works and merits be the cause of predestination, when it is the other way around, since works and merits are effects of predestination and divine will is its cause, as we have said above.]

Two key words here are evident in Ariosto's later phrasing in the *Orlando furioso*: *meriti* and *grazia* (*Fur.*, XIV 72, 1, 5). The passage reliably dates to 1493, when Savonarola was preaching on Psalm 73 (*Quam bonus*; 72 in the Septuagint numbering), but would have not been published until 1528. Later, in his exposition of Psalm 51 (*Miserere*; 50 in the Septuagint numbering), dated to

1498 and already published in 1499, Savonarola stated more peremptorily that "non ex meritis eorum, non ex operibus eorum salvati sunt, ne quis gloriari possit, sed quoniam ita placitum est coram te" (not by their own merits; not by works were they saved, lest any man should boast, but because it seemed good in Thy sight).[39] Ariosto was more than likely quite familiar with reflections such as these.

But rather than being identified as strictly Lutheran or Savonarolian affirmations, claims in favor of justification by faith alone and predestination at the time of the gestation of the *Furioso* are to be regarded primarily as a syncretic contamination between pre-Lutheran stances and humanistic methodologies, as emphasized in a broader context by Delio Cantimori when discussing humanist approaches to religion.[40]

It should not seem surprising, then, that Ariosto inserted such a reflection on justification by faith alone into a passage that is apparently dedicated to the religious war between Christians and Muslims.[41] Rather than a faithful emperor opposing his external enemies, Charlemagne here looks more like a fellow humanist reflecting upon a much-debated issue in contemporary Christendom. Ariosto is clearly winking at his audience in order to meet their expectations of a poem able to deal with current issues rather than merely addressing the opposition of Christians and Muslims. The external framework of the *Orlando furioso* works as a means to include more contemporary and fewer medieval religious concerns, so as to move beyond what had become a rather static tradition and in order to engage more closely with the poet's intended audience of Ferrarese humanists. Ariosto clearly asserts his membership in this group, constructing a sense of affiliation around shared questions, which is the mechanism of how collective memory operates, as shown in particular by Maurice Halbwachs and Jan Assman in their studies.[42]

As a consequence, we should not overlook Ariosto's involvement in religious debates, marked, in an increasingly conscious way, by criticism of the teachings of the Roman Church and aimed at reforming horizons, in which Luther's teaching played an important part. This engagement, despite a willingness to listen to Luther, did not imply a break with the institutional Church but rather aimed at acting within it, to fertilize its pastoral action, to patiently guide the theological knowledge and ethical behavior of the faithful. Rather than focusing on the Eastern Other, Ariosto is clearly more interested in debates over the identity and mission of the Church, issues much closer to his and his contemporaries' immediate concerns, as one might expect of a sixteenth-century citizen of the Papal States.

6. Platonism, Hermetism, and Natural Philosophy

On another level, there is little doubt that religion works as an offshoot of the narrative machine when we look at the consequences of Charlemagne's prayer. God sends the archangel Michael to support the Christians with the intended help of Silence and to hinder the Saracens with the assistance of Discord. Expecting to find Silence in churches and monasteries, Michael visits them, to discover, to his surprise, only Discord, given that Pity, Quiet, Humility, Love, and Peace no longer dwelt there, having been replaced by Gluttony, Avarice, Wrath, Pride, Envy, Sloth, and Cruelty:

> Né Pietà, né Quiete, né Umiltade,
> né quivi Amor, né quivi Pace mira.
> Ben vi fur già, ma ne l'antiqua etade;
> che le cacciar Gola, Avarizia ed Ira,
> Superbia, Invidia, Inerzia e Crudeltade.
> Di tanta novità l'angel si ammira:
> andò guardando quella brutta schiera,
> e vide ch'anco la Discordia v'era.
> —*Fur.*, XIV 81
>
> [Piety was not to be seen either, nor were Tranquillity or Meekness, Love or Peace. They used to be found here in days of old, but have since been driven out by Gluttony, Avarice and Wrath, Pride, Envy, Sloth and Cruelty. The angel was amazed at this turn of affairs; he looked here and there among this hideous throng and noticed that Discord was here too.]

Ascoli has highlighted the interplay between Silence and Discord that leads to their ambiguity and interchangeability: by replacing Silence with Discord, "Ariosto shows how (apparently angelic) Silence might signify Truth and devotion, but might as easily mask Fraud and treachery."[43] A game of mirrors thus opens up a further reading of Ariosto's religious engagement, which creates a space for reading beyond the surface of the text. Silence, in its turn, will be found in Arabia, in between Sloth and Laziness, because it has abandoned the sacred place it had previously occupied to make company with Treachery and Murder:

> Domanda a costei l'angelo, che via
> debba tener, sì che 'l Silenzio truove.
> Disse la Fraude:—Già costui solia
> fra virtudi abitare, e non altrove,

con Benedetto e con quelli d'Elia
ne le badie, quando erano ancor nuove:
fe' ne le scuole assai de la sua vita
al tempo di Pitagora e d'Archita.

Mancati quei filosofi e quei santi
che lo solean tener pel camin ritto,
dagli onesti costumi ch'avea inanti,
fece alle sceleraggini tragitto.
Cominciò andar la notte con gli amanti,
indi coi ladri, e fare ogni delitto.
Molto col Tradimento egli dimora:
veduto l'ho con l'Omicidio ancora.
—*Fur.*, XIV 88–89

[Michael asked Fraud which road was most likely to lead him to Silence, and was told: "He used to dwell exclusively among the virtues, with Benedict, and with the disciples of Elias the hermit, at the time when the monasteries were still in their infancy. Much of his time he spent in the schools back in the days of Pythagoras and Archytas.

"When there were no philosophers or holy men left to keep him on the straight and narrow path, he forsook his virtuous propensities and threw in his lot with the wicked. He began consorting with lovers at night, then with thieves; he was party to every sort of crime. Now he frequents Treachery a great deal, and I have seen him keep company with Murder."]

The episode is clearly critical of the customs of contemporary clergy and would become suspect to inquisitors later in the century, precisely because the angel finds Discord in the friars' convents ("de Angelo qui invenit discordia in convento fratruum").[44] Focusing only on the allusion to Arabia, however, Cavallo has argued that "the fact that Silence is found lying between fat, indolent Sloth and inert Laziness carries over the moral censure of the previous scene, suggestively presenting idleness as a distinct characteristic of the Orient."[45] Yet Cavallo overlooks the fact that Ariosto's interest in religion derives from a sixteenth-century Christian perspective rather than from our own contemporary religiously divided world. Once again, in my view, Ariosto exploits the Christian/Muslim conflict to introduce into his poem issues from contemporary religious debates in Christian humanist circles. Stefano Prandi and Gianluca Genovese have recently noted that Silence must necessarily be associated with Ariosto's hermetic interests,[46] as also demonstrated by the coupling of philosophers and saints in this passage, the former in the likes of Pythagoras and Archytas and the latter in those of Benedict and Elias the hermit. Pythagoras is the Greek pre-Socratic philosopher whom Renaissance humanists regarded as a predecessor of Plato in matters related to cosmology, psychology, and natural and moral philosophy. Archytas is one of his followers, reputed to be a good friend of Plato. Benedict and Elias the hermit are cited as exemplars of perfect monastic life. The pairing of the two couples alerts the reader to the Christianization of ancient philosophy that points to the core of Marsilio Ficino's philosophy.[47]

These references can best be explained taking into consideration Ariosto's early adulthood in the literary establishment of Ferrara at the end of the fifteenth century, as testified by a letter he wrote when he was twenty-four years old to the Venetian publisher Aldo Manuzio (1449/1452–1515) on behalf of his fellow Ferrarese humanists. The letter is dated January 5, 1498, and contains a request to Aldo to send the *corpus platonicum* translated by Ficino:

> Since Sebastiano Aquila, devoted cultivator of the liberal arts—who has a public charge to teach medicine here and also dedicates himself to Platonic philosophy—is lecturing on Plato's Timaeus during our holidays to a large audience, there is significant interest among the scholars to have the books of Marsilio Ficino and however much has been translated into Latin from the pages of Greek Platonists. And since you more than any other person are able to satisfy them (I learned this from, among others, most recently Alberto Pio, well-known and extremely learned, who, returning from Venice, brought us a volume in which writings by Platonic philosophers have been collected together with other books), in order to follow through with the requests of these scholars and also bearing in mind what is best for you, assuming that it is not inconsequential if more of your books are sold, I have considered it my duty to insist with this letter that you indulge our legitimate desire.[48]

Ariosto mentions two key figures in the spread of natural philosophy and unorthodox intellectual currents in Ferrara: a senior scholar, Sebastiano dell'Aquila (ca. 1440–1510), professor of medicine and philosophy at the University of Ferrara and a protagonist of the 1497 Ferrarese dispute about the *mal francese* (or syphilis); and a fellow humanist, Alberto Pio (1475–1531), prince of Carpi, the nephew of Giovanni Pico della Mirandola (1463–1494), educated by Manuzio and a close friend of Ariosto, later suspected of heterodox ideas.

The Platonic and humanist focus of the group opens up an entirely new field of investigation for Ariosto's religious culture, as already suggested in part by Gennaro Savarese and Peter Vincent Marinelli.[49] Ariosto's full immersion in natural philosophy might be considered among the reasons he decided to collaborate with Mazzocchi's printing press, which was founded and directed by a practicing natural philosopher, Lodovico Bonaccioli (1475–1536), scientist, humanist, and the gynecologist of Lucrezia Borgia.[50]

It is significant that Mario Equicola (ca. 1470–1525)—among the closest acquaintances of Ariosto and one of the figures who had the greatest impact on his cultural formation (Equicola had moved to Ferrara from Naples in 1498, accompanying his patron, Sigismondo Cantelmo)—made his literary debut with several interesting religious pamphlets, all published in Ferrara between 1498 and 1501. These pamphlets were linked to the official installation of Ippolito d'Este (later Ariosto's patron) as archbishop of Milan in 1498 and combine religious and humanist thinking: *De religione libellus*, in which Equicola argues in favor of natural religion; *Oratio dicta Papiae*, an oration made at the University of Pavia in 1498 that discusses the fields of theology, physics, and law; and *De Passione Domini*, an oration made in Milan in 1499 in the presence of Ippolito.[51]

It should also be noted that Pietro Pomponazzi, another important heterodox thinker, lectured in two different periods at the University of Ferrara on Aristotle's *De anima* (On the soul), a treatise on biopsychology and entelechy that argues in favor of both the soul's mortality and predestination. Pomponazzi delivered the first of these lectures during Ariosto's student days in 1496–1497 and then in 1509–1510 while Ariosto was writing the *Orlando furioso*.[52] Pomponazzi was the tutor of Alberto Pio, one of Ariosto's closest friends, to whom Pomponazzi dedicated his 1514 *De intensione et remissione formarum* (On the intension and remission of forms).[53] I argue that all this background is far more important to Ariosto's religion than the rift between Christian and Muslim. Far from sitting comfortably within either humanist circles or the courtly world, the *Furioso* works as a collector of and reactor to contemporary debates in order to foster the reader's engagement and, ironically, to suggest the multiplication of viewpoints.

It is no coincidence, I would contend, that Ariosto's interest in religious controversy emerges specifically when the Christian/Muslim conflict is at center stage. It is as if Ariosto were diverting his informed readers from the traditional matter of Christian epic to a more insightful understanding of contemporary religious issues. In so doing, he shows his ability to shift attention from the religious wars of chivalric epic to other, more recent and more urgent, religious questions. Less astute, superficial, or hasty readers could, of course, remain satisfied with skimming the surface of the narrative, never moving beyond the traditional framework of Christian epic. In other words, Ariosto's religious engagement needs contextualizing before proclaiming that he is in tune with either the crusading spirit or stereotypical views of the Orient.[54]

7. Classicism, Humanism, and Praying

The second prayer I wish to focus on is that of Medoro to the moon in canto XVIII (AB XVI):

> O santa dea, che dagli antiqui nostri
> debitamente sei detta triforme;
> ch'in cielo, in terra e ne l'inferno mostri
> l'alta bellezza tua sotto più forme,
> e ne le selve, di fere e di mostri
> vai cacciatrice seguitando l'orme;
> mostrami ove 'l mio re giaccia fra tanti,
> che vivendo imitò tuoi studi santi.
> —*Fur.*, XVIII 184
>
> [Holy Goddess, rightly are you invoked under three names by our ancestors: in heaven, on earth, and in the underworld you reveal your supreme beauty under different guises, and in the forests you are a huntress chasing monsters and wild beasts! Show me where my king lies among so many dead: as he lived he was devoted to your sacred pursuits.]

This is a typical pagan rather than Muslim prayer, as confirmed by the fact that it is imbued with classical sources, including Nisus's prayer in Virgil's *Aeneid* (9.403–409), Medea's invocation in Ovid's *Metamorphoses* (7.194–195), and Dymas's prayer in Statius's *Thebaid* (10.365–370).[55] Medoro invokes the moon as Trivia, triform, which is the classical formula inclusive of Diana/Cynthia or Artemis on earth, as the goddess of hunting, Lucina or Selene in heaven, and Hecate or Persephone in the underworld.

It would be simplistic to read Medoro's prayer as a means of constructing the enemy, to use Eco's idea. This is clearly not the case. Medoro looks rather more like a humanist competing with his classical sources than a Saracen dominated by anti-Christian sentiment. As it happens, however, Medoro's prayer is answered, whether, Ariosto underlines, by chance or through his great faith:

La luna a quel pregar la nube aperse
(o fosse caso o pur la tanta fede),
bella come fu allor ch'ella s'offerse,
e nuda in braccio a Endimion si diede.
—*Fur.*, XVIII 185, 1–4
[The Moon breached the clouds at this prayer (whether by chance or in answer to such faith)
and disclosed herself, beautiful as the night when she gave herself naked into the arms of Endymion.]

The prayers of both Charlemagne and Medoro are therefore answered, apparently on the assumption that praying in itself deserves fulfillment. But is this to be understood as miracle, chance, or natural magic?

The issue of the fulfillment of prayers was much debated at the time, and an ongoing discussion of the topic involved, among others, Ficino, Pico della Mirandola, and Pomponazzi.[56] In his *De naturalium effectuum admirandorum causis, sive de incantationibus* (On the causes of marvelous natural effects, or on incantations), completed around 1520, Pomponazzi explained that prayers are part of the divinely ordered structure of the universe and do not depend on religious affiliation; as long as they are uttered with "recta et ordinata dispositio" (upright and orderly intent), they are part of the order of the universe granted by God. When they are sincere, prayers are always answered: "numquam frustrari potest, si ardenti mente fit" (it can never be prevented, if done with an ardent mind).[57]

Ariosto would therefore be in line with contemporary teaching about natural magic, as suggested by Franco Picchio: the power of prayer causes prayers to be heard, independently of whether they are addressed to the Christian God, the Muslim Allah, or the pagan gods.[58] Since the names of Ficino, Pico, and Pomponazzi have already come up in this discussion, it looks clear to me, once again, that the Christian/Muslim dialectic in the poem works for Ariosto as a means to address his intended readers' humanist interpretation of religious matters rather than as a way to explore otherness and identity.

8. Double Truth

I move now to my third and final example. In canto XXV, octave 44, of the *Orlando furioso*, Fiordispina prays fervently to her Muslim gods (*Macone e . . . tutti i dei*)[59] that Bradamante be transformed into the "better sex":

> Quanti prieghi la notte, quanti voti,
> offerse al suo Macone e a tutti i dei,
> che con miracoli apparenti e noti
> mutassero in miglior sesso costei!
> ma tutti vede andar d'effetto voti,
> e forse ancora il ciel ridea di lei.
> —*Fur.*, XXV 44
>
> [How many prayers and vows did she not offer that night to Mahomet and all the gods, asking them to change Bradamant's sex for the better by a clear and self-evident miracle! But she saw that all her prayers were vain; perhaps Heaven even mocked her.]

This prayer is paradoxical in many respects: not only is it a prayer to the "false" gods of Islam, apparently unworthy of being satisfied in itself, but it is also absurd and immoral in its content, because it requests a sexual transformation that would have been considered unnatural at the time. Yet the prayer of Fiordispina will be fulfilled; thanks to Ricciardetto's deception, her beloved will indeed be transformed from female into male, but through magic rather than divine intervention—at least, this is what Fiordispina is eager to believe.

The story comes from Boiardo's *Inamoramento de Orlando.*[60] It recounts that the Spanish princess Fiordispina, a Saracen, falls in love with someone she believes to be a man but who proves, in fact, to be Bradamante. Distraught at finding herself in love with a woman, Fiordispina nevertheless insists on inviting Bradamante to share her bed. During the night, she desperately explores whether Bradamante has changed into *il miglior sesso*, but in vain. The following morning, Bradamante returns home and tells her family what has happened. Her twin brother, Ricciardetto, seizes the opportunity to take advantage of the situation and goes to Fiordispina's castle pretending to be his sister. Fiordispina does not hesitate to share with him the same bed she had shared with his sister, but this time all to her advantage, because Ricciardetto makes clear that a nymph has transformed "her" into a male, thus paving the way to the heterosexual triumph of the final "joust."

The paradox is that, though undeserving of love because her desire is unnatural and hence undeserving of satisfaction and because her prayer is addressed to the wrong God, Fiordispina achieves both satisfaction and love. A number of interpreters of the episode have addressed issues of gender, personal and sexual identity, and humanist knowledge, but no one has yet, as far as I can determine, stressed Fiordispina belonging to the world of the Saracens in the poem.[61]

Ariosto's ambiguity in the treatment of religious matters here could not be more intriguing. Is the heaven that laughs at Fiordispina's prayer Christian or Muslim? As her request is unorthodox, it could easily be both. If we were to take things from a Christian perspective, this prayer would be even more ridiculous, as it includes an absurd request and is addressed to nonexistent pagan gods. And yet it is satisfied. But is it satisfied by the Muslim "gods"[62] or by a fatal coincidence? There can be no right answer, because Ariosto is purposely playing with double truth here. On the one hand, Fiordispina's prayer is undeserving of recognition, being both heretical and unnatural; on the other hand, it deserves to be rewarded because it is born of love, which is a human rather than supernatural force. In being human, in other words, Fiordispina overcomes the traditional, ideological opposition between Christian and Muslim. The paradoxical nature of her story is that every given truth can be questioned—including the prejudice that a prayer to Allah cannot be heard.[63]

9. Orientalism and Otherness

In 1932, the German novelist Hermann Hesse (1877–1962), one of the champions of German Orientalism, identified Ariosto's opening to canto VII of *Orlando furioso* as a gateway to modern Orientalism:

> I see that I am already coming up against one of the greatest obstacles in my account. The heights to which our deeds rose, the spiritual plane of experience to which they belong might be made proportionately more comprehensible to the reader if I were permitted to disclose to him the essence of the League's secret. But a great deal, perhaps everything, will remain incredible and incomprehensible. One paradox, however, must be accepted and this is that it is necessary to continually attempt the seemingly impossible. I agree with Siddhartha, our wise friend from the East, who once said: "Words do not express thoughts very well; everything immediately becomes a little different, a little distorted, a little foolish. And yet it also pleases me and seems right that what is of value and wisdom to one man seems nonsense to another." Even centuries ago the members and historians of our League recognized and courageously faced up to this difficulty. One of the greatest of them gave expression to it in an immortal verse:
>
> He who travels far will often see things
> Far removed from what he believed was Truth.
> When he talks about it in the fields at home,
> He is often accused of lying,
> For the obdurate people will not believe

> What they do not see and distinctly feel.
> Inexperience, I believe,
> Will give little credence to my song.
>
> This inexperience has also created the position where, now that publicity is being given to our journey which once roused thousands to ecstasy, it is not only forgotten but a real taboo is imposed upon its recollection.[64]

Ariosto is made to champion here an imaginary League, including, among others—and in an eclectic mixture of historical and fictional characters—Pythagoras, Plato, Don Quixote, Puss in Boots, Mozart, and Baudelaire, whose aim is to discover the "ultimate truth." The passage is particularly striking in that Ariosto had not yet been associated with Orientalism in literary criticism and would not come to be so identified for quite some time. Yet the *Orlando furioso* could be read as a key to the investigation of issues of otherness and spiritual journey in Hesse's 1930s Germany, to the extent that the poem's discourse on fiction makes way for the discovery of another world via the literary imagination, as Hesse suggests.

This other world, however, does not need to be situated in the reassuring dichotomy between West and East. It is a matter of journeying, in which religious divisions have little place. After all, Ariosto is more concerned with alternative literary worlds than with the fight between two rival ones. What interested him most, in conclusion, is literary fiction as a space to explore whatever might be relevant to himself and his readers rather than as a way to establish a relationship with either a specific poetic tradition (chivalric romance) or an ideological position (Christian truth). He appears to exploit the Christian/Muslim partition to highlight the problematic nature of truth and fiction, to develop an engagement with his audience in terms of contemporary religious arguments, and to subvert all traditional stereotypes. Rather than remaining strictly within his Christian milieu, Ariosto—a Christian who by culture and formation could not have been anything but a Christian—is also eager to promote a more nuanced view of religious conflict and open up the discussion, pointing toward an entirely new, unexplored world. Ariosto is part of the broader framework of humanist innovation in which religious themes were at the core of its debates and cultural identity. He is certainly more interested in intellectual dispute than in ideological approaches to the Orient. Seen in this light, Ariosto's religion would thus coincide with what Cantimori has identified as the pillars of the humanist approach to religion: critical reason, rejection of doctrine and dogma in the name of justification by faith alone, and critique against claims of authority.[65]

Notes

1. For references to the first edition of the poem, see Dorigatti's critical edition (Ariosto 2006).

2. On the Western tradition of the legend, see D'Ancona 1889; Casari 2003; Di Cesare 2012.

3. Gregory 2006, p. 132.

4. See Ricci 2002. On early modern processes of construction of religious otherness, see also Zatti 1998; Ricci 2008; and Formica 2012. On issues of conflict and otherness in chivalric literature before Ariosto, see Pagliardini and Fuchs 2006; Pagliardini 2008; De Capitani 2015; Perrotta 2017.

5. A useful critical perspective here could be drawn from anticipating for the *Orlando furioso* Zatti's analysis of "Christian Uniformity, Pagan Multiplicity" in Tasso's later poem, the *Gerusalemme liberata*; see Zatti 2006, pp. 135–159.

6. Fornari 1549, p. 34.

7. Everson 2005, p. 60.

8. For a reading of the *Orlando furioso* as "Christian epic," see Fichter 1982.

9. Pavlova 2015; 2020. See also Pavlova's chapter in this volume.

10. De Sanctis 2018, p. 563; English translation in De Sanctis 1930, p. 436.

11. Croce 1920; English translation, slightly modified, in Croce 1966, p. 64.

12. Calvino 1970; English translation in Cavallo 2013, p. 5.

13. Zatti 2018, p. 105; my translation.

14. Cavallo 2013.

15. Schwarz Lausten 2014, p. 262; my translation.

16. Pavlova 2014, p. 478.

17. Beer 2012. See also Jossa 2016; Dalmas 2018.

18. Dalmas 2019.

19. Dolce 1564, c. 448*v*; my translation. See also Hempfer 2004, p. 219; Dalmas 2019, p. 211.

20. Emilio Bigi (1982, p. 31), in his introduction to the poem, had already suggested that Ariosto's religious engagement should be examined in the following episodes: Charlemagne's prayer in XIX, 68–72 and subsequent allegory; Medoro's prayer in XVIII 184–185; the allegory of heresy in XXVI 31–53; Astolfo's descent to hell in XXXIV 4–92; Saint John's discourse in XXXIV 54–67; the attempted conversion of Agramante in XLI 37–45; the conversions and baptisms of Ruggiero in XLI 47–67 and Sobrino in XLIII 193–194.

21. Jameson 1986, p. 40.

22. Crusade propaganda was widespread at the time, moving from the legacy of the humanist Pope Pius II (Aeneas Sylvius Piccolomini) to Baldassare Castiglione's invitation to Christians "to devote their power to subjugating the infidels" (Castiglione 2002, p. 233). On this, see Moudarres 2012.

23. Hampton 1993.

24. Eco 2011, p. 10; English translation in Eco 2012, p. 2. For a similar approach in an epic-chivalric context, see also Quint 1993, pp. 213-247 (on Tasso's *Gerusalemme liberata*).

25. For further discussion of the episode, see Ascoli 2001; Ritrovato 2016; Di Gesù 2020.

26. Villa 2011.

27. The notion "horizon of expectations" was coined by the German critic Hans Robert Jauss (1970) to frame readers' approach to texts, taking into consideration the cultural codes readers bring to texts based on their previous reading. For the horizon of expectations of Ariosto's readers, based less on chivalric romance than on cultural debates within early-sixteenth-century Italian courts, see Jossa 2019.

28. For a reading of the full canto, see Bucchi 2016.

29. Gregory 2006, p. 149.

30. Cavallo 2013, p. 198.

31. See Ascoli 1987, pp. 352–353.

32. Quint 1993, p. 45.

33. See, e.g., *Inam.*, 2.24.18, where Charlemagne prays for divine aid.

34. Fragnito 1992; 2010; 2019.

35. For Ariosto's citation of Luther, see *Satira VI*: "Se Nicoletto o fra Martin fan segno / d'infedele o d'eretico, ne accuso / il saper troppo, e men con lor mi sdegno: / perché, salendo lo intelletto in suso / per veder Dio, non de' parerci strano / se talor cade giù cieco e confuso" (vv. 43–48). ("If Nicolet or Martin

seems to be / An atheist or heretic, I'm not inclined / To think he knows too much (a fault in me); / For when the intellect aspires to find / A straighter sight of God, there's nothing strange / if it should trip at times, confused and blind"; Ariosto 1977, p. 49). *Satira VI* can be dated to 1524–1525: see Paoli 2000 and Campeggiani 2017. On Ariosto's "loosely evangelical religion," see Mayer 1993, pp. 295–296.

36. For the location of Ariosto in contemporary debates and within his publisher's cultural program, see Marinelli 1987; Looney 2003; Jossa 2016; Jossa 2019.

37. Zarri 2006; Herzig 2008; Lazzerini 2013. On Ferrarese Savonarolism, see also Fragnito and Miegge 2001. Furthermore, Mazzocchi made explicit that Savonarola was from Ferrara; and Ariosto deliberately and prominently promoted his own Ferrarese heritage in the paratextual editorial strategy of the 1516 *Orlando furioso* (see Richardson 2018).

38. Savonarola 1846, p. 302; my translation.

39. Savonarola 1970, p. 200; for the English translation, Savonarola 1889, p. 11. The *Miserere* was included in one of the texts published by Mazzocchi; see Jossa 2019, pp. 154–157.

40. Cantimori 1975, p. 291.

41. Other references to justification by faith alone can be found in *Fur.*, XXXIII 117; XXXIV 56; and *Cinque Canti*, IV 76 and 82. See Fragnito 1992, p. 320; Fragnito 2019, p. 195.

42. See especially Halbwachs 1980; Assman 2005.

43. Ascoli 1987, p. 352.

44. Fragnito 2010, pp. 109, 124. On censorship on the *Orlando furioso*, see also Helm 2012. For further discussion on both censorship and the relevant episode here, see also Dalmas 2019, pp. 197–199, 205–207.

45. Cavallo 2013, p. 199.

46. Prandi 2006; Genovese 2012.

47. On Pythagoras's relevance in Renaissance thinking, see Celenza 1999; Allen 2014.

48. "Cum Sebastianus Aquila, vir bonarum artium sedulus cultor, qui apud nos praeter medicinam, quam publico stipendio docet, academicum dogma profitetur, Platonem in Timaeo diebus festis maxima audientia legat, non mediocre desiderium studiosis incidit habendi libros Marsilii et aliorum qui aliquid de hac secta a Graecis scriptum latine transtulerunt. Et cum tu possis illos potissimum explere: nam id cum ex aliis tum superioribus diebus ex Alberto Pio, viro magnifico ac literatissimo, cognovi, qui abs te rediens ad nos volumen inter caeteros attulit, in quo platonicorum quorundam opera quaedam congesta sunt; ego, ut his doctis viris qui ad id hortantur morem geram, et tuae utilitati consulam, quam non minima existimo si quae imprimenda curasti a pluribus emantur, meum ufficium duxi te litteris obsecrare, ut nostro huic honesto desiderio obsequi velis" (Ariosto 1965, p. 3). The English translation is from Ariosto 2010, p. 25. For the identification of the volume requested by Ariosto with Aldo's 1497 collection of Ficino's translations of hermetic and Neoplatonic texts, see Benedetti 2001, p. 211.

49. Savarese 1984; Marinelli 1987. For a more nuanced view of Ariosto's cultural environment, see also Ascoli 1987.

50. On Mazzocchi's press, see Everson 1994, pp. 66–67; Nuovo 1998, pp. 93–100; Azzini 2008; Everson 2011; Richardson 2018. On Bonaccioli's importance for Mazzocchi's printing enterprise, see Jossa 2019.

51. Kolsky 1991, pp. 50–60. On the relationship between Ariosto and Equicola, see Regan 2005.

52. Martin 2017. On Pomponazzi's lectures in Ferrara, see Zambelli 1994.

53. On the role played by Alberto Pio in Renaissance Aristotelianism, see Schmitt 1984. Ariosto dedicated three of the Latin poems of his youth to Alberto Pio; see Ariosto 2018.

54. Ariosto's "Orientalism" would rather lie in his bond with figures interested in Egyptian antiquities, Pythagoreanism, Orphism, and Oriental philosophy, such as his master Celio Calcagnini in Ferrara and his friend Pierio Valeriano in Rome (both mentioned in the list of friends awaiting the conclusion of the poem in the last canto of the *Orlando furioso*); see Curran 2007.

55. On Medoro's prayer, see Javitch 2016.

56. On Renaissance philosophy of prayer, see Walker 1958.

57. For Pomponazzi's philosophy of prayer, see Douglas 1910, pp. 291–300.

58. Picchio 2007, p. 209.

59. It was typical of the medieval chivalric tradition to include Mahomet in a triad of divinities together with Apollon and Trivigant, as if this corresponded to the Christian Holy Trinity but also reminiscent of pagan polytheism; see De Capitani 2015. Ariosto was, understandably, rather uninformed about Islam and relied mostly on literary tradition for his ideas about it; see Pavlova 2014; Pavlova 2020.

60. Boiardo, *Inam.*, III 9, 26.

61. Orazio Ariosto, the great-nephew of the poet, mentioned in his defense of the *Orlando furioso* that Fiordispina "è donna di diversa religione e nimica" (is a woman of another religion and an enemy; Ariosto 1585, p. 75) but did not make much use of this. For interpretations of the episode, see Ferroni 1982; Finucci 1992, pp. 199–225; Shemek 1998, pp. 111–116; Mac Carthy 2007, pp. 146–151; Primo 2007; DeCoste 2009; Mac Carthy 2019; Strologo 2019a and 2019b, as well as Pavlova's chapter in this volume.

62. See note 59 above.

63. On Pomponazzi and double truth, see Pine 1968. Although Ariosto cannot be linked with such complex philosophical speculation, there is nevertheless a sense of a shared cultural relationship that merits further consideration.

64. Hesse 1933, pp. 6–7.

65. Cantimori 1975, p. 283.

Bibliography

Allen 2014

Allen, M. J. B. "Pythagoras in the Early Renaissance." In *A History of Pythagoreanism*, edited by Carl A. Huffman, pp. 435–453. Cambridge: Cambridge University Press, 2014.

Ariosto 1585

Ariosto, Orazio. *Difese dell'*Orlando furioso (1585). In Giuseppe Venturini, *Orazio Ariosti e la polemica intorno alla superiorità del Tasso sull'Ariosto*. Ferrara: Deputazione Provinciale Ferrarese di Storia Patria, 1972.

Ariosto 1965

Ariosto, Ludovico. *Lettere*, edited by Angelo Stella. Milan: Mondadori, 1965.

Ariosto 1974

Ariosto, Ludovico. *Orlando furioso*, translated by Guido Waldman. Oxford: Oxford University Press, .1974.

Ariosto 1977

Ariosto, Ludovico. *The Satires*, translated by Rudolph B. Gottfried. Bloomington, IN: R. B. Gottfried, 1977.

Ariosto 2006

Ariosto, Ludovico. *Orlando furioso di Ludovico Ariosto secondo la princeps del 1516*, edited by Marco Dorigatti, with Gerarda Stimato. Florence: Olschki, 2006.

Ariosto 2010

Ariosto, Ludovico. *"My Muse Will Have a Story to Paint": Selected Prose of Ludovico Ariosto*, translated by Dennis Looney. Toronto: University of Toronto Press, 2010.

Ariosto 2018

Ariosto, Ludovico. *Latin Poetry*, translated by Dennis Looney and D. Mark Possanza. Cambridge, MA: Harvard University Press, 2018.

Ascoli 1987

Ascoli, Albert Russell. *Ariosto's Bitter Harmony: Crisis and Evasion in the Italian Renaissance*. Princeton, NJ: Princeton University Press, 1987.

Ascoli 2001

Ascoli, Albert Russell. "Ariosto and the 'Fier Pastor': Form and History in *Orlando Furioso*." *Renaissance Quarterly* 54, no. 2 (2001): pp. 487–522. doi:10.2307/3176785. https://www.jstor.org/stable/3176785.

Assman 2005

Assman, Jan. *Religion and Cultural Memory: Ten Studies*, translated by Rodney Livingstone. Stanford, CA: Stanford University Press, 2005.

Azzini 2008

Azzini, Eleonora. "Mazzocchi, Giovanni (Giovanni Mazzocco di Bondeno)." *DBI* 72 (2008).

Beer 2012

Beer, Marina. "Osservazioni sull'*Orlando Furioso* e le Sacre Scritture." In *Religion et littérature à la Renaissance:* Mélanges en l'honneur de Franco Giacone, edited by François Roudaut, pp. 457–472. Paris: Classiques Garnier, 2012.

Benedetti 2001

Benedetti, Stefano. *Itinerari di Cebete: Tradizione e ricezione della* Tabula *in Italia dal XV al XVIII secolo.* Rome: Bulzoni, 2001.

Bigi 1982

Bigi, Emilio. "Introduzione." In Ludovico Ariosto, *Orlando furioso*, pp. 7–70. Milan: Rusconi, 1982.

Bucchi 2016

Bucchi, Gabriele. "Canto XIV." In *Lettura dell'"Orlando furioso,"* Vol. 1, edited by Gabriele Bucchi and Franco Tomasi, pp. 361–384. Florence: Edizioni del Galluzzo, 2016.

Calvino 1970

Calvino, Italo. *Orlando Furioso di Ludovico Ariosto raccontato da Italo Calvino.* Turin: Einaudi, 1970.

Campeggiani 2017

Campeggiani, Ida. *L'ultimo Ariosto: Dalle Satire ai Frammenti autografi.* Pisa: Scuola Normale Superiore, 2017.

Cantimori 1975

Cantimori, Delio. *Umanesimo e religione nel Rinascimento.* Turin: Einaudi, 1975.

Casari 2003

Casari, Mario. "Percorsi tematici nel viaggio euro-asiatico dei testi." In *Lo Spazio letterario del Medioevo* 3: *Le culture circostanti*, Vol. 2, *La cultura arabo-islamica*, edited by Mario Capaldo, Franco Cardini, Guglielmo Cavallo, and Biancamaria Scarcia Amoretti, pp. 459–498. Rome: Salerno Editrice, 2003.

Castiglione 2002

Baldesar Castiglione. *The Book of the Courtier*, edited by Daniel Javitch, translated by Charles Singleton. New York: Norton, 2002.

Cavallo 2013

Cavallo, Jo Ann. *The World beyond Europe in the Romance Epics of Boiardo and Ariosto.* Toronto: University of Toronto Press, 2013.

Celenza 1999

Celenza, Christopher S. "Pythagoras in the Renaissance: The Case of Marsilio Ficino." *Renaissance Quarterly* 52, no. 3 (1999): pp. 667–711. doi:10.2307/2901915. https://www.jstor.org/stable/2901915.

Croce 1966

Croce, Benedetto. *Ariosto, Shakespeare and Corneille*, translated by Douglas Ainslie. New York: Russell & Russell, 1966.

Curran 2 007

Curran, Brian. *The Egyptian Renaissance: The Afterlife of Ancient Egypt in Early Modern Italy.* Chicago: University of Chicago Press, 2007.

Dalmas 2018

Dalmas, Davide. "Ariosto apocalittico." *Italique: Poésie italienne de la Renaissance* 21 (2018): pp. 29–58.

Dalmas 2019

Dalmas, Davide. "Dibattiti religiosi e polemica anticlericale nei poemi di Boiardo e Ariosto." In *Verso la riforma: Criticare la chiesa, riformare la chiesa (15.–16. secolo)*, edited by Susanna Peyronel Rambaldi, pp. 197–214. Turin: Claudiana, 2019.

D'Ancona 1889

D'Ancona, Alessandro. "La leggenda di Maometto in Occidente." *Giornale Storico della Letteratura Italiana* 13 (1889): pp. 199–281.

De Capitani 2015

De Capitani, Patrizia. "Les 'musulmans' dans quelques narrations chevaleresques italiennes des XIVe et XVe siècles: Entre persistances et changements." *Cahier d'études italiennes* 21 (2015): pp. 55–84.

DeCoste 2009

Mary-Michelle DeCoste. *Hopeless Love: Boiardo, Ariosto, and Narratives of Queer Female Desire.* Toronto: University of Toronto Press, 2009.

De Sanctis 1930
De Sanctis, Francesco. *History of Italian Literature*, translated by Joan Redfern. Oxford: Oxford University Press, 1930 (Vol. 1), 1932 (Vol. 2).
De Sanctis 2018
De Sanctis, Francesco. *Storia della letteratura italiana*, introduction by René Welleck. Milan: Rizzoli, 2018.
Di Cesare 2012
Di Cesare, Michelina. *The Pseudo-historical Image of the Prophet Muhammad in Medieval Latin Literature: A Repertory*. Berlin: De Gruyter, 2012.
Di Gesù 2020
Di Gesù, Matteo. *L'*Orlando furioso*, l'Italia (e i Turchi). Note su identità, alterità, conflitti*. Macerata: Quodlibet, 2020.
Dolce 1564
Dolce, Lodovico. *Modi affigurati e voci scelte et eleganti della volgar lingua: Con un discorso sopra a' mutamenti e diversi ornamenti dell'Ariosto*. Venice: Gio. Battista et Marchio Sessa, 1564.
Douglas 1910
Douglas, Andrew Halliday. *The Philosophy and Psychology of Pietro Pomponazzi*. Cambridge: Cambridge University Press, 1910.
Eco 2011
Eco, Umberto. *Costruire il nemico e altri scritti occasionali*. Milan: Bompiani, 2011.
Eco 2012
Eco, Umberto. *Inventing the Enemy: Essays*, translated by Richard Dixon. Boston: Houghton Mifflin Harcourt, 2012.
Everson 1994
Everson, Jane E. *Bibliografia del* Mambriano *di Francesco Cieco da Ferrara*. Alessandria: Edizioni dell'Orso, 1994.
Everson 2005
Everson, Jane E. "The Epic Tradition of Charlemagne in Italy." *Cahiers de Recherches Médiévales et Humanistes* 12 (2005): pp. 45–81. https://journals.openedition.org/crm/2192.
Everson 2011
Everson, Jane. "Il Mambriano di Francesco Cieco da Ferrara—fra tradizione cavalleresca e mondo estense." In *L'uno e l'altro Ariosto: In corte e nelle delizie*, edited by Gianni Venturi, pp. 153–173. Florence: Olschki, 2011.
Ferroni 1982
Ferroni, Giulio. "Da Bradamante a Ricciardetto: Interferenze testuali e scambi di sesso." In *La parola ritrovata: Fonti e analisi letteraria*, edited by Costanzo Di Girolamo and Ivano Paccagnella, pp. 137–159. Palermo: Sellerio, 1982.
Fichter 1982
Fichter, Andrew. *Poets Historical: Dynastic Epic in the Renaissance*. New Haven, CT: Yale University Press, 1982.
Finucci 1992
Finucci, Valeria. *The Lady Vanishes: Subjectivity and Representation in Castiglione and Ariosto*. Stanford, CA: Stanford University Press, 1992.
Formica 2012
Formica, Marina. *Lo specchio turco: Immagini dell'altro e riflessi del sé nella cultura italiana d'età moderna*. Rome: Donzelli, 2012.
Fornari 1549
Fornari, Simon. *La spositione sopra l'Orlando furioso di M. L. Ariosto*. Florence: Lorenzo Torrentino, 1549 (Vol. 1), 1550 (Vol. 2).
Fragnito 1992
Fragnito, Gigliola. "Intorno alla 'religione' dell'Ariosto: I dubbi del Bembo e le credenze ereticali del fratello Galasso." *Lettere Italiane* 34 (1992): pp. 208–239. (Also in *Cinquecento italiano: Religione, cultura e potere dal Rinascimento alla Controriforma*, pp. 289–323. Bologna: Il Mulino, 2011.)
Fragnito 2010
Fragnito, Gigliola. "'Vanissimus et spurcissimus homo': Ariosto all'esame dei censori." In *Dalla biblio-*

grafia alla storia: Studi in onore di Ugo Rozzo, edited by Rudj Gorian, pp. 115–129. Udine: Forum, 2010.

Fragnito 2019

Fragnito, Gigliola. *Rinascimento perduto: La letteratura italiana sotto gli occhi dei censori (secoli XV–XVII)*. Bologna: Il Mulino, 2019.

Fragnito and Miegge 2001

Fragnito, Gigliola, and Mario Miegge, eds. *Savonarola da Ferrara all'Europa, Atti del Convegno internazionale (Ferrara, 30 marzo–3 aprile 1998)*. Florence: Sismel–Edizioni del Galluzzo, 2001.

Genovese 2012

Genovese, Gianluca. "'Quel c'ha detto, non può far non detto': Il silenzio nell'*Orlando furioso*." In *Silenzio: Atti del Terzo Colloquio Internazionale di Letteratura Italiana*, edited by Silvia Zoppi, pp. 145–165. Rome: Salerno Editrice, 2012. (Also reprinted as "Il Silenzio, tra icona e figura morale." In *Le vie del Furioso*, pp. 97–118. Naples: Guida, 2017.

Gregory 2006

Gregory, Tobias. *From Many Gods to One: Divine Action in Renaissance Epic*. Chicago: University of Chicago Press, 2006.

Halbwachs 1992

Halbwachs, Maurice. *The Collective Memory*, edited, translated, and with an introduction by Lewis A. Coser. Chicago: University of Chicago Press, 1992.

Hampton 1993

Hampton, Timothy. "'Turkish Dogs': Rabelais, Erasmus, and the Rhetoric of Alterity." *Representations* 41 (Winter 1993): pp. 58–82.

Helm 2012

Helm, Jennifer. "Literary Censorship: The Case of the *Orlando furioso*." *Dimensioni e problemi della ricerca storica*, 1 (2012): pp. 193–214. doi: 10.7376/71412.

Hempfer 2004

Hempfer, Klaus W. *Letture discrepanti: La ricezione dell'*Orlando furioso *nel Cinquecento: Lo studio della ricezione storica come euristica dell'interpretazione*. Modena: Franco Cosimo Panini, 2004. Original edition *Diskrepante Lektüren: Die Orlando-Furioso-Rezeption im Cinquecento: Historische Rezeptionsforschung als Heuristik der Interpretation*, n.p., 1987.

Herzig 2008

Herzig, Tamar. *Savonarola's Women: Visions and Reform in Renaissance Italy*. Chicago: University of Chicago Press, 2008.

Hesse 1933

Hesse, Hermann. *The Journey to the East*, translated by Hilda Rosner. London: Peter Owen, Vision Press, 1933. (Original edition *Die Morgenlandfahrt*, n.p., 1932.)

Jameson 1986

Jameson, Fredric. "Religion and Ideology: A Political Reading of *Paradise Lost*." In *Literature, Politics, and Theory*, edited by Francis Barker. London: Methuen, 1986.

Jauss 1970

Jauss, Hans Robert. "Literary History as a Challenge to Literary Theory," translated by Elizabeth Benzinger. *New Literary History* 2, no. 1 (1970): pp. 7–37. doi: 10.2307/468585. https://www.jstor.org/stable/468585.

Javitch 2010

Javitch, Daniel. "Reconsidering the Last Part of *Orlando Furioso*: Romance to the Bitter End." *Modern Language Quarterly* 71, no. 4 (2010): pp. 385–406.

Javitch 2016

Javitch, Daniel. "Canto XVIII." In *Lettura dell'"Orlando furioso,"* Vol. 1, edited by Gabriele Bucchi and Franco Tomasi, pp. 441–456. Florence: Edizioni del Galluzzo, 2016.

Jossa 2016

Jossa, Stefano. "'A difesa di sua santa fede': Il poema cristiano dell'Ariosto (*Orlando furioso*, XXXIV 54–67)." In *Chivalry, Academy, and Cultural Dialogues: The Italian Contribution to European Culture, Essays in Honour of Jane E. Everson*, edited by Stefano Jossa and Giuliana Pieri, pp. 32–42. Cambridge: Legenda, 2016.

Jossa 2019
Jossa, Stefano. "L'*Orlando Furioso* nel suo contesto editoriale." In *"Dreaming Again on Things Already Dreamed": 500 Years of Orlando Furioso (1516–2016)*, edited by Marco Dorigatti and Maria Pavlova, pp. 147–172. Oxford: Peter Lang, 2019.

Kolsky 1991
Kolsky, Stephen. *Mario Equicola: The Real Courtier*. Geneva: Librairie Droz, 1991.

Lazzerini 2013
Lazzerini, Luigi. *Teologia del Miserere: Da Savonarola al "Beneficio di Cristo" 1490–1543*. Turin: Rosenberg & Sellier, 2013.

Looney 2003
Looney, Dennis. "Ariosto and the Classics in Ferrara." In *Ariosto Today: Contemporary Perspectives*, edited by Donald Beecher, Massimo Ciavolella, and Roberto Fedi, pp. 18–31. Toronto: University of Toronto Press, 2003.

Mac Carthy 2007
Mac Carthy, Ita. *Women and the Making of Poetry in Ariosto's Orlando Furioso*. Leicester, UK: Troubador, 2007.

Mac Carthy 2019
Mac Carthy, Ita. "Fiordispina's English Afterlives: From Harington to Ali Smith." In *Ariosto, the Orlando Furioso and English Culture*, edited by Jane E. Everson, Andrew Hiscock, and Stefano Jossa, pp. 125–143. Oxford: Oxford University Press, 2019.

Marinelli 1987
Marinelli, Peter V. *Ariosto and Boiardo: The Origins of* Orlando Furioso. Columbia: University of Missouri Press, 1987.

Martin 2017
Martin, Craig. "Pietro Pomponazzi." In *The Stanford Encyclopedia of Philosophy Archive* (Winter 2017),edited by Edward N. Zalta. https://stanford.library.sydney.edu.au/archives/win2017/entries/pomponazzi.

Mayer 1993
Mayer, Thomas F. "Ariosto Anticlerical: Epic Poetry and the Clergy in Early Cinquecento Italy." In *Anticlericalism in Late Medieval and Early Modern Europe,* Proceedings of an *International Colloquium Held Sept. 20–22, 1990, at the University of Arizona, Tucson*, edited by Peter Alan Dykema and Heiko Augustinus Oberman, pp. 283–297. Leiden: Brill, 1993.

McLaughlin 2019
McLaughlin, Martin. "The Furioso in Translation: 'Lascivious' Ariosto in Two Modern English Versions." In *Ariosto, the Orlando Furioso and English Culture*, edited by Jane E. Everson, Andrew Hiscock, and Stefano Jossa, pp. 246–267. Oxford: Oxford University Press, 2019.

Moudarres 2012
Moudarres, Andrea. "The Geography of the Enemy: Old and New Empires between Humanist Debates and Tasso's *Gerusalemme liberata*." In *New Worlds and the Italian Renaissance: Contributions to the History of European Intellectual Culture*, edited by Andrea Moudarres and Christiana Purdy Moudarres, pp. 291–332. Leiden: Brill, 2012.

Nuovo 1998
Nuovo, Angela. *Il commercio librario a Ferrara tra XV e XVI secolo: La bottega di Domenico Sivieri*. Florence: Olschki, 1998.

Pagliardini 2008
Pagliardini, Angelo. "Cristiani e pagani nell'epica cavalleresca cristiana." *Carte di viaggio: Studi di lingua e letteratura italiana* 1 (2008): pp. 1–24.

Pagliardini and Fuchs 2006
Pagliardini, Angelo, and Fuchs, Gerhild. "La rappresentazione del pagano/musulmano nell'epica cavalleresca rinascimentale." In *Italia e Europa: Dalla cultura nazionale all'interculturalismo, Atti XVI Congresso dell'A.I.P.I. Cracovia 26–29 agosto 2004*, edited by Bart Van den Bossche, Michel Bastiaensen, Corinna Salvadori Lonergan, and Stanislaw Widłak, Vol. 2, pp. 579–587. Florence: Cesati, 2006.

Paoli 2000
Paoli, Michel. "*'Quale fu la prima satira che compose'*: Storia vs. letteratura nelle satire ariostesche." In *Fra Satire e Rime ariostesche*, edited by Claudia Berra, pp. 35–63. Milan: Cisalpino, 2000.

Pavlova 2014
Pavlova, Maria. "Ariosto." In *Christian-Muslim Relations: A Bibliographical History*, Vol. 6, *Western Europe (1500–1600)*, edited by David Thomas and John Chesworth, pp. 469–483. Leiden: Brill, 2014.
Pavlova 2015
Pavlova, Maria. "'Il fior de Pagania': Saracens and Their World in Boiardo and Ariosto." PhD diss., Oxford University, 2015.
Pavlova 2020
Pavlova, Maria. *Saracens and Their World in Boiardo and Ariosto*. Cambridge: Legenda, 2020.
Perrotta 2017
Perrotta, Annalisa. *I cristiani e gli Altri: Guerre di religione, politica e propaganda nel poema cavalleresco di fine Quattrocento*. Rome: Bagatto Libri, 2017.
Picchio 2007
Picchio, Franco. *Ariosto e Bacco due: Apocalisse e nuova religione nel* Furioso. Cosenza: Pellegrini, 2007.
Pine 1968
Pine, Martin. "Pomponazzi and the Problem of 'Double Truth.'" *Journal of the History of Ideas* 29, no. 2 (1968): pp. 163–176. https://www.jstor.org/stable/2708574.
Prandi 2006
Prandi, Stefano. "Premesse umanistiche del 'Furioso': Ariosto, Calcagnini e il Silenzio (*O.F.* XIV, 78–97)." *Lettere Italiane* 58, no. 1 (2006): pp. 3–32. https://www.jstor.org/stable/26267052.
Primo 2007
Primo, Novella. "Ariosto, Ovidio e la 'favola' di Fiordispina." *Carte Italiane* 2, nos. 2–3 (2007). http://escholarship.org/uc/item/7wc6r5t6.
Quint 1993
Quint, David. *Epic and Empire: Politics and Generic Form from Virgil to Milton*. Princeton, NJ: Princeton University Press, 1993.
Regan 2005
Regan, Lisa K. "Ariosto's Threshold Patron: Isabella d'Este in the 'Orlando Furioso.'" *Modern Language Notes* 120, no. 1 (2005): pp. 50–69. www.jstor.org/stable/3252027.
Ricci 2002
Ricci, Giovanni. *Ossessione turca: In una retrovia cristiana dell'Europa moderna*. Bologna: Il Mulino, 2002.
Ricci 2008
Ricci, Giovanni. *I Turchi alle porte*. Bologna: Il Mulino, 2008.
Richardson 2018
Richardson, Brian. "The 1516 Edition of Ariosto's *Orlando Furioso*: The Opening." *Modern Language Review* 113, no. 1 (2018): pp. 80–106. www.jstor.org/stable/10.5699/modelangrevi.113.1.0080.
Ritrovato 2016
Ritrovato, Salvatore. "Canto XVII." In *Lettura dell'"Orlando furioso,"* Vol. 1, edited by Gabriele Bucchi and Franco Tomasi, pp. 421–440. Florence: Edizioni del Galluzzo, 2016.
Savarese 1984
Savarese, Gennaro. "Il progetto del poema tra Marsilio Ficino e 'adescatrici galliche.'" In Gennaro Savarese, *Il Furioso e la cultura del Rinascimento*, pp. 15–37. Rome: Bulzoni, 1984.
Savonarola 1846
Sermoni e prediche di F. Girolamo Savonarola de' predicatori. Prato: Ranieri Guasti, 1846.
Savonarola 1889
Savonarola, Girolamo. *An Exposition of the Psalm Miserere Mei Deus*, translated by F. C. Cowper. Milwaukee: Young Churchman, 1889.
Savonarola 1970
Savonarola, Girolamo. "Expositio in Psalmum '*Miserere mei, deus*.'" In *Operette spirituali*, edited by Mario Ferrara, Vol. 2, pp. 195–234. Rome: Belardetti, 1970.
Schmitt 1984
Schmitt, Charles B. "Alberto Pio and the Aristotelian Studies of his Time." In Charles B. Schmitt, *The Aristotelian Tradition and Renaissance Universities*, pp. 43–64. London: Variorum, 1984.
Schwarz Lausten 2014
Schwarz Lausten, Pia. "Saraceni e Turchi nell'*Orlando Furioso* di Ariosto." In *Studi di Italianistica nordica*,

Atti del X Convegno, edited by Marco Cargiulo, Margareth Hagen, and Stefano Rosatti, pp. 261–286. Rome: Aracne Editrice, 2014.

Shemek 1998
Shemek, Dianna. *Ladies Errant: Wayward Women and Social Order in Early Modern Italy*. Durham, NC: Duke University Press, 1998.

Strologo 2019a
Strologo, Franca. "Canto XXV." In *Lettura dell'"Orlando furioso,"* Vol. 2, edited by Annalisa Izzo and Franco Tomasi, pp. 55–84. Florence: Edizioni del Galluzzo, 2019.

Strologo 2019b
Strologo, Franca. "Trasgressione, travestimento e metamorfosi nel *Furioso*: Intorno alla storia di Ricciardetto e Fiordispina." In *"Dreaming Again on Things Already Dreamed": 500 Years of Orlando Furioso (1516–2016)*, edited by Marco Dorigatti and Maria Pavlova, pp. 173–198. Oxford: Peter Lang, 2019.

Villa 2011
Villa, Alessandra. "Variazioni sull'idea di barbarie nell'*Orlando furioso*." *Chroniques italiennes* 19, no. 1 (2011): pp. 1–20. http://chroniquesitaliennes.univ-paris3.fr/PDF/web19/Villaweb19.pdf.

Walker 1958
Walker, Daniel Pickering. *Spiritual and Demonic Magic: From Ficino to Campanella*. London: Warburg Institute, 1958.

Zambelli 1994
Zambelli, Paola. "Pomponazzi, i greci e Ferrara." In *Alla corte degli Estensi: Filosofia, arte e cultura a Ferrara nei secoli XV e XVI*, edited by Marco Bertozzi, pp. 41–64. Ferrara: Università degli Studi, 1994.

Zarri 2006
Zarri, Gabriella. *La religione di Lucrezia Borgia*. Rome: Roma nel Rinascimento, 2006.

Zatti 1998
Zatti, Sergio, ed. *La rappresentazione dell'altro nei testi del Rinascimento*. Pisa: Pacini-Fazzi, 1998.

Zatti 2006
Zatti, Sergio. *The Quest for Epic: From Ariosto to Tasso*, edited by Dennis Looney, introduction by Albert Russell Ascoli, translated by Sally Hill and Dennis Looney. Toronto: University of Toronto Press, 2006.

Zatti 2016
Zatti, Sergio, *Lettura dell'*Orlando furioso. Bologna: Il Mulino, 2016.

PART II

Textual Contexts: Around the *Furioso*

Literary Life in Mamluk Egypt and Syria (1250–1517): A Forgotten Heyday of Arabic Culture

Thomas Bauer

1. Meanwhile in the East . . .

In January 1517, a few months after Ariosto had published the first version of his *Orlando furioso*, the Mamluk army suffered its ultimate defeat at the battle of Raydāniyya outside Cairo. Henceforth, Egypt, Syria, and the Ḥijāz ended up as mere provinces of the Ottoman Empire. The Ottoman conquest led to the end of one of the most glorious eras in the history of Egypt and Syria, both politically and culturally.

With the exception of the conspicuously stunning architecture, the cultural achievements of the Mamluk period have been utterly neglected by modern scholarship. The backwardness of Islamic regions in the nineteenth and twentieth centuries was attributed to a long period of stagnation and decline that lasted for almost a millennium. Improbable as such an idea might seem, this narrative was well suited to the interests of colonialism with its promise to restore the Arabian lands to their former glory. Consequently, literature of the Mamluk period was rarely read and almost never studied until recent decades.[1] Despite the short history of Mamluk literary studies, it does not overstate the case to say that the period from the twelfth century to the Ottoman conquest (the period largely covered by the dynasties of the Ayyubids and Mamluks) was one of the most productive, vibrant, and multifarious periods in the history of Arabic literature.[2] At one end of the spectrum, elite poets and prose authors created some of the most sophisticated and elegant texts in the entire Arabic literary tradition, while at the same time, popular poets and storytellers flourished in Syria and Egypt, where a larger segment of the population than ever before engaged in the literary marketplace as producers and/or consumers.

At the time of Ariosto, the Mamluk Empire was the uncontested center of Arabic literature. But did Ariosto know of it, and could Arabic literature of this period have had any influence on him when he wrote about his *arabi* and *saraceni*? Arabic influence is visible in several ways in Ariosto's work, but it is highly improbable that it originated from contemporary connections. Rather, Ariosto was benefiting from contacts between Arabic and Romance literatures from earlier periods that had left their traces in Italian literature. It has since been established that the first of such contacts dates back to the beginning of the twelfth century, when Occitanian troubadours took inspiration from singers of Arabic strophic poetry. The troubadours, in their turn, most likely together with indigenous Arabic traditions, shaped the poetry of the Sicilian School in the thirteenth century. These currents, directly and/or indirectly, influenced poetry in Italian, French, and Spanish. Petrarch and his followers and even Spanish baroque poetry still owe much to Arabic love poetry.[3] The influence of *petrarchismo* is evident in the work of Ariosto, though he was most certainly unaware of its Arabic tint.

After the Arabs had lost Sicily and with the end of Arabic predominance over al-Andalus (Islamic Iberia), influence from the western part of the Arab territories lost its significance. Claudia Ott, however, offers an interesting perspective on parallels to *Orlando furioso* in the collection of *One Hundred and One Nights*, which points to a "Western" connection in the field of prose.[4] It is more difficult to identify influence in prose than in poetry, since themes and motifs traveled orally in ways that can hardly be retraced.

As for the eastern part of the Arab world, it is obvious that the Crusades were a major inspiration for *Orlando furioso*. However, this is again an inspiration from the past, since Latin presence in the Levant had ended when the Mamluk sultan al-Ashraf Khalīl conquered ʿAkkā (Acre) in 1291. Since the Arabs of this region were no longer immediate enemies, Ariosto could portray the *arabi* and *saraceni* in a not entirely negative way but even grant them real heroism—contrary to the *turchi*, the Ottomans, who constituted a menace to the Italian powers and the nemesis of the Mamluk Empire.

Given the fact that these many threads of almost exclusively indirect Arabic influence in Ariosto's *Orlando* are virtually inextricable, it seems more rewarding for the moment to engage in synchronic comparison of different literary traditions without attempting to determine specific influences. A comparison of this kind not only might point to parallel or contrary developments but could also highlight phenomena and raise questions that would otherwise be overlooked or considered less relevant were the focus to be with one particular literary tradition alone. In this regard, the following three points could merit further investigation.

First, a contrasting development seems to take place as concerns the importance of the courts as centers of literary life, in relation to that of the towns. Whereas Italy at the time of Ariosto witnessed the growing importance of the courts, it was the *Bürgertum* ("bourgeoisie") of the cities that came to dominate the field of literature in the Mamluk period.

Second, a similar development, though with different results, is the growing importance of vernacular literature. In the Mamluk period, the *zajal*, strophic poetry in the *volgare*, was even composed and enjoyed by the educated elite, and epics in colloquial Arabic formed a major part of popular oral tradition and began to be written down as literature. But whereas in Italian literature, the *volgare* gradually replaced Latin and ultimately led to the creation of a national language, for various reasons, Classical Arabic has remained the language of literature up to the present day.

Finally, it is remarkable that the epic in the vernacular witnessed a heyday both in Arabic and in the Italian vernacular around the period of Ariosto's lifetime. Both differed greatly in their origin as well as in their character. The Arabic epic seems to be much older (though sources are comparatively late), drawing from traditions such as stories about the wars and skirmishes of Arab tribes in pre-Islamic times and ancient Persian narratives. The setting of the Arabic epics ranges from the Maghreb and Islamic Spain, Himyaritic southern Arabia, and the Sassanian Empire far into Asia, and it stretches from the time of Alexander the Great, almost up to contemporary events in the Mamluk Empire. Miracles and magic play a crucial role in some of the epics but are almost absent in others. Apart from these differences, most epics share a fascination with the exotic and focus around the subjects of love and, especially, heroism, often depicting the hero moving from one battle to the next. It is also here that a striking similarity between the Arabic and Romance epics is conspicuous: their focus on the heroic and the fascination with fantastic places, in which the encounter with the stranger is almost always hostile and a challenge to the hero's valor. The "Fremdraum," as Thomas Herzog calls them, are Islamic territories from al-Andalus to Egypt in the case of Ariosto's *Orlando*, where the Christian heroes struggle with the *saraceni*, while they consist of Genoa, Catalonia, and Portugal in the *Sīrat Baybars*, where Baybars engage in battle with the Francs.[5] The reason for this convergence is less likely to be the result of direct influence than due to similar audience expectations and predilections. A striking parallel phenomenon is the *donne guerriere* such as Bradamante and Marfisa in *Orlando furioso*. In the more or less contemporary popular Arabic epics, they find an intriguing parallel in the "warrior women of Islam," as Remke Kruk titled her study on the subject.[6]

In order to trigger ideas for comparisons of this kind, it seems worthwhile to cast a glance over the eastern shores of the Mediterranean to gather an impression about what was happening in Arabic literature at the period between the beginnings of Italian literature and the death of Ariosto in the West. Inevitably, such a short overview will be somewhat superficial and partial, not only as a consequence of its brevity but also due to the incomplete state of scholarship. After all, to attempt such an overview would have been completely impossible only fifteen years ago.

2. A Post-Decline Society

Copying books can be dangerous. The Cairene poet and scholar Badr al-dīn al-Bashtakī (1347–1427) earned his living by copying books, and he was an especially talented copyist. As his biographer, Ibn Ḥajar al-ʿAsqalānī (1372–1449) informs us, he could copy ten quires per day. He would write the first five quires while sitting up, and when he got tired, he would lie down on his side and write another five quires in that position. He was bound to burn out eventually. As Ibn Ḥajar says: "In sum, in terms of his intellectual brilliance and quick comprehension, al-Bashtakī was unique. In the end, however, he became stultified by copying so much."[7] During his lifetime, al-Bashtakī must have copied many thousands of books. Unfortunately, it cost him his mind. Nevertheless, the example of al-Bashtakī is a good indication of a period in which literary culture was thriving at an unprecedented level.

But was it really thriving? Until recently, scholars in both the West and the Arab world were convinced that this period during which al-Bashtakī lost his mind copying books was a period of stagnation and decline. As a result, hardly anyone bothered to study Ayyubid and Mamluk literature. Michael Meinecke (1941–1995), the great scholar of Mamluk architecture, once asked a specialist in Arabic literature about Mamluk literature. "You know," he said, "Mamluk architecture is doubtless one of the greatest achievements of Islamic culture. Could it possibly be that nothing comparable was being achieved simultaneously in literature?" The literature specialist could only reply with a shrug of his shoulders.[8]

The situation has improved considerably since then. The decline paradigm proves less and less tenable as we learn more about Ayyubid and Mamluk literature. This becomes even more evident when, apart from analyzing single texts, we start looking at literature as a system constructed by various participants. There is the producer (poet, prose writer), the consumer (reader, audience), the disseminator (such as the unfortunate copyist al-Bashtakī), and the theorist and critic. An analysis of this system can tell us a great deal about the role and importance of literature at a certain period, and it can indicate much about its vigor and vitality and offer possible starting points for intercultural comparison.

The first result of applying this approach to our period is the surprising fact that we are dealing with a post-decline literary epoch, which had its onset after the end of the eleventh century, a period in which the Islamic world was completely reshaped. Until about the year 1000, Islamic societies in the Middle East followed an almost seamless continuation from late antique societies.[9] After the catastrophic eleventh century, they reappeared as early modern societies. In a way, the eleventh century constitutes the real and only Islamic "Middle Ages." As Ronnie Ellenblum has shown, Egypt, Syria, and Iraq underwent an economic crisis of unprecedented vehemence due to climatic causes. In its wake and due to political mismanagement, urban culture dwindled away. Smaller towns such as Ramla were almost completely lost. Large towns that were integrated with long-distance trading networks, such as Cairo, Damascus, and Aleppo, fared somewhat better but still lost much of their former vigor. Bedouin dynasties exploited large parts of the region, causing a further deterioration of agriculture and economy. Turkish nomads fled from drought in their original pasture grounds and flooded the already crisis-ridden regions of the Middle East.[10] Small wonder that this was not a great time for literature. The only exceptions were the western and eastern fringes of Arabic culture. In the West, al-Andalus was spared from the crisis and saw some of its finest poets, such as Ibn Zaydūn (1003–1070) and Ibn Khafāja (1058–1139). In the East, two different developments of literary relevance occurred, one of them detrimental for Arabic literature, the other beneficial. Through the first of these, poets living to the east of Iraq gradually switched from Arabic to Persian, while during the second, what is generally called the "Sunni revival," the educational canons of the *udabāʾ* and the *ʿulamāʾ* merged. The *udabāʾ* (singular *adīb*) were poets and litterateurs and representatives of courtly culture and administration. The *ʿulamāʾ* (singular *ʿālim*) were scholars specializing in law, religion, and related disciplines. By the onset of the eleventh century, the border between *ʿulamāʾ* and *udabāʾ* blurred. The great religious scholar al-Zamakhsharī (1075–1144), who spent most of his life in what is today Uzbekistan, was one of the first men of primarily religious learning who also composed a volume of poetry in the Arabic language.

In the meantime, the central Arab lands recovered from the crisis of the eleventh century. Ironically, the Crusaders arrived at what was the last phase of this crisis, which is why they were initially so successful. But their arrival also coincided with a time that Stefan Heidemann has reasonably called the "renaissance of the towns in Syria and northern Iraq."[11] The economy improved considerably, and so did urban life and culture, and energetic rulers such as the Zangid dynasty brought a certain level of stability. Saladin (d. 1193), the founder of the Ayyubid dynasty, took a decisive step when he managed to unite

Syria and Egypt under a single dynasty. The Arabic-speaking world had found new political and cultural centers: Cairo and Damascus were the new Baghdad. Urban culture not only recovered but positively exploded, as did literary life. There are two names that are closely associated with the beginning of what was probably the most productive period ever of Arabic literature. Two intellectuals in the service of Saladin shaped the new literary style that would influence elite literature for the centuries to come. Not coincidentally, both bore the title of *qāḍī* (judge). The first is al-Qāḍī al-Fāḍil (1135–1200), who became the model for literary prose. The second is Ibn Sanāʾ al-Mulk, also called al-Qāḍī al-Saʿīd (1155–1211), who was more influential in the field of poetry.

The literary system of the Ayyubid and Mamluk period was more complex and manifold than that of earlier periods. In order to illustrate its complexity, the following sections give a virtual tour of a Mamluk town, taking in the various places where one would have been highly likely to encounter literary activity.

3. Courts

The tour starts with the court. For many centuries, courts had been the centers of literary activity. Every poet dreamed of being welcomed at the court of the highest-ranking ruler, vizier, or general to dedicate his panegyric odes to him. The pinnacle for composers of panegyrics was, of course, to praise the caliph, and many caliphs were not only connoisseurs but also themselves poets. The literary taste of courtiers, high dignitaries of the administration and the army, set the standards even for those outside elite circles.

By the Mamluk period, two decisive developments had occurred: the Turkification of the ruling class and the *adab*-ization of the *ʿulamāʾ*. To begin with the first of these, in the main, Arabic societies came to be ruled by leaders of Turkic or Circassian origin, many of whom did not master Arabic well enough to comprehend the subtleties of sophisticated literature. Instead, they preferred architecture, calligraphy, and other art forms as their main instruments of representation. Though a number of Mamluks had received good training in different fields of Arabic culture, only a few rulers combined power with refined literary taste.[12] Such rulers were eagerly sought after, however, since ambitious poets were keen to prove their talent in the traditional genre of courtly panegyrics. Fortunate in this respect were Ṣafī al-dīn al-Ḥillī (1278–1350), who found his Maecenas in the Artuqid rulers of Mardin, and Ibn Nubāta al-Miṣrī (1287–1366), whose close relationship with the Ayyubid sultan of Ḥamā, al-Malik al-Muʾayyad, awoke remembrances of the most famous Arab poet, al-Mutanabbī (ca. 915–965) and his relationship with the Ḥamdānid ruler of Aleppo, Sayf al-Dawla (916–967). A generation later, Ibn Ḥajar al-ʿAsqalānī went as far as Yemen to find rulers appreciative of his poetry. He was welcomed at the court of the Rasūlids but finally decided that a career as scholar in the fields of *ḥadīth* and law would be more promising.

This leads us to the second development, the *adab*-ization of the *ʿulamāʾ*.[13] As al-Zamakhsharī's example shows, religious scholars during and after the Sunni revival had good training in *adab*, language and literature, and many of them engaged themselves as poets or, at least, as recipients of poetry. When al-Mutanabbī was still young and had not yet found an illustrious patron, he was obliged to compose panegyric poems dedicated to judges and scholars, and this he did with obvious aversion. After all, the two major subjects of a panegyric poem were to praise the dedicatee first for his generosity and second for his military prowess. Even in the best cases, the second point constituted a problem with scholars. In his poem for the judge al-Mughīth al-ʿIjlī, al-Mutanabbī dedicated one single line to the intellectual achievements of al-Mughīth but five lines to the military prowess of his ancestors, since al-Mughīth himself did not have any martial experience whatsoever. Two hundred years later, poets, many of whom were scholars themselves, had learned to praise scholars, who had never held a sword in their hands, simply for their scholarship.

As a result of these developments, the courts lost their power to define literary standards. Literature became primarily the domain of the educated middle classes, the *Bildungsbürgertum*, to use a German term. This does not mean that courts were not interested in literature; there were even Mamluk sultans who cared about poetry. The penultimate Mamluk sultan, Qānṣūh al-Ghawrī (r. 1501–1516), even left two *dīwāns* (collections of poetry) of his own poetry, one in Arabic and one in Turkish, which shows that Arabic was not the only literary language in Arab lands.[14] The most important sultan for Arabic literature, however, was al-Nāṣir Ḥasan (r. 1347–1351 and 1354–1361), to whom Ibn Abī Ḥajala (1325–1375) dedicated three literary anthologies and who invited the senior poet and prose writer Ibn Nubāta to Cairo.[15] To give weight to his invitation, he asked the best Egyptian writer, al-Qīrāṭī (1326–1379), who adored Ibn Nubāta, to accompany his edict with a letter of invitation. This letter of about forty pages is an overwhelming, even miraculous example of Arabic epistolography.[16] It shows how the courts in the Mamluk period had to have recourse to the literary standards of the *Bildungsbürgertum*, the educated civil elite, whenever they wanted to engage in their own literary game. This is an instructive example of the *Verbürgerlichung* (a German term meaning something like "bourgeoisification") of Arabic literature after the Sunni revival.

4. Mosques, Chanceries, Madrasas, and Pyramids

Let us turn now to the *Bildungsbürgertum* of the Mamluk Empire and the places where they met. The civilian elite of the Mamluk Empire consisted mainly of two groups: on the one hand, the *ʿulamāʾ* (singular *ʿālim*), scholars, especially judges and law experts; and on the other hand, the *udabāʾ* (singular *adībʾ*), poets, litterateurs, and experts on language. Unlike in earlier periods, both groups shared a largely common canon of scholarly and literary education, and in many cases, the borders between the two were blurred, even though people associated each group with a different lifestyle. So we hear that the *adīb* al-Samanhūdī (d. 1320) loved wine and the company of young men, as was typical of the *udabāʾ*, whereas the famous poet and prose writer al-Qīrāṭī was firm in his religion and devoted to worship *despite* being a proficient *adīb*.[17] Obviously, it was not self-evident that a litterateur was also a pious man. Nevertheless, the mosque was a place where one could meet *ʿulamāʾ* and *udabāʾ* alike, since mosques were and still are not only places of worship but also general meeting points, where discussion and the exchange of literary texts can take place. Every evening, after the afternoon prayer, al-Ṣafadī (1297–1363) and Ibn Nubāta used to meet for discussions at a certain window of the Umayyad mosque in Damascus. When al-Ṣafadī failed to show up one evening, Ibn Nubāta was disappointed and sent him an epigram.[18]

As in earlier periods, Mamluk belles lettres were predominantly secular. Religious literature, however, gained importance, especially in the form of poems in praise of the Prophet and the celebration of his birthday. Again, these genres were treated both in (often extremely) sophisticated form and in simpler, more immediate form for a broader public. The same is true for Sufi poetry which found its final apogee during the Mamluk period in the mystical poems of the poetess ʿĀʾisha al-Bāʿūniyya, who died in 1517, the same year as the end of the Mamluk Empire.[19]

Moreover, a good deal of teaching was still going on in mosques, and so were public readings of both secular and religious texts. Konrad Hirschler has traced the sessions at which members of the Ibn ʿAsākir family publicly read ʿAlī ibn ʿAsākir's multivolume *Taʾrīkh madīnat Dimashq* (*History of Damascus*) at the Umayyad mosque in Damascus but also at other places during the twelfth and thirteenth centuries, and he concludes that "'aurality,' in the sense of reading aloud a written text to a group of listeners, remained a prominent praxis throughout the Middle Period."[20] These sessions were attended not only by scholars but also by traders, craftsmen, workers, and slaves and thus contributed to raising the general level of education in the town.[21]

The next place to visit in the Mamluk town is the chancery, where one would be more likely to meet *udabāʾ* than *ʿulamāʾ*. There were quite a number of chanceries in the empire. In addition to the great state chanceries in Cairo and Damascus, there were chanceries in regional towns such as Ḥamā and local ones in mosques such as the Umayyad mosque in Damascus. State chanceries issued official letters and appointment decrees, whereas local ones issued marriage contracts and similar documents of a more private character. For Ibn Nubāta, the chancery of Damascus was at least as important as the court of Ḥamā. Though for a long time he did not aspire to a position in the chancery, he was in close contact with its directors and did not refrain from criticizing its clerks, sometimes even provoking them. Only in the year 1342, after the end of the sultanate of Ḥamā, at a point when his father was no longer willing to finance his life as a freelance intellectual, did Ibn Nubāta enter the chancery as one of its clerks. He was already fifty-five years old at that time and, as a beginner, was not appointed to a rank that befitted his achievements as the best stylist in the whole country. In reaction to this embarrassing situation, he published his complete output of letters and documents from his first two chancery years in book form.[22] There is no doubt that he and his peers considered the documents they created in the chancery not only as pragmatic texts but also as works of art displaying a highly refined style and striking literary concepts and ideas. In Mamluk literary life, where borders were everywhere blurred, even boundaries between pragmatic and literary texts were no longer clear-cut.[23] Naturally, the chancery was also a place of competition among secretaries vying to express the best style and the best ideas.[24] The style that was developed in the chancery came to exert a heavy influence on the style of literary prose and even that of poetry.

Let us turn to a place where there was greater likelihood of encountering *ʿulamāʾ* rather than *udabāʾ*. This was the *madrasa*, an institution of learning closely connected to the Sunni revival. The number of madrasas had impressively increased since the "renaissance of the towns" in the twelfth century. During the Ayyubid period alone, close to three hundred teaching institutions were founded in Egypt and Syria.[25] In the subsequent Mamluk period, an even larger number were added. This not only added to the availability of books, since these madrasas had libraries, but especially to a soaring rise of education and knowledge. Madrasas were not only attended by regular students in search of academic careers or the position of a judge; they were also open to the larger public so that even craftsmen and workers might stop at a madrasa nearby to learn a bit about grammar or law. Furthermore, each madrasa needed auxiliary personnel such as an imam, a muezzin, a housekeeper, a librarian, and so on. This group of "petty scholars" came to form a sediment of semieducated, substandard scholars, who nonetheless contributed something to the level of education in towns. Sometimes they even evolved into scholars in their own right. The *adīb* Khālid ibn ʿAbdallāh al-Azharī (ca. 1434–1499) is a good example. As a young man, he had a job as lamplighter in a madrasa. Once, wax dropped from one of his lamps and hurt a scholar, who offended him in the harshest way. Struck by the scholar's arrogance, he decided to become a scholar himself, and so it came about.[26]

Finally, one may ask how the pyramids come in. The story is as follows. Scholars and litterateurs were not only continually contacting one another, but they also chronicled their contacts. Huge, multivolume biographical dictionaries provided ample information about who was who, what his (or sometimes her) achievements were, and with whom he or she was in contact and which texts they exchanged. Most of the exchanges were in written form. When they took the form of a personal encounter, a man like al-Ṣafadī, the most assiduous biographer of his age, would note the exact place. Hence, we know that al-Ṣafadī found pleasure in exchanging riddles while sitting on the pyramids (which at this time were still largely buried in sand). The riddles were exchanged in written form,[27] and answers to them, too, had to be given in the form of a riddle. Here is one of al-Ṣafadī's answers:

> baʿathta lughzan badīʿan / mithla n-nasīmi laṭāfa
> lākinnahū fī musamman / qad ḥāza baʿḍa kathāfa[28]
> [You sent me a wonderful riddle, gentle like a soft breeze.
> Yet it's about a word in which is some (a part of) thickness.]

For talking about literature, I chose a riddle whose solution is "book." The Arabic word for it, *kitāb*, contains part of the Arabic word for thickness, *kathāfa*, which is the opposite of fineness, *laṭāfa*, with which the partner's riddle is characterized.

5. Scholars' Homes

In the Mamluk period, the representational function of literature, though still persistant, relinquished its leading role to the communicative function of literature.[29] Instead of primarily addressing princes and caliphs, most poems and prose texts were now addressed to equals, to people of an only slightly higher position, or even to those with a lower social standing. These groups made up a larger segment of the middle- and upper-class population than ever before. Nevertheless, all members of them had a similar educational background and were familiar with more or less the same literary canon.

Despite the continuing importance of the oral (and aural) form, most communication took place in written form. Most commonly, a written text was sent from the home of one scholar and litterateur to that of another. These texts had manifold forms and functions, among them entertainment. Countless witty, often funny epigrams of an entertaining character were devised. Riddles of all kinds were more popular as a game in this period than ever before. More complex poems and prose texts were intended to ensure the reader's aesthetic and emotional edification. The form of the *maqāma*, which combined elegant rhymed prose with poetry, was used for both entertaining and educational texts, for highbrow literature as well as for popular humorous amusement.

Another important task of literature is the creation and strengthening of social bonds. Sometimes a specific concern, such as the request for a present, a favor, or a better position, was behind the production of literary texts. At other times, the writer only wanted to remind the recipient of himself and their mutual ties. Since epigrams are an especially appropriate means of witty and pointed communication, it is no coincidence that the Ayyubid and Mamluk periods witnessed an unprecedented flourishing of this literary form.[30] A typical occasion for a conversation in literary form was the exchange of presents. Of course, a present had to be accompanied by a poem, if not by a long letter that included a poem. The recipient had to answer the poem with a poem of his own, using the same rhyme and meter. When the scholar Badr al-dīn ibn Mālik (d. 1287) could not find a proper answer and when it became known that he had asked his neighbors to compose the answer poem in his stead, the entire literary world ridiculed him.[31]

This leads us to a third function, the construction of social groups and group identities. In the Mamluk Empire, hierarchies were almost inexistent outside the military (and, to a certain extent, the chancery), teaching institutions did not issue official diplomas, and there were no hereditary titles of nobility. Under these circumstances, social rank had to be constructed in informal ways. At the same time, learning and education burgeoned to an extraordinary extent, and the percentage of people who had acquired at least a basic literary and scholarly education reached unprecedented levels. Consequently, it became especially important for elite litterateurs and scholars (or those who reckoned themselves among them) to find some means of distinction and delimitation. A primary way to achieve this was the creation and maintenance of networks. To become a member of such a network, one had to convince the others that one was equal in education and competence. To do this, one had to send them scholarly papers, stylistically elaborate letters in ornate prose, and poems of all kinds, displaying linguistic and stylistic excellence, comprehensive knowledge, and originality of ideas. In turn, the recipient was expected to answer the text at least at the same level as the sender.[32]

This was one of the reasons the period between the eleventh and fifteenth centuries was the (still largely unstudied) apogee of Arabic epistolography. However, in concluding this chapter, I will introduce a literary genre that was especially invented for networking: the *taqrīẓ*. A *taqrīẓ* (commendation) is a text in ornate prose and/or poetry, in which a member of the literary or scholarly establishment praises another person for his achievement, mostly on the occasion of one of his recent works. Young writers, who wanted to make their debuts on the literary stage, went in search of *taqārīẓ*, which they subsequently published as appendixes to the text that had presented them with the occasion. A number of such debut *taqārīẓ* have come to light, and it seems very probable that Ibn Nubāta was the originator of this practice. In the year 1317, he had finished an anthology, in which he explained the duties of an *adīb*. In order to secure a good start for his career in Syria, he sent the book to exponents of scholarship and literature and asked them for a *taqrīẓ*, in which they commended his own work but also praised his Maecenas, the prince of Ḥamā. Eleven of them responded to his request and sent remarkable texts.[33]

The final question is: what happened to all these texts that were sent from one home to another? The answer is: sooner or later, most of them ended up in books, which consisted of collections of poems or anthologies of the author's own texts or of the texts of others. This is one of the reasons the Mamluk period was also the golden age of the anthology.[34] These collections may have continued to circulate as such, but often they were intended for publication. For this purpose, they would usually have been revised thoroughly. Chapters were added, expressions changed, the name of the original recipient or dedicatee anonymized, and so forth. This is exactly what Ibn Nubāta did with the *taqārīẓ* he had received. He collected them and added praise to each of the contributors as well as further letters and poems he had exchanged with their authors. He prefaced the book with a copious introduction, gave it a title, and published it in book form in 1319. Eventually, that book became one of his most famous publications.[35]

As in this case, most of these texts ended up in the book market, reason enough to visit this dangerous place—where al-Bashtakī had lost his mind by copying too many books—a second time.

6. Book Market

After the book revolution brought about by the increased availability of paper in the ninth century—by the way, a media revolution much more important than the introduction of printing—a "reading revolution" followed, "where the written word became increasingly central and spread to wider sections of society." Hirschler is certainly correct when he states that the ubiquity of reading suggests that the literacy rate "became a two-digit number in the cities of Egypt and Syria."[36]

At that time, many books were equipped with bibliographies and cross-references to other books. Their authors must have been optimistic that their readers could get hold of the books mentioned. For authors, perhaps especially for litterateurs, who had less access to the madrasa network, book markets also provided income for copyists. A number of books were even composed to meet the demands of the book market. A typical example is al-Nawājī (d. 1455), who covered all fields of poetry, prose, and linguistic scholarship in order to prove that he was an all-around *adīb*. His most successful titles, still extant in a large number of manuscripts, were anthologies with little scholarly ambition. One, an anthology of wine and nature poetry and related subjects, and another, an anthology of homoerotic poetry, are testimony to his vast knowledge, fine discernment, and, most important, his instinct for appealing to the taste of a potential readership.

However, as we have already learned, the book market was a dangerous place, and al-Nawājī was not to be spared its hazards. As he was a combative character, he accumulated enemies. One of them decided to take revenge by assembling satires against him. A number of such texts, both by that enemy and by others, were collected and published under the title *Qubḥ al-ahājī fī l-Nawājī* (The Disgrace of Satires against al-Nawājī). Thereupon he ordered a broker to make his rounds among the booksellers on the pretense of selling them the book, knowing that al-Nawājī was present at the market. When the broker passed by a shop that al-Nawājī happened to be visiting, al-Nawājī asked to cast a glance at the book and immediately realized what it was about. He was shocked but had to hand the book back to the broker, who returned it to its author, who apparently never published it. The affair, however, had a lasting effect on al-Nawājī and even caused a serious deterioration of his health.[37]

7. Public Libraries

Let us now move to a safer place: the library. The decline paradigm has been especially powerful in library studies. Impressed by reports about the destruction of libraries and the obvious demise of the grand caliphal libraries, common opinion was that the availability of books had decreased significantly by the post-Mongol period. Nevertheless, Hirschler has adduced persuasive evidence that the exact the opposite was the case. The era of monumental royal libraries—to which probably only a small elite ever had access—was now ended, yet people from all walks of society had access to a vast number of smaller public libraries in all larger towns of the Ayyubid and Mamluk Empires. In general, these libraries were endowments and formed parts of madrasas, mosques, or Sufi convents. They were open to the public, and people could borrow the books. Libraries of this kind therefore played a significant role in the education of the middle classes in Cairo, Damascus, and elsewhere.

In the 1270s, a dedicated librarian compiled a catalogue of the holdings of the Ashrafiyya madrasa in Damascus. This was a madrasa of minor importance and employed only a single professor for Koran reading. Its library housed about 2,100 books. Significantly, more than half of the library's books belonged to the fields of poetry, *adab*, and philology. Even Shiite theology and the sciences were well represented. Unfortunately, this is the only library catalogue of the period that has come down to us. Nevertheless, it is obvious that "a reader in Damascus would have had access to tens of thousands of books in libraries alone."[38] In sum, one can conclude with Hirschler that "Arabic societies, at least those in Syria and Egypt, arguably belonged to the most literate and bookish societies worldwide when the Ashrafiya library was founded in the seventh/thirteenth century."[39]

8. Streets and Marketplaces

Bibliocentric as this society undoubtedly was, oral literature still played an enormous role, but thanks to the centrality of books, much of it eventually found its way back into book form. Consequently, we know much more about "popular literature" of the Mamluk period than for any other period before. What was first recited and performed in the streets and markets of Cairo, Damascus, and other urban centers was again multifold and heterogeneous in form, content, and level. In general, it is obvious that even people without formal education, who could barely write, were capable of understanding and enjoying literary texts of rather high complexity (which may have been one of the reasons the *volgare* never became the standard language for literature). The same is true for authors of popular literature, among them craftsmen, merchants, and service personnel of mosques and madrasas, many of whom were capable of composing texts of a level almost equal to that of elite poets.[40] On the other hand, several elite poets tried their hands at popular forms of poetry, using a dialectal form of Arabic. Especially popular was the *zajal*, strophic poetry in a language heavily influenced by the vernacular.[41] Many litterateurs shunned it. After all, their elitist standing depended on their mastery of faultless and elegant Classical Arabic. Other highbrow litterateurs such as Ṣafī al-dīn al-Ḥillī and even Ibn Nubāta had fewer problems with this form of poetry. However, it is not true that elite literature became closer to popular literature in general, as has occasionally been stated. Because the borders between elite and popular literature were blurred, those litterateurs who wanted to be accepted as members of the upper echelon had to present poems and letters of extreme complexity.

The unquestionable fact that borders between the popular and the highbrow became blurred does not mean that they did not exist at all. Instead, several topics and forms were peculiar to one of them. A few examples of what was more typical in popular literature will conclude this overview.

A major popular poet was Ibrāhīm al-Miʿmār (d. 1348 or 1349), who was a stonemason and builder by profession but gained lasting fame as a poet, among both his peers and the elite.[42] His poems were collected and written down by others, sometimes even in magnificent manuscripts. Many of his epigrams cannot be distinguished from those composed by elite poets; Ibn Nubāta even adopted a number of his ideas. However, some of his epigrams are so daring and obscene that they would have endangered the social standing of those belonging to the elite. In the following epigram, al-Miʿmār complains about a futile attempt to remedy his overactive libido by masturbating. The subject would have been not be a strict taboo for highbrow poets. What makes it really audacious is the fact that the penis quotes from the Holy Koran, God's uncreated speech, grossly altering its meaning. In the Koranic verse in question, God speaks through the Prophet to say that people visiting him should return home after their meal and not seek to engage in conversation.

> fa-ʾidhā ṭaʿimtum fa-ntashirū wa-lā mustaʾnisīna li-ḥadīthin
> [When you have taken your meal, then disperse and do not seek familiar conversation]

The verb *intashara* used here in the meaning "disperse" can also mean "spread out." It is this meaning that it assumes in al-Miʿmār's penis epigram:

> aṭʿamtu ʾayrī kay yanāma wa-qultu qarri fa-mā staqarr
> bal qāma yasʿā qāʾilan: ana man ʾidhā ṭuʿima ntashar[43]

> [I fed my penis in order to make him sleep and said: "Rest!"—But he did not rest. Instead, he rose again zealously and said: "I am one of those who spread out after taking their meal!"]

Today, the author of an epigram like this would certainly get into serious trouble. In his own time, al-Miʿmār attracted the admiration of even the highest-level religious scholars such as Ibn Ḥajar al-ʿAsqalānī. It is clear, however, that due to his social position, Ibn Ḥajar could never publish an epigram like this, whereas a stonemason could.

Al-Miʿmār was especially successful with his strophic poems in a stylized form of Arabic close to the vernacular. This form, the *zajal* (plural *azjāl*), had its origins in al-Andalus but soon spread to the East. Al-Miʿmār raised the Eastern *zajal* to a new level. We do not know how *azjāl* were performed in al-Miʿmār's time. It could well be that it was not very different from a modern tradition that lives on in contemporary Lebanon and Syria. A number of recordings from *zajal* performances by prominent *zajal* poets such as Zayn Shuʿayb (1922–2005) and Ṭalīʿ Ḥamdān (b. 1944) can give an impression of the way *azjāl* were performed in the 1970s and later.[44]

There are no videos displaying another form of popular literature, the shadow play (*khayāl al-ẓill*), because this dramatic form is no longer alive in the Arab world. This was a form of popular entertainment for the masses, in which no elite authors took part. The most important author in this genre was Ibn Dāniyāl (d. 1310), an oculist by main profession. He was also a composer of highbrow poems, but his fame is founded on his plays, three of which have survived—the only shadow plays of the period whose text has come down to us.[45] To read them is to understand why no other texts survived and why the shadow play was disdained by elite authors. The plays were written at a time that was especially tolerant of ribaldries and obscenities; the obscenities in shadow plays, however, were too crude even for this period. In Arab countries, the tradition has died out, although perhaps a tame echo of it persists in the Turkish *Karagöz*.

It is often said that Arabic literature did not have drama, romance, or epic. This is not true, especially if we consider popular Arabic literature in the Mamluk period. We have already touched on the drama, which is only poorly preserved. Romances fared better. The collection of *One Thousand and One Nights* (*alf layla wa-layla*) contains texts of almost all genres: highbrow and popular poems, fables, stories of all kinds, fairy tales, and romances of considerable length. Their language is not the stylized vernacular of the *zajal* but standard Arabic with a considerable but unintentional influence of the spoken language.

The Mamluk period was crucial for the formation of the corpus of the *Nights*. By then, many stories were already many hundreds of years old, but a number of them were added in the Fatimid, Ayyubid, and Mamluk periods in Egypt. The oldest surviving manuscript of the first part of the *Nights* dates from around the year 1450. Furthermore, it seems that the stories united in the collection of the *Nights* are, so to speak, the tip of the iceberg. Many more such stories have come to light and are gradually being edited, translated, and studied. Nevertheless, much still remains to be done.[46]

A search for themes and motifs parallel to those in the *Orlando furioso* will probably be most successful if focused on the popular epics. More than a dozen of these folktales have been preserved, some of them of extraordinary length.[47] Over the centuries, before the arrival of modern mass media, they were central for public entertainment. Today, only the *Sīrat Banī Hilāl* is still performed in Egypt, sung in verse accompanied by the spike fiddle (*rabāba*).

The three most famous and longest epics (*sīra*, plural *siyar*) are the *Sīrat ʿAntar*, a chivalrous romance about a pre-Islamic poet and hero, which took shape around the thirteenth century (the oldest manuscript dates to the fifteenth century); the *Sīrat Banī Hilāl*, describing the migration of the Bedouin tribe of the Banū Hilāl from the Ḥijāz to North Africa from the tenth to the twelfth centuries; and the *Sīrat Baybars*, which tells of the legendary adventures of the Mamluk sultan Baybars (r. 1260–1277). The language of the *siyar* varies from dialect to a form closer to the standard language, as in the *Sīrat ʿAntar*. The literary form and the manner of performance are equally varied.[48] The old preconceptions about the age of the Ayyubids and Mamluks as a period of decline have been more or less discarded, and scholarship in this field progresses continually. This development will lay fertile ground for a broader, intercultural perspective on the literatures of the Mediterranean.

Notes

1. See Bauer 2007, esp. pp. 141–146.
2. See Bauer 2006; Bauer 2007; Bauer 2013a.
3. Despite its focus on Spanish poetry, El Omari 2014 is also crucial in relation to Italian literature, esp. pp. 61–102. On the relation between Arabic strophic poetry and troubadour poetry, see Schoeler 1990.
4. See Ott's contribution in this volume.
5. See Herzog 2006, pp. 233–238.
6. Kruk 2014.
7. Ibn Ḥajar 1975, p. 133.
8. Personal communication by Gregor Schoeler, Basel.

9. See Bauer 2018.
10. See Ellenblum 2012.
11. Heidemann 2002.
12. See Mauder 2012.
13. See Bauer 2004, p. 710.
14. On works in Persian in the Ashrafiyya library in Damascus, see Hirschler 2016, p. 114.
15. See Papoutsakis and von Hees 2017.
16. See Bauer 2017.
17. On al-Samanhūdī, see Ibn Ḥajar 1929, p. 363; on al-Qīrāṭī, see Bauer 2017, p. 340.
18. See al-Ṣafadī 1961, p. 326.
19. See Homerin 2011.
20. Hirschler 2012, p. 15.
21. Hirschler 2012, pp. 32–70.
22. See Bauer 2009a, p. 197.
23. See Bauer 2013b, pp. 23–26.
24. See Bauer 2013b, pp. 39–44.
25. See Hirschler 2016, p. 14.
26. See Bauer 2008 with further references.
27. See al-Ṣafadī 2005, p. 210.
28. See al-Ṣafadī 2005, p. 215.
29. See Bauer 2013a, pp. 9–10.
30. See Talib 2018.
31. See Bauer 2013b, p. 32; al-Ṣafadī 1961, p. 204.
32. See Bauer 2013a, pp. 14–20; Bauer 2013b.
33. See Bauer 2013b, pp. 44–50; Bauer 2014.
34. See Bauer 2003.
35. See Bauer 2013b, pp. 46–50.
36. Hirschler 2016, p. 2.
37. See Bauer 2009b, pp. 326–327.
38. Hirschler 2016, p. 14.
39. Hirschler 2016, p. 2.
40. On popular poetry, see Larkin 2007.
41. See the comprehensive study by Özkan 2020.
42. See al-Miʿmār 2018.
43. Epigram 244, al-Miʿmār 2018, p. 154.
44. See, e.g., https://www.youtube.com/watch?time_continue=17&v=roMoL3blSyc.
45. On Ibn Dāniyāl and the shadow play, see Guo 2011.
46. For a first overview, see Marzolph 2007.
47. Studies of the epics are plentiful. It may suffice here to mention Lyons 1995; Heath 2007; Kruk 2007; Reynolds 2007.
48. See Dwight Reynolds's chapter in this volume.

Bibliography

Bauer 2003

Bauer, Thomas. "Literarische Anthologien der Mamlūkenzeit." In *Die Mamlūken: Studien zu ihrer Geschichte und Kultur, zum Gedenken an Ulrich Haarmann (1942–1999)*, edited by Stephan Conermann and Anja Pistor-Hatam, pp. 71–122. Hamburg: EB-Verlag, 2003.

Bauer 2004

Bauer, Thomas. "Shāʿir (Poet): From the ʿAbbāsid Period to the Nahḍa." In *Encyclopaedia of Islam, New Edition*, Vol. 12 (Supplement), pp. 717–722. Leiden: Brill, 2004.

Bauer 2006
Bauer, Thomas. "Mamluk Literature: Misunderstandings and New Approaches." *Mamlūk Studies Review* 9, no. 2 (2005): 105–132.
Bauer 2007
Bauer, Thomas. "In Search of 'Post-Classical Literature.'" *Mamlūk Studies Review* 11, no. 2 (2007): pp. 137–167.
Bauer 2008
Bauer, Thomas. "Al-Azharī, Khālid b. ʿAbdallāh." In *Encyclopaedia of Islam, Three*, pp. 176–178. Leiden: Brill, 2008.
Bauer 2009a
Bauer, Thomas. "Jamāl al-Dīn Ibn Nubāta." In *Essays in Arabic Literary Biography*, edited by Joseph E. Lowry and Devin J. Stewart, pp. 184–202. Wiesbaden: Harrassowitz, 2009.
Bauer 2009b
Bauer, Thomas. "Al-Nawājī." In *Essays in Arabic Literary Biography*, edited by Joseph E. Lowry and Devin J. Stewart, pp. 321–331. Wiesbaden: Harrassowitz, 2009.
Bauer 2013a
Bauer, Thomas. "'Ayna hādhā min al-Mutanabbī!' Toward an Aesthetics of Mamluk Literature." *Mamlūk Studies Review* 17 (2013): pp. 5–22.
Bauer 2013b
Bauer, Thomas. "Mamluk Literature as a Means of Communication." In *Ubi sumus? Quo vademus? Mamluk Studies: State of the Art*, edited by Stephan Conermann, pp. 23–56. Göttingen: V&R Unipress, 2013.
Bauer 2014
Bauer, Thomas. "How to Create a Network: Zaynaddīn al-Āṯārī and His Muqarriẓūn." In *Everything Is on the Move: The Mamluk Empire as a Node in (Trans-)Regional Networks*, edited by Stephan Conermann, pp. 205–221. Göttingen: V&R Unipress, 2014.
Bauer 2017
Bauer, Thomas. "'Extremely Beautiful and Extremely Long': Al-Qīrāṭī's Exuberant Letter from the Year 761/1360." In *Arabic Humanities, Islamic Thought: Essays in Honor of Everett K. Rowson*, edited by Joseph E. Lowry and Shawkat M. Toorawa, pp. 338–360. Leiden: Brill, 2017.
Bauer 2018
Bauer, Thomas. *Warum es kein islamisches Mittelalter gab: Das Erbe der Antike und der Orient*. Munich: C. H. Beck, 2018.
Ellenblum 2012
Ellenblum, Ronnie. *The Collapse of the Eastern Mediterranean: Climate Change and the Decline of the East, 950–1072*. Cambridge: Cambridge University Press, 2012.
El Omari 2014
El Omari, Dina. *Das arabische Element in der spanischen Dichtung des 15. bis 17. Jahrhunderts: Eine vergleichende Studie anhand der Schönheitsbeschreibung*. Würzburg: Ergon, 2014.
Guo 2011
Guo, Li. *The Performing Arts in Medieval Islam: Shadow Play and Popular Poetry in Ibn Dāniyāl's Mamluk Cairo*. Leiden: Brill, 2011.
Heath 2007
Heath, Peter. "Other Sīras and Popular Narratives." In *Arabic Literature in the Post-Classical Period*, edited by Roger Allen and D. S. Richards, pp. 319–339. Cambridge: Cambridge University Press, 2007.
Heidemann 2002
Heidemann, Stefan. *Die Renaissance der Städte in Nordsyrien und Nordmesopotamien: Städtische Entwicklung und wirtschaftliche Bedingungen in ar-Raqqa und Ḥarrān von der Zeit der beduinischen Vorherrschaft bis zu den Seldschuken*. Leiden: Brill, 2002.
Herzog 2006
Thomas Herzog. *Geschichte und Imaginaire: Entstehung, Überlieferung und Bedeutung der Sīrat Baibars in ihrem sozio-politischen Kontext*. Wiesbaden: Harrassowitz, 2006.
Hirschler 2012
Hirschler, Konrad. *The Written Word in the Medieval Arabic Lands: A Social and Cultural History of Reading Practices*. Edinburgh: Edinburgh University Press, 2012.

Hirschler 2016
Hirschler, Konrad. *Medieval Damascus: Plurality and Diversity in an Arabic Library: The Ashrafīya Library Catalogue.* Edinburgh: Edinburgh University Press 2016.
Homerin 2011
Homerin, Th. Emil. *Emanations of Grace: Mystical Poems by ʿĀʾisha al-Bāʿūnīyah.* Lousiville, KY: Fons Vitae, 2011.
Ibn Ḥajar 1929
Ibn Ḥajar al-ʿAsqalānī. *Al-Durar al-kāmina fī aʿyān al-miʾa al-thāmina.* 4 vols. Hyderabad: Dāʾirat al-Maʿārif al-ʿUthmāniyya, 1348–1350/1929–1931.
Ibn Ḥajar 1975
Ibn Ḥajar al-ʿAsqalānī. *Inbāʾ al-ghumr bi-abnāʾ al-ʿumr,* Vol. 8, edited by Muḥammad ʿAbd al-Wahhāb al-Bukhārī. Hyderabad: Dāʾirat al-Maʿārif al-ʿUthmāniyya, 1395/1975.
Kruk 2007
Kruk, Remke. "Sīrat ʿAntar ibn Shaddād." In *Arabic Literature in the Post-Classical Period,* edited by Roger Allen and D. S. Richards, pp. 292–306. Cambridge: Cambridge University Press, 2007.
Kruk 2014
Kruk, Remke. *The Warrior Women of Islam: Female Empowerment in Arabic Popular Literature.* London: I.B. Tauris, 2014.
Larkin 2007
Larkin, Margaret. "Popular Poetry in the Post-Classical Period." In *Arabic Literature in the Post-Classical Period,* edited by Roger Allen and D. S. Richards, pp. 191–242. Cambridge: Cambridge University Press, 2007.
Lyons 1995
Lyons, Malcolm Cameron. *The Arabian Epic: Heroic and Oral Storytelling,* 3 vols. Cambridge: Cambridge University Press, 1995.
Marzolph 2007
Marzolph, Ulrich. "Arabian Nights." In *Encyclopaedia of Islam, Three,* pp. 137–145. Leiden: Brill, 2007.
Mauder 2012
Mauder, Christian. *Gelehrte Krieger: Die Mamluken als Träger arabischsprachiger Bildung nach al-Ṣafadī, al-Maqrīzī und weiteren Quellen.* Hildesheim: Olms, 2012.
al-Miʿmār 2018
Bauer, Thomas, Anke Osigus, and Hakan Özkan, eds. *Der Dīwān des Ibrāhīm al-Miʿmār (gest. 749/1348–49): Edition und Kommentar.* Baden-Baden: Ergon, 2018.
Papoutsakis and von Hees 2017
Papoutsakis, Nefeli, and Syrinx von Hees, eds. *The Sultan's Anthol ogist: Ibn Abī Ḥağalah and His Work.* Baden-Baden: Ergon, 2017.
Reynolds 2007
Reynolds, Dwight F. "Sīrat Banī Hilāl." In *Arabic Literature in the Post-Classical Period,* edited by Roger Allen and D. S. Richards, pp. 307–318. Cambridge: Cambridge University Press, 2007.
al-Ṣafadī 1961
Ṣafadī, Khalīl ibn Aybak al-. *Al-Wāfī bi-l-wafayāt,* Vol. 1, edited by Helmut Ritter. Wiesbaden: Franz Steiner, 1962.
al-Ṣafadī 2005
Ṣafadī, Khalīl ibn Aybak al-. *Al-Rawḍ al-bāsim wa-l-ʿurf al-nāsim,* edited by Muḥammad ʿAbdalmajīd Lāshīn. Cairo: Dār al-Āfāq al-ʿArabiyyah, 1425/2005.
Özkan 2020
Özkan, Hakan. *Geschichte des östlichen zağal: Dialektale arabische Strophendichtung aus dem Osten der arabischen Welt—von den Anfängen bis zum Ende der Mamlukenzeit.* Baden-Baden: Ergon, 2020.
Schoeler 1990
Schoeler, Gregor. "Muwaššaḥ und Zağal. Einfluss auf die Troubadour-Dichtung?" *Neues Handbuch der Literaturwissenschaft, Band 5, Orientalisches Mittelalter,* edited by Wolfhart Heinrichs, pp. 440–464. Wiesbaden: AULA, 1990.
Talib 2018
Talib, Adam. *How Do You Say "Epigram" in Arabic? Literary History at the Limits of Comparison.* Leiden: Brill, 2018.

From al-Barqā to Albracca: *Orlando furioso* and the World of the *Arabian Nights*

Claudia Ott

This chapter provides a new investigation into the long-debated matter of the relationship between some fragments of the *Orlando furioso* and the Arabic tradition of the *Arabian Nights* narrative cycle. It shows that the connection between the famous story of Astolfo and Iocondo in Ariosto's poem and the frame story of the *Arabian Nights* should be oriented more toward the less well-known *One Hundred and One Nights*, rather than toward the celebrated *One Thousand and One Nights*. Besides this narrative episode, the case of the toponym *Albracca*, which is discussed here in detail for the first time, suggests that other textual features may mark a significant connection between the *Hundred and One Nights* and the *Orlando* tradition. The exact path of the transmission of these motifs to Italy—perhaps via translations into Spanish or other Romance languages—is not yet clear and may be impossible to establish definitively. But the recent discovery of a thirteenth-century Andalusian manuscript of the *Hundred and One Nights* represents a milestone in the reconstruction of this textual route, due to the chronological and geographical context of its production, in a cultural environment where many other works of Classical Arabic literature followed the same trajectory.

1. Hundreds and Thousands of Nights

> The transmitter of this story tells the following tale: There was once a king of India. He ruled over his people with might and was held in high esteem by his contemporaries. He directed the fate of his kingdom well and was just to his subjects. His justice protected them, and they were enfolded in his goodness.
>
> Every year, this king staged a holiday, on which he wined and dined his people. When his subjects had eaten the food and drunk the wine, and everyone had had his fill, the king retired to his palace for a little while, only to appear before

> his subjects sometime later, dressed in regal splendor, with a crown on his head, his servants to his right and to his left and attired in the most magnificent garments.
>
> Adorned in this way, he would then go into his throne room. He would sit down on his royal throne, and his viziers and his royal court were allowed to sit down, too. Then the king would ask for a mirror, and this was placed before him. The king would look at his face in the mirror and then ask: "Do you know of anyone in the world who is more beautiful than I?"—"But of course not, by God," they used to reply, "we don`t know anyone of the kind." And the king rejoiced and was content.
>
> This was how he behaved, and he was pleased with himself until, one day, an elderly shaykh came to him and addressed him: "Beware of vanity, O King, as long as women have children. I have visited every country and district; I have traveled across the land and over the seas. In the town of Khorasan I met a young man, one of the merchant's sons, who is heartrendingly beautiful and who shines like a beaming light!"[1]

This is the beginning of the frame story of the *Hundred and One Nights*, after a thirteenth-century Andalusian manuscript held by the Aga Khan Foundation (fig. 1).[2] Through the various tales contained within this frame story, this very significant manuscript—whose presumed date (1234–1235) makes it roughly two and a half centuries older than *Orlando innamorato* and three centuries before *Orlando furioso*—recounts tales of the merchants of Kairouan as well as of the cannibals of the Camphor Island. In the stories of the *Hundred and One Nights*, we catch cunning wives at play with their passionate lovers and, in the next moment, witness virgin-eating lindworms at battle with knights and warriors. Centuries before Leonardo da Vinci, the *Hundred and One Nights* describes an ebony horse flying machine with a takeoff and landing propeller and probably the oldest motion detectors in the history of literature.[3]

Of course, the *Hundred and One Nights* was not the first and only collection of tales of its kind. The larger and much better-known *Thousand and One Nights* was already in existence in the East of the Islamic world long before the presumed production period of this manuscript.[4] Already in the tenth century, Arabic literary scholars, librarians, and historians had reported on a collection of stories, *The Thousand Tales* (*Alf khurāfa*, in Persian *Hezār Afsāne*, then *Thousand Nights*, *Alf layla*), which was translated from Persian and then completed

Fig. 1. *Kitāb Mi'at layla wa-layla* (One Hundred and One Nights), dated 622/1234-5. Toronto, Aga Khan Museum, Ms. AKM 513

in Arabic. The title *One Thousand and One Nights*, which is still used today, was first documented around 1150, but references from the tenth and eleventh centuries make it probable that the work acquired that title long before this date and that the title *Thousand Nights, Alf layla*, might have been used as an abbreviation for *Thousand and One Nights, Alf layla wa-layla*.[5] The oldest preserved manuscript fragment of the *Thousand Nights* is even older, dating from around 800.[6] But while the *Thousand and One Nights* flourished in the eastern part of the Arabic world, the *Hundred and One Nights* was transmitted independently in the West, that is, in the Maghreb and al-Andalus.

2. Frame Stories of the *Nights*

As is well known, the frame story for these two works, the *Hundred and One Nights* and the *Thousand and One Nights*, is organized around the same basic idea. A king, upset by the discovery of his wife's infidelity, seeks vengeance on all women, by sleeping with one each night and killing her at dawn of the following day. The daughter of the king's minister, the world-famous Shahrazād (Scheherazade), finds herself in the same position as the other women but astutely implements a stratagem of narration in order to save her own life every day and cure the king, who will eventually marry her. Besides the different timescales (101 or 1,001 nights), there are some differences in detail between the two works, the most important of which is the way the king arrives at his infamous purpose. After the incipit cited above, the frame story of the *Hundred and One Nights* can be summarized as follows:

> The king of India—who, as we have seen in the beginning, regards himself as the most beautiful person in the world—invites the young man of Khorasan to his court to compare their beauty. But the envoy who has been sent out to bring him has to wait for him an entire year, since the young man is just about to marry and will have to spend the first year of marriage at home. After that year, the young man can set out on his journey to India. Soon after his departure, he returns to his city because he has forgotten something in his home. There he finds his wife in bed with a black slave. He kills both of them and then continues his journey but is deeply distressed and his beauty disappears. From a tower in the palace where he is lodged to recover from his sickness, he happens to witness the king's wife having intercourse with an ugly and ill-mannered black slave. Only then, he overcomes his own misfortune and is comforted. His beauty returns and he wins the beauty contest. The king notices the change in his appearance, insists on knowing what had happened, and the young man makes him see the scene with his own eyes. The king then kills his wife and her lover and decides to marry a new woman every night and kill her the following morning—until Shahrazād appears.[7]

The most ancient model of this story has been traced back to the *Tripitaka*, a collection of Indian Buddhist canonical writings, translated into Chinese in the year 251. Here the story goes as follows:

> A king looks at himself in a mirror, then asks his ministers present whether they know of a more beautiful person in the world than he. They tell him they have heard of the unparalleled beauty of a young man in his kingdom. The king has the young man sent for, under the pretext that he wants to invite him on the grounds of his great wisdom. Shortly after setting out, the young man returns home again to fetch some excerpts from his books. There he finds his

> wife in the arms of another man. As a result, the young man finds himself in a crisis; his appearance changes and his beauty disappears. After reaching the king, who knows nothing of this experience, he is first isolated, so that he can recover from his strenuous journey. During this time, the young man chances to see the king's wife amusing herself with a stable lad. Comforted from his own fate to such a degree, the young man immediately recovers and his former beauty is restored. When the king questions him about this, the young man tells him what he has experienced himself and what he has observed. Like him, the king is outraged at the licentiousness of the female sex. Both men decide to withdraw to the mountains and turn their backs on the world.[8]

What is the difference between this *Hundred and One Nights* frame story and its literary source, on the one hand, and the more widely known frame story of the *Thousand and One Nights*, on the other hand?

In the *Thousand and One Nights*, the beauty contest motif is entirely missing. Here, the two men who suffer marital infidelity are two brothers, Shāhriyār, the elder, and Shāhzamān, the younger, who meet at the former's court for a family reunion after some years of separation. Then, after their own personal unpleasant discoveries, they travel around the world to confirm their conviction of the inevitable infidelity of women. Finally, Shahriyār ends up making the same decision to marry a new woman every night and kill her the following morning—until Shahrazād appears.

The motif of the beauty contest, however, is particularly relevant when we look at the connection between *Orlando furioso* and the world of the *Arabian Nights*, as various scholars over the last two centuries have already shown.

3. The Story of Astolfo and Iocondo

At the end of canto XXVII of Ariosto's *Orlando furioso*, a benevolent innkeeper tries to lift the spirits of the Saracen hero Rodomonte, embittered by the decision of Doralice, who had chosen his rival Mandricardo instead of him. The innkeeper decides to tell him a story about the infidelity of women, which he happened to hear at his inn:

> Un gentilomo di Vinegia poi,
> che qui mia buona sorte già condusse,
> seppe far sì con veri esempi suoi,
> che fuor de l'ignoranza mi ridusse.
> Gian Francesco Valerio era nomato;

> che 'l nome suo non mi s'è mai scordato.
> —*Fur.*, XXVII 137, 3–8
> [A gentleman from Venice whom good fortune brought to my door, was able, with true instances of his own, to draw me out of my ignorance. I have never forgotten his name: Gian Francesco Valerio.]

The greater part of the following canto, XXVIII, is taken up by the report of this dramatic and comic story that can be summarized as follows (*Fur.*, XXVIII 4–74):[9]

> King Astolfo of the Longobards regards himself as the most beautiful person of his day. His courtier Fausto informs him that his brother Iocondo in Rome is as beautiful as he is. The king invites Iocondo to compare their beauty, but it is hard for Fausto, the envoy, to convince him to leave his wife for some time, since she is so much in love with him. Shortly after having set out for his journey, Iocondo returns home because he has forgotten a precious cross that his wife had given him as a token of her love. He discovers his wife in bed with a stable boy. In consequence, he is overwhelmed by sadness and his beauty disappears. When he arrives in Pavia, and is lodged in a palace to recover from his sickness, he happens to witness the king's wife having intercourse with an ugly dwarf. Iocondo is comforted by this scene and his beauty is restored. The king notices the change in his appearance and asks him to explain what had occurred. After having witnessed the betrayal with his own eyes, the king decides that both of them should leave the palace at once and roam the world in order to seduce a thousand women. In the course of this enterprise, however, they grow more and more bored with the fact that they can procure every woman they want. Given that a faithful woman cannot be found, they then try to find one and the same woman for both of them; that woman, they suggest, should have no reason to deceive them. The beautiful Fiammetta, a poor innkeeper's daughter of Valencia, meets their expectations, and they take her along with them, treating her as their common mistress. But when they come to Zattiva (today Xàtiva), Fiammetta happens to meet her former lover Greco and manages to allow him in to sleep with her that night, with her two lovers lying beside her. Each of the two thinks that the other is having intercourse with Fiammetta and therefore refrains from disturbing them. In the morning they discover the deceit, but instead of becoming enraged once again, they laugh at what had happened, decide to help Fiammetta marry her lover, and return to their spouses in (presumed) total awareness of what awaits them.

4. Patterns and Transmission

The affinity between this story and the frame story of the *Thousand and One Nights* was explored by several scholars during the nineteenth and twentieth centuries,[10] while the role of intermediary was tentatively attributed to the Venetian gentleman Giovan Francesco Valier, a friend of Ariosto, mentioned by the innkeeper as the reporter of the story.[11] Other experts have highlighted the presence of a similar narrative pattern in contexts as different as Hungarian and Belorussian folklore, in tales that it would be difficult to date and associate with any specific literary trajectory.[12] In the last decades of the nineteenth century, Pio Rajna was probably the first to identify a possible predecessor to Ariosto's tale in a novella by Giovanni Sercambi, in which two of the protagonists bear the names Astolfo and Fiammetta, as in Ariosto's tale, although in different roles. For Rajna, the relationship between Sercambi's novella and Ariosto's narrative implied the existence of an older Italian source, preceding both, but it left open the question of the entry of this narrative into Italian literature. Rajna thought that the dependency on the frame story of the *Thousand and One Nights* was the primary route to track, although he found it difficult to square the comparison with the theme of the beauty contest, lacking in both the Arabic work and Sercambi's novella.[13] Now that the text of the *Hundred and One Nights* has been made more widely available, it seems evident that the similarity lies more with this latter Arabic text than with the former.

Two further points help to substantiate this hypothesis: the relative antiquity of the Aga Khan manuscript of the *Hundred and One Nights* and the Western, that is, Maghrebinian-Andalusian origin and transmission of the whole work. Both points merit attention here in some detail.

To date, we know of seven manuscripts of the *Hundred and One Nights*; six of them are from the eighteenth or nineteenth century, the oldest of these dating from 1776.[14] The Andalusian manuscript from the Aga Khan Museum, which was discovered in 2010, stands out in the group both for the condition of the text and possibly by virtue of a much older date of origin. In fact, although further research is required, this manuscript might be dated by the colophon of another manuscript text with which it is bound, a copy of the *Kitāb al-Jaʿrāfiyya* (Book of Geography) by the Andalusian author Muḥammad ibn Abī Bakr al-Zuhrī (d. ca. 1150). As research on paper, ink, and calligraphy has shown, the scribe ʿAbdallāh ibn ʿAbd al-Mawlā al-Najjūm is responsible for both parts of the manuscript.[15] If we do not consider the entire manuscript as a more recent copy or even as a forgery,[16] the Aga Khan version of the *Hundred and One Nights* would therefore be dated around 1234/1235 (Islamic year 632), thus representing a very significant milestone in the transmission of this narrative. Irregardless of the date of the Aga Khan manuscript, all scholars agree that at least some parts of the *Hundred and One Nights* should be considered quite old, and in particular, the frame story in this work may be considered older than its equivalent in the *Thousand and One Nights*, on the basis of narrative investigation.[17]

The second element regarding the *Hundred and One Nights* is the high probability of its place of origin being the western side of the Islamic world. Not only have all the manuscripts that we know of today been produced either in al-Andalus or in the Maghreb, but also many of the stories are set in North Africa or al-Andalus, and many of their protagonists are suggestive—either directly or indirectly—of Andalusian history; moreover, dialectal features of Maghrebi and Andalusi Arabic are frequent. Although this assertion also requires further examination, the circulation of this work (and its frame) in the west of Europe certainly favors an hypotheses of transmission—at least of sections of it, possibly through an oral route—related to the Romance languages.

5. The Malice of Women: Assertions, Qualms, and Effects

A central theme of the Astolfo and Iocondo story is without doubt that of the malice of women, a ubiquitous medieval motif in both the Christian and Islamic contexts. In this investigation of the relationship between the worlds of the *Arabian Nights* and the *Orlando furioso* tradition, it is worthwhile comparing the different approaches and the different consequences that the texts offer with regard to this loaded subject.

As we have seen, in Ariosto's *Orlando furioso*, the story of Astolfo and Iocondo is related by the innkeeper to the misogynistic Saracen Rodomonte as an example of the "malice of women." However, Ariosto as author finds the story so disrespectful that he distances himself from its misogynistic content:[18]

> Donne, e voi che le donne avete in pregio,
> per Dio, non date a questa istoria orecchia,
> a questa che l'ostier dire in dispregio
> e in vostra infamia e biasmo s'apparecchia;
> ben che né macchia vi può dar né fregio
> lingua sì vile, e sia l'usanza vecchia
> che 'l volgare ignorante ognun riprenda,
> e parli più di quel che meno intenda.

Lasciate questo canto, che senza esso
può star l'istoria, e non sarà men chiara.
Mettendolo Turpino, anch'io l'ho messo,
non per malivolenza né per gara.
Ch'io v'ami, oltre mia lingua che l'ha espresso,
che mai non fu di celebrarvi avara,
n'ho fatto mille prove; e v'ho dimostro
ch'io son, né potrei esser se non vostro.

Passi, chi vuol, tre carte o quattro, senza
leggerne verso, e chi pur legger vuole,
gli dia quella medesima credenza
che si suol dare a finzioni e a fole.
Ma tornando al dir nostro, poi ch'udienza
apparecchiata vide a sue parole,
e darsi luogo incontra al cavalliero,
così l'istoria incominciò l'ostiero.
—*Fur.*, XXVIII 1–3

[Ladies (and ladies' devotees), by all means disregard this tale which the innkeeper is preparing to relate to the disparagement, to the ignominy and censure of your sex—not that a tongue as common as his can either sully or embellish your image. The ignorant herd will always carp at everything; the deeper their ignorance, the more they will talk.

Skip this canto: it is not essential—my story is no less clear without it. As Turpin included it, so have I, but in no spirit of malevolence or provocation. That I dote upon you my tongue has confessed—it has never stinted your praises—and I have proved it, furthermore, in a thousand ways; I have demonstrated to you that I am, and can only be, yours.

Those who wish, then, may skip three or four pages without reading a line of them; those who prefer to read them must regard the story in the same light as legends and fables. But, as we were saying, when he saw that everyone was ready to listen to his words and room was made for him facing Rodomont, the innkeeper began his story as follows.]

Furthermore, after the story is told, the innkeeper receives Rodomonte's approval but is reproached by an old man, who maintains that this wickedness was the fruit of a negative experience suffered personally by its first narrator. The unidentified elder goes on to claim that the resulting wrath had made the fault of one woman a general disease, when in reality, it is men who fall more easily into temptation. Rodomonte does not, however, want to hear these truths and immediately silences the old man with threats (*Fur.*, XXVIII 75–84).

More generally, it is interesting to note that the three principal versions of the story that we have been looking at result in different outcomes on male attitudes and decision-making, which call for further exploration.[19] In the ancient Buddhist narrative, the two men's disappointment with women leads them toward a choice of asceticism and renunciation of worldly life. In the Italian Renaissance courtly poem, a sense of what might almost be described as proportion dawns upon the two companions after their disappointing exploration of various aspects of female infidelity, to the extent that they consider it worth going back to their wives (more or less the same ending characterizes the two Hungarian and Belorussian folktales mentioned above).

It seems that the Arabic tradition conveys the harshest consequences for these narrated events, with the king undertaking to kill all women in order to punish them for their (even potential) betrayal. This outcome is closely connected to the significant role of the theme of the "malice of women" in Arabic literature.

Within the frame of its universal popularity in the medieval Eurasian context, we can assert that the "craft and malice of women" (in Arabic *makr al-nisāʾ* or *kayd al-nisāʾ*, *kayd* and *makr* being synonyms) was a particularly frequent subject in Arabic literature. A wide variety of books, anthologies, treatises, story collections, and even poetry deal with the subject, which is already alluded to in the Koranic legend of Joseph and Potiphar's wife. When Potiphar realizes that his wife has falsely accused Joseph of having seduced her, he states: "The guile of you (women) is immense" (*inna kaydakunna ʿaẓīm*; Sura 12, v. 28). This Koranic verse is repeated verbatim by the two kings Shāhriyār and Shāhzamān in the frame story of the *Thousand and One Nights* immediately after they discover the deceit of the woman in the glass chest.[20] Often, it is used in literature to condemn women in general and associate the female sex with cunning. In the stories collected in the *Arabian Nights*, *makr al-nisāʾ* is also known as the alternative title of the section including the so-called *Book of Sindbad the Wise* or *Book of the Seven Viziers*, another famous Eurasian narrative cycle, which was included in a compact form within the frame of the *Arabian Nights* cycle, at an undetermined stage of its development.[21] The earliest testimony to date of this insertion should be identified in the Aga Khan manuscript of the *Hundred and One Nights* (Nights 56–75).[22] The title *makr al-nisāʾ* also has acquired such a general value in relation to the *Arabian Nights* cycle that it even served as a pseudo-title for a *Thousand and One Nights* manuscript preserved at Kayseri in Turkey.[23]

6. The Case of Albracca

If, from what has been said so far, it is possible to trace an indirect connection between the Astolfo and Iocondo story and the frame story of the *Hundred and One Nights*, another detail may suggest that a wider relationship between the two literary works should be taken into consideration.

Over the years, many hypotheses have been made about the etymology of the toponym *Albracca*, the home and refuge of Princess Angelica in Cathay (China, or India), which enters the *Orlando furioso* straight out of Boiardo's *Orlando innamorato* (I v, 72).[24] Against the various unsatisfactory hypotheses that have been proposed, the name's shape and its Asian location may well be tied to the text of the *Hundred and One Nights*.

In the world of the *Arabian Nights*, India and China often stand for the extreme Orient, the furthest edges of the known world, and sources of treasures as well as of wisdom and stories. It is the image of an Orient that is far away, unfamiliar, exotic, and, for that reason, particularly attractive. One such fantastical story is the "Story of the Camphor Island." It is part of the *Hundred and One Nights* but does not appear in the *Thousand and One Nights*. In this story, a three-hundred-year-old globetrotter tells the king of Persia about his travels. The remotest place on earth he had ever reached, as he relates, was in China, a city named al-Barqā. The globetrotter then describes in detail the castle of al-Barqā, with its marvelous palace gardens full of walls, pillars, fruits and trees, canals built of pure gold, and a golden pavilion with a peacock made of jewels adorning its roof.[25]

The name Albracca may possibly be traced back to this Arabic toponym. Al-Barqā (*al-barqā*) is the feminine gender of the adjective *al-ʾabraq*, with the variant meanings of "multicolored, black and white, stony ground," and is used more than once in Arabic geography and poetry as a place name.[26] Due to the absence of signs for most vowels in the normal Arabic script, the Arabic letters البرقى can be easily misread as *al-braqā*, respectively, "Albraca/Albracca." This would mean a shift in one vowel only, at the graphic level just a small sign (*fatḥa*) that does not normally appear in Arabic script. Moreover, even a correct reading could easily have been misunderstood or misspelled in subsequent transmission.

The passage with the name of the city *al-Barqā* is part of the thirteenth-century Aga Khan manuscript of the *Hundred and One Nights* (fig. 2),[27] but it seems to have vanished in the course of transmission, possibly being regarded as an unimportant detail. The more recent manuscripts of the *Hundred and One Nights*, which form the textual basis for both the Arabic editions of 1979 and 2016 and for the latter's English translation, do not mention it.[28] And, as noted above, the *Thousand and One Nights* does not transmit the "Story of the Camphor Island" at all.

The case of al-Barqā/Albracca seems to be another significant link between the early Arabic *Hundred and One Nights and the Orlando furioso* tradition. In the course of the circulation of narrative cycles throughout Eurasia during the late antique and medieval eras, the juxtaposition of terms (especially proper names) from different languages, without respect for fictional or real geography, was a fairly common occurrence, in which can be seen the casual convergence of mistakes, exoticism, euphony, textual crossing, and so on, as opposed to any meaningful logic. More to the point, it is sometimes the case that these terms suggest the participation of one particular text or another in the creation and transmission of a story, and hence the principal interest of the case of Albracca.

7. Conclusion

The question of the sources of Ariosto's *Orlando furioso*—with their various degrees of intermediation—remains a very complex literary puzzle, and even in the case of an isolated story such as that concerning Astolfo and Iocondo, it is not possible to trace the exact path that the various motifs followed before merging into the shape that this narrative forms in the Italian poem. However, the outline of the themes and motifs network presented here suggests that the role of the frame story from the *Hundred and One Nights* has most probably been central to the formation and transmission of the episode.

The western Arabic context of this work and the antiquity of the recently discovered manuscript allow for the hypothesis that the story was translated quite early—in written or oral form—from Arabic into Spanish or other Romance languages, at a time when many other works of Classical Arabic literature took the same route. It is possible that this process does not concern the frame story alone but is also behind other consistent parts of the book in its earliest form. And if the trope of the craft and malice of women, which was shared by many cultures, went through varied developments in the movement of the narrative from one language to others, certain details, such as the linguistic issue regarding the toponym *Albracca*, suggest that the relation between the *Furioso* and its literary world and the world of the *Arabian Nights* should be explored more thoroughly, pivoting on the more compact text of the *Hundred and One Nights*.

Fig. 2. *Kitāb Miʾat layla wa-layla* (One Hundred and One Nights), fol. 9b, dated 622/1234-5. Toronto, Aga Khan Museum, Ms. AKM 513. The espression *madīnat al-Barqā* (the city of al-Barqā) is at line 18

Notes

1. Ott 2012, pp. 5–6. English translation by Bridget Ineichen.

2. *Kitāb Mi'at layla wa-layla*, MS AKM 00513, fol. 1b. See Marzolph and Chraïbi 2012.

3. For this latter case, see Bottigheimer and Ott 2014.

4. On the question of the creation and transmission of the *Hundred and One Nights*, see below.

5. Cf. Chraïbi 2016, 21.

6. For general overviews of the complex literary history of the *Thousand and One Nights*, see Irwin 1994; Marzolph and van Leeuwen 1994; Chraïbi 2008; Chraïbi 2016.

7. See Ott 2021.

8. Summary of the Buddhist story quoted by Chavannes 1910, I, no. 107.

9. For an interesting case of the figurative fortune of this tale, see Monica Preti's contribution in this volume.

10. See Rajna 1975, 436–455; Spampinato Beretta 1999; Minervini 2009.

11. One of the sixteenth-century commentators of Ariosto reported that a very entertaining book by Giovan Francesco Valier, titled *Inganni delle mogli fatti ai mariti; et d'altre donne verso altri huomini usati*, had circulated widely in Italian courts, although it apparently was never officially published: Toscanella 1574, p. 217.

12. See the discussions in Scaglione 1958; Lemos Horta 2015.

13. Rajna 1975, pp. 436–455.

14. Three are conserved in Paris, at the National Library of France (BNF 3660; 3661; 3662, the oldest among these six); two are kept in the Tunis National Library (04576; 18260); one is held in a private collection in Algeria. Paris BNF 3662 was used as the basis for two editions: Ṭarshūna 1979; Fudge 2016. A third Arabic edition was based on the nineteenth-century manuscript preserved in Algiers: Shuraybiṭ 2005. Two other manuscript versions, which were mentioned as existing in France at the beginning of the twentieth century, are now apparently lost. For all further bibliography and references, see Ott 2020.

15. See the detailed discussion in Ott 2012, pp. 252–255 and appendix with facsimiles.

16. This opinion is expressed in the "Note on the Text" in Fudge 2016.

17. For discussion on this, see Cosquin 1909; Marzolph and Chraïbi 2012; Fudge 2016.

18. Cf. Finucci 1999, pp. 215, 217.

19. Discussions in Finucci 1999; Izzo 2012; Lemos Horta 2015.

20. English translation, e.g., Haddawy 1990, p. 10.

21. See Marzolph and van Leeuwen 1994, pp. 160–161, s.v. "Craft and Malice of Women"; Krönung 2016.

22. Ott 2012, pp. 141–181; see the Italian translation *Cento e una notte* 2017, pp.158–203.

23. See Ott 2016, p. 378.

24. E.g., from *Acbalec Manzi*, mentioned by Marco Polo, possibly a Mongol toponym (Blochet 1908, pp. 346–349); or from the city of Bukhara, again through Marco Polo's *Bocara* with the addition of the Arabic article *al-* (see Boiardo 1995, p. 121 n 72).

25. German translation in Ott 2012, p. 44; Italian translation in *Cento e una notte* 2017, p. 48.

26. Cf. Ott 2012, p. 263.

27. MS AKM 513, fol. 9b, line 18.

28. Cf. Ṭarshūna 1979, p. 125; Fudge 2016, p. 71.

Bibliography

Blochet 1908
Blochet, Edgar. "Notes de géographie et d'histoire d'Extrême Orient." *Revue de l'Orient chrétien* 13 (1908): pp. 346–366.

Boiardo 1995
Boiardo, Matteo Maria. *Orlando innamorato*, 2 vols, edited by Riccardo Bruscagli. Turin: Einaudi, 1995.

Bottigheimer and Ott 2014
Bottigheimer, Ruth, and Claudia Ott. "The Case of the Ebony Horse." *Gramarye* 5 (2014): pp. 8–20.

Cento e una notte 2017
Cento e una notte, edited by Claudia Ott, translated by Isabella Amico di Meane, Italian edition edited by Elisabetta Benigni. Turin: Einaudi, 2017.

Chavannes 1910
Chavannes, Édouard. *Cinq cents Contes et apologues du Tripitaka chinois*. Paris: Librairie Ernest Leroux, 1910.

Chraïbi 2008
Chraïbi, Aboubakr. *Les mille et une nuits: Histoire du texte et classification des contes*. Paris: L'Harmattan, 2008.

Chraïbi 2016
Chraïbi, Aboubakr. *Arabic Manuscripts of the Thousand and One Nights: Presentation and Critical Editions of Four Noteworthy Texts, Observations on Some Osmanli Traditions*. Paris: Espaces & Signes, 2016.

Cosquin 1909
Cosquin, Emmanuel. "Le prologue cadre des *Mille et une nuits*, les légendes perses et le livre d'Esther." *Revue Biblique* 6 (1909), pp. 7–49.

Fudge 2016
A Hundred and One Nights, edited and translated by Bruce Fudge. New York: New York University Press, 2016.

Finucci 1999
Finucci, Valeria. "The Masquerade of Masculinity: Astolfo and Jocondo in *Orlando furioso*, canto 28." In *Renaissance Transactions: Ariosto and Tasso*, edited by Valeria Finucci. Durham, NC: Duke University Press, 1999.

Haddawy 1990
The Arabian Nights, translated by Husain Haddawy based on the text edited by Muhsin Mahdi. New York: Norton, 1990.

Irwin 1994
Irwin, Robert. *The Arabian Nights: A Companion*. London: Allen Lane, 1994.

Izzo 2012
Izzo, Annalisa. "Misoginia e filoginia nell'*Orlando furioso*." *Chroniques italiennes web* 22 (2012): pp. 1–25.

Krönung 2016
Krönung, Bettina. "Fighting with Tales 1: The Arabic Book of Sindbad the Philosopher." In *Fictional Storytelling in the Medieval Eastern Mediterranean and Beyond*, edited by Carolina Cupane and Bettina Krönung, pp. 365–379. Leiden: Brill, 2016.

Lemos Horta 2015
Lemos Horta, Paulo. "Beautiful Men and Deceitful Women: The One Hundred and One Nights and World Literature." *Narrative Culture* 2, no. 2 (2015): pp. 190–207.

Marzolph and Chraïbi 2012
Marzolph, Ulrich, and Chraïbi, Aboubakr. "The Hundred and One Nights: A Recently Discovered Old Manuscript." *Zeitschrift der Deutschen Morgenländischen Gesellschaft* 162 (2012): pp. 299–316.

Marzolph and van Leeuwen 1994
Marzolph, Ulrich, and Richard van Leeuwen. *The Arabian Nights Encyclopaedia*, 2 vols. Santa Barbara, CA: ABC-CLIO, 1994.

Minervini 2009
Minervini, Laura. "Le 'Mille e una notte' e le letterature romanze medievali: Un bilancio alla luce dell'edizione Mahdi." In *Medioevo romanzo e orientale sulle orme di Sharazàd: Le "Mille e una notte" fra Oriente e*

Occidente, edited by Mirella Cassarino and Soveria Mannelli, pp. 193–203. Catanzaro: Rubbettino, 2009.

Ott 2012

101 Nacht. First translated into German, and with extensive commentaries, by Claudia Ott. after the Andalusian Manuscript of the Aga Khan Museum, with facsimile illustrations of the original. Zurich: Manesse, 2012.

Ott 2016

Tausendundeine Nacht—Das glückliche Ende. After the manuscript of the Raşid-Efendi-Bibliothek Kayseri, first translated into German by Claudia Ott. Munich: C. H. Beck, 2016.

Ott 2021

Ott, Claudia. "Miʾat Layla wa-Layla (A Hundred and One Nights)." In *Encyclopedia of Islam, Three.* Leiden: Brill, 2021.

Rajna 1975

Rajna, Pio. *Le fonti dell'*Orlando Furioso*: Ristampa della seconda edizione 1900 accresciuta d'inediti*, edited by Francesco Mazzoni. Florence: Sansoni, 1975.

Scaglione 1958

Scaglione, Aldo. "Shahryar, Giocondo, Koterviky: Three Versions of the Motif of the Faithless Woman." *Oriens* 2 (1958): pp. 151–161.

Shuraybiṭ 2005

Ḥājj al-Bāhī al-Būnī, al-. *Miʾat layla wa-layla . . . wa-ḥikāyāt ukhrā*, edited by Shuraybiṭ Aḥmad Shuraybiṭ. Algiers: Al-Maktaba al-waṭaniyya al-jazāʾiriyya, 2005.

Spampinato Beretta 1999

Spampinato Beretta, Margherita. "La cornice delle Mille e una notte ed il canto XXVIII dell'*Orlando furioso.*" In *Medioevo romanzo e orientale: Il viaggio dei testi, III Colloquio internazionale, Venezia, 10-13 ottobre 1996*, edited by Antonio Pioletti and Francesca Rizzo Nervo, pp. 229–249. Catanzaro: Rubbettino, 1999.

Ṭarshūna 1979

Kitāb Miʾat layla wa-layla, edited by Maḥmūd Ṭarshūna. Tunis: Al-Dār al-ʿarabiyya lil-kitāb, 1399H/1979.

Toscanella 1574

Toscanella, Orazio. *Bellezze del Furioso di M. Lodovico Ariosto.* Venice: Pietro dei Franceschi, 1574.

Jews and Judaism in Ariosto's Literary Production

Fabrizio Lelli

1. Jews in Ferrara

The Rothschild Miscellany of the Israel Museum in Jerusalem is universally known as the most elegantly and lavishly executed Hebrew manuscript of the Italian Renaissance. It was planned as a sumptuous work that would encompass, in detail, almost every custom of religious and secular Jewish life of the Italian region where its wealthy patron lived. Its fanciful landscapes, spatial perspective settings, and human and animal representations echo the style of the best artists who worked for the court of the Este in Ferrara in the third quarter of the fifteenth century. Indeed, the illuminators of this glorious masterwork may have been associated with the workshop that decorated the famous Latin Bible of Borso d'Este.[1]

At the end of the book of Job that the Miscellany displays in its entirety, we find a full-page miniature in which the eponymous character of the biblical book is represented in the garb of a Northern Italian Renaissance *signore* (fig. 1). This scene emphasizes the fact that Mosheh ben Yequti'el ha-Kohen, the patron of this manuscript, intentionally chose to identify with a victorious Job, whose dynamic vitality is more relevant than the various ordeals he overcame.[2] Moses was most probably a member of the Jewish banking elite of Ferrara.

The politics of the Este were expensive, entailing costs such as urban development programs, armed conflicts, the draining of the Po Valley, and contributing to the splendors of the court. All this caused an ongoing demand for ready cash and long-term loans to which Jewish moneylenders might well provide a partial solution; this was certainly the main reason behind the Ferrara princes' eagerness to welcome Jews from all over Europe and the Mediterranean. As a result, the Jewish population of Ferrara grew dramatically at the turn of the sixteenth century, after the massive expulsions of Jews from Spain and Portugal (1492, 1497) and the various waves of migration of thousands of exiles from Southern Italy (between 1495 and 1510), when the kingdom of Naples was absorbed into the Spanish territories. Ercole I (1431–1505) reigned as

Fig. 1. Illustration of the book of Job (Job 42:12), *The Rothschild Miscellany*, fol. 65v, ca. 1460–1480. Jerusalem, The Israel Museum, B61.09.0803o.s.; 180/051

duke of Ferrara from 1471. His wife, Eleonora of Naples, was from the royal family of Aragon, who sheltered Jewish Iberian exiles in their kingdom. In Ercole's lands, Jews were accepted in all trades, were allowed to collect taxes, and could own pharmacies; the duke also extended to them a papal permission to practice medicine among Christians.[3] Such excellent conditions attracted to Ferrara new waves of exiles throughout the Cinquecento. Among these were also crypto-Jews or Marranos from Portugal,[4] who often reverted to Judaism after their arrival in Italy.[5] Besides the traditional activities of loan banking, usually run by Italian or Ashkenazi Jewish families, new industries, especially in silk weaving, were established by the newcomers, who traded with the Iberian Peninsula and the Spanish colonies in the East. Jews likewise stimulated the export trade through their transactions with *conversos* in Flanders and France, in Rome, Naples, and Venice.[6]

In Ariosto's time (1474–1533), the Jewish population of Ferrara numbered around two thousand souls, making up a large segment of the total population of the city, around thirty thousand people.[7] Ariosto lived, then, in a period when the Jewish component of Ferrara's society could be seen by everyone, everywhere. Jews were present at court, in the streets, and in the markets; their daily activities could not have possibly escaped the poet's sharp eyes.

In Ariosto's day, there were at least three Jewish pawnshops in Ferrara. One had been founded around 1434 by a certain Bonaventura, along with Salamon Zudio, the son of Manuele Norsa. The shop was known as the *banco della Ripa* (or *Riva*) or the *banco da Po* because of the branch of the river that used to run in the south of the city. The second pawnshop was run by Davide di Consiglio and took its name from the *strada dei Sabbioni* (present-day via Mazzini), on which it stood. The third shop, owned by the same family of Davide, was known as *a la bocha del Canal, del borgo Vecchio,* or *dei Carri*. We find all three in Ariosto's comedy *La Lena* (1529), where one of the characters, Flavio, affirms that the fastest way to obtain cash is from the *banco de' Sabbioni*,[8] but only later on do we learn that this was a Jewish bank. The names of its main agents are mentioned by the character Corbolo, "Isaac e Beniamin," [Isaac and Benjamin][9] and the use of first names suggests familiarity.[10] The two other pawnshops are mentioned soon after: "Dai Sabbioni ho avvisato: ora vuo' volgermi / a i Carri; quei da Riva saran gli ultimi" [I've warned Isaac and Benjamin at the Sabbioni; now I'm going to the Carri. Those at the Riva will be the last.][11] Corbolo says he trusts Jewish bankers as reliable; this is why it would be better to give advance notice to them: "Non saria buon che i rigattieri fossino / avvisati, e gli Ebrei che se venissero / questi assassini ad impegnare, o vendere / le robe, tanto a bada li tenessino, / che voi foste avvisato, sì che andandovi / le riaveste, e lor faceste prendere?" [Don't you think it would be a good idea to warn the secondhand dealers and the Jews? In case these assassins come to pawn or sell the clothes, they could hold them at bay until you got there to recover the goods and have them arrested.][12] But his interlocutor Ilario replies:

Cotesto più giovar potria, che nuocere:
Pur non ci spero; che questi che prestano
A usura, esser ribaldi non è dubbio,
E quest'altri, che compran per rivendere,
Son fraudolenti, e 'l ver mai non ti dicono:
Né l'altre cose più volentier pigliano
Delle rubate, perché comperandole
Costan lor poco; e se danar vi prestano
Sopra, fanno che mai non si riscuotono.

Fig. 2. Bartolomeo Veneto, *Portrait of a Man (Abraham Farissol?)*, oil on panel, ca.1525–1530. Madrid, Thyssen-Bornemisza National Museum, inv. no. 30 (1930.8)

> [This could be more useful than harmful. / Yet I'm not very hopeful, for those who lend money / at interest are undoubtedly scoundrels themselves. / Those others, the secondhand dealers, / are fraudulent and never tell you the truth; / and they accept nothing more readily / than stolen goods, for they can buy them / very cheaply. If they lend you money on an item, / they see to it that you never get it back.][13]

Ilario's words reflect the most common attitude of non-Jewish society toward Jewish loan bankers, or pawnbrokers; they also indicate Ariosto's opinion. In a letter of 1509 from Ariosto to Cardinal Ippolito d'Este, the sender reports that "currently in Ferrara there's much rumor about Benjamin the Jew of [the bank of] Riva who went bankrupt for 14 thousand ducats. . . . Marco Marighella . . . told me, in addition, that many silver objects belonging to Your Excellency are still deposited in that pawn bank, and since the Lord Duke signed a laissez-passer for Benjamin, those pieces are not safe, as sooner or later Benjamin might flee."[14]

This remark suggests that Ariosto's attitude toward Jews was nothing remarkable in contemporary Ferrara; he wrote his comedies for an audience who wanted a lively representation of daily life, not a theological debate. Indeed, Ariosto's writings never mention the complex intellectual discussions—on both religious and scientific subjects—that occurred when learned Christians encountered learned Jews in Renaissance Ferrara. I am thinking, for instance, of the important theological disputation between Avraham ben Mordekhay Farissol (1452–ca. 1528), born in Provence (fig. 2), and Pietro Palagano from Trani; the debate took place at the court of Ercole I around 1487 and sparked more polemics.[15] At a later period, the *converso* physician Amatus Lusitanus (1511–1568), born in Portugal and the author of *Curationum medicinalium centuriae septem* (1556), noted that several Jewish scholars would meet with converts and Christians in public and private spaces in Ferrara in order to discuss theological and philosophical issues.[16]

2. Ariosto in Jewish Renaissance Culture

Although there has been no study of direct relations between Ariosto and contemporary Jewish intellectuals, recent scholarship has investigated his role in the literary education of late-Renaissance Jews—and not just in Italy; versions of the *Orlando furioso* were produced either in Hebrew or in other languages spoken by European Jews, and some were written in Hebrew characters. A manuscript now at the Bodleian Library in Oxford contains the first

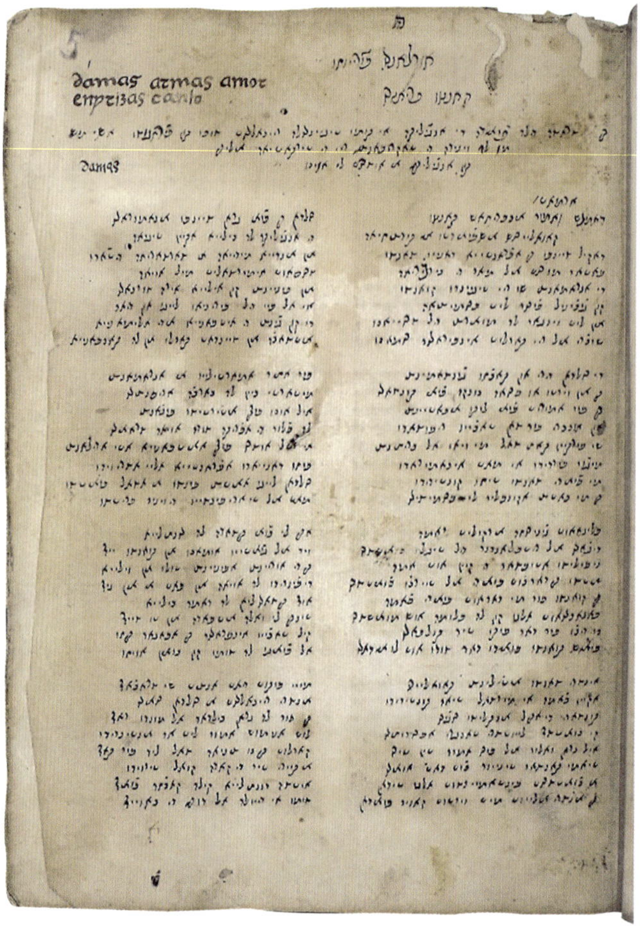

Fig. 3. *Orlando furioso*, in Judeo-Spanish, fol. 5r, late sixteenth century. Oxford, Bodleian Library MS Canonici Or. 6

thirty-six cantos of the *Furioso* in a late-sixteenth-century Castilian translation in Hebrew script (fig. 3).[17] Many lists of books compiled in the same period attest to the presence of the *Furioso* in private collections of Northern Italian Jews.[18] At the end of the sixteenth century, one of the most important Italian rabbis of the early modern era, Leone da Modena (1571–1648), translated two cantos (I and XXVIII) of the *Furioso* into Hebrew. In the previous generation, another Leone, the Mantuan Leone de' Sommi Portaleone (1525–1592), based a play of his own on Ariosto's comedy *Lena*. Leone's comedy, written in Hebrew, is *Ṣaḥot Bediquta De-Qiddushin*; the title is an Aramaic formula, "A stylish farce on engagement / or betrothal." This was the first comedy written in Hebrew that made use of classical patterns; it was recently translated into English as *A Comedy of Betrothal*.[19]

The direct influence of Ariosto's *Furioso* on Jewish Renaissance culture is evident, and no less significant is its indirect effect on literary models widely known in sixteenth-century Jewish society. Jews in Northern Italy, especially Ashkenazi Jews, adapted the popular chivalric genre to biblical narrative. We still have lengthy poems on the books of Kings in four-line strophes of two rhyming couplets, also a poetic version of the books of Samuel dating to the end of the fifteenth century. In the manner of de' Sommi's drama, these epic poems merged motifs from non-Jewish sources with rabbinic texts, which made them more authoritative.[20] Eliyyah Levita (1469–1549)—best known for his intellectual collaboration with non-Jews, especially the famous Cardinal Egidio Antonini da Viterbo (1469–1532)—adapted two traditional chivalric stories, *Buovo d'Antona* and *Paris e Vienna* into Yiddish. The first, titled *Bovo-Buch*, dates to the first decade of the sixteenth century, making it one of the oldest monuments of Yiddish literature.[21] Each story is told in about seven hundred *ottava rima* stanzas—the first use of this format in Germanic literature.[22] *Pariz un Wiene*, composed around 1530, is based on an Italian version of a tale of chivalry from the thirteenth century; in this case, Levita sticks closer to Ariosto's model, injecting himself frequently into the narrative "and confessing that he is a frustrated lover hoping his beloved's heart will be more lenient with him after she hears the story of the two famous lovers." Levita feels free to speak satirically mainly in the prologues to the ten books of poetic narrative.[23]

Levita's Yiddish works display grotesque and burlesque elements that characterize a subgenre of Italian chivalric romances. This special feature reflects the inversion of traditional values in the culture of Carnival. Northern Italian Hebrew manuscripts abound with *Purimspielen*, plays for the Purim festival, in *ottava rima*; the most important is Mordekhay Dato's *Istoria de Purim*, or *The Account of Purim*, dating to the second half of the sixteenth century and composed in the Ferrara region.[24] The intercultural transactions are notable. Plays performed during the Jewish festival of Purim, more or less corresponding to Christian Carnival, followed patterns of theatrical performance common among Christians. We should not forget that many Renaissance comedies "all'antica," like Ariosto's, were performed during the pre-Lent Carnival period.[25]

In Northern Italy, many actors were Jewish. The history of Jews as public entertainers dates back at least to the late Middle Ages, a time when they were forced to play the Fool in pre-Lent celebrations. In "sacred" dramas from fifteenth-century Italy, Jewish characters are often portrayed in such a way as to ridicule and vilify them. Throughout the sixteenth century, however, as secular entertainments began to replace religious performances, Jews with stage talent were increasingly requested as actors, dancers, and musicians on state and civic occasions. In 1520, for instance, Duke Ercole Gonzaga of Mantua invited two Jewish players from Ferrara, Solomon and Jacob, to perform at court. In 1563, a mainly Jewish troupe presented Ariosto's *Suppositi* (The substitutes) at the Gonzaga court to honor the visit of two archdukes of Austria.[26]

We may wonder whether Jews cherished Ariosto's writing only because of its immense popularity or also because of themes or allusions that could be traced back to their own traditions. Italian Renaissance Jews often highlighted affinities between their own culture and trends current in the non-Jewish culture. At the end of the fifteenth century, for example, Yoḥanan Alemanno (ca. 1435–ca. 1504)—a Jewish intellectual who visited Ferrara and lived for a longer time in Medici Florence—drew inspiration from the humanist revival of classical biography to compose a life of King Solomon in Hebrew.[27] He wanted to show that a Jewish scholar would have no trouble building from records of an ancient Jewish monarch to create something comparable to ancient biographies (like Plutarch's *Lives*) of illustrious Greeks and Romans. Introducing his story of Solomon, Alemanno addressed his ideal reader as

> a wise and understanding man, a Jew who is not used to such long stories about a man and his deeds, and who might say that listening to the bleating of this flock of Solomon's virtues wearies the mind. You may say, "All these virtues are already recorded in the book of Chronicles. Why must you recount his statutes and teachings? Praise the Lord with grateful, noble words for He is awesome and praiseworthy." Listen, therefore, to my replies to anyone who would seal his ears from hearing more. First, I greatly envied those among all the nations who praise their idols and compose about a single man whole hosts of books as long as the chronicles of the kings of Israel and Judah combined; while we the community of Jews, do not know how to give two or three particles of praise to one of the holy men of our people. I have, therefore, opened my mouth to glorify and praise King Solomon, may he rest in peace, with many praises. I took it upon myself to put them into a book in an order that will make apparent to all the nations that we have a heart like them.[28]

Alemanno's views can be compared with those of de' Sommi, who lets a personification of "Wisdom" introduce his Hebrew play with these words:

> Now some playwrights among the gentiles have looked down upon the Jews because they seem to lack this literary facility. It is for this reason that I have this day resolved to show that the Hebrew language is not inferior to its artistic power. In-

deed, what is a crowning glory for other languages is but a glitter of a shoe-buckle for Hebrew. Hence, men should not deem it a defect in that language because they have not seen it cast, ere now, into a pleasing comedy. Rather, it is because the words that constitute this holy tongue are of most ancient and wondrous origin, and it has seemed unworthy for such sacred words to be said solely for human pleasure. But what other languages can do, Hebrew can do better. The very proof of this statement I shall soon place before your eyes. For if the play form is novel for Hebrew, its capacity for creating parables and proverbs is well-known, and so can make it even more marvelous as a medium for theatrical entertainment.[29]

3. Wisdom and Languages

While Jews were inspired by such classical literary genres as biography, epic,[30] or drama,[31] their Christian contemporaries were investigating Jewish approaches to biblical hermeneutics in order to find a basis for universal knowledge shared by all religious and philosophical systems.[32]

Such wisdom, grounded in the notion of a hidden language that encodes divine secrets, is at the core of the *Orlando furioso*, a sort of magical box containing every field and tool of human learning.[33] In Ariosto's poem, language plays a large role. Speech and writing have arcane and occult properties. Readers of Ariosto will do well to bear in mind the links detected by learned people between natural forces in the universe and the magical powers of words; this connectedness was a favorite topic of speculation in the Renaissance and afterward. The magical component had also been part and parcel of the medieval literature that inspired Ariosto and his literary predecessors, but Renaissance scholars sought a deeper philosophical understanding of language as a path to hidden forces thought to rule the sublunary world.[34] The notion that the heavens above are closely connected with lower earthly bodies was not new. But Marsilio Ficino (1433–1499), Giovanni Pico della Mirandola (1463–1494), and their followers in the Cinquecento found new ways to uncover forces hidden in nature and evoke these magical powers by manipulating language.[35] On this issue, see, for instance, Ariosto's words in *Orlando furioso*, canto XXXV, octave 18. Here it is Saint John the Evangelist himself who explains to Astolfo:

Tu déi saper che non si muove fronda
là giù che segno qui non se ne faccia.
Ogni effetto convien che corrisponda
in terra e in ciel, ma con diversa faccia.
—*Fur.*, XXXV 18, 1–4

> [Understand that not a bough moves down on earth but its motion is remarked up here. There must be a correspondence, albeit under different guise, between every effect on earth and in heaven.]

Note that Saint John the Evangelist is the only Christian authority quoted by Leone Ebreo[36] in his Neoplatonic *Dialogues on Love*, written in a very high Tuscan vernacular and first published in 1535. Leone Ebreo, whose original name was Yehudah Abravanel (ca. 1460–ca. 1530), came from a wealthy family of exiled Spanish Jews. After leaving the Iberian Peninsula, the Abravanels first settled in Aragonese Naples, where the Neapolitan rulers welcomed them before they moved to Venice, Florence, and Ferrara.[37]

Leone Ebreo's Neoplatonic ideas[38] parallel the views of his Florentine contemporary Francesco Cattani da Diacceto (1466–1522), a disciple of Ficino. Like most of their contemporaries, both Francesco and Leone held that linguistic formulas could awaken magical powers in natural objects and sometimes produce unusual effects by changing the course of terrestrial events. This ancient theory was prominent in Renaissance learning, notwithstanding strict ecclesiastical (rabbinic, in the case of Judaism) prohibitions on binding charms and harmful spells.[39]

Jews, commonly thought to possess arcane wisdom, were renowned for practical applications of religious magic such as amulets containing verses of Scripture.[40] In the region of Ferrara, where magical texts were plentiful after the large migration of Sephardic Jews at the end of the fifteenth century, occult learning became part of regular education and gained recognition at the Este court.[41] Members of the Spanish Zacuto family, active in Ferrara in the early sixteenth century, published annual prognostications in Latin that became a popular basis for astral horoscopes.[42]

A later response to the prominence of Jewish magic in Renaissance Ferrara conversations is preserved in a text of the early eighteenth century, whose author, Girolamo Baruffaldi (1675–1755), was a native of the region and an expert in Ariosto's poetry. Baruffaldi wrote an anti-Jewish pamphlet, "Rabbi Talass, profeta al Ghetto di Ferrara," in which the "rabbi prophet" himself underwrites an anti-Jewish slur: that gravestones inscribed with Hebrew characters will be used sacrilegiously to restore a Christian monument in Ferrara's cathedral square. The prophetic rabbi exclaims:

> Toccherà a noi pregar la medicina,
> né già per virtù d'erbe, e d'arte maga,

ma per virtù del nostro Cimitero
sorgerà la Colonna, altera e vaga.
[It will be upon us [the Jews] to seek for the medicament:
not by virtue of herbs or magic,
but by means of our cemetery
(Borso's) column will stand in its severe beauty.][43]

Baruffaldi has in mind gravestones removed from the Jewish cemetery to restore the fifteenth-century monument erected in honor of Borso d'Este after the 1716 fire. He may also be thinking of a magical ritual that plays out in canto XXII (octave 23) of *Orlando furioso,* where Astolfo eventually succeeds in destroying Atlante's magic castle.[44] After consulting his grimoire, he digs up and removes a heavy slab of stone carved with mysterious characters and images:

Astolfo, poi ch'ebbe cacciato il mago,
levò di su la soglia il grave sasso,
e vi ritrovò sotto alcuna imago,
ed altre cose che di scriver lasso:
e di distrugger quello incanto vago,
di ciò che vi trovò, fece fraccasso,
come gli mostra il libro che far debbia;
e si sciolse il palazzo in fumo e in nebbia.
—*Fur.*, XXII 23
[Having expelled the magician, Astolfo lifted the heavy slab from the threshold; under it he found some images and other objects which I'll not describe. Eager to break the spells, he smashed everything the way the book instructed him. The palace dissolved into smoke and mist.]

Could the mystical marks on the foundation stone of Atlante's castle be Hebrew script? We know that during the 1960 restoration of the pillar supporting Borso's monument, Jewish funerary stones were found inside the thick column. Although scholars wanted these artifacts to go to the local Jewish museum, citizens of Ferrara thought they should be put back inside the column. Out of sight, out of mind. Or maybe they thought the column would collapse like Atlante's castle without those "magical stones" inside it?

Informed by Baruffaldi, we can conclude that Jews in eighteenth-century Ferrara served as physicians (Borso's restored column is described as a cure) who used botanical magic to heal their patients. For Baruffaldi, the magic is a silly joke, but in Renaissance Ferrara—where Platonism permeated the teaching of Guarino da Verona (1374–1460)—theories of magic advertised by Ficino and others attracted wide attention. The celebrity of magic in Ferrarese culture created a context of esteem, quite unlike Baruffaldi's mockery, for traditional Jewish lore. In light of this background, we can reconsider one of Ariosto's earliest works, his fragmentary poem *De laudibus Sophiae ad Herculem Ferrariae ducem II* (On Sophia's praises to Ercole, second duke of Ferrara).

The Latin hexameters in praise of *Sophia*, or Wisdom, were written in 1495 to embellish the opening of the academic year at the University of Ferrara. Ariosto maintains that Wisdom was born in ancient Egypt. This Neoplatonic-Hermetic conception of tracing the origins of universal wisdom back to Egypt is associated by Ariosto with Mosaic wisdom, even older and revealed directly by God: Hermes Trismegistus and Moses are primordial voices of divine knowledge. This patristic notion of a primeval ancient theology (*prisca sapientia),* revived by Ficino and propagated by his admirers,[45] appealed to Ariosto, even while he praised Ercole's good government with literary stereotypes from courtly literature. But when the poet sees traditional debates on poetry as revealing concealed wisdom, he updates the chivalric commonplaces by surrounding them with Neoplatonic fantasies prized by his own generation. The same ideas, likewise inspired by Ficino, were well known to Leone Ebreo, who used the Renaissance topos of Moses as an ancient Egyptian philosopher.[46] One of the two interlocutors in Leone's *Dialogues on Love* is Sophia, and these are Ariosto's words:[47]

> deseruit clarae urbis opus ter maximus Hermes;
> legifer hinc Moses, illinc pia turba frequentat,
> casta quidem, sed rara tamen; namque inclyta virtus
> neglegit infausti foedata examina vulgi.
> [Hermes Trismegistos left behind his famous city's work; from one direction comes Moses the lawgiver, from another comes the devoted throng, pure indeed, but nonetheless few in number because renowned virtue ignores the filthy hordes of the accursed mob.][48]

4. Jewish Magicians and the *Negromante*

Descending from the heights of Wisdom intellectualized, Ariosto popularized the identification of Judaism with magic in his *Negromante*. A first version dates roughly to 1509, but the play was completed only in 1520, when it was dedicated to Pope Leo X and eventually staged in Ferrara for the 1528 Carnival. The protagonist is a necromancer—strictly speaking, "someone who is able to call a dead man back to life"—but he is a general-purpose wizard, an astrologer, and a Jew,[49] one of many Sephardic Jewish exiles who lived in Northern Italian cities when Ariosto was writing.

A monologue by the wizard's attendant—Nibbio, the Kite—reviews his master's deeds and character to open the second act of the play. The audience hears the necromancer's name for the first time from Nibbio. He is Giacchelino or Iacchelino, a vernacular diminutive of the Hebrew Yeḥi'el[50] and a very common name, especially among Italian Jews of the time. Nibbio calls him *mastro*, or master, corresponding to *magister* in Latin and reserved in official documents for healers allowed to practice by public authorities; addressing the wizard as *mastro Giacchelino* was tantamount to calling him Dr. Giacchelino. These are Nibbio's words:

> Per certo, questa è pur gran confidenzia,[51]
> che mastro Giacchelino ha in se medesmo,
> che, mal sapendo leggere e mal scrivere,
> caccia professione di filosofo,
> d'alchemista, di medico, di astrologo,
> di mago, e di scongiurator di spiriti;
> e sa di queste e dell'altre scienzie,
> quanto l'asino e 'l bue di sonar gli organi;
> benché si faccia nominar lo astrologo
> per eccellenza, sì come Virgilio
> il poeta, e Aristotile il filosofo.
> Ma con un viso più che marmo immobile,
> ciance, menzogne, e non con altra industria,
> aggira et avviluppa il capo agli uomini;
> e gode, e fa godere a me (aiutandoci
> la sciocchezza, che al mondo è in abbondanzia)
> l'altrui ricchezze. Andiamo come zingani
> di paese in paese; e le vestigie
> sue tuttavia, dovunque passa, restano,
> come de la lumaca, o per più simile
> comparazion, di grandine, o di fulmine;
> sì che di terra in terra, per nascondersi,
> si muta nome, abito, lingua e patria.
> Or è Giovanni, or Pietro; quando fingesi
> greco, quando d'Egitto, quando d'Africa;

> ed è, per dire il ver, Giudeo d'origine,
> di quei che fur cacciati di Castilia.
> [My master, Jachelino, / certainly has great confidence in himself; / for while he hardly knows how to read and write, / he nevertheless professes to be a philosopher, an alchemist, / a doctor, an astrologer, a magician, / and even a conjurer of spirits. / Although he's called the Astrologer par excellence, / just as Vergil is known as the Poet / and Aristotle as the Philosopher, / he knows as much about these and other sciences as a donkey / or an ox knows about playing an organ. / But with a face as motionless as marble, / with stories and lies, and no other skills, / he swindles people and confounds their minds. / Thus, he benefits and makes me benefit / from the riches of others / —with the help of folly, which abounds in the world. / Like gypsies, we go from place to place, / and wherever he passes he leaves his imprint like a snail or, / for a more fitting comparison, like fire or lightning; / and in each place, in order to disguise himself, / he changes his name, his dress, and his country. / Now he calls himself Peter, now John; / now he pretends to come / from Greece, now from Egypt, now from Africa. / In reality, he's a Jew, / and he was among those who were expelled from Castile.][52]

Even though Nibbio seems unsure about the actual skills of his *mastro*, the servant describes his master's pretensions in grand language: the wizard claims "professione di philosopho, / d'alchimista, di medico, di astrologo / di mago, e di scongiurator di spiriti" [to be a philosopher, an alchemist, a doctor, an astrologer, a magician, and even a conjurer of spirits]. Nibbio names job descriptions ascribed to Jews at the turn of the sixteenth century. When the list is compared to similar remarks by contemporary Jews—such as Alemanno or Joseph Israel of Forlì (early sixteenth century)—the similarity is striking: what a Christian thinker like Ariosto expected to find in educated Jews was astrological and magical medicine loosely framed by Aristotelian natural philosophy and Platonic metaphysics.[53]

When Ariosto was young, Alemanno addressed a handbook on rhetoric to young Jewish students, thinking of rhetoric as a tool for making magic seem presentably scientific to contemporary society. Here are Alemanno's words:

> It is well-known to every wise man that really knowledgeable people fully understand the object of their scientific research by performing many operations and by acting on the nature of existents, by connecting the latter and by creating interactions between one another. Thus they will cause much good to themselves and to the others.[54]

Alemanno then explains that the practical basis of this universal expertise is virtuous behavior, made reflective and theoretical by philosophy, alchemy, astrology, the science of plants and talismans and of magic formulas and divine and angelic names.[55]

Just at the time when the final version of the *Negromante* was staged, Eliyyah Menaḥem Ḥalfan (ca. 1480–ca. 1551) was writing about Christian perceptions of kabbalah as a Jewish magic more arcane than the knowledge described by Alemanno. Ḥalfan was a Venetian Jew who had studied near Ferrara with a Spanish-born kabbalist in the early sixteenth century.[56] He wrote this in a short statement on the *Transmission of Kabbalistic Knowledge*:

> Especially after the rise of the sect of Luther, many of the nobles and scholars of the land [i.e., non-Jewish Italians] sought to obtain a thorough knowledge of this glorious science. They have exhausted themselves in this search, because among our people there are but a few experts in this science, for after the great number of troubles and expulsions but a few remain. Thus, seven learned men grasp a Jewish man by the hem of his garment and say: "Be our master in this science."[57]

So curious were non-Jews about Jewish knowledge that they stopped Jews on the street to ask about these hidden traditions.

Ariosto's Nibbio lets the audience know that Giacchelino, like many other Jews, fled Castile for Italy; after traveling to Cremona, he wandered like a vagabond through other Northern Italian cities, utterly unlike the non-Jews who live permanently in the same city for generations. Everything about him is obscure: his profession, his name, his language, and even his religion. But in the first act of the comedy, the audience learns about the wizard from other characters; now he is an astrologer, now a physician, now a conjuror. Nibbio warns the audience that Giacchelino's name, dress, language, and religion change from place to place and time to time: "Or è Giovanni, or Pietro; quando fingesi / Greco, quando d'Egitto, quando d'Africa" [Now he calls himself Peter, now John; now he pretends to come from Greece, now from Egypt, now from Africa]. Versatility was a practical matter for Jews, suddenly forced to leave their native land, change names and religion, and adopt different habits. In fact, Alemanno advised his students to change residence frequently, because getting to know a variety of traditions would strengthen them.[58] Many Jews exiled from the Iberian Peninsula as converts reverted to their original religion in Ferrara or Venice, as Nibbio seems to have realized: "Fate a mio senno, padron;

come avuti li / avete, andiamo a Ferrara, o a Vinegia" [Take my advice, Master. As soon as you get them let's head for Ferrara or Venice].[59]

What non-Jews, as Ariosto presents them, see in Jews is the paradox of constant mutability:[60] Giacchelino is a dissimulator whose vaunted magic trades on incomprehensible spells. On the other hand, it is Giacchelino's linguistic power of persuasion that eventually helps him untangle the oppressive bonds in which Jews are knotted up by non-Jews. Giacchelino's special talent is to cast light on obscure mysteries that ground a "steady" society. He solves hard problems by recreating a primeval order, by returning the characters of the comedy to pristine conditions, before they were changed for the worse by the abstruse social games of their parents.

Giacchelino's rhetoric,[61] following Italian Jewish tradition, aims to persuade customers and patients to trust him. He behaves like Atlante, the wizard in the *Furioso*, who convinces prisoners to trust him. Atlante shows others a reality that does not exist. He reads from a secret book that has the same power as the Bible, whose words, when God utters them, are the magic of creation itself—according to midrash and kabbalah. On one hand, then, Ariosto's reality is Platonizing poetic illusion. Jews, like magicians, are expert mediators between different levels of reality. Art, like poetry, is fiction, hence deceitful,[62] and poetry, like magic, makes its own reality.[63] The goal is positive, to restore the original order of creation, lost by human intervention in God's primordial plan. On the other hand, a Renaissance magus will also learn from Aristotle to strengthen his imaginative faculty in order to concoct his fakery; Diacceto writes that "through the vehemence of his imagination the magus becomes pregnant with the kindred power of the heavens."[64]

Occult arts of magic, like the redemptive devotions of kabbalah, were attractive to Renaissance Jews and Christians, encouraging citizens of an ideal state to revive a golden age—and yet an illusory age conjured up by spells and incantations. The magical city of the sun celebrated by thinkers of the Italian Renaissance—like the labyrinthine Cremona of the *Negromante* or Atlante's castle[65]—had already appeared in medieval texts produced by Jews and Muslims and then circulated by Jews living in the north of Italy during the Renaissance.[66]

Another theme of fluctuating reality is the primeval motif of changing humans into animals. Any competent wizard can turn a prince into a frog or make someone invisible, like Giacchelino:

> De le donne e de gli uomini
> sa trasformar, sempre che vuole, in varii

animali e volatili e quadrupedi.
[Whenever he likes he can change
men and women into various
winged animals and quadrupeds.][67]
Vi farò prendere
forma, s'io voglio, d'un cane domestico
o di gatto. Or che direste, vedendovi
trasformare in un topo, che è sì piccolo?
[If I want to, I can make you take
the form of a dog
or a cat. Now, what would you say if you found yourself
transformed into something very small like a mouse?][68]

Ovid's influence, ubiquitous in medieval and post-medieval Latin texts, was also felt in the Hebrew literature of Renaissance Italy.[69] Another way to track transitions between different levels of creation—where the very idea of a "level" of being had excited many Platonists—was to explain them by metempsychosis, a notion as familiar to Jews as it was to Socrates and his pupils.[70] But Ariosto's approach to metamorphosis was more literary than philosophical or religious, though fables with this motif can be found in the Aggadic genre of ancient and medieval Hebrew literature. In yet another way, Renaissance thinkers (like Gorgias and Socrates again) saw metamorphosis as a function of rhetoric, since one task of the orator was to alter concepts by altering sounds and signs, just as magicians and alchemists worked to transform bodily objects and natural phenomena. When Giulio Camillo Delminio (ca. 1480–1544)—named one of the best scholars of the day by the *Furioso*—describes three kinds of metamorphosis, one is linguistic or rhetorical.[71]

Giacchelino conducts his necromantic ritual at night. The wizard must turn eastward to aim his enchantments in that direction:

ma dire orazioni, e leggere
certe scongiurazioni potentissime,
da far che tutti qui in casa di Massimo,
insino a i topi, eccetto Emilia, dormano.
[I'll say prayers and recite
certain powerful exorcisms
that will make everyone in Massimo's house,
except Emilia, sleep—even the mice.][72]

Demonic rituals require special garments and particular tools:

> Bisogna far la stola e dua manipuli
> di drappo nero, e porne a piè del camice,
> dui quadri, e due nel petto, e in fronte all'amito
> un terzo, come i sacerdoti gli usano,
> quando alle feste solenni s'apparano.
> [We also have to make the stole and two maniples out
> of black silk; and we have to put
> two squares [of black silk] at the bottom of the surplice,
> two on the chest, and another on the front of the amice,
> just as priests wear on religious holidays.][73]

The magic apparel is traditional: one or two silver *baccini* (basins),[74] torches and candles, fragrant herbs and incense call the heavenly choirs down to earth or invoke spirits of the dead: "Ci bisognano / due torchi, assai candele, ed erbe varie, / e varie gomme per li suffumigi" [We also need two torches, plenty of candles, various herbs, and gums for the fumigation].[75] A specific talisman is needed, bearing a pentacle:[76] "Ah, quasi che'l pentacolo / m'era scordato" [Ah! I almost forgot the pentacle].[77]

All the fuss is amusing in the comedy, but such rites were really used in ceremonies where Jewish know-how was valued. To keep curious people away from a box thought to contain a corpse, Giacchelino warns that when someone who failed to trust him touched a similar box, "arse in guisa, che né pur in cenere / ne restò" [he burned in such a way that not even the ashes were left].[78] This recalls an episode in 1 Samuel of the punishment of Philistines who stole a much more sacred box, the Ark of the Covenant.[79] Another punishment for violating sacred space happened, according to Nibbio, "In Andrenopoli, / voi trovereste in Vinegia un par d'uomini / che san la cosa appunto, e così in Genova" [At Adrianople. Perhaps you'll come across a couple of men in Venice, and also in Genoa, who know the story in detail].[80] The Ottoman East was a safe harbor for Jews who fled Spain in 1492, and this is the destination envisaged by the astrologer and his assistant when they wrap up their adventures in Italy.[81] Many Iberian Jews who settled first in Ferrara moved later to the Ottoman Empire but remained in touch with Italian communities.

5. Agramante's Jewish Lineage

One final suggestion: I wonder whether the name of the Moorish king Agramante in the *Furioso* reflects Jewish influence. Ariosto took it from Boiardo. The Latin original would be something like Agramas, perhaps a king of demons, Agramas or Agrimas, who appears in many *midrashim*. According to a few medieval texts, possibly from the Italian peninsula, Adam's firstborn was not Cain but Agrimas. According to an older tradition, Adam's first wife was the demonic Lilith, and Agrimas was their son. He was an ancestor of other demons—though a story about Methuselah, one of Adam's descendants, says that the patriarch used a magic spell and a sword inscribed with divine names to exterminate the progeny of Agrimas. As his name suggests, this mighty demon was the Persian Ahrīmān in Jewish garb.[82] The connection is salient because the Agramante of the epic is a bad Muslim king. He is also related to Ruggieri, an ancestor of the Este dukes—a Christian who was kidnapped, lost his religious identity, and waged war on the Muslim side before being re-christened, recovering his original faith, and producing the Este line. This game of changing faiths and recovering lost identities was part and parcel of a composite society in sixteenth-century Ferrara.

To conclude, although Ariosto almost never mentioned his Jewish contemporaries, Jews were active in his society and were conspicuous—noted as scholars, merchants, bankers, physicians, and astrologers. Like many Christians, Ariosto probably saw them as neighbors, not as strangers or infidels. The wizard Giacchelino, nonetheless, is his Christian presentation of a type—the learned Renaissance Jew who deals in arcane and exotic matters. This common portrayal, known from many sixteenth-century depictions of Jews in Christian literary and pictorial art, was certainly motivated by the scholarly excitement of Italian humanism, an environment where Christian intellectuals sought out arcane Jewish wisdom not only by studying kabbalist exegesis of the Bible but also by investigating magical interpretations of divinity and the divine creation produced and put into practice by Jews.[83]

Notes

1. See Séd-Rajna 1987, pp. 140–141. For a description of this codex, see Beit-Arié 1993, pp. 181–215.

2. A view that contrasts with the most common medieval interpretation of Job as an afflicted man; see Lelli 2008a, p. 233.

3. See Ioly Zorattini 1993.

4. See Bonfil 1993; Di Leone Leoni 2011.

5. A case in point is that of the physician Amatus Lusitanus (1511–1568), on whom see Gutwirth 2004.

6. See Bonfil 2005; Graziani Secchieri 2014; Magrini 2015.

7. See Traniello 2017, pp. 207–208.

8. This and the following quotes from Ariosto's plays are derived from Ariosto 1936, *La Lena*, Act I, scene 2, p. 434; English translation in Ariosto 1975, p. 166: [Lena] "If your friends won't lend it to you ask the brokers, for they're always dealing with a hundred moneylenders. Take off this velvet gown, remove your cap, and send them to the Jew: you have other clothes to wear." . . . [Flavio] ". . . go to the Sabbioni's exchange and pawn them for twenty-five florins."

9. Ariosto 1936, *La Lena*, Act III, scene 6, p. 468; Ariosto 1975, p. 178.

10. See below on Ariosto's *Letters*.

11. Ariosto 1936, *La Lena*, Act III, scene 6, p. 468; Ariosto 1975, p. 178.

12. Ariosto 1936, *La Lena*, Act III, scene II, p. 463; Ariosto 1975, p. 177.

13. Ariosto 1936, *La Lena*, Act III, scene II, p. 464; Ariosto 1975, p. 177.

14. *Ariosto* 1887, Letter II to Cardinal Ippolito d'Este (1509): "Al presente si parla assai per Ferrara di Beniamin ebreo da Riva che ha fallito di 14 mila ducati che avea da altri ebrei forastieri a guadagno, e questo per avere esso credito col conte Rinaldo Sacrato e col conte Jeronimo Roverella e con altri di qualche migliaro di ducati che non può esigere. A Ferrara sopra di questo si dicono molte ciancie: che è stato il Duca che avendo inteso che avea molti denari di cristiani ad interesse, ha voluto sapere chi sono questi che per suo mezzo prestano ad usura, e ha voluto torgli tutti questi denari che erano di cristiani usurari; e la fama sovvertendo la veritade, dice che'l conte Rinaldo prefato avea su quel banco duemila ducati a guadagno, e così molti altri che si nominano. Pur Marco Marighella, al quale in queste cose si può dar fede, mi ha certificato esser così come prima ho scritto, e m'ha detto ancora che molti argenti di V. S. sono su quel banco; e avvenga che'l signor Duca abbia fatto il salvo condotto a Beniamin, pur non vi sono molto sicuri, perchè un giorno se ne potrebbe fuggire." Benjamin da Riva was a prominent Ferraran moneylender who was instrumental in financing the wars against Venice. In Letter III to Cardinal Ippolito, we read: "Venuto in questa terra, ho trovato due Siciliani. . . . Un Marino da la Maitina ha chiamato un Francesco Salamone per provargli di certa causa matrimoniale . . . e questo è che quel Marino ha scritto volere provare a quel Francesco quattro cose . . . la terza che questo Francesco non avrà ardire di venire in campo perchè è codardo e che è un giudeo." This letter witnesses the existence of native Sicilian (or Southern Italian) people in Ferrara who were suspected of being converted Jews, mainly on the basis of their family names.

15. See Herzig 2012. On Abraham Farissol, see Ruderman 1981.

16. See Gutwirth 2004; Lelli 2004b.

17. See Minervini 1993.

18. See the lists of books owned by Mantuan Jews at the end of the sixteenth century that reveal the extraordinary circulation of the *Orlando furioso* in their collections: Baruchson-Arbib 2001, pp. 163–182.

19. De' Sommi 1988.

20. Bikard 2012. I am grateful to Mario Casari for this bibliographic reference.

21. Bikard 2012, p. 33; Rosenzweig 2016.

22. Bikard 2012, p. 33.

23. Against such a sociocultural background, we better understand the opening words of Abraham Farissol's treatise *Sefer Orḥot ʿOlam* (The book of the ways of the world, written in Ferrara in 1524), where the author warns his reader against the *meshalim*, that is, the fictional literature or belles lettres that he describes as mainly consisting of "love songs or historical books of ancient wars" (see MS Philadelphia, University of Pennsylvania, LJS 499, fol. 1*r*).

24. See Busi 1987; English translation in Tennen 2008.

25. However, the Purim festival being grounded in the biblical book of Esther, the Jewish plays in *ottava rima* had both a comic and an epic component: they were cheerful productions in a tragic or dramatic mood.

26. De' Sommi 1988, pp. 16–17.

27. See Lesley 1976; Lesley 1988.

28. English quote from Lesley 1976, p. 53. See also Lelli 2004a, p. 29.

29. De' Sommi 1988, p. 68.

30. On Esther as an epic heroine in sixteenth- and seventeenth-century Ferrara and Venice, see Arbib 2003.

31. By the end of the sixteenth century, Terence's play *Eunuchus* was printed in the holy language in Mantua, as well as *The Story of Joseph* (apparently a dramatization of the biblical narrative); see de' Sommi 1988, p. 21. De' Sommi wrote several plays in Italian.

32. On this complex issue, see, e.g., Lelli 2004c.

33. On Ariosto and magic, see Kisacky 2000 and Jossa's essay in this volume.

34. See, e.g., Beitchman 1998; Lelli 2008b.

35. On Ariosto's attitude toward Neoplatonism, see Dell'Aia 2013; on the poet's critique of contemporaneous Neoplatonic thinkers, see Looney 2013.

36. Even though the mention of a Christian saint could be an addition of the editor of the Roman 1535 edition of the *Dialogues*; see Leone Ebreo 2009, pp. 264, 403n154.

37. See Netanyahu 1953, pp. 61–87. On Leone's stay in Ferrara in 1516, see Fontanesi 1934, pp. 21–28.

38. On the influence of Leone Ebreo's *Dialogues on Love* on the elaboration of Olimpia's character in Ariosto's *Furioso*, see Bonadeo 1968, pp. 56–57.

39. See Copenhaver 1988; Perrone Compagni 2008.

40. See Halbronn 1985.

41. See Biondi 1977; Vasoli 1977.

42. See Flórez Miguel 2007.

43. Baruffaldi 1794. I owe this reference to the kindness of Gianmarco Sinisi. See also Magrini 2015, pp. 165–166.

44. On this episode, see Quint 1979; Ascoli 1987, pp. 176–199.

45. See Lelli 2000.

46. See Veltri 2004, p. 57.

47. It might be worthy of mention that Leone's father, Yiṣḥaq Abravanel (1437–1508), possibly to counteract the authority of the pagan theologians, not only identified Hermes with the biblical patriarch Enoch but also ascribed to Moses a genealogy that could easily compete with the claims of Renaissance non-Jewish trends of thought; see Idel 2011, pp. 171–172.

48. Ariosto 2018, pp. 13-14. On Moses as a legislator, on his Egyptian formation, and on the alleged contemporaneity of Moses and Hermes Trismegistus according to Renaissance authors, see Lelli 2004c, pp. 51–57; Lelli 2019.

49. In the first version of the play, Giacchelino is given the title of *Fisico* (Physicist); he becomes an *Astrologo* (Astrologer) only in the second version.

50. The name *Yeḥi'el* was usually translated into Italian as *Vitale* (Latin *Vitalis*).

51. On this expression, see Scorrano 1971.

52. Ariosto 1936, *Il negromante*, Act II, scene 1, pp. 330–331; English translation in Ariosto 1975, p. 116.

53. See Lelli 1996.

54. Lelli 1996, p. 128.

55. Lelli 1996, pp. 128–132.

56. See Lelli 2011b.

57. See the Hebrew text of the letter, accompanied by an Italian translation, in Lelli 2011a, p. 493.

58. See Lelli 1997.

59. Ariosto 1936, *Il negromante*, Act II, scene 2, p. 332; Ariosto 1975, p. 117. Nibbio's assumption is that, once settled in Ferrara or Venice, his master will lead a safer life.

60. On mobility versus stability in Ariosto's late work *Erbolato*, see Looney 2013, p. 32.

61. See Alemanno 1995, pp. 29–55.

62. As stated earlier, the play was performed at Carnival, a festival of deception and subversion. On the Italian comedy as deeply related to Carnival celebrations, see Toschi 1955.

63. See Lelli 2008c.

64. See Walker 1958, pp. 32–33.

65. See Ansani 2016.

66. See Idel 2011, pp. 344–348.

67. Ariosto 1936, *Il negromante*, Act I, scene 3, p. 321; Ariosto 1975, p. 112.

68. Ariosto 1936, *Il negromante*, Act III, scene 3, pp. 357–358. Ariosto 1975, p. 129.

69. See the case of David Messer Leon's treatise *Shevaḥ Nashim* (Women's praise): Tirosh-Rothschild 1991, pp. 73–77.

70. On metempsychosis in Renaissance Judaism and Christianity, see Ogren 2009.

71. See Bolzoni 2000.

72. Ariosto 1936, *Il negromante*, Act III, scene 3, p. 360; Ariosto 1975, p. 130.

73. Ariosto 1936, *Il negromante*, Act III, scene 4, p. 364; Ariosto 1975, p. 133.

74. Ariosto 1936, *Il negromante*, Act III, scene 4, p. 366; Ariosto 1975, p. 133.

75. Ariosto 1936, *Il negromante*, Act III, scene 4, p. 366; Ariosto 1975, p. 133–134.

76. The word *pentacle* is misunderstood by Massimo, who at first understands it as *pentole* (pots), then *pennacchi* (crests) and *spantacchio* (a meaningless funny-sounding word; Ariosto 1936, *Il negromante*, Act III, scene 4, pp. 365–66; Ariosto 1975, p. 133).

77. Ariosto 1936, *Il negromante*, Act III, scene 4, p. 364; Ariosto 1975, p. 133.

78. Ariosto 1936, *Il negromante*, Act III, scene 4, p. 368; Ariosto 1975, p. 134.

79. 1 Sam. 4:1–11.

80. Ariosto 1936, *Il negromante*, Act III, scene 4, p. 369; Ariosto 1975, p. 135. Another such episode may be also reminiscent of the biblical text of Exodus: *In rane trasformaronsi, / e tuttavia alla porta dietro gracchiano / a i forastier, che inanzi e indietro passano* (They were transformed into frogs and they're still at the gates croaking at foreigners who pass back and forth; Ariosto 1936, *Il negromante*, Act III, scene 4, p. 368; Ariosto 1975, pp. 134–135).

81. Ariosto 1936, *Il negromante*, Act III, scene 4, p. 371; Ariosto 1975, p. 136.

82. Idel 2016, pp. 60–74.

83. See Lelli 2006.

Bibliography

Alemanno 1995

Alemanno, Yoḥanan. *Ḥay ha-'olamim* (The immortal), *Parte I: La retorica*, edited by Fabrizio Lelli. Florence: Olschki, 1995.

Ansani 2016

Ansani, Antonella. "Questioning Poetry in Ariosto's *Negromante*." *Northeast Modern Language Association Italian Studies* 38 (2016): pp. 67–99.

Arbib 2003

Arbib, Marina. "The Queen Esther's Triangle: Leon Modena, Ansaldo Cebà, and Sara Copio Sullam." In *The Lion Shall Roar: Leon Modena and His World*, edited by David Malkiel, pp. 103–135. Jerusalem: Hebrew University/Ben-Zvi Institute, 2003.

Ariosto 1887

Lettere di Lodovico Ariosto, edited by Antonio Cappelli. Milan: Ulrico Hoepli Editore, 1887. http://www.gutenberg.org/files/57780.

Ariosto 1936

Ariosto, Lodovico. *Opere minori*. Florence: Adriano Salani Editore, 1936.

Ariosto 1975

The Comedies of Ariosto, translated and edited by Edmond M. Beame and Leonard G. Sbrocchi. Chicago: University of Chicago Press, 1975.

Ariosto 2018

Ariosto. Ludovico. *Latin Poetry*, translated by Dennis Looney. Cambridge, MA. Harvard University Press, 2018.

Ascoli 1987
Ascoli, Albert R. *Ariosto's Bitter Harmony: Crisis and Evasion in the Italian Renaissance*. Princeton, NJ: Princeton University Press, 1987.
Baruchson-Arbib 2001
Baruchson-Arbib, Shifra. *La culture livresque des juifs d'Italie à la fin de la Renaissance*. Paris: CNRS, 2001.
Baruffaldi 1794
Baruffaldi, Girolamo. *Rime serie, e giocose: Opere postume dell'Arciprete Baruffaldi, in aggiunta alla raccolta stampata in Ferrara da Francesco Pomatelli*. Ferrara: n.p., 1794.
Beit-Arié 1993
Beit-Arié, Malachi. *The Making of the Medieval Hebrew Book: Studies in Paleography and Codicology*. Jerusalem: Magnes, 1993.
Beitchman 1998
Beitchman, Philip. *Alchemy of the Word: Cabala of the Renaissance*. Albany: State University of New York Press, 1998.
Bikard 2012
Bikard, Arnaud. "Elia Levita's Yiddish Works: Echoes of the Italian Renaissance in the Poetical Creation of a Jewish Humanist." In *Jewish Migration: Voices of the Diaspora, Italianistica Ultraiectina VII*, edited by Raniero Spelman, Monica Jansen, and Silvia Gaiga, pp. 32–39. Utrecht: Igitur, 2012.
Biondi 1977
Biondi, Albano. "Streghe ed eretici nei domini estensi all'epoca dell'Ariosto." In *Il Rinascimento nelle corti padane: Società e cultura*, edited by Paolo Rossi, pp. 165–199. Bari: De Donato, 1977.
Bolzoni 2000
Bolzoni, Lina. "Notes on Giordano Bruno and Ariosto." *Rinascimento* 40 (2000): pp. 19–43.
Bonadeo 1968
Bonadeo, Alfredo. "Olimpia." *Italica* 45 (1968): pp. 47–58.
Bonfil 1993
Bonfil, Robert. "Ferrara: Un puerto seguro y apacible para la diáspora sefardí." In *Los judíos de España: Historia de una diáspora, 1492–1992*, edited by Henry Méchoulan, pp. 291–298. Madrid: Editorial Trotta, 1993.
Bonfil 2005
Bonfil, Robert. "Judeo-Christian Cultural Reflections in Cinquecento Ferrara." In *Phaeton's Children: The Este Court and Its Culture in Early Modern Ferrara*, edited by Dennis Looney and Deanna Shemek, pp. 385–410. Tempe: Arizona Center for Medieval and Renaissance Studies, 2005.
Busi 1987
Busi, Giulio. *La istoria de Purim io ve racconto . . . Il libro di Ester secondo un Rabbino Emiliano del Cinquecento*. Rimini: Luisè Editore, 1987.
Copenhaver 1988
Copenhaver, Brian P. "Astrology and Magic." In *The Cambridge History of Renaissance Philosophy*, edited by Charles B. Schmitt and Quentin Skinner, pp. 274–285. Cambridge, MA: Harvard University Press, 1988.
De' Sommi 1988
Leone de' Sommi. *A Comedy of Betrothal (Tsahoth B'dihutha D'Kiddushin)*, translated with introduction and notes by Alfred S. Golding. Ottawa: Dovehouse Editions Canada, 1988.
Dell'Aia 2013
Dell'Aia, Lucia. "Il platonismo di Ariosto." *Enthymema* 9 (2013): pp. 241–256.
Di Leone Leoni 2011
Di Leone Leoni, Aron. *La nazione ebraica spagnola e portoghese di Ferrara (1492–1559) e i suoi rapporti col governo ducale e la popolazione locale ed i suoi legami con le nazioni portoghesi di Ancona, Pesaro e Venezia*, 2 vols., edited by Laura Graziani Secchieri, Florence: Olschki, 2011.
Flórez Miguel 2007
Flórez Miguel, Cirilo. "Zacut: Abraham ben Samuel Zacut." In *The Biographical Encyclopedia of Astronomers*, edited by Thomas Hockey, Virginia Trimble, Thomas R. Williams, Katherine Bracher, Richard A. Jarrell, Jordan D. Marché, F. Jamil Ragep, JoAnn Palmeri, and Marvin Bolt, pp. 1255–1256. New York: Springer, 2007.
Fontanesi 1934
Fontanesi, Giuseppina. *Il problema dell'amore nell'opera di Leone Ebreo*. Venice: Libreria Emiliana, 1934.

Graziani Secchieri 2014
Aspetti culturali, economici e sociali della presenza ebraica a Ferrara, edited by Laura Graziani Secchieri. Florence: Giuntina, 2014.
Gutwirth 2004
Gutwirth, Eleazar. "Amatus Lusitanus and the Location of Sixteenth-Century Cultures." In *Cultural Intermediaries: Jewish Intellectuals in Early Modern Italy*, edited by David B. Ruderman and Giuseppe Veltri, pp. 216–238. Philadelphia: University of Pennsylvania Press, 2004.
Halbronn 1985
Halbronn, Jacques. *Le monde juif et l'astrologie: Histoire d'un vieux couple*. Milan: Archè, 1985.
Herzig 2012
Herzig, Tamar. "Anti-Jewish Polemics and Female Stigmatization in Renaissance Ferrara." *Archivio Italiano per la Storia della Pietà* 25 (2012): pp. 113–138.
Idel 2011
Idel, Moshe. *Kabbalah in Italy, 1280–1510: A Survey*. New Haven, CT: Yale University Press, 2011.
Idel 2016
Idel, Moshe. *Il male primordiale nella Qabbalah*, translated by Fabrizio Lelli. Milan: Adelphi, 2016.
Ioly Zorattini 1993
Ioly Zorattini, Piercesare. "Sephardic Settlement in Ferrara under the House of Este." In *New Horizons in Sephardic Studies*, edited by Yedida K. Stillman and George K. Zucker, pp. 5–13. Albany: State University of New York Press, 1993.
Kisacky 2000
Kisacky, Julia M. *Magic in Boiardo and Ariosto*. New York: Peter Lang, 2000.
Lelli 1996
Lelli, Fabrizio. "L'educazione ebraica nella seconda metà del '400: Poetica e scienze naturali nel *Ḥay ha-'olamim* di Yoḥanan Alemanno." *Rinascimento* 36 (1996): pp. 75–136.
Lelli 1997
Lelli, Fabrizio. *Umanesimo laurenziano nell'opera di Yoḥanan Alemanno*. In *La cultura ebraica all'epoca di Lorenzo il Magnifico*, edited by Dora Liscia Bemporad and Ida Zatelli, pp. 49–67. Florence: Olschki, 1997.
Lelli 2000
Lelli, Fabrizio. "*Prisca Philosophia* and *Docta Religio*: The Boundaries of Rational Knowledge in Jewish and Christian Humanist Thought." *Jewish Quarterly Review* 91 (2000): pp. 53–100.
Lelli 2004a
Lelli, Fabrizio. "Biography and Autobiography in Yoḥanan Alemanno's Literary Perception." In *Cultural Intermediaries: Jewish Intellectuals in Early Modern Italy*, edited by David B. Ruderman and Giuseppe Veltri, pp. 2–38. Philadelphia: University of Pennsylvania Press, 2004.
Lelli 2004b
Lelli, Fabrizio. "Gli Ebrei e le terme." In *Gli Umanisti e le Terme*, edited by Paola Andrioli Nemola, Olga S. Casale, and Paolo Viti, pp. 31–48. Lecce: Conte, 2004.
Lelli 2004c
Lelli, Fabrizio. "Jews, Humanists, and the Reappraisal of Pagan Wisdom, Associated with the Conception of *Dignitas Hominis*." In *Hebraica Veritas? Christian Hebraists and the Study of Judaism in Early Modern Europe*, edited by Allison P. Coudert and Jeffrey S. Shoulson, pp. 49–70. Philadelphia: University of Pennsylvania Press, 2004.
Lelli 2006
Lelli, Fabrizio. "Intellectual Relationships of Fifteenth-Century Jewish and Christian Scholars in Light of Contemporary Art." *Cadernos de Estudos Sefarditas* 6 (2006): pp. 149–170.
Lelli 2008a
Lelli, Fabrizio. "Christian and Jewish Iconographies of Job in Fifteenth-Century Italy." In *Jewish Biblical Interpretation and Cultural Exchange*, edited by Natalie B. Dohrmann and David Stern, pp. 214–235. Philadelphia: University of Pennsylvania Press, 2008.
Lelli 2008b
Lelli, Fabrizio. "Il linguaggio di Dio: La Cabala in Occidente." In *Il Rinascimento italiano e l'Europa* V, *Le scienze*, edited by Antonio Clericuzio and Germana Ernst, pp. 129–147. Vicenza: Fondazione Cassamarca/Angelo Colla Editore, 2008.

Lelli 2008c
Lelli, Fabrizio. "Poetic Theology and Jewish Kabbalah in Fifteenth-Century Florentine Speculation: Giovanni Pico della Mirandola and Elijah Hayyim ben Benjamin of Genazzano." *Studia Judaica* 16 (2008): pp. 144–152.
Lelli 2011a
Lelli, Fabrizio. "L'interpretazione teosofica della storia d'Israele nell'*Epistola sulla storia della Cabbalà* di Eliyyà Menaḥem ben Abba Mari Ḥalfan." In *Adorare caelestia, gubernare terrena, Atti del colloquio internazionale in onore di Paolo Lucentini (Napoli, 6–7 Novembre 2010)*, edited by Pasquale Arfé, Irene Caiazzo, and Antonella Sannino, pp. 475–505. Turnhout: Brepols, 2011.
Lelli 2011b
Lelli, Fabrizio. "Ricezione e interpretazione della Cabbalà nel pensiero di Eliyyà Menaḥem Ḥalfan." *Rivista di Storia e Letteratura Religiosa* 47, no. 3 (2011): pp. 547–572.
Lelli 2019
Lelli, Fabrizio. "Moses as Legislator in Fifteenth-Century Italian Jewish and Christian Authors." *Intellectual History Review* 29 (2019): pp. 35–52.
Leone Ebreo 2009
Leone Ebreo. *Dialogues of Love*. translated by Damian Bacich and Rossella Pescatori. Toronto: University of Toronto Press, 2009.
Lesley 1976
Lesley, Arthur M. "The 'Song of Solomon's Ascents' by Yoḥanan Alemanno: Love and Human Perfection According to a Jewish Associate of Giovanni Pico della Mirandola." PhD diss., University of California, Berkeley, 1976.
Lesley 1988
Lesley, Arthur M. "Jewish Adaptation of Humanist Concepts in 15th and 16th Century Culture." In *Renaissance Rereadings, Intertext and Context*, edited by Maryanne C. Horowitz, Anne J. Cruz, and Wendy A. Furman, pp. 51–66. Chicago: University of Chicago Press, 1988.
Looney 2013
Looney, Dennis. "Ariosto's Dialogue with Authority in the 'Erbolato.'" *Modern Language Notes* 128 (2013): pp. 20–39.
Magrini 2015
Magrini, Silvio. *Storia degli ebrei di Ferrara: Dalle origini al 1943*. Livorno: Salomone Belforte, 2015.
Minervini 1993
Minervini, Laura. "Una versione giudeo-spagnola dell'*Orlando furioso*." *Annali di Ca' Foscari* 32–33 (1993): pp. 35–45.
Netanyahu 1953
Netanyahu, Benzion. *Don Yiṣḥaq Abravanel: Statesman and Philosopher*. Ithaca, NY: Cornell University Press, 1953.
Ogren 2009
Ogren, Brian. *Renaissance and Rebirth: Reincarnation in Early Modern Italian Kabbalah*. Leiden: Brill, 2009.
Perrone Compagni 2008
Perrone Compagni, Vittoria. "Maritare il mondo: Magia naturale ed ermetismo." In *Il Rinascimento italiano e l'Europa* V, *Le scienze*, edited by Antonio Clericuzio and Germana Ernst, pp. 97–110. Vicenza: Fondazione Cassamarca/Angelo Colla Editore, 2008.
Quint 1979
Quint, David. "The Figure of Atlante: Ariosto and Boiardo's Poem." *Modern Language Notes* 94 (1979): pp. 77–91.
Rosenzweig 2016
Rosenzweig, Claudia. *Bovo d'Antona by Elye Bokher. A Yiddish Romance: A Critical Edition with Commentary*. Leiden, Brill, 2016.
Ruderman 1981
Ruderman, David B. *The World of a Renaissance Jew: The Life and Thought of Avraham ben Mordekhay Farissol*. Cincinnati: Hebrew Union College Press, 1981.
Scorrano 1971
Scorrano, Luigi. "La 'gran confidenzia' di mastro Iachelino e altre osservazioni sul *Negromante*." *Annali*

della Facoltà di Magistero dell'Università degli Studi di Lecce 1 (1971), pp. 39–71.

Séd-Rajna 1987

Séd-Rajna, Gabrielle. *The Hebrew Bible in Medieval Illuminated Manuscripts*, translated by. J. Bacon. New York: Rizzoli, 1987.

Tennen 2008

Tennen, Debra. "*Megillat Ester in Ottava Rima*: Mordecai Dato's Poetry regarding Sixteenth-Century Italian Jewish Women." *Renaissance Studies* 22, no. 4 (2008): pp. 507–541.

Tirosh-Rothschild 1991

Tirosh-Rothschild, Hava. *Between Worlds: The Life and Thought of Rabbi David ben Judah Messer Leon*. Albany: State University of New York Press, 1991.

Toschi 1955

Toschi, Paolo. *Le origini del teatro italiano*. Turin: Einaudi, 1955.

Traniello 2017

Traniello, Elisabetta. "Reti sovrapposte: Ipotesi per la presenza ebraica composita di Ferrara nel XVI secolo." In *Storia economica e storia degli ebrei: Istituzioni, capitale sociale e stereotipi (secc. XV–XVIII)*, edited by Maria Romani, pp. 207–221. Milan: Franco Angeli, 2017.

Vasoli 1977

Vasoli, Cesare. "L'astrologia a Ferrara tra la metà del Quattrocento e la metà del Cinquecento." In *Il Rinascimento nelle corti padane: Società e cultura*, edited by Paolo Rossi, pp. 469–494. Bari: De Donato, 1977.

Veltri 2004

Veltri, Giuseppe. "*Philo* and *Sophia*: Leone Ebreo's Concept of Jewish Philosophy." In *Cultural Intermediaries: Jewish Intellectuals in Early Modern Italy*, edited by David B. Ruderman and Giuseppe Veltri, pp. 55–66. Philadelphia: University of Pennsylvania Press, 2004.

Walker 1958

Walker, Daniel P. *Spiritual and Demonic Magic: From Ficino to Campanella*. London: Warburg Institute/ University of London, 1958.

"A un giovine Aphrican si donò in tutto": The Marriage of Africa and India in Ariosto and Camões

Vincent Barletta

In critical discussions of Islam and the work of Ludovico Ariosto, it is perhaps logical to place special emphasis on the marriage of Ruggiero and Bradamante, the former's conversion to Christianity, and the implications of this union for the Este family in Ferrara. Of somewhat less importance, but significant still, is the union between Angelica and her Muslim lover, Medoro. While these two admittedly depart for Asia long before the end of *Orlando furioso*, one sees their impact on Ariosto's readers in the many reworkings of their affair in European art, music, and literature well into the nineteenth century.[1] Denis Diderot, to take a prominent example, devotes an entire section of his *Salons de 1765* to a mordant critique of François Boucher's 1763 painting of Angelica and Medoro, while early-nineteenth-century Slovenian painter Mihael Stroj adds something like domestic warmth (with notable Orientalist touches) to his own treatment of the motif.[2] As late as 1860, no less a figure than Eugène Delacroix would portray Angelica walking alongside a wounded Medoro in free and vigorous lines that anticipate the early Impressionism of Alfred Sisley and Pierre-Auguste Renoir.

For readers of sixteenth-century Portuguese literature, and specifically those familiar with the work of Luís de Camões (1524?–1580), the figures of Angelica and Medoro signify in particular ways. This is so, it bears mentioning, not primarily due to the improbable couple's status as non-Christians or to their Asian/African origins. On the contrary, Iberian literature from the medieval period through the seventeenth century is all but filled with such characters, in genres that range from epic poetry and theater to fictional prose and popular ballads. Even in the aftermath of the various edicts of expulsion that came at the end of the fifteenth century, the almost constant drumbeat of war against the Turks, and the establishment of state inquisitions, the kingdoms of the Iberian Peninsula would remain somewhat fixated on at least the fictional idea of non-Christians in love. What is, in fact, most compelling about Angelica and Medoro from the perspective of Ariosto's early modern Portuguese readers—a small group of mostly cultural elites that had its origins in 1526 or 1527, with

Francisco de Sá de Miranda's return from a five-year stay in Rome—is the pair's explicit, practically insistent whiteness.[3]

The enormous geographic scope of Portugal's overseas empire made the physical appearance of North Africans and Asians (the latter from the Indian subcontinent or farther east) much more than a matter of abstract literary imagination. To imagine a beautiful North African, for example, Portuguese readers needed not to close their eyes but rather to open them: this concrete, strangely familiar, and unabashedly dark beauty was all around them, whether across the strait or much closer to home. Even more to the point, the steady migration and intermarriage of peoples from North Africa and the Iberian Peninsula from the eighth century onward meant that finding such beauty could just as easily mean looking in a mirror.[4] Asians were logically on a somewhat different footing, but here again, there was enough familiarity with Gujarati, Goan, Burmese, Chinese, and Indonesian bodies that fictional accounts such as Ariosto's were readily understood to be fanciful. Put another way, while the physical beauty of North Africans and Asians (especially women) finds ample expression within Portuguese literature from the sixteenth century, this beauty is based more on familiarity and marked difference than on the paradoxically exotic "sameness" or the metapoetic and Ovidian play one finds in Ariosto.[5] Camões himself, who lost an eye fighting in Morocco and spent seventeen years serving the empire in Asia (from Muscat to Macau), works quite consciously, in both his epic and lyric poetry, to question the learned principles of white beauty that he had inherited at once from the classical tradition and newly Europeanist ideologies of empire.

1. Cathay-on-Po

Matteo Boiardo first establishes the pale beauty of Angelica in *L'inamoramento de Orlando*, pointing almost simultaneously to her whiteness and her Eastern origins:

> Essa sembrava matutina stella
> e ziglio d'orto e rosa di verzeri;
> in soma, a dir di lei la veritate,
> non fu veduta mai tanta beltade.
> —*Inam.* I 1 21, 4–8
> [She resembled the morning star,
> The lily and the garden rose;
> In short, to tell the truth of her,
> Never before was so much beauty seen.]

Boiardo here employs images of feminine light and beauty that had become more or less common by the end of the fifteenth century—the *matutina stella* refers to the planet Venus, which rises in the East, white and shimmering, hours before the sun, while *giglio d'orto* is, through the double meaning of *orto*, at once a reference to a garden flower and an index of sunrise and the East—but that had found their earliest and most widespread expression in the lyric poetry of Guido Guinizzelli, two centuries earlier:

> Io voglio del ver la mia donna laudare,
> ed assembrarli la rosa e lo giglio:
> più che la stella diana splende e pare,
> e ciò ch' è lassú bello a lei somiglio.[6]
> [I wish honestly to praise my beloved,
> and compare her to the rose and the lily:
> she shines and seems more than the morning star,
> and I equate her with all that is beautiful above.]

Later in the same canto, Boiardo presents a sleeping Angelica, just outside her brother Argalia's tent, in the following way:

> Angelica, non troppo a lui lontana,
> la bionda testa in sul'erba posava,
> sotto il gran pino, a lato ala fontana;
> quattro giganti sempre la guardava.
> Dormendo non parìa già cosa humana,
> ma ad angelo de il ciel rasumigliava;
> —*Inam.* I 1 42, 1–6
> [Not far away Angelica
> Laid her blond head upon the grass
> beneath the large pine by the spring,
> four giants ever vigilant.
> Asleep she seemed no human thing,
> An angel, rather—heavenly.]

Ariosto follows Boiardo in presenting Angelica as a luminous beauty, but he also extends this quality to Medoro. In a strange parallel, Ariosto partially mirrors Boiardo's description of the sleeping Angelica in his own account of the North African soldier's beauty, presenting Medoro as a blond-headed angel:

> Medoro avea la guancia colorita
> e bianca e grata ne la età novella;
> e fra la gente a quella impresa uscita
> non era faccia più gioconda e bella:
> occhi avea neri, e chioma crespa d'oro:
> angel parea di quei del sommo coro.
> —*Fur.*, XVIII 166, 3–8
> [Medoro had rosy cheeks and he was white and graceful in youth. Of all the people engaged in that campaign, there was none with a more joyful and beautiful face: he had black eyes and curly golden hair, and he resembled an angel of the supreme choir.]

Ariosto repeats this formula in his description of Cupid's assault on Angelica's heart:

> Assai più larga piaga e più profonda
> nel cor sentì da non veduto strale,
> che da' begli occhi e da la testa bionda
> di Medoro aventò l'Arcier c'ha l'ale.
> —*Fur.*, XIX 28, 1–4
> [She felt a much wider and deeper wound in her heart from the unseen arrow, which from Medoro's beautiful eyes and blond head the Archer had given wing.]

While Ariosto mostly relies on Boiardo to establish Angelica's whiteness, he works deliberately to do the same for Medoro, who is at once Angelica's husband and, in many senses, her twin.[7]

2. Some Portuguese Conventions

It is worth mentioning here that Iberian poets and readers were, in spite of their history and lived experience, well aware of the broader European aesthetic traditions that found no apparent contradiction in the stylized representation of African and Asian characters as fair-skinned and blond. Writing during Camões's lifetime, for example, the Castilian poet Francisco de Aldana (who died fighting for the Portuguese at al-Qaṣr al-Kabīr in 1578) would write a string of octaves in which he speaks explicitly of Medoro's "white, tender chest" and the couple's flowing golden hair:

Con el siniestro brazo un nudo hecho
por el cuello a su sol tiene Medoro,
ciñe la otra el blanco y tierno pecho
que es del cielo y amor alto tesoro;
acá y allá, sobre el dichoso lecho
vuela el rico, sutil cabello de oro
y al caluroso aliento que salía
un poco ventilando se movía.
—vv. 25–32
[Medoro's left arm forms a knot
encircling the neck of his sun,
he embraces the white, tender chest
that is a treasure to heaven and love;
here and there, on the happy bed,
their rich and exquisite golden hair runs,
moving in rhythm with the warm breath
that escapes from each of them.]

Lyric images of pale beauty—even if not directly connected to *Orlando furioso*—find expression in sixteenth-century Portugal as well. Taking as an example Diogo Bernardes's third eclogue, one finds the following lament by the shepherd Dellio:

Quando Liarda minha desencolhe
o seu longo cabello, louro, e ondado
o sol d'enveja pura se recolhe
corrido de se ver menos dourado;
não há pastor tão livre, que tal olhe
que nelle não fique preso, e enlaçado.
Não soltes ora, Ninfa, os teus cabellos,
pois tantos prendem quantos ousão vellos.[8]
[When my Liarda lets down
her long and wavy blond hair
the sun, out of pure envy, recoils,
ashamed to see itself less golden;
there is no shepherd so free, that on seeing such hair,
he is not captured and caught in it.
Do not loosen now, Nymph, your hair,
as it imprisons all those who dare look upon it.]

One also finds the following description of the nymph Galatea in Camões's eighth eclogue: *Arde por Galatea branca e loura / sereno pescador pobre, forçado / d'uma estrella, que quer á mingoa moura* (Burning for white and blond Galatea is a serene and poor fisherman, forced by a star to wither away). Both of the preceding examples are pastoral in nature and so follow conventions specific to that mode of poetic production; however, they nonetheless serve to provide concrete evidence of a familiarity in Portugal with the more or less conventional link between whiteness and beauty in classical and Renaissance European letters.

Beyond the literary conventions of elite Iberian culture (never wholly separate from their Italian sources), there are also imperial matters to consider.[9] Iberian readers were well aware of the histories and legends of whiteness associated with Alexander the Great, Scipio Africanus, Saint Sebastian, and the founding of Rome from the ruins of Troy. These functioned from the start as desirable albeit unattainable ideals for the Portuguese, many of whom spent decades in North Africa and Asia and underwent profound physical, mental, and spiritual changes while there. Such an imperial ideal finds pointed expression in, for example, Portuguese playwright Gil Vicente's *Auto da Índia* (India play, 1509). In this farce, a husband returns from two years in India to find himself immediately rejected by his wife, who over time had come to dread his homecoming. When he enters the house, she greets him: *Jesu! Quam negro e tostado! Nam vos quero! Nam vos quero!* (Jesus! How black and tanned! I do not love you! I do not love you!; vv. 420–421). As Josiah Blackmore has argued, the blackness that lingers upon the husband from his Asian journey is not simply the effect of overexposure to the sun but rather a symptom of contact with the melancholic humors associated with the Orient (Blackmore 2009). In essence, the husband has returned from the East, but he has brought the humoral ill effects of that region back to Portugal with him. The Virgilian return, at least as far as Vicente and his courtly audience understood it, thus carried with it a lingering contagion associated with the Orient and framed as a loss of whiteness. Turning back to Ariosto, it bears mentioning again that his Portuguese readers would, of course, recognize the purely literary connections he sought to make through his angelic and pale African/Asian lovers; beyond this, however, they would also labor to see themselves connected to them. That is, this whiteness—also linked *ex post facto* within the poetics of empire to epic figures such as Scipio Africanus and Alexander—served at once as a poetic and imperial ideal for the Portuguese (Barletta 2010).

Why precisely was whiteness such an issue for the Portuguese? To a large extent, the essentialized divisions of labor upon which their empire rested revolved around it (Quijano 2000). Beyond this, however, there are also thorny matters of genealogy (and even phenotype) to address and overcome. As is well known, Portugal, Castile, and the Crown of Aragon were kingdoms formed out of centuries of conversion and intermarriage between Muslims and Christians, and it was no secret that Iberian lineages (even those of the noble classes) were in many cases largely indistinguishable from those of their North African counterparts. Even well into the sixteenth century, the Iberian Peninsula and the Maghreb were a continuum separated by only fifteen kilometers of water, and this fact made necessary a good deal of rhetorical hand-wringing for an imperial power looking to legitimate its conquests in Africa and Asia through a broader, now wholly "European" evangelical project. Not that this was a universally accepted fact. Turning once again to Vicente's *Auto da Índia*, the question remains whether the darkness the wife sees in her husband is wholly the product of his journey to India or something that has been within him all along—not a *loss* of whiteness but rather a phylogenetic distance from it made more acute (and visible) through the maritime passage around the Cape of Good Hope. This speaks, in other words, to difference as a matter of degree rather than kind. Portuguese and other Iberian authors, in fact, spill rivers of ink throughout the sixteenth century to blot out their cultural, linguistic, and blood ties to the Maghreb and to emphasize (or simply fabricate) lines of descent that point to France and England rather than Morocco and Tunis. In essence, while no one could really deny that the Portuguese past, like its Castilian and Aragonese counterparts, was to a significant degree always linked to Africa, this same past—as in the case of Medoro (for which see below)—was consistently presented as an accident or unfortunate interruption that could never fully obscure the essential, foundational (Gothic) whiteness of the Iberian Peninsula and the two world empires that almost simultaneously emerged from it.

The final layer of complexity that Angelica and Medoro present to readers in sixteenth-century Portugal has to do with the fact that Portuguese literati tended to see the Mediterranean as a decidedly parochial framework. In text after text, from Macau to Goa to Mozambique to Brazil, Portuguese writers took great pains to present Roman conquest—and the Mediterranean itself—as something of relatively little consequence. Camões himself participates in this rhetoric, the point of which is to place the Portuguese above the Romans as an imperial power and to call attention to the relative paucity of contemporary writing on that power. If the Romans covered very little actual territory, the argument went, they made up for it with an incontestably fine literary corpus;

the Portuguese, on the other hand, had extended their dominion over lands (and seas) unknown to the Romans, yet they wrote relatively little about it. The Portuguese effort to transcend the Mediterranean was, of course, only partially successful. In most cases, they managed only to bring it with them. To give an example, it is a historical fact that when Vasco da Gama first reached India (thanks to a Muslim Gujarati pilot supplied by the Muslim sultan of Malinde), his first contact was with two (Muslim) Tunisian traders proficient in Genoese and Castilian. In popular chronicles, these traders become a single person, and in Camões's epic, *Os Lusíadas* (The Lusiads, 1572), this person (now called Monçaide) saves the expedition from ruin before promising to convert to Christianity and returning to Lisbon with Gama and his crew.

While it is true that Ariosto inherits Ruggiero, along with his European lineage, from Boiardo, he also develops the character's origins much further. There is really no question, after all, that this supposed North African Muslim is primarily Franco-Italian. Ariosto, in fact, celebrates the marriage of Bradamante and Ruggiero as a *nuovo nodo* (new knot) that joins the Mongrana and Chiaramonte lines mutually descended from Beuve d'Antone. Ruggiero's status as a Muslim is, as it turns out, somewhat accidental, and his conversion to Christianity plays as the happy resolution to a longer story of forced exile and alienation.[10] And as I have just suggested, such stories would fall on particularly receptive ears in the Iberian Peninsula.

For Portuguese readers, Medoro would likely have been even more compelling than Ruggiero. As a white-skinned, rosy-cheeked, and blond African endowed with something akin to classical Greek beauty, his status as a Muslim would, in fact, be secondary for Portuguese readers (at least to cultural and political elites) to his role as an organic link between Greek and Portuguese conquest in Asia. He, like the Portuguese themselves (at least in their imperial imaginary), is at once an orphan of Alexander and a harbinger of a new, global imperial order—one built on equal measures of violence, lyric, and erotic desire. His presence in Asia and marriage to a princess of Cathay (situated either in China or India, depending on one's map) is, one might say, icing on the cake.

3. Camões

In turning to Camões, it is useful to pivot from Ariosto's epic theorization of African/Asian whiteness to what amounts to a new lyric formulation of blackness. This formulation is linked to Ariosto in significant ways (as well as to Petrarch, as Rita Marnoto has pointed out).[11] It is, one might say, a kind of lyric riposte both to the marriage of Medoro and Angelica and to the parodic and monstrous accounts of black alterity in the *Furioso* and elsewhere.[12] The poem at the center of Camões's intervention is an *endecha* (a traditional Iberian song form associated with the *planto*, or lament) commonly referred to as *Aquela cativa* (That Captive) or, alternatively, *Bárbora escrava* (Barbarous [or Barbara the] Slave). This poem speaks of the unshakable, erotic love that the poetic subject has for an enslaved woman whose dark beauty, he claims, surpasses that of any white European woman. Fernão Rodrigues Soropita includes the poem in the fifth part of his 1595 anthology of Camões's collected lyric, devoted to *redondilhas*, *motes*, *esparsas*, and *grosas*, all of which are traditional song forms. In Portuguese poetics, *redondilhas* are compositions of varying length that consist of verses of either five (*redondilha menor*) or seven syllables (*redondilha maior*). Camões's *Aquela cativa* is made up of verses of five syllables, and this is likely why Soropita includes it with the *redondilhas*.[13] Beyond its formal classification, Soropita also provides the following rubric: "Endechas, a hũa catiua com quẽ andaua d'amores na Índia, chamada Barbora" (*Endechas* to a slave, named Barbara, with whom he had an affair in India; 1595, f. 159*r–v*). A good deal of scholarship has attempted to draw out the historical details of Camões's possible relationship in Goa with an African slave named Barbara, but with little success. And given that much larger questions regarding Camões's life remain enshrouded in mystery, the fact that a micro-detail such as this remains uncertain comes as little surprise. It is plausible that Camões had some interaction with such a woman during his time in Goa, as there were, in fact, numerous enslaved Africans present in Portuguese India throughout the sixteenth century (commonly referred to in the historical record as *cafres*). However, the fact that Camões seems to have spent much of his time in Goa on the brink of absolute penury argues somewhat forcefully against the idea that he owned any slaves himself.

Beyond the question of Camões's biography, there is an even larger mimetic question that is worth addressing, albeit briefly. Perhaps the most popular reading of *Aquela cativa* leaves open the question of Camões's biography, seeing the poem instead as a dense representation of the Portuguese empire's racialized economy of sex. This economy, referred to as Lusotropicalism by early-twentieth-century Brazilian social scientist Gilberto Freyre, posits (inter alia) that the Portuguese, due to their high degree of social malleability, were more inclined to miscegenation than other European imperial powers: "Mas independente da falta ou escassez de mulher branca o português sempre pendeu para o contato voluptuoso com mulher exótica. Para o cruzamento e miscigenação. Tendência que parece resultar de plasticidade social, maior no português que em qualquer outro colonizador europeu" (Independent of the absence or scarcity of white women, the Portuguese always tended toward sexual contact with exotic women. For breeding and miscegenation. A tendency that seems to result from greater social plasticity in the Portuguese than in any other European colonizer).[14] The discourse of Lusotropicalism reached its apex in Portugal during the later stages of António Salazar's fascist dictatorship (1926–1974), and poems such as Camões's *Aquela cativa* were commonly trotted out at this time as confirmation of Portugal's enduring and quite literal love for its African colonial subjects. While its arguments have largely disappeared from serious scholarly work, Lusotropicalism remains surprisingly resilient in the popular (and political) imaginary in both Portugal and Brazil. One might say that many readers in these countries (and throughout the Portuguese diaspora) tend still to understand Camões's poem as a probable biographical fiction that nonetheless reveals a more general (and not coincidentally flattering) truth about themselves.

A reading of *Aquela cativa* that focuses explicitly on Ariosto will necessarily be less concerned with questions of mimesis (biographical or otherwise) and more focused on issues of metapoetics. This is so, to begin with, because one rarely gets the sense while reading Camões, whether his epic or lyric poetry, that he is primarily concerned with *representing* a world. Even in *Os Lusíadas*, which is ostensibly an epic retelling of da Gama's first voyage to India, the events of the journey are frequently subordinated to lyric episodes that pause temporal movement and narration in favor of lyric performance and prophecy.[15] The entire ninth canto of *Os Lusíadas*, one might justifiably argue, is itself *outside* of the world and, toward its end, even time. This is not to say that things do not happen within the canto, of course. The story is, in fact, quite straightforward. On their way back to Portugal from India, da Gama and his men arrive at an island conjured up out of nothing by Venus. Once ashore, they engage in an explicitly allegorical sexual escapade with a group of compliant nymphs (made so by Cupid's arrows). Afterward, the nymph Tethys takes Gama to see the future by means of a wondrous "world machine." Despite this narrative skeleton, it is difficult to see the crew's animalistic orgy on Venus's island as in any sense mimetic, given that Camões himself frames it as an allegorical aside. Even when this fantasy subsides, Camões moves quite literally outside of time and world into the realm of prophecy. It is, of course, true that the events that Tethys foretells have already occurred for Camões's readers; however, what most matters here is the poetic/generic reframing of history (i.e., representation) as prophecy (i.e., performance).[16]

Beyond the fine-grained complexities of referentiality in *Os Lusíadas*, it is also true that Camões's lyric and epic poetry both maintain a practically obsessive concern with poetry itself, as well as the act of composing it. This alone does not set Camões apart from other sixteenth-century poets, including Ariosto himself, and it is undeniable that part of Camões's (meta)poetic project stems from his commitment to classical literature and thought. It is true that he was never officially a student at the University of Coimbra; however, he did receive in that city a highly sophisticated understanding of the Greco-Roman foundations of Renaissance thought and expression: Homer, Virgil, Horace, Propertius, and Ovid, as well as Cicero, Plato, Aristotle, Quintus Curcius, and Quintilian, to name but a few sources. There is also Camões's seventeen years of service to the Portuguese Empire in Asia, an experience that influenced his art in different ways and at levels that have yet to be fully considered. What did Camões encounter in Goa and Macau? And what of his two-year layover in Mozambique as he made his way back to Portugal? It seems implausible that the rich philosophical, poetic, and musical traditions of these regions would not have given at least partial shape to Camões's understanding in meaningful ways. They would have intensified and complicated, at the very least, his concern for alterity, temporality, and bondage (his own and that of others), a concern that could not but place in doubt Renaissance ideas of harmony and facile whiteness. *Aquela cativa* offers a relatively clear view of this tension in Camões's poetics, even as he makes use of a traditional Iberian song form to do so.

The poem begins with its primary conceit: *Aquela cativa / que me tem cativo, / porque nela vivo / já não quer que viva* (That captive who holds me captive, because I live in her, [she] no longer wants me alive). This is a Petrarchan idea, and the notions of amorous bondage and the beloved's power over life and death are common enough throughout the Iberian sixteenth century. What Camões does to this conceit, however, matters a great deal. As Marnoto has argued, Camões is working here in an explicitly mannerist vein to push Petrarchan notions of both white feminine beauty and harmony off their foundation just a bit.[17] He is also taking a traditional Iberian song form and pushing it into new conceptual and contextual territory. But there is, of course, much more to the poem than even this.

In the fourth stanza (out of five), Camões begins to develop a discussion of "blackness" and bondage that is at once rooted in experience, poetic tradition, and more troubling ontological concerns:

Pretidão de Amor,
tão doce a figura,
que a neve lhe jura
que trocara a cor.
Leda mansidão
que o siso acompanha:
bem parece estranha,
mas bárbara não.
[Blackness of love,
so sweet the figure,
that the snow swears to it
that it would trade color.
Happy docility
accompanied by wisdom:
it does seem strange,
but not barbarous.][18]

What to make of the construction *pretidão de Amor*? What is this blackness of love that Camões links to the body (*figura*) of his beloved? It is a disturbing construction, in that it both emphasizes and openly eroticizes the beloved's physical blackness, even as it frames this blackness as an abstract (nominative) essence rather than as a merely adjectival accident. One might well attempt to explain this as a gloss on Song of Songs 1:5–6, in which a woman whose skin has been darkened by outdoor work (in the vineyards of another) speaks to the elite "daughters of Jerusalem":

> Sh'chora ani, ve-nava, bnot Yerushalayim, ke-ohale Kedar, k-iriyot Shelomo.
>
> Al tir-uni she-ani sh'charchoret she-shezafatni ha-shamesh. Bne imi, nicharu-vi, samuni notera et ha-keramim. Karmi sheli, lo natarti.
> [I am black, but lovely, oh daughters of Jerusalem, as the tents of Kedar, as the curtains of Solomon.
>
> Do not stare at me because I am black, because the sun has darkened me. My mother's sons were angry at me and made me keeper of the vineyards. My own vineyard I had to neglect.]

Here there is beauty, to be sure, but it exists *despite* the fact that the sun has darkened the woman's skin; and this darkness, she is quick to point out, is associated with her work conditions and not with her essence. The poetic subject is not elite like the daughters of Jerusalem (*bnot Yerushalayim*), and she wears this class habitus on her skin. In this, however, we are far from the modern idea of racial identity.

Is there truly something novel in Camões's talk of essentialized *blackness*? It is worth pointing out that the word *pretidão* would certainly have sounded strange to the ears of Camões's audience; there is evidence of this in the fact that one finds only two other examples of the word in sixteenth-century Portuguese texts. The first of these is João de Barros's description of the black skin of Akan king Kwamin Ansah, and the second is Jerónimo Cardoso's 1569 Latin-Portuguese dictionary, with *pretidão* serving as the translation for *pullīgo* (dark color). I have no knowledge of any instances of the term prior to the sixteenth century, and I have likewise found no examples of it in any seventeenth- or eighteenth-century Portuguese texts. My search has almost certainly not been comprehensive; however, it nonetheless remains clear that while *preto* (black) was a common adjective used to describe people's skin in sixteenth-century Portuguese, *pretidão*—as an abstract noun—was still a learned neologism in sixteenth-century Portugal.

To speak of blackness as an essence rather than a condition—especially in relation to the color of a person's skin—in early modern Portuguese is extremely rare and estranging, even though the adjectives *preto* and *negro* are certainly common during the same period. And it is not that contact with sub-Saharan Africans was necessarily uncommon in Portugal's colonies or even in Portugal itself: by 1550, it is estimated that the African population of Lisbon, due most directly to the large-scale enslavement and sale of people from western Africa, was roughly ten thousand (or ten percent of the city's population).[19] Despite this contact, and an almost universal recognition of African otherness in early modern Portugal (and the overseas empire), the question of blackness as an essence (or whiteness, for that matter) was not yet part of the conceptual landscape.

What does Camões mean when he speaks of blackness? More precisely, what does he do through its use? In speaking of the "blackness of Love," ostensibly as a trope for the beloved herself, he transforms a common adjectival form (*preto*) into an abstract noun through the addition of a suffix (*pretidão*). This move from *black* to *blackness*, one might argue, represents an early and somewhat tentative move in the development of modern Western notions of race: it speaks of blackness as *ousía*, an innate form of being. On another, more poetic level, however, Camões dramatically expands and recontextualizes a common Petrarchan conceit that would find ample development during the early modern period. Petrarch does, in fact, speak of *il nero* and *il bianco* in the *Canzoniere*, but when these are not merely figurative references to Laura's eyes, they speak to moods or forms of suffering: a figurative darkness or lightness that intersects with modern notions, such as the "blackness of eternity" or the "black prison of suffering." In this Petrarchan vein, Camões's *pretidão de Amor* points most directly and conventionally to the figurative darkness of amorous bondage.

For Camões, both domains are in play. He is sincerely concerned, as sixteenth-century Iberian lyric poets tended to be, with reworking Petrarch in ways that speak to new realities and anxieties, amorous and otherwise. Beyond this, he quite consciously links this explicitly poetic project to the (newly) essentialized and inescapable blackness (as an innate form of otherness) of his lyric beloved's skin and hair.

In the end, what is formed is a kind of monstrous conceit (Camões refers to it as *estranha*, or strange) that brings harmony and excess into an unresolved tension. The enslaved black woman has enslaved the (white) poet, both bringing an end to his customary *jouissance* and giving him form, expressed as life. How do we understand this tension? As I have just hinted, it is most clearly seen as a spiritual, poetic, and physical bondage that gives form to and *orders* the poetic subject even as it threatens to end his life. He is, in a very strict and philosophical sense, her captive. And it is Camões's linking of poesis and bondage that serves to trouble the triumphalist poetics of empire while likewise inverting classical and Renaissance ideals of angelic whiteness.

Camões's reference to the "blackness of Love" speaks of bondage at many levels. There is, of course, amorous bondage; there are the perverse power asymmetries of colonial rule that paradoxically bind colonizers along with the colonized and bind masters along with their slaves; there is the unresolved disharmony of sublime blackness as an abstract essence; there is also the impossibility of poetry, encoded in the "blackness" of love but also in the third and fourth lines of the final stanza: *nela, enfim, descansa / toda a minha pena* (in her, finally, rests all of my suffering [also: pen]). Here Camões exploits the double meaning of *pena*, as he does in many other poems, to speak of a respite from suffering and the end of poetry itself and, ultimately, of poetry (and language more generally) as the most oppressive and cruel form of bondage that he faced.

There is, in the end, no resolution to Camões's *Aquela cativa*; it remains strangely discordant, a song that speaks to how love, sex, empire, and human bondage condition and delimit the lyric subject. This is not the felicitous miscegenation of Freyre's Lusotropicalism; rather, it is a relation that results in dispossession, the colonizing subject turned to ash, to paraphrase Castilian poet Garcilaso de la Vega (1501?–1536). In this sense, Camões's *endecha* speaks to the warped realities of Portuguese empire and specifically the Estado da Índia while also offering a metapoetic response to Medoro and Angelica's whiteness that subverts the very possibility of harmony. This is, in a very concentrated form, Camões's poetics, developed throughout his lyric and epic poetry and intertwined here with colonial economies of desire that run both parallel to and up against theories of poetic expression—in both Italy and the Iberian Peninsula—at the end of the sixteenth century, but it also offers a metapoetic break with numerical order and harmony.

Notes

1. For an account of the Angelica and Medoro motif in the visual arts, see Molinaro 1954; Lee 1977.

2. On Boucher's painting, Diderot 1821, p. 119 writes: "Voyez, ou plutôt ne voyez pas le Médor, ses jambes surtout; elles sont d'un petit garçon qui n'a ni goût ni étude. L'Angélique est une petite tripière: ô le vilain mot ! D'accord; mais il peint: dessin rond, mou et chairs flasques. Cet homme ne prend le pinceau que pour me montrer des tetons et des fesses. Je suis bien aise d'en voir, mais je ne veux pas qu'on me les montre" (Consider, or rather do not consider [Boucher's] Medoro, especially his legs; they are of a little boy with neither taste nor study. Angelica is a little tripe vender: oh, ugly word! Fine, he paints: rounded lines, soft and flabby flesh. This man takes up the brush only to show me breasts and buttocks. I'm comfortable seeing them, but I don't want someone showing them to me). Unless otherwise specified, all translations are my own.

3. Sá de Miranda first refers to Ariosto in two poetic letters, the first to António Pereira, Senhor de Bastos: "líamos pelos amores / do bravo e furioso Orlando" (we would read of the loves / of the fierce and furious Orlando; 1885, p. 242). The second letter, a Castilian panegyric to fellow poet Jorge de Montemor, speaks of "Rogel, del ingenioso ferrarés / tanto alabado en tan sabroso estilo; / Astolfo, aventurero i vano inglés" (Ruggiero, of the ingenious Ferraran / so praised in such exquisite style; / Astolfo, adventurer and vain Englishman; 1885, p. 457). For more on Sá de Miranda and Ariosto, see Marnoto 2012. While there were no Portuguese translations of *Orlando furioso* during the sixteenth century, there were at least three Castilian translations produced at the middle of the century; these likely had a readership in Portugal that extended slightly beyond humanists such as Sá de Miranda (Marnoto 2012, p. 38). For later readers of Ariosto in Portugal, especially Jerónimo Corte-Real, see Alves 2001.

4. While it is true that an edict of expulsion for all Jews and Muslims living in Portugal went into effect in 1497, the presence of Christian converts from both religions remained constant throughout the early modern period. This was even more the case for the Iberian crowns of Castile and Aragon, which did not effectively expel its Muslim converts to Christianity (the so-called Moriscos) until the start of the seventeenth century. For more on this, see Barletta 2005; Barletta 2011; Harvey 1986; Harvey 2005; Lopes 1897; Ribas 2004.

5. See James 2019.

6. Guinizzelli 2002, p. 52.

7. For more on Medoro as a mirror of Angelica, and what this means for questions of subjectivity in *Orlando furioso*, see Ascoli 1987, p. 317.

8. Bernardes 1596.

9. For an in-depth account of the influence of Italian literature in Renaissance Portugal, see Earle 2013; Marnoto 1997.

10. For more on the dynastic union between Bradamante and Ruggiero, see Fichter 1982; Stoppino 2012.

11. See Marnoto 2002; 2007.

12. See James 2019; Pavlova 2013.

13. As for the rest, *esparsas* are normally melancholic single-stanza poems, adapted from troubadour lyric, of anywhere from eight to sixteen verses; *motes* are motifs or refrains that can serve as the basis for longer compositions; and *grosas* or *glosas* are songs in which each stanza ends with one of the verses of a given *mote*.

14. Freyre 2002, p. 213.

15. Gil 2009.

16. There are similarities here to the prophecies of the witch Melissa regarding the Este family in canto III of *Orlando furioso*; however, unlike Melissa, Tethys otherwise takes no active role in the Portuguese imperial project, leaving all support for the Portuguese to Venus. In fact, the prophecy (and sex) that Tethys offers to da Gama stems directly from the spell that Venus has Cupid cast over Tethys and other sea nymphs in canto IX. In any case, the most direct source for the prophecies of canto X is almost certainly the underworld scene with the Cumaean Sibyl in canto VI of Virgil's *Aeneid*.

17. Marnoto 2002; 2005; 2007.

18. Barletta, Bajus, and Malik 2013, pp. 226–227.

19. Couto 2003.

Bibliography

Alves 2001

Alves, Hélio J. *Camões, Corte-Real e o sistema da epopeia quinhentista*. Coimbra: Universidade de Coimbra, 2001.

Ariosto 2012

Ariosto, Ludovico. *Orlando furioso*, introduction and commentary by Emilio Bigi, edited by Cristina Zampese. Milan: Rizzoli, 2012.

Ascoli 1987

Ascoli, Albert Russell. *Ariosto's Bitter Harmony: Crisis and Evasion in the Italian Renaissance*. Princeton, NJ: Princeton University Press, 1987.

Barletta 2005

Barletta, Vincent. *Covert Gestures: Crypto-Islamic Literature as Cultural Practice in Early Modern Spain*. Minneapolis: University of Minnesota Press, 2005.

Barletta 2010

Barletta, Vincent. *Death in Babylon: Alexander the Great and Iberian Empire in the Muslim Orient*. Chicago: University of Chicago Press, 2010.

Barletta 2011

Barletta, Vincent. "Pulsações do império: Aljamia portuguesa e a nova filologia." *Tágides* 1 (2011): pp. 70–88.

Barletta, Bajus, and Malik 2013

Barletta, Vincent, Mark L. Bajus, and Cici J. Malik, eds. and trans. *Dreams of Waking: An Anthology of Iberian Lyric Poetry, 1400–1700*. Chicago: University of Chicago Press, 2013.

Bernardes 1596

Bernardes, Diogo. *O Lyma*. Lisbon: Simão Lopes, 1596. www.cervantesvirtual.com/nd/ark:/59851/bmc4t6v8.

Blackmore 2009

Blackmore, Josiah. *Moorings: Portuguese Expansion and the Writing of Africa*. Minneapolis: University of Minnesota Press, 2009.

Camões 1595
Camões, Luís de. *Rhythmas de Luís de Camões: Divididas em cinco partes*, edited by Fernão Rodrigues Lobo Soropita. Lisbon: Manuel de Lira, 1595.
Camões 1985
Camões, Luís de. *Lírica de Camões: Éclogas e sextina*, edited by Leodegário Amarante Azevedo Filho. Lisbon: Imprensa Nacional–Casa da Moeda, 1985.
Camões 2006
Camões, Luís de. 2006. *Os Lusíadas*, edited by Emanuel Paulo Ramos. Porto: Porto Editora, 2006.
Couto 2003
Couto, Dejanirah. *História de Lisboa*. Lisbon: Gótica, 2003.
Diderot 1821
Diderot, Denis. *Salons*, Vol. 1. Paris, Brière, 1821.
Earle 2013
Earle, Thomas F. *Estudos sobre cultura e literatura portuguesa do Renascimento*. Coimbra: Universidade de Coimbra, 2013.
Fichter 1982
Fichter, Andrew. *Poets Historical: Dynastic Epic in the Renaissance*. New Haven, CT: Yale University Press, 1982.
Freyre 2002
Freyre, Gilberto. *Casa-grande e senzala*. Nanterre: Allca XX, 2002.
Gil 2009
Gil, Fernando. "The Expression of Poetry and the Impasses of Empire." *Portuguese Literary and Cultural Studies* 9 (2009): pp. 79–94.
Guinizzelli 2002
Guinizzelli, Guido. *Rime*, edited by Luciano Rossi. Turin: Einaudi, 2002.
Harvey 1986
Harvey, Leonard Patrick. "Aljamia Portuguesa Revisited." *Portuguese Studies* 2 (1986): pp. 1–14.
Harvey 2005
Harvey, Leonard Patrick. *Muslims in Spain, 1500 to 1614*. Chicago: University of Chicago Press, 2005.
James 2019
James, Heather. "An Aethiopian Sodomite, Aesop, and Ovid: The Undoing of Dynastic Epic in Ariosto's *Orlando furioso*." *Modern Philology* 117, no. 2 (2019): pp. 163–193.
Lee 1977
Lee, Rensselaer Wright. *Names on Trees: Ariosto into Art*. Princeton, NJ: Princeton University Press, 1977.
Lopes 1897
Lopes, David. *Textos em aljamía portuguesa: Documentos para a história do domínio português em Safim*. Lisbon: Imprensa Nacional, 1897.
Marnoto 1997
Marnoto, Rita. *O petrarquismo português do renascimento e do maneirismo*. Coimbra: Universidade de Coimbra, 1997.
Marnoto 2002
Marnoto, Rita. "'Bárbora escrava': Canon, Beauty and Color: An Embarrassing Contradiction." *Portuguese Literary and Cultural Studies* 9 (2002): pp. 49–61.
Marnoto 2005
Marnoto, Rita. "Petrarca em Portugal: *ad eorum littus irem*," in *Petrarca: 700 anos*, pp. 251-7. Edited by Rita Marnoto. Lisbon, Universidade de Coimbra, 2005.
Marnoto 2007
Marnoto, Rita. "Laura Bárbora." In *Sete ensaios camonianos*, pp. 35–106. Coimbra: Centro Interuniversitário de Estudos Camonianos, 2007.
Mechon Mamre 2016
Mechon Mamre. "Song of Songs." *A Hebrew-English Bible According to the Masoretic Text and the JPS 1917 Edition*. https://www.mechon-mamre.org/p/pt/pt0.htm/.
Molinaro 1954
Molinaro, Julius A. "Angelica and Medoro: The Development of a Motif from the Renaissance to the

Baroque." PhD diss., University of Toronto, 1954.
Pavlova 2013
Pavlova, Maria. "Rodomonte e Ruggiero: Una questione d'onore." *Rassegna Europea di Letteratura Italiana* 42 (2013): pp. 135–177.
Quijano 2000
Quijano, Aníbal. "Coloniality of Power and Eurocentrism in Latin America." *International Sociology* 15, no. 2 (2000): pp. 215–132.
Ribas 2004
Ribas, Rogério de Oliveira. "'Cide Abdella': Um Marabuto na Corte de D. João III." In *D. João III e o Império*, edited by Roberto Carneiro and Artur Teodoro de Matos, pp. 621–626. Lisbon: Centro de História de Além-Mar and Centro de Estudos dos Povos e Culturas de Expressão Portuguesa, 2004.
Ribas 2005
Ribas, Rogério de Oliveira. "Filhos de Mafoma: Mouriscos, cripto-islamismo e inquisição no Portugal quinhentista." PhD diss., Universidade de Lisboa, 2005.
Sá de Miranda 1885
Sá de Miranda, Francisco de. *Poesias de Francisco de Sá de Miranda*, edited by Carolina Michaëlis de Vasconcellos. Halle: Max Niemeyer, 1885.
Stoppino 2012
Stoppino, Eleanora. *Genealogies of Fiction: Women Warriors and the Dynastic Imagination in the* Orlando Furioso. New York: Fordham University Press, 2012.
Vicente 1986
Vicente, Gil. *Auto da Índia: Farsa*, edited by Mário Fiúza. Porto: Porto Editora, 1986.

PART III

Geographical and Visual Contexts

"Popul la più parte circonciso": Ariosto in Ferrara and the Muslim World of His Time

Giovanni Ricci

"Infidels"—Muslims, or Saracens as they are called in Western chivalric literature—did not figure only in the pages of the *Orlando furioso*. Beyond the stanzas of Ariosto's narrative poem, these figures were part and parcel of the poet's world, close at hand and at times numerous, a source of both private reflection and public discourse. The interpenetration of current events and imaginative literature was a challenge vigorously embraced by many European Renaissance poets.[1] What, then, for Ariosto, was the Muslim world of his time? In search of an answer, this chapter will be divided into two parts: the first examines traces of the most significant religious and political dynamics of the period within the *Furioso*; the second moves beyond the poetic text in order to account for the Muslim presence in Ferrara, the city where Ariosto lived the better part of his life and wrote his poem. These two levels—the poetic imaginary with regard to the Orient and its encompassing Oriental reality—are to some extent interdependent but at the same time autonomous, a dynamic that must be accounted for in any early modern Mediterranean history worthy of the name.[2]

1. Conversions in the *Furioso*

Religious conversion, at times under compulsion, is among the significant issues of the early modern Mediterranean world. In the *Furioso*, there is one historical allusion to conversions to Christianity and one to conversions to Islam. With regard to the first event, a minor episode in the Italian Wars of 1511–1512 had as its protagonist the captain of the Este fortress of Bastia (now the village of San Biagio; the remains of the fortress were destroyed in the Second World War), which was strategically situated midway between Ferrara and Ravenna at the confluence of a tributary of the Po (known today as the Reno) and Santerno rivers with the Zaniolo canal. This soldier, Vestidello Pagano, fought valiantly to defend the Este stronghold, but upon surrender and in violation of the peace agreement, he was murdered by several of the Spanish troops:

gente cordovese e di Granata . . .
popul la più parte circonciso.
—*Fur.*, LXII 4, 8; 5, 8
[Cordovans and Granadans . . . for the most part circumcised peoples.]

Through these circumcised Spanish soldiers, we encounter the general theme of the Spanish New Christians following the fall of Granada and the end of the Reconquista. The indelible bodily mark signaled by the poet here—intended as an insult but exacerbated by the contemporary confusion in the West between circumcision, castration, and sodomy[3]—associates these Spanish soldiers with Muslim origins. But Spanish troops in this period were required to possess *limpieza de sangre* (purity of blood),[4] and as others were forbidden to bear arms, it is unclear whether Ariosto was ignorant of this constraint or if he intentionally meant to impugn the Spanish forces by accusing them all of being mongrels. We have to remember that the Renaissance Este dukes were systematically allied with the French and never hesitated to defame the Spanish. Francesco Guicciardini also testifies to this offense leveled at Spaniards: during the battle of Ravenna in 1512, the Roman captain Fabrizio Colonna, at odds with his Spanish commander Pedro Navarro (who had seized the fortress at Bastia) about the conduct of combat operations, decried "la malignità di quel marrano" (the malevolence of that Marrano), the term used by the Spanish against recently converted Jews and Muslims (though not true in the case of Navarro).[5] In addition to the citation above, Granata (Granada) is mentioned eight other times in the *Furioso*, primarily with regard to the Saracen lady Doralice and her father, Stordilano, king of Granata (*Fur.*, XIV 13, 40, 49, 54, 114; XVI 67; XXVII 5, 51). As for the other earlier capital of Muslim Spain, Cordova (Córdoba), it is the subject of only two generic references in Ariosto's poem (*Fur.*, XIV 12; XXXIII 97).

The violent Christianization of Spain between the fifteenth and sixteenth centuries is thus tangentially reflected in the *Furioso*. But an inverse process, the Islamicization of Catholic individuals or groups, is also registered in the poem. Here our attention moves to the eastern Mediterranean, and in particular to Cairo, the greatest metropolis of the early modern Middle East. Ariosto's Cairo is immense: *diciotto mila gran contrade* (eighteen thousand principal streets); with houses *che . . . hanno tre palchi* (that . . . are three floors high); a huge population, *e ancora ne dormono infiniti in su le strade* (and even so thousands have to sleep in the streets); while the castle of the Mamluk sultan watches over everything, *mirabil di grandezza, e ricco e bello* (remarkable for its size, beauty, and splendor) (*Fur.*, XV 63, 4–8). But most of all, Cairo was considered to be a den of converts to Islam, figures whose anthropology made Christians particularly anxious. The sultan amasses and protects those converts there:

> quindici mila suoi vasalli,
> che son cristiani rinegati tutti,
> con mogli, con famigli e con cavalli
> ha sotto un tetto sol quivi ridutti.
> —*Fur.*, XV 64, 1–4
> [fifteen thousand of his subjects, all of them renegade Christians, with their wives, families, and horses, he has all housed under one roof.]

Published initially in the 1516 edition of the *Furioso*, this brief account of the Egyptian capital is inserted between the episodes of Astolfo's defeat of the giant Caligorante and that of the thief Orrilo (*Fur.*, XV 43–62; 64, 5–90, 8), situated in an Egypt contemporary with the principal action of Ariosto's poem, when

> Non era grande il Cairo così allora,
> come se ne ragiona a nostra etade.
> —*Fur.*, XV 63, 1–2
> [Cairo was not as large then as we are told it is today.]

Here the city is described as it would have been closer to the poet's own time.[6] The subsequent 1521 and 1532 editions of the *Furioso*—rich in topical news[7]—did not alter the substance of these stanzas; it appears not to have mattered to Ariosto that the Ottoman Selīm I had dethroned the last Mamluk sultan, Ṭūmān Bāy, in 1517, so Cairo remains in the final version of the poem the capital of an independent political power that no longer existed. This misreading of the situation suggests that Ariosto (like many in Italy at the time) had not fully appreciated the seriousness of the Egyptian defeat,[8] which—consolidating the earlier Ottoman conquest of the Byzantine Empire in 1453—effectively reestablished the eastern Mediterranean as the "Sea of the caliphs,"[9] dealing a mortal blow to the naval dominance of Italian city-states in the area.

2. Dogs on Either Side

It was not a process of conversion but an incipient Islamicization that involved the Second Rome:

> Perché Constantinopoli e del mondo
> la miglior parte occupa il Turco immondo?
> —*Fur.*, XVII 75, 7–8
> [Why is Constantinople, and the better part of the world, occupied by the unclean Turk?]

Such regret for the fall of the Christian metropolis was a well-established topos in Ariosto's time,[10] when contemporary conflicts would often be read as the latest episodes of the collision between Europe and Asia that had its archetype in the ancient Greco-Persian Wars.[11] But the struggle of the medieval paladins against the Saracens could also be rendered current, in the form of the struggle of Christian Europe against the Turks.[12] The use of Ariosto's poem in a decidedly anti-Turkish key, however, was a subsequent development: a collection of encomiums about the battle of Lepanto published in Venice by Valvassori in 1572, *Varii componimenti di diversi auttori sopra la vittoria dell'armata della santissima lega*, employed the frontispiece of the 1554 edition of the *Furioso* issued by the same publisher, with the addition of decorative elements from the *princeps* edition of 1516.[13]

For the whole of Christian Europe, the Turks constituted a grand synecdoche. The terms *Saracen*, *Moor*, and *Arab* might also, generically, be substituted with *Turk* (this is the descending order of frequency with which these terms appear in the *Furioso*).[14] The analogy was even certified at the linguistic level by the Accademia della Crusca, according to which not only the subjects of the Ottomans were designated as Turks but also all followers of the "Mohammedan sect."[15] In evoking Constantinople, Ariosto uses a heavily laden adjective for the Turks: *immondo* (unclean), typical of the lexicon of infamy that Christians and Muslims hurled at one another in this period, each reciprocally vilified by the other as unclean, like a dog. This stereotype was regularly employed by early modern European authors, from Petrarch (animated by anti-Arab sentiment)—

> Gite superbi, o miseri Cristiani,
> consumando l'un l'altro, e non vi caglia
> che 'l sepolcro di Cristo è in man de' cani.
> —*Triumphus Fame* II 142–144

[Destroy each other, miserable Christians,
with your arrogant disputes, and pay no heed
that the tomb of Christ is in the hands of dogs.][16]

—to Miguel de Cervantes's *gente perra* (doglike people) in *Don Quixote*,[17] and the same slur informed entire treatises dedicated to the infamy of the Turks.[18] Even humanist culture, despite its vaunted universalism, cultivated a negative rhetoric of canine otherness.[19] Muslims, for their part, did not shrink from portraying Christians as animals. One example of this reciprocal attitude is revealed in two parallel sources relating to the Turkish conquest of Otranto (1480–1481): the Ottoman historiographer Kemāl Paşa-zāde called the people of Otranto "infernal dogs," "pigs," "scorpions," and so forth;[20] while the Apulian scholar Michele Laggetto, well aware of the terror inspired by the infidels at home, cursed "the rabid dogs, our enemies."[21]

Within the Ferrarese context, expressions such as "Saracen dogs" are peppered throughout the account of the journey of Niccolò III d'Este to the Holy Land in 1413.[22] And the same is true of the descriptions of the Holy Land made by a great-uncle of the poet, Alessandro Ariosto, who was a missionary there in several periods between 1463 and 1478.[23] But over the whole of the *Furioso* (38,736 lines in the final edition of 1532), dedicated to the struggle of Christians against the infidels, we find the doglike nature of the infidels invoked only three times. The first of these occurs when Charlemagne recommends his faithful supporters to God:

che 'l tuo sepolcro hanno purgato e mondo
da' brutti cani.
—*Fur.*, XVI 71, 6–7
[that have cleansed your sepulchre and purged it of brutish dogs.]

The second instance is when Charlemagne exhorts his followers to fight against Rodomonte:

Mostrate a questo can vostra prodezza,
a questo can che gli uomini devora.
—*Fur.*, XVII 15, 3–4
[Show this dog what you can do, this man-eating dog.]

And finally, concerning the holy places that Ariosto's own narrative voice invokes:

> Che ora i superbi e miseri cristiani,
> e con biasmo lor, lasciano in man de' cani.
> —*Fur.*, XVII 73, 7–8
> [Nowadays to their shame, Christians the arrogant wretches, leave these places in the hands of dogs.]

These are the only such examples in Ariosto's poem, although one analogous instance from the other side of the conflict is given by the young Dardinello, king of Zumara,[24] who nobly invites the Saracen troops under his command to fight to the bitter end:

> Molto è meglio morir qui, ch'ai supplici
> darsi e a discrezion di questi cani.
> —*Fur.*, XVI 51, 1–2
> [Far better is it to die here than to yield ourselves to the dubious mercies of these dogs.]

Given the extremely limited occurrence of the term in Ariosto's poem as well as the only slightly disproportionate balancing act he effects in its use by Christians and a single Muslim within the space of only two cantos of the *Furioso*, the poet demonstrates here as elsewhere an atypical restraint with regard to his contemporaries.

3. Ariosto and the Prophet

For Ariosto, Machon (Muḥammad) is the epitome of the religion of the Saracens. In accordance with a common misconception of the time, Ariosto attributes divine characteristics to him, rather than those of a prophet: *dove Machon s'adori* (where Mohamed [be] worshiped; *Fur.*, XXXVIII 18, 6). Muḥammad appears ten times in the poem, but there is no mention of Allah. His believers make vows to the Prophet (*Fur.*, XVIII 55, XXV 42), but there is also the raging Ferraù, who gives vent to his feelings against him, *biastemmiando Machone* (cursing Muḥammad, *Fur.*, XII 59). Despite the good faith of some of his followers, this is represented as a false god and therefore incapable of answering their prayers. Dardinello promises to offer him a trophy: *al suo Machon, s'udir lo puote* (swearing to Muḥammad, if [he] had ears, *Fur.*, XVIII 55); and

Dentro a Biserta i sacerdoti fanti
supplicando col populo dolente,
battonsi il petto, e con dirotti pianti
chiamano il lor Machon che nulla sente.
—*Fur.*, LX 13, 1–4
[In Biserta the holy priests prayed with their grieving flock, beating their breasts and sobbing as they invoked their Muḥammad, who hears nothing.]

Here, with both "holy priests" and the depiction of the grief of their faithful followers, we might be tempted to see the affirmation of the so-called ethic of intention, in which moral purpose matters more than the result, respect for the ritual form of the law rather than its substance. But there is no equivalence between Ariosto's attitude in the *Furioso* and the violence of Dante in his depiction of Muḥammad in *Inferno* XXVIII 22–63.[25] As with the characterization of infidels as canine, Ariosto appears to have been unfazed when faced with a religion that was considered to be a deviant Christian sect.[26] Could this have been a further motive providing fodder for the subsequent misgivings of inquisitors regarding his piety?[27]

But for Ariosto, it is enough that the paladins devote themselves to a simple religious apostolate. Brandimarte declares that *Cristo conobbi Dio, Maumette stolto* (I knew Christ for God, Muḥammad for a dupe], *Fur.*, LXI 39, 5, while Bradamante exhorts Ruggiero in the 1516 edition of the poem, *lasci Maumete e battizar si deggia* (leave Muḥammad and be baptized, you must); *Fur.* (A XX 34, 7).[28]

The baptism of infidels that emerges here was, in fact, a subject that the earlier epic tradition had already developed.[29] In Boiardo, at the end of a bloody duel, Orlando converts the ferocious Agricane, who immediately makes his profession of Christian faith:

Io credo nel tuo Dio che morì in croce,
bategiami barone ala fontana.
—*Inam.,* I xix 12, 8; 13, 1
[I believe in your God who died on the cross,
baptize me, baron, at the fountain.]

A tireless evangelist, Boiardo's Orlando also brings Brandimarte, *anima perdita* (lost soul), to the Christian faith after explaining the sacred texts to him in outline.[30]

In the *Furioso,* there are numerous characters predestined for baptism due to their personal virtue. At the mercy of the waves, it is said of Ruggiero that:

> A Dio, ch'ivi punir non lo volesse,
> pentito disse quattro volte e diece;
> e fece voto di core e di fede
> d'esser cristian, se ponea in terra il piede.
> —*Fur.*, LXI 48, 5–8
> [He asked God not to punish him now, penitently time and again; and swore faithfully from the bottom of his heart to become a Christian if he set foot on shore.]

Saved on an island inhabited by a hermit, the conclusion for Ruggiero is inevitable and speedy, anticipating the pattern of later Tridentine conversions:

> Imparò poi più ad agio in questo loco
> de nostra fede i gran misterii tutti;
> et alla pura fonte ebbe battesmo
> il dí seguente dal vecchio medesmo.
> —*Fur.*, LXI 59, 5–8
> [He learned here at greater leisure all the mysteries of our faith and in the pure spring he was baptized the next day by the old man.]

Contractual religious sentiment, based on the system of *do ut des* (I give in order that you may give), is typical of chivalrous literature, as are the topoi of the island and the hermit.[31] The Saracen Sobrino, following a miraculous recovery, also changes his life:

> si dispon di lasciar Macon da canto,
> e Cristo confessar vivo e potente:
> e domanda con cor di fede attrito,
> d'iniciïarsi al nostro sacro rito.
> —*Fur.*, LXIII 193, 5–8
> [he decided to renounce Muḥammad, and confess Christ living and powerful. His heart touched with faith, he asked to be initiated in our sacred rite.]

There is no corresponding conversion to Islam among the principal characters of the poem. But what of the fifteen thousand renegades comfortably settled in Cairo? Ariosto could not have ignored this widely known reality. The abundant baptisms in the remainder of the *Furioso*, however, serve nothing other than a consolatory function with regard to the very real frequency of Christians converting to Islam in the period and the rarity of movement in the opposite direction.[32]

Ariosto barely names the Koran. Muḥammad's followers swear on their holy book as Christians do on the Gospels:

In quel del nostro è la vita perfetta
scritta di Christo; e l'altro è l'Alcorano.
—*Fur.*, XXXVIII 81
[In ours is written the perfect life of Christ; and the other is the Koran.]

It would appear that the poet did not know the holy book of Islam directly, though the more or less complete Latin translation—actually a somewhat distorted paraphrase with a highly polemical hue—by Robert of Ketton (Rodbertus Ketenensis) around 1141–1142 was included by Peter the Venerable, abbot of Cluny, in the *Collectio toletana* (Toledan Collection) that he supervised, which gathered various texts on the Muslim religion and circulated in manuscripts throughout Europe (more than thirty of these survive today) until their publication in print by Theodor Bibliander in Basel in 1543. The first Italian translation, based on the Bibliander edition, was published in Venice in 1547.[33] The Italian translation of *Confusión de la secta mahomética y del Alcoran* by the Spanish converso Juan Andrés, was dedicated in 1537 to Duke Ercole II, four years after Ariosto's death, though the work's original edition from 1515 may well have been known in an Italy increasingly dominated by Spain in the early sixteenth century.[34]

4. Muslims in Ferrara

So far, we have seen what Ariosto says explicitly about Muslims and the Muslim world, all of which was nourished by fragments of information and suggestions from various sources lodged in the prevailing *immaginario* of his time and place. Ariosto can at best be considered a tangential intermediary with the contemporary Muslim,[35] Ferrara having been less exposed to intercultural exchange than frontier capitals, such as Venice or Dubrovnik. Nevertheless, the threat of the "infidels"— actual persons or their specters—weighed significantly on the social and political life of Ariosto's city, as well as on its artistic production.

In the first place, there were slaves. From 1382 to 1522, some forty such individuals, mostly designated as "Moors," can be identified in Ferrarese documents. Limiting ourselves only to documents from Ariosto's lifetime, two Turks are mentioned in 1476 among the staff of the castle's wood storehouse; a short time later, Duchess Eleonora of Aragon, wife to Ercole I, obtained a pregnant "Moorish" woman from the market in Venice so as "to establish a race of Moors" in Ferrara; in 1491, Anna Sforza, the future first wife of Alfonso I, had a young black female slave of her own; and in 1522, Isabella d'Este, marchioness of Mantua, was offered by her native Ferrara a sixteen-year-old "Moorish" servant who was very expensive because she was a virgin. But in addition to the Este court, private households also held slaves, and here we come closer to our poet's own antecedents: in 1403, a certain Aldovrandino Ariosti bought a Bosnian female of twenty-six in Venice at the price of forty-eight ducats; in 1441, Taddeo Ariosti sold a young female slave to a fellow citizen for thirty-two ducats; and in the meantime, Giovanni Ariosti had a child by an unknown slave who was baptized with the name of Pietro and who in 1448 was accused of stealing liturgical objects from the cathedral.[36] While the Bosnian may have been an Islamicized Slav, we have no information about the others.

In addition to housing these "resident" slaves, Ferrara was also a transit route for slavery in this period. Sixteen Turks in chains were seen there in 1459, sent by the despot of Morea, Thomas Palaiologos, to the congress of Mantua as part of his campaign for the gathered princes to launch a new Crusade. This vision of shackled Turks—defeated and vulnerable—partially compensated for the terror of Turkish power that Byzantine accounts had disseminated in Ferrara two decades earlier, during the Council of Ferrara-Florence (1438–1439), despite the recent Ottoman conquest of Constantinople.

In 1483, there was a massive but short-lived passage of Turks through the city. Alfonso, the duke of Calabria—son of Ferdinand, the king of Naples (subsequently his successor), and brother of Eleonora of Aragon, the duchess of Ferrara—the man who had driven the Turks from Otranto, arrived in Ferrara. Boiardo dedicated lines of gratitude to him:

> sì com'è Italia da' Turchi diffesa
> per sua prodecia sola e suo valore.
> —*Inam.,* II xxvii 57, 3-5
> [thus is Italy from the Turks defended only by his prowess and valor.]

Alfonso brought five hundred Turks with him, captured at Otranto and hired for the war against Venice, but one night, the Turks crossed over to the Venetian camp in the hope that the republic would take them back to their homeland.

What kind of reception would these Turkish soldiers have had in a city with which they were such half-hearted allies? The fact that they stripped the empty houses of the Borgo dei Leoni district of firewood would not have won them much affection.[37] The young Ludovico Ariosto would certainly have seen these captive Turks in Ferrara and formed some idea of them.

A merchant dealing in carpets originally from Cairo worked in the city, a certain "Master Sabadino, upholsterer," also called "Syro," "Negro," and "Moro," but it is unclear whether he was a Muslim or a Christian. We know that Duke Ercole I was a passionate collector of Oriental rugs, and in 1481, having seen several exempla supplied by another merchant, from Dubrovnik, in the Palazzo Bevilacqua, he acquired a number of them. Given that there was a regular flow of caravans from Constantinople to the Dalmatian city,[38] these rugs were probably of Turkish origin. But while the name of the Egyptian merchant features in Ferrarese documents between the 1480s and up to 1528, not a single piece acquired from him by Este patrons has survived. Images of such precious objects, however, were first included in fifteenth-century Ferrarese painting; there are knotted carpets from western Anatolia in the frescoes attributed to Francesco del Cossa in Palazzo Schifanoia, while the frescoes of Garofalo in Palazzo Costabili contain what appear to be prayer rugs.[39] There is no information about other objects arriving in Ferrara from the Muslim world in this period except for a piece mentioned in the Guardaroba Estense in 1494: "a round shield of Moorish style covered with silk of several colours in a leather case."[40] Who knows how it came to be there?

5. Fear and Prophecy

During Ariosto's youth, most of the news about the Turks reaching Ferrara came from Venice, as was to be expected; but such reports also arrived from Naples, thanks to the presence there of the duchess Eleonora of Aragon. Events of primary interest were recorded in 1481 by Bernardino Zambotti, the Ferrarese chronicler. Zambotti (later a close associate of Ariosto's), rejoiced at the death of Meḥmed II (*el magno Octomano*), the terror of Christianity: "processions in praise of the omnipotent God were made, and [there were] bonfires and fireworks of joy."[41] Meanwhile, however, the Bosnian cavalry raged across Friuli, which was poorly defended by the Venetian militias: "The news came that . . . in the city of Udine, the Turks have assaulted the Christians and killed most of them." Rhodes was besieged in 1480 but saved by a miracle: "Saint John appeared to the inhabitants above the walls when they were fighting with the Turks." Cem, the brother and rival of Meḥmed's successor, Bāyezīd II, landed in

Italy in 1481, and Ferrara was perhaps indirectly involved. A young man who had allegedly received a commission to murder Cem from Bāyezīd, according to some sources, had been "groom to Duke Borso"[42] of Ferrara; he was later condemned to be dismembered in Rome. In 1499, interest turned to the Levant when the Venetian fortress of Lepanto fell "following considerable bloodshed." Subsequently, attention was focused on Modone (Methoni) in Morea, "which cost the deaths of 20,000 Christians." At this point, having relayed the body count, a feeling of exhaustion overtook the Ferrarese chronicler: "the danger for Christians is extreme, I fear that we will fall into the hands of infidels." New "powerful" Turkish threats loomed against Friuli in 1500. But news arrived in 1501 of a Christian league, because the Turk "was advancing continuously to the harm of the Christians."[43] And so on in a similar vein, following the stages of the great conflict.

Diplomacy and war were accompanied by prognostication, in which Ferrarese astrology played a significant role. At the end of the fifteenth century, the medical doctor Carlo Sosenna kept a spirit at home; this *diabolus* revealed both knowledge of the future and hidden aspects of the present, to the extent that Duke Ercole I was in the habit of consulting him. In 1494, among other predictions, the spirit announced that Turkish conquests in the Balkans would soon be avenged by the Holy Roman Emperor.[44] The most celebrated Ferrarese prophetic text is, however, by the local astrologer Antonio Arquato, *De eversione Europae prognosticon*, heavily influenced by Joachinism;[45] it bears a dedication to Matthias Corvino, king of Hungary.[46] Its first edition was published in 1534, but the prophecy declared itself to have been made in 1480, announcing, in the wake of many hardships, the conversion of the Muslims and the end of the "Mohammedan sect."[47] Would Ariosto have subscribed to this belief—it had circulated for decades before its publication—at a time when he was writing his long narrative poem engaged with the conflict between Muslims and Christians in earlier centuries?

Notes

1. Miotti 2017.
2. See Trivellato 2010; Cavallo 2013; Jossa 2017.
3. See Bennassar 1989, pp. 426–432.
4. See Greenwood 1978.
5. Guicciardini 1971, p. 997.
6. Bigi (Ariosto 2012, p. 502) suggests that Ariosto probably depended on travel literature, particularly Lionardo Frescobaldi's fourteenth-century *Viaggio in Egitto e in Terrasanta*, for this information about Cairo.
7. See Scianatico 2005; Le Gall 2018.
8. See Ricci 2013.
9. The title of Picard 2015, a study of the seventh-century Muslim struggle for dominance of the entire Mediterranean basin.
10. See Centro Italiano 2008.
11. See Meserve 2008, pp. 65–116.
12. See Bisaha 2004, pp. 30–42; Matarrese 2004, pp. 19–31; Pavlova 2013.
13. See Paul 2011, pp. 80–82.
14. See Ricci 2018b; Lausten 2019.
15. Accademia della Crusca 1691, p. 1736.
16. Petrarca 1996.
17. See Meier 2007; Cervantes 1998, I, p. 1151. It must also be noted, however, that Cervantes's position toward both Muslims and dogs is multidimensional; among the most telling examples of the former, all of part I of Don Quixote is said by the author to be translated from a putative Arabic manuscript; and two speaking dogs in "El coloquio de los perros" (the last of the *Novelas ejemplares*) are made into expositors of Cervantes's own poetics.
18. See Schnapp 2010.
19. See Hampton 1993, pp. 67, 80.
20. See Kreiser 2008; Cassetta and Ercolino 2002.
21. Antonaci 1955, pp. 52–56, 68. See Tommasino 2015.
22. Dal Campo 2011, pp. 202–203.
23. See Ariosto 2007.
24. His father, Almonte, had been killed in battle by Orlando, who then appropriated the defeated Sarcen king's helmet and his sword, Durindana. Dardinello, killed in turn by Rinaldo, is buried by his subject Medoro in the episode in *Fur.*, XIX 17–42 in which the humble Saracen soldier first meets Angelica, and it is their relationship that provokes Orlando's titular madness in the central cantos of the poem, *Fur.*, XXII–XXIV.
25. See Gabrieli 1965, pp. 20–22.
26. See Conconi 2001.
27. See Fragnito 2010.
28. More clearly expressed in the first edition, in *Fur.* (C, XXII 34, 7-8) this is trimmed to prima si battezzi [first be baptized]; see Ariosto 2006.
29. See Rajna 1975, pp. 564–567; Pavlova 2014.
30. *Inam.*, I xix 12–16); II xii 11–14).
31. See Klettke 2017.
32. See Bennassar 1989; Rostagno 1983.
33. See Felici 2011; Tommasino 2013.
34. Andrea 1537, pp. 1–3. See Gorris 1996, pp. 73–80; D'Ascia 2001, pp. 24–25; Tommasino 2013, pp. 161–188. On the entirely new but never completed translation of the Koran initiated in humanist circles in the late fifteenth century, see Casari in this volume.
35. He is not, for instance, cited in Contadini and Norton 2013, a collection of essays dealing with the material, intellectual, and commercial exchanges between the Ottomans and Europe.
36. See Ricci 2011.
37. See Ricci 2002, pp. 35–37.
38. See Bertelli 2004, pp. 51–101; Rakić 2019.

39. See Boralevi 1989; Curatola 2014.
40. See Campori 1870, p. 34.
41. Zambotti 1934–1937, pp. 93–96.
42. See İnalcik 1979; Ricci 2018a, pp. 48–49.
43. Zambotti 1934–1937, pp. 41, 47–48, 83, 204, 217, 292, 299, 301, 307.
44. See Bacchelli 2000.
45. Joachim de Fiore's *Expositio in Apocalypsim* has plentiful references to Islam and the Third Crusade; on the reception of Joachim de Fiore's works and Joachinism, see Reeves 1977.
46. Ippolito d'Este—the future dedicatee of the *Furioso*—was named cardinal at the age of seven by Corvino, and, though the appointment would not take effect until he was eighteen, Ippolito's commitments in Hungary subsequently complicated Ariosto's career when the poet refused to join the cardinal there in 1518.
47. See Garin 1969, pp. 105–111; Gollner 1978, p. 341.

Bibliography

Accademia della Crusca 1691
Vocabolario degli Accademici della Crusca. Florence: Accademia della Crusca, 1691.

Andrea 1537
Andrea, Giovan [Juan Andrés]. *Opera chiamata confusione della setta machumetana*. Seville [Venice]: n.p., 1537.

Antonaci 1955
Antonaci, Antonio. *Otranto: Testi e monumenti*. Galatina: Congedo, 1955.

Ariosto 2006
Ariosto, Ludovico. *Orlando furioso secondo la princeps del 1516*, edited by Marco Dorigatti. Florence: Olschki, 2006.

Ariosto 2007
Ariosto, Alessandro. *Itinerarium, 1476–1479*, edited by Fabio Uliana. Alessandria: Edizioni dell'Orso, 2007.

Ariosto 2012
Ariosto, Ludovico. *Orlando furioso*, with comments by Emilio Bigi (1982), edited by Cristina Zampese. Milan: Rizzoli, 2012.

Bacchelli 2000
Bacchelli, Franco. "Magia e astrologia a Ferrara tra Quattrocento e Cinquecento." In *Storia di Ferrara*, edited by Adriano Prosperi, VI, pp. 236–244. Ferrara: Corbo, 2000.

Baldissone 2016
Baldissone, Riccardo. "With Teeth and Nails: The Embodied Inservitude of Étienne de la Boétie." In *Performing the Renaissance Body. Essays on Drama, Law, and Representation*, edited by Sidia Fiorato and John Drakakis, pp. 157–181. Berlin: De Gruyter, 2016.

Bennassar 1989
Bennassar, Bartolomé. *Les Chrétiens d'Allah: L'histoire extraordinaire des renégats. XVIe et XVIIe siècles*. Paris: Perrin, 1989.

Bertelli 2004
Bertelli, Sandro. *Trittico: Lucca, Ragusa, Boston: Tre città mercantili tra Cinque e Seicento*. Rome: Donzelli, 2004.

Bisaha 2004
Bisaha, Nancy. *Creating East and West: Renaissance Humanism and the Ottoman Turks*. Philadelphia: University of Pennsylvania Press, 2004.

Boralevi 1989
Boralevi, Alberto. "I tappeti." In *Atlante di Schifanoia*, edited by Ranieri Varese, pp. 217–220. Ferrara: Panini, 1989.

Campori 1870
Campori, Giuseppe. *Raccolta di cataloghi ed inventarii inediti*. Modena: Vincenzi, 1870.
Cassetta and Ercolino 2002
Cassetta, Ilenia Romana, and Elettra Ercolino. "La prise d'Orante (1480–81), entre sources chrétiennes et turques." *Turcica: Revue d'études turques* 34 (2002): pp. 255–275.
Cavallo 2013
Cavallo, Jo Ann. *The World beyond Europe in the Romance Epics of Boiardo and Ariosto*. Toronto: University of Toronto Press, 2013.
Centro Italiano 2008
Centro Italiano di Studi sul Basso Medioevo (Accademia Tudertina). *L'Europa dopo la caduta di Costantinopoli: 29 maggio 1453, Atti del XLIV Convegno Storico Internazionale, Todi, 7–9 ottobre 2007*. Spoleto: Fondazione Centro italiano di studi sull'alto Medioevo, 2008.
Cervantes 1998
Cervantes, Miguel de. *Don Quijote de la Mancha*, edited by Francisco Rico. Barcelona: Instituto Cervantes, 1998.
Conconi 2001
Conconi, Bruna. "Chrétiens et Turcs: La comparaison des religions à la Renaissance." In *L'Europa e il Levante nel Cinquecento: Cose turchesche*, edited by Luigia Zilli, pp. 113–144. Padua: Unipress, 2001.
Contadini and Norton 2013
Contadini, Anna, and Claire Norton, eds. *The Renaissance and the Ottoman World*. Surrey, UK: Ashgate, 2013.
Curatola 2014
Curatola, Giovanni. "Tappeti ottomani nella pittura: Dalla devozione mariana all'uso profano." In *Incontri di civiltà nel Mediterraneo: L'Impero ottomano e l'Italia del Rinascimento*, edited by Alireza Naser Eslami, pp. 75–88. Florence: Olschki, 2014.
Dal Campo 2011
Dal Campo, Luchino. *Viaggio del marchese Nicolò d'Este al Santo Sepolcro (1413)*, edited by Caterina Brandoli. Florence: Olschki, 2011.
D'Ascia 2001
D'Ascia, Luca. *Il corano e la tiara: L'epistola a Maometto II di Enea Silvio Piccolomini (papa Pio II)*. Bologna: Pendragon, 2001.
Felici 2011
Felici, Lucia. "Una nuova immagine dell'Islam (e del cristianesimo) nell'Europa del XVI secolo." In *Encountering Otherness: Diversities and Transcultural Experiences in Early Modern European Culture*, edited by Guido Abbattista, pp. 43–66. Trieste: Editrice dell'Università di Trieste, 2011.
Fragnito 2010
Fragnito, Gigliola. "'Vanissimus et spurcissimus homo': Ariosto all'esame dei censori." In *Dalla bibliografia alla storia: Studi in onore di Ugo Rozzo*, edited by Rudj Gorian, pp. 115–137. Udine: Forum, 2010.
Gabrieli 1965
Gabrieli, Francesco. *Letture e divagazioni dantesche*. Bari: Edizioni del Centro Librario, 1965.
Garin 1969
Garin, Eugenio. *L'età nuova: Ricerche di storia della cultura dal XII al XVI secolo*. Naples: Morano, 1969.
Gollner 1978
Gollner, Carl. *Turcica: Die Türkenfrage in der öffentlichen Meinung Europas im 16. Jahrhundert*, III. Bucharest: Academiei Republicii Socialiste Romania–Heitz, 1978.
Gorris 1996
Gorris, Rosanna. *Alla corte del principe: Traduzione, romanzo, alchimia, scienza e politica tra Italia e Francia nel Rinascimento*. Ferrara: Università degli Studi, 1996.
Greenwood 1978
Greenwood, Davydd J. "Pureza de sangre y nobleza en el País Vasco y Castilla: Conceptos naturistas, variedades del orden social y autonomía de la naturaleza." *Ethnica: Revista de antropología* 14 (1978): pp. 161–182
Guicciardini 1971
Guicciardini, Francesco. *Storia d'Italia*, edited by Silvana Seidel Menchi. Turin: Einaudi, 1971.

Hampton 1993
Hampton, Timothy. "'Turkish Dogs': Rabelais, Erasmus and the Rhetoric of Alterity." *Representations* 41 (1993): pp. 58–82.

İnalcik 1979
İnalcik, Halil. "A Case Study in Renaissance Diplomacy: The Agreement between Innocent VIII and Bâyezîd on Djem Sultan." *Journal of Turkish Studies* 3 (1979): pp. 209–223.

Jossa 2017
Jossa, Stefano. "Ariosto Redivivus in 2016: A Year of Centenary Celebration and Critical Reassessment of *Orlando Furioso*." *The Italianist* 38, no. 1 (2017): pp. 134–149.

Klettke 2017
Klettke, Cornelia. "L'archipel dans le Roland furieux de l'Arioste: Hybridité du savoir cartographiqueet de l'imaginaire géographique." In *Îles et Insulaires (XVIe–XVIIIe siècles)*, edited by Frank Lestringant and Alexandre Tarrête, pp. 225–242. Paris: Presses de l'Université Paris-Sorbonne, 2017.

Kreiser 2008
Kreiser, Klaus. "La conquista turca di Otranto nella cronaca di Kemalpascia Zâde. 1468/69–1534." In *La conquista turca di Otranto tra storia e mito*, edited by Hubert Houben, I, pp. 159–175. Galatina: Congedo, 2008.

Lausten 2019
Lausten, Pia Schwarz. "Saracens and Turks in Ariostos's *Orlando Furioso*: Sheer Imagination or Allusions to Reality." *Nordic Journal of Renaissance Studies* 16 (2019): pp. 97–126.

Le Gall 2018
Le Gall, Jean-Marie. "La figure de l'ennemi chez l'Arioste." *Schifanoia* 54–55 (2018): pp. 177–192.

Matarrese 2004
Matarrese, Tina. *Parole e forme dei cavalieri boiardeschi*. Novara: Interlinea, 2004.

Meier 2007
Meier, Franziska. "Francesco Petrarcas Orient und die Idee Europas." *Romanische Forschungen* 119 (2007): pp. 38–72.

Meserve 2008
Meserve, Margaret. *Empires of Islam in Renaissance Historical Thought*. Cambridge, MA: Harvard University Press, 2008.

Miotti 2017
Miotti, Mariangela. *Rappresentare la storia: Letteratura e attualità nella Francia e nell'Europa del XVI secolo*. Perugia: Aguaplano, 2017.

Paul 2011
Paul, Benjamin. "'And the moon has started to bleed': Apocalypticism and Religious Reform in Venetian Art at the Time of the Battle of Lepanto." In *The Turk and Islam in the Western Eye, 1450–1750: Visual Imagery before Orientalism*, edited by James Harper, pp. 80–82. Farnham, UK: Ashgate, 2011.

Pavlova 2013
Pavlova, Maria. "Rodomonte e Ruggiero: Una questione d'onore." *Rassegna europea della letteratura italiana* 42 (2013): pp. 142–177.

Pavlova 2014
Pavlova, Maria. "I saraceni nella letteratura cavalleresca del Quattrocento, dai rifacimenti di storie medievali all'*Inamoramento de Orlando*." In *Epic Connections / Rencontres épiques, Proceedings of the Nineteenth International Conference of the Société Rencesvals*, edited by Marianne J. Ailes, Philip E. Bennett, and Anne E. Cobby, pp. 579–599. Edinburgh: Société Rencesvals British Branch, 2014.

Petrarca 1996
Petrarca, Francesco. *Trionfi, Rime Estravaganti, Codice Degli Abbozzi*, edited by Vinicio Pacca and Laura Paolino, introduction by Marco Santagata. Milan: A. Mondadori, 1996.

Picard 2015
Picard, Christophe. *La mer des califes: Une histoire de la Méditerranée musulmane (VIIe–XIIe siècle)*. Paris: Seuil, 2015.

Rajna 1975
Rajna, Pio. *Le fonti dell'Orlando Furioso*. Florence: Sansoni, 1975.

Rakić 2019

Rakićv, Ivana Čapeta. "Islamic Rugs in the Painting of the Eastern Adriatic." In *Jews and Muslims Made Visible in Christian Iberia and Beyond, 14th to 18th Centuries*, edited by Borja Franco Llopis and Antonio Urquízar-Herrera, pp. 213–233. Leiden: Brill, 2019.

Reeves 1977

Reeves, Marjorie. *Joachim of Fiore and the Prophetic Future.* New York: Harper & Row, 1977.

Ricci 2002

Ricci, Giovanni. *Ossessione turca: In una retrovia cristiana dell'Europa moderna.* Bologna: Il Mulino, 2002.

Ricci 2011

Ricci, Giovanni. "Les derniers esclaves domestiques: Entre Ferrare, Venise et Mantoue." In *Les musulmans dans l'histoire de l'Europe*, edited by Jocelyne Dakhlia and Bernard Vincent, I, pp. 443–455. Paris: Albin Michel, 2011.

Ricci 2012

Ricci, Giovanni. "Fra Costantinopoli, Gerusalemme e Mistrà: Sedici schiavi turchi al tempo della Dieta di Mantova del 1459." In *Le due Muse: Scritti d'arte, collezionismo e letteratura in onore di Ranieri Varese*, edited by Francesca Cappelletti, Anna Cerboni Baiardi, Valter Curzi, and Cecilia Prete, pp. 403–407. Ancona: Il Lavoro Editoriale, 2012.

Ricci 2013

Ricci, Giovanni. "L'opinion italienne sous-évalue-t-elle la conquête de l'Égypte?" In *Conquête ottomane de l'Égypte (1517)*, edited by Benjamin Lellouch and Nicolas Michel, pp. 329–338. Leiden: Brill, 2013.

Ricci 2018a

Ricci, Giovanni. *Appeal to the Turk: The Broken Boundaries of the Renaissance.* Rome: Viella, 2018.

Ricci 2018b

Ricci, Giovanni. "Gli infedeli dell'Ariosto." *Schifanoia* 54–55 (2018): pp. 177–192.

Rostagno 1983

Rostagno, Lucia. *Mi faccio turco: Esperienze e immagini dell'islam nell'Italia moderna.* Rome: Istituto per l'Oriente, 1983.

Schnapp 2010

Schnapp, Joël. "Antichrist et Antichrists turcs au XVe siècle." In *Italien und das Osmanische Reich*, edited by Franziska Meier, pp. 14–167. Herne: Schäfer, 2010.

Scianatico 2005

Scianatico, Giovanna. "Le 'moderne cose': Storia contemporanea nel Furioso." In *Il principe e la storia*, edited by Tina Matarrese and Cristina Montagnani, pp. 223–238. Novara: Interlinea, 2005.

Tommasino 2013

Tommasino, Pier Mattia. *L'Alcorano di Macometto: Storia di un libro del Cinquecento europeo.* Bologna: Il Mulino, 2013.

Tommasino 2015

Tommasino, Pier Mattia. "Otranto and the Self." *I Tatti Studies in the Italian Renaissance* 18, 2015: pp. 147–155.

Trivellato 2010

Trivellato, Francesca. "Renaissance Italy and the Muslim Mediterranean in Recent Historical Work." *Journal of Modern History* 82, no. 1 (March 2010): pp. 127–155.

Zambotti 1934–1937

Zambotti, Bernardino. *Diario ferrarese dall'anno 1476 sino al 1504*, edited by Giuseppe Pardi. Bologna: Zanichelli, 1934–1937.

Ariosto, the Arabs, and the Geo-cartographic Culture of the Este Court

Massimo Rossi

Italo Calvino, one of the principal Italian author/critics of the twentieth century, has defined the *Furioso* as "the poem of movement . . . movement in broken, zigzagging lines. We could trace the general design of the poem by following the continuous intersection and divergence of these lines on a map of Europe and Africa."[1] Calvino understood chivalric romance as "an immense game of chess played on the geographic map of the world, a huge game that is subdivided into many simultaneous games. [But] the world map is much more variegated than a chessboard."[2] And again, "in each canto of the *Orlando furioso* the map of the world unfolds simultaneously under the reader's eye."[3]

While well aware of the altered literary-critical paradigm now operative in the analysis of Ariosto's masterpiece with respect to its earlier "Calvinization"—a condensed and demystified vision employed by Calvino in his reading of the poem—that recent scholarship has rejected in emphasizing the complexity of the *Furioso* and its accordingly multivalent interpretations,[4] it nevertheless seems useful and productive here to put into practice Calvino's suggestion to relate the geographic space of the poem with the values of the contemporary maps familiar to Ariosto.

But what were these maps of the world? Which maps, atlases, or travel writing could Ariosto have profitably had at his disposal in Ferrara, the capital of the Este dynasty, whose court was particularly attentive to and eager for news in the great period of the age of geographical exploration?

1. Geography at Court

When Ariosto began to compose his poem, the geo-cartographic resources present in the Este library and in the learned tradition of geographical knowledge at court—under Borso and at the time of Ercole I—would have provided fruitful intellectual stimulus for the poet. The ready availability of a considerable number of geographical texts provided Ariosto the opportunity to acquire practical knowledge for establishing the descriptive peculiarities of the places evoked in his narrative verse: from the treatises of Pliny, Strabo, and Pomponio Mela to a considerable number of editions of Ptolemy:

> descrizioni di regioni particolari, dell'Irlanda, dell'Inghilterra, della Germania, della Terra Santa e dell'India; relazioni di viaggi in Spagna, in Francia, in Inghilterra, nei Paesi bassi, in Terra Santa, compiuti dai duchi estensi con splendidi cortei.[5]
> [descriptions of particular regions, of Ireland, England, Germany, the Holy Land, and India; reports about the journeys to Spain, France, England, the Netherlands, and the Holy Land made by the Este dukes and accompanied everywhere they traveled by splendid pageants.]

The "library" of Ercole I was housed in the Este Castle in the Rigobello tower, and Pellegrino Prisciani was the manager, archivist, and librarian who oversaw its complex reorganization. Books and maps circulated among courtiers, as shown by Este archival documents attesting to both the purchase and borrowing of cartographic materials.

On December 27, 1463, under the reign of the marquis Borso d'Este, "unum Mapamundi secundum tabulas Ptholomei" (a world map according to the tables of Ptolemy) was purchased; on March 30, 1466, the "Exc.mo Cosmographo D. Nicolao Germanico" (most Excellent Cosmographer Lord Nicolaus Germanus) dedicated his *Cosmographia* to Borso, who rewarded him with one hundred gold florins;[6] in 1459–1460, a globe was sent "a Belfiore al magn. Conte Lorenzo [Strozzi]" (to Belfiore to the magnificent Count Lorenzo Strozzi)," together with a navigational map.

In an inventory of the library of Duke Ercole I, we find the following annotation: "uno mapamondi in una guaina de cuoio. Die XJ Julij1488: magister Galeatius Trottus habuit de Commissione lli.mi D. Duci nostra et in ejus presentia pro imponendo in studio sue Excel.tiae"[7] (a map of the world in a large leather casing. July 11, 1488: master Galeazzo Trotti received from the authority of the Most Illustrious Lord Duke and in his and our presence to hang it in the study of His Excellency). This is the *Mappamondo catalano estense* (Catalan–este world map) preserved today in Modena, of Majorcan origin and contemporary with the Venetian *mappamondo* (world map) of Fra Mauro.[8]

In the library of Borso and Ercole, there were also classical texts such as Pliny's *Historia naturalis*; Strabo's *Geografia*; the geographical work of Pomponio Mela; the principal university text for the teaching of astronomy, the *Sphaera mundi* of Giovanni Sacrobosco; the *Libro* of Marco Polo;[9] the *Cosmographia* of

Fig. 1. *Carta del navicare per le isole novamente trovate in parte de l'India,* 1502. Modena, Biblioteca Estense Universitaria, Ms. c.g.a.2

Claudius Ptolemy; and the imaginative journeys of Sir John of Mandeville. The contemporary faculty of the University of Ferrara included the court scientists and astrologers Giovanni Bianchini and Pietro Bono dell'Avogaro (involved in the elaboration of the Bolognese edition of Ptolemy published in 1477),[10] and Nicolaus Copernicus completed his Italian education there in 1503 as *doctoratus* in canon law.[11]

But the most significant example of Ercole I's interest in news regarding recent geographical findings is the so-called *Carta del Cantino* (Cantino map) (figs. 1 and 2), which demonstrates that just over six months after Columbus's arrival in what are now called the Bahamas, the court at Ferrara was already informed about the first voyage of the Genoese navigator. Through the work of Alberto Cantino, the cartographic heritage of the ducal library acquired a document of the highest scientific and artistic value. An Este agent in Lisbon, Cantino wrote five letters to the duke of Ferrara between June 7, 1501, and November 19, 1502, and in the last, he communicated the theft of a "charta del navicare" (navigational map),[12] updated with the latest Portuguese discoveries and including the third voyage of Amerigo Vespucci which had gone as far as Tierra del Fuego. The map, measuring 2,200 by 1,050 millimeters, for which Cantino had paid twelve gold ducats, traveled via Genoa before reaching Ferrara, where, in 1597, it appeared in the inventory of Alfonso II's assets;[13] after being transported to Modena following the Este loss of Ferrara in 1598, the map disappeared in 1859

Fig. 2. *Carta del navicare per le isole novamente trovate in parte de l'India*, 1502. Detail. Modena, Biblioteca Estense Universitaria, Ms. c.g.a.2

during the civil strife that eventually led to Italian unification and was only rediscovered in 1870 in a butcher's shop, attached to a screen, by Giuseppe Boni, who later donated it to the Biblioteca Estense in Modena.

The Ferrarese court was thus an active participant in this initiative of significant cartographic innovation between the late fifteenth and early sixteenth centuries, an investment that also had an impact on the design of the Este capital itself.[14] In 1492, the year of Columbus's first voyage, work began on the Barco neighborhood north of the old city, where the Belfiore residence of the Este was located. The area that hosted this addition, its principal contours built over the course of twenty years, came to be named *terra nova* (new world); in the center of its *piazza nova* (new square), an equestrian monument to Hercules supported by two columns was to have been realized, a mythological admonition but at the same time a symbol of courage, resourcefulness, and imperishable glory, as the epitaphs engraved on the plaques at the foot of the never-completed monument testified.[15] These stimuli are to be noted not so much for crediting the court with an awareness of the historical significance of the Columbian explorations but for suggesting that the geographical culture of the Este establishment may well have encouraged the collective imagination in this period of the city's material transformation.

It was Pellegrino Prisciani, working in his capacity as cartographer, who documented the moment of transition from the old to the new city with a splendid colored map. Executed in 1498, this map, oriented with the south pointing upward, represents the first topographical survey of the Este capital realized by perch (pole or rod) measurement, corresponding to a scale of approximately 1:8000.[16] In his own *Historiae*, the librarian, astrologer, historian, and philosopher also prepared space to accommodate four other chorographies. Three of these were to have depicted the Ferrara area before, during, and after the *rotta di Ficarolo*, a disastrous flood that affected the course of the Po River at the town of Ficarolo, about twelve miles northeast of Ferrara, in 1152; and a fourth would have shown the region in Prisciani's own time.[17]

Knowledge of classical geographic works in Ferrara, combined with humanist confidence in the practical utility of geography for understanding territorial changes and developing new measures to face them (urban planning and reclamation), can already be found in the third decade of the fifteenth century. The cartographic survey became a particularly refined and important tool for the reclamation of the marshy lands of the vast depressions in the various wetlands into which the region was divided. In fact, it was precisely through substantial capital investments to drain the waters from the countryside that, especially toward the middle of the sixteenth century, the states of the Po Valley engaged a wide array of technicians to plan and execute the reclamation of huge tracts of the territory. One of the first such measures worth mentioning here is the reclamation of the Diamantina (ca. 1513), 1,622 hectares (4,008 acres) located in the Polesine di Casaglia, northwest of Ferrara.[18]

2. "With Ptolemy, Bounding over Maps"

As he writes in *Satira* III—dedicated to his cousin Annibale Malaguzzi—Ariosto traveled over Ptolemy's maps, offering Renaissance cartography as the backdrop to the narrative engine of the *Furioso* and the adventures of its cast of characters:

> Chi vuole andare a torno, a torno vada:
> vegga Inghelterra, Ongheria, Francia e Spagna;
> a me piace abitar la mia contrada.
>
> Visto ho Toscana, Lombardia, Romagna,
> quel monte che divide e quel che serra
> Italia, e un mare e l'altro che la bagna.
>
> Questo mi basta; il resto de la terra,
> senza mai pagar l'oste, andrò cercando
> con Ptolomeo, sia il mondo in pace o in guerra;
>
> e tutto il mar, senza far voti quando
> lampeggi il ciel, sicuro in su le carte
> verrò, più che sui legni, volteggiando.
> —*Satira* III, 55–66[19]
>
> [Who wishes to wander, go, wander. See England, Hungary, France, and Spain. I am content to live in my neck of the woods. I have seen Tuscany, Lombardy, Romagna; the mountains that divide and those that close off Italy, the one sea and the other that bathe her. This is enough for me; the rest of the earth, without ever paying the innkeeper, I shall with Ptolemy go in search of, be the world at peace or war. And over the vast sea, without making vows when the heavens flash lightning, safer on maps than on boats I shall go, bounding.]

The place names recorded in the imaginary universe of medieval and early modern romance occur with considerable frequency on Ptolemaic maps, and the innovative edition assembled by the German geographer Martin Waldseemüller and others confirms this relationship. The Strasbourg edition of 1513 was the first modern edition of Ptolemy, and in addition to its twenty-seven canonical Ptolemaic maps, there are twenty new ones redrawn on the basis of contemporary sources, updated in their layouts and toponymies.[20] It should also be noted that in 1507, the same geographer published a *Universalis Cosmographia secundum Ptholemaei traditionem et Americi Vespucii aliorumque lustrationes* (Universal cosmography according to Ptolemaic tradition and the discoveries of Amerigo Vespucci and others), destined to become a monument in the history of cartography. In it, Waldseemüller invented the American continent, deriving its name from the Florentine Amerigo Vespucci, and demonstrated that he knew, or in any case had borrowed, his own sources from those used by the Portuguese master cartographer author of the *Carta del Cantino* (Cantino map, 1502).

The humanist Matthias Ringmann, friend of Waldseemüller and member of the "Gymnasium Vosagense" of Saint-Dié-des-Vosges, dealt with the translation from Greek into Latin of Ptolemy's *Geography* on the basis of a Greek codex provided to him by Giovanni Francesco Pico della Mirandola, with whom he was on good terms. In the edition of Ptolemy's *Geography* published in Strasbourg in 1513, both the dedication to and a letter by Giovanni Francesco Pico, dated 1508, are published, praising the inclusion of new maps illustrating the recently explored lands. The edition furthermore bears witness to the relationship between Ringmann and another friend of Pico, the Ferrara humanist Lilio Gregorio Giraldi, who, in another letter dated 1508, explains the Greek system of whole numbers and fractions.[21] An interesting study posits the hypothesis of the arrival in Ferrara of Waldseemüller's *Universalis Cosmographia* precisely through Ringmann.[22]

But at this point, it is necessary to briefly contextualize the importance of the rediscovery of the second-century CE work of the Alexandrian geographer Claudius Ptolemy by the fifteenth-century Florentine humanist circle, eager, as historian of geographic thought Patrick Gautier Dalché has pointed out, to reconstruct ancient space, to understand the geography of the Roman Empire and "reconstitute in the smallest details the spirit evoked in the ancient texts that they admired."[23]

The *Geographike hyphegesis* (Guide to Geography) is Ptolemy's most famous work, brought to Florence from Constantinople by the Greek scholar Manuel Chrysoloras in 1397 and then translated into Latin by his pupil Jacopo Angelo da Scarperia in 1406. With scientific criteria, the text fixes places on the earth's surface through a rigorous grid of meridians and parallels and provides instructions on how to construct maps by enumerating and dividing thousands of

Fig. 3. Claudius Ptolomaeus, *Cosmographia*, fol. 74r, 1471, ex libris of Borso d'Este. Paris, Bibliothèque nationale de France, Département des manuscrits, Latin 4801

locations within geographical and ethnographic regions according to their respective astronomical coordinates.

The geo-astronomical organization of Ptolemy's cumulative scientific work is useful for framing the interests that guided the scientist, directly aimed at understanding the physical-mathematical and geometric relationships between the structure of the universe, the terrestrial globe, and the restricted geographical space in which human life takes place. Knowledge of the earth necessarily came from the study of the heavens and astronomy; astrology and geography were considered substantially synonymous. After having synthesized the astronomical knowledge of his time in the treatise *Syntaxis mathematike*, better known as the *Almagest* (translated in the twelfth century from Arabic into Latin by Gerard of Cremona), Ptolemy organized a systematic table of the astral influences that link the sky to the earth with the *Tetràbiblos* or *Opus quadripartitum* (Four books), also translated first into Arabic in the ninth century and then into Latin in the eleventh. With the *Geographia*, Ptolemy achieved for the earth what he had already done for the sky.

The critical object of study for the Alexandrian geographer was the space inhabited by humans, as effectively illustrated in the Latin manuscript codex 4801 (f. 74*r*), preserved in the Bibliothèque nationale in Paris and having belonged to Borso d'Este (fig. 3).

3. Relations with the Arab World

As we have seen, the evidence of the transmission of Ptolemaic ideas in Arab geographical culture is clear, and the work compiled by the traveler and geographer al-Idrīsī for the Norman king Roger II of Altavilla represents one of the best early descriptions of the inhabited world after the *Geographia* of Ptolemy. The *Nuzhat al-mushtāq fi'khtirāq al-āfāq*, better known as *La delizia di chi desidera attraversare la terra* (The delight of those who wish to cross the earth) or *Kitāb Rujār* (The book of Roger), was produced in Sicily in 1154. This compendium is divided into seven climates or regions, and each climate is further divided into ten sections. Its texts describe each region from a physical, cultural, political, social, and economic point of view on the basis of information drawn from accurately verified written and oral sources. Maps were created for each of the seventy sections, which assembled together form a large planisphere, the so-called *Tabula rogeriana* (The map of Roger).[24] In some manuscript versions of the work, there is also a circular map of the world, oriented with the south at the top, in which the influence of the Alexandrian geographer is evident (fig. 4).[25]

Fig. 4. Al-Idrīsī, *Mappamundi*, in *Nuzhat al-mushtaq fi'khtiraq al-'afaq*, fols. 3v-4r, 1250-1325. Paris, Bibliothèque nationale de France, Département des manuscrits, Arabe 2221

There is no extant archival or literary evidence that would allow us to attribute direct knowledge on the part of the Este court of several important Venetian geographical works, but it will nevertheless be useful to expand our sense of the Ferrarese context to nearby Venice, where, already at the beginning of the fourteenth century, the works of Marin Sanudo, Paolino Veneto, and Pietro Vesconte played a fundamental role in the transmission of a geographic vision of the world strongly oriented toward the reconquest of the Holy Land and the resumption of mercantile traffic hindered by the Muslim presence there. Sanudo's *Liber secretorum fidelium crucis super Terrae Sanctae recuperatione et conservatione* was presented to Pope John XXII in Avignon in 1321.[26] A traveler well acquainted with Middle Eastern territories and their markets, Sanudo initially aimed to promote a new Crusade for the reconquest of the holy places in the manuscript *Conditiones terre sancte*, presenting it to Pope Clement V in 1309. The Venetian then continued to expand the work, incorporating the *Conditiones* into the more extensive *Liber secretorum*, promoting knowledge of the text "to the Pope, to various Cardinals, and Princes with the objective of inflaming their support of the great enterprise of the recovery and conservation of the Holy Land"[27] and, of course, also for the purpose of reactivating commercial traffic in the eastern Mediterranean.

In *Liber*, Sanudo elaborated a sophisticated strategic-military project accompanied by a wealth of cartographic knowledge encompassing "quator mappas mundi: unas de mari Mediterraneo; Secundam de mari et de terra; Tertiam de terra Sancta; Quartam vero de terra Aegypti," as well as the topographies of Jerusalem and Acre.[28]

Here we are interested in the function of the *mappa mundi*, the planisphere, explained by Sanudo at the bottom of the figure, where he writes that "bisogna sapere che questa *mappa mundi* non ha lo scopo di contenere tutti i dettagli, perché così sarebbe impossibile disegnarla. Ma è stata realizzata al fine di rendere comprensibile a coloro che non sanno come è fatto il mondo, con questa raffigurazione concreta, gli avvenimenti d'Oltremare inseriti nel libro intitolato *Secreta fidelium crucis*"[29] (it is essential to understand that this *mappa mundi* does not mean to contain all details [of the world], because otherwise it would be impossible to draw it. But it was created for those who do not know how the world is arranged in order to make clear, via a tangible image, the distant events included in the book entitled *Secreta fidelium crucis*). This circular planisphere is oriented to the east and divides the continents surrounded by the ocean into three parts: Asia, Europe, and Africa;[30] for the region of the Mediterranean, it is in close dialogue with navigational charts, an innovative development of medieval Mediterranean culture.[31]

The relationship between Sanudo and the Franciscan Paolino Veneto (ca. 1270–1344) likely dates to the years in which the *Liber secretorum* was subjected to the scrutiny of a papal commission, which included the future bishop of Pozzuoli (also known as Paolino Minorita). The friar wrote three universal chronicles: *Epithoma*, *Compendium*, and *Satirica Hystoria*, the last two of which contain the same maps reproduced in Sanudo's *Liber* as well as several textual passages that suggest at the very least a common source (fig. 5).[32] The maps are attributed to the Genoese Pietro Vesconte, active in Venice in the second and third decades of the fourteenth century, with the exception of a manuscript in the Vatican Library, Vat. Lat. 1960, ascribed to Paolino Veneto and containing maps of Italy and topographical surveys of Rome and Ferrara, this latter accounting for the relevance of Veneto's work to the argument of this chapter.[33]

The central role in the history of the medieval cartographic representation of the Mediterranean was played by two Genoese, Vesconte and Angelino Dulcert (or Dalorto).[34] In a recent study, the Catalan historian Ramon Pujades i Bataller assigned to both men the early diffusion of nautical charts by exporting to Venice and Mallorca—the two centers of mapmaking to which each had respectively emigrated, forcibly or by choice—the cartographic production technique that had been developed in Genoa.[35] According to Bataller, Vesconte's relocation from Genoa to Venice around 1311 initiated the production of nautical charts in the lagoon city, previously unattested there.[36]

As we have noted, medieval *mappaemundi* have an intimate relationship with nautical charts and bear traces of familiarity with Ptolemy's *Geographia*. In particular, the fourteenth- and fifteenth-century world maps of the Genoese Vesconte, the Majorcan Jew Abraham Cresques, and the Venetians Andrea Bianco, Albertin di Virga, and Fra Mauro are closely related to the great maritime and mercantile traditions of the period.[37] In the Venetian area, this tradition generated pioneering cartographic work that, from the nautical chart of the Mediterranean basin, the Aegean, and the Black Sea, and later of the northern European coasts, navigated and consequently known in their smallest details, expanded its borders toward the east, producing a "hybrid" globe, defined as such because it encompasses the mixed nautical influences of the Vescontean and Majorcan models as well as those of the ancient Ptolemaic tradition transmitted by Arab culture, clearly visible in the still-unexplored eastern coastal zones derived from the geography of Ptolemy.

The *Mappamondo catalano estense* is an important example of this Majorcan production that hybridizes the most up-to-date nautical charts of the Mediterranean and northern Europe (excluding the British Isles and Scandinavia), North Africa, the Aegean, and the Black Sea, while still relying on the Ptolemaic maps for delineating the coastal contours of the Indian Ocean as far as China. The relationship with the Arab world is visible in the drawing of an African continent still largely unknown but theoretically circumnavigable (contrary to Ptolemy), populated, with one exception, by Saracen rulers portrayed in sumptuous tents, its eastern coast in the process of being explored by Portuguese ships. Two sites present in Ariosto's chivalric romance stand out in this planisphere (fig. 6): the kingdom of the legendary Prester John (Ariosto calls him Senapo, in canto XXXIII), Ethiopia, whose adherence to Christianity

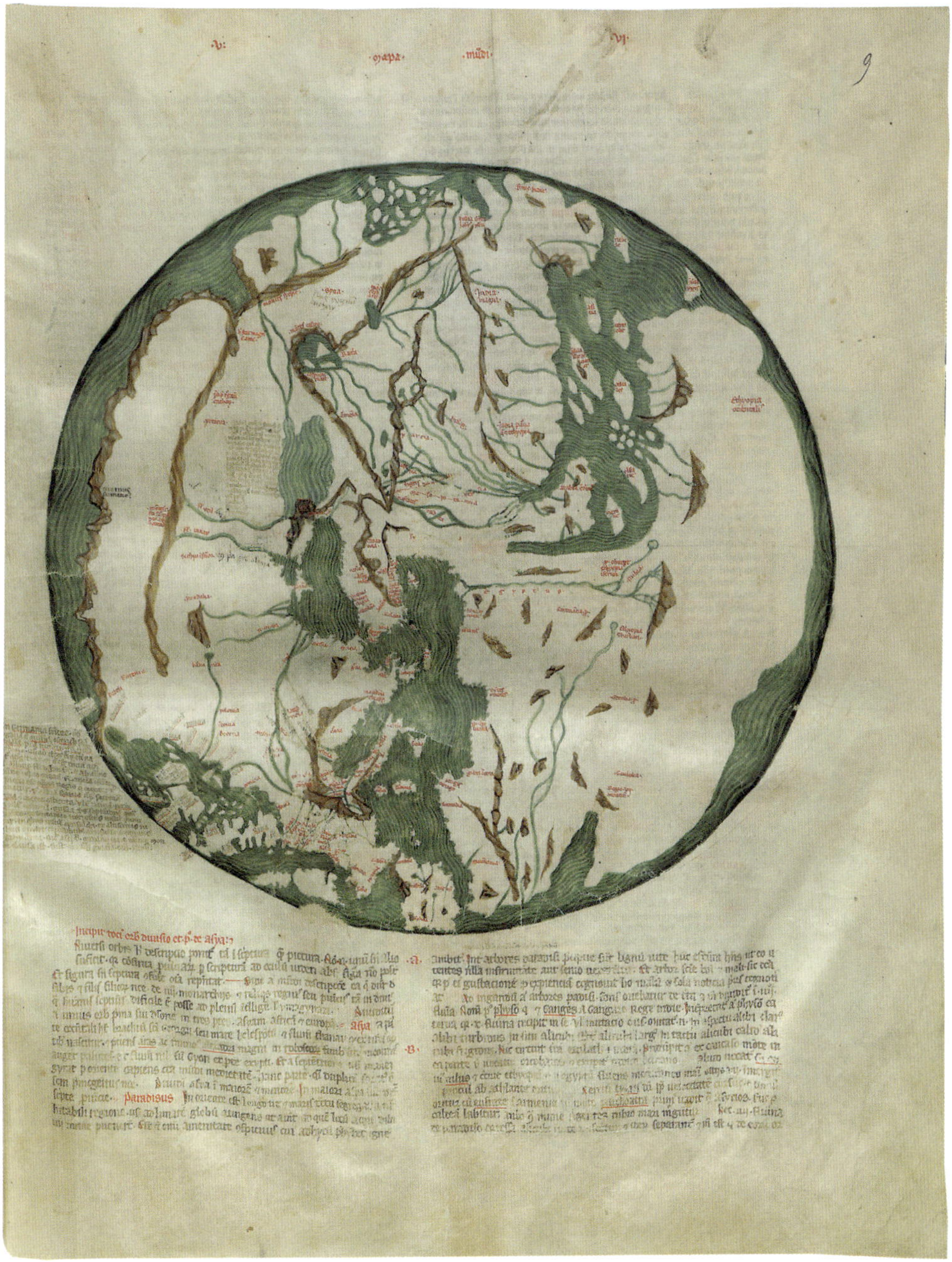

Fig. 5. Paolino Veneto, *Mapa mundi*, in *Chronologia magna*, fol. 9r, 1328–1343. Paris, Bibliothèque nationale de France, Département des manuscrits, Latin 4939

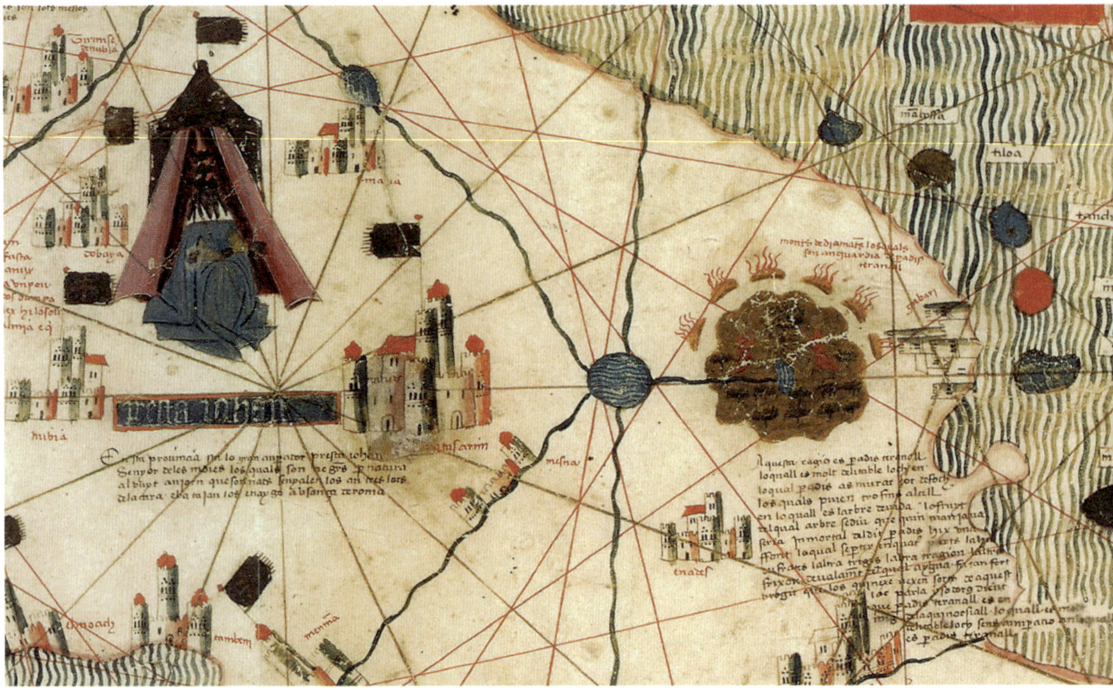

Fig. 6. *Mappamondo catalano estense,* ca. 1460. Detail with "Preste Iohan" and "Heaven on Earth." Modena, Biblioteca Estense Universitaria, Ms. c.g.a.1

had been the source since the distant Middle Ages of fantastical tales exalting its refined modus vivendi and culture, stories that also expressed hope that its people might one day be liberated from the centuries-old Saracen threat that surrounded them; and the "Earthly Paradise," surrounded by a wall of fire (from which, in canto XXXIV, Astolfo flies to the moon to recover Orlando's sanity).

4. "Words to Watch": The Geographic Itineraries of Ariosto's Characters

In previous studies, I have mapped out the itineraries traced by several of the extraordinary travelers who are characters in Ariosto's poem, in whom the cognitive restiveness and spirit of adventure that sparked Renaissance exploration seem to fully express themselves.[38] Ruggiero's Atlantic journey astride the hippogriff in the wake of the voyages of Columbus and Vespucci

> prende la via verso ove cade a punto
> il sol, quando con Granchio si raggira.
> —*Fur.*, IV 50, 3–4

[set course to where the Sun sets when its circle lies in Cancer.]

Lasciato avea di gran spazio distante
tutta l'Europa, et era uscito fore
per molto spazio il segno che prescritto
avea già ai naviganti Ercole invitto.
—*Fur.*, VI 17, 5–8
[He had left the European mainland far behind him, and had passed way out beyond the bounds which matchless Hercules had set for mariners.]

And his return to Europe and flying over the Asian territories described by Marco Polo and the Franciscan travelers Giovanni da Pian del Carpine and Guglielmo da Rubruck

finir tutto il cominciato tondo,
per aver, come il sol, girato il mondo.

Quinci il Cataio, e quindi Mangiana
sopra il gran Quinsaì vide passando:
volò sopra l'Imavo, e Sericana
lascio a man destra; e sempre declinando
da l'iperborei Sciti a l'onda ircana,
giunse alle parti di Sarmazia: e quando
fu dove Asia da Europa si divide,
Russi e Pruteni e la Pomeria vide.

Ben che di Ruggier fosse ogni desire
di ritornare a Bradamante presto;
pur, gustato il piacer ch'avea di gire
cercando il mondo, non restò per questo,
ch'alli Pollacchi, agli Ungari venire
non volesse anco, alli Germani, e al resto
di quella boreale orrida terra;
e venne al fin ne l'ultima Inghilterra.
—*Fur.*, X 70, 7–8; 71; 72
[complete the circle he had started, so as to girdle the Earth, like the Sun. / On his journey he saw Cathay to one side and to the other Mangiana, as he passed over great Quinsai. He flew over the Himavian range, and skirted Sericana to his

> right. From the hyperborean land of the Scythians, he turned in towards the Hyrcanian sea and reached Sarmatia; then, arriving at the point where Europe and Asia meet, he beheld the lands of the Russians and Prussians, and came to Pomerania. / For all his pressing desire to return to Bradamant, Ruggiero was unwilling to forgo the pleasure of discovering the world, but had perforce to pass by way of the Poles, Hungarians, and Germans and the rest of those bleak northern lands. Finally he arrived in far-off England.]

Ruggiero's flight reproduces, in fictional terms, Magellan's circumnavigation of the globe exalted by Ariosto in the octaves added to canto XV in the 1532 *Furioso*, with the "prophecy of Andronica" that reveals to Astolfo the great geographical discoveries of the fifteenth and early sixteenth centuries.

The words of Andronica reecho the latest news of the journeys of exploration contemporary with the revisions to the third edition of the *Furioso*, taking into account the time lag resulting from the challenges to the circulation of this type of information:

> Ma volgendosi gli anni, io veggio uscire
> da l'estreme contrade di ponente
> nuovi Argonauti e nuovi Tifi, e aprire
> la strada ignota infin al dí presente:
> altri volteggiar l'Africa, e seguire
> tanto la costa de la negra gente,
> che passino quel segno onde ritorno
> fa il sole a noi, lasciando il Capricorno;
>
> e ritrovar del lungo tratto il fine,
> che questo fa parer dui mar diversi;
> e scorrer tutti i liti e le vicine
> isole d'indi, d'Arabi e di Persi:
> altri lasciar le destre e le mancine
> rive che due per opra Erculea fèrsi;
> e del sole imitando il camin tondo,
> ritrovar nuove terre e nuovo mondo.
>
> Veggio la santa croce, e veggio i segni
> imperïal nel verde lito eretti:
> veggio altri a guardia dei battuti legni,

altri all'acquisto del paese eletti:
veggio da dieci cacciar mille, e i regni
di lá da l'India ad Aragon suggetti;
e veggio i capitan di Carlo quinto,
dovunque vanno, aver per tutto vinto.
—*Fur.*, XV 21–23

[But with the passage of time I see new Argonauts, new Tiphyses hailing from the lands which lie furthest to the West, who shall open routes unknown to this day. Some of them shall round Africa, following the shores of the black peoples right on past the limits whence the sun returns to us after leaving Capricorn; / they shall discover the limit of the long stretch of land which makes us imagine two separate seas. They shall sail along every shore and past the neighbouring islands of the Indians, Arabians, and Persians. Others shall leave to their left and right the Pillars established by Hercules, and, following the circuit of the sun, discover new lands, a new world. / I see the Holy Cross and the imperial standards set up on the verdant shore; some guard the storm-tossed ships, others are taking possession of the territory; they are chosen men—I see ten of them routing a thousand, and kingdoms beyond the Indies being subjected to Aragon; and I see Charles V's captains sweeping all before them.]

Accompanied by Andronica, Duke Astolfo (fig. 7), son of the king of England, travels a sea route in canto XV closely linked to emerging Renaissance scientific knowledge. They follow a coastal path toward the west that proceeds along the southern flank of the Asian continent and the chain of Eastern and Middle Eastern Portuguese trading bases, retracing the return journey of Marco Polo from China to Persia, where he had escorted a Mongolian princess to Hormuz before returning to Venice after almost twenty years of absence (*Fur.*, XV 16–17; 37).

After having passed beyond the Pillars of Hercules—*la meta che pose ai primi naviganti Ercole invitto* (the boundary set for the first sailors by invincible Hercules; *Fur.*, XXXIII 98)—Astolfo also flies over the principal African coastal centers well known in Ptolemaic (fig. 8) and nautical cartography, carefully reproduced in the medieval *mappaemundi*, and then on to Ethiopia and the kingdom of Senapo. A study by the distinguished Italian twentieth-century Orientalist Enrico Cerulli (who had lived, and worked in Ethiopia, even briefly governing the country) aimed to coherently reconstruct the path of the knight errant by comparing it with the itineraries of the Genoese religious and commercial missions sent to that part of Africa.[39]

In his *Lezioni americane: Sei proposte per il prossimo millenio* (Six memos for the

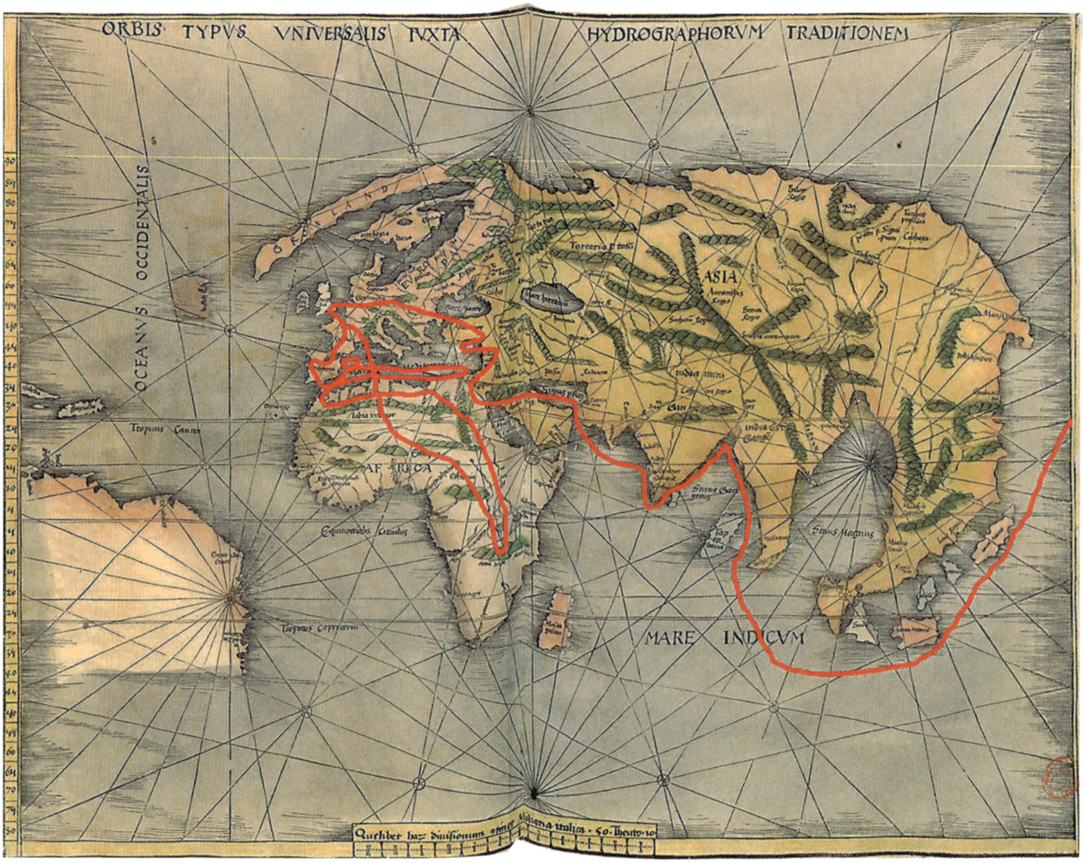

Fig. 7. *Itinerary of Astolfo*, elaboration by Massimo Rossi on the cartographic basis of the 1513 Ptolemaic edition of Strasbourg

next millennium), first published posthumously in 1988, Calvino identified five literary values to be preserved in the next millennium, standards that he wished to transmit to future generations of readers: lightness, quickness, exactitude, visibility, and multiplicity.[40] The critic and writer—native of Sanremo—brought these "categories" of narrative knowledge to light in focusing on the contrast with their respective opposites, while at the same time valorizing the latter. I am of the opinion that these benchmarks—not to be taken as strict "methods" of academic analysis—can provide constructive critical stimuli for investigating the informational capacity of historical maps.

The search for "lightness," Calvino's first value, signals a change in approach, to "guardare il mondo con un'altra ottica, un'altra logica, altri metodi di conoscenza e di verifica" (look at the world from another perspective, with a different logic, and with fresh methods of cognition and verification),[41] among which, I would suggest, is the cartographic document with its equally "light," comprehensive, and direct graphic result. The second value evoked is "quickness," understood as narrative time. In proposing this category, Calvino cites a novella by Boccaccio in which a knight, in telling a story, ruins both its rhythm and its style. Every cartographic document has its own lexicon and its own syntax, and respect for both leads to the immediate result of the intelligibility of the signs contained in it. Anything that impedes the agility of expression hinders both the reading and the perception of that document; the symbolic endeavor characteristic of cartography, graphic adherence to the pattern of reality, allows for a rapid and unmediated understanding of the nature of the object represented.

Yet another value is "exactitude." Calvino is unambiguous in this regard: To my mind exactitude means three things above all: 1. a well-defined and well-calculated plan of the work in question; 2. the evocation of clear, incisive, memorable visual images . . .; 3. a language as precise as possible both in choice of words and in expression of the subtleties of thought and imagination.[42]

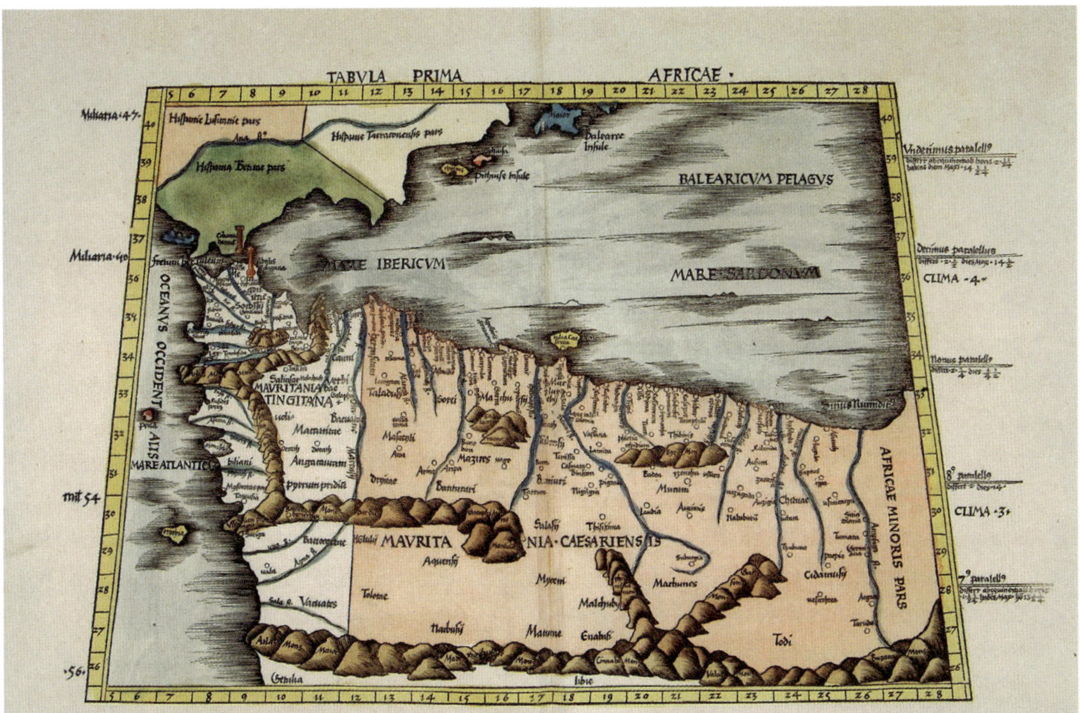

Fig. 8. *Claudii Ptolemaei viri Alexandrini Geographiae*, Strasbourg 1513, detail with Africa and Columns of Hercules

I believe that this further value, perhaps even more clearly than the others, is particularly apposite to the cartographic document, not only for the obvious considerations relating to its geometric accuracy but also for its surprising congruity with the third point: despite the variability of the graphic sign, even if encoded, we can see in the different maps taken into consideration above, but also more generally, the tension in the use of a common language for a universal understanding.

As for "visibility": "Possiamo distinguere due tipi di processi immaginativi: quello che parte dalla parola e arriva all'immagine visiva e quello che parte dall'immagine visiva e arriva all'espressione verbale" (We may distinguish two types of imaginative process: the one that starts with the word and arrives at the visual image, and the one that starts with the visual image and arrives at its verbal expression).[43] Here Calvino probes the relationship between the generation of images and discursive thought, literature and figural stimulus, and I am convinced that this is the foundation, indeed, the constitutive power of cartography, its principal duty to transform narration into images, and vice versa. To stay briefly on the subject, a projected map is designed to guide the potential reader/user along reliable interpretive tracks. Textual apparatuses serve the purpose of accompanying the reading of maps on a guided tour of the image. In this sense, texts become, to use the happy formulation of Svetlana Alpers, "words to look at,"[44] capable of creating a kind of shortcut between image and verbal description, translating space into writing.

The final value is "multiplicity." The theme of Calvino's concluding "memo" concerns the "romanzo contemporaneo come enciclopedia, come metodo di conoscenza, e soprattutto come rete di connessione tra i fatti, tra le persone, tra le cose del mondo" (contemporary novel as an encyclopedia, as a method of knowledge, and above all as a network of connection between the events, the people, and the things of the world).[45] The construction of a map responds to the necessity—vital for literature, essential for the cartographic document—of setting "obiettivi smisurati, anche al di là d'ogni possibilità di realizzazione" (immeasurable goals, far beyond all hope of achievement).[46] What more boundless objective than to portray the world according to a rigorous geometric scale?

In my view, the cartographic document, if reconnected to the historical and cultural context that produced it, is by its very nature a hospitable vehicle for these values, which are not limited only to the "literary," because it contains within itself a spontaneous narrative faculty directly proportional to the sensibilities of both its creator and its user. The matrix of relationships that cartography establishes is cultural. The map manages to transmit information the more its visual interlocutor establishes a dialogue of transversal knowledge with it:

not only technical or geographical knowledge but also historical, philological, literary, artistic, and so on. In composing the *Furioso*, Ariosto drew on literary sources from previous eras, classical and medieval, written in Latin, Catalan, and Old French, and in so doing, he transformed the chivalric romance into a contemporary novel in verse. Drawing on the geographical knowledge available to him at court, the poet established a system of multidisciplinary relationships, which in their deepest, hybrid, nature are an expression of the diverse civilizations of a specific geographical region, the Mediterranean, frequented for millennia by mutually permeable cultures in dialogue with one another, as demonstrated by the uninterrupted transmission of common practices and expertise well represented by the nautical charts appropriated in the world maps of Pietro Vesconte and Fra Mauro, in the *Mappamondo catalano estense*, and in the *Atlas catalan* by Cresques, these, in turn, elaborated through a consolidated web of maritime-mercantile, technical, and intellectual exchanges.

Nautical charts—as well as hybrid *mappaemundi* or nautical atlases—represent not only technical knowledge, as is evident in their paradigmatic role relative to their depictions of urban centers. Absent in Vesconte, which only reports place names perpendicular to the coastline, we find outsized representations of the first "vertical" cities in the Genoese and Majorcan maps of the early fifteenth century that portray the most important trading centers of the Mediterranean: Genoa and Venice.[47] Heraldic-vexillological decorative motifs introduced by Sanudo in the Vescontean maps help to outline an articulated political and economic geography of the Mediterranean.[48] Furthermore, invaluable textual tools describe the wonders of places and the customs of peoples often borrowed from literary sources that amplify the sense of the marvelous of a number of symbolic sites famous for their wealth.

See, for instance, these annotations in the *Mappamondo catalano estense*:

> prouincia laquall tania lareyna sabba ara es de sarains alarps . . . a questa terra es abundada detots bens delmo[n] en esta terra se fa vn aucell quisapella Fenix. . . . Enla antrade de lamar roga a vn castell loqual seapella adem aquij prenan la desena part deles species les quals vena[n] deles jindies abnaus, and puys de aqui van anlaciutat de cos. . . . A questi solda dababilonia es gran epoderos and senyoraia tota egipta e la terra sancta fins autauris.[49]
> [Province ruled by the Queen of Sheba. Now it belongs to the Arab Saracens. . . . This land is rich in all the goods of the world. In this land there is a bird called phoenix. . . . At the entrance to the Red Sea there is a castle called Aden. Here they take the tenth part of the spices that arrive from the Indies by ship and

> then from here they go to the city of Cos. . . . This sultan of Babylon is great and powerful and governs all of Egypt and the Holy Land up to Tauris.]

And in Fra Mauro's *Mappamondo*, we find "Arabia Sabea. Provincia nobilissima, ne la qual nasce mira, cinamomo e incenso e pietre pretiose e metali"[50] (Sabean Arabia, a most noble province, in which grow myrrh, cinnamon, and incense, and precious stones and metals). The Camaldolese friar demystifies the cliché of the presence of monstrous men and animals in Africa:

> Perché sono molti cosmographi e doctissimi homeni i qual scriveno che in questa affrica, maxime ne le mauritanie, esservi molti monstruosi homeni e animali, parme neccessario qui notar el parer mio . . . e per tuti queli regni de negri non trovi mai alguno me ne sapesse dar aviso de quelo io trovo scripto da queli; vunde non ne sapiando altro non ne posso testificar.[51]
> [Because there are many cosmographers and most learned men who write that in Africa, and above all in Mauritania, there are many human and animal monsters, I consider it necessary to give my opinion. . . . And in all these kingdoms of the negroes I have never found anyone who could give me information on what those men have written. Thus, not knowing anything, I cannot bear further witness to the question.]

The geographer al-Idrīsī never visited Rome, but his careful description of the capital of Christianity testifies to the derivation of information from Arabic and Persian texts that had a wide circulation:[52]

> Rome is one of the pillars of Christendom because it is seat of a patriarchate. . . . The perimeter of Rome is huge. . . . Inside the city we notice a huge church, built under the invocation of St. Peter and St. Paul . . . the length of this building is three hundred cubits, its width two hundred, and the height of the ceiling one hundred. The columns have been cast in copper, and the ceiling is covered with yellow copper. There are twelve hundred churches in Rome; the markets and streets are paved with white or blue marble. There are a thousand baths in this city.

The description of the city of Jerusalem exalts its beauty and its historical importance:

> Jerusalem is an illustrious city, of immemorial and eternal construction . . . we

reach the prison where the Lord Messiah was detained and the place where he was crucified.[53]

In the *Furioso,* as for its dueling heroes, Mohammedans or Christians, undifferentiated champions of courtly values, the toponyms of the poem's narrative also appear as symbols on a map, a series of uniform circles (obtained, moreover, from the punch used for musical notation), appearing in a seemingly endless list that traces continuous lines on a homogeneous plane, a succession of cities within an isomorphic Ptolemaic geography.

Vide Marocco, Feza, Orano, Ippona,
Algier, Buzea, tutte cittá superbe,
c'hanno d'altre cittá tutte corona,
corona d'oro, e non di fronde o d'erbe.
Verso Biserta e Tunigi poi sprona:
vide Capisse e l'isola d'Alzerbe
e Tripoli e Bernicche e Tolomitta,
sin dove il Nilo in Asia si tragitta.
—*Fur.*, XXXIII 99

[He saw Morocco, Fez, Oran, Bône, Algiers, Bougie, all proud cities, all possessing the crowns of other cities—crowns of gold, not of leaves or grass. Then he spurred toward Bizerta and Tunis, visited Gabes and the island of Djerba; he saw Tripoli, Benghazi, Tolmeta, right to where the Nile crosses into Asia.]

To contextualize, using a similar example from Arab culture, we can consider the cosmographical treatise entitled *Kitāb Gharā'ib al-funūn wa-mulaḥ al-'uyūn* (Book of the curiosities of the sciences and wonders for the eyes) from the late-fourteenth-/early-fifteenth-century manuscript copy, now preserved in the Bodleian Library at the University of Oxford, of an original created in Egypt in the first half of the eleventh century.[54] Chapter XII of the second book, in particular, contains an extensive account of Sicily entitled "Brief Description of the Largest Islands in These Seas and a Map."[55] Analysis of the text accompanying the map reveals that it is a compendium of the treatise by the Baghdad geographer Ibn Hawqal:[56] the schematic and serial arrangement of place names in the drawing betrays its source, a written itinerary, clearly visible in the almost mechanical transposition of localities (fig. 9).

Without reducing Ariosto's poem to a Renaissance travel book, in my opinion, the conscious use of cartographic works provided with textual apparatus,

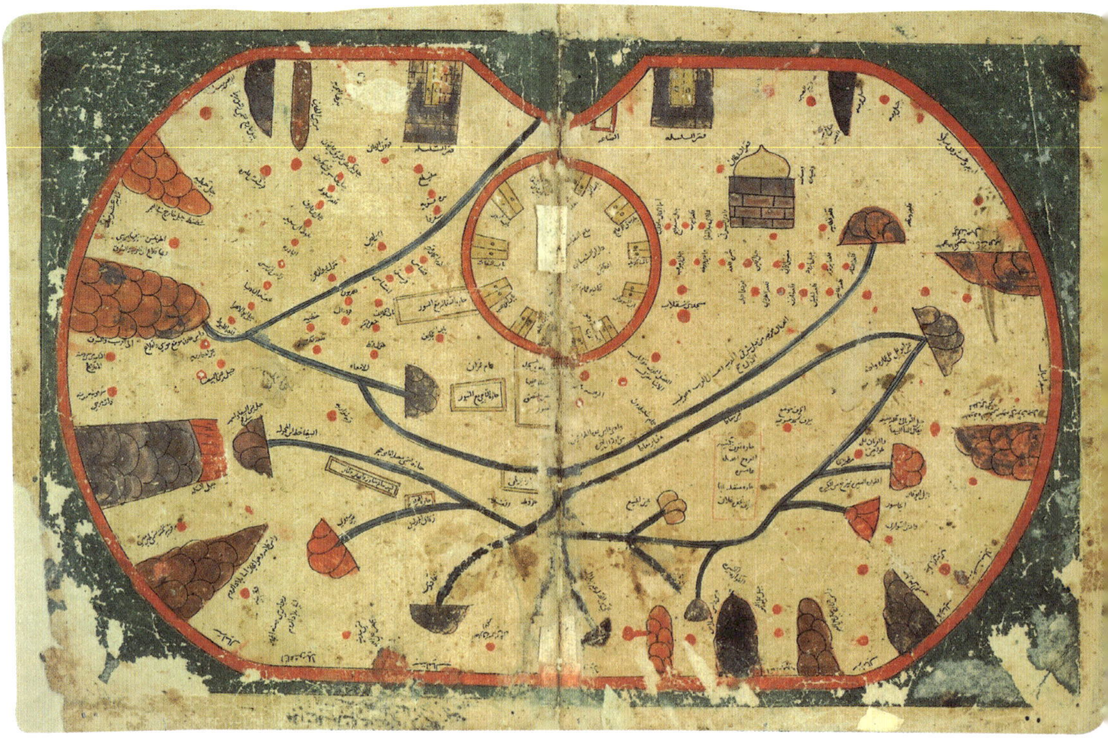

Fig. 9. Map of Sicily, late thirteenth to early fourteenth century. Oxford, Bodleian Library, Ms. Arab., c. 90

writings, and toponyms, redacted in several languages, belonging to different cultures and geographical regions, originating in antiquity (the *Geographia* of Ptolemy) or in more contemporary sources (nautical charts, hybrid globes, Venetian and Majorcan nautical atlases) contributed, tout court, to a radical revision of the chivalric genre in updating the concept of *ventura* (fortune), making the knight-travelers—Arabs or Christians, without distinction between them—traverse new and unanticipated scenarios, reinforcing the innovative thrust that Ariosto sought to impart to the chivalric tradition.[57]

This geographical reading of the *Furioso*, a discipline barely engaged with by literary scholars, can usefully contribute to countering the perception of an Ariosto in "fuga dai contrasti e dalle passioni della realtà per rifugiarsi in un regno di quiete e di fantasia" (flight from the conflicts and disorder of reality in order to take refuge in a kingdom of withdrawal and fantasy), as the historian of modern Italy Rosario Romeo could still sustain in the 1950s.[58] This commonplace unfortunately lives on in certain academic quarters, and within the context of the recent five-hundredth anniversary of the first edition of the

Furioso, it was considered necessary to assert that Ariosto was not merely a poet of "fables" . . . (an affirmation that) should without delay become an incontrovertible critical assumption. The stereotype far too widely disseminated at the scholastic and journalistic levels of a poet of mere fantasy, fabrication, and escape, should now definitively be rejected in favor of the premise of an intellectually committed writer, attentive to contemporary cultural and religious debates.[59]

Notes

1. "Il poema del movimento . . . movimento a linee spezzate, a zig-zag. Potremmo tracciare il disegno generale del poema seguendo il continuo intersecarsi e divergere di queste linee su una mappa d'Europa e d'Africa": Calvino 1995, p. 23.

2. "Un'immensa partita di scacchi che si gioca sulla carta geografica del mondo, una partita smisurata che si dirama in tante partite simultanee. La carta del mondo è ben più varia d'una scacchiera": Calvino 1995, p. 75.

3. "In ogni canto dell'Orlando furioso la mappa del mondo si dispiega tutta contemporaneamente sotto l'occhio del lettore": Calvino 1995, p. 81.

4. Jossa 2017. See also the contribution by Stefano Jossa in this volume, which invites us to reflect on Ariosto's religious motivations, entirely dismissed by the earlier criticism of De Sanctis, Croce, and Calvino, suggesting instead a more nuanced reading of the opposition between Christians and Muslims, necessary to advance the narrative movement of the poem rather than to create an ethical and ideological divide.

5. Vernero 1916, p. 63; see also Nori 1982, pp. 233–246. Regarding these questions, see my earlier study, Rossi 2006.

6. Biblioteca Estense Universitaria di Modena (hereafter BEU), codice estense miscellaneo α.H .L13 (= It. 844), cart, in folio, sec. XVIII, app. E, section dedicated to *Libri copiati, comprati, donati, dedicati sotto Leonello, Borso, Ercole*, cc. 193–198. Cited by Milano 1991, p. 88.

7. Bertoni 1903, p. 261; Milano 1991, p. 90.

8. *Mappamondo catalano estense*, BEU, c.g.a.1., ms., ca. 1460; about which see Bini 2002, pp. 25–32. The *mappamondo* of Fra Mauro, ca. 1459, is preserved in the Biblioteca Nazionale Marciana in Venice.

9. Bertoni 1903 notes the presence of a manuscript copy in Latin of Marco Polo's travel accounts in the libraries of Borso and Ercole I in the respective catalogs of 1467 (62, *Marcus Paulus de Venetjs de conditionibus et Consuetudinibus de Orientai. Regionu*) and 1495 (319, *Marcopollo in latino*).

10. See Rossi 2016.

11. See Pepe 1993.

12. *Carta del navicare per le isole novamente trovate in parte de l'India*, Modena, BEU, c.g.a.2, ms., sec. XVI (1502); Milano 1991, pp. 96–97.

13. Milano 1991, p. 98.

14. Folin 2006, pp. 51–174.

15. The inscriptions, transcribed by Giovan Battista Aleotti, glorified the works that Ercole realized in Molinella: the construction and restoration of the palaces of Belriguardo and Belfiore, the great work of reclamation, the "recovery" of the ancient theater, and the expansion of the city; see Tuohy 1996, p. 123; Rossi 1999, p. 853; Rossi 2000, pp. 241–243.

16. Pellegrino Prisciani, *Historiae Ferrarienses*, Modena, Archivio di Stato, Biblioteca, ms. 130, IV, cc. 20*v*–21*r*; in Folin 2010, pp. 99–120.

17. Pellegrino Prisciani, *Historiae* . . . cit., ms. 129, I, c. 41*r*; in Bondanini 1981, pp. 34–35: "Et prima tabularum: in prima aetate illa, loca iam dieta reprasentabit, altera ad scissurae Ficaroli tempora, illa deducet, tertia autem, post fracturam tantam, regionem nostram figurabit. Quarta et ultima, diebus nostris apartentem agrum ferrariensem omnem continebit" (The first of the maps will initially represent the places already mentioned above; the second will represent the time of the *rotta di Ficarolo*; and the third will then depict our region after this event. The fourth and last will encompass the entirety of the Ferrarese countryside in our own day). For Prisciani, see Rotondò 1960; Bacchi 1988; Remondini 1988; Rossi 1990, p. 164.

18. Archivio di Stato di Modena, *Mappe e disegni, Topografia e territori*, I, n. 21, perg. 560 x 300 mm, scale 1:21,950; see Bondanini 1981, p. 53.

19. Ariosto 2019, pp. 105-06.

20. *Claudii Ptolemaei viri Alexandrini Geographiae opus novissima traductione Graecorum archetypis castigatissime pressum: Ceteris ante lucubratorum multo prestantius. Anno Christi Opt. Max. MD XIII. Marci XII. Pressus hic Ptolemaeus Argeniinae vigilantissima castigatione, industriaque Ioannis Schotti urbis indigenae*. It should be noted that the 1513 Strasbourg edition does not bear the names of either Martin Waldseemüller or Matthias Ringmann, only that of Johann Schott (Ioannis Schotti); see Broc 1986, p. 10; and Battini 2002, p. 180.

21. Nordenskiöld 1973, p. 20. Unfortunately, the biographical entry on Lilio Gregorio Giraldi, Foà 2001, entirely neglects Giraldi's relationship with Ringmann.

22. Doroszlaï 1998, p. 40, though archival evidence is completely missing.

23. Gautier Dalché 2009, p. 161. Jossa (2019, p. 159) suggests thinking of Ariosto's cultural formation as more humanistic than chivalric: "curioso verso le novità della cultura più recente, soprattutto di area fiorentina, interessato alla filologia e alla filosofia, sulla scia delle lezioni di Poliziano, da un lato, e Ficino, dall'altro" (curious about the most recent cultural innovations, especially those emanating from Florence, interested in philology and philosophy, in the wake of Poliziano's thinking, on the one hand, and Ficino's, on the other), an observation that would appear to confirm Ariosto's interest in Ptolemy's geographical work as not limited only to utilitarian or targeted uses.

24. The silver disc weighing more than 100 kilograms (220 pounds) that was supposed to represent the image of the world on the basis of individual maps has not come down to us. For reasons of space, it is not possible to make here the necessary theoretical references to the geographical school of Balchkī and to the Ptolemaic components present in the works of Arab geographers, including Ibn Hawqal, al-Muqaddasī, and, of course, al-Idrīsī. See Tibbets 1992; and Ahmad 1992, in the foundational Harley and Woodward 1992.

25. According to the Turkish scholar Fuat Sezgin, al-Idrīsī, in fact, produced a map derived from those commissioned in the ninth century by the calif al-Ma'mūn; see Sezgin 2000, p. vii; Miller 1926. The image to which I refer is preserved in the Bibliothèque nationale de France, Département des manuscrits, Arabe 2221.

26. On cosmography and cartography in Venice during the humanist period, see Rossi forthcoming. On the *Liber secretorum fidelium crucis*, see Motzo 1947, pp. xx–xxii; Almagià 1980, p. 3.

27. Zurla 1818, p. 306.

28. *Liber Secretorvm Fidelivm Crvcis Super Terræ Sanctæ Recvperatione et Conservatione . . . Cuius Auctor Marinvs Sanvtvs dictus Torsellvs, Tomus Secundus*, Hanoviæ, Typis Wechelianis, apud heredes Ioannis Aubrii, MDCXI, p. 1.

29. Bouloux 2002, p. 62.

30. https://digi.vatlib.it/view/MSS_Vat.lat.2972, cc. 107*r*–113*r*.

31. Gautier Dalché 2001, pp. 17–18.

32. Bouloux 2002, p. 50. On Paolino Veneto, see also Huellant-Donat 1993. On relations between Vesconte and Sanuto, see Kretschmer 1891; Kretschmer 1909, pp. 110ff.; Almagià 1980, p. 3. The image to which I refer here is in Bibliothèque nationale de France, Département des manuscrits, Latin 4939, f. 9.

33. The most careful study of the maps of the city of Ferrara and its surrounding territories is still that of Andrea Bondanini, who nevertheless does not address the question of the possible knowledge of this manuscript on the part of the Ferrarese court; see Bondanini 1973.

34. Biographical information for this cartographer is scarce; see Quaini and Rossi 2007, pp. 48–49.

35. An assumption already proposed by Alberto Magnaghi with regard to Angelino Dulcert/Dalorto; see Magnaghi 1909, p. 127; Almagià 1980, p. 3.

36. Pujades i Bataller 2013, pp. 82–83. For a useful résumé of the origins and development of the nautical chart, see Sáenz-López Pérez 2015, esp. fig. 12, p. 25.

37. Abraham Cresques, *Atlas catalan*, 1375, Paris, Bibliothèque nationale de France, ms. Espagnol 30;

Andrea Bianco, *Atlante*, 1436, Venice, Biblioteca nazionale Marciana, ms. IT Z, 76 = 4783. Albertin di Virga elaborated a *mappamondo*, now lost, datable to 1410–1419; the *mappamondo* of Fra Mauro, ca. 1459, is preserved in the Biblioteca nazionale Marciana in Venice.

38. Rossi 2006.

39. Cerulli 1932, p. 20. See also Milanesi 1984, pp. 235–251.

40. Calvino 2002. See also my discussion of the text, Rossi 2007, pp. 120–128.

41. Calvino 2002, p. 12; translation in Calvino 1988, p. 7.

42. "Esattezza vuol dire per me soprattutto tre cose: 1. un disegno dell'opera ben definito e calcolato; 2. l'evocazione d'immagini visuali nitide, incisive, memorabili . . . 3. un linguaggio il più preciso possibile come lessico e come resa delle sfumature del pensiero e dell'immaginazione": Calvino 2002, pp. 65–66; translation in Calvino 1988, pp. 55–56.

43. Calvino 2002, p. 93; translation in Calvino 1988, p. 83.

44. Alpers 1984, chap. 5.

45. Calvino 2002, p. 116; translation in Calvino 1988, p. 105.

46. Calvino 2002, p. 123; translation in Calvino 1988, p. 112.

47. Pujades i Bataller 2013, pp. 228–229.

48. Pujades i Bataller 2007, pp. 140–143.

49. Milano and Battini 1995, p. 184.

50. Falchetta 2006, p. 267n407.

51. Falchetta 2006, p. 387n1043.

52. Casari 2011, p. 535.

53. *La Géographie d'Idrîsî* 2000, Climate 5, section 2, for Rome; Climate 3, section 5, for Jerusalem; see the description of al-Idrīsī's *Nuzhat al-mushtaq* on p. 205 for an explanation of these divisions of the text.

54. Savage-Smith and Rapoport 2007; see also Rossi 2015.

55. Map of Sicily, in *Kitāb Gharā'ib*, late thirteenth–early fourteenth century, Book 2, chap. XII, fol. 32b–33a.

56. The geographer and merchant Ibn Hawqal traveled for roughly thirty years in Islamic territories. His work *Kitāb al-masālik wa l-mamālik* (The book of routes and kingdoms) contains a description of Sicily, which he visited in 973.

57. The perception of a different alignment, and therefore a different vision of the world, on Ariosto's part would be significant should we interpret *il lato destra della terra*" (the right side of the earth; *Fur.*, XXII 24, 8) as the northern hemisphere (among other things, congruent with the use of the *Mappamondo catalano estense*) and not as the eastern hemisphere, thus rendering the poetic line an empirical-spatial reference to its protagonists in motion rather than a cartographic indication oriented to the north, as claimed by Spinelli 2015.

58. Romeo 1989, p. 36.

59. "Ariosto non fosse solo un poeta di 'fole' . . . dovrebbe presto diventare acquisizione condivisa. Lo stereotipo troppo divulgato a livello scolastico e giornalistico del poeta della fantasia, dell'invenzione e dell'evasione, andrà ormai definitivamente abbandonato, a favore dell'ipotesi di uno scrittore intellettualmente impegnato, attento ai dibattiti culturali e religiosi contemporanei": Jossa 2019, p. 159.

Bibliography

Ahmad 1992
Ahmad, S. Maqbul. *Cartography of al-Sharif al-Idrisi.* In Harley and Woodward 1992, pp. 156–174.

Almagià 1980
Almagià, Roberto. *Monumenta italiae cartographica: Riproduzione di carte generali e regionali d'Italia dal secolo XIV al XVII raccolte e illustrate.* Florence: Istituto Geografico Militare, 1929; reprint Sala Bolognese: Arnaldo Forni Editore, 1980.

Alpers 1984
Alpers, Svetlana. *Arte del descrivere: Scienza e pittura nel Seicento olandese.* Turin: Bollati Boringhieri, 1984.

Ariosto 2002
Ariosto, Ludovico. *Satire,* edited by Alfredo D'Orto. Milan: Fondazione Pietro Bembo; Parma: Guanda, 2002.

Aujac 1993
Aujac, Germaine. *Claude Ptolémée astronome, astrologue, géographe connaissance et représentation du monde habité.* Paris: Éditions du CTHS, 1993.

Bacchi 1988
Bacchi, Teresa. "Pellegrino Prisciani e la sua vocazione cartografica." *Schifanoia* 6 (1988): pp. 187–191.

Barlusconi 1977
Barlusconi, Giovanna. "L'*Orlando Furioso* poema dello spazio." In *Studi sull'Ariosto,* edited by Enzo Noè Girardi, pp. 39–130. Milan: Vita e Pensiero, 1977.

Battini 2002
Battini, Annalisa. "Gli atlanti del Cinquecento: Mercatore e la cartografia moderna." In *Alla scoperta del mondo: L'arte della cartografia da Tolomeo a Mercatore,* edited by Mauro Bini and Ernesto Milano, pp. 171–239. Modena: Il Bulino, 2002.

Bertoni 1903
Bertoni, Giulio. *La Biblioteca Estense e la coltura ferrarese ai tempi del Duca Ercole I (1471–1505).* Turin: Loescher, 1902.

Bini 2002
Bini, Mauro. "Dalla cosmografia classica alla cartografia del Quattrocento." In *Alla scoperta del mondo: L'arte della cartografia da Tolomeo a Mercatore,* edited by Mauro Bini and Ernesto Milano, pp. 11–63. Modena: Il Bulino, 2002.

Bini and Milano 2002
Bini, Mauro, and Ernesto Milano, eds. *Alla scoperta del mondo: L'arte della cartografia da Tolomeo a Mercatore.* Modena: Il Bulino, 2002.

Bondanini 1973
Bondanini, Andrea. "La pianta di Ferrara di Fra Paolino minorita." *Atti e Memorie della Deputazione Provinciale Ferrarese di Storia Patria,* ser. 3, 13 (1973): pp. 33–89.

Bondanini 1981
Bondanini, Andrea. "Contributi per la storia della cartografia ferrarese: Cinque studi." *Atti e memorie della Deputazione Provinciale Ferrarese di Storia Patria,* ser. 3, 29 (1981).

Bordin and Trovato 2006
Bordin, Michele, and Paolo Trovato, eds. *Lucrezia Borgia: Storia e mito.* Florence: Olschki, 2006.

Bouloux 2002
Bouloux, Nathalie. *Culture et savoirs géographiques en Italie au XIVe siècle.* Turnhout: Brepols, 2002.

Broc 1986
Broc, Numa. *La geografia del Rinascimento,* edited by Claudio Greppi. Ferrara: Istituto di Studi Rinascimentali; Modena: Panini, 1986.

Calvino 1995
Calvino, Italo. *Orlando furioso di Ludovico Ariosto raccontato da Italo Calvino.* Milan: Arnoldo Mondadori, 1995 [1970].

Calvino 2002
Calvino, Italo. *Lezioni americane: Sei proposte per il prossimo millennio.* Turin: Einaudi, 2002.

Casari 2011
Casari, Mario. "Decoding the Labyrinth: Rome in Arabic and Persian Medieval Literature." In *Rome Re-imagined: Twelfth-century Jews, Christians and Muslims Encounter the Eternal City*, edited by Louis I. Hamilton and Stefano Riccioni, pp. 534–565. Boston: Brill, 2011.
Cerulli 1932
Cerulli, Enrico. "Il volo di Astolfo sull'Etiopia nell'*Orlando Furioso*." *Atti dell'Accademia dei Lincei: Rendiconti della classe di Scienze morali*, sixth ser., 8 (1932): pp. 19–38.
Doroszlaï 1998
Doroszlaï, Alexandre. *Ptolemée et l'hippogriffe: La géographie de l'Arioste soumise à l'épreuve des cartes*. Alessandria: Edizioni dell'Orso, 1998.
Falchetta 2006
Falchetta, Piero. *Fra Mauro's World Map*. Turnhout: Brepols, 2006.
Farinelli 1992
Farinelli, Franco. *I segni del mondo: Immagine cartografia e discorso geografico in età moderna*. Florence: La Nuova Italia, 1992.
Foà 2001
Foà, Simon. "Giraldi, Lilio Gregorio." In *Dizionario biografico degli Italiani*, Vol. 6, pp. 452–455. Rome: Istituto della Enciclopedia Italiana, 2001.
Folin 2010
Folin, Marco, ed. *Rappresentare la città: Topografie urbane nell'Italia di Antico Regime*. Reggio Emilia: Diabasis, 2010.
Folin 2006
Folin, Marco, ed. *Sistole e diastole: Episodi di trasformazione urbana nell'Italia delle città*. Venice: Istituto Veneto di Scienze, Lettere ed Arti, 2006.
Gautier Dalché 2001
Gautier Dalché, Patrick. *Cartes marines, représentation du littoral et perception de l'espace au Moyen Âge: Un état de la question*, pp. 9–32. Rome: École française de Rome & Casa de Velazquez, 2001.
Gautier Dalché 2009
Gautier Dalché, Patrick. *La géographie de Ptolémée en Occident (IVe–XVIe siècle)*. Turnhout: Brepols, 2009.
La Géographie d'Idrîsî 2000
La Géographie d'Idrîsî: Un atlas du monde au XIIe siècle, translated by A. Nef and E. de la Vaissière. Paris: Bibliothèque nationale de France (CD-ROM of Oriental ms. 2221, Département des manuscrits), 2000.
Harley and Woodward 1992
Harley, John Brian, and David Woodward, eds. *The History of Cartography*, Vol. 2, Book 1, *Cartography in the Traditional Islamic and South Asian Societies*. Chicago: University of Chicago Press, 1992.
Huellant-Donat 1993
Huellant-Donat, Isabelle. "Entrer dans l'histoire: Paolino da Venezia et les prologues de ses Chroniques universelles." *Mélanges de l'école française de Rome* 105, no. 1 (1993): pp. 381–442.
Jossa 2017
Jossa, Stefano. "Con Ariosto, senza Calvino." *Doppiozero* (January 7, 2017). https://www.doppiozero.com/materiali/con-ariosto-senza-calvino.
Jossa 2019
Jossa, Stefano. "L'Orlando furioso nel suo contesto editoriale." In *"Dreaming Again on Things Already Dreamed": 500 Years of Orlando Furioso (1516–2016)*, edited by Marco Dorigatti and Maria Pavlova, pp. 147–172. Oxford: Peter Lang, 2019.
Kitāb Gharā'ib late thirteenth–early fourteenth century.
Kitāb Gharā'ib al-funūn wa-mulaḥ al-'uyūn. Ms. Arab. c. 90, Bodleian Library, Oxford.
Kretschmer 1891
Kretschmer, Konrad. "Marin Sanudo der Aeltere und die Karten des Petrus Vescont." *Zeitschrift der Gesellschaft für Erdkunde zu Berlin* 26 (1891): pp. 352–370.
Kretschmer 1909
Kretschmer, Konrad. *Die italienischen Portolane des Mittelalters*. Berlin: Ernst Siegfried Mittler, 1909.
Magnaghi 1909
Magnaghi, Alberto. "Sulle origini del Portolano normale nel Medio Evo e della cartografia dell'Europa occidentale." *Memorie Geografiche* 8 (1909): pp. 115–186.

Milanesi 1984
Milanesi, Marica. *Tolomeo sostituito: Studi di storia delle conoscenze geografiche nel XVI secolo.* Milan: Unicopli, 1984.
Milano 1991
Milano, Ernesto. *La carta del Cantino e la rappresentazione della Terra nei codici e nei libri a stampa della Biblioteca Estense e Universitaria.* Modena: Il Bulino, 1991.
Milano and Battini 1995
Milano, Ernesto, and Annalisa Battini. *Il Mappamondo catalano estense.* Zurich: Urs Graf, 1995.
Miller 1926
Miller, Konrad. *Mappae Arabicae.* Stuttgart: Selbstverlag des Herausgebers, 1926.
Motzo 1947
Motzo, Bacchisio Raimondo, ed. *Il compasso da navigare: Opera italiana della metà del secolo XIII, prefazione e testo del Codice Hamilton 396.* Cagliari: Università di Cagliari, 1947.
Nordenskiöld 1973
Nordenskjöld, Adolf Erik. *Facsimile-Atlas to the Early History of Cartography, with Reproductions of the Most Important Maps Printed in the XV and XVI Centuries,* translated from the Swedish original by Johan Adolf Ekelof and Clements R. Markham. Stockholm: Norstedt & Soner, 1889. Reprint New York: Dover, 1973.
Nori 1982
Nori, Gabriele. "La corte itinerante: Il pellegrinaggio di Niccolò III in Terrasanta." In *La corte e lo spazio: Ferrara estense,* Vol. 1, edited by Giuseppe Papagno and Amedeo Quondam, pp. 233–246. Rome: Bulzoni, 1982.
Papagno and Quondam 1982
Papagno, Giuseppe, and Amedeo Quondam, eds. *La corte e lo spazio: Ferrara estense,* 3 vols. Rome: Bulzoni, 1982.
Pepe 1993
Pepe, Luigi, ed. *Copernico e la questione copernicana: Opere della Pubblica Biblioteca di Ferrara.* Ferrara: Gabriele Corbo Editore, 1993.
Pujades i Bataller 2007
Pujades i Bataller, Ramon J. *Les cartes portolanes: La representació medieval d'una mar solcada,* pp. 415–418. Barcelona: Institut Cartogràfic de Catalunya, Lunwerg Editores, 2007.
Pujades i Bataller 2013
Pujades i Bataller, Ramon J. *De Génova a Venecia y Mallorca: La emigración de cartógrafos ligures y la expansión mediterránea de las cartas de navegar (s. XIV), ventitreesimo convegno internazionale di studi, Circolazione di uomini e scambi culturali tra città (secoli XII–XIV).* Rome: Viella, 2013.
Quaini and Rossi 2007
Quaini, Massimo, and Luisa Rossi, eds. *Cartografi in Liguria (secoli XIV–XIX), Dizionario storico dei cartografi italiani.* Genoa: Brigati, 2007.
Remondini 1988
Remondini, Anna Rosa. "Pellegrino Prisciani e il *Ferrariae Regiminis liber primus.*" *Schifanoia* 6 (1988): pp. 180–186.
Romeo 1989
Romeo, Rosario. *Le scoperte americane nella coscienza italiana del Cinquecento.* Bari: Editori Laterza, 1989 [1954].
Rossi 1990
Rossi, Massimo. "La cartografia del Ferrarese." In *Il Parco del Delta del Po,* edited by Carlo Bassi, pp. 163–193. Ferrara: Spazio Libri, 1990.
Rossi 1999
Rossi, Massimo. "Il contributo della cartografia storica per lo studio del paesaggio ferrarese nell'epoca del Tasso." In *Torquato Tasso e la cultura estense,* Vol. 2, edited by Gianni Venturi, pp. 829–841. Florence: Olschki, 1999.
Rossi 2000
Rossi, Massimo, ed. *Della scienza et dell'arte del ben regolare le acque di Giovan Battista Aleotti.* Modena: Panini, 2000.

Rossi 2006
Rossi, Massimo. "La geografia del Furioso: Sul sapere geo-cartografico alla corte estense." In *Lucrezia Borgia: Storia e mito*, edited by Michele Bordin and Paolo Trovato, pp. 97–138. Florence: Olschki, 2006.
Rossi 2007
Rossi, Massimo. *L'officina della Kriegskarte: Anton von Zach e le cartografie degli stati veneti, 1796–1805*. Treviso: Fondazione Benetton Studi Ricerche, Grafiche V. Bernardi, 2007.
Rossi 2015
Rossi, Massimo. "Conca d'oro: Mappe per una storia di lunga durata." In *Maredolce–La Favara*, edited by Giuseppe Barbera and Luigi Latini, pp. 88–100. Treviso: Fondazione Benetton Studi Ricerche, Grafiche Antiga, 2015.
Rossi 2016
Rossi, Massimo. "Riflessioni sulla riscoperta di Tolomeo e su alcune 'anomalie' del canone nella cultura geografica padana tra XV e XVI secolo." *Schifanoia* 50–51 (2016): pp. 63–78.
Rossi forthcoming
Rossi, Massimo. "Cosmografia e cartografia a Venezia nell'età dell'Umanesimo (XIV–XV secolo)." *Humanistica* (forthcoming).
Rotondò 1960
Rotondò, Antonio. "Pellegrino Prisciani (1435 ca.–1518)." *Rinascimento* (1960): pp. 69–110.
Sáenz-López Pérez 2015
Sáenz-López Pérez, Sandra. *La cartografía náutica bajomedieval y el arte de su realización*. Potes, Spain: Casa de Cultura de Potes, 2015.
Savage-Smith and Rapoport 2007
Savage-Smith, Emilie, and Yossef Rapoport, eds. *The Book of Curiosities: A Critical Edition* [of Bodleian Library, ms. Arab 90]. www.bodley.ox.ac.uk/bookofcuriosities, 2007.
Sezgin 2000
Sezgin, Fuat. *Mathematical Geography and Cartography in Islam and Their Continuation in the Occident*, Vol.3. Frankfurt am Main: Institute for the History of Arabic-Islamic Science, Johann Wolfgang Goethe University, 2000.
Spinelli 2015
Spinelli, Alice. "Intorno al 'lato destro de la terra': Nuove proposte esegetiche sull'immaginario cosmografico e geoculturale di Ariosto." *Babel* 32 (2015): pp. 1–18.
Tibbets 1992
Tibbets, Gerald R. "The Balchi School of Geographers." In Harley and Woodward 1992, pp. 108–129.
Tuohy 1996
Tuohy, Thomas. *Herculean Ferrara: Ercole d'Este, 1471–1505, and the Invention of a Ducal Capital*. Cambridge: Cambridge University Press, 1996.
Vernero 1913
Vernero, Michele. *Studi critici sopra la geografia nell'*Orlando Furioso. Turin: Tip. Palatina di Bonis e Rossi, 1913.
Vernero 1916
Vernero, Michele. "I concetti cosmografici e le cognizioni geografiche dell'Ariosto in rapporto a quelle del suo tempo." *Geografia* 4, no. 3 (1916): pp. 62–73.
Zurla 1818
Zurla, Placido. *Di Marco Polo e di altri viaggiatori veneziani*. Venice: G. G. Fuchs, 1818.

The Middle Eastern Intellectual and Artistic Context at the Time of Ariosto

Anna Contadini

This chapter discusses the aspects of Ariosto's environment that involve connections with the Middle East.[1] What is meant by environment is both the intellectual milieu—what was or could be thought about at the time, whether derived from scholarly inquiry, the transmission of personal experience, or inherited prejudice and myth—and the material world, the artifacts obtained from the Middle East, what they represented, and what reverberations they had over time in the new cultural environment. In both areas, we are confronted with processes: scholarly research enlarges the historical and linguistic horizons, allowing texts to be discovered or reclaimed, while the reports of merchants and diplomats add a leavening of realism with regard to contemporary understandings. Beyond the constants of sustained trading relationships, intermittent armed conflict, and religious antagonism, there is an increasing awareness in the Estense circles to which Ariosto belonged, as elsewhere in Europe, of the nature of Middle Eastern polities and cultures. With regard to material culture, we find both continuing acquisition and the circulation of objects and an interest in ornaments of Middle Eastern origin that is reflected, for example, in the bindings made for texts studied and written by humanists. In addition, objects acquired from the Middle East provide models that enrich the worlds of design and engineering and are gradually formed into collections that constitute a cultural vision.

Integral to the humanist endeavor is exploration of the classical past and, with all due caution, I should like to suggest certain parallels with the interests and patronage of the Ottoman sultan Meḥmed II the Conqueror. Indeed, further parallels might be glimpsed with the interest of the Jewish communities under Estense protection in early philosophical and scientific works in Arabic that were translated into Hebrew or preserved in Judeo-Arabic form.

1. Intellectual and Visual World

The Este courts of Ferrara and Modena typify the multifaceted engagement of Renaissance Europe with the Middle Eastern world, relating not only to the constants of trade, diplomacy, and sporadic warfare but also to the intellectual domain. Earlier contacts had resulted in the acquisition (and exchange) of goods and ideas, and these relationships were to continue to evolve through the fifteenth and later centuries. The conquest of Constantinople in 1453 and, less than a century later, the first siege of Vienna may have inspired fear of the Ottomans but did not end the peaceful interchanges that went alongside armed conflict. Trade was maintained, with its own circuits of knowledge, and further information, along with material goods, was circulated by diplomatic envoys. Others, too, attended the Ottoman court. A captive contemporary of Ariosto, Giovan Maria Angiolello (1452–1525) from Vicenza, even became a treasurer there and accompanied palace officers on various military campaigns. His historical works are important for the insight they give into the cosmopolitanism of the capital, Istanbul, and of the international circulation of people of different professions.[2]

The exploration of the Greek legacy that was part of Ariosto's intellectual environment was not exclusive to western Europe, for it also had its counterpart at the Ottoman court, more precisely that of Meḥmed II (H 836–886/1432–1481), where Greek administrators had prominent roles and where, under his patronage, a scriptorium operated alongside intellectuals active in preserving Greek scholarship.[3] Works on various subjects, not just in Turkish and Greek but also in Arabic, Persian, and Latin, were produced for the imperial library, and manuscripts continued to be produced there under the aegis of Meḥmed II's bibliophile son Bāyezīd II (H 851–918/1447–1512), including illuminated and illustrated manuscripts.[4] An eclectic variety of copies and translations were commissioned by Meḥmed II, who, in parallel with the humanist movement, evinced an interest in Greek learning and Grecian antiquities. A polyglot who knew Greek as well as Arabic, Persian, and his native Turkish,[5] he also had a cultural breadth that allowed acceptance of Byzantine and other modes of representation in art and architecture.[6] Indeed, he engaged Italian artists; and, as Ariosto might well have been aware, these included artists such as his contemporaries Gentile Bellini (ca. 1429–1507) and Costanzo da Ferrara (or Costanzo de Moyses, active 1474–1524), who were asked to paint Meḥmed's portrait.[7] As Costanzo worked in Ferrara as well as Naples, married a Ferrarese lady, and had his family there, Ariosto may well have known him personally.

Italian modes of representation were taken up by Ottoman artists. The

Fig. 1. Sinān Bey (attr.), *Bust Portrait of Meḥmed II*, Album H. 2153, fol. 145v, ca. 1478–1481. Istanbul, Topkapı Palace Museum Library

bust portrait of Meḥmed II attributed to the leading court portrait painter, Sinān Bey (fig. 1), dated to ca. 1478–1481, is interesting in this context. A close copy of Costanzo da Ferrara's medal of ca. 1478 now in Washington (fig. 2), the portrait resembles it in being rendered fairly naturalistically but is set against a uniform gold background that recalls those of Byzantine paintings and mosaics in its abstract quality.[8]

Meḥmed II's interest in portraiture was to be developed further by, for example, his grandson Selīm I (r. H 918–927/1512–1520) and in the 1579 portrait series by the court artist Naqqāş ʿOthmān.[9] This is mirrored, in Europe, by an anonymous follower of Veronese producing no fewer than twelve oil on canvas portraits of Ottoman sultans around 1578.[10]

Fig. 2. Costanzo da Ferrara, bronze medal of Meḥmed II, ca. 1478. Washington, DC, National Gallery of Art, Samuel H. Kress Collection, 1957.14.695

A parallel to this interest is provided by Italian humanists such as the Comasque physician and historian Paolo Giovio (1483–1552), a contemporary of Ariosto, whose writings on the Ottomans are among the most informative of the period.[11] Giovio's large collection of portraits of historical figures included several Middle Eastern rulers of various times, such as Saladin, and contemporary figures such as Meḥmed II and also the corsair Kheyr el-dīn Barbarossa (ca. H 871–953/1466–1546) together with his captain Yahūd Sinān (fig. 3).[12]

Fig. 3. Follower of Gentile Bellini, *Kheyr el-dīn Barbarossa and Yahūd Sinān*, ca. 1535. Chicago, Art Institute of Chicago, Worcester Collection, inv. no. 1947.53 (from the collection of Paolo Giovio)

Giovio included these prominent Ottomans in his *Elogia virorum bellica virtute illustrium*, and although the first 1551 Florence edition was unillustrated, a 1575 Basel edition published after his death contains woodcuts by Tobias Stimmer (1539–1584) that were based on Giovio's paintings.[13]

The Barbarossa–Yahūd Sinān portrait, previously attributed to Gentile Bellini but actually by an unknown painter, is particularly interesting in the present context, as it was the object of negotiations with Rodolfo da Carpi, nephew of Ariosto's friend Alberto III Pio (see below). In writing to Rodolfo in 1535, Giovio offered to exchange it for a portrait of Alberto III Pio.[14] It may be added that in the preceding part of the volume, entitled *Elogia veris clarorum virorum imaginibus apposita*, Giovio also mentions Ariosto and includes a portrait of him by Stimmer (fig. 4).[15]

In addition to portraiture, European curiosity about the Muslim world received increasing visual expression in paintings that frequently include elements (artifacts, items of clothing) drawn from the cultures of the Middle East.[16] Toward the end of the fifteenth century, the growth of trade and diplomatic links promoted by Venetian communities in Mamluk Egypt and Syria led to a widening of the visual range to include views of places and costumes of those regions.[17] Depictions of Mamluk dress and heraldic emblems,[18] for instance, appear in paintings by Gentile Bellini and his pupil Giovanni Mansueti (ca. 1465–1527), such as Mansueti's *The Arrest and Trial of St. Mark* of 1499, where we find Mamluk dresses and headgear.[19] Later, following the Ottoman conquest of those regions, Ottoman costume becomes prevalent, as in Jacopo Tintoretto's (1518–1594) *Miracle of the Slave* (1548), which inserts into his European setting figures in Ottoman dress.[20]

A widening range of geographical references is also characteristic of Ariosto. The "outside" world of the *Orlando furioso* is very large, extending from China to Syria to Spain, and has much to do with Turkish and North African lands.[21] Could this be a reflection of Ariosto's awareness of the threat from the Ottoman Empire and of continuing conflict along the North African littoral, where there were battles between Christian knights and "Moors," and various naval assaults on port cities?[22]

Fear of Muslims was generated primarily, however, by Ottoman expansion in eastern Europe, reflected in numerous visual representations in the form of printed images, woodcuts, and etchings, prominent among them portrayals of the "Turk" as a type. The printing presses were beginning to produce visual material, notably by Albrecht Dürer, that promoted alarmist stereotypes, and the heightened level of fear caused by the siege of Vienna in 1529 led to an increase in production of, for example, the depictions of atrocities in the woodcuts of Erhard Schön.[23] The "Turks" were perceived as successors to the Mongols, and scholarly speculation in Renaissance humanistic writings on the origins of the "Turk" invoked the feared image of the Asian steppe nomad. Conscious of the Ottoman danger, Renaissance scholars could emphasize, in some of their writings, that the "Turks" were bloodthirsty and cruel, a view given powerful expression in Ariosto's *Orlando furioso*: *di Dio turbata la serena*

DOCTORVM VIRORVM 157

Ludouicus Arioſtus.

LVDOVICVS Arioſtus nobili genere Ferrariæ natus, cum paterna hæreditas inter numeroſam fratrum ſobolem diducta, ipſi pertenuis obuenisſet, ingenium in literis vigilāter exercuit, vt certo nobilique præſidio familiæ nomen tueretur. Sed vti pari prope neceſsitatis, & gloriæ ſtimulo vehementer excitatus, feliciore certè iudicio inter primos Etruſcæ linguæ poetas celebrari, quā inter Latinos in ſecundis gradibus conſiſtere maluit: quod eius induſtriæ labor, cū eruditis ac idiotis latisſimè diſpenſatus, vberiorem præſentis præmij, & diffuſæ laudis fructum oſtēderet. Adhæſit comes Hippolyto Ateſtino cardinali in Pannoniam profecto: quū ille erudito ac illuſtri comitatu apud reges Hungaros ambitioſè gauderet: ſed iterū euntem, quū ſequi recuſaſſet, vſq; adeò grauiter offendit, vt penè implacabilis odij diſcrimen adierit. Receptus inde eſt ab

Fig. 4. Tobias Stimmer, "Ludovico Ariosto," in Paolo Giovio, *Elogia virorum literis illustrium* (Basel: Pietro Perna, 1577), p. 157. Regensburg, Staatliche Bibliothek, 999/2Hist. pol.792

fronte, / che scórse ogni lor luogo il Turco e'l Moro/ con stupri, uccision, rapine ed onte (must have vexed the serene face of the Almighty, for the Turks and Moors had overrun all their lands, committing rape and murder, pillage and outrage; *Fur.*, XVII 6, 2–4); and also *Perché Costantinopoli e del mondo / la miglior parte occupa il Turco immondo?* (Why is Constantinople and the better part of the world occupied by unclean Turks?; *Fur.*, XVII 75, 7–8).

They could also be seen as usurpers, to be contrasted therefore with legitimate neighboring rulers who might be potential allies against them. For Aeneas Sylvius Piccolomini (1405–1464), who became Pope Pius II in 1458, their barbarous nature was expressed through the epithet "Scythian," for the presumption of a Scythian origin could be related to a complex of inherited notions about barbarous races that were thought to represent a potentially apocalyptic threat to civilization and to Christianity itself.[24]

It is interesting, however, that Pius II also wrote a letter (not sent) in 1461 addressed to Meḥmed II the Conqueror, in which he praised the bravery of the Scythians, suggested that they had been lured into an alliance by the weaker, non-war-inclined Arabs, and argued that it would be advantageous for them to form an alliance with the equally courageous Christians.[25] Recognition of the valor of an enemy is a topos reminiscent of the equality in bravery and courage of the various opposed knights in Ariosto's *Orlando furioso*, especially Rodomonte, king of Sarza (Algeria), and Ruggiero, a "Saracen" knight who converted to Christianity and married Bradamante, a female knight of equal valor, thereby giving rise to the House of Este, the patrons of Ariosto (and of Boiardo before him).

At the same time, there was a continuing intellectual engagement with philosophy, medicine, science, technology, theology—and with Arabic and the other Middle Eastern languages in which they were expressed—that was part of the curriculum in Modena, Ferrara, and Bologna. Although Ariosto himself seems to not have attempted Arabic or any other Middle Eastern language, or to have traveled to the Middle Eastern and North African regions, there were people close to him who had personal knowledge of these places or languages and were intellectually engaged with the Islamic world. Besides the humanists mentioned above, it was at the University of Ferrara that his predecessor Matteo Maria Boiardo (1441–1494), who wrote the *Inamoramento de Orlando*, learned Middle Eastern languages alongside Latin and Greek, while the Este family had members who made the pilgrimage to the Holy Land.[26]

Manuscripts with classical texts of interest to the humanists were sought out, as well as translated or retranslated, by scholars such as Andrea Alpago (ca. 1450–1522) from Belluno, a physician at the Venetian embassy in Damascus and professor of medicine at the University of Padua (1521–1522).[27] Alpago is famous for his revision, published in 1527, of Gerard of Cremona's late-twelfth-century Latin translation of Ibn Sīnā's (Avicenna, H 370–429/980–1037) *Qānūn fī l-ṭibb* (Canon of medicine). In addition, as we learn from his nephew Paolo Alpago, he engaged in an extensive and arduous search for Arabic manuscripts, traveling to Cyprus, Syria, and Egypt, and found some of Avicenna's lesser-known treatises, which he then translated for the first time.[28] The role of such scholars was complemented by the expertise of émigré Greek teachers, who provided the linguistic competence and training needed to tackle classical texts. A major figure in this process was Cardinal Basilios Bessarione of Trebizond (1395?–1472), who participated as a Catholic advocate in the Council of Ferrara (1438) and the Council of Florence (1439–1445). A translator and commentator himself, he promoted humanistic learning, supported refugee Greek scholars, and, in 1468, presented his library, which contained several hundred Greek and Latin manuscripts, to the Republic of Venice, becoming the nucleus of the Biblioteca Marciana.[29]

Ariosto's intellectual milieu was further enriched by scholars who were also great travelers and had dealings with the Ottoman court. Like the characters in the *Orlando furioso,* they covered great distances around the eastern and western Mediterranean and had encounters with Europeans, Ottoman Turks, and Arabs. The merchant and chronicler Benedetto Dei of Florence (1418–1492), for example, visited Tunis and Cartagena and even ventured as far south as Timbuktu. He traveled through the Balkans to Anatolia and the Black Sea and stayed at the court of Meḥmed II from 1460 until 1467, when he returned to Italy, where he continued mercantile activities and frequented the courts of the Este. He wrote a *Cronaca* in which he records his various experiences and travels, including those in Turkey and at the Ottoman court, and his observations on them.[30]

Such scholarly activity, which also involved a network of corresponding humanists across the continent, was the extension of a long-standing tradition of intellectual inquiry. A major translation project was under way in Toledo in the twelfth century, providing Latin versions of important philosophical texts in Arabic and involving Jewish as well as Christian scholars, while major medical texts such as those by Dioscorides, Ibn Buṭlān, and Ibn Sīnā were being studied and translated from Arabic into Latin at the Schola Medica Salernitana already during the eleventh century.[31] From the early twelfth century, the Normans in Sicily were commissioning translations from Greek into Latin, from Arabic into Latin, or from Arabic to Greek and then into Latin.[32]

2. The Manuscript as a Whole and the Translation of Ornament

These texts, in their Latin versions, translated either from Arabic or from Greek, were to remain standard medical sources at least until the end of the sixteenth century, accompanied by the increasingly voluminous commentaries of doctors such as the renowned Sienese physician and botanist Pietro Andrea Mattioli (1501–1578), who was in contact with Erasmus and other humanists.[33] In particular, he added many comments and further material to Dioscorides's text and published first Italian and then Latin translations of it.[34] An impressive example of his Latin translation printed in Venice in 1565 and illustrated by Giorgio Liberale, is in the Estense Library in Modena (fig. 5).[35] It has a splendid red morocco leather binding executed in the same year in Venice in Ottoman style, with very deep mold-pressured medallions that give it a three-dimensional effect. It is a type of *cuoridoro*, a leather with decoration in gold, various colors, and varnishes and the whole surface then covered with a further light, transparent varnish.[36] The doublures are also decorated, but this time in a European fashion with, at the center, the coat of arms and blazon (*armi e impresa*) of Alfonso II d'Este (1533–1597), for whom the book was made. He was the grandson of Alfonso I d'Este, the second patron of Ariosto (the first having been Ippolito d'Este). Alfonso II was the patron, among others, of Torquato Tasso, who, following in Ariosto's footsteps, wrote the *Gerusalemme liberata*.

The Mattioli volume arrived too late for Ariosto to handle, but he may well have been familiar with a book that is fundamental to the understanding of the humanist endeavor in relation to Arabic: the *Hypnerotomachia Poliphili*. Published in 1499 by Manuzio with the Aldine Press, it is an allegorical work of

a

b

Fig. 5. (a) Upper cover in Ottoman style; (b) doublure with coat of arms and blazon of Alfonso II d'Este. Dioscorides, *De Materia Medica*, translated by Pietro Andrea Mattioli (Venice: Valgrisi, 1565). Modena, Biblioteca Estense Universitaria, Alfa Y.3.8

uncertain authorship (Francesco Colonna?) that contains the first Arabic printed inscriptions.[37] The visions (*hypnerotomachia*) of the young Polifilo are linked to explorations of ancient sites and monuments, with an emphasis on marble slabs containing a vast epigraphic repertoire. This imposing scriptural and multilinguistic manifestation is one of the most important elements in the work; most of the inscriptions are in Latin and Greek, but they also include four in Arabic and three in Hebrew (fig. 6).[38] They reflect the fifteenth- and sixteenth-century humanist endeavor to learn Arabic in order to explore Greek philosophical and medical knowledge mediated through Arabic translations. During the Renaissance, we witness, accordingly, a growing awareness of the importance of Arabic alongside the biblical Semitic languages. Indeed, we find already in the late fourteenth to early fifteenth century that Middle Eastern manuscripts were being acquired, for example, by the bibliophile Niccolò de' Niccoli (1364–1437), a Florentine humanist, collector, and member of the intellectual circle of Cosimo de' Medici, whose private library is now in the Laurenziana and Riccardiana libraries in Florence.[39]

This interest in manuscripts also extended to their bindings, which humanists collected, sponsored, or indeed produced. By the mid-fifteenth century, decorated bindings in Middle Eastern style were produced in Italy for manuscripts that celebrated the revival of classical literature and learning, in a new style of writing, the "humanistic script," the first exponent of which was, perhaps, Poggio Bracciolini (1380–1459) and which was developed by the abovementioned Niccolò de' Niccoli.[40] The bindings were characterized both by technological innovations coming from the Middle East and by innovations in the vocabulary of ornament.

The transfer of ornament could be effected indirectly through pattern books, which came into vogue in the early sixteenth century. Francesco di Pellegrino's *La fleur de la science de pourtraicture: Patrons de brolierie, façon arabicque et ytalique* (1530) contains, for example, a printed drawing of an almond medallion that could have inspired an imitation design from which recent technological advances allowed a large stamp to be cut for pressure molding.[41] Such a process may have been involved in creating the pattern of the central medallion of the Venetian binding in the Chatsworth Library, the 1520–1530 Fra Giocondo *Syllogie*, which closely resembles the field of a binding by the influential Turkmen binder Ghiyāth al-Dīn in 1477.[42] The pattern books of Francesco di Pellegrino, Peter Flötner, and others include multiple "Oriental" motifs (called *moresque* by Flötner and *façon arabicque* by Pellegrino). Undifferentiated with regard to origin, they are integrated into the European vocabulary of ornament, becoming

Sopra qualũque delle quale, di charactere Ionico. Romano. Hebræo. & Arabo, uidi el titulo che la Diua Regina Eleuterilyda haueami prædicto & pronosticato, che io ritrouerei. La porta dextra hauea sculpta questa parola. THEODOXIA. Sopra della sinistra q̃sto dicto. COSMODOXIA. Et la tertia hauea notato cusi. EROTOTROPHOS.

Da poscia che nui quiui applicassimo ĩmediate, le Damigelle comite incominciorono ad interpretare, disertamente, & elucidare gli notandi tituli, Et pulsando alle resonante ualue dextere occluse, di metallo, di uerdaceo rubigine infecte, sencia dimorare furon aperte.

Fig. 6. Three inscriptions in Arabic, Hebrew, Greek, and Latin above each of the three doors (from left to right): "Glory of God", "Mother of love", "Glory of the world". Francesco Colonna (attr.), *Hypnerotomachia Poliphili*, fol. h8r (Venice: Aldo Manuzio, 1499)

available to craftsmen working in different media to be creatively adapted and recombined.[43] Indeed, styles and techniques derived from Mamluk and Ottoman bindings, first adopted by Italian bookbinders, would spread throughout Europe. They included the introduction of pasteboards in place of wooden boards, pressure molding, the layout of ornament within a frame, the use of gold tooling and filigree, and even the adoption of more recent innovations such as panel stamping.[44]

Suitable models were provided by the Arabic and Turkish manuscripts in collections such as those of King Rene of Anjou (1409–1480); the Italian philosopher Giovanni Pico della Mirandola (1463–1494), who was of the Estense circle; and Diego Hurtado de Mendoza (ca. 1503–1575), the Spanish ambassador to Venice.[45] Yet the enthusiastic response to Mamluk and Ottoman bindings did not take the form of blind imitation, and although the resemblances are sometimes close enough to have led to erroneous ascriptions, there are identifiable differences in both design and decoration. For example, the Bodleian Library binding of 1460–1470 covering Petrarch's *Canzoniere*, previously thought to be Italian, has now been shown, by analyses of the sewing, by its tooling, and by the organization of its design, to be Mamluk.[46] It is of a type that could have served as a model for the doublures of Leonardo Bruni's *Rerum in Italia suo tempore gestarum commentarius* (1464–1465) in the Marciana Library; its organization is of Mamluk derivation, although in elements of its design, such as the cloud collar, the binding appears to be inspired by Ottoman bindings of the first half of the fifteenth century.[47] But the little resin pearls covering the filigree of the doublures are a decorative feature not found on Middle Eastern bindings (fig. 7).

Books may even have been sent to the Middle East to be bound. For example, Hobson has suggested that a volume in the Biblioteca Marciana, later owned by the Venetian historian Marin Sanudo the Younger (1466–1536), which has a Mamluk or North African–style binding (with a flap), was bound in Egypt.[48] He also identified two European books (a copy of the Aldine Press edition of Catullus, Tibullus, and Propertius (1502) and the *Horae Beata Mariae Virginis*, printed in Paris in 1505) as having Ottoman sewing and bindings; presumably, then, they were bound in Istanbul.[49]

It is also possible to identify a group of humanists who were interested in covering their translations or transcriptions of classical works with Middle Eastern–inspired bindings. One was Felice Feliciano (1433–1479) from Verona, who knew Leonardo Bruni, Poggio Bracciolini, and many other scholars, a humanist interested in the archaeology of Roman antiquities, of which he made drawings, including epigraphical ones. He was also a scribe, illuminator,

Fig. 7. Filigree doublure in early Ottoman style, probably made in Bologna. Leonardo Bruni, *Rerum in Italia suo tempore gestarum commentarius*, 1464–1465. Venice, Biblioteca Marciana, Lat. X, 117 (= 3844)

bookbinder, and wood carver who worked in several important centers such as Ferrara, Venice, Rome, Bologna, and Padua.[50] To Feliciano may be attributed the bindings of the Bruni manuscript in the Marciana, mentioned above, and of the *Collectio Antiquitatum* of Giovanni Marcanova (1418–1467), another of the humanist group in Bologna, in the Estense Library in Modena.[51] To Feliciano is also attributable the calligraphy, in the "humanistic script", of the beginning of the text of the Bruni manuscript, written while he was in Bologna between 1464–1465, so it is probable that both bindings were made there and at that time. In the sumptuous Modena codex, carried out by an atelier of copyists probably guided by Feliciano, the date given in the frontispiece is 1465.[52] A collection of beautiful pen drawings and watercolors of antiquities, on parchment, its binding is also extraordinary, providing a second rare example, alongside the Bruni binding, of plates decorated using a Middle Eastern layout and

a

b

c

Fig. 8. (a) Upper cover; (b) filigree doublure; (c) detail of filigree. Binding in early Ottoman style, probably made in Bologna. Giovanni Marcanova, *Collectio Antiquitatum*, 1465. Modena, Biblioteca Estense Universitaria, Alfa L.5.15

design, with the interior ones in filigree with dots of resin on the cutouts (while the exterior ones are decorated with both blind and gold tooling) (fig. 8). They constitute a Renaissance prototype, as they are the earliest European bindings with filigree in Middle Eastern style.

Further testimony of a diffusion of taste in Middle Eastern style is given by the fifteenth-century binding that covers the parchment translation into Latin of *Dionysius Areopagita* by Ambrosius Monachus (from Florence), whose name appears on the back plate (fig. 9).[53] The binding, decorated with blind and gold tooling (gold leaf) and with a layout approximating that of a Mamluk binding, has the Hungarian coat of arms at the center of both medallions, as it was done for King Matthias Corvinus (1443–1490). The Este had a close relationship with Hungary, especially through Corvinus's wife, Beatrice d'Aragona, who strongly supported her nephew Ippolito d'Este, Ariosto's first patron.[54] This is another

Fig. 9. Upper cover with blind and gold tooling in Mamluk style with the Hungarian coat of arms in the center. Ambrosius Monachus, *Dionysius Areopagita*, fifteenth century. Modena, Biblioteca Estense Universitaria, Alfa U.5.24

example of a non-precise copy of a Middle Eastern binding and at the same time an instance of the humanist interest in classical works that goes beyond Italy to emerge as a pan-European concern.

Ornament in Middle Eastern style becomes integral to European vocabulary but does not retain distinctive features that would associate it with specific Middle Eastern localities and objects. The binding that covers a musical manuscript of motets demonstrates this point (fig. 10).[55] Datable to the sixteenth century, it is an exquisite example of pressed design gilded with gold leaf that incorporates elements often labeled *arabesche* or *alla moresca*, which are now integrated into the global vocabulary of ornament and can be creatively combined with other

Fig. 10. Upper cover with layout and gilded design inspired by Middle Eastern bindings, with the eagle of the Este in the center. *Mottetti a quattro voci di autori diversi*, early sixteenth century. Modena, Biblioteca Estense Universitaria, Mus. C.313.1–4

design features in new ways by Italian and other Western artists. This process is further exemplified in the *Collectio Antiquitatum* of Giovanni Marcanova in the Estense Library of 1465, mentioned above. It contains several decorations that are obviously inspired by Middle Eastern models, such as the beautiful interlace on folio 114 (fig. 11a), which I would associate with, for example, the gold interlace in the fresco on the ceiling of the Sala delle Asse painted by Leonardo da Vinci in around 1498 (fig. 11c) and with the interlace painted on certain majolica plates, such as the example decorated *alla moresca* in Siena in 1525 (fig. 11b).[56] It is thus testimony to the transmateriality of these types of ornament: freed from one medium, they can be applied to others.

a b c

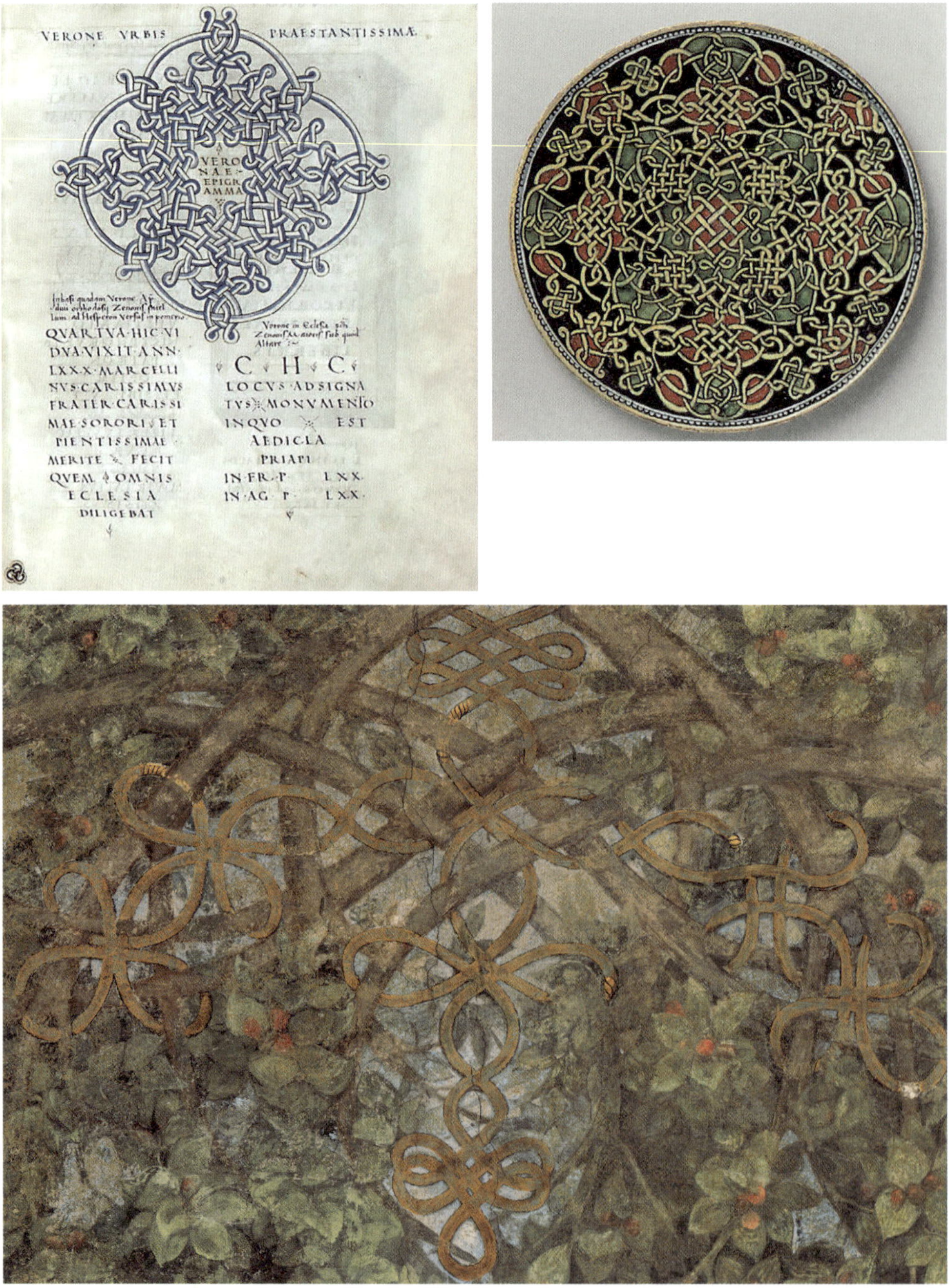

Fig. 11. (a) Interlace ornament in Giovanni Marcanova, *Collectio Antiquitatum*, fol. 114, 1465. Modena, Biblioteca Estense Universitaria, Alfa L.5.15. (b) Interlace on majolica plate decorated *alla moresca*, Siena, 1525. Amsterdam, Rijksmuseum, inv. no. BK-NM-13136. (c) Detail of interlace on mural painting by Leonardo da Vinci and/or workshop, Sala delle Asse, ca. 1498, restored and repainted in 1902 (Edoardo Rusca), restored in 1955 (Ottemi della Rotta). Milan, Castello Sforzesco

Such types of decoration are to be found not only in pattern books but also in various embroidery books, further contributing to the circulation of ornament, ranging from those in the Victoria and Albert Museum by the Venetians Lunardo Ferro and Amadio Novello, both dated 1559, to the *Libro dei ricami* in the Museo del Tessuto in Prato, dated 1570.[57] Having the outlines pricked for the transfer of the design by pouncing, the *Libro dei ricami* contains material similar to Pellegrino's drawings and points to the long-lasting success of Middle Eastern–inspired designs. Along with the manuscripts, publications of this nature are testimony to a taste for Middle Eastern design among humanist intellectuals of fifteenth- and sixteenth-century Italy, not least in the environment with which Ariosto was familiar.

His patrons, the Este family, included among their number bibliophiles, with the result that a large library, also containing books on Asia and the outside world, had been accumulated, starting from the family's early days.[58] Beginning with classical, geographical sources such as Ptolemy's (100 CE–ca. 170 CE) *Geography*, translated into Latin by Jacopo Angelo da Scarperia and made for Borso d'Este in 1466, and Strabo's (63 BCE–23 CE) *Geography*, translated by the humanist Guarino da Verona in Ferrara,[59] it then expanded to include actual "Oriental" manuscripts collected by Alberto III Pio, prince of Carpi (1475–1531), becoming one of the most important libraries of the period. Educated in Ferrara, where he was a student companion of Ariosto, he had tutors of the stature of the humanist Giovanni Pico della Mirandola (1463–1494) and Aldo Manuzio (1449–1515), who was later to establish the famous Aldine Press (Tipografia Aldina) in Venice, with projects funded by Alberto.[60]

Although Alberto's collection of objects seems not to contain Middle Eastern items,[61] a number of Middle Eastern manuscripts appear alongside books on Asia and a great number of Greek and Latin works in his vast collection of manuscripts and printed books. The range of the "Oriental" manuscripts suggests that in addition to his knowledge of Latin, Greek, and Hebrew, Alberto probably wanted to learn Arabic and Syriac, too.[62] His collection is now dispersed in various libraries, above all the Vatican Library,[63] but here attention will be primarily on the "Oriental" manuscripts held in the Biblioteca Estense.

3. Middle Eastern Manuscripts and Artifacts in the Estense and Other Collections

Alberto's intellectual humanist friendship with Ariosto is worth highlighting here, as it is his imposing library collection that contained the original nucleus of the "Oriental" part of the Estense library, collected during their lifetimes.

Fig. 12. Al-Bukhārī, *Ṣaḥīḥ*, vol. 4, fol. 1v., Spain, dated 1466. Modena, Biblioteca Estense Universitaria, Alfa S.7.11

Of this first nucleus, six manuscripts have been identified as Arabic, five as Judeo-Arabic, five as Hebrew, and two as Syriac.[64] Unfortunately, in the course of subsequent rebindings, all the original bindings had been detached and lost. The nucleus does not appear to be the fruit of a particular policy of acquisition. The Hebrew manuscripts presumably came from the Jewish community of Ferrara (or Bologna), which prospered between the thirteenth and fifteenth centuries under the protection of the dukes of Este, who, in 1451, refused to expel the Jews as demanded by a papal decree.[65]

Fig. 13. Leo Africanus, Epistles of St. Paul, fols. 1v and 2r, in Arabic, 1521. Modena, Biblioteca Estense Universitaria, Alfa J.6.3

Prominent among the Arabic manuscripts is al-Bukhārī's *Ṣaḥīḥ* (an authoritative collection of the sayings and doings of the Prophet Muḥammad) in Maghribi script, the fourth volume of which has a colophon that mentions al-Bukhārī's authorship and the date H 870/1466 (fig. 12).[66] Others of note include a translation from Coptic into Arabic of the Epistles of Saint Paul, dated H 927/1521, made for Alberto III Carpi by Leo Africanus (fig. 13).[67] It may be placed within a humanistic environment where the Epistles inspired an interest in Eastern Christianity and provided a point of intersection between three faiths and their diverse linguistic forms of expression.[68] Likewise, a manuscript of the Gospels in Syriac, written for Alberto in Rome in 1518,[69] may be considered a further expression of the interest in Middle Eastern languages that characterized the religious-intellectual humanist approach.

The Hebrew first nucleus, later enriched by the addition of further manuscripts, including scrolls, some illustrated,[70] reflects a European concern with language as a branch of biblical studies. One, for example, is a commentary on Isaiah,[71] while another contains the Pentateuch and the Prophets.[72]

But the collection also represents a Jewish parallel to humanist inquiries, as

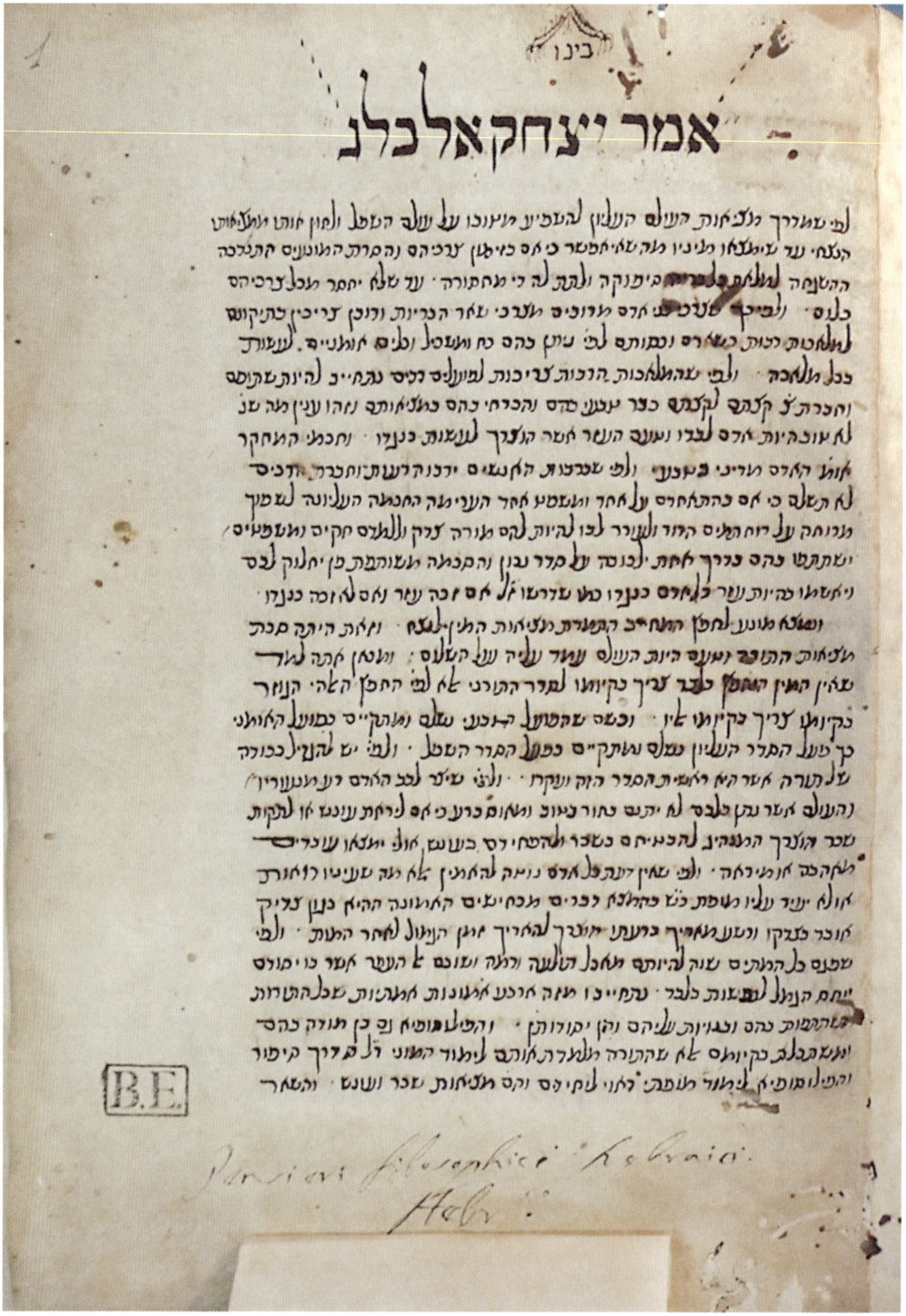
בינו

אמר יצחק אלבלג

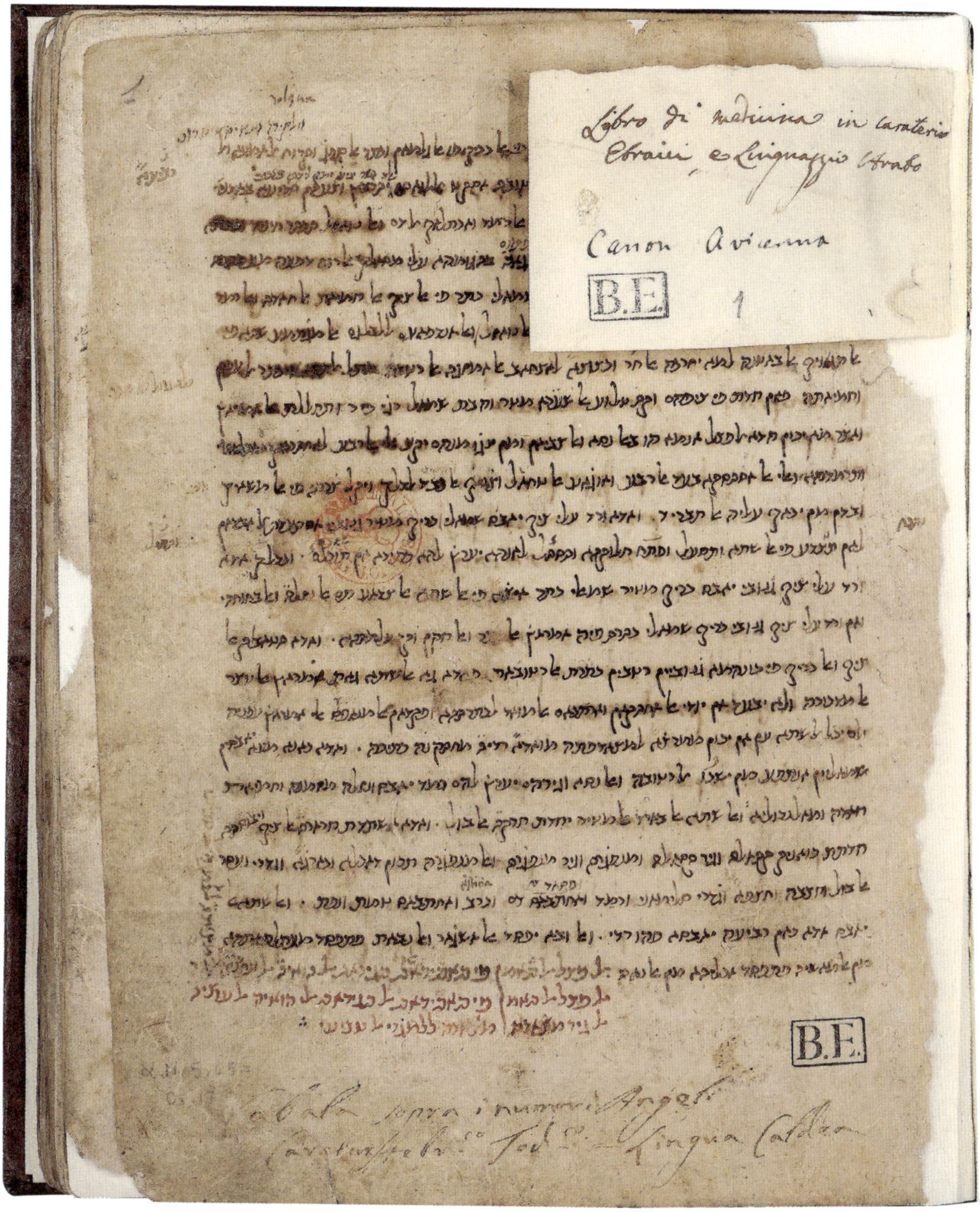

Facing page
Fig. 14. Hebrew translation of al-Ghazālī, *Maqāṣid al-falāsifa* (The aims of philosophers), fol. 1r, late fifteenth century. Modena, Biblioteca Estense Universitaria, Alfa N.8.14

Above
Fig. 15. Fragment of Ibn Sīnā's *Qānūn fī l-ṭibb* (Canon of medicine), fol. 1r, in Judeo-Arabic, (Arabic written in Hebrew script), Spain(?), date uncertain. Modena, Biblioteca Estense Universitaria, Alfa N.5.15

Fig. 16. Episode at the Schola Medica Salernitana. From an illustrated Hebrew translation from the Arabic of Ibn Sīnā's *Qānūn fī l-ṭibb* (Canon of medicine), fol. 210r, produced in Ferrara or Venice, first half of the fifteenth century. Bologna, Biblioteca Universitaria, ms. 2197

it includes Hebrew translations of the *Qānūn* of Ibn Sīnā, mentioned above, and other texts, most probably produced in 1487;[73] of the commentary on Aristotle's treatise on meteorology by Ibn Rushd (Averroes, H 520–595/1126–1198);[74] and of the *Maqāṣid al-falāsifa* (The aims of philosophers), by al-Ghazālī (ca. H 450–505/1058–1111), datable to the late fifteenth century (fig. 14).[75]

The Hebrew translation of Ibn Sīnā's *Qānūn* in the University Library in Bologna is a further confirmation.[76] This parchment manuscript, datable to the first half of the fifteenth century, is a full translation of all five books of the *Qānūn*, completed in 1279 by a well-known translator, Natan ben Eliʿezer ha-Meʾati. The manuscript is exceptional, being lavishly illuminated and illustrated. According to Tamani, the patron and the scribe(s) were Jews, while the painters were not, as it was the custom among Jewish bankers and doctors to have their books decorated in workshops of Christian artists.[77] The paintings have been attributed to different artistic centers, with Ferrara or Venice as the most recent suggestions. The painting on fol. 210r (fig. 16) is particularly relevant here: it is a representation of the Schola Medica Salernitana and of a specific episode linked to it.[78] While the lateral, smaller panels represent the four ages of man and the four seasons, the subject matter of the central, larger panel, enacted in front of the Schola Medica, with, in the background, the Gulf of Salerno, is the farewell of King Robert II, duke of Normandy from the doctors who treated him, while the corpse of his wife, Sibylla, who had heroically saved his life by sucking the poison out of his wound, is represented naked (but with a crown on her head) in the lower left corner, ready to be placed in a coffin.

It is striking that alongside the Hebrew translations, we also find texts in Judeo-Arabic that further demonstrate a continuing interest in Arabic scholarship within the Jewish communities. They are either Arabic texts or classical texts in Arabic translation but in Hebrew script. They include, for instance, Ibn Rushd's commentary on Aristotle's *De generatione et corruptione*, dated 1356,[79] and fragments of the *Qānūn* of Ibn Sīnā, of uncertain date,[80] both in scripts associated with Spain (according to Bernheimer) (fig. 15). They constitute, in other words, a Jewish parallel to the humanist preservation of source knowledge.

These intensive scholarly activities and intellectual exchanges took place within a social world where objects of Middle Eastern provenance were commonplace. Interesting work has been done on the agency that paintings contemporary with Ariosto might have had in his descriptions of women, people, and knights in the *Orlando furioso*,[81] but in the absence of any comparable textual trace responses to the parallel question, whether awareness of the cultural origins of such objects could also have colored Ariosto's imagination can only remain at the level of reasonable conjecture. It has been suggested, for example, that he might have thought of his "Saracen" knights as wielding sword of the Boabdil type.[82] Likewise, the horn, *il corno*, could reflect acquaintance with an actual oliphant, a type of ivory elephant tusk richly carved in relief, many of which are of medieval Southern Italian or Middle Eastern provenance,[83] although it could equally well be an intertextual element of a literary tradition going back to the *Chanson de Roland*, whose hero is asked to sound his to summon help:

Cumpainz Rollant, l'olifan car sunez!
Si l'orrat Carles, ferat l'ost returner
—LXXXIV, 1059-1060
[Roland, my friend, it's time to sound your horn,
King Charles will hear, and bring his army back]

Fig. 17. Lid of perfume burner. Egypt or Syria, late thirteenth or early fourteenth century. Modena, Galleria Estense, inv. no. 2065

Two Middle Eastern metal objects from the Galleria Estense have actually been noted in the literature surrounding Ariosto: a lid for a perfume burner elaborately shaped and inlaid with silver and gold (fig. 17), and the famous Khurasani ewer (fig. 18).[84] Their significance, however, is not literary but social and cultural; they are material instances of a pervasive presence, associated with the intense relationships the Este had with the Middle East and North Africa, beginning in the Middle Ages and relating both to pilgrimage to the Holy Land and to diplomacy. Borso d'Este (1413–1471), for example, duke of Ferrara and first duke of Modena, maintained connections with the region of "Barbaria," in particular the Tunisian court, which involved sending gifts such as arms, carved ivories, and Murano glass, and objects such as inlaid metalwork could have been given in return, together with Arab horses.[85]

In 1882, Venturi recorded that together with objects of antiquity, "Oriental" objects were also transported from Ferrara to the Galleria Estense in Modena. These are metal objects, some chiseled, others with inlay decoration.[86] It is not known exactly how they had arrived in Ferrara, but this was most probably either directly from the Middle East and North Africa or through Venice. Relationships between Ferrara and Venice were close, even before the beginnings of the Este family power in the early thirteenth century.[87] The Este themselves had a major and important palace in Venice, eventually to become the so-called Fondaco (from the Arabic *funduq*) dei Turchi. It was constructed in the first half of the thirteenth century, and the Venetian Republic purchased it in 1381 for Niccolò II d'Este, the marquess of Ferrara. During its early history, it served as a residence for many international visiting dignitaries. It became the Fondaco dei Turchi from the early seventeenth century through to 1838, serving Venice's Ottoman Turkish population as a combined residence, warehouse, and market for traders.[88]

Indeed, Venice played a fundamental role in trade with the Middle East from the Middle Ages on, with carpets a major and lucrative import. Also significant was the import of inlaid metalwork, which survived the general downturn of imports from the Middle East during the fifteenth century and influenced Venetian metal production, especially in the late fifteenth and the sixteenth century. Such metalwork imports are predominantly of Mamluk manufacture, as they are described as *di Damasco* or *domaschini*, and were generally shipped from Alexandria.[89]

Fig. 18. Ewer. Khurasan, probably Herat, late twelfth to early thirteenth century. Modena, Galleria Estense, inv. no. 6921

The decline in the import of metalwork is matched by an increase in the Italian production of metalwork *alla damaschina*,[90] replacing the earlier *da* or *di Damasco* reference to imports. It indicated production *in loco* in the manner of Damascus and reflected the widespread fashion for ornament of Middle Eastern origin across various materials. It is important to highlight that the use of these design features was not necessarily taken directly from objects coming from the Middle East, for they had already been mediated through a culture of ornament developed in Italy. For example, designs found on sixteenth-century Venetian or Bolognese bookbindings, metalwork, and textiles are closer to those produced by the abovementioned Francesco di Pellegrino in the early sixteenth century than to those on Middle Eastern objects. A further complication comes from the presence of Muslim as well as Jewish communities in Venice, Ferrara, and Modena, which opens up the possibility of inlaid metal objects and others being produced by Middle Eastern craftsmen working in Italy.

But whether featuring on imported or locally produced Middle Eastern artifacts or recombined in Italian ones, such design features were ubiquitous in Ariosto's environment. They were appreciated, for example, by the influential Isabella d'Este (1474–1539), sister of both of Ariosto's patrons, Ippolito and Alfonso d'Este.[91] A major cultural figure who grew up in Ferrara, she was the first to recognize the merits of the *Orlando furioso*, within which Ariosto characterizes her as *liberale e magnanima*, and to relish the adventures it relates.[92] The correspondence she had in 1511 with Lorenzo da Pavia, residing in Venice,[93] in which she asked for a pair of nail scissors decorated with gold inlay (*alla damaschina*), is revelatory with regard to the production of inlaid metalwork in Italy. In his answer, and in a previous letter to Isabella, Lorenzo explains the stages of manufacture of such objects. The artisan who makes the scissors is not the same as the one who decorates them; first, the scissors are made and tempered, and then they are sent to a master (*maestro*) who works on them with the gold inlay. He also mentions the presence of a very accomplished *azzemino* (from *agemina*, this term denotes an artist specialized in inlaid metalwork) in Mantua and adds that he had a pupil in Venice who had surpassed the master ("che lavora ecelentemente, melio de l'Azemino ch'è a Mantova, ancora che el sia sta' suo disipolo, e l'à più desegno"). From a document discussed by Bertolotti, we may assume that the master *azzemino* was a certain Andrea,[94] and from a different document dated 1563 in the Archivio Storico in Florence, Spallanzani has hypothesized that his pupil was a certain Antonio Surian, thirty-five years of age, who had studied mathematics in Damascus and was now working in the port of Venice to recover sunken artillery. But he was also a very accomplished *azzemino* and produced work better than any Italian ("Qui è uno damaschino. . . . Lavora di sua mano di azimino meglio che homo di Italia"). Spallanzani adds that although he did not know Italian well, he could have taught pupils, in the same way that Andrea did.[95] This document has important implications for the debate on the so-called Veneto-Saracenic metalwork, as it confirms, unlike what Hans Huth had suggested, that people from the Middle East could work as metalworkers in Venice and that the picture is more complicated than previously thought.[96]

4. Antiquarian and Contemporary Appreciation

Isabella's correspondence also highlights a familiar humanist theme, that of antiquarian appreciation, and gives it a particular emphasis, valuing the ancient above the modern. Lorenzo da Pavia tells her of a large inlaid damascene vase, of beautiful form and with a beautiful inlaid inscription with letters in gold and silver, the best he has ever seen ("le più bele che abia maie visto"), and he also describes it as one of the antique pieces ("lavori antegi") to which contemporary ones are inferior ("ché adesso non lavorano così bene"). However, not all present-day craftsmanship from the Middle East is dismissed; he is also going to send, for Isabella's consideration, a modern object, a smaller vase with a lid, worked in the same way and decorated by the best master in Damascus ("de mano del meliore mastro che sia a Damascho").[97]

The documentation related to Isabella d'Este is significant for the fact that it confirms that Middle Eastern objects circulated in Italy and that their designs were imitated, becoming part of a broader vocabulary of ornament, especially in the period in question. Together with a multitude of other objects collected in a *studiolo* or library, such artifacts would have been familiar to Ariosto.

The two vases mentioned in the letter recall items of Middle Eastern metalwork kept at the Galleria Estense in Modena. The beautiful inlaid inscription on the "antique" vase was most probably very similar to that on bowl no. 2062, probably produced in Syria, in the late thirteenth or early fourteenth century (fig. 19a).[98] This is a magnificent bowl with both gold and silver inlay. Its interior surface has an inlaid decoration, at the bottom of which, within a polylobed medallion, are depicted numerous fish; on the exterior base is a large polylobed medallion with, in the center, a twelve-petaled flower. It contains a multitude of ducks, symbols of purity and for Sufis also of spirituality and enlightenment, flying or extending their wings.[99] Still toward the base but above the polylobed medallion is depicted a magnificent series of fourteen animals running in a circle, including a unicorn, a griffin, and a camel, together with lions, cheetahs, hares, and deer. This is a wonderful rendition in keeping with the iconography of such borders of running animals on other Middle Eastern metalwork and

Fig. 19. (a) Bowl; (b) detail. Syria, late thirteenth or early fourteenth century. Modena, Galleria Estense, inv. no. 2062

Fig. 20. (a) Spherical perfume burner; (b) view of the top. Syria, first half of the fifteenth century. Modena, Galleria Estense, inv. no. 2066

Fig. 21. Spherical perfume burner with a receptacle inside mounted on a gimbal device. Syria, first half of the fifteenth century. Bologna, Museo Civico Medievale, inv. no. 2116

in illustrated manuscripts of the period.[100] Higher on the body of the bowl is a band of inscription in large silver-inlaid letters, divided into four rectangular cartouches by four round medallions. Two contain the lotus flower, rendered in the typical Mamluk style, surrounded by smaller four-, five-, and six-petaled flowers, while the other two have at the center a human head wearing a three-pointed crown and with a crescent under the chin, a *hilāl* motif representing the moon that is found both in series of astronomical imagery and in isolation, as here, where the crown and the crescent are gold-inlaid and the symbolism has princely connections (fig. 19b).[101] Instead of the expected list of epithets related to the sultan (whether named or not), the inscription is a list of epithets related to the royal seat of authority.

Middle Eastern objects were frequently represented in paintings, together with carpets, textiles, ceramics, glass, and metalwork of various types, including perfume burners, of which a splendid large spherical one, probably produced in Syria in the first half of the fifteenth century, is held in Modena's Galleria Estense, no. 2066 (fig. 20).[102] Like the example in Modena, they are intricately decorated, with silver and at times also gold inlay, and often also have inscriptions in Arabic of a benedictory or augural type.[103] The substance burning inside a little semispherical receptacle could be ambergris, musk, or aloe wood, and a gimbal device ensured that the receptacle always remained horizontal, so that the burner could be rolled. The receptacle and the mechanism are well preserved in one of the perfume burners in the Museo Civico Medievale in Bologna, also datable to the first half of the fifteenth century and probably manufactured in Syria (fig. 21).[104] Indeed, as the twelfth-century poet Ibn Ḥamdīs describes, they could be made to run over carpets, letting out smoke through the many small perforations in the metal.[105]

The large example represented in the 1532 portrait of Georg Gisze by Hans Holbein, hanging by a chain from a hook on a shelf, has an inscription in the Roman alphabet and is presumably of Western manufacture but is indebted to Middle Eastern models in its ornamentation (fig. 22).[106] The painting also shows a Turkish carpet on the table, of a type known as "Holbein," very much in vogue in Italy in the fifteenth and early sixteenth centuries, with bigger or smaller medallions and a pseudo-Arabic inscription around the border.[107] In the Bargello museum in Florence, two brass perfume burners with inlay decoration are kept, from the Medici collections, produced in Syria, one in the fourteenth century and the other, very similar to the ones in Modena and Bologna, in the first half of the fifteenth century.[108] But, interestingly, the ones in the Bargello have chains, an indication that they were to be suspended, as in the

Fig. 22. Hans Holbein, *Georg Gisze*, 1532. Berlin, Staatliche Museen zu Berlin, Gemäldegalerie, inv. no. 586

Holbein painting and in Persian miniatures.[109] The wonderful perfume burners in Modena and Bologna represent a type that could very well have been found in Ariosto's environment.

5. Conclusion

Ariosto's intellectual world was saturated with awareness of the Middle East, and his visual and tactile environment contained, in addition to their representations in paintings, numerous artifacts from the Middle East, ranging from carpets to ceramics to metalwork, as well as bookbindings and other objects with designs incorporating features of Middle Eastern origin. Humanist communities had a scholarly awareness of, and engagement with, classical texts as transmitted through Arabic and actively sought both Arabic translations and commentaries and original works produced by Middle Eastern scholars. Some of these, most notably the medical works of Avicenna, would, when rendered into Latin, for centuries remain central to European understanding and teaching. Equally pervasive was the presence of artifacts from the Middle East, some of which were war trophies, although the majority were acquired peacefully through complex trading networks that represented the competing mercantile ambitions of the Italian city-states. The agency of such objects and that of the designs inscribed on them were to have a profound impression on the style world of European design. For Ariosto, then, the Islamic Middle East was a perpetual background presence, a mediated contributor to the imaginary within which his literary achievements were conceived.

Notes

1. I would like to thank Alina Payne and Monica Preti for inviting me to participate in this exciting project and also for their support and advice. I am also grateful to Martina Bagnoli, director of the Galleria Estense in Modena, and her team for permission and support to study the Middle Eastern metalwork items in their care, both those on display and those in storage; and to Nadia De Lutio, director of the Biblioteca Estense Universitaria, for permission to study the Oriental manuscripts held there, and to her team, especially Elga Disperdi, for their continuing assistance. I also thank Norihito Hayashi, professor of Islamic Art at Kyoto University, with whom I share a collaborative project funded by the Research Committee of Japan (JSPS KAKENHI Grant number 16KK0044), which made possible a research trip to Modena, and for his photography, opinions and comments on the material studied there. I am grateful to Giuliano Tamani for providing me with research material at a time when there was no access to libraries. I am also grateful to the anonymous readers for their useful comments.

2. Although the authorship of the *Historia Turchesca* is disputed, it contains material from Angiolello, who is also mentioned there as the author. See Necipoğlu 2012, n. 8, for reference to a list of passages attributable to Angiolello. Another important historical work by Angiolello is his *Viaggio di Negroponte*, Angiolello 1982. Also see Babinger 1978, pp. 45, 285, 312, 331, 411; and Necipoğlu 2012, p. 2, and n. 6 on the name of Istanbul.

3. Raby 1983. One such Greek scholar and historian was Michael Kritovoulus of Imbros (ca. 1410–ca. 1470), who was one of the main sources for the fall of Constantinople in 1453 in his *History of Meḥmed the Conqueror*, dedicated to Meḥmed II (Kritovoulus 1954).

4. Kafescioğlu 2013, p. 487; and *Muqarnas Supplements* 14, 2019, 2 vols. For the illuminated and illustrated manuscripts, see esp. Atbaş 2019; Tanındı 2019.

5. Patrinelis 1971; Raby 1983, pp. 23–24.

6. Necipoğlu 2012, pp. 37–38; see also Necipoğlu 2010.

7. On these two artists at the Ottoman court, see Campbell and Chong 2005. The Bellini family was invited and commissioned to produce a series of portraits of the sultans, of which one is extant: Gentile Bellini, *Meḥmed II*, 1480, London, National Gallery, inv. no. NG3099. For this portrait, see also Rodini 2020. In Naples, Costanzo da Ferrara was at the court of King Ferrante (King Ferdinand I), and in a letter written by Battista Bendidio, the Ferrarese ambassador in Naples, to Eleonora of Aragon, duchess of Ferrara, dated August 24, 1485, we learn that King Ferrante sent Costanzo to the court of Meḥmed II, who had asked for an artist to be sent to him; see Campbell and Chong 2005, p. 126.

8. On Costanzo da Ferrara's medal in Washington, D.C., National Gallery of Art, inv. no. 1957.14.695, see Raby 1987, pp. 176–177, fig. 5; Campbell and Chong 2005, pp. 71–72, cat. 16; Necipoğlu 2012, pp. 30–32, fig. 17a. Costanzo stayed in Istanbul probably between 1477 and 1479; see Campbell and Chong 2005, pp. 126–127. The portrait is in Istanbul, Topkapı Palace Museum Library, Album H. 2153, fol. 145v; see Necipoğlu 2012, p. 36, fig. 19, and p. 31, where it is suggested that Meḥmed II's portrait on the medal recalls the verbal description of the sultan's features by Angiolello; also see Raby 2000a; Campbell and Chong 2005, pp. 88, 90, fig. 34.

9. These were included in the *Şemā'ilnāme* by the imperial panegyrist Loqmān; see Necipoğlu 2000, pp. 31–42; Çağman 2000. On Ottoman royal portraiture, see Kangal 2000 and esp. Raby 2000a and Raby 2000c.

10. For these and the several other portraits by the anonymous follower of Veronese, see Raby 2000b, pp. 150–163; Raby 2007; Kynan-Wilson 2019.

11. *Commentario delle cose dei Turchi*, dedicated to Charles V, published in 1532 (Giovio 1532). On Giovio, see Zimmermann 2001.

12. Art Institute of Chicago, Worcester Collection, inv. no. 1947.53; see Klinger and Raby 1989. Giovio's portrait collection, which was housed in his museum in Como, was later dispersed, but copies commissioned by Cosimo de' Medici are now in the Uffizi Gallery in Florence. For a discussion of his collection, especially with regard to Ottoman subjects, see Raby 2000b, pp. 141–150; see also Smith 2014, pp. 116–117, 161–162.

13. Giovio 1575; for Saladin, pp. 29–31; Meḥmed II, pp. 164–166; Barbarossa and Yahūd Sinān, pp. 343–343. A translation in Italian is in Giovio 2006; see also Milwright 2014–2015.

14. Klinger and Raby 1989, p. 48; Giovio 2006, pp. 244–246n1.

15. First published in 1546 without illustrations, later republished in 1577 as *Elogia virorum literis illustrium*: Giovio 1546, fols. 52*v*–53*v*; Giovio 1577, pp. 101–102; Giovio 2006, pp. 247–249.

16. Contadini 2013.

17. Raby 1989, pp. 41–42; see also Raby 1982, pp. 35–53.

18. Raby 1982, pp. 35–53.

19. Giovanni Mansueti, *The Arrest of St. Mark from the Synagogue*, Venice, dated 1499, oil on canvas; Vienna, Sammlungen des Fürsten von und zu Liechtenstein, inv. no. GE 857; see Schmidt Arcangeli 2007, esp. pp. 126–127.

20. Venice, Gallerie dell'Accademia, inv. no. 45; see Echols and Ilchman 2018. For images of the "Other" in early modern Venetian painting, see Ch'ien 2021.

21. Mac Carthy 2007; Cavallo 2013.

22. Such as the Knights Hospitaller, who had left Rhodes in 1522 and moved to Tripoli. Barbarossa captured Algiers in 1516 and Tunis in 1534 (although it was to be captured in the following year by a navy of the Holy Roman Empire). For the Ottomans in North Africa, see Soucek 2013.

23. Raby 1989, p. 42; Smith 2014, pp. 41–68.

24. See Meserve 2008, pp. 3, 22, and, for views of the Scythians pp. 79–80. For negative humanist views about the "Turks" and their construction of a cultural and religious "Other", see also Bisaha 2004; for positive views of Islam and the Ottomans in the sixteenth century, see Malcolm 2013.

25. Piccolomini 1990, p. 74 (paragraph 143); Akasoy 2013, pp. 248–250.

26. See Cavallo 2013, p. 11.

27. For Andrea Alpago, see Lucchetta 1964.

28. Burnett 1999, pp. 190–191 and n. 26.

29. See Ficcadori 1994; also Campbell and Chong 2005, pp. 36–38.

30. Benedetto Dei, *Cronaca*, Archivio di Stato di Firenze, Manoscritti 119; see Orvieto 1969; also Azzi 1952.

31. Burnett 2009. For a summary of the transmission of medical knowledge from the Islamic world to the West, see Siraisi 1990, pp. 12–16.

32. Metcalfe 2013, p. 106; see also Burnett 1994.

33. Employed in the service of the prince-bishop Bernardo Cles in 1528 at Trento, Mattioli came to be in contact with Italian and European humanists, which his knowledge of Latin and classical Greek facilitated; see Preti 2008.

34. *Di Pedacio Dioscoride Anazarbeo libri cinque. Della historia et materia medicinale tradotti in lingua volgare italiana*, the first edition of which, without illustrations, was published in Venice by Nicolò de Bascarini in 1544; see Ferri 1997, pp. 17–21. Mattioli produced the first edition in Latin in 1554; see Fausti 2004, p. 17.

35. Modena, Biblioteca Estense Universitaria, Alfa Y.3.8, printed in Venice by V. Valgrisi and dated January 1565, with the addition of an essay (and accompanying illustrations) on the distillation of water. For the binding, see Fumagalli 1913, pp. 7–8, no. 12, and tabs. XVII and XVIIbis.

36. Contadini 1989.

37. Colonna 1499. For the work and its connections with humanist circles, see Griggs 1998. For a useful bibliography on the *Hypnerotomachia Poliphili* up to 2014, see Barcaioli 2015. A 1499 *incunabulum* is in Modena, Biblioteca Estense Universitaria, Alfa C.4.3, a gift to the library by Alfonso Gioia from Ferrara in 1687.

38. For the Arabic inscriptions, see Piemontese 1999.

39. For Niccoli's library, see Ullman and Stadter 1972; see also Schiaparelli 1871, pp. xii, xx–xxi.

40. Ullman 1960.

41. Pellegrino 1908.

42. The Venetian binding of Fra Giocondo's *Syllogie* is in the Chatsworth Library, Chatsworth House, Derbyshire; see Ohta 2013, p. 229, fig. 11.3. The binding by Ghiyāth al-Dīn is in Istanbul, Museum of Turkish and Islamic Art, ms. 2031; see Raby and Tanındı 1993, cat. no. 33; see also Contadini 2014, pp. 70–71, figs. 14–16; Contadini 2016, pp. 302–303, fig. 23.9.

43. Contadini 1999, pp. 9–11.

44. Ohta 2013; see also Gacek 1990–91.

45. Hobson 1989, pp. 22, 148.

46. Petrarch, *Canzoniere e trionfi*, Florence, 1460–1470. Oxford, Bodleian Library, Ms. Canon. Ital. 78: Ohta 2013, p. 223, fig. 11.1.

47. Venice, Biblioteca Marciana, Marc. Lat. X, 117 (= 3844); see Valentinelli 1873, p. 109. These were once considered to be glass, but they seem to be made of resin. For an example of an Ottoman filigree binding with the cloud-collar design from the first half of the fifteenth century, see Raby and Tanındı 1993, p. 42 and figs. 40 and 41. For filigree bindings and their origins in the Middle East, see Ohta 2004.

48. Venice, Biblioteca Marciana, Lat. VI 270 (= 3671); see Hobson 1989, pp. 22–23.

49. Hobson 1989, p. 148.

50. For Felice Feliciano, see Mitchell 1961; Hobson 1989, pp. 3–12, 41–50; Granzotto 1995.

51. But see the reservations of Granzotto 1995, p. 224; and for the Bruni manuscript, see n. 48. Giovanni Marcanova, *Collectio Antiquitatum*, dated 1465. Modena, Biblioteca Estense Universitaria, Alfa L.5.15; see Fava and Salmi 1973, no. 121, pp. 44–48; see also Huelsen 1907, p. 46. For the binding, see Fumagalli 1913, pp. 58–61, no. 252, and tabs. IV, IVb. For the binding of the Bruni, see Ohta 2013, plate 42; Contadini 2016, fig. 23.8a.

52. Hobson 1989, p. 43; Ohta 2013, p. 228.

53. Translation into Latin by Ambrosius Monachus, *Dionysius Areopagita*, fifteenth century. Modena, Biblioteca Estense Universitaria, Alfa U.5.24; see Fava and Salmi 1973, pp. 71–72, no. 138 and tab. XXVIII, 1; Ricci 2002. For the binding, see Fumagalli 1913, p. 3, no. 1 and tab. III; Gnoli 1939, p. 19, no. 13 and tab. XI.

54. For the relationships with Hungary, see Mikó 2011. For connections between the court of Matthias Corvinus, Beatrice, and Italian humanists, see Pajorin 1994, pp. 186–187.

55. *Mottetti a quattro voci di autori diversi*, paper, early sixteenth century. Modena, Biblioteca Estense Universitaria, Mus. C.313.1–4. For the binding, see Fumagalli 1913, p. 6, no. 5 and tab. XIV.

56. For Leonardo's frescoes in the Sala delle Asse, see Salsi 2016; for the majolica plate now held in the Rijksmuseum, Amsterdam, inv. no. BK-NM-13136, see Mack 2002, fig. 101; Contadini 2014, fig. 12. It has been suggested that there is a conceptual link between this visual interlace and the parallel narrative technique used in the *Orlando furioso*: see Montagnani 2016, pp. 286–295 and fig. 44; and for the literary technique of interlacement, see also Regan 2005, p. 54n7.

57. Contadini 2016, p. 302 and fig. 23.10. For the transfer of ornament in an Ottoman context and its international ramifications, routes, and exchanges, see Necipoğlu 1990, pp. 155, 169n49; Necipoğlu 2014, pp. 340–354.

58. Lach 1977, pp. 48–50; Cavallo 2013, p. 7 and nn. 10 and 11.

59. Ptolemy: Modena, Biblioteca Estense Universitaria, Alfa X.1.3; see Fava and Salmi 1973, pp. 69–70, no. 136 and tabs. XXVI, 4, XXVII, 1; Federzoni and Battini 2006. Strabo: Modena, Biblioteca Estense Universitaria, Alfa X.1.10; see Fava and Salmi 1973, p. 78, no. 144 and tab. XXXI; Di Pietro Lombardi 2002. See also Rossi's chapter in this volume.

60. For Alberto III Pio, see Vasoli 1978, who presents him as a multifarious personage—prince, diplomat, and humanist. See also Casari's chapter in this volume. For Aldo Manuzio and the Aldine Press, see Dionisotti 1975, pp. xxxvi–xxxvii; and for Manuzio and Alberto III Pio, see Balsamo 1983; Nuovo 1999. For printing in general, see also Eisenstein 2005; Brotton 2002, pp. 77–79.

61. For Alberto's and his nephew Rodolfo's collection, see Rossi 2004, pp. 9–10; Franzoni 2004.

62. Di Pietro Lombardi 2004, p. 226.

63. Urbini 2004.

64. Bernheimer 1960.

65. Pope Callisto III (1455–1458); see Di Leone Leoni 2011, Vol. 1, pp. 13–14. The Este family welcomed Jewish refugees from Spain in 1492, the Marranos in 1524, and refugees from Germany in 1530, Milan in 1540, Naples in 1541, and the papal state of Bologna in 1569; see Balletti 1930, pp. 76–78. See also Lelli in this volume.

66. Modena, Biblioteca Estense Universitaria, Alfa S.7.11; see Bernheimer 1960, p. 63, no. 53.

67. Modena, Biblioteca Estense Universitaria, Alfa J.6.3; see Bernheimer 1960, pp. 68–69, no. 65. Leo Africanus (b. 1495 in Granada, d. in Tunis ca. 1550), a Moroccan diplomat and author, known for his *Descrittione del'Africa* (published in Venice by Giovanbattista Ramusio in 1550), focused on the Maghreb and the Nile Valley. On converting to Christianity, he took the name Yuḥannā al-Asad al-Gharnaṭī, given that he was born in Granada (Spain), in place of his original name al-Ḥasan b. Muḥammad al-Wazzān al-Zayātī or al-Fāsī. He studied at Fez, at the Qarawiyyīn University. For Leo Africanus, see Pouillon 2009.

68. Piemontese 1999.

69. Modena, Biblioteca Estense Universitaria, Alfa W.9.23; see Bernheimer 1960, pp. 73–74, no. 68.

70. Puliatti 1960, esp. p. xi.

71. Modena, Biblioteca Estense Universitaria, Alfa Q.6.20, a commentary on Isaiah by Joseph b. Simeon Qara. Bernheimer 1960, p. 21, no. 14, attributes it to the fourteenth century.

72. Modena, Biblioteca Estense Universitaria, Alfa W.5.14; see Bernheimer 1960, pp. 16–19, no. 8.

73. Modena, Biblioteca Estense Universitaria, Alfa R.8.8; see Bernheimer 1960, pp. 42–43, no. 36. The scribe was Jaqub Grechi, who must be the same person as Alfa N.8.14 (see below).

74. Modena, Biblioteca Estense Universitaria, Alfa Q.6.16; Bernheimer 1960, pp. 37–38, no. 32.

75. Modena, Biblioteca Estense Universitaria, Alfa N.8.14; Bernheimer 1960, pp. 40–41, no. 34. The scribe is again Jaqub Grechi, as per Alfa R.8.8, which was most probably produced in 1487.

76. Bologna, University Library, ms. 2197, first half of the fifteenth century. The manuscript has been reproduced in facsimile edition: Ibn Sīnā 2002. For an ample discussion of this manuscript, its context, and its illustrations, see Tamani 1988.

77. Tamani 1988, p. 65 n34.

78. Tamani 1988, pp. 67, 73; see also Pazzini 1943.

79. Modena, Biblioteca Estense Universitaria, Alfa J.6.23; see Bernheimer 1960, pp. 55–56, no. 41.

80. Modena, Biblioteca Estense Universitaria, Alfa N.5.15; see Bernheimer 1960, pp. 57–58, no. 43.

81. See esp. Gnudi 1994 (who interestingly calls for the Middle Eastern art context to be researched, p. 28) and the more recent Collareta 2016.

82. One such sword is illustrated in Beltramini and Tura 2016, pp. 126–127, no. 46 (entry by Olivier Renaudeau). For swords associated with famous personages, see Huynh 2011.

83. One such ivory oliphant, probably carved in Southern Italy, is illustrated in Beltramini and Tura 2016, pp. 42–43, no. 5 (entry by Flora Dennis). For the oliphants and their classification, see the monumental work by Kühnel 1971; see also more recently Shalem and Glaser 2014.

84. They are illustrated in Bentini 1994, pp. 196–197, no. 146; p. 155, no. 66, which, however, does not represent the object described but a European vase in the collection. For the lid of the perfume burner, see also Venturi 1882, pp. 89–90; for the Khurasani ewer, see, among others, Curatola 1993, pp. 234–237, no. 125 (entry by Michele Bernardini); and Canby et al. 2016, p. 143, no. 73 (entry by Deniz Beyazit).

85. Foucard 1881; Ricci 2008, p. 153.

86. Venturi 1882, p. 83.

87. Cittadella 1872.

88. Turan 1968, esp. p. 261; Preto 1975, pp. 126–143; Constable 2001; Constable 2003.

89. Spallanzani 1989, p. 86.

90. On the difference in terminology and its implications, see Spallanzani 2010, pp. 10–11.

91. For Isabella d'Este, see IDEA: Isabella d'Este Archive, http://isabelladeste.web.unc.edu; an edition of a selection of her letters is Isabella d'Este 2017, edited by Deanna Shemek.

92. *Fur.* XIII 59; see Ariosto 2012, p. 109; see also Marek 1976, pp. xiii, 95; and Regan 2005.

93. In two letters kept in Mantua, Gonzaga Archive, Busta 2996, 29, c. 79*v*; Busta 1446, c. 76; see Brown 1982, documents 162 and 163, pp. 124–125, and E11, pp. 242–243; Spallanzani 2010, p. 11n21.

94. This artisan is mentioned in Bertolotti 1974, pp. 140–141, where he hypothesizes, however, a Spanish origin of Andrea.

95. Spallanzani 2010, p. 12 and n. 22.

96. Huth 1970. For a revision of Huth's hypothesis and a more detailed discussion, see esp. Auld 2004, pp. 7–9, 36–43, and chap. 7. The term "Veneto-Saracenic" would be best abandoned, as the objects in this "category" are actually varied and from different geographical production, that is, Egypt and Syria, Western Iran/Anatolia, and Italy; see Contadini 2006, pp. 309–315.

97. See Brown 1982, p. 122; also Spallanzani 2010, p. 4.

98. Brass bowl with gold and silver inlay, h. 8.5 cm, d. 13 cm (mouth), d. 18 cm (body). Modena, Galleria Estense, inv. no. 2062; see Venturi 1882, pp. 84–88. This object, together with the other metalwork in the Modena and Bologna collections, is part of a project that I am conducting and that will culminate in a series of publications.

99. For the symbolism of the duck based on literary sources, see Daneshvari 1986, pp. 83–86.

100. See, e.g., the *Kitāb manāfi' al-ḥayawān* (Book of the usefulness of animals) of H 755/1354 in San Lorenzo del Escorial, Biblioteca Real, Ar. 898; see Contadini 1988–1989.

101. See Rice 1957, where the *hilāl* is discussed, esp. p. 321. See also Ettinghausen 1971, and fig. 14, which is a detail in black-and-white of the *hilāl* from the bowl in Modena.

102. Spherical perfume burner with gold and silver inlay, pierced. Syria, first half of the fifteenth century. Brass, h. 13.5 cm, d. 13 cm. Modena, Galleria Estense, inv. no. 2066; see Venturi 1882, pp. 90–91. There is a type also manufactured in Europe, although usually smaller in size, that may also have been used as hand warmers; see Auld 2004, p. 110.

103. For Arabic and Persian inscriptions on objects, see Contadini 2017, especially pp. 124–125.

104. Spherical perfume burner with iron receptacle and gimbal device inside. Syria, first half of the fifteenth century. Brass with silver inlay, pierced, d. 9.5 cm, weight 440 g. Bologna, Museo Civico Medievale, inv. no. 2116; see Auld 2004, pp. 119–120; Franzoni and Nardoni 2019, pp. 190–191, no. 95. There are several such spherical perfume burners that preserve the internal mechanism; another one is in the Museo Correr in Venice, Cl. XII, 11, for which see Contadini 2006, fig. 21.1.

105. Ibn Ḥamdīs al-ʿAzdī al-Ṣiqillī (ca. 1056–ca. 1133), Arab poet of Sicily, who describes this use in a poem in honor of ʿAlī ibn Yaḥyā, Zirid prince of Mahdia; see Amari 1876; also Scerrato 1967, p. 29.

106. Berlin, Gemäldegalerie, Staatliche Museen zu Berlin, inv. no. 586; see Buck 1999, fig. 83; Sternthal 2007, p. 197.

107. We have documents that testify to the diffusion of this type, called *a ruote*; see Spallanzani 2007, pp. 60–64.

108. Florence, Museo Nazionale del Bargello, inv. nos. 292 and 299; see Spallanzani 1980, plates 27, 28; Curatola and Spallanzani 1981, pp. 7–9, no. 1; Auld 2004, pp. 108, 123, no. 1.16; Spallanzani 2010, p. 58, plates 42, 43.

109. Marchal 1971, cat. no. 173 (entry by Assadullah Souren Melikian-Chirvani).

Bibliography

Akasoy 2013

Akasoy, Anna. "Meḥmed II as a Patron of Greek Philosophy." In *The Renaissance and the Ottoman World*, edited by Anna Contadini and Claire Norton, pp. 245–256. Farnham, UK: Ashgate, 2013.

Amari 1876

Amari, Michele. "Epigrafia: Decrizioni di lavori orientali con iscrizioni arabiche." *Bollettino italiano degli studii orientali*, series 1, 7–8 (1876): pp. 122–133.

Angiolello 1982

Angiolello, Giovan Maria. *Viaggio di Negroponte*, edited by Cristina Bazzolo. Vicenza: N. Pozza, 1982.

Ariosto 2012

Ariosto, Ludovico. *Orlando furioso*, with commentary by Emilio Bigi, edited by Cristina Zambese. Milan: BUR, 2012.

Atbaş 2019

Atbaş, Zeynep. "Artistic Aspects of Sultan Bāyezīd II's Book Treasury Collection: Extant Volumes Preserved at the Topkapı Palace Museum Library." In *Treasures of Knowledge: An Inventory of the Ottoman Palace Library (1502/3–1503/4)*, 2 vols., edited by Gülru Necipoğlu, Cemal Kafadar, and Cornell H. Fleischer, Vol. 1, pp. 161–211. [*Muqarnas Supplements* 14 (2019).]

Auld 2004

Auld, Sylvia. *Renaissance Venice, Islam and Mahmud al-Kurd: A Metalworking Enigma*. London: Altajir World of Islam Trust, 2004.

Azzi 1952

Azzi, Giustiniano Degli. "Un frammento inedito della Cronaca di Benedetto Dei." *Archivio Storico Italiano* 110, no. 1 (1952): pp. 99–113.

Babinger 1978

Babinger, Franz. *Meḥmed the Conqueror and His Time*, edited by William C. Hickman, translated by Ralph Manheim. Princeton, NJ: Princeton University Press, 1978.

Balletti 1930

Balletti, Andrea. *Gli Ebrei e gli Estensi*. Reggio-Emilia: Anonima Poligrafica Emiliana, 1930.

Balsamo 1983

Balsamo, Luigi. "Editoria e mecenatismo fra '400 e '500: Il caso di Aldo Manuzio e Alberto Pio." In *Produzione e circolazione libraria in Emilia (XV–XVIII sec.): Studi e ricerche*, edited by Luigi Balsamo, pp. 101–132. Parma: Casanova, 1983.

Barcaioli 2015

Barcaioli, Linda. "Una banca dati per il *Polifilo*: La catalogazione dei contributi." *Bibliothecae.it* 4, no. 1 (2015): pp. 123–147.

Beltramini and Tura 2016

Beltramini, Guido, and Adolfo Tura, eds. *Orlando Furioso 500 Anni*. Ferrara: Sate, 2016.

Bentini 1994

Bentini, Jadranka, ed. *Signore cortese e umanissimo: Viaggio intorno a Ludovico Ariosto*. Venice: Marsilio, 1994.

Bernheimer 1960

Bernheimer, Carlo. *Catalogo dei manoscritti Orientali della Biblioteca Estense*. Rome: Istituto Poligrafico dello Stato, 1960.

Bertolotti 1974
Bertolotti, Antonino. *Le arti minori alla corte di Mantova nei secoli XV, XVI e XVII (Ricerche Storiche negli Archivi Mantovani)*. Milan: Arnaldo Forni Editore, 1889; 2nd printing Bologna: Arnaldo Forni Editore, 1974.

Bisaha 2004
Bisaha, Nancy. *Creating East and West: Renaissance Humanists and the Ottoman Turks*. Philadelphia: University of Pennsylvania Press, 2004.

Brotton 2002
Brotton, Jerry. *The Renaissance Bazaar: From the Silk Road to Michelangelo*. Oxford: Oxford University Press, 2002.

Brown 1982
Brown, Clifford M., with Anna Maria Lorenzini. *Isabella d'Este and Lorenzo da Pavia: Documents for the History of Art and Culture in Renaissance Mantua*. Geneva: Librairie Droz, 1982.

Buck 1999
Buck, Stephanie. *Hans Holbein*. Cologne: Könemann, 1999.

Burnett 1994
Burnett, Charles. "Michael Scot and the Transmission of Scientific Culture from Toledo to Bologna via the Court of Frederick II Hohenstaufen." *Micrologus* 2 (1994): pp. 101–126. (Reprinted in Burnett 2009.)

Burnett 1999
Burnett, Charles. "The Second Revelation of Arabic Philosophy and Science: 1492–1562." In *Islam and the Italian Renaissance*, edited by Charles Burnett and Anna Contadini, pp. 185–198. London: Warburg Institute, 1999.

Burnett 2009
Burnett, Charles. *Arabic into Latin in the Middle Ages: The Translators and Their Intellectual and Social Context*. Farnham, UK: Ashgate, 2009.

Çağman 2000
Çağman, Filiz. "Portrait Series of Naqqāş ʿOthmān." In *The Sultan's Portrait: Picturing the House of Osman*, edited by Selmin Kangal, pp. 164–1878. Istanbul: Işbank, 2000.

Campbell 2013
Campbell, Caroline. "The 'Reception of the Venetian Ambassadors in Damascus': Dating, Meaning and Attribution." In *The Renaissance and the Ottoman World*, edited by Anna Contadini and Claire Norton, pp. 109–122. Farnham, UK: Ashgate, 2013.

Campbell and Chong 2005
Campbell, Caroline, and Alan Chong. *Bellini and the East*. London: National Gallery, 2005.

Canby et al. 2016
Canby, Sheila R., Deniz Beyazit, Martina Rugiadi, and A. C. S. Peacock. *Court and Cosmos: The Great Age of the Seljuqs*. New York: Metropolitan Museum of Art, 2016.

Cavallo 2013
Cavallo, Jo Ann. *The World beyond Europe in the Romance Epics of Boiardo and Ariosto* . Toronto: University of Toronto Press, 2013.

Ch'ien 2021
Ch'ien, Letha. "Polytopos in Early Modern Venetian Imagery." In *Cultures and Practices of Coexistence from the Thirteenth through the Seventeenth Centuries: Multi-ethnic Cities in the Mediterranean World*, Vol. 1, edited by Marco Folin and Antonio Musarra. New York: Routledge, 2021.

Cittadella 1872
Cittadella, Luigi Napoleone. *Notizie relative a Ferrara*. Ferrara: Taddei, 1872.

Collareta 2016
Collareta, Marco. "Le arti visive negli scritti di Ariosto: Opere, idee, protagonisti." In *Orlando Furioso 500 Anni*, edited by Guido Beltramini and Adolfo Tura, pp. 212–221. Ferrara: Sate, 2016.

Colonna 1499
Colonna, Francesco (attr.). *Hypnerotomachia Poliphili*. Venice: Aldo Manuzio, 1499.

Constable 2001
Constable, Olivia Remie. "Funduq, Fondaco and Khan in the Wake of Christian Commerce and Crusade." In *The Crusades from the Perspective of Byzantium and the Muslim World*, edited by Angeliki E. Laiou

and Roy Parviz Mottahedeh, pp. 145–156. Washington, DC: Dumbarton Oaks, 2001.

Constable 2003

Constable, Olivia Remie. *Housing the Stranger in the Mediterranean World: Lodging, Trade and Travel in Late Antiquity and the Middle Ages*. Cambridge: Cambridge University Press, 2003.

Contadini 1988–1989

Contadini, Anna. "The *Kitāb Manāfi al-Ḥayawān* in the Escorial Library." *Islamic Art* 3 (1988–1989): pp. 33–57 and color plate III.

Contadini 1989

Contadini, Anna. "'Cuoridoro': Tecnica e decorazione di cuoi dorati veneziani e italiani con influssi islamici." In *Arte veneziana e arte islamica: Atti del primo simposio internazionale sull'arte veneziana e l'arte islamica*, edited by Ernst J. Grube, Stefano Carboni, and Giovanni Curatola, pp. 231–251. Venice: L'Altra Riva, 1989.

Contadini 1999

Contadini, Anna. "Artistic Contacts: Present Scholarship and Future Tasks." In *Islam and the Italian Renaissance*, edited by Charles Burnett and Anna Contadini, pp. 1–65. London: Warburg Institute, 1999.

Contadini 2006

Contadini, Anna. "Middle Eastern Objects." In *At Home in Renaissance Italy*, edited by Marta Ajmar-Wollheim and Flora Dennis, pp. 308–321. London: V&A Publications, 2006.

Contadini 2013

Contadini, Anna. "Sharing a Taste? Material Culture and Intellectual Curiosity around the Mediterranean, from the Eleventh to the Sixteenth Century." In *The Renaissance and the Ottoman World*, edited by Anna Contadini and Claire Norton, pp. 23–61. Farnham, UK: Ashgate, 2013.

Contadini 2014

Contadini, Anna. "L'ornamento nel mondo ottomano e nell'Italia del Rinascimento: Trasmissione e congiunzione." In *Incontri di civiltà nel Mediterraneo: L'Impero Ottomano e l'Italia del Rinascimento: Storia, arte e architettura*, edited by Alireza Naser Eslami, pp. 57–73. Florence: Olschki, 2014.

Contadini 2016

Contadini, Anna. "Threads of Ornament in the Style World of the Fifteenth and Sixteenth Centuries." In *Histories of Ornament: From Global to Local*, edited by Gülru Necipoğlu and Alina Payne, pp. 290–308 and notes on p. 397. Princeton, NJ: Princeton University Press, 2016.

Contadini 2017

Contadini, Anna. "Text and Image on Middle Eastern Objects: The Palmer Cup in Context." In *A Rothschild Renaissance: A New Look at the Waddesdon Bequest in the British Museum*, edited by Pippa Shirley and Dora Thornton, pp. 124–145. The British Museum Research Publication 212. London: British Museum, 2017.

Curatola 1993

Curatola, Giovanni, ed. *Eredità dell'Islam: Arte islamica in Italia*. Cinisello Balsamo: Silvana Editoriale, 1993.

Curatola and Spallanzani 1981

Curatola, Giovanni, and Marco Spallanzani. *Metalli islamici dalle collezioni Granducali / Islamic Metalwork from the Grand Ducal Collection*. Florence: Museo Nazionale del Bargello, 1981.

Daneshvari 1986

Daneshvari, Abbas. *Animal Symbolism in Warqa wa Gulshāh*. Oxford Studies in Islamic Art II. Oxford: Oxford University Press, 1986.

Di Leone Leoni 2011

Di Leone Leoni, Aron. *La Nazione Ebraica Spagnola e Portoghese di Ferrara (1492–1559)*, 2 vols. Florence: Olschki, 2011.

Dionisotti 1975

Dionisotti, Carlo. "Introduzione." In *Aldo Manuzio editore: Dediche, prefazioni, note ai testi*, 2 vols., translated by Giovanni Orlandi, Vol. 1, pp. ix–1. Milan: Il Polifilo, 1975.

Di Pietro Lombardi 2002

Di Pietro Lombardi, Paola. "Strabo: Geographia a Guarino (Veronensi) in Latinum translata." In *Nel segno del Corvo libri e miniature della biblioteca di Mattia Corvino re d'Ungheria (1443–1490)*, edited by Nicola Bono, Gábor Görgey, Francesco Sicilia, and István Monok, pp. 142–143, cat. 2. Modena: Il Bulino, 2002.

Di Pietro Lombardi 2004
Di Pietro Lombardi, Paola. "I codici greci e orientali di Alberto III Pio." In *Alberto III e Rodolfo Pio da Carpi collezionisti e mecenati*, edited by Manuela Rossi, pp. 215–227. Tavagnacco: Arti Grafiche Friulane, 2004.

Echols and Ilchman 2018
Echols, Robert, and Frederick Ilchman, eds. *Tintoretto: Artist of Renaissance Venice*. Washington, DC: National Gallery of Art, 2018.

Eisenstein 2005
Eisenstein, Elizabeth. *The Printing Revolution in Early Modern Europe*. 2nd ed. Cambridge: Cambridge University Press, 2005.

Ettinghausen 1971
Ettinghausen, Richard. "*Hilāl*, ii.—In Islamic Art." In *Encyclopaedia of Islam, Second Edition*, Vol. 3, edited by P. Bearman, Th. Bianquis, C. E. Bosworth, E. van Donzel, and W. P. Heinrichs, pp. 381–385. Leiden: Brill, 1971.

Fausti 2004
Fausti, Daniela. "La tradizione dell'erbario illustrato: qualche esempio." In *La complessa scienza dei Semplici: Atti delle celebrazioni per il V Centenario della nascità di Pietro Andrea Mattoli, Siena, 12 marzo–19 novembre 2001*, edited by Daniela Fausti, pp. 17–36. Siena: Accademia dei fisiocritici onlus, 2004.

Fava and Salmi 1973
Fava, Domenico, and Mario Salmi. *I manoscritti miniati della biblioteca Estense di Modena*, Vol. 2. Milan: Electa Editrice, 1973.

Federzoni and Battini 2006
Federzoni, Laura, and Annalisa Battini. *L'atlante di Borso d'Este: La Cosmographia di Claudio Tolomeo della Biblioteca estense universitaria di Modena: Commentario all'edizione in facsimile del codice miniato α.X.1.3. = Lat. 463*. Modena: Il Bulino, 2006.

Ferri 1997
Ferri, Sara. "Il 'Dioscoride,' i 'Discorsi,' i 'Commenrarii': Gli amici e i nemici." In *Pietro Andrea Mattioli: Siena 1501–Trento 1578: La vita, le opere, con l'identificazione delle piante*, edited by Sara Ferri, pp. 15–48. Perugia: Quattroemme, 1997.

Ficcadori 1994
Ficcadori, Gianfranco, ed. *Bessarione e l'Umanesimo*. Naples: Vivarium, 1994.

Foucard 1881
Foucard, Cesare. *Relazione dei Duchi di Ferrara e di Modena coi re di Tunisi*. Modena: Tipografia Sociale, 1881.

Franzoni 2004
Franzoni, Claudio. "Quindici anni di una collezione." In *Alberto III e Rodolfo Pio da Carpi collezionisti e mecenati*, edited by Manuela Rossi, pp. 61–84. Tavagnacco: Arti Grafiche Friulane, 2004.

Franzoni and Nardoni 2019
Franzoni, Claudio, and Pierluca Nardoni, eds. *What a Wonderful World: La lunga storia dell'ornamento tra arte e natura*. Milan: Skira, 2019.

Fumagalli 1913
Fumagalli, Giuseppe. *L'arte della legatura alla corte degli Estensi, a Ferrara e a Modena, dal secolo XV al XIX*. Florence: T. de Marinis, 1913.

Gacek 1990–1991
Gacek, Adam. "Arabic Bookmaking and Terminology as Portrayed by Bakr al-Ishbīlī in His *Kitāb al-taysīr fī ṣināʿat al-tasfīr*." *Manuscripts of the Middle East* 5 (1990–1991): pp. 106–113.

Giovio 1532
Giovio, Paolo. *Commentario de le cose de' Turchi*. Rome: Antonio Blado, 1532.

Giovio 1546
Giovio, Paolo. *Elogia veris clarorum virorum imaginibus apposita*. Venice: Tramezzino, 1546.

Giovio 1575
Giovio, Paolo. *Elogia virorum bellica virtute illustrium*. Basel: Pietro Perna, 1575.

Giovio 1577
Giovio, Paolo. *Elogia virorum literis illustrium*. Basel: Pietro Perna, 1577.

Giovio 2006
Giovio, Paolo. *Elogi degli uomini illustri*, edited by Franco Minonzio and Andrea Gasparri. Turin: Einaudi, 2006.
Gnoli 1939
Gnoli, Tomaso. *Mostra delle legature artistiche esistenti a Modena*. Modena: Società Tipografica Modenese, 1939.
Gnudi 1994
Gnudi, Cesare. "L'Ariosto e le arti figurative." In *Signore cortese e umanissimo: Viaggio intorno a Ludovico Ariosto*, edited by Jadranka Bentini, pp. 13–47. Venice: Marsilio, 1994.
Granzotto 1995
Granzotto, Orfea. "Alcune note su Felice Feliciano legatore." In *L'"antiquario" Felice Feliciano Veronese: Tra epigrafia antica, letteratura e arti del libro, Atti del convergno di studi, Verona, 3–4 giugno 1993*, edited by Agostino Contò and Leonardo Quaquarelli, pp. 221–229. Medioevo e Umanesimo 89. Padua: Editrice Antonore, 1995.
Griggs 1998
Griggs, Tamara. "Promoting the Past: The *Hypnerotomachia Poliphili* as Antiquarian Enterprise." *Word and Image* 14, nos. 1/2 (January–June 1998): pp. 17–39.
Hobson 1989
Hobson, Anthony. *Humanists and Bookbinders: The Origin and Diffusion of the Humanistic Bookbinding*. Cambridge: Cambridge University Press, 1989.
Huelsen 1907
Huelsen, Christian. *La Roma antica di Ciriaco d'Ancona*. Rome: Ermanno Loescher, 1907.
Huth 1970
Huth, Hans. "'Sarazenen' in Venedig?" In *Festschrift für Heinz Ladendorf*, edited by Peter Block and Gisela Zick, pp. 58–68. Cologne: Böhlau.
Huynh 2011
Huynh, Michel, ed. *L'epée, usages, mythes et symboles*. Paris: Musée de Cluny, 2011.
Ibn Sīnā 2002
Ibn Sīnā. *Qānūn fī l-ṭibb*, Hebrew translation. Facsimile edition of ms. 2197, Bologna, University Library. Madrid: AyN Ediciones, 2002.
Isabella d'Este 2017
Isabella d'Este. *Selected Letters*. Edited and translated by Deanna Shemek. Toronto: Iter, 2017.
Kafescioğlu 2013
Kafescioğlu, Çiğdem. "The Visual Arts." In *The Cambridge History of Turkey*, Vol. 2, *The Ottoman Empire as a World Power, 1453–1603*, edited by Suraiya N. Faroqhi and Kate Fleet, pp. 457–547. Cambridge: Cambridge University Press, 2013.
Kangal 2000
Kangal, Selmin, ed. *The Sultan's Portrait: Picturing the House of Osman*. Istanbul: Işbank, 2000.
Klinger and Raby 1989
Klinger, Linda, and Julian Raby. "Barbarossa and Sinan: A Portrait of Two Ottoman Corsairs from the Collection of Paolo Giovio." In *Arte veneziana e arte islamica: Atti del primo simposio internazionale sull'arte veneziana e l'arte islamica*, edited by Ernst J. Grube, Stefano Carboni, and Giovanni Curatola, pp. 47–59. Venice: L'Altra Riva, 1989.
Kritovoulus 1954
Kritovoulus, Michael. *History of Meḥmed the Conqueror*, translated by Charles T. Riggs. Princeton, NJ: Princeton University Press, 1954.
Kühnel 1971
Kühnel, Ernst. *Die Islamischen Elfenbeinskulpturen VIII–XIII Jahrhundert*, 2 vols. Berlin: Deutscher Verlag für Kunstwissenschaft, 1971.
Kynan-Wilson 2019
Kynan-Wilson, William. "School of Veronese (around 1548–1588), *A Portrait of Sultan Bayezid I*." In *Inspired by the East: How the Islamic World Influenced Western Art*, edited by William Greenwood and Lucien de Guise, p. 117, cat. 8. London: British Museum Press, 2019.

Lach 1977
Lach, Donald F. *Asia in the Making of Europe*, Vol. 2, Book 2. Chicago: University of Chicago Press, 1977 (paperback edition 1994).
Lucchetta 1964
Lucchetta, Francesca. *Il medico e filosofo bellunese Andrea Alpago (±1522), traduttore di Avicenna: Profilo biografico*. Padua: Editrice Antenore, 1964.
Mac Carthy 2007
Mac Carthy, Ita. "Ariosto the Traveller." *Modern Language Review* 102, no. 2 (2007): pp. 397–409.
Mack 2002
Mack, Rosamond E. *Bazaar to Piazza: Islamic Trade and Italian Art, 1300–1600*. Berkeley: University of California Press, 2002.
Malcolm 2013
Malcolm, Noel. "Positive Views of Islam and of Ottoman Rule in the Sixteenth Century: The Case of Jean Bodin." In *The Renaissance and the Ottoman World*, edited by Anna Contadini and Claire Norton, pp. 197–217. Farnham, UK: Ashgate, 2013.
Marchal 1971
Marchal, Henri, ed. *Arts de l'Islam, des origines à 1700, dans les collections publiques françaises*. Paris: Réunion des Musées Nationaux, 1971.
Marek 1976
Marek, George R. *The Bed and the Throne: The Life of Isabella d'Este*. New York: Harper & Row, 1976.
Meserve 2008
Meserve, Margaret. *Empires of Islam in Renaissance Historical Thought*. Cambridge, MA: Harvard University Press, 2008.
Metcalfe 2013
Metcalfe, Alex. *Muslims and Christians in Norman Sicily: Arabic-Speakers and the End of Islam*. Abingdon, UK: Routledge, 2013.
Mikó 2011
Mikó, Árpád. "Beatrice D'Aragona e il primo rinascimento in Ungheria." In *Italy and Hungary: Humanism and Art in Early Renaissance*, edited by Péter Farbaky and Louis A. Waldman, pp. 409–425. Florence -Milan: Villa I Tatti Officina Libraria, 2011.
Milwright 2014–2015
Milwright, Marcus. "An Ayyubid in Mamluk Guise: The Portrait of Saladin in Paolo Giovio's *Elogia virorum bellica virtute illustrium* (1575)." *Mamluk Studies Review* 18 (2014–2015): pp. 187–217.
Mitchell 1961
Mitchell, Charles. "Felice Feliciano *Antiquarius*." *Proceedings of the British Academy* 47 (1961): pp. 197–221, plates XXVI–XLI.
Montagnani 2016
Montagnani, Cristina. "Autore e lettore: La partita truccata dell'intreccio." In *Orlando Furioso 500 Anni*, edited by Guido Beltramini and Adolfo Tura, pp. 285–295. Ferrara: Sate, 2016.
Necipoğlu 1990
Necipoğlu, Gülrü. "From International Timurid to Ottoman: A Change of Taste in Sixteenth-Century Ceramic Tiles." *Muqarnas* 7 (1990): pp. 136–170.
Necipoğlu 2000
Necipoğlu, Gülrü. "The Serial Portraits of Ottoman Sultans in Comparative Perspective." In *The Sultan's Portrait: Picturing the House of Osman*, edited by Selmin Kangal, pp. 22–61. Istanbul: Işbank, 2000.
Necipoğlu 2010
Necipoğlu, Gülrü. "From Byzantine Constantinople to Ottoman Konstantiniyye: Creation of a Cosmopolitan Capital and Visual Culture under Sultan Meḥmed II." In *From Byzantion to Istanbul: 8000 Years of a Capital*, edited by Koray Durak, pp. 262–277. Istanbul: Sakıp Sabancı Museum, 2010.
Necipoğlu 2012
Necipoğlu, Gülrü. "Visual Cosmopolitanism and Creative Translation: Artistic Conversations with Renaissance Italy in Meḥmed II's Constantinople." *Muqarnas* 29 (2012): pp. 1–81.
Necipoğlu 2014
Necipoğlu, Gülrü. "Connectivity, Mobility and 'Portable Archaeology': Pashas from the Dalmatian Hin-

terland as Cultural Mediators." In *Dalmatia and the Mediterranean: Portable Archaeology and the Poetics of Influence*, edited by Alina Payne, pp. 313–381. Leiden: Brill, 2014.

Nuovo 1999
Nuovo, Angela. "Alberto Pio e Aldo Manuzio." In *Carpi: Una sede principesca del Rinascimento*, edited by Luisa Giordano, pp. 353–356. Pisa: ETS, 1999.

Ohta 2004
Ohta, Alison. "Filigree Bindings of the Mamluk Period." In "Essays in Honor of J. M. Rogers," edited by Doris Behrens-Abouseif and Anna Contadini, *Muqarnas* 21 (2004): pp. 267–276.

Ohta 2013
Ohta, Alison. "Binding Relationships: Mamluk, Ottoman and Renaissance Bookbindings." In *The Renaissance and the Ottoman World*, edited by Anna Contadini and Claire Norton, pp. 221–230. Farnham, UK: Ashgate, 2013.

Orvieto 1969
Orvieto, Paolo. "Un esperto orientalista del '400: Benedetto Dei." *Rinascimento*, 2nd series, 9 (1969): pp. 205–275.

Pajorin 1994
Pajorin, Klára. "La rinascita del simposio antico e la corte di Mattia Corvino." In *Italia e Ungheria all'epoca dell'umanesimo Corviniano*, edited by Sante Graciotti and Cesare Vasoli, pp. 179–228. Florence: Olschki, 1994.

Patrinelis 1971
Patrinelis, Christos G. "Mehmet II the Conqueror and His Presumed Knowledge of Greek and Latin." *Viator* 2 (1971): pp. 349–354.

Pazzini 1943
Pazzini, Adalberto. "Probabile raffigurazione della 'Schola salernitana' in una miniatura del secolo XV." *Accademie e biblioteche d'Italia* 17 (1943): pp. 316–324.

Pellegrino 1908
Pellegrino, Francesco di. *La fleur de la science de pourtraicture, patrons de broderie, facon arabique et ytalique, 1530*. Facsimile edition with introduction by Gaston Migeon. Paris: J. Schemit, 1908.

Piccolomini 1990
Piccolomini, Aeneas Silvius. *Epistola ad Mahomatem (*Epistle to Mohammed II*)*, edited and translated by Albert R. Baca. New York: Peter Lang, 1990.

Piemontese 1999
Piemontese, Angelo Michele. "Le iscrizioni arabe nella *Poliphili Hypnerotomachia*." In *Islam and the Italian Renaissance*, edited by Charles Burnett and Anna Contadini, pp. 199–220. London: Warburg Institute, 1999.

Pouillon 2009
Pouillon, François, ed. *Léon l'Africain*. Paris: Karthala and IISMM, 2009.

Preti 2008
Preti, Cesare. "Mattioli, Pietro Andrea." In *Dizionario biografico degli italiani*, Vol. 72. Rome: Istituto dell'Enciclopedia Italiana Treccani, 2008.

Preto 1975
Preto, Paolo. *Venezia e i Turchi*. Florence: Sansoni, 1975.

Puliatti 1960
Puliatti, Pietro. "Profilo storico del fondo dei manoscritti orientali della Biblioteca Estense." In Carlo Bernheimer, *Catalogo dei manoscritti Orientali della Biblioteca Estense*, pp. vii–xiii. Rome: Istituto Poligrafico dello Stato, 1960.

Raby 1982
Raby, Julian. *Venice, Dürer, and the Oriental Mode*. N.p.: Islamic Art Publications, 1982.

Raby 1983
Raby, Julian. "Meḥmed the Conqueror's Greek Scriptorium." *Dumbarton Oaks Papers* 37 (1983): pp. 15–34.

Raby 1987
Raby, Julian. "Pride and Prejudice: Meḥmed the Conqueror and the Italian Portrait Medal." In *Italian Medals*, edited by J. Graham Pollard, pp. 171–194 Studies in the History of Art 21. Washington, DC: National Gallery of Art, 1987.

Raby 1989

Raby, Julian. "The European Vision of the Muslim Orient in the 16th Century." In *Arte veneziana e arte islamica: Atti del primo simposio internazionale sull'arte veneziana e l'arte islamica*. Edited by Ernst J. Grube, Stefano Carboni and Giovanni Curatola. Venice: L'Altra Riva, 1989, pp. 41–46.

Raby 2000a

Raby, Julian. "Bust Portrait of Meḥmed II." In *The Sultan's Portrait: Picturing the House of Osman*, edited by Selmin Kangal, p. 90, cat. 7. Istanbul: Işbank, 2000.

Raby 2000b

Raby, Julian. "From Europe to Istanbul." In *The Sultan's Portrait: Picturing the House of Osman*, edited by Selmin Kangal, pp. 136–163. Istanbul: Işbank, 2000.

Raby 2000c

Raby, Julian. "Opening Gambits." In *The Sultan's Portrait: Picturing the House of Osman*, edited by Selmin Kangal, pp. 64–79. Istanbul: Işbank, 2000.

Raby 2007

Raby, Julian. "The Serenissima and the Sublime Porte: Art in the Art of Diplomacy 1453–1600." In *Venice and the Islamic World, 828–1797*, edited by Stefano Carboni, pp. 90–119 and cat. 35–38. New York: Metropolitan Museum of Art; New Haven, CT: Yale University Press, 2007 (1st ed. in French, 2006).

Raby and Tanındı 1993

Raby, Julian, and Zeren Tanındı. *Turkish Bookbinding in the 15th Century*. London: Azimuth Editions, 1993.

Ricci 2002

Ricci, Milena. "[Pseudo-]Dionysius Areopagita: Opera e graeco in latinum traducta per Ambrosium monachum florentinum." In *Nel segno del Corvo libri e miniature della biblioteca di Mattia Corvino re d'Ungheria (1443–1490)*, edited by Nicola Bono, Gábor Görgey, Francesco Sicilia, and István Monok, pp. 179–82, cat. 15. Modena: Il Bulino, 2002.

Ricci 2008

Ricci, Giovanni. *I Turchi alle porte*. Bologna: Il Mulino, 2008.

Rice 1957

Rice, D. S. "Inlaid Brasses from the Workshop of Aḥmad al-D̲h̲akī al-Mawṣilī." *Ars Orientalis* 2 (1957): 283–326.

Rodini 2020

Rodini, Elizabeth. *Gentile Bellini's Portrait of Sultan Meḥmed II: Lives and Afterlives of an Iconic Image*. London: I.B. Tauris, 2020.

Rossi 2004

Rossi, Manuela. "Rodolfo Pio e Carpi: Tracce di un legame." In *Alberto III e Rodolfo Pio da Carpi collezionisti e mecenati*, edited by Manuela Rossi, pp. 9–13. Tavagnacco: Arti Grafiche Friulane, 2004.

Salsi 2016

Salsi, Claudio A. M. "Il progetto di restauro della Sala delle Asse nel Castello Sforzesco di Milano." In *Leonardo da Vinci: Metodi e tecniche per la costruzione della conoscenza*, edited by Pietro C. Marani and Rodolfo Maffeis, pp. 115–116. Busto Arsizio: Nomos Edizioni, 2016.

Scerrato 1967

Scerrato, Umberto. *Arte Islamica a Napoli*. Naples: Istituto Universitario Orientale di Napoli, 1967.

Schiaparelli 1871

Schiaparelli, C. *Vocabulista in Arabico*. Florence: Tipografia dei Successori Le Monnier, 1871.

Schmidt Arcangeli 2007

Schmidt Arcangeli, Catarina. "'Orientalist' Painting in Venice, 15th–17th Centuries." In *Venice and the Islamic World, 828–1797*, edited by Stefano Carboni. New York: Metropolitan Museum of Art; New Haven, CT: Yale University Press, 2007 (1st ed. in French 2006), pp. 120–139.

Shalem and Glaser 2014

Shalem, Avinoam, and Maria Glaser. *Die mittelalterlichen Olifante*. Berlin: Deutscher Verlag für Kunstwissenschaft, 2014.

Siraisi 1990

Siraisi, Nancy G. *Medieval and Early Renaissance Medicine: An Introduction to Knowledge and Practice*. Chicago: University of Chicago Press, 1990.

Smith 2014
Smith, Charlotte Colding. *Images of Islam, 1453–1600: Turks in Germany and Central Europe*. Abingdon, UK: Routledge, 2014.
Soucek 2013
Soucek, Svat. "The Ottoman Conquests of Egypt and Algeria." *Conquête ottomane de l'Égypte (1517): Arrière-plan, impact, échos*, edited by Benjamin Lellouch and Nicolas Michel, pp. 79–98. Leiden: Brill, 2013.
Spallanzani 1980
Spallanzani, Marco. "Metalli islamici nelle raccolte medicee da Cosimo I a Ferdinando I." In *Le arti del Principato Mediceo*, pp. 95–115 Florence: SPES, 1980.
Spallanzani 1989
Spallanzani, Marco. "Fonti archivistiche per lo studio dei rapport fra l'Italia e l'Islam: Le arti minori nei secoli XIV–XVI." In *Arte veneziana e arte islamica: Atti del primo simposio internazionale sull'arte veneziana e l'arte islamica*, edited by Ernst J. Grube, Stefano Carboni, and Giovanni Curatola, pp. 83–100. Venice: L'Altra Riva, 1989.
Spallanzani 2007
Spallanzani, Marco. *Oriental Rugs in Renaissance Florence*. Florence: SPES, 2007.
Spallanzani 2010
Spallanzani, Marco. *Metalli islamici a Firenze nel Rinascimento*. Florence: SPES, 2010.
Sternthal 2007
Sternthal, Barbara. *Kreuz Ritter: Pilger, Krieger, Abenteurer*. Schallaburg: Schallaburg Kulturbetriebsges, 2007.
Tamani 1988
Tamani, Giuliano, ed. *Il* Canon medicinae *di Avicenna nella tradizione ebraica*. Padua: Studio Editoriale Programma, 1988.
Tanındı 2019
Tanındı, Zeren. "Arts of the Book: The Illustrated and Illuminated Manuscripts Listed in ʿAtufi's Inventory." In *Treasures of Knowledge: An Inventory of the Ottoman Palace Library (1502/3–1503/4)*, 2 vols., edited by Gülru Necipoğlu, Cemal Kafadar, and Cornell H. Fleischer, Vol. 1, pp. 213–239. [*Muqarnas Supplements* 14 (2019).]
Turan 1968
Turan, Şerafettin. "Venedik'te Türk ticaret merkezi (Fondaco dei Turchi)." *Belleten* 32 (1968): pp. 247–283.
Ullman 1960
Ullman, Berthold L. *The Origin and Development of Humanistic Script*. Rome: Edizioni di Storia e Letteratura, 1960.
Ullman and Stadter 1972
Ullman, Berthold L., and Philip A. Stadter. *The Public Library of Renaissance Florence: Niccolò Niccoli, Cosimo de' Medici and the Library of San Marco*. Padua: Editrice Antenore, 1972.
Urbini 2004
Urbini, Silvia. "Immagini evocate, incise, miniate nei libri di Alberto Pio." In *Alberto III e Rodolfo Pio da Carpi collezionisti e mecenati*, edited by Manuela Rossi, pp. 195–214. Tavagnacco: Arti Grafiche Friulane, 2004.
Ursu 1909
Ursu, Ion, ed. *Historia turchesca (1300–1514)*. Bucharest: Editiunea Academiei Romane, 1909.
Valentinelli 1873
Valentinelli, Giuseppe. *Bibliotheca manuscripta ad S. Marei Venetiarum*, Vol. 6. Venice: Typographia Commercii, 1873.
Vasoli 1978
Vasoli, Cesare. *Alberto III Pio da Carpi*. Carpi: Assessorato ai Servizi Culturali, 1978.
Venturi 1882
Venturi, Adolfo. *La R. Galleria Estense in Modena*. Modena: Paolo Toschi, 1882.
Zimmermann 2001
Zimmermann, T. C. Price. "Giovio, Paolo." In *Dizionario biografico degli italiani*, Vol. 56. Rome: Istituto dell'Enciclopedia Italiana Treccani, 2001.

Images of Rodomonte: The Ambiguous Allure of the Enemy in the *Furioso* and in the Ariostan Figurative Tradition

Vincenzo Farinella

1. Rodomonte in Boiardo

In Matteo Maria Boiardo's *Inamoramento de Orlando,* Rodomonte (or, rather, Rodamonte, as he is always called by the earlier Este poet) appears in the first canto of the second book (II i 52), in the great collective scene set in the palace of Biserta, where Agramante welcomes thirty-two Saracen kings summoned to discuss the impending war in France.[1] We are in a huge room decorated with scenes from the life of Alexander the Great.[2] This should not be surprising, since Alexander was considered the progenitor of the African kings and, consequently, through the figure of Ruggiero, also of the Este family. A given (poetic) fact, this Muslim lineage present in Este blood, usually ignored in favor of a Trojan pedigree, cannot be completely neglected or effaced. Ruggiero, in fact, even if he will subsequently discover that both of his parents were Christians and will convert thanks to Bradamante's love, is to all effects and purposes a Saracen knight.[3]

Rodamonte, king of Sarza, son of Ulieno, king of Algiers, is immediately presented as the most daring young man present at this royal assembly, but at the same time, he is endowed with such pride as to drive him to despise the whole world:

> Il re de Sarza fo un giovene arguto:
> questo era il figlio del forte Ulieno,
> magior assai di patre, e più membruto.
> nul'altro fo d'ardir più colmo e pieno,
> ma fo superbo e orgoglioso tanto
> che dispregiava il mondo tuto quanto.
> —*Inam.* II i 52
> [The king of Sarza was a bold
> Young man, stout Ulieno's son,
> Who passed his father's size and strength.

The brimming valor he could vaunt
None matched; but he was arrogant,
And he despised the whole wide world.]

He accuses the old and prudent kings of cowardice and betrayal, challenging them to a duel. We are faced with a ferocious young man, endowed with a formidably fierce spirit and a hugely powerful body, capable of each and every feat, feared by all. The literary models from which Boiardo draws vary from Capaneus to the *Thebaid* of Statius (IX, 548–550) to the Virgilian Mesenzius (*Aeneid* X, 773–774) or even to Ulieno of the anonymous epic poem of the fifteenth century *Aspramonte*[4]—famous archetypes of the impudent hero, inevitably destined by his own hubris to ruin. The elderly king of Garamanta predicts, in the event of a war in France, the defeat of the Saracen army and the death of Rodamonte, but the young man replies in a booming voice, arrogantly challenging the soothsayer and swearing allegiance to King Agramante.

In the third canto of the second book (II iii 22), the image of Rodamonte is enriched with a contemptuous and scandalous "profession of faith," based on the conception of a god isolated in the heavens and indifferent to human passions—similar to the deity present in *De rerum natura* of Lucretius ("rediscovered" by Poggio Bracciolini at the Benedectine monastery of Fulda in 1417 and well known in Italy during the fifteenth century)—on the part of an antihero who essentially despises the divinity, trusting only in himself and in his own indomitable courage:

Se egli è alcun dio nel ciel (ch'io nol sciò certo)
là stassi ad alto e di qua già non cura;
omo non è che l'abbia visto esperto,
ma la vil gente crede per paura.
Io de la mia fede vi ragiono aperto,
che sol il mio bon brando e l'armatura
e la maza ch'io porto al destrier mio
e l'animo ch'io ho son il mio dio!
—*Inam*. II iii 22
[If there's a God, which I don't know,
His care's above, not here below.
There's no one who has witnessed him,
But craven men believe from fear.
I'll tell you my faith openly:

It's just my armor, my good sword,
My horse, the club I carry, and
The heart I have—I'm my own god.]

At this point, Rodamonte crashes through the inertia, deciding to go it alone, with his army, to France to defeat Charlemagne and wrest the crown from his head. But leaving aside Boiardo's poem and moving on to Ariosto's "junction" to it, in the group of cantos (XIV–XVIII) that witness the subject matter of war erupting into the poem, we take up the thread of the story of the siege of Paris, broken off in *Inam.* III viii.

2. Rodomonte in Ariosto

Ariosto presents Rodomonte for the first time in *Orlando furioso* XIV, where the long description of the siege of Paris begins (compared, due to its bloody outcome, to the dramatic battle of Ravenna [1512], exalting the decisive role played there by Duke Alfonso I d'Este). Rodomonte is a true antihero, characterized by unbridled strength and audacity but also by an insatiable aversion to Christianity (which tends toward a more general loathing of religion).[5] His image is confused with that of the banner, already described twice in *Inam.* II vii 28, and II xiv 20, almost as if Ariosto wanted to blatantly pick up the thread of the story left suspended by Boiardo. The lion harnessed by the beloved lady (Doralice) allows Ariosto, before launching into a description of the contradictory aspects of the character and physical appearance of this antihero, to emphasize that Rodomonte *cortesia e valor per lei mostrava* (showed courtesy and valor for her; *Fur.*, XIV 115, 5). We are faced with a courteous and at the same time cruel hero, who despises danger but blasphemes God, a sort of new Nimrod (both the biblical and the Dantesque giant who became an example of pride and revolt against God), indomitable, proud, and furious as a wild boar, despising the heavens and easily capable of massacring Christian knights (there are eighteen names of those he has already killed in the fighting around Paris), a champion of strength and dexterity, power and agility, but unfit for command (all of his soldiers will perish in this battle, and only he will manage to save himself).

Ariosto is clearly fascinated by this grandiose (for better or for worse) character, invented by Boiardo, for his overbearing and irrepressible vitality. The classical models evoked by the fifteenth-century poet from Scandiano allowed Ariosto to create an extreme example of reckless audacity, of haughty and uncontrollable arrogance: "E come Boiardo e più di lui, che affiancava a Rodomonte altri personaggi . . ., Ariosto isola al centro della narrazione questa figura che si staglia sull'immenso clamore degli eserciti" (And as Boiardo and other [chivalric poets] flanked Rodomonte with other characters . . ., Ariosto isolates this figure, who stands out against the immense clamor of the armies, at the center of his narrative.)[6] The poet, however, seduced by the allure exerted by this immense figure, offers a much more chiaroscuro portrait of Rodomonte than Boiardo does, sketching his defects and virtues with greater flexibility, in order to create not a horrible and inhuman monster but a dramatic figure, exalted and overwhelmed by his own excesses.

The victory of Cardinal Ippolito at the battle of Polesella (1509) is praised in canto XV because it was obtained almost without damage to Este weaponry, in contrast to the bold but ill-advised actions of Rodomonte between the inner and outer walls of Paris. The Saracen king indeed manages to save himself from the consuming fire in the space below with a *mirabil salto* (marvelous leap; *Fur.*, XV 5, 2) but, while he *bestemmia il cielo con spaventoso grido* (curses the sky with a terrifying cry; *Fur.*, XV 5, 8), unwittingly condemns his soldiers to a terrible death in the burning pit. Although the Saracen king here embodies the negative example of the captain *troppo in suo danno audace* (too much to his daring damage; *Fur.*, XV 3, 1) we are far from the "giocosa indifferenza con cui Rodomonte vede perire quasi tutto il suo esercito nella battaglia sulla costa francese, nel sesto canto del libro II dell'*Inamoramento*" (playful indifference with which Rodomonte sees almost all his army perish in the battle on the French coast, in the sixth canto of book II of the *Inamoramento*).[7]

In the sixteenth canto, Ariosto makes use of a new model, the Virgilian Turnus, committed to perpetrating a massacre in the Trojan camp (*Aeneid* IX, 728ff.) and considerably more noble and dramatic than the purely negative examples of Capaneus and Mesenzius used by Boiardo. Rodomonte, even more terrifying and hideous, has become *l'africano Marte* (the African Mars; *Fur.*, XV1 19, 6), absolutely sure of himself in the memorable leap that has kept him—the singularly atrocious and rugged Saracen—safe from the Christian flames. Like a tiger or a wolf, he effects immense slaughter, putting all on the run and showing pity for no one; his greatest value is inextricably linked to his enormous cruelty. *L'empio re, capo e signor de li empi* (The wicked king, chief and lord of the wicked; *Fur.*, XV1 26, 2), he burns houses and temples, destroys walls more effectively than a cannon. Practically like a new Satan, surrounded by horrible signs of his cruelty (bodies torn to pieces, human limbs scattered everywhere), he almost wins the battle and destroys Paris entirely on his own. Here, too, with respect to Boiardo's model, it is possible to "ammirare nella dismisura dell'eroe pagano una maggiore potenza letteraria, un tono acre e oscuro dalle radici virgiliane" (admire in the excess of the pagan hero a greater literary force, an acrid and dark tone with Virgilian roots).[8]

Canto XVII opens with a catalogue of ancient and modern *tiranni atrocissimi e mostri* (fearful tyrants and monsters; *Fur.*, XVII 1, 5)—Gaius Marius and Sulla, Nero and Caligula, Domitian, Elagabalus and Maximinus Thrax, Creon and Mezentius, Attila and Ezzelino III da Romano—in order to introduce the fury of Rodomonte, *d'orgoglio e d'ira pazzo* (Of pride and mad anger; *Fur.*, XVII 9, 5), a lone man remarkably destroying Paris all on his own, a city that now appears in the eyes of Charlemagne as a *terra desolata* (wasteland; *Fur.*, XVII 7, 3). In Rodomonte's act of unhinging the doors of the palace, Ariosto mentions a further illustrious Virgilian model, Pyrrhus Neoptolemus, the son of Achilles, committed to slaughtering the Trojans in the tragic night sung of in the second book of the *Aeneid*. Rodomonte is a brutal man, but in his heroic solitude, he nevertheless reveals signs of tragic grandeur; Charlemagne and seven paladins together hurl themselves against him (not, it must be admitted, in the highest chivalric manner) to collectively wound him in the chest, hips, and forehead.

The attack of these eight Christians against the *crudo Moro* (crude Moor; *Fur.*, XVIII 9, 4) results in a stalemate in canto XVIII. His *scagliosa scorza* (scaly rind; *Fur.*, XVIII 9, 3) not only easily rebuffs the assault but allows Rodomonte to magnify his solitude even further in a majestic visual metaphor, like a ship whipped by the wind. Fourteen other paladins join the fight (they now make twenty-two), raging *tutti intorno al Saracin crudele* (all around the cruel Saracen; *Fur.*, XVIII 9, 3), who shudders with pride and indignation. No one manages to hurt him, he suffers not even a scratch, while the whole populace of Paris, heartened by the arrival of Charlemagne, rushes against him. At this point, impious Rodomonte, with eyes as horrible as a furious bull, having already effected a sizable massacre, decides to save himself. With dozens of his enemies torn to pieces, the square filled with human limbs cut off from their bodies, *tutto di sangue il fier pagano asperso* (all the blood the proud pagan had spilled; *Fur.*, XVIII 20, 5), he retreats without manifesting any fear and heads toward the river in a storm of arrows (taking up again the analogy with Virgil's Turnus, similarly engaged within the Trojan camp in the ninth book of the *Aeneid*). Three times he returns from the banks of the Seine, to throw himself back into the fray, killing more than a hundred of the opposing forces, but in the end, reason sees the better of anger and rage, and Rodomonte dives into the Seine, showing no difficulty whatsoever in swimming away under the weight of his armor and weapons. At this point, at long last, the Ariostan celebration unfolds: Africa has never generated such a valorous giant, neither the mythical titan Antaeus nor the great Carthaginian strategist Hannibal are worthy of being compared to him. But arriving safely on the other shore, Rodomonte is desperate for not having completed the destruction of the French city, and pride and anger for a moment almost compel him back to complete the work. "Il grande eroe che contempla la città, un attimo prima nelle sue mani, è un passo che veramente ricrea l'antico" (The great hero who contemplates the city, a moment before in his hands, is a passage that truly recreates the ancient).[9]

But at this point, the intervention of Discord, Pride, and Jealousy suddenly alters the image of Rodomonte; "le gesta 'virgiliane' dell'eroe saraceno si trasformano nell'ira furiosa di un innamorato tradito" (the "Virgilian" deeds of the Saracen hero are transformed into the furious anger of a betrayed lover).[10] Rodomonte all but becomes a Saracen counterpart to Orlando, driven mad by love and jealousy. The Saracen hero learns from a dwarf that Mandricardo has kidnapped Doralice, and he suddenly abandons the battlefield, forgetting Paris and the glory of war, in order to set out in search of his beloved, thus involuntarily contributing to the defeat of the pagan troops. The Virgilian model of Turnus is momentarily abandoned, to transform Rodomonte into an incarnation of the furious insanity provoked by unbridled amorous passion.

The clash between Mandricardo and Rodomonte—*duo pagani, senza pare in terra* (two pagans, without equal on earth; *Fur.*, XXIV 100, 1)—takes place in stanzas 94–115 of canto XXIV. But Doralice convinces them to suspend their duel and rush to the rescue of the Saracen camp, besieged by Christian arms, thus allowing Love to temporarily prevail over Discord and Pride. In canto XXVI, it is actually Rodomonte who interrupts the fight that breaks out between Mandricardo and Marfisa, reminding them that Agramante needs their help and becoming, at least momentarily, an example of the chivalrous virtue of fidelity. But in the following canto, Rodomonte's wild nature explodes again. Confronted with Doralice's unexpected decision to favor Mandricardo, Rodomonte indignantly abandons the Saracen camp, while at the same time he considers rescuing his own king Agramante, in order to help him regain his kingdom after he had lost it, demonstrating the value of true friendship.[11]

Rodomonte meets Isabella in canto XXVIII and immediately falls hopelessly in love with the unblemished young woman. In the face of her determination to abandon the world and dedicate herself to God, *Ride il pagan altier che in Dio non crede, / d'ogni legge inimico e d'ogni fede* (The presumptuous pagan who does not believe in God laughs, enemy of every law and faith; *Fur.* XXVIII 100, 7–8). But it is in the following canto that the negative image of Rodomonte reaches its culmination. He first brutally casts away the hermit who had accompanied

Isabella and kept her safe; he then makes an agreement with the young woman, never doubting that he can break the pact as he pleases:

> Ma 'l suo pensiero è poi rompere il patto,
> perché non ha timor né reverenzia
> di Dio o di santi; e nel mancar di fede
> tutta a lui la bugiarda Africa cede"
> —*Fur.*, XXIX 18, 4-8
> [But his thought is to break the covenant, because he has no fear or reverence of God or of saints; and in the lack of faith all to him the liar Africa yields].

And finally, after shamelessly getting drunk, he falls into a moral and rhetorical trap, unwittingly killing Isabella, transforming himself into a merciless *nuovo Breusse* (new Brehus; *Fur.* XXIX 30, 8), a negative character in Breton romance, an "anti-courteous" knight par excellence. But immediately after, Rodomonte resolves to seek redemption through erecting a monument to Isabella's memory, as grandiose as the emperor Hadrian's mausoleum in Rome, and consecrating his life as a sign of expiation to the memory of his beloved. It is at this point that the clash with Orlando on the bridge takes place, and the two oversized heroes, both turned mad for love and fiercely embraced in conflict, plunge into the river.[12] From this point forward, in the final third of the *Furioso*, the figure of Rodomonte gradually becomes more and more marginal, before suddenly reappearing, larger than life, in the final stanzas of the poem.

After the duel on the bridge with Brandimarte, taken prisoner by the Saracen king (A XXIX 64–75), Rodomonte, refusing the offers made to him to return to fight in the army of Agramante (A XXX 5), also clashes with Bradamante, and, defeated and humiliated, he retreats to a cave (A XXXII 42–54), disappearing for a long stretch from the plot of the *Furioso*. But at the apex of the last canto, the boundless nature of Rodomonte—even for evil—reemerges, together with the indisputably ambiguous allure he exercised over the poet (the same enigmatic fascination that the great Saracen sovereigns exercised—as we shall see—on the imaginations of Western princes, intellectuals, and artists). The death of the great pagan rebel is, in fact, clearly modeled on that of Turnus, which closes the *Aeneid*:

> hoc dicens ferrum adverso sub pectore condit
> fervidus; ast illi solvuntur frigore membra
> vitaque cum gemitu fugit indignata sub umbras.

—*Aeneid* 12.950–952
[Incensed, he thrust his sword through Turnus's chest.
His enemy's body soon grew cold and helpless,
While the indignant soul flew down to Hades.]

Alle squalide ripe d'Acheronte,
lasciando il corpo più freddo che giaccio,
biastemmiando fuggì l'alma sdegnosa,
che fu sì altiera al mondo e sì orgogliosa.
—*Fur.* LXVI 140, 5–8
[Released from its body, now ice-cold, the angry spirit, which, among the living, had been so proud and insolent, fled cursing down to the dismal shores of Acheron.]

The citation is so explicit here—it is for all intents and purposes a translation of Virgil's Latin text—that it can be taken as a striking example of "allusive art." The reader is thus not only compelled to appreciate the ability of the early modern poet to rewrite and update in his own vernacular the famous Virgilian verses but is also prompted to grasp the kinship between Turnus and Rodomonte, the two antiheroes with which both poems conclude, driven by fate toward death but nevertheless defined by a sense of undeniable grandeur.[13]

3. Rodomonte and Contemporary History

The figure of Rodomonte stands apart in the *Furioso* and reveals, on the part of the poet, a patent fascination with a character who seems to synthesize the defects and merits of the great antiheroes of literature, among the most memorable "villains" of our collective imagination. Ariosto is beguiled by the equivocal charm of an evil hero, unparalleled in the Muslim camp and with whom there are very few analogues even in the Christian one. In considering the sources that inspired the Ferrarese poet, beyond the obvious literary models, we must ask ourselves whether in this case, as in others, the events and protagonists of contemporary history have not left their mark on the text. It is well known, for example, that behind the figure of Isabella, the chaste heroine who voluntarily chooses death in order not to betray the memory of her beloved, is the historical figure of Isabella d'Este, the marquise of Mantua honored in the poem not only explicitly, in the passages in which she is remembered and praised as a great protector of the arts and literature, but also implicitly, as she is assimilated into one of the noblest protagonists of the *Furioso* (A XXVII 29).[14] This is a question of the encomiums implicit within the the poem, of its subterranean relations—but as such no less evident to the first readers of the *Furioso*—with contemporaneity, an interpretative trail that does not seem to me adequately addressed by scholars of the Ariostan cosmos. Contemporary history left its mark as never before in this chivalric romance (as recently reiterated by Alberto Casadei),[15] but it also appears to have transfigured itself under the guises of the heroes and heroines of the poem, positive or negative as they may be.

As a case in point, I have been wondering for some time, rereading the *Furioso* in its various editions, if behind the figure of the "grand duke" Astolfo—a profoundly transformed character in Ariosto with respect to the ridiculous swaggerer of the *Inamoramento*, who has now become a veritable deus ex machina of the poem's narrative action—there might not be a celebratory undercurrent of the virtues of the Este duke Alfonso I, who, with his brother Ippolito, shared the role of protector and patron of the poet. In this case, not the homonymous Isabella but the onomastic assonance Astolfo/Alfonso and the repetition of the title of "duke" could well have constituted significant clues for the contemporary reader.

I would rather not, at least for now, venture too far into a field in which it would be easy to lose one's way in the pursuit of perhaps overly facile analogies. But before examining how visual artists reacted to the stimuli embodied in Ariosto's Rodomonte, I would like to merely pose the question of whether with regard to this character, apart from the clearly literary models (Nimrod, Capaneus, Mesenzius, Turnus, Pyrrhus Neoptolemus, Brehus), we might not advance the hypothesis, with all due caution (i.e., in the absence of objective and incontrovertible evidence), that the poet's imagination was fertilized by the suggestive example of a protagonist of contemporary history. Provisionally admitting the possibility and considering the moment in which the first redaction of the *Furioso* was completed, one turns almost inevitably to Selīm I, called *Yāvūz*, the Strong (or Audacious) or the Cruel (or Severe), sultan of the Ottoman Empire from April 24, 1512, to September 21, 1520. A historical figure whose vices and virtues fascinated the West, he was remarkably effective in vastly extending the borders of his empire with a series of lightning-fast military campaigns in Persia, Syria, and Egypt but also capable of brutal and apparently inhuman "political" crimes in order to avoid problems of succession.[16] After forcing his father to abdicate, Selīm exterminated his brothers, other potential usurpers, and even his own children, with the exception of his designated heir, Süleymān Şāh bin Selīm Şāh Khān, who would come to be known in the West as Süleymān the Magnificent. A grandiose and disturbing "antihero," Selīm was made the protagonist and idealized recipient of an anonymous Italian poem written in *ottave* between 1515 and 1517, inspired by Pulci and Boiardo: eight thousand verses divided into twelve cantos that celebrate a character who is anything but execrated, treated even as "un principe europeo del Rinascimento"[17] (a European Renaissance prince). After effecting the fall of Constantinople (1453) and the end of the Eastern Roman Empire, Selīm's grandfather Meḥmed II the Conqueror had assumed the title of *Qayṣer-i Rūm* (Caesar of the Romans) that was inherited by successive Ottoman sultans and maintained for nearly half a millennium, until 1922. Furthermore, it was Selīm I, "per dominar il mondo al mondo nato" (born into the world to dominate it), who would be the Muslim conqueror of the Mamluk kingdom, unleashing, between 1516 and 1517, a war against his own coreligionists. In Ariosto's poem, Rodomonte similarly had no fear of blaspheming the divinity and proudly declaring his essential absence of religious faith.

In this context, the ambiguous allure exercised by Islam on the mentality of Renaissance Italy must be taken into account: an Other—enemy—culture, and not only for religious motives but with which it was nevertheless possible to establish "dangerous relations" as well as explicit political and military alliances (even on the part of the Roman papacy). In the Turkish-Venetian war of 1499–1502 , for example, Milan and Naples were allies of Sultan Bāyezīd II against Venice, while in 1509, during the war of Venice against the League of Cambrai, it was a group of Venetian senators who proposed calling on the Turks for help.[18] The flaunted, even if never realized, desire to launch a new Crusade to liberate Constantinople and Jerusalem together with simultaneous secret negotiations with the Turks emerge, for example, from a famous document of Amico Aspertini, now in the British Museum (fig. 1), where the parody of Julius II (expelled from Bologna in the second half of 1511) also touches on the Islamic "problem," as demonstrated by the "portrait" of the sultan that appears, unexpectedly, embroidered on the pope's chest.[19]

A number of artists in these years demonstrated an affinity for the Muslim world. According to the trustworthy Condivi,[20] Michelangelo—an artist whose deep religious faith can hardly be doubted—is said to have planned, in the most bitter moment of his dispute with Julius II, to move to Constantinople. He was to have built a bridge over the Bosphorus Strait for the sultan but was only convinced to abandon the project through the providential intervention of Piero Soderini, as shown in a painting by Mirabello Cavalori, now at the National Gallery in London, and in another, by Giovanni Biliverti, in the seventeenth-century biographical cycle in Casa Buonarroti in Florence, in which the sultan's ambassadors are shown trying to convince the artist to move to

Fig. 1. Amico Aspertini, *Political Allegory* (at the center a portrait of Julius II and an image of a Turk on his chest), 1511. London, British Museum, Department of Prints and Drawings, inv. 1939-10-14-148

the East. There is an earlier letter, dated July 3, 1503, from Leonardo da Vinci to Bāyezīd II (lost but translated into Turkish and copied by the sultan's chancellery, in Topkapi Palace), wherein the artist, evidently in search of new job opportunities shortly before obtaining the prestigious Florentine commission for the *Battle of Anghiari*, offers his skills as architect and hydraulic engineer, declaring himself ready to design a bridge capable of connecting Galata to Istanbul, the two banks of the Golden Horn, and an innovative drawbridge over the Bosphorus.[21] Although neither Leonardo nor Michelangelo ever realized these Ottoman prospects, there were many Western engineers and architects who worked in the territories of the Muslim Empire, following the peace treaty signed by Venice with the Turks in December 1502.[22]

It is too complex a story to be summarized here, but the studies of Giovanni Ricci have taught us how in those years, Italy was "divisa fra il terrore del Turco, la speranza nel suo arrivo e l'attesa di schierarsi col vincitore, chiunque egli fosse"[23] (divided between terror of the Turk, hope for his arrival, and the expectation to side with the winner, whoever he was to be).

4. The Iconography of Rodomonte

The problem I would like to pose here is whether this ambiguous allure of the enemy, the covert fascination for the figure of Rodomonte that is perceived in Ariosto's poem, can also be perceived in the figurative tradition that emerged from the *Furioso* over the course of the sixteenth century.[24]

In the fifteen years between 1516 and 1532, which saw the *Orlando furioso* gradually establish itself—from its debut as a Ferrarese poem addressed to the Este court to its canonization as a masterpiece of Italian literature—the only figurative text unquestionably inspired by Ariosto's poetry is the painting by Battista Dossi now in the collection of Wadsworth Atheneum in Hartford, Connecticut, datable to the mid-twenties of the sixteenth century (fig. 2),[25] when the second edition of the text (1521) was then available. A painting of less than overwhelming quality, it has consequently often been underestimated by scholars, considered only as a simple, flat illustration of a famous passage from the poem (which has also known, over the centuries, other figurative translations, such as the one provided in 1838 by Giuseppe Bisi (fig. 3), notable for its Oriental interpretation of the mausoleum of Isabella and Zerbino, built by Rodomonte and therefore imagined as an Islamic mosque complete with a minaret).[26] The relevant verses of the poem see Orlando, reduced through his own madness to a bestial and antiheroic nudity, fighting furiously against the Saracen Rodomonte, who stood guard over a bridge near the mausoleum of Isabella, created by the king of Algiers to atone for the involuntary murder of his beloved.

Placar o in parte satisfar pensosse
a l'anima beata d'Issabella,
che, poi che a morte il corpo le percosse,
desse almen vita alla memoria d'ella.
Trovò per mezo (aciò che così fosse)
di convertirle quella chiesa, quella
dove abitava e dove ella fu uccisa,
in un sepolcro; e vi dirò in che guisa.

Di tutti i luochi intorno fe' venire
mastri, chi per amore e chi per tema;
e più di se' mila uomini fe' unire;
con questi i monti dei gran sassi scema,
e ne fa una gran massa stabilire,
che da la cima era alla parte estrema

Fig. 2. Battista Dossi, *Duel of Orlando and Rodomonte*, ca. 1527, Hartford, Conn., Wadsworth Atheneum

Fig. 3. Giuseppe Bisi, *Orlando and Rodomonte Fight in the Presence of Fiordiligi*, 1838. Brescia, Musei Civici di Arte e di Storia

novanta braccia; e vi rinchiude dentro
la chiesa, che i due amanti avea nel centro.

Imita quasi la superba mole
che fe' Adriano all'onda tiberina.
Presso al sepolcro una torre alta vuole;
ch'abitarvi alcun tempo si destina.
Un ponte stretto e di due braccia sole
fece su l'acqua che correa vicina:
lungo il ponte, ma largo era sì poco,
che dava a pena dui cavalli luoco;

a dui cavalli che venuti a paro,
o che insieme si fussero scontrati;
e non avea né sponda né riparo,
e si potea cader da tutti i lati.
Il passar quindi vuol che costi caro
a guerrieri o pagani o battezati;
che de le spoglie lor mille trofei
promette al cimiterio di costei.
—Fur. (A XXVII 31-34)[27]

[He considered how to placate or in part to satisfy Isabel's blessed soul: that though he had slain her body, at least he could give life to her memory. To this end he converted the chapel in which he was living–the site of her death–into a tomb for her. This is how he did it. / He assembled masons from the whole vicinity, some with blandishments, others with threats; and more than six thousand men he brought together, with these he deprived the hills of many huge rocks, had these compacted as a great mound, ninety yards from top to bottom, which encased the chapel containing the pair of lovers. / It almost copied the imposing mound thrown up by Hadrian on the Tiber's bank. Beside the tomb he had a tall tower built in which he planned to live awhile. Over the nearby river he built a narrow bridge, but two yards wide. The bridge was long, but so narrow that it scarcely allowed room for two horses, / whether approaching it abreast or arriving from opposite ends. The bridge had no parapet of any kind: it was possible to fall off either side. He meant to exact a high toll from every knight who crossed the bridge, whether pagan or Christian—he promised their spoil as trophies for the couple's tomb.][28]

The painting depicts a clash between two heroes, one standing for good, the other for evil, both of them otherwise driven "mad" for their lost loves. It should be noted, in this context, that of the two protagonists, Rodomonte maintains intact his chivalrous identity, entirely abandoned and forgotten by the bestial Orlando. Rodomonte, clad in splendid armor and an elegant cloak, indeed appears to be nobly engaged in the fight, and as he crushes Orlando's bare foot with his steel-shod foot, he seems almost surprised at not being able to contain the feral madness of his contender. Of the two entwined figures, the one that preserves his humanity (ignoring the poet's verses, which compare him to a stolid bear that rages against the tree from which it fell; see below, stanza 46, 5–8) is precisely Rodomonte. This contest can only end, however, with a crazed entangled flight of both figures into the swirling waves of the river:

A caso venne il furioso conte [Orlando]
a capitar su questa gran riviera,
dove (come io vi dico) Rodomonte
far in fretta facea, né finito era
il sepolcro e la torre e il stretto ponte:
di tutte l'arme, fuor che la visera,
a quell'ora il pagan si trovò in punto,
ch'Orlando al fiume e al ponte è sopraggiunto.

Orlando (come el suo furor lo caccia)
salta la sbarra e sopra il ponte corre.
Ma Rodomonte con turbata faccia,
a piè, come era innanzi a la gran torre,
gli grida di lontano e gli minaccia,
né si gli degna con la spada opporre:
—Ritorna, temerario asino, indrieto,
importuno villan poco discreto!

Sol per signori e cavallieri è fatto
il ponte, non per te, bestia balorda.—
Orlando, ch'era in gran pensier distratto,
vien pur inanzi e fa l'orecchia sorda.
—Bisogna ch'io castighi questo matto—
disse il pagano; e con la voglia ingorda
se ne venìa per traboccarlo in l'onda,
non pensando trovar chi gli risponda.

. . .

Per far del ponte l'un l'altro cadere
a por tutta lor forza sono intenti.
—Come è che un pazzo debbia sì valere?—
seco il fiero pagan dice tra' denti;
e qua e là si volge e si raggira,
pieno di sdegno e di superbia et ira.

Con l'una e l'altra man va ricercando
far nuova presa, ove il suo meglio vede;
or tra le gambe, or fuor gli pone quando
con arte il destro, e quando il manco piede.
Simiglia Rodomonte intorno a Orlando
il stolido orso che sveller si crede
l'arbor onde è caduto; e come n'abbia
quello ogni colpa, odio gli porta e rabbia.

Orlando, che l'ingegno aveva immerso
io non so dove, e sol la forza usava,
l'estreme forze a cui per l'universo
nessuno o raro paragon di dava,
cader dal ponte si lasciò riverso
col pagano abbracciato come stava.
Cadon nel fiume e vanno al fondo insieme:
ne salta in aria l'onda, e il lito geme.[29]
—*Fur.* (A XXVII 40–42; 45, 3–8; 47)

[If those he overthrew were pagans, he contented himself with despoiling them and taking their arms on which, before hanging them on the marble of the tomb, he clearly inscribed the name of their erstwhile owner. The Christians he held prisoner, and I believe he later sent them all to Algiers. The building work was not yet completed when who should arrive but mad Orlando. / The raving count chanced to arrive at the wide river where Rodomont, as I've said, was urgently building but had not yet finished the tomb, the tower, or the narrow bridge. Except for his visor the pagan was fully armed at the moment when Orlando came to the river and the bridge. / Impelled by his madness, Orlando jumped over the barrier and ran onto the bridge. Rodomont glowered as he waited on foot in front of the great tower, and yelled threats at him from a distance: he would not deign to use his sword against him. "Go back, far away, reckless ass, unwelcome, inconsiderate, villain: / this bridge is for lords and knights, not for the like of you!" Now Orlando, who was in a daydream, did not listen but simply kept on. "I'll have to punish the idiot," said the pagan; and with an insatiable urge, he made to hurl him into the water, never imagining he would meet resistance. / At this point a gentle maiden arrived at the bridge to cross the river. She was dainty in her dress, her face comely and her manner studiedly modest. She was Fiordiligi, the damsel (you may remember, my Lord) who was looking for the traces of her lover Brandimart, in every place except where he actually was, in Paris. / She reached the bridge at the moment when Orlando came to grips with Rodomont, who wanted to throw him into the river. Now she was well acquainted with the count and recognized him at once. She was astonished at the folly that possessed him to go about naked. / She stopped to see what would result from the fury of two men as strong as these. Each was intent on putting all his might into heaving the other off the bridge. "How can a madman be so strong?" the pagan muttered between his teeth as he twisted and turned this way and that, full of bile, contempt, and rage. / He tried out new holds with either hand, looking for the best grip, and skillfully advanced his right foot or his left, now between the other's legs, now outside them. Rodomont at grips with Orlando looked like the sturdy bear expecting to uproot the tree out of which he has fallen—as though the tree were wholly to blame and he were furious with it. / Orlando, whose wits were already soaked, I know not where, and who was relying solely on his massive strength (which few, if any, could match), dropped backwards off the bridge still clasping the pagan. They fell into the river with a mighty splash and sank to the bottom together, while the banks groaned.]

But in fact, as suggested several years ago by Andrea Marchesi,[30] this painting—seemingly disappointing in its flatly illustrative appearance, interesting at first glance perhaps only for its chronological proximity to the second edition of the *Furioso*—reveals a significant impulse to update and interpret the Ariostan verses still hot off the press, only a few years following their publication. Various elements of the landscape background (the still-unfinished turreted palace, only partially covered with marble slabs, the box hedges as fences for fallow deer and roe deer, the small country church, the wooden bridge) seem, ideally, to situate the scene in the Belvedere of Alfonso I d'Este, the paradisiacal *delizia* built on an islet in the middle of the Po River, an arrow's shot from the walls of Ferrara, which constituted a veritable *paradiso del principe* (princely paradise), a setting for courtly *otium* (leisure) and refreshment, but at the same time a spectacular cultural manifesto of the Este regime, after the difficult and dramatic years of the wars with Venice and with Julius II.[31] Given that the Belvedere *delizia* was still under construction when Ariosto completed the first draft of the poem in October 1515 and thus goes unmentioned in those passages of the poem dedicated to encomiastically celebrating the protagonists and the works of the Este court, it is no coincidence that the site should come to occupy a significant space in the definitive version of the 1532 *Furioso* (XLIII 56–59), there celebrated on a par with other sites of pleasure in the ancient world (the Homeric island of the Phaeacians, the villa of Tiberius on Capri, the mythical garden of the Hesperides, the palace of Circe) and destined to welcome even Venus, after abandoning Cyprus and Cnidus, in the company of the Graces and Cupid.[32]

In Dossi's painting, most likely executed for a member of the Este family or for a member of the court (as seems pointedly suggested by the allusions to the courtly context of the Belvedere), Ariosto's verses have been visually interpreted not only to tell a drama of love and madness, in which the two greatest heroes of the opposing camps, Christian and Moor, collide—both of them overwhelmed and united by unfortunate and fatal loves—but also to set these distant events in the contemporary context of Ferrara, as if the islet of Belvedere, with its architecture, its fountains, its gardens, and its exotic fauna, could offer a suggestive background for staging the stories of medieval heroes before the eyes of its patrons, in an open-air theatrical setting. There are, moreover, other well-known examples of "actualization" of the ancient chivalric legends in the extended Este context: Pisanello's fresco cycle in the Palazzo Ducale in Mantua, depicting the episode of Lancelot du Lac at the tournament of the Chateau de la Marche, likely contains figures representing contemporary protagonists (Leonello and Borso d'Este, Gianfrancesco Gonzaga), alluding, as hypothesized by Maria Luisa Meneghetti, to dynastic problems within the Este court; the detail of the lion with the lioness and the two lions could refer to Leonello, to his wife, Margherita Gonzaga, and the offspring born of this marriage.[33]

The backstory of the showdown between Rodomonte and Orlando, the tragic (albeit involuntary) beheading of Isabella, is shown in another famous visual interpretation of the poem (fig. 4). Located in the ducal palace of Sassuolo, in the room dedicated to "Marital Fidelity" within the duchess's apartment, the court painter of Francesco I d'Este, Jean Boulanger, painted this exemplum of extreme faithfulness to one's love and of *continentia* (continence), the sacrifice

Fig. 4. Jean Boulanger, *Isabella Leads Rodomonte to Kill Her*, before 1640. Sassuolo, Palazzo Ducale, Apartment of the Duchess, Room of "Marital Fidelity"

of Isabella offering her neck to the sword of Rodomonte, deceiving the Saracen king after declaring her magical invulnerability to his weapon.[34] In this fresco, Rodomonte is depicted three times: first on the right in the background, in a pose that expresses pride and arrogance, while he watches as the Galician princess gathers the herbs necessary to prepare the magical potion; then on the left, in the background, while, at a banquet and indifferent to religious prescription, he recklessly drinks wine; and finally, drunk and foolishly sure of himself, busily testing the edge of his sword on the neck of his beloved. The shape of these frescoes depicting the scene of Isabella's murder-suicide was determined by the illustration of canto XXIX in the edition of the poem published by Giovanni Varisco in Venice in 1568, where, in the background, the subsequent episode of the duel between Orlando and Rodomonte on the bridge also appears, in miniature.[35]

By this time in the seventeenth century, Ariosto's alluring Rodomonte seems to have completely vanished. The Saracen king as depicted in Sassuolo perfectly

Fig. 5. Ludovico Ariosto, *Orlando furioso*, illustration of canto XIII. (Venice: Zoppino, 1530)

Fig. 6. Ludovico Ariosto, *Orlando furioso*, illustration of canto XV. (Venice: Zoppino, 1530)

incarnates the vice of incontinence—unable to control himself, overwhelmed by wine, and by the beauty of Isabella, he commits a heinous act—the negative protagonist of a story entirely aimed at enhancing the noble and virtuous figure of the female heroine. But returning to the sixteenth century, closer to the years in which the poem was published, we can see how the character of Rodomonte is presented in the illustrated editions of the *Furioso* that accompanied and disseminated the fame of Ariosto's poetry.

In the first illustrated edition of the poem in 1530, Zoppino and his xylographer seem clearly fascinated by Ariosto's verse and by the grandeur of the figure of Rodomonte in their representation of him in canto XIII (fig. 5), where the siege of Paris begins. Here the larger-than-life image of the king of Sarza, with a lighted torch in his hand, colossally dominates the walls of the burning city. Rodomonte is an antihero who appears to have transformed himself into a gigantic demon committed to roasting the whole world, unstoppable by any human effort. Even the woodcut that illustrates canto XV in 1530 (fig. 6) reiterates the image of Rodomonte alone in the enemy city, set aflame by the fury of a giant, observed by Charlemagne and his paladins, who rush to save Paris from a saboteur glorified in his heroic solitude. The two woodcuts are

Fig. 7. Ludovico Ariosto, *Orlando furioso,* illustration of canto XVII. (Venice: Valvassori, 1553)

repeated without changes (slipping only in cantos XV and XVI) by Zoppino in the new illustrated edition prepared in 1536 to take into account the definitive redaction of the poem printed four years earlier.

In the edition of Valvassori (1553), canto XVII is illustrated by a woodcut marked by the image of Rodomonte attacked by Charlemagne and seven of his paladins (fig. 7). In the total disparity of the skirmish (only one fighter on foot armed with a sword, who heroically confronts eight knights armed with spears, who throw themselves against him), it is clear where the sympathy of the illustrator and the reader will inevitably be directed. In the edition of Valgrisi (1556), the same canto is accompanied by a large

Fig. 8. Ludovico Ariosto, *Orlando furioso,* illustration of canto XVII. (Venice: Valgrisi, 1556)

synoptic illustration (fig. 8), which, despite aiming to visually recapitulate all Ariostan stanzas, reserves a place for the character of Rodomonte as protagonist. Here as earlier, is the image of the Saracen king attacked over and above the strictures of the chivalric code by eight Christian knights acting in unison but Rodomonte is also depicted attacking, in Virgilian mode, the doors of the Parisian palace, focusing the attention of the observer on him, and obscuring the appearance of Charlemagne in the foreground.

That in the Italy of the first decades of the sixteenth century the literary character of Rodomonte, even with all of his excesses, could be viewed sympathetically seems to me also demonstrated by the historical figure of Luigi Gonzaga "di Gazolo" (1500–1532), the Mantuan military leader endowed with uncommon poetic skills and nicknamed from his childhood on as "Rodomonte" for his extraordinary physical strength. This is a period preceding the appearance in print of Ariosto's *Furioso* in 1516, and so the referent here would have been the character invented by Boiardo that had made such a strong impression on the *immaginario* of early-sixteenth-century Italy. It is striking that in 1527 it would be this contemporary "Rodomonte" who, after having participated in the Sack of Rome with a Mantuan contingent alongside the imperial troops, would rescue Pope Clement VII, imprisoned in Castel Sant'Angelo, and escort him to Orvieto. This is an astonishing intercultural *translatio*: the chivalric reincarnation of a Saracen king committed to freeing the Roman pontiff from the hands of the Protestant *lanzichenecchi* sent to Italy by the Catholic Holy Roman Emperor! In April 1532, Luigi "Rodomonte" Gonzaga went to Ferrara to visit Ariosto, in the run-up to the publication of the definitive edition of the *Furioso*, delighted by the two encomiastic citations concerning him now incorporated into the poem (in cantos XXVI and XXVIII). His stanzas in praise of Ariosto were printed in 1542 in the Giolito edition.[36]

Between 1565 and 1566, there was a further episode of the sixteenth-century *fortuna* of the character of Rodomonte, evoked several years ago by Lina Bolzoni: Giordano Bruno, then a Dominican novice in Naples, while engaged in playing "lots" by randomly extracting a verse from the *Furioso*, came across the noted Ariostan definition "d'ogni legge nimico e d'ogni fede" (hostile to every law, to every faith; *Fur.*, XXVIII 99, 8), seeing in this characterization of Rodomonte, "il pagan altier ch'in Dio non crede" (the haughty pagan who does not believe in God; *Fur.*, XXVIII 99, 7), an emblem of his own character and the foreshadowing of the destiny of an eccentric thinker. During the trial of Giordano Bruno, one of his fellow prisoners testified that "di questo lui si gloriava assai dicendo che gl'era toccato il verso conforme alla sua natura" (he

Fig. 9. Antonio Tempesta, *The Mighty Rodomonte, the Very Gracious Isabella*, ca. 1600. Milan, Civica Raccolta delle Stampe "A. Bertarelli"

took great pride in this, saying that he had picked a verse that resonated with his nature conforming to his nature). Giordano Bruno found in these words, dedicated to a character "così barbaro e così vitale" (as barbaric and vibrant) as Rodomonte, an incentive to continue to interrogate Ariosto's poem for his entire lifetime, until his tragic death by fire on January 1, 1600.[37]

Sympathy for Rodomonte seems to me still suggested at the beginning of the seventeenth century by the series of "caricature couples" engraved by Antonio Tempesta (fig. 9).[38] Here, *il fortissimo Rodomonte* and *la vaghissima Isabella* (the mighty Rodomonte and the very gracious Isabella) can be treated as a joke as the artist uses grotesque heads of distant Leonardesque memory, in a sequence of portraits of Ariosto's heroines and knights where no difference is made between Christians and Saracens, between real heroes and antiheroes.

I would like to conclude this rapid foray into the iconography of Rodomonte—after first noting Monica Preti's essay in this volume regarding another interesting seventeenth-century occurrence of this antihero—with a

Fig. 10. Grazia Nidasio, plate of *The Death of Rodomonte*, in *Orlando furioso di Ludovico Ariosto raccontato da Italo Calvino*, Milan, 2009

very recent image that demonstrates how even today Ariosto's poem can kindle the imagination of artists, in this particular instance cloaking the figure of the Saracen king in epic grandeur: the illustration created in 2009 by Grazia Nidasio (1931–2018) for an edition of the *Orlando Furioso di Ludovico Ariosto raccontato da Italo Calvino* (*Orlando Furioso recounted by Italo Calvino*) (fig. 10).[39] Here, in a sudden burst of fantasy, this remarkable Milanese illustrator imagined the death of Rodomonte by projecting it onto the iconography of the Homeric scene of the blinding of Polyphemus and reusing, at the same time, the compositional scheme of the famous photograph taken in 1945 at Iwo Jima by the American war photojournalist Joe Rosenthal. Rodomonte, in this illustration, is made into a huge Polyphemus and at the same time, occupying the place at the top of the Japanese mountain Suribachi, the symbol of the end of a devastating global war, thus consecrating the negative figure of the Saracen king in the pantheon of the greatest characters of Western literature.

Notes

1. On Rodamonte in Boiardo, see Cavallo 2002; Cavallo 2013, pp. 112–118; Pavlova 2013, pp. 145–150.

2. Farinella 2018, pp. 212, 217–219.

3. As argued in Pavlova 2018, p. 197.

4. Regarding this latter model, see Pavlova 2013, pp. 141–146.

5. On Rodomonte in Ariosto, see Weaver 1977; Horse 2002; Giudicetti 2010, pp. 149–185; Horse 2013, pp. 118–123; Morato 2013, who cites De Sanctis, pp. 83–84: "Rodomonte is the spirit of the individual driven to madness." Pavlova 2013, pp. 135–141, reviews a series of critical studies concerning Ariosto's Rodomonte. The characterization of Rodomonte by Italo Calvino (2015, p. 301) is still quite effective: "the boldest, the most immoderate, the most testy, the most unfortunate, the most pitiful of all our heroes . . . Rodomonte who embodies the multifarious spirit of the poem, its sonorous audacity, its melancholy, its inexhaustible reserves of energy"

6. Matarrese and Praloran, in Ariosto 2016, Vol. 1, p. 383.

7. Matarrese and Praloran, in Ariosto 2016, Vol. 1, p. 413.

8. Matarrese and Praloran, in Ariosto 2016, Vol. 1, p. 443.

9. Matarrese and Praloran, in Ariosto 2016, Vol. 1, p. 546.

10. Javitch 2016, p. 446.

11. On this theme, and for citations from Galileo Galilei and Ludovico Antonio Muratori in praise of Rodomonte's behavior, see Pavlova 2013.

12. Roncaccia 2016, p. 417: "A fine canto, nella zuffa tra Rodomonte e Orlando si confrontano per un momento, oltre ai maggiori campioni degli schieramenti nemici, le due follie più estreme del poema" (At the end of the canto, in the brawl between Rodomonte and Orlando, both the two principal champions of the opposing camps and the most extreme deliria of the poem briefly collide with each other).

13. Jossa (2016, p. 194) notes that following his death, Rodomonte will reappear, to overturn Charon's boat, in the *Marfisa* of Pietro Aretino (1532).

14. Güntert 1982; Regan 2005.

15. Casadei 2016.

16. Le Thiec 2012.

17. Lippi 2001, p. 51.

18. Cavallo 2013, pp. 272–273.

19. Farinella 2014, p. 171 (with preceding bibliography); Rospocher 2015, p. 202.

20. Condivi 1998, pp. 27–28; also p. xxii, for the corroborating annotation: *Fu vero, e ne haveva già fatto uno modello [del ponte sul Bosforo], mi disse* (It was true, and he had already made a model [of the bridge over the Bosphorus], he told me).

21. Villata 1999, pp. 158–159n177.

22. Corso 2018, pp. 185–186.

23. Ricci 2011, p. 28; see also Ricci 2002; Ricci 2008; Ricci 2018.

24. On the image of Rodomonte, and particularly his confrontation with Orlando, see Bondi 2014.

25. Ballarin, Pattanaro, and Romani 1995, p. 335, cat. 429 (ca. 1523; entry by Vittoria Romani); Humfrey and Lucco 1998, pp. 250–252, cat. 50 (ca. 1527–1530; entry by Peter Humfrey); Bondi 2014, pp. 75–76, 96–97 (but with an unacceptable dating of the painting "negli anni Quaranta del Cinquecento" [in the 1540s]); Caneparo 2015, pp. 29–31.

26. Cogotti, Farinella, and Preti 2016, pp. 264–265, cat. 68 (entry by Cecilia Ghibaudi).

27. Ariosto 2016, Vol. 2, pp. 930–931. This citation and the next are from the first edition of the *Orlando furioso* (1516), given that these verses are compared here with a painting from ca. 1527, earlier than the third edition (1532).

28. As in the rest of this volume, this English prose translation of the *Furioso* is by Guido Waldman, adapted here and in the subsequent citation to correspond to the differences between the 1516 edition and that of 1532 used by Waldman.

29. Ariosto 2016, Vol. 2, pp. 932–934.

30. Marchesi 2011, pp. 176–177.

31. On the *delizia* of the Belvedere, see most recently Marchesi 2015, pp. x–xi, 34–145.

32. Farinella 2011, pp. 216–217.

33. Meneghetti 2015, pp. 154–159.
34. Caneparo 2015, pp. 46–49; Zampetti 2017.
35. Zampetti 2017, p. 141.
36. Benzoni 2001.
37. Bolzoni 2012.
38. Cogotti, Farinella, and Preti 2016, pp. 199–201, cat. 31 (entry by Alessia Alberti).
39. Bacci 2014, p. 570.

Bibliography

Ariosto 2016
Ariosto, Ludovico. *Orlando furioso secondo l'editio princeps del 1516*, edited by Tina Matarrese and Marco Praloran. 2 vols. Turin: Einaudi, 2016.

Bacci 2014
Bacci, Giorgio. "'Un'immagine carica di significato': Illustrazioni novecentesche." In *L'*Orlando furioso *nello specchio delle immagini*, edited by Lina Bolzoni, pp. 567–610. Rome: Istituto dell'Enciclopedia Treccani, 2014.

Ballarin, Pattanaro, and Romani 1995
Ballarin, Alessandro, Vittoria Romani, and Alessandra Pattanaro, eds. *La pittura a Ferrara negli Anni del Ducato di Alfonso I*, 2 vols. Cittadella: Bertoncello Arti Grafiche, 1995.

Benzoni 2001
Benzoni, Lina. "Gonzaga, Luigi, detto Rodomonte." In *Dizionario biografico degli italiani*, Vol. 58, pp. 817–824. Rome, 2001.

Bolzoni 2012
Bolzoni, Lina. "Come Giordano Bruno legge l'Ariosto." In Lina Bolzoni, *Il lettore creativo: Percorsi cinquecenteschi fra memoria, gioco, scrittura*, pp. 59–82. Naples: Guida, 2012.

Bondi 2014
Bondi, Fabrizio. "'In furore e matto': Rappresentazioni della follia nelle immagini del Furioso." In *L'*Orlando furioso *nello specchio delle immagini*, edited by Lina Bolzoni, pp. 74–77. Rome: Istituto dell'Enciclopedia Treccani, 2014.

Calvino 2015
Calvino, Italo. *Orlando Furioso di Lodovico Ariosto raccontato da Italo Calvino, Con una scelta del poema*. Turin: Einaudi, 2015 [1970].

Caneparo 2015
Caneparo, Federica. *"Di molte figure adornato": L'Orlando furioso nei cicli pittorici tra Cinque e Seicento*. Milan: Officina Libraria, 2015.

Casadei 2016
Casadei, Alberto. "Storia." In *Lessico critico dell'Orlando furioso*, edited by Annalisa Izzo, pp. 387–403. Rome: Carocci, 2016.

Cavallo 2002
Cavallo, Jo Ann. "The Pathways of Knowledge in Boiardo and Ariosto: The Case of Rodamonte." *Italica* 79, no. 3 (2002): pp. 305–320.

Cavallo 2013
Cavallo, Jo Ann. *The World beyond Europe in the Romance Epics of Boiardo and Ariosto*. Toronto: University of Toronto Press, 2013.

Cogotti, Farinella, and Preti 2016
Cogotti, Marina, Vincenzo Farinella, and Monica Preti, eds. *I voli dell'Ariosto: L'*Orlando furioso *e le arti*. Milan: Officina Libraria, 2016.

Condivi 1998
Condivi, Ascanio. *Vita di Michelagnolo Buonarroti*, edited by Giovanni Nencioni, with essays by Michael Hirst and Caroline Elam. Florence: SPES, 1998.

Corso 2018
Corso, Michela. *Leonardo: Una vita*. Milan: Officina Libraria, 2018.

Farinella 2011
Farinella, Vincenzo. "*Venere sull'Eridano* di Battista Dossi e Girolamo da Carpi: Un nuovo dipinto ariostesco per la delizia del Belvedere?" In *L'uno e l'altro Ariosto, in corte e nelle delizie*, edited by Gianni Venturi, pp. 215–226. Florence: Olschki, 2011.

Farinella 2014
Farinella, Vincenzo. *Alfonso I d'Este, le immagini e il potere: Da Ercole de' Roberti a Michelangelo*. Milan: Officina Libraria, 2014.

Farinella 2018
Farinella, Vincenzo. "Le arti figurative nell'Innamoramento de Orlando: Boiardo prima di Ariosto." *Schifanoia* 54–55 (2018), pp. 207–226.

Giudicetti 2010
Giudicetti, Gian Paolo. *Mandricardo e la melanconia: Discorsi diretti e sproloqui nell'*Orlando furioso. Brussels: Peter Lang, 2010.

Güntert 1982
Güntert, Georges. "Le imprese di Isabella d'Este Gonzaga e l'*Orlando furioso*." In *Il Rinascimento: Aspetti e problemi attuali, Atti del X congresso dell'Associazione Internazionale per gli Studi di Lingua e Letteratura Italiana*, edited by Vittore Branca, pp. 445–454. Florence: Olschki, 1982.

Humfrey and Lucco 1998
Humfrey, Peter, and Mauro Lucco, eds. *Dosso Dossi: Pittore di corte a Ferrara nel Rinascimento*. Ferrara: Ferrara Arte, 1998. Exhibition catalogue.

Javitch 2016
Javitch, Daniel. "Canto XVIII." In *Lettura dell'"Orlando furioso" diretta da Guido Baldassarri e Marco Praloran*, Vol. 1, edited by Gabriele Bucchi and Franco Tomasi. Florence: Edizioni del Galluzzo per la Fondazione Ezio Franceschini, 2016.

Jossa 2016
Jossa, Stefano. "Ironia." In *Lessico critico dell'Orlando furioso*, edited by Annalisa Izzo, pp. 177–197. Rome: Carocci, 2016.

Le Thiec 2012
Le Thiec, Guy. "Portraits d'un conquérant: Selim Ier au miroir de la culture artistique italienne de la Renaissance (1517–1575)." In *Conquête ottomane de l'Égypte: Arrière-plan, impact, échos*, edited by Benjalmn Lellouch and Nicolas Michel, pp. 339–379. Boston: Brill, 2012.

Lippi 2001
Lippi, Emilio. "1517: L'ottava al servizio del sultano." *Quaderni Veneti* 34 (2001): pp. 49–88.

Marchesi 2011
Marchesi, Andrea. "Oltre il mito letterario, una mirabolante fabbrica estense: Protagonisti e significati nel cantiere di Belvedere (e dintorni)." In *L'uno e l'altro Ariosto, in corte e nelle delizie*, edited by Gianni Venturi, pp. 175–214. Florence: Olschki, 2011.

Marchesi 2015
Marchesi, Andrea. *Delizie d'archivio: Regesti e documenti per la storia delle residenze estensi nella Ferrara del Cinquecento*, Vol. 1, *Dimore urbane*. Ferrara: Le Immagini, 2015.

Meneghetti 2015
Meneghetti, Maria Luisa. *Storie al muro. Temi e personaggi della letteratura profana nell'arte medievale*. Torino: Einaudi, 2015.

Morato 2013
Morato, Nicola. "La scomparsa delle donne e la follia degli eroi: Lettura del canto XXIX dell'*Orlando Furioso*." *Stilistica e metrica italiana* 13 (2013): pp. 71–98.

Pavlova 2013
Pavlova, Maria. "Rodomonte e Ruggiero: Una questione d'onore." *Rassegna europea di letteratura italiana* 42 (2013): pp. 135–177.

Pavlova 2018
Pavlova, Maria. "L'Africa nell'*Orlando furioso*." *Schifanoia* 54–55 (2018): pp. 193–205.
Regan 2005
Regan, Lisa K. "Ariosto's Threshold Patron: Isabella d'Este in the *Orlando furioso*." *Modern Language Notes* 120, no. 1 (2005): pp. 50–69.
Ricci 2002
Ricci, Giovanni. *Ossessione turca: In una retrovia cristiana dell'Europa moderna*. Bologna: Il Mulino, 2002.
Ricci 2008
Ricci, Giovanni. *I turchi alle porte*. Bologna: Il Mulino, 2008.
Ricci 2011
Ricci, Giovanni. *Appello al Turco: I confini infranti del Rinascimento*. Rome: Viella, 2011.
Ricci 2018
Ricci, Giovanni. "Gli infedeli nell'Ariosto." *Schifanoia* 54–55 (2018): pp. 171–176.
Roncaccia 2016
Roncaccia, Alberto. "Struttura." In *Lessico critico dell'Orlando furioso*, edited by Annalisa Izzo, pp. 402–425. Rome: Carocci, 2016.
Rospocher 2015
Rospocher, Massimo. *Il papa guerriero: Giulio II nello spazio pubblico europeo*. Bologna: Il Mulino, 2015.
Villata 1999
Villata, Edoardo, ed. *Leonardo da Vinci: I documenti e le testimonianze contemporanee*. Milan: Castello Sforzesco, 1999.
Weaver 1977
Weaver, Elissa Barbara. "Lettura dell'intreccio dell'*Orlando furioso*: Il caso delle tre pazzie d'amore." *Strumenti critici* 34 (1977): pp. 384–406.
Zampetti 2017
Zampetti, Monica. "L'*Orlando Furioso* nel palazzo ducale di Sassuolo." In *Galassia Ariosto: Il modello editoriale dell'"Orlando Furioso" dal libro illustrato al web*, edited by Lina Bolzoni, pp. 139–145. Roma: Bolzoni, 2017.

Intercultural Threads in the Figurative Legacy of the *Orlando furioso*: Two Ariostan Plates of Otto Vaenius on the Chastity and Indecency of Women

Monica Preti

It has long been recognized that among the numerous strands that make up the composite fabric of Ariostan narration, there are several that originate in the Oriental tradition. It appears that some of the earliest commentators on the *Orlando furioso* were aware of these sources, which gave rise to the suspicion that the poem had early on been translated into Arabic[1] (which would have been a unique case in the pre-modern European literary tradition, though Cervantes in Book I of *Don Quixote* played with the opposite scenario: that his text had been translated from an Arabic original). For centuries, two *novelle* placed side by side in the poem despite their disparate origins have attracted the attention of scholars in this regard: the tale of Astolfo and Iocondo narrated by the innkeeper of Aigues-Mortes in canto XXVIII and the episode of Isabella's suicide provoked by Rodomonte's attempted seduction at the beginning of canto XXIX. Particularly following the publication of Antoine Galland's translation of the *Thousand and One Nights* (1704–1717), French and German Orientalists gave rise to a heated debate on the apparent analogies between the story of Astolfo and Iocondo and those of the brothers Shāhriyār and Shāhzamān that frame the inexhaustible fantasy of Shahrazād.[2] Subsequently, it was above all Pio Rajna who opened new horizons of research, singling out among possible Ariostan sources a series of textual intermediaries—the short stories of Giovanni Sercambi and Francesco Barbaro's *De re uxoria*, the universal chronicle of Georgios Kedrenos and the "Saracen stories" by Jirjis al-Makīn[3]—through which the *disiecta membra* from the other side of the Mediterranean could have passed through the court of Ferrara and then scattered among the thousand byways of European folklore; an entire branch of research ensued, with notable results up to the present day.[4]

Here I would like to examine two little-known plates by the Dutch artist and humanist Otto van Veen, or Vaenius (1556–1629), in which the two episodes cited above are once again paired, a little less than a century after the publication of the final edition of *Orlando furioso*. In them, as I aim to show, come together not only earlier Oriental traces and their Ariostan adaptation but also further cues related to the "canonization" of the poem in illustrated editions of it from the second half of the sixteenth century, the visual imagination of Vaenius, several trends prevalent in the printing market in the Netherlands of the late sixteenth century, and an unexpected epilogue in the India of the Mughal emperors of the early seventeenth century. As far as I have been able to determine, the two plates in question are the only ones in the whole of Vaenius's artistic production inspired by the *Furioso*; that they have to do specifically with the two episodes of most manifest "Arab" origins seems to me all the more interesting in the context of this volume. Their unique character has led me to explore distinct textual and iconographic traditions on which they drew that nevertheless also demonstrate a number of reciprocal intersections; and although the precise connections between these different traditions are not always clear, there seems evident to me the existence of a "landscape of intercultural relations" fueled by the illustrated editions of *Orlando furioso* and more generally by the imaginary of which Ariosto's poetry became the vehicle.

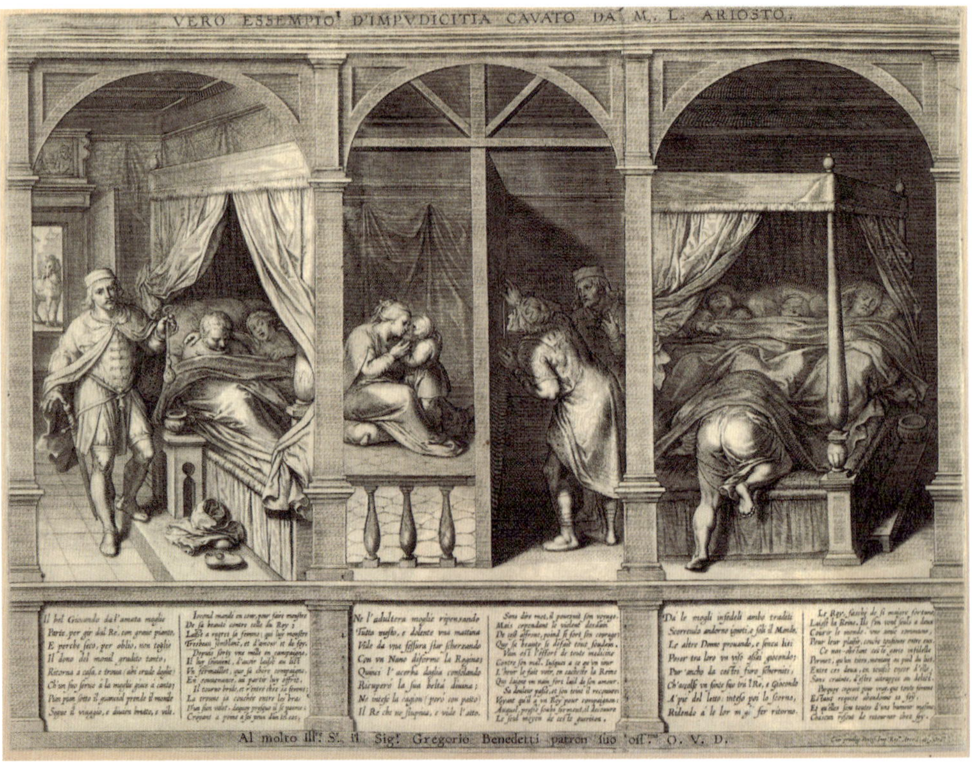

Fig. 1. Engraver unknown, after Otto van Veen (Vaenius), *Vero essempio d'impudicitia cavato da M. L. Ariosto*, ca. 1590–1625. London, British Museum, Department of Prints and Drawings

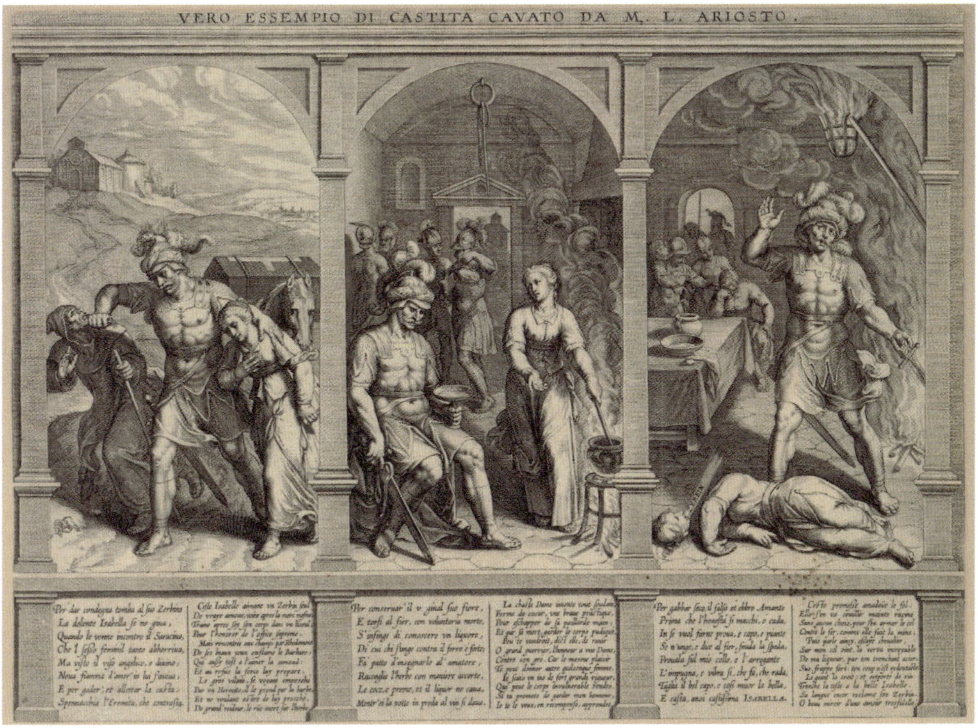

Fig. 2. Engraver unknown, after Otto van Veen (Vaenius), *Vero essempio di castità cavato da M. L. Ariosto*, ca. 1590–1625. London, British Museum, Department of Prints and Drawings

1. *Vero essempio d'impudicitia* and *Vero essempio di castità*: Two Ariostan plates by Otto Vaenius

The two plates by Vaenius—*Vero essempio d'impudicitia cavato da M. L. Ariosto* (True example of indecency taken from M. L. Ariosto) and *Vero essempio di castità cavato da M. L. Ariosto* (True example of chastity taken from M. L. Ariosto) (figs. 1–2)—are constructed as mirrors of each other, a matching pair. Both are articulated in triptychs in a simple architectural frame that also serves to separate the columns of text below, a loose adaptation in Italian with a French gloss of the verses of the *Furioso* to which the images refer.[5] The plates are anonymous, but there is no doubt about the identity of their author, which can be deduced from the monogram with which the dedication is signed, repeated under both tables next to the reference of the printing privilege: "Al molto Ill.re S.r il Sig.r Gregorio Benedetti patron suo oss.mo O.V.D." (i.e., Otto Van Veen) (To the most Illustrious Mr. Gregorio Benedetti patron, his esteemed O.V.D.).[6] We know nothing—at least, I could find no information—regarding the dedicatee, whom we can only suppose to have been a relative of the Pietro Benedetti who was the

Fig. 3. Otto van Veen (Vaenius), *Isabella and Rodomonte*. Paris, Musée du Louvre, Département des Arts graphiques

principal Italian collaborator of Vaenius from 1612 onward, if not earlier (there is a poem of his at the beginning of Vaenius's 1608 *Amorum emblemata*). We could reasonably infer that Pietro—a Genovese "mercator doctus" transplanted to Antwerp, where for many years he played an important role of cultural mediation—was the author of the verse adaptations that accompany the plates.[7]

The preparatory drawing of the *Vero essempio di castità* is now preserved in the Louvre (fig. 3). Made in pen and pencil, with shaded brown ink and white lead strokes, it corresponds in most respects to the engraved plate, except that here the image is inverted and lacks the plate's textual apparatus.[8] Conversely, we only have the engraved version of the *Vero essempio d'impudicitia*, of which three different impressions are known—as is the case with its companion piece—though undated and without the name of the engraver (except for the final one, printed in Coburg by Johannes Monmartius). Frits Lugt believes the plates to have been published after 1606 but provides no support for the claim; the British Museum is more prudent, situating its copies in a wider period between 1590 and 1625.[9]

1.*1. The Novella of Iocondo and Astolfo*

We begin with the plate that illustrates the opening octaves of canto XXVIII, a story within a story—similar to a typical narrative practice in Arabic literature but also prevalent in Boccaccio and other pre-modern Italian authors—told by the innkeeper of a tavern in Aigues-Mortes to the "silent and pensive" king of Algiers, the proud Rodomonte, distraught following the betrayal of his beloved Doralice.[10] In order to console the humiliated king but also to warn his guests of the general inconstancy of women, always prone to infidelity, Ariosto's host recalls a story he says he heard from a *gentilomo di Vinegia* (gentleman of Venice), Gian Francesco Valerio, demonstrating that *mai donne pudiche / non si trovaro, o povere o di conto* (chaste women, whether poor or well-to-do, never did exist; *Fur.*, XXVII 137, 3; 138, 6–7). This is the story of the young Iocondo, called to the court of Pavia by Astolfo, king of the Lombards, eager to compare Iocondo's much-vaunted beauty to his own.[11] Apparently desperate at the departure of her husband, Iocondo's wife gives him a jewel-encrusted cross as a token of her love, which the young man nevertheless forgets at home; returning quickly to retrieve it, he finds the woman asleep in the arms of a young man. This is the episode depicted by Vaenius in the first of the three scenes that make up this triptych; we see Iocondo with the pendant in his hand, stunned after discovering his wife's adultery. But while the love that Iocondo still retains for his wife prevents him from killing the two faithless lovers, on his subsequent journey to Pavia, the resulting pain inevitably corrodes his handsome features: *segue il viaggio, e divien brutto, e vile* (he continues the journey, and becomes ugly, and base), we read in the Italian verses that accompany the scene in Vaenius's plate.

In illustrating the scene, Vaenius does not follow the accompanying text to the letter, rather referring to the verses of the *Furioso* which he demonstrates that he knows directly.[12] The detail of the bed curtain—recalling similar moments in Boccaccio—voyeuristically drawn open so as to reveal a scene that Annalisa Izzo has rightly defined as "theatricalized," can only have been inspired by the Ariostan original (there is no trace of it in Sercambi or in the *Thousand and One Nights*):[13]

> La cortina levò senza far motto
> E vide quel che men veder credea,
> che la sua casta e fedel moglie, sotto
> la coltre in braccio a un giovene giacea.
> —*Fur.*, XXVIII 21, 2–4
> [He lifted the curtains without a word—and was no little surprised by what he saw: his chaste and loyal wife under the covers in a young man's arms.]

Fig. 4. (a) Augustan gravestone (First century CE), *Fidei simulacrum*. Vatican City, Musei Vaticani, Galleria Lapidaria. (b) Unknown roman sculptor (second half of the fifteenth century), tomb of Stefano Satri de Baroniis, his wife Maddalena degli Arlotti, and son Giovan Battista. Rome, Church of Sant'Omobono, left wall. (c) Engraver unknown, after Otto van Veen (Vaenius), *Vero essempio di castità cavato da M. L. Ariosto*, ca. 1590–1625 (detail). (d) *Fidii simulacrum*, emblem 9 in the book *Emblemata* by Andrea Alciato (Padua: Paolo Tozzi, 1618)

Another important element in Vaenius's plate is the pendant that Iocondo holds in his hand—a token of love but at the same time an involuntary cause of the discovery of the adultery—described by Ariosto as a reliquary that a Bohemian pilgrim had brought back from Jerusalem (an ironically veiled dig at forms of external devotion toward which the poet never failed to show himself resistant):[14]

> Dal collo un suo monile ella si sciolse,
> Ch'una crocetta avea ricca di gemme,
> E di sante reliquie che raccolse
> In molti luoghi un peregrin boemme;
> Ed il padre di lei, ch'in casa il tolse
> Tornando infermo, di Ierusalemme,
> Venendo a morte poi ne lasciò erede:
> Questa levossi ed al marito diede.
> —*Fur.*, XXVIII 15
>
> [She wore a necklace from which hung a cross encrusted with jewels and holy relics collected in many places by a pilgrim from Bohemia. Her father had brought it home when he returned, a sick man, from Jerusalem; at his death he bequeathed it to her. This she now slipped off and gave to her husband.]

The jewel depicted by Vaenius does not correspond precisely to Ariosto's description, but the effigy of the Agnus Dei that can be seen on it clearly distinguishes it as a devotional artifact, in use for centuries by pilgrims.

The scene glimpsed in the overdoor takes up instead an iconographic schema known as *Fidei simulacrum* or *Fidei symbolum* (representation or symbol of faithfulness) which was derived from a famous Roman relief now in the Vatican Museums (Lapidary Gallery, 80A) and which enjoyed a considerable fortune in sixteenth-century emblematics from Andrea Alciato to Pierio Valeriano and from Guillaume du Choul to Vicenzo Cartari (fig. 4).[15]

The central scene of the triptych illustrates the continuation of the story: despite Astolfo's festive welcome, Iocondo does not recover from his shock until he sees, through a chink in the wall of his room, the beautiful wife of the king submissive to the pleasures of a "deformed" dwarf. He feels obliged to tell Astolfo of the shocking betrayal, and the king, in turn, does not hesitate to witness the scene together with Iocondo. Vaenius uses visual artifice (the representation of a sectional wall) to simultaneously show Astolfo and Iocondo peeking from a chink in the wall in one room and in the other the queen's adultery, all the more reprehensible for having been committed with a repulsive being.

The stigmatization signaled here is not only the infidelity of Astolfo's wife—a general prerogative of the female sex, according to Ariosto's narrator—but also the perversion that had led her to lie with a monstrous lover.[16]

Thus united by the same fate, Iocondo and Astolfo decide to travel the world and to do with the wives of others what the young man and the dwarf had done with theirs. The last scene depicts the moment when the two come to share, in a startling ménage à trois, the beautiful Fiammetta; she, in turn, one night welcomes a third young man, Greco, into her bed, leaving each of her earlier lovers to imagine that in those hours she had taken her pleasure with the other. Also in this case, Vaenius shows his direct dependence on the *Furioso* as evidenced by the way in which the young Greek is portrayed slipping into the bed, literally glossing Ariosto's octave:

> va brancolando infin che'l letto trova:
> di là dove gli altri avean le piante,
> tacito si cacciò col capo inante.
> —*Fur.*, XXVIII 63, 6–8
> [he groped his way till he found the bed—into which, at the point where the sleepers had their feet, he quietly intruded head first.]

The conclusion and moral of the story are deduced instead from the bilingual verses situated below the images. When Astolfo and Iocondo become aware of the deception, they have no other choice but to laugh and return to their wives, fully aware that infidelity pertains to all women, not only theirs: "inteso poi lo scorno, / Ridendo à le lor moglie fer ritorno" (having understood then the scorn, / Laughing at their wives they returned to them); "Croyant pour vray, que toute femme / Estant requise abandonne sa foy, / Et qu'elles sont toutes d'une humeur mesme; / Chacun resout de retourner chez soy" (Believing it true, that all women / Under pressure abandon their vows / And as they are all of the same disposition / Each man resolved to return home).

1.*2. Rodomonte and Isabella*

The final octaves of canto XXVIII and the initial ones of canto XXIX are dedicated to one of the most famous episodes of the *Furioso*, the subject of Vaenius's second plate: the meeting between Rodomonte and the beautiful daughter of the Saracen king of Galicia, the young Isabella, who would subsequently position herself to be killed through her own deception in order to preserve her chastity. Rajna, as noted above, had initially identified some of the Oriental sources of the story; and Enrico Cerulli, taking up the insights of Giorgio Levi della Vida, retraced their peregrinations in the vast sea of cultural transmission against the background of a very broad spatial-temporal span, from Jerusalem conquered by the Persians (614 CE) to Baghdad occupied by the Mongols (1258), from Arab-Christian Egypt to Georgian-Armenian literature, to reach the Lithuanian-Polish border in the fourteenth century.[17] But as was likely the case with the story of Astolfo and Iocondo, so, too, here the actual sources of the Ferrarese poet were probably much closer to home; if, as regards the earlier story, they were drawn (at least, according to what the innkeeper of Aigues-Mortes had declared) from the *novelluzze* of Giovan Francesco Valier on the deceptions of women, the most immediate Ariostan source for Isabella and Rodomonte seems to have been Francesco Barbaro's *De re uxoria* (1416), in which the original plot of oriental origin—a parable of female martyrdom—is transformed into an episode of conjugal fidelity.[18]

What is certain is that also in this second plate, Vaenius closely follows the *Furioso*, beginning from the background that linked the matter of Isabella's death to the previous episode. In the first scene, we see Rodomonte, who, after his stop at the tavern in Aigues-Mortes, had taken up residence in an abandoned church near Montpellier (visible in the background, on the upper left); it is here that the meeting with Isabella—accompanying the coffin of her beloved Zerbino (who had died in canto XIV)—and a hermit takes place. The outrage against all women is immediately forgotten—"a modo / che da l'asse si trae chiodo con chiodo" (the way one nail drives out another; *Fur.* XXVIII 98, 7–8), Ariosto comments wryly—and Rodomonte finds himself ensnared by the beauty of the young Saracen, whom he tries to seduce. Determined that the friar not get in the way of his designs, Rodomonte grabs the man angrily by his beard and furiously casts him away: "Con man lo stringe a guise di tanaglia; / E poi ch'una e due volte raggirollo, / Da sé per l'aria e verso il mar lo scaglia" (He closed his fingers round the other's neck like pincers and, whirling him about a couple of times, tossed him up into the sky, towards the sea; *Fur.*, XXIX 6, 1–4).

In the second scene, the focus shifts to the sad Isabella, who, in order not to break the vow of chastity with which she intended to honor the memory of Zerbino, eludes Rodomonte's desires thanks to an expedient that will provoke her own death: she promises the king of Algiers a liquor that will make him invulnerable in exchange for the promise that he not attack her virtue. We see her as she prepares her herbal potion beside a Rodomonte dazed by alcohol, consumed in contravention of the rules of his religion, proof of his personal villainy, as Ariosto had already pointed out:

> Non era Rodomonte usato al vino,
> perché la legge sua lo vieta e danna:
> e poi che lo gustò, liquor divino
> gli par, miglior che 'l nettare o la manna;
> e riprendendo il rito saracino,
> gran tazze e pieni fiaschi ne tracanna.
> —*Fur.*, XXIX 22, 1–6
>
> [But Rodomont was unaccustomed to wine, which Moslem law forbids and condemns. And it tasted to him like the liquor of the gods, better than nectar or manna; so, repudiating Saracen custom, he drank it by the bumper-full, flasks at a time.]

Having concluded her preparations, Isabella proposes to the now-drunk knight that she be the first to sample the tonic's powers, and after anointing her whole body with the herbal extract, she offers her neck to Rodomonte, asking him to cut off her head. In the third scene, Vaenius depicts "the brute," who becomes aware of the deception only when it is too late: *del bel capo, già d'Amore albergo, / fé tronco rimanere il petto e il tergo*" (he lopped her fair head, once the abode of love, clean from her shoulders; *Fur.*, XXIX 25, 5–8). Isabella thus dies beheaded, pronouncing in extremis the name of Zerbino; and Vaenius, faithful to Ariosto's text, visually translates the detail of the severed head that continues to speak, absent in all previous versions of the story, depicting a sequence of letters that issue from the young woman's mouth: *Quel fé tre balzi; e funne udita chiara / voce ch'uscendo nominò Zerbino* (Her head bounced thrice: from it a voice could be clearly heard pronouncing the name of Zerbin; *Fur.*, XXIX 26, 1–2).

The posture of the decapitated body seems particularly significant, in that Vaenius appears to have freely drawn inspiration from a visual cue of a completely different origin: the corpse reclining on one side, legs stretched out, arms and hands sprawled to hint at one final spiritual appeal, recalls the forms carved by Stefano Maderno to record the precise position in which the remains of Saint Cecilia were discovered during excavations in the eponymous church in Trastevere, in 1599.[19] The exhumation had aroused enormous clamor, also conveyed through a series of artistic works of a strongly Counter-Reformational stamp, beginning with Maderno's statue placed over the tomb of the martyr, widely reproduced in prints engraved respectively by Cornelis Galle I after the drawing of Francesco Vanni (1601) and later by Hieronymus Wierix from the painting by Vanni himself for the Church of Santa Maria in Trastevere (1603–1605) (fig. 5).[20] Given the notoriety of the event and the circulation of the

Fig. 5. H. Wierix, after F. Vanni, *Death of St. Cecilia*, ca. 1599–1605. New York, The Metropolitan Museum of Art

iconography invented by Maderno in Dutch artistic-editorial circles precisely in the years in which our Ariostan *essempi* were produced, it would not seem improbable to hypothesize some influence of these models that could well have come to the attention of Vaenius, particularly as both Cornelis Galle I and Hieronymus Wierix were among his collaborators. In this way—and without its author necessarily having been aware of the association—the chaste Isabella beheaded by Rodomonte evokes the form of the young martyr of the faith that had initially denoted this character in the Oriental tradition.

2. The Illustrative Tradition of the *Orlando furioso*

From a certain point of view, we can consider the two prints by Vaenius as testimony to the enormous editorial fortune of the *Orlando furioso*, the first real best seller of Italian and European literature in the age of printing, the first "classic" of contemporary literature, which, soon after its definitive edition, saw countless illustrated versions issued, accompanied by an increasingly rich and refined iconographic apparatus which contributed to the extraordinary diffusion of Ariosto's dramatis personae in the European visual—and artistic—imagination.[21] From 1542 onward, or rather from the first Giolito edition edited by Ludovico Dolce, the illustrations used to recapitulate the main narrative threads of each canto of the *Furioso* were accompanied by textual tools ("Allegories"), which were used not only to identify characters and clarify the plot but also to elucidate its allegorical, moral significance (fig. 6).[22] As is widely recognized, it was also through this insistent and widespread moral allegorization that the success of the poem and its canonization as a classic of world literature were established—equated to the great masterpieces of Greco-Latin culture, transformed into a handbook of edifying maxims and exemplary teachings, stripped of any problematic or controversial elements, and rendered consonant with the ethical-religious principles of the Counter-Reformation. Thus, in the Valvassori edition (Venice 1553), our two *canti* are summarized and interpreted as follows:

> Nella moglie di Giocondo, che piangendo mostra di voler morire per la lontananza di lui, ma non così tosto s'è partito, ch'ella si giace con un ragazzo, si fa chiaro, che molte non si contentano del marito solo, tuttoché s'infingano di portargli grandissimo amore. . . . Nella regina, la quale ha il marito bellissimo, pur tuttavia si prende amoroso piacere col nano contraffatto, si vituperano le donne maritate a uomini belli e di alto affare, che si danno in potere d'amanti brutti e vilissimi. . . .
>
> Nella Fiammetta, la quale si gode insieme col suo amante, mentre due giace-

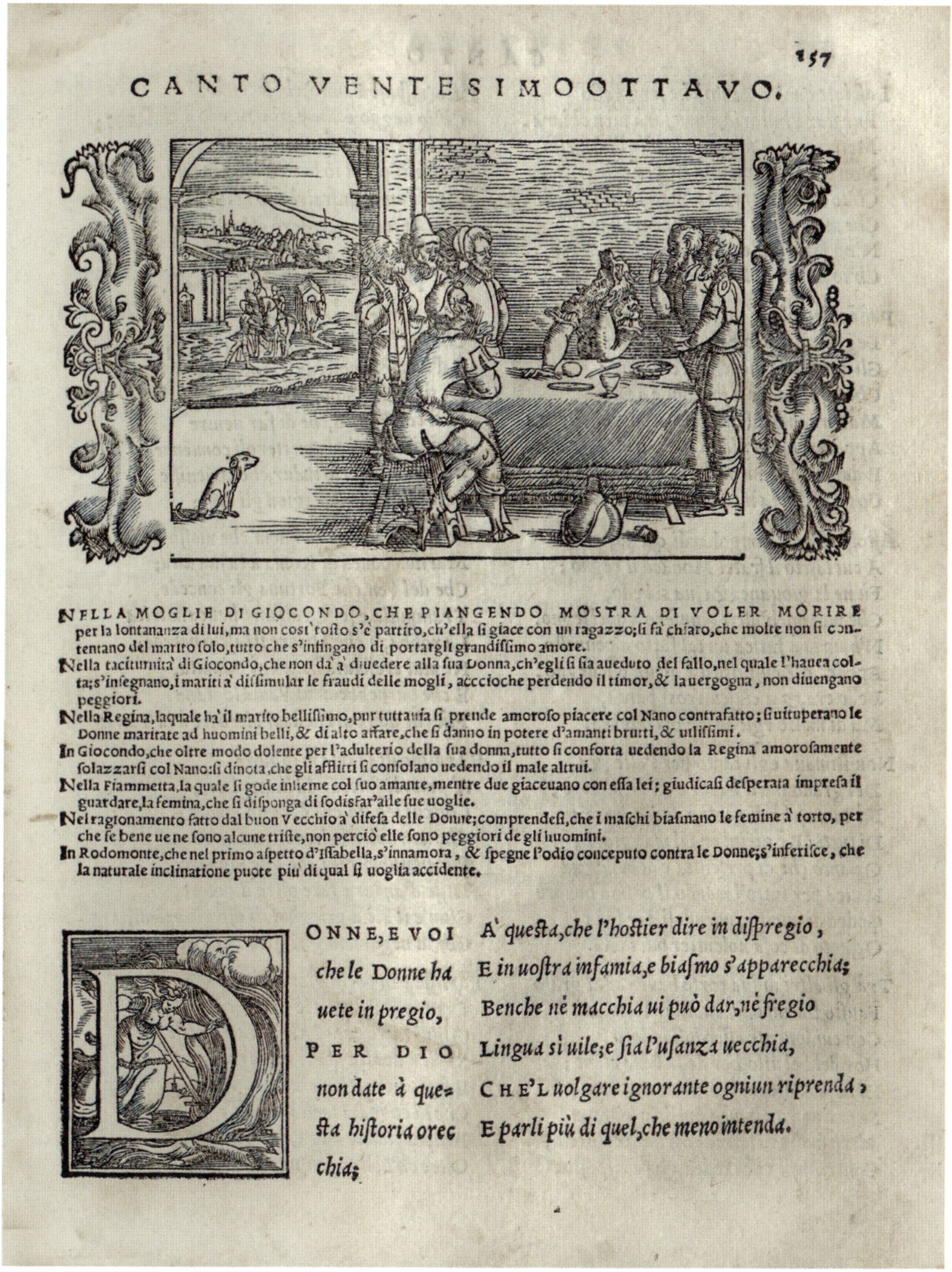
157

CANTO VENTESIMOOTTAVO.

NELLA MOGLIE DI GIOCONDO, CHE PIANGENDO MOSTRA DI VOLER MORIRE per la lontananza di lui, ma non così tosto s'è partito, ch'ella si giace con un ragazzo; si fà chiaro, che molte non si contentano del marito solo, tutto che s'infingano di portargli grandissimo amore.

Nella taciturnità di Giocondo, che non dà à diuedere alla sua Donna, ch'egli si sia aueduto del fallo, nel quale l'hauea colta; s'insegnano, i mariti à dissimular le fraudi delle mogli, accioche perdendo il timor, & la uergogna, non diuengano peggiori.

Nella Regina, laquale hà il marito bellissimo, pur tuttauia si prende amoroso piacere col Nano contrafatto; si uituperano le Donne maritate ad huomini belli, & di alto affare, che si danno in potere d'amanti brutti, & uilissimi.

In Giocondo, che oltre modo dolente per l'adulterio della sua donna, tutto si conforta uedendo la Regina amorosamente solazzarsi col Nano: si dinota, che gli afflitti si consolano uedendo il male altrui.

Nella Fiammetta, la quale si gode insieme col suo amante, mentre due giaceuano con essa lei; giudicasi desperata impresa il guardare, la femina, che si disponga di sodisfar'alle sue uoglie.

Nel ragionamento fatto dal buon Vecchio à difesa delle Donne; comprendesi, che i maschi biasmano le femine à torto, per che se bene ue ne sono alcune triste, non perciò elle sono peggiori de gli huomini.

In Rodomonte, che nel primo aspetto d'Issabella, s'innamora, & spegne l'odio conceputo contra le Donne; s'inferisce, che la naturale inclinatione puote più di qual si uoglia accidente.

DONNE, E VOI
che le Donne ha
uete in pregio,
PER DIO
non date à que-
sta historia orec
chia;

À questa, che l'hostier dire in dispregio,
E in uostra infamia, e biasmo s'apparecchia;
Benche nè macchia ui può dar, nè fregio
Lingua sì uile; e sia l'usanza uecchia,
CHE'L uolgare ignorante ogniun riprenda,
E parli più di quel, che meno intenda.

Fig. 6. Ludovico Ariosto, *Orlando furioso di M. Lodovico Ariosto, ornato di nove figure, e allegorie in ciascun Canto*, first page of canto XXVIII (Venice: Valvassori, 1553)

vano con essa lei, giudicasi disperata impresa il guardare la femmina che si disponga di soddisfar alle sue voglie.[23]

[In Giocondo's wife, who through her tears shows that she wants to die because of her husband's impending departure but not so much so that once he has indeed gone she does not hesitate to lie with a boy, it becomes clear that many wives are not satisfied merely by their husbands, though they pretend to bear them great love. . . . In the queen, who has a handsome husband but nevertheless takes her pleasure with the hideous dwarf, all women married to attractive and well born men who give themselves over to ugly and vile lovers are reproached. . . . In Fiammetta, who enjoys her lover while two others lie with her, it should be considered a hopeless cause the prospect of any female capable of satisfying her desires.]

. . . Nella costanza d'Isabella, la quale, per servar castità, con arte meravigliosa procurò la propria morte, comprendono le donne che doverebbono più tosto caste morire, che disonestamente vivere. In Rodomonte, il quale, avendo troppo bevuto, scioccamente s'indusse ad ammazzar Isabella, dimostrasi come il vino, preso senza misura, abbarbaglia gli occhi dell'intelletto. . . . Che Iddio riguardando l'atto stupendo d'Isabella, l'esalta sì fattamente ch'ella sempre ne sia lodata da scrittori, appare che la donna può con l'onestà acquistarsi eterna e chiarissima fama.[24]

. . . In the constancy of Isabella, who in order to serve chastity procured her own death with marvelous art, are also to be counted those women who would prefer to die chaste rather than live dishonestly. In Rodomonte, who having drunk too much was led into killing Isabella, it is proven how wine taken without measure blinds the eyes of the intellect. . . . That God, with regard to Isabella's astonishing deed, exalts her so emphatically that she is always praised by writers, it seems that women can through honesty acquire eternal and perspicuous fame.]

The reading of the poem in a moral key, the strong link between text and image, the use of the latter to point out and reaffirm the exemplary values of the episode—between the tools developed by sixteenth-century publishers and their subsequent revisitation by Vaenius, the family resemblance is palpable.

Nevertheless, the two prints we are dealing with clearly distinguish themselves from the iconographic apparatus of the illustrated editions of Ariosto, so much so that in other respects, they represent an *unicum* in the sixteenth- and seventeenth-century figurative fortune of the *Furioso*. They do not appear to fit into any comprehensive project of illustrating the text, nor do they seem to belong to a more integral series of plates; the evidence suggests that they constitute an isolated pair, conceived to be marketed independently (and, as such, an anomaly in Vaenius's production). Their relationship with the poem is very different from that established by book illustrations; if these latter were essentially configured as commentary in the margins of the text, a visual paraphrase that was intended to guide the reading of it, the two "true examples" of Vaenius are presented as an autonomous work, with a self-contained meaning, the significance of which is not so much derived from the specific romance plot that provided their bearings as from the universal, apodictic value of the truths they represent. Their narrative coordinates and adherence to the Ariostan source notwithstanding, the function of Vaenius's plates is essentially exemplary, didactic. These images were not intended to elucidate Ariosto's text; rather, the two Ariostan episodes provided the artist with prompts for the subjects he depicted and for the exposition of general truths.

It is, therefore, no coincidence that at the iconographic level, the engravings by Vaenius have little in common with the previous illustrative tradition of the *Furioso*, in which the same episodes appear rarely and in radically different forms.[25] Although occupying a good part of canto XXVIII, the *novella* of Astolfo and Iocondo never appears among the illustrations that accompany the principal Italian editions of Ariosto in the sixteenth century; the story would have been considered too scandalous to be explicitly translated into images in Italy, and Italian publishers were always concerned in this period not to fall into the crosshairs of the Congregation of the Index. Even when we find the episode included in a summary plate—as in the Valgrisi (1556) and De Franceschi (1584) editions—the conjugal debaucheries remembered by the innkeeper of Aigues-Mortes are only evoked indirectly,[26] while the scene foregrounded in the image is Rodomonte's stop at the tavern and his conversations with the host and the other patrons (fig. 7).[27]

It is clear that the *novella* enjoyed a certain figurative fortune apart from the integral editions of the *Furioso*; there remains a trace of it in a pamphlet, freely adapted with the title *Historia del re di Pavia*.[28] The woodcut illustrating the first page is divided into two sections: on the left, Astolfo and Iocondo spy on the queen and the dwarf; on the right, the latter give themselves to their lovemaking on a chair, while situated in the background, forgotten, lie the nuptial bed and crown. Even here, the image is not lacking in allegorical implications, which in some versions of the text were made explicit: in the copy of the Brera Library in Milan, the scene is framed by a suggestive inscription, CHI VUOL VEDERE / VEDERA COSSA / MOLTO MARAVIGLIOSA (Who wishes to see / Will see a thing / Quite marvelous) (fig. 8).[29] Other than their suggestive bipartite structure

VENTESIM'OTTAVO.
XXVIII
VALENZA
VIENNA
LION
ROD
La sonna fiume
ROD.
HOSTO.

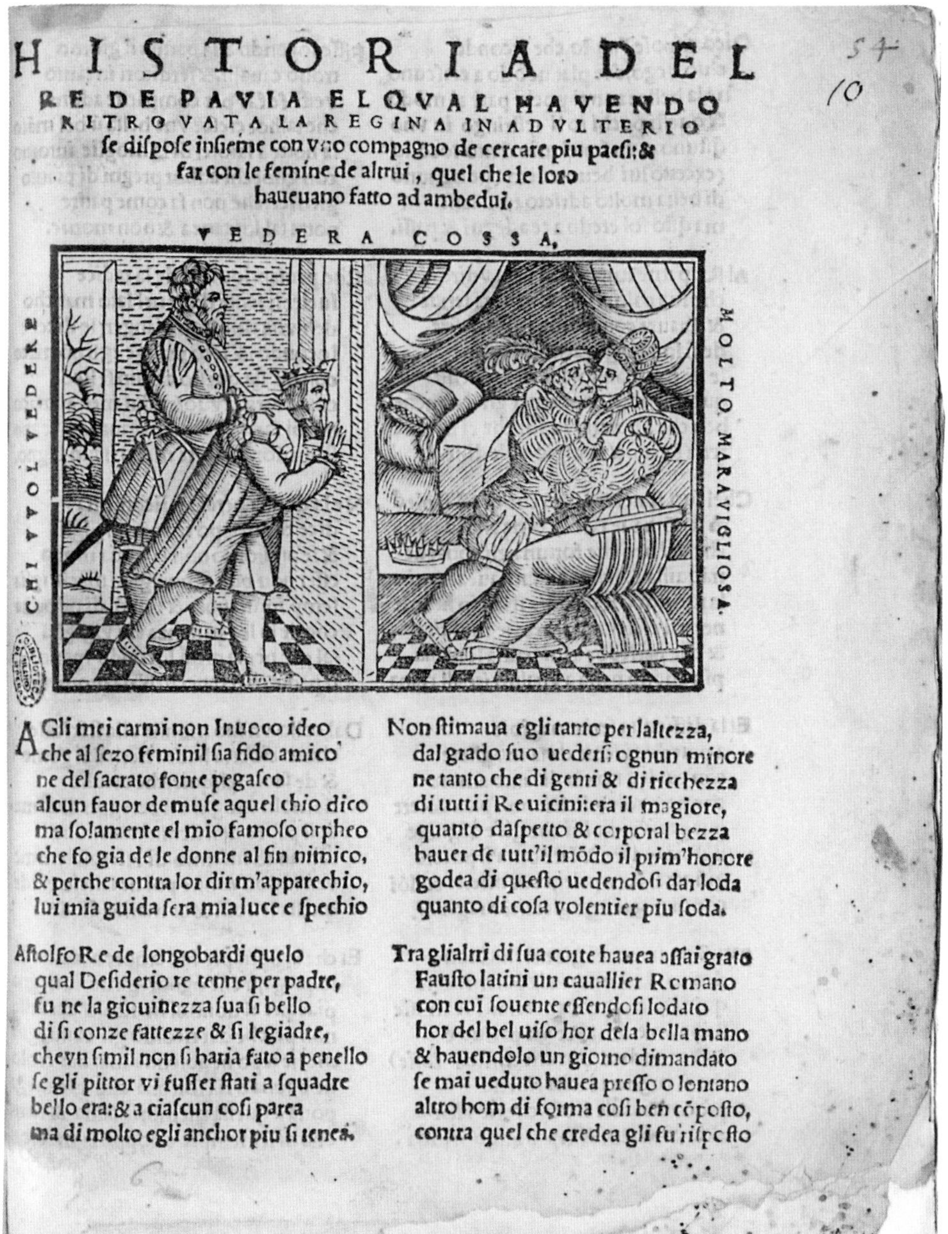
HISTORIA DEL
RE DE PAVIA EL QVAL HAVENDO
RITROVATA LA REGINA IN ADVLTERIO
se dispose insieme con vno compagno de cercare piu paesi:&
far con le femine de altrui, quel che le loro
haueuano fatto ad ambedui.

VEDERA COSSA,

AGli mei carmi non Inuoco ideo
che al sezo feminil sia fido amico'
ne del sacrato fonte pegasco
alcun fauor de muse aquel chio dico
ma solamente el mio famoso orpheo
che fo gia de le donne al fin nimico,
& perche contra lor dir m'apparechio,
lui mia guida sera mia luce e spechio

Astolfo Re de longobardi quelo
qual Desiderio re tenne per padre,
fu ne la giouinezza sua si bello
di si conze fattezze & si legiadre,
che vn simil non si haria fato a penello
se gli pittor vi fusser stati a squadre
bello era:& a ciascun cosi parea
ma di molto egli anchor piu si tenea.

Non stimaua egli tanto per laltezza,
dal grado suo uedersi ognun minore
ne tanto che di genti & di ricchezza
di tutti i Re uicini:era il magiore,
quanto daspetto & corporal bezza
hauer de tutt'il mõdo il prim'honore
godea di questo uedendosi dar loda
quanto di cosa volentier piu soda.

Tra glialtri di sua corte hauea assai grato
Fausto latini un cauallier Romano
con cui souente essendosi lodato
hor del bel uiso hor dela bella mano
& hauendolo un giorno dimandato
se mai ueduto hauea presso o lontano
altro hom di forma cosi ben cõposto,
contra quel che credea gli fu risposto

Facing page
Fig. 7. Ludovico Ariosto, *Orlando furioso di M. Lodovico Ariosto nuovamente adornato di figure di rame da Girolamo Porro . . .*, illustration of canto XXVIII (Venice: Francesco de Franceschi, 1584)

Above
Fig. 8. *Historia del re de Pavia.* (Venice: Matio Pagan in Frezaria) n.d.

Above
Fig. 9. Ludovico Ariosto, *Orlando furioso di M. Lodovico Ariosto, tutto ricorretto, et di nuove figure adornato . . .*, illustration of canto XXIX (Venice: Valgrisi, 1558)

Facing page
Fig. 10. Ludovico Ariosto, *Orlando furioso di M. Lodovico Ariosto nuovamente adornato di figure di rame da Girolamo Porro . . .*, illustration of canto XXIX (Venice: Francesco de Franceschi, 1584)

324
CANTO
XXVIIII
ROD.
ISABELLA.

and a certain measure of grotesquery in the portrait of the dwarf, however, these rather crude prints intended for a popular readership do not seem to have served as models for Vaenius.

As for images of the unfortunate meeting of Rodomonte and Isabella—which we find portrayed more often and with a greater range of expressive possibilities in sixteenth-century editions of Ariosto's poem—similarities with Vaenius's engravings are negligible and limited to aspects of their details, such as Zerbino's coffin marked by a cross or the hermit whom Rodomonte attacks and grabs by the beard represented in the opening plates of canto XXIX in the Valgrisi (1556) and De Franceschi (1584) editions (figs. 9–10). The presence of these not particularly relevant details only serves to make even more tangible the striking differences that distinguish—with regard to the intrinsic logic of the images—the illustrative apparatus of editions of *Orlando furioso* on one side and Vaenius's plates on the other. In the latter, the scenes depicted are found to be extrapolated from the overall plot of the poem to become emblems (examples) of general truths; and their universal value lies precisely in their being detached from their respective contexts of origin. On the contrary, the attempt to connect each character to the thread of his or her particular story is quite evident in the images of the editions just cited: to the "before" and "after" of the events narrated in the canto, through iconographic solutions that have been defined as "pluri- or multi-narrative" or "poly-episodic," and precisely for their intent to combine in a single composite image different narrative segments distributed seamlessly over the space of the page.

3. The *Emblemata* of Vaenius

As already noted, the two plates under consideration here are undated, so we do not know exactly to which phase of the rich and diversified activity of their author they can be ascribed. What is certain is that, beyond their subject matter, the emblematic matrix that characterizes them fits coherently into the scope of the editorial genre to which Vaenius had increasingly dedicated himself from the last years of the sixteenth century onward: emblem books. His first collection of *Emblemata Horatiana* dates from 1607 (though we know he had worked on it for almost ten years); published in Antwerp in Latin, it was enormously successful and was immediately reissued in various polyglot editions.[30] Subsequently, the *Amorum emblemata* (1608)—illustrated compilations of maxims based on amorous-courteous subjects and taken from classical authors—and the *Amoris divini emblemata* (Veen 1615), in which amatory themes are parsed in spiritual terms, were all books that saw numerous editions

Fig. 11. Otto van Veen (Vaenius), *Amorum emblemata: Officit officio* (86), Antwerp, 1608

and reprintings, and they continued to circulate widely between the seventeenth and eighteenth centuries, carving out a recognized position in the context of the Renaissance emblem.[31]

It is not only in their "exemplary" character that our plates show a certain affinity with this copious and varied production but also in their overall structure, the result of a well-proven interweaving of texts and figures; their articulation in title, together with underlying image and verse, closely resembles the canonical structure of Andrea Alciato's emblems (*inscriptio, pictura,* and *subscriptio*), which between the sixteenth and seventeenth centuries had established itself as an essential point of reference throughout Europe.[32] And there are also precise correspondences with Vaenius's own *emblemata*; the torch that illuminates the scene of Isabella's beheading, for example, is practically identical to the "flame of Love" that burns in the emblem "Officit officio" "Soccorso mi nuoce" / "Loves fyre is unquencheable"), and the correspondence is all the more significant since in both scenes, the torch is clearly invested with the same symbolic implications (fig. 11).

There are, nevertheless, many aspects in which the two Ariostan plates remain very different from Vaenius's other work. First of all, as we have seen, they do not belong to any collection or series but were one-offs, fully intended to stand on their own; their meaning self-contained, it goes no further than the recollection of two exemplary events. These autonomous works do not display the ambitions of their author's books, nor do the plates demonstrate the element that most distinguished the *emblemata* on the European publishing scene: the complex intertextual dialogue in which *picturae* found themselves inserted (quotations and paraphrases taken from various classical sources, assembled together with editorial comments and translations), determining, among other things, the marked multilingualism of their pages, in which no fewer than seven different ancient and modern languages were juxtaposed, a completely different operation with respect to the "simple" reinterpretation of the Ariostan verses in French and Italian.[33] The typographical composition of the pages is also significantly different in these two cases: images and texts in the *emblemata* never coexist on the same page—as in the *veri essempi*—but face each other on separate sheets.

Regarding the more specifically iconographic dimensions of these two cases, the differences are no less significant than those already noted. The men and women who populate the two plates taken from *Orlando furioso* are fully formed personae, and they maintain all of the distinctive features of their literary referents: personalities, drives, particular and defining sentiments. In the *emblemata*, however, we largely see abstract personifications of concepts and states of mind at play (attitudes and inclinations, vices and virtues, impulses and temperaments), purely allegorical affectations, so stylized as to be almost interchangeable, to the point of being reduced to the recurring figure of the winged cupid in the *Amorum emblemata*. Moreover, it is the very structure of the *picturae* in the plates and the emblems that is completely different: in the latter, the images are never divided into several squares or compartments but rather occupy more or less the entire space of the page with a single scene of a distinctly unitary character, and precisely as such legible in an emblematic key. But the two plates "quarried from M. Ludovico Ariosto" are framed by an architectural structure that divides them into triptychs, like altarpieces. We are clearly dealing here with a completely different rubric, which seems to be derived from another iconographic-editorial tradition that at that time continued to enjoy great fortune in the Netherlands, namely, that of the *Bibliae pauperum* and the *Specula humanae salvationis* (fig. 12).[34] Here we are dealing with a prototype widely used

Fig. 12. *Biblia pauperum*, Netherlands, fol. 2r, ca. 1460–1463. Paris, Bibliothèque nationale de France, Réserve des livres rares, XYLO-3

since the late Middle Ages, particularly wherever the aim was to juxtapose a series of episodes from the Old and New Testaments (the former presented as prefigurations of the latter) combined according to typological or analogical criteria, which were then employed as proof of the respective allegorical correspondences. We can probably attribute to this same dichotomous structure the idea of a pair of specular plates, each conceived as pendant of the other.

In the absence of other documents—particularly regarding information about the dedicatee, Gregorio Benedetti—we can advance the hypothesis that our plates belong to the first phase of Vaenius's interest in the emblematic, a phase in which we can suppose that the Dutch artist was experimenting in various directions with the potential of the juxtaposition of text and image that would be codified, once the solutions that convinced him most were identified, in formulas substantially different from those essayed in his encounter with *Orlando furioso*.

4. Vaenius and Ariosto: Elective Affinities in the Shadow of Horace

If in interpreting the vicissitudes of Astolfo, Iocondo, Isabella, and Rodomonte through a moralizing lens Vaenius did nothing more than conform to a general trend typical of late-sixteenth-century illustrated editions of the *Furioso*, he nevertheless adopted a completely original strategy in extrapolating the two episodes from the thread of the Ariostan narrative to make of them emblems of universal import; and, as we have seen, he achieved this result in breaking not only from the practices of the time but also from those he himself utilized in his best-known works. At this point, the time has come to ask ourselves what might have been the reasons for Vaenius's particular interest in *Orlando furioso* and what might have prompted him to isolate the two episodes taken from cantos XXVIII and XXIX in order to elevate them to the rank of "true examples" of the vices and virtues typical of women.

An initial element for which Ariosto would have represented a privileged interlocutor in the eyes of Vaenius is undoubtedly the fact that the Ferrarese poet was credited throughout sixteenth-century Europe as a recognized authority in matters of love and their various repercussions. We find Ariosto cited in this capacity in treatises beginning with the *Trattato d'amore* by Benedetto di Falco (1538), which situated aphorisms of the author of the *Furioso* alongside those of earlier illustrious writers such as Theocritus, Plato, or Petrarch in order to examine the different effects of "divine" and "profane" love.[35] This was an approach that would have been irresistible to Vaenius, who had made the theme of love one of his chosen, if not defining, subjects;[36] the opinions attributed to Ariosto in this area by many of the sixteenth- and seventeenth-century *trattatisti*—who identified in him the champion of a robust idea of sensual love, alien to the abstract sublimations of Platonism—must have seemed particularly kindred to one who never hesitated in declaring his hostility toward both the *bullati greges* (flock of bulls) and the *serious viri* (serious man), dedicating his *Amorum emblemata* to *iuvenes . . . lepidasque puellas* (charming young girls; c. 4*v*).[37]

Further common ground on which Vaenius might have sought to establish a dialogue with Ariosto was their shared love for Horace. For both, the Roman poet was not only a canonical author frequently engaged as a source of inspiration (for the Ferrarese poet in both his *Satires* and the *Furioso*; for the Dutch artist in his *Emblemata Horatiana*) but also a benchmark whose authority extended considerably beyond the literary sphere, a master of life, whose teachings endowed the moral dimension with an *aurea mediocritas* (golden mean) tinged not only with Stoic or neo-Stoic elements but also—as has been suggested by many scholars—with religious disquietude.[38] It would seem that for both Vaenius and Ariosto, declaring oneself a follower of the Horatian model was a way of assuming a nom de plume as fellow men, artists, and poets; accordingly, both figures appear to have become spokesmen for wider circles, linked—in addition to analogous philosophico-literary taste and inclination—through shared attitudes in terms of devotion and spirituality, attributable in both cases to the galaxy of Erasmian Christian humanism.[39] In passing, we can also note that these circles included the same Gian Francesco Valier—a multifaceted individual, scholar, and diplomat, hanged by the Serenissima in 1542 as a spy in the service of Francis I and his pro-Turkish policy—expressly remembered by Ariosto among his interlocutors of choice (*Fur.*, XLVI 16, 5–8), as well as one of the sources of the story told by the innkeeper of Aigues-Mortes, which some decades later would have so fascinated Vaenius.[40]

It is in this context that the specific questions with which our two plates are concerned acquire particular significance: "around the squalid table of an eighth-century tavern in the *Aiguemortaise*," Annalisa Izzo writes, "one of the most lively rituals within the culture of Renaissance Europe is celebrated, the intellectual dispute over the question of women and the prerogative of their amorous desires."[41] With respect to this *querelle*, Ariosto's position is revealed to be—under the facetious and witty guise of literary fiction—surprisingly open and undogmatic, thus giving an unusually positive inflection to the account of the uninhibited wives of Astolfo and Iocondo:

> Io farei (se a me stesse il darla e torre)
> tal legge, ch'uom non vi potrebbe opporre.
>
> Saria la legge, ch'ogni donna colta
> in adulterio, fosse messa a morte,
> se provar non potesse ch'una volta
> avesse adulterato il suo consorte:
> se provar lo potesse, andrebbe asciolta,
> né temeria il marito né la corte.
> Cristo ha lasciato nei precetti suoi:
> non far altrui quel che patir non vuoi.
> —*Fur.*, XXVIII 81, 7–8; 82
> [If it fell to me to make and suspend laws, I would enact a law to which no man could object: / every woman caught in adultery would be put to death unless she could prove that her husband had once done so too. If she could prove it,

she would be absolved—she would need fear neither her husband nor the court. Christ left us among his precepts: Do not do to others what you would not endure yourself.]

The word and, to some extent, even the concept of "tolerance" did not yet exist in the early-sixteenth-century European lexicon. But in the arguments of the "sincere and just old man" to whom Ariosto entrusted his own thinly veiled sentiments, the attentive reader can perceive a desire for balance and sober-mindedness, of measure and common sense, that resonates with the equanimity with which "Moors" and "Saracens" are described in the *Furioso*. Alternately enslaved to their debaucheries yet capable of acts of heroism and virtue, eager for love and bewitched by petty greed, devoted to honor but susceptible to fragile dispositions and easily distracted, these Others show themselves to be no different, whether men or women, from the "most Christian" Carolingian knights and their beloveds.[42]

There is no reason to be surprised at such benevolent skepticism in Vaenius, officially Catholic but stranger to any position of a too openly confessional nature, so much so as to provoke the question of whether his moderation was the result of a marketing strategy or a certain religious indifference (the two were not necessarily in contradiction).[43] Born in Leiden in 1556 on the eve of the insurrection against Spanish rule, Vaenius soon left his homeland for the Loyalist provinces; but he remained deeply attached to his native soil and maintained throughout his life, as evidenced by his *Liber amicorum*, correspondents of all faiths—Domenico Lampsonio, Justus Lipsius, and the "Christian Horace" Laevinus Torrentius, to name but a few—accustomed, as he was, to stoically negotiating opposing extremisms and inclined to distancing themselves from zealotry in the name of other, higher values.[44]

5. Epilogue: Transcultural Encounters at the Mughal Court

Texts and images are not static objects; the former stimulate new readings, and the latter give rise to new interpretations. At every shift in time and space, the course of intercultural exchange proceeds without pause, conveying reverberations, reflections, and recastings into the most diverse milieus. This is the case of the aforementioned print of the *Martyrdom of St. Cecilia* by Hieronymus Wierix made from the painting by Francesco Vanni, from which, as we have seen, Vaenius may have been inspired to portray the Ariostan Isabella. Wierix's image was copied shortly after it was first published, in a completely different context (fig. 13).[45] This painting, signed by the Mughal artist Nīnī (active at the

Fig. 13. Nīnī, *Martyrdom of St. Cecilia*, after an engraving by Hieronymus Wierix, ca. 1600–1650. Mounted with calligraphy by Sulṭān ʿAlī Mashhadī. London, Victoria and Albert Museum

beginning of the seventeenth century), was subsequently inserted into one of the pages of an album made for Emperor Shāh Jahān (1628–1658), mounted inside a frame decorated with floral motifs and calligraphic inscriptions that reproduce a *ghazal* by the Indo-Persian poet Amīr Khusraw Dihlavī (1253–1325) dedicated to the tribulations of poetic creation likened to the deliriums of love.[46]

Nīnī's painting does not explicitly allude to the theme of Christian martyrdom (neither the title of Wierix's print nor its accompanying text is mentioned, and the wounds on the neck of Saint Cecilia are barely visible). We can nevertheless consider it a particularly meaningful testimony to the opening toward Western culture that characterized Mughal artistic workshops during the reigns of Akbar (1556–1605) and Jahāngīr (1605–1627). In this context, as Rice has observed, the encounter between the graphic layout of the European print—essentially composed of lines—on the one hand, and traditional Persian pictorial-calligraphic practices, on the other, favored the birth of a highly composite aesthetic, based on the notions of imitation, replication, and reworking.[47] From this point of view, several Mughal album leaves created between the end of the sixteenth and the first half of the seventeenth century, such as the one on which the painting of Nīnī was glued, can be considered an extraordinary transcultural site of encounter, where text and image combine to bring together a formal sense of taste and speculative meanings of various and occasionally dissimilar origins.

Nīnī conceived his painting not as an illustration of the accompanying verses but as a free variation on their theme: the words of the poem evoke the travails of writing; the image stages a young woman wounded by the pains of love.[48] The original iconography—attenuated of any reference to the original story of martyrdom—was thus reimagined in a new erotic-literary context.

The story of Shahrazād took root in the Indo-Persian world centuries before reaching that of the *Orlando furioso* via a long sequence of verbal echoes, subsequently hybridized by Vaenius together with visual cues of varied provenance within the restless climate of the Spanish Netherlands. Maderno's profile of Saint Cecilia—who, in Vaenius's hands, lent her features to chaste Isabella beheaded by Rodomonte—would have alighted on Indian shores through the print of Wierix in the wake of the first Jesuit missions welcomed by the court of the Mughal emperors.[49] And here at the dawn of a new day, perhaps, as in the *Thousand and One Nights*, the story might have begun again.

Notes

The preparation for and writing of this article were made possible thanks to a stay at I Tatti as director's appointee from January to June 2019.

1. See Pigna 1554, p. 69; and additionally Pellegrino 1584, p. x; Accademia della Crusca 1584, p. 11v; Oddi 1587, p. 46. In this regard, see also Rajna 1975, p. 439n2; Pavlova 2014, p. 47; and the contribution of Mario Casari in this volume.

2. See Silvestre de Sacy 1829; Schlegel 1846, pp. 1–23 (the published letter of August Wilhelm von Schlegel to Antoine Isaac Silvestre de Sacy, dated Bonn, January 20, 1833, is now available in the digital correspondence of Schlegel: https://august-wilhelm-schlegel.de/briefedigital/); Ariosto 1839, Vol. 2, pp. 399–402; and additionally Rajna 1975, pp. 439–440, as well as the bibliography indicated there.

3. Rajna 1975, pp. 436–455.

4. On the different versions of this account and Ariosto's possible sources for them, see Scaglione 1958; Sercambi 1995, pp. 949–952n1; Spampinato Beretta 1999; Minervini 2009; Izzo 2012; Lemos Horta 2015.

5. Hollstein 1988, pp. 166–167nn12–13.

6. For the identification of the monogram, see Brulliot 1833, p. 293n2190. The attribution to van Veen is further corroborated, were there the need, by the third reprint of the two plates, published in Coburg, with the indication "Otho Vaenius pinxit" (Hollstein 1988, p. 167). Regarding the printing privilege ("Cum privileg. Pontif. Imp. reg.m Archid. atq. Ord.m"; that is, "Cum privilegiis pontificis, imperatoris, regum, archiducum atque Ordinum"), this is one of the most generous allowed within the context of the Low Countries at this time; see Stijnman 2012, pp. 413–418.

7. On the figure of Pietro Benedetti and his collaboration with Vaenius, see Montone 2001; Montone 2003; Selmi 2012. More generally, on the Genovese community in Antwerp, of which Benedetti was a prominent member, see Maggiore 1998.

8. Paris, Musée du Louvre, Département des Arts Graphiques, inv. 21258, *recto*. Brush and off-white and light brown oil, and pen and brown ink, 22.3 x 77.5 cm.

9. Lugt 1949, pp. 72–73n1360; London, the British Museum, V, 3.63 and V, 3.64. The copy of *Vero essempio di castità* owned by British Museum (V, 3.64) is cut at the bottom of the sheet and does not contain the dedication.

10. On the role of *novelle* and second-degree narration in the *Furioso*, see most recently Sangirardi 2009; Izzo 2008; Izzo 2013; Izzo 2016, with the bibliography indicated there. As for the relation with Boccaccio, see Barbirato 1987; Sangirardi 1992; Verzini 2017. For the figure of Rodomonte and his iconographic legacy, see the Vincenzo Farinella's chapter in this volume (and its bibliography).

11. As Rajna observed, the motif of the beauty contest is absent in both the *Thousand and One Nights* and Sercambi; we find it again, however, in a version of the story that circulated between Andalusia and the Maghreb incorporated into the collection *Mi'at layla wa-layla* (*One Hundred and One Nights*, known through several manuscripts, among which is one recently rediscovered in the collections of the Aga Khan Museum. See Marzolph and Chraïbi 2012; Ott 2016; Ott and Benigni 2017; and the contribution of Claudia Ott in this volume.

12. The title of the two plates seems both an implicit and direct citation of canto XXVII of *Orlando furioso*, where the *novella* of Iocondo and Astolfo is presented to the host at Aigues-Mortes as one of the *veri esempi* (true instances) that he happens to hear: *Un gentilomo di Vinegia poi, / che qui mia buona sorte già condusse, / seppe far sì con* veri esempi *suoi, / che fuor de l'ignoranza mi ridusse. / Gian Francesco Valerio era nomato; / che 'l nome suo non mi s'è mai scordato* (a gentleman from Venice whom good fortune brought to my door, was able, with true instances of his own, to draw me out of my ignorance. I have never forgotten his name: Gian Francesco Valerio; *Fur.*, XXVII 137, 3–8; emphasis mine).

13. Cf. Izzo 2012, pp. 6–8; Izzo emphasizes how the image of the bed curtain is completely missing from Sercambi, referring to Rajna's idea that both Ariosto and Sercambi had acquired it from a common progenitor (Rajna 1975, p. 448), while also posing the question of a possible invention on Ariosto's part of this detail or of the use of another model (that would seem to be the *Decameron*, in which the bed curtain is typical). In both Sercambi and the *Thousand and One Nights*, the adulterer is simply discovered between the sheets with her lover.

14. For other possible barbs directed at pilgrimages to the Holy Land (which had a specific Ferrarese history; see Luchino da Campo 2011; Ariosto 2007), see Picchio 2007.

15. Among various Renaissance reinterpretations, strikingly similar to the Vaenius overdoor is the one found on the tomb of Stefano Satri in Rome (fig. 4b). For the history of the ancient bas-relief and its Renaissance appropriations, see Williams 1940–41; Weiss 1961; Wirth 1984; Cavallaro 2015.

16. In general, on the figure of the dwarf between the Middle Ages and the Renaissance, see Spila 2009; more specifically, regarding Gonzaga clowns, dwarves, and slaves and the nonchalance with which Isabella d'Este made use of them, see Luzio and Renier 1891.

17. Rajna 1975, pp. 459–463; Cerulli 1946; Cerulli 1947; Levi della Vida 1959; Cerulli 1975.

18. On Francesco Barbaro and *De re uxoria*, see Kravina 2018 (and its bibliography). As for Valier—who remains a little-known figure, in part due to the *damnatio memoriae* suffered following his death sentence, a fate suffered also by his manuscripts—see esp. Ordine 1992; Rebecchini 2013; Allonge 2017.

19. Among recent contributions to this argument, see Montanari 2005; Lirosi 2010. Thanks to Marco Folin for having brought this similarity to my attention.

20. See New Hollstein 2004, pp. 4–6nn1413–1414. As for the print of Cornelis Galle I, the related design of Francesco Vanni is preserved in the Albertina Library in Vienna (inv. 782), about which see Boorsch 2012.

21. On the artistic legacy of the Ariostan imaginary, see Paoli and Preti 2012; Bolzoni 2014; Caneparo 2015; Cogotti, Farinella, and Preti 2016; Bolzoni 2017. On the figurative reception of the poem—and specifically regarding the *novella* of Iocondo—in Elizabethan England, see Degli Innocenti 2019.

22. On the process of the "canonization" of *Orlando furioso* and its visual and moral interpretations, see the classic study Javitch 1991 and, more recently, Modano 2017. More specifically, on the illustrated editions, see Bolzoni, Pezzini, and Rizzarelli 2011; Bolzoni and Girotto 2012 (and the bibliography cited therein).

23. Ariosto 1553, canto XXVIII, "Allegoria."

24. Ariosto 1553, canto XXIX, "Allegoria."

25. For a repertory of the illustrations published in sixteenth-century editions of the *Furioso*, see the valuable digital archives realized by the CTL of the Scuola Normale Superiore in Pisa under the direction of Lina Bolzoni: *L'*Orlando furioso *e la sua traduzione in immagini* (http://www.ctl.sns.it/furioso/apps_v3/mastro_furioso/intro.php) and *Galassia Ariosto: Un archivio digitale dei poemi narrativi illustrati tra Cinque e Seicento* (http://www.galassiaariosto.sns.it).

26. They are, however, explicitly inserted into the image prefacing the canto in the 1591 English translation by John Harington, whose plates were taken—and, as in this instance, occasionally reworked—from those done by Girolamo Porro for De Franceschi, which Vaenius might well have known, given the already considerable circulation of English books in the Netherlands in this period. See Degli Innocenti 2019, pp. 61–64. Thanks to Michael Wyatt for reminding me about the Harington plates.

27. On the particular iconographic formulas adopted in the Valgrisi (1556) and De Franceschi (1584) editions, see Andreoli 2011; Preti 2012; Andreoli 2013.

28. See Agnelli and Ravegnani 1933, Vol. 1, pp. 182–185; Modano 2017, pp. 225–226; Degli Innocenti 2019, pp. 61–64.

29. Edit16, CNCE, 22608.

30. Veen 1607. There is an excellent online edition available at the site of the University of Utrecht: *Emblem Project Utrecht: Dutch Love Emblems of the Seventeenth Century*, http://emblems.let.uu.nl.

31. The bibliography of Vaenius's emblematic work has been greatly enriched in recent years; among others, see Gerards-Nelissen 1971; Porteman 1996; Montone 2003; Thøfner 2003; McKeown 2012; Dekoninck, Guiderdoni, and Smeesters 2018; Enenkel 2018, pp. 365–438.

32. On the European dimension of emblem production in the Low Countries, see Adams and Weij 2003.

33. On Vaenius's textual pastiches, see Montone 2003.

34. On biblical iconography in the early centuries of printing, see Engammare 1994; Melion 2009. More generally, regarding the different means for assembling images for mnemonic, didactic, or devotional ends in Netherlands publishing between the fifteenth and sixteenth centuries, see Dekoninck 2017.

35. Genovese 2011, p. 346.

36. Melion 2012.

37. Veen 1608, *Ad librum*, n.p. On the figure of Ariosto in sixteenth-century love treatises, see Favaro 2008.

38. On the relationship between Horace and Ariosto, see, most recently, Alhaique Pettinelli 2004; Villa 2017. On the *Emblemata Horatiana* as an "ethics manual," see Gerards-Nelissen 1971; and esp. Enenkel 2018, pp. 365–438.

39. On the complex question of Ariosto and religion, and especially his ties to Erasmian circles, see Fragnito 1992; Prandi 2006; Jossa 2016; and esp. the chapter by Stefano Jossa in this volume.

40. On the figure of Valier and about his possible heterodoxy, see the bibliography cited above in note 17.

41. Izzo 2012, p. 3.

42. On the philogyny of Ariosto, see Izzo 2012; Weaver 2016. The equivalence between Christian and Saracen knights in *Orlando furioso* was a thesis proposed by Italo Calvino but discussed in a more complex, and—to an extent—critical, manner by Maria Pavlova. See Pavlova 2014; Pavlova 2020; and her chapter in this volume. For a reading of *Orlando furioso* as a "Stoic comedy," see Carroll 1997.

43. In this regard, see Visser 2007, pp. 35–40; Dekoninck, Guiderdoni, and Smeesters 2018, pp. 18–19.

44. For a biographical profile of Vaenius, see Porteman 2011; more specifically, on his politico-religious positions, see Dekoninck, Guiderdoni, and Smeesters 2018; Morford 2001; De Brézé 2015.

45. On the *Saint Cecila* of the female painter Nīnī, copied from the print by Wierix, see Stronge 2002, pl. 70, p. 104; Rice 2017; Natif 2018, pp. 68–109.

46. See Natif 2018, p. 85n40.

47. Rice 2017.

48. See Natif 2018, p. 88, who subtly notes that in the final verse, Dihlavī metaphorically associates bleeding and the amorous gaze—"bloodshed and the amorous glance of the beloved"—in order to describe his deeply anguished state of mind, playing on the double significance of the same word in Persian.

49. Rice 2017.

Bibliography

Accademia della Crusca 1584

Degli Accademici della Crusca difesa dell'Orlando furioso dell'Ariosto: Contra 'l dialogo dell'epica poesia di Camillo Pellegrino, Stacciata prima. Florence: Per Domenico Manzani Stampator della Crusca, 1584.

Adams and Weij 2003

Adams, Alison, and Marleen van der Weij, eds. *Emblems of the Low Countries: A Book Historical Perspective.* Paris: Droz, 2003.

Agnelli and Ravegnani 1933

Agnelli, Giuseppe, and Giuseppe Ravegnani. *Annali delle edizioni ariostee.* 2 vols. Bologna: Zanichelli, 1933.

Alciati 1618

Alciati, Andrea. *Emblemata . . . cum imaginibus plerisque restitutis ad mentem Auctoris: Adiecta compendiosa explicatione Claudij Minois Divionensis et notulis extemporarijs Laurentij Pignorij Patavini.* Padua: Pietro Paolo Tozzi, 1618.

Alhaique Pettinelli 2004

Alhaique Pettinelli, Rosanna. "'Ma grandemente commendava Orazio . . .': Presenza oraziana nel *Furioso.*" In *Forme e percorsi dei romanzi di cavalleria da Boiardo a Brusantino,* edited by Rosanna Alhaique Pettinelli, pp. 19–44. Rome: Bulzoni, 2004.

Allonge 2017

Allonge, Guillaume. "Evangelismo ed eterodossia nella diplomazia franco-turca di Francesco I." *Mélanges de l'École française de Rome: Italie et Méditerranée modernes et contemporaines* 129, no. 2 (2017): pp. 433–444.

Andreoli 2011

Andreoli, Ilaria. "L'*Orlando furioso* 'tutto ricorretto et di nuove figure adornato': L'edizione Valgrisi (1556) nel contesto della storia editoriale e illustrativa del poema tra Italia e Francia nel Cinquecento." In *Routes du livre ancien italien en Normandie, Actes du colloque (Caen, 2010)*, edited by Silvia Fabrizio-Costa, pp. 41–131. Bern: Peter Lang, 2011.

Andreoli 2013
Andreoli, Ilaria, ed. *Exercices furieux: À partir de l'*Orlando furioso *de Franceschi (Venise, 1584)*. Bern: Peter Lang, 2013.

Ariosto 1553
Ariosto, Ludovico. *Orlando furioso di M. Lodovico Ariosto, ornato di nove figure, e allegorie in ciascun canto.* Venice: Giovanni Andrea Valvassori, 1553.

Ariosto 1839
Ariosto, Ludovico. *Roland furieux, nouvelle traduction, avec la vie de l'Arioste et des notes sur les romans chevaleresques, les traditions orientales, les chroniques, les chants des trouvères et des troubadours comparés au poème de l'Arioste par A. Mazuy.* Paris: F. Knab, 1839.

Ariosto 2007
Ariosto, Alessandro. *Itinerarium (1476–1479)*, edited by Fabio Uliana. Alessandria: Edizioni dell'Orso, 2007.

Barbirato 1987
Barbirato, Giorgio. "Elementi decameroniani in alcune novelle ariostesche." *Studi sul Boccaccio*, 26 (1987): pp. 329–360.

Bolzoni 2014
Bolzoni, Lina, ed. *L'*Orlando furioso *nello specchio delle immagini*. Rome: Istituto dell'Enciclopedia Treccani, 2014.

Bolzoni 2017
Bolzoni, Lina, ed. *Galassia Ariosto: Il modello editoriale dell'"Orlando furioso" dal libro illustrato al web.* Rome: Bolzoni, 2017.

Bolzoni and Girotto 2012
Bolzoni, Lina, and Carlo Alberto Girotto, eds. *Donne, cavalieri, incanti e follie: Viaggio attraverso le immagini dell'*Orlando furioso. Lucca: Pacini Fazzi, 2012. Exhibition catalogue.

Bolzoni, Pezzini, and Rizzarelli 2011
Bolzoni, Lina, Serena Pezzini, and Giovanna Rizzarelli, eds. *"Tra mille carte vive ancora": Ricezione del Furioso tra immagini e parole*. Lucca: Pacini Fazzi, 2011.

Boorsch 2012
Boorsch, Suzanne. "Cornelis Galle I and Francesco Vanni." In *Ein privilegiertes Medium und die Bildkulturen Europas: Deutsche, französische und niederländische Kupferstecher und Graphikverleger in Rom von 1590 bis 1630, Akten des Internationalen Studientages der Bibliotheca Hertziana, Rom, 10.–11. November 2008*, edited by Sybille Ebert-Schifferer, Elisabeth Kieven, and Eckhard Leuschner, pp. 163–176. Munich: Hirmer, 2012.

Bruilliot 1833
Brulliot, François. *Dictionnaire des monogrammes, marques figurées, lettres initiales, noms abrégés etc. avec lesquels les peintres, dessinateurs, graveurs et sculpteurs ont désigné leurs noms*, Vol. 2, *Contenant les lettres initiales*. Munich: Institut Littéraire Artistique de la Librairie de J. G. Cotta, 1833.

Caneparo 2015
Caneparo, Federica. *"Di molte figure adornato": L'*Orlando furioso *nei cicli pittorici tra Cinque e Seicento*. Milan: Officina Libraria, 2015.

Carroll 1997
Carroll, Clare. *The* Orlando Furioso*: A Stoic Comedy*. Tempe, AZ: Medieval and Renaissance Texts and Studies, 1997.

Cavallaro 2015
Cavallaro, Anna. "Un'indagine storico-artistica delle sepolture femminili nel Rinascimento romano." *Mélanges de l'École française de Rome–Moyen Âge* 127, no. 1 (2015). http://journals.openedition.org/mefrm/2604.

Cerulli 1946
Cerulli, Enrico. "'La conquista persiana di Gerusalemme' ed altre fonti orientali cristiane di un episodio dell'*Orlando furioso*." *Orientalia*, n.s. 15 (1946): pp. 439–481.

Cerulli 1947
Cerulli, Enrico. "Nuovi testi sulla 'Conquista persiana di Gerusalemme' come fonte di un episodio dell'*Orlando furioso*." *Orientalia*, n.s. 16 (1947): pp. 377–390.

Cerulli 1975
Cerulli, Enrico. "L'Orlando furioso nella storia culturale." In *Atti del Convegno Internazionale Ludovico Ariosto, Roma, Lucca, Castelnuovo di Garfagnana, Reggio Emilia and Ferrara, 27 settembre–5 ottobre 1974*, pp. 11–21. Rome: Accademia Nazionale dei Lincei, 1975.
Cogotti, Farinella, and Preti 2016
Cogotti, Marina, Vincenzo Farinella, and Monica Preti, eds. *I voli dell'Ariosto: L'*Orlando furioso *e le arti*. Milan: Officina Libraria, 2016.
Cosquin 1909
Cosquin, Emmanuel Georges. *Le prologue-cadre des Mille et une nuits, les légendes Perses et le livre d'Esther*. Paris: V. Lecoffre, 1909.
De Brézé 2015
De Brézé, Nathalie. "Les implications politiques d'Otto Vaenius dans les Pays-Bas." In *Acta Conventus Neo-Latini Monasteriensis: Proceedings of the Fifteenth International Congress of Neo-Latin Studies (Münster 2012)*, edited by Astrid Steiner-Weber, pp. 134–149. Leiden: Brill, 2015.
Degli Innocenti 2019
Degli Innocenti, Luca. "Reading the Poem 'in the Very Picture': New Evidence on Harington's Original Sin." In *Ariosto, the Orlando Furioso and English Culture*, edited by Jane E. Everson, Andrew Hiscock, and Stefano Jossa, pp. 50–68. Oxford: Oxford University Press, 2019.
Dekoninck 2017
Dekoninck, Ralph. "Le montage des images comme outil méditatif dans la gravure anversoise des XVIe et XVIIe siècles." *Archivio italiano per la storia della pietà* 19 (2017), pp. 153–169.
Dekoninck, Guiderdoni, and Smeesters 2018
Dekoninck, Ralph, Agnès Guiderdoni, and Aline Smeesters, eds. *Physicae et theologicae conclusiones by Vaenius (1621)*. Turnhout: Brepols, 2018.
Enenkel 2018
Enenkel, Karl A. E. *The Invention of the Emblem Book and the Transmission of Knowledge, ca. 1510–1610*. Leiden: Brill, 2018.
Engammare 1994
Engammare, Max. "Figures de la Bible: Le destin oublié d'un genre littéraire en image (XVIe–XVIIe s.)." In *Mélanges de l'École française de Rome: Italie et Méditerranée* 106, no. 2 (1994): pp. 549–591.
Favaro 2008
Favaro, Maiko. "Ariosto nella trattatistica amorosa del Cinquecento e del primo Seicento." *Italianistica* 37, no. 3 (2008): pp. 133–146.
Fragnito 1992
Fragnito, Gigliola. "Intorno alla 'religione' dell'Ariosto: I dubbi del Bembo e le credenze ereticali del fratello Galasso." *Lettere Italiane* 44, no. 2 (1992): pp. 208–239.
Genovese 2011
Genovese, Gianluca. "Ariosto a Napoli: Vicende della ricezione del Furioso negli anni Trenta e Quaranta del Cinquecento." In *"Tra mille carte vive ancora": Ricezione del Furioso tra immagini e parole*, edited by Lina Bolzoni, Serena Pezzini, and Giovanna Rizzarelli, pp. 339–356. Lucca: Pacini Fazzi, 2011.
Gerards-Nelissen 1971
Gerards-Nelissen, Inemie. "Otto van Veen's *Emblemata Horatiana*." *Simiolus* 5 (1971): pp. 20–63.
Historia del re di Pavia ca. 1520
Historia del re di Pavia el qual *havendo ritrovata* la *regina* in *adulterio* se dispose insieme con un compagno cercar più paesi: *Et far con le femine daltrui quel* che loro havean fatto ad ambedui. Venice: Agustino Bindoni, n.d.
Hollstein 1988
Hollstein's Dutch and Flemish Etchings, Engravings and Woodcuts ca. 1450–1700, Vol. 32, *Petrus Valck to Esaias Van de Velde*, compiled by Ger Luijten, edited by D. de Hoop Scheffer. Amsterdam: Van Gendt, 1988.
Izzo 2008
Izzo, Annalisa. "Il racconto di secondo grado nel Furioso." *Italianistica* 3 (2008): pp. 77–85.
Izzo 2012
Izzo, Annalisa. "Misoginia e filoginia nell'Orlando furioso." *Chroniques italiennes web* 22 (2012): pp. 1–25.

Izzo 2013
Izzo, Annalisa. "Discorso diretto e 'entrelacement' nel romanzo cavalleresco: Boiardo e Ariosto." In *"D'un parlar ne l'altro": Aspetti dell'enunciazione dal romanzo arturiano alla "Gerusalemme liberata,"* edited by Annalisa Izzo, pp. 113–140. Pisa: Edizioni ETS, 2013.
Izzo 2016
Izzo, Annalisa. "Racconti." In *Lessico critico dell'Orlando furioso*, edited by Annalisa Izzo, pp. 367–385. Rome: Carocci, 2016.
Javitch 1991
Javitch, Daniel. *Proclaiming a Classic: The Canonization of Orlando Furioso*. Princeton, NJ: Princeton University Press, 1991.
Jossa 2016
Jossa, Stefano. "A 'difesa di sua santa fede': Il poema cristiano dell'Ariosto (*Orlando furioso*, XXXIV 54–67)." In *Chivalry, Academy, and Cultural Dialogues: The Italian Contribution to European Culture*, edited by in Stefano Jossa and Giuliana Pieri, pp. 32–42. Oxford: Legenda, 2016.
Kravina 2018
Kravina, Chiara. "Tradizione e fortuna del *De re uxoria* di Francesco Barbaro." In *Acta Conventus Neo-Latini Vindobonensis: Proceedings of the Sixteenth International Congress of Neo-Latin Studies (Vienna 2015)*, edited by Astrid Syeiner-Weber and Fraz Römer, pp. 412–422. Leiden: Brill, 2018.
Lemos Horta 2015
Lemos Horta, Paulo. "Beautiful Men and Deceitful Women: *The One Hundred and One Nights* and World Literature." *Narrative Culture* 2, no. 2 (2015): pp. 190–207.
Levi della Vida 1959
Levi della Vida, Giorgio. "Fonti orientali dell'Isabella ariostesca." In Giorgio Levi della Vida, *Aneddoti e svaghi arabi e non arabi*, pp. 170–190. Milan: R. Ricciardi, 1959.
Lirosi 2010
Lirosi, Alessia. "Il corpo di santa Cecilia (Roma, III–XVII secolo)." *Mélanges de l'École française de Rome: Italie et Méditerranée modernes et contemporaines* 122, no. 1 (2010): pp. 5–51.
Luchino da Campo 2011
Luchino da Campo. *Viaggio del marchese Nicolò d'Este al Santo Sepolcro (1413)*, edited by Caterina Brandoli. Florence: Olschki, 2011.
Lugt 1949
Lugt, Fritz. *Inventaire général des dessins des écoles du Nord: Publié sous les auspices du Cabinet des dessins*, Vol. 1, *École flamande*. Paris: Musées Nationaux, 1949.
Luzio and Renier 1891
Luzio, Alessandro, and Rodolfo Renier. "Buffoni, nani e schiavi dei Gonzaga ai tempi d'Isabella d'Este." *Nuova Antologia* 118 (1891): pp. 618–650; 119 (1891): pp. 112–146.
Maggiore 1998
Maggiore, Luca. *De Italiaanse kolonie te Antwerpen (1598–1648)*. PhD diss., KU Leuven, 1998.
Marzolph and Chraïbi 2012
Marzolph, Ulrich, and Aboubakr Chraïbi. "The Hundred and One Nights: A Recently Discovered Old Manuscript." *Zeitschrift der Deutschen Morgenländischen Gesellschaft* 162, no. 2 (2012): pp. 299–316.
McKeown 2012
McKeown, Simon, ed. *Otto Vaenius and His Emblem Books*. Glasgow: University of Glasgow, 2012.
Melion 2009
Melion, Walter S. "Bible Illustration in the Sixteenth-Century Low Countries." In *Scripture for the Eyes: Bible Illustration in Netherlandish Prints of the Sixteenth Century*, edited by James Clifton and Walter S. Melion. London: Giles, 2009. Exhibition catalogue.
Melion 2012
Melion, Walter S. "Venus/Venius: On the artistic identity of Otto Vaenius and His Doctrine of the Image." In *Otto Vaenius and His Emblem Books*, edited by Simon McKeown, pp. 1–53. Glasgow: University of Glasgow, 2012.
Minervini 2009
Minervini, Laura. "Le 'Mille e una notte' e le letterature romanze medievali: Un bilancio alla luce dell'edizione Mahdi." In *Medioevo romanzo e orientale sulle orme di Sharazàd: Le "Mille e una notte" fra Oriente e*

Occidente, edited by Mirella Cassarino, pp. 193–203. Catanzaro: Rubbettino, 2009.

Modano 2017

Modano, Stefania. "La ricezione dell'Ariosto 'visualizzato' tra letteratura delle immagini e filosofia morale." PhD diss., Université de Lorraine/Università degli Studi di Perugia, 2017.

Montanari 2005

Montanari, Tomaso. "Una nuova fonte per l'invenzione del corpo di Santa Cecilia: Testimoni oculari, immagini e dubbi." *Marburger Jahrbuch für Kunstwissenschaft* 32 (2005): pp. 149–165.

Montone 2001

Montone, Tina. "*Il Magico Legato*: Una pastorale italiana ad Anversa nel 1607." *Filologia e Critica: Rivista quadrimestrale* 26, no. 2 (2001): pp. 263–277.

Montone 2003

Montone, Tina. "'Dolci ire, dolci sdegni, e dolci paci': The Role of the Italian Collaborator in the Making of Otto Vaenius's *Amorum emblemata* (1608)." In *Emblems of the Low Countries: A Book Historical Perspective*, edited by Alison Adams and Marleen van der Weij, pp. 45–62. Glasgow: University of Glasgow, 2003.

Morford 2001

Morford, Mark. "Theatrum hodiernae vitae: Lipsius, Vaenius, and the Rebellion of Civilis." In *Recreating Ancient History: Episodes from the Greek and Roman Past in the Arts and Literature of the Early Modern Period*, edited by Karl A. E. Enenkel et al., pp. 57–74. Leiden: Brill, 2001.

Natif 2018

Natif, Mika. *Mughal Occidentalism: Artistic Encounters between Europe and Asia at the Courts of India, 1580–1630*. Leiden: Brill, 2018.

New Hollstein 2004

New Hollstein's Dutch and Flemish Etchings, Engravings and Woodcuts: 1450–1700, compiled by Zsuzsanna van Ruyven-Zeman with Marjolein Leesberg, edited by Jan van der Stock and Marjolein Leesberg. Rotterdam: Sound & Vision; Amsterdam: Rijksprentenkabinet Rijksmuseum, 2004.

Oddi 1587

Oddi, Niccolò degli. *Dialogo di don Nicolo de gli Oddi padouano in difesa di Camillo Pellegrini: Contra gli Academici della Crusca*. Venice: Fratelli Guerra, 1587.

Ordine 1992

Ordine, Nuccio. "Giovan Francesco Valier, homme de lettres et espion au service de François Ier." In *La circulation des hommes et des œuvres antre la France et l'Italie à l'époque de la Renaissance*, pp. 225–246. Paris, 1992.

Ott 2016

Ott, Claudia, ed. and trans. *Tausendundeine Nacht: Das glückliche Ende*. Munich: C. H. Beck, 2016.

Ott and Benigni 2017

Ott, Claudia, and Elisabetta Benigni, eds. *Cento e una notte*, translated by Isabella Amico di Meane. Turin: Einaudi, 2017.

Paoli and Preti 2012

Paoli, Michel, and Monica Preti, eds. *L'Arioste et les arts*. Milan: Officina Libraria; Paris: Musée du Louvre, 2012.

Pavlova 2014

Pavlova, Maria. "Ludovico Ariosto." In *Christian-Muslim Relations: A Bibliographical History*, Vol. 6, *Western Europe, 1500–1600*, edited by David Thomas and John Chesworth, pp. 469–483. Leiden: Brill, 2014.

Pavlova 2020

Pavlova, Maria. *Saracens and Their World in Boiardo and Ariosto*. Cambridge: Legenda, 2020.

Pellegrino 1584

Pellegrino, Camillo. *Il Carrafa, o vero della epica poesia: Dialogo di Camillo Pellegrino, all'Illustrissimo Signor Marco Antonio Carrafa*. Florence: Stamperia del Sermartelli, 1584.

Picchio 2007

Picchio, Franco. *Ariosto e Bacco due: Apocalisse e nuova religione nel Furioso*. Cosenza: L. Pellegrini, 2007.

Pigna 1554

Pigna, Giovan Battista. *I romanzi di M. Giovan Battista Pigna, al S. Donno Luigi da Este, vescovo di Ferrara, divisi in tre libri: Ne quali della poesia, e della vita dell'Ariosto con nuovo modo si tratta*. Venice: Bottega d'Erasmo, Vincenzo Valgrisi, 1554.

Porteman 1996

Porteman, Karel. "Introduction." In *Amorum Emblemata / Otto Vaenius*. Aldershot, UK: Scolar, 1996, pp. 1–21.

Porteman 2011

Poteman, Karel. "*Veen*, Otto (Octavio) van, ook V(a)enius, tekenaar, schilder en Schrijver." In *Nationaal biografisch woordenboek* 20 (2011): pp. 1060–1087.

Prandi 2006

Prandi, Stefano. "Premesse umanistiche del Furioso: Ariosto, Calcagnini e il silenzio (O.F. XIV, 78–97)." *Lettere italiane* 58, no. 1 (2006): pp. 3–32.

Preti 2012

Preti, Monica. "'Tacendo parla molte lingue': Girolamo Porro illustrateur de l'*Orlando furioso*." In *L'Arioste et les arts*, edited by Michel Paoli and Monica Preti, pp. 199–221. Paris: Musée du Louvre; Milan: Officina Libraria, 2012.

Rajna 1975

Rajna, Pio. *Le fonti dell'*Orlando furioso*: Ristampa della seconda edizione 1900 accresciuta d'inediti*, edited by Francesco Mazzoni. Florence: Sansoni, 1975.

Rebecchini 2013

Rebecchini, Guido. "Les débuts de Jean Du Bellay à Rome, la cour d'Hippolyte de Médicis et le rôle de Giovan Francesco Valier." In *Jean du Bellay: Diplomatie et culture dans l'Europe de la Renaissance*, edited by Cédric Michon and Loris Petris, pp. 269–281. Rennes: Presses Universitaires de Rennes; Tours: Presses Universitaires François Rabelais de Tours, 2013.

Rice 2017

Rice, Yael. "Lines of Perception: European Prints and the Mughal Kitābkhāna." In *Prints in Translation, 1450–1750: Image, Materiality, Space*, edited by Suzanne Karr Schmidt and Edward H. Wouk, pp. 201–223. London: Routledge, 2017.

Sangirardi 1992

Sangirardi, Giuseppe. "La presenza del *Decameron* nell'*Orlando furioso*." *Rivista di letteratura italiana* 10 (1992): pp. 25–67.

Sangirardi 2009

Sangirardi, Giuseppe. "Les nouvelles du *Roland furieux*." *Cahiers d'études italiennes* 10 (2009): pp. 115–128.

Scaglione 1958

Scaglione, Aldo. "Shahryar, Giocondo, Koterviky: Three Versions of the Motif of the Faithless Woman." *Oriens* 2 (1958): pp. 151–161.

Schlegel 1846

Schlegel, August Wilhelm von. *Œuvres de M. Auguste-Guillaume de Schlegel écrites en français et publiées par Édouard Böcking*, Vol. 3, *Essais littéraires et critiques: Littérature orientale*. Leipzig: Librairie de Weidmann, 1846.

Selmi 2012

Selmi, Elisabetta. "Nodo d'amore e d'eroismo: Riscrittura e allegoria nelle pastorali del primo Seicento." In *Tra boschi e marine: Varietà della pastorale nel Rinascimento e nell'Età barocca*, edited by Daria Perocco, pp. 353–394. Bologna: Clueb, 2012.

Sercambi 1995

Sercambi, Giovanni. *Novelle: Nuovo testo critico con studio introduttivo e note*, edited by Giovanni Sinicropi. Florence: Le Lettere, 1995.

Silvestre de Sacy 1829

Silvestre de Sacy, Antoine-Isaac. *Recherches sur l'origine du recueil de contes intitulé Les Mille et une nuits: Mémoire lu à la séance publique de l'Académie royale des Inscriptions et Belles-Lettres, le 31 juillet 1829*. Paris: Académie Royale des Inscriptions et Belles-Lettres, 1829.

Spampinato Beretta 1999

Spampinato Beretta, Margherita. "La cornice delle Mille e una notte ed il Canto XXVIII dell'*Orlando furioso*." In *Medioevo romanzo e orientale: Il viaggio dei testi, III Colloquio internazionale, Venezia, 10–13 ottobre 1996*, edited by Antonio Pioletti and Francesca Rizzo Nervo, pp. 229–249. Catanzaro: Rubbettino, 1999.

Spila 2009
Spila, Cristiano. *Mostri da salotto: I nani fra Medioevo e Rinascimento*. Naples: Liguori, 2009.
Stijnman 2012
Stijnman, Ad. *Engraving and Etching 1400–2000: A History of the Development of Manual Intaglio Printmaking Processes*. London: Archetype; Houten: Hes & De Graaf, 2012.
Stronge 2002
Stronge, Susan. *Painting for the Mughal Emperor: The Art of the Book 1560–1660*. London: V&A Publications, 2002.
Thøfner 2003
Thøfner, Margit. "Making a Chimera: Invention, Collaboration and the Production of Otto Vaenius's *Emblemata Horatiana*." In *Emblems of the Low Countries: A Book Historical Perspective*, edited by Alison Adams and Marleen van der Weij, pp. 17–44. Glasgow: University of Glasgow, 2003.
Veen 1607
Veen, Otto van (Otto Vaenius). *Quinti Horatii Flacci emblemata: Imaginibus in aes incisis, notisq[ue], illustrata*. Antwerp: Hieronymus Verdussen, 1607.
Veen 1608
Veen, Otto van [Otto Vaenius]. *Amorum emblemata figuris aeneis incisa*. Antwerp: Hieronymus Verdussen, 1608.
Veen 1615
Veen, Otto van (Otto Vaenius). *Amoris divini emblemata, studio et aere Othonis Vaenii concinnata*. Antwerp: Martini Nutii & Joannis Meursii, 1615.
Verzini 2017
Verzini, Martina. "Echi decameroniani nell'*Orlando furioso*." PhD diss., Università degli Studi di Padova, 2017.
Villa 2017
Villa, Alessandra. "L'Arioste qui voulait être Horace." In *L'invention de la vie privée et le modèle d'Horace: Rencontres, 261, Colloques, congrès et conférences sur la Renaissance européenne 93*, edited by Bénédicte Delignon, Nathalie Dauvois, and Line Cottegnies, pp. 299–320. Paris: Classiques Garnier, 2017.
Visser 2007
Visser, Arnoud. "Commonplaces of Catholic Love: Otto van Veen, Michel Hoyer and St. Augustin between Humanism and the Counter Reformation." In *Learned Love: Proceedings of the Emblem Project Utrecht Conference on Dutch Love Emblems and the Internet (November 2006)*, edited by Els Stronks and Peter Boot, pp. 33–48. The Hague: DANS, 2007.
Weaver 1977
Weaver, Elissa Barbara. "Lettura dell'intreccio dell'*Orlando furioso*: Il caso delle tre pazzie d'amore." *Strumenti critici* 34 (1977): pp. 384–406.
Weaver 2016
Weaver, Elissa Barbara. "Filoginia e misoginia." In *Lessico critico dell'Orlando furioso*, edited by Annalisa Izzo, pp. 81–97. Rome: Carocci, 2016.
Weiss 1961
Weiss, Roberto. "A note on the so-called 'Fidei Simulacrum.'" *Journal of the Warburg and Courtauld Institutes* 24 (1961): p. 128.
Williams 1940–1941
Williams, Phyllis L. "Two Roman Reliefs in Renaissance Disguise." *Journal of the Warburg and Courtauld Institutes* 4 (1940–1941): pp. 47–66.
Wirth 1984
Wirth, Karl-August. "Fides III: 'Fidei Simulacrum' (und 'Fidei Symbolum'). *Reallexikon zur deutschen Kunstgeschichte* 8 (1984): pp. 831–876.

PART IV

Performative Contexts

"And of these things a dream was left behind called ʿAntar": Arabic Performance Traditions of Heroic Poetry

Dwight F. Reynolds

Lengthy Arabic heroic tales in oral and written tradition have survived for some fifteen hundred years in many forms and in many different performance modes: sung in verse to the accompaniment of musical instruments, declaimed in coffeehouses from written manuscripts, narrated in public squares by oral storytellers, recited at Sufi *mūlid*[1] festivals, recounted as folktales in domestic settings, printed as cheap chapbooks sold in marketplaces and on blankets spread on urban sidewalks, told against painted backgrounds scrolled through the *ṣandūq al-dunyā* (Box of the World) or *ṣandūq al-ʿajāʾib* (Box of Wonders), marketed on cassettes, portrayed in films and soap operas, even preserved in proverbs and riddles.[2]

Many of these stories are anchored in a distant but historical (rather than mythic) past. They are peopled by central figures who actually lived and left their imprint on history, accompanied by fictional and even supernatural characters that storytellers have conjured up over the centuries.[3] Their geographies are half real (including well-known sites such as Baghdad, Cairo, Cyprus, Jerusalem, and China) and half imaginary (Mount Qāf, the Isle of Wāqwāq, the land of Shīrīnbāt and ʿAlam, etc.). Their roster of characters includes chivalric heroes, archvillains, beautiful maidens, female warriors, comic figures of all sorts, as well as trickster figures (or "men of wiles," as Lyons has termed them) who challenge accepted norms and morals.[4]

As in Jorge Luis Borges's "Ariosto y los Árabes" (Ariosto and the Arabs), these half-real, half-imaginary tales of heroic feats, dramatic loves, victories, and defeats exist in a space between "dreams" and "books"—in the performance space. Although Borges wrote *y de esas cosas quedó un sueño: Arturo* ([of these things was] left behind a dream: Arturius)[5], he could well have substituted the Arabic ʿAntar (as I have done in the chapter title above), the name of the legendary pre-Islamic hero of one of the most famous of the Arabic folk epics, equally famed for his chivalry, his exploits in battle, and his magnificent poetry.[6] The many echoes and reflections of Arabic heroic narratives in Borges and

Ariosto's *Orlando furioso* would argue for multiple points of cultural contact over several centuries. Rather than attempt to pin down the precise historic moments and venues of that contact, however, this essay describes the many different forms of transmission and performance modes that have promulgated the Arabic heroic narrative traditions, starting with the earliest-known examples and then examining the fascinating and rich written and oral medieval traditions of lengthy chivalric folk epics known as *siyar* (singular *sīra*) in the light of modern ethnographic accounts.[7]

1. Early Arabic Heroic Narrative

Arabic literature quite literally begins with heroic narrative. The corpus of tales and poems known as the *Ayyām al-ʿArab* (Days of the Arabs), dating to the fifth and sixth centuries CE, are generally recognized as the oldest Arabic literary material to have come down to us.[8] Several of the key characteristics of these ancient tales have remained surprisingly constant in the Arabic heroic tradition from pre-Islamic times to modern live performances and are worth noting here. The first is that these narratives are usually prosimetric, meaning that the narratives unfold in alternating passages of prose and verse. For anyone familiar with Arabic literature, this is obvious and scarcely causes any comment, but in fact, it should. For in a comparative perspective, this is a rather rare form in world literature. In European literatures, for example, there are relatively few extended narratives in mixed prose and verse, and these are almost all medieval.[9]

Another key characteristic of the Arabic heroic narrative tradition is that the poems are often either quotations by characters within the narrative or poems composed after the fact placed at the end of the story. A description of a tribal raid or battle is periodically interrupted by a statement along the lines of "And this is when so-and-so composed the following verses." It is clear that the inclusion of these verses is meant to substantiate the truth of what has been recounted in prose: "Here is the proof that what I have told you in this story is true!" A key element here is that poetry in preliterate contexts was often deemed more truthful than prose, and this is, in fact, a very rational claim. When words are composed using patterning techniques such as rhythm, meter, rhyme, alliteration, or assonance, an oral "text" is far more likely to be remembered and later performed verbatim than a prose message, because intense linguistic patterning facilitates memorization. The early Arabic terms for poetry and prose reflect this understanding: poetry was referred to as "organized" or "strung" speech, using the ancient metaphor of *manẓūm* (strung like pearls on a string), in opposition to prose, which was referred to as "scattered" (*manthūr*) speech (i.e., unstrung pearls).

Later literate authors dubbed ancient poetry *dīwān al-ʿArab* (the archive of the ancient Arabs, in the sense of "the preserver of historical records").[10] It was widely recognized that poetry played a very significant role in preserving the memory of great deeds and significant events in the absence of written records. The intellectual polymath Ibn Qutayba (d. 889), for example, expressed this idea as follows:

> He who does not have a single line of poetry to record his nobility and the noble deeds and laudable actions he claims for his forebears—his achievements will fade away, even if they are well-known, and will become effaced in the course of time. But whoever binds [his deeds] with the rhymes of poetry and lends firmness to them with its meters, and makes them well-known by means of an unusual line of poetry, or a saying that becomes proverbial, or a poetical idea of great elegance, he will make them outlast time.[11]

These ancient stories and poems of Arab tribal raids, battles, conquests, and so forth, collectively known as the "Days of the Arabs," were set down in writing at various times and places during the eighth and ninth centuries CE from oral sources, and it is as written texts that they are, and have been for centuries, studied and analyzed. The question arises, however, as to how these narratives and poems were performed in ancient times. Early Arabic sources give us a fair amount of information about the performance of other genres such as long poems—*qaṣīdas* (odes)—in the pre-Islamic market of ʿUkkāẓ and other settings, and there are also references to the *quṣṣāṣ* (storytellers) who appear to have specialized in tales of the ancient prophets and tales referred to as the *Isrāʾīliyyāt* (tales of the ancient Israelites), but much less information is available about how and when the ancient prosimetric heroic narratives were performed. As Werner Caskel noted in his 1930 study, smaller pieces of poetry were typically inserted into the narrative itself, while longer poems, especially those said to have been composed *after* the events of the narrative, and are therefore more commentary on the story rather than part of it, are typically placed at the end of the story. Is this the work of the literate compilers, or was there an oral performance tradition similar to the structure of these texts? One informative account is found in a collection known as *Akhbār ʿUbayd* (ʿUbayd's Accounts) and tells how the aged ʿUbayd ibn Sharya al-Jurhumī was summoned to the court of the Umayyad caliph Muʿāwiya (r. 644–656) in Damascus to tell him stories of pre-Islamic times:

> After each of ʿUbayd's accounts, Muʿāwiya would say: "Has any poetry been composed about this?" ʿUbayd would invariably answer: "Yes" (never: "Sorry, I don't recall any"), whereupon the caliph would command, "Let me hear it then!" Then, after the recital of the poems, Muʿāwiya would state: "You have indeed brought the proof (*burhān*) for your story, O 'Ubayd!"[12]

In one place, Muʿāwiya and ʿUbayd even discuss the appropriate placement for the post hoc "commentary poems":

> Muʿāwiya said: "Has any poetry been composed about that?"
> ʿUbayd said: "Yes, O Muʿāwiya, the Arabs composed poems about that. If you want, I will recite them to you; but if you prefer [to hear them] at the end of the story, that would be more appropriate." Muʿāwiya said, "Let me hear them at the end of the story, for that is better."[13]

Heinrichs concludes that such performances grew out of the dialogue-like storytelling sessions termed *musāmara*, and that after a story had been told, listeners would ask for poetic proof, and they could now understand the verses because they knew the story: "There is a dialectic between prose and poetry: the poetry cannot really be understood without the prose, and the prose is not considered trustworthy without the poetry to corroborate it."[14]

A remarkable modern echo of this idea is cited in *Nationalism and the Genealogical Imagination*, by Andrew Shryock. Shryock conducted ethnographic fieldwork among Bedouin in Jordan, who were becoming more and more sedentarized and who were also beginning to record their oral tribal histories in written form. Their oral histories are remarkably similar in form and even content to the ancient *Ayyām al-ʿArab* tales. At one point, he is interviewing a shaykh about a historical event and mentions that another tribe narrated the event differently. The shaykh immediately retorts that the other tribe's version is false—lies!—and the proof that their version is false is that they do not have any poems to back up their narratives. He admonishes Shryock, "You go and ask them for their poems and you will see—they don't have any! *il-qiṣṣa illay ma 'indhā qaṣīd kidhib*" (The story that does not have a poem is a lie!).[15]

Another study of modern Arabic oral poetry among Bedouin tribes of the Arabian Peninsula, by Saad Sowayan, contains very similar narratives and ideas:

> Although nomadic poetry deals mainly with tribal raids and forays, it is not straightforward historical narrative. Poets make only allusions and cryptic ref-

> erences to the incidents celebrated in their poems. Therefore, a poetic reference usually alternates with a prose narrative which recounts the raids and battles celebrated in the poetry and serves to put the poetry into its proper context and to illuminate its allusions. The poetry does, however, serve as an authentic document substantiating the incidents in the narrative and enhancing their circulation and preservation in public memory.[16]

This particular symbiotic interplay between prose and verse emerged before the advent of Islam in the early seventh century CE but has been maintained in oral contexts, such as the Bedouin examples cited by Shryock and Sowayan and also in some forms of written literature. These ancient Arabic stories and those narrated by modern Bedouin, however, never achieved the extraordinary length or narrative complexity of the vast heroic narratives that emerged in the early Middle Ages.

2. Medieval Arabic "Epics"

At some point in the eleventh century or soon thereafter, a new genre of written heroic narrative appeared that later was termed *sīra shaʿbiyya*, often translated as "folk epic."[17] The genre has variously been referred to in European languages as epic, romance, geste, saga, and other terms, but none of these Western terms is an exact equivalent for the Arabic genre *sīra*. The written literary genre almost certainly had its roots in the orally transmitted legends of pre-Islamic and early Islamic heroes, but the exact nature of that relationship is difficult to determine. Over the period of a very few centuries, from the eleventh to the fourteenth, more than a dozen such mega-narratives emerged, often numbering thousands of pages in written form.[18]

A fascinating passage that gives some indication of the growth of these lengthy heroic narratives in popular written literature appears in a text by a twelfth-century Jewish convert to Islam, Samawʾal al-Maghribī (d. 1174). In the opening autobiographical chapter of his *Ifḥām al-Yahūd* (Silencing the Jews), a polemical treatise that attempts to demonstrate the validity of Islam and the errors of Judaism, he writes that as a young person, he was much given to reading books of legendary histories, but his tastes later matured, and he subsequently rejected them for more serious works of history:

> when I was twelve and thirteen years old I was much taken with tales and stories and was devoted to reading about ancient times and knowing about what had happened in previous centuries. So I read the various types of collected works of

> stories and anecdotes, then I moved on to a love of lengthy tales and fictional stories, then to the great compilations of tales such as the book of *The Epic of ʿAntar* [*dīwān akhbār ʿAntar*], and the *Epic of Dhī al-Himma and al-Baṭṭāl*, and the *Tales of Alexander the Two-Horned*, and the *Tales of the Phoenix*, and the *Tales of al-Taraf ibn Ludhan*, and others. Then it became clear to me while I was studying these works, that most of them were written by historians, and I began to ask for true accounts [*akhbār ṣaḥīḥa*] and my interest turned to books of history.[19]

Samawʾal clearly wishes to portray the path of a developing mind. At first taken with shorter fictional stories, he later moved on to larger works of fiction, then to the very lengthy mixed prose-and-poetry epics, and finally to works of true history. He has thereby also provided us with a brief typology of the popular fictional literature of his era. His general attitude toward popular texts is not markedly negative but rather suggests that they are more appropriate for young people or for the less educated classes and not for mature adults and scholars. Samawʾal's account provides some of the earliest evidence for the rather sudden and widespread appearance of the Arabic prosimetric folk epics (*siyar*) in written form during the twelfth century; he, however, refers to each of them as a *dīwān*, a term more often applied to collections of poetry, which may indicate that the term *sīra* in reference to these works had not yet become widespread.[20] This wonderful passage also provides testimony to something rather important: a solitary reader consuming these books alone, not in oral performance, not as part of his studies, but for personal leisure in the twelfth century. It would seem, therefore, that from very early on, these popular epics existed in both oral and written forms.

After the twelfth century, references to the folk *sīra* genre are found in a variety of different sources. Religious figures at times chide copyists for producing these popular texts since they have nothing to do with religion:

> It is best for the copyist not to copy anything from books that lead [their readers] astray, such as the books of heretics or sectarians. Likewise, he should not copy books in which there is no benefit for God, such as the *sīra of ʿAntar* and other diverse subjects that waste time and in which there is nothing of religion.[21]

The historian Ibn Kathīr (d. 1373 CE), on the other hand, denounced the popular *siyar* for their mendacity:

> As for what the masses recount about the hero al-Baṭṭāl in the *sīra* of Dalhimma . . . it is nothing but lies, falsehood, stupid writings, complete ignorance, and shameless prattle that is only in demand by fools and lowly ignoramuses. The same is true of the fabricated *sīra of ʿAntar*.[22]

These attacks from religious figures and other scholars, however, did nothing to slow down the copying of these works or the spread of their popularity. Not only did professional copyists in the marketplace produce manuscripts for sale, but it appears that some learned persons developed a strong personal interest in the folk epics, such as the physician who acquired the nickname "al ʿAntarī," which is explained as follows in a biography compiled by Ibn Abī Uṣaybiʿa (d. 1270):

> Al-ʿAntarī: His real name was al-Muʾayyad Muḥammad ibn al-Mujallī ibn al-Ṣāʾigh al-Jazarī. He was a famous physician, a noted scholar, a good diagnostician, provided excellent treatment, was of noble qualities, a philosopher, and particularly devoted to the field of literature. He wrote much poetry on wisdom and other themes. The scholar Ṣadad al-Dīn Maḥmūd ibn ʿUmar—may God have mercy upon him—told me that al-ʿAntarī as a young man was so given to copying out tales of ʿAntar al-ʿAbsī that he became known for this, hence his nickname.[23]

Did these massive folk epics emerge first as lengthy oral traditions performed by specialized reciters and singers using techniques similar to those documented by Milman Parry and Albert Lord, or did the oral traditions consist of shorter episodes that were then compiled and woven together by literate copyists?[24] For most of the dozen and a half Arabic folk epics that first appear in the Middle Ages, so little documentation exists about how they were performed before, or even contemporaneous with, their appearance as written texts that it is impossible to say for certain. One notable exception is the *sīra* of the Banū Hilāl Bedouin tribe (*Sīrat Banī Hilāl*) for which we have a fascinating glimpse of the interface between written and oral traditions from the fourteenth century.

Unlike many of the other epics, that of the Banū Hilāl focuses not on one central hero but rather on a constellation of central characters, and the central story line recounts the remarkable migration of this large Bedouin tribe in the tenth and eleventh centuries from their homeland in the Najd region of the Arabian Peninsula, westward through Egypt, to North Africa. They then conquered and ruled much of the North African littoral (though not all of the urban centers) for about one century and were then in turn defeated and all but obliterated in a series of battles with the Moroccan Almohad dynasty in the mid-twelfth century. Remnants of the Banū Hilāl tribal confederation, however, were still to be found in the desert areas around the city of Tunis two centuries later, when the late medieval historian Ibn Khaldūn (1332–1406) wrote his great history of the Arabs and Berbers, *Kitāb al-ʿIbar* (The Book of Lessons), and its famous *al-Muqaddima* (Introduction).[25] Ibn Khaldūn collected oral stories and poems from the descendants of the Banū Hilāl tribe which he then incorporated into his scholarly writings. At one point in the *al-Muqaddima,* he argues that oral poetry in vernacular dialects can be as beautiful as poetry written in Classical Arabic, and to prove this point, he includes poems from the Banū Hilāl. In another section, in the *Kitāb al-ʿIbar*, where he discusses the use of oral sources in the writing of history, he includes several oral narratives he had collected from them, which, however, he often deems of doubtful veracity.[26]

The remarkable thing about these stories and poems in the fourteenth century is that they are identifiable as passages parallel to what later came to be known as *Sīrat Banī Hilāl* and can be compared to sections of oral performances recorded in the nineteenth and twentieth centuries. What remains unclear, however, is whether the fragments recorded by Ibn Khaldūn were already part of a larger epic narrative at that point, or whether the process of weaving these discrete tales and poems into a larger entity had not yet taken place. In any case, by the nineteenth century, Western travelers and ethnographers, along with Arab writers, attest that tales of the Banū Hilāl and the other folk epics were known and performed throughout the Arab Middle East.[27]

Sadly, information about the oral performances of these heroic narratives in pre-modern times is almost nonexistent, so it is to modern ethnographic accounts that we must turn for an understanding of these performance traditions. One of the most detailed accounts of how the folk epics were performed is found in the writings of Edward Lane, an Englishman who lived in Cairo in the 1830s. His remarkable account of Egypt includes three chapters devoted the public recitation of what he termed "romances" in coffeehouses (fig. 1):

> The reciter generally seats himself upon a small stool on the *maṣṭabah*, or raised seat, which is built against the front of the coffee-shop: some of his auditors occupy the rest of that seat, others arrange themselves upon the *maṣṭabahs* of the houses on the opposite side of the narrow street, and the rest sit upon stools or benches made of palm-sticks; most of them with pipe in hand; some sipping their coffee; and all highly amused, not only with the story, but also with the lively and dramatic manner of the narrator.[28]

Fig. 1. Egyptian storyteller. From Edward Lane, *An Account of the Manners and Customs of the Modern Egyptians*, vol. 2 (London: Charles Knight and Co., 1836)

Lane estimated that some fifty professional singers specialized in performing the epic of the Banū Hilāl in the coffeeshops of Cairo. They performed without a written text, alternately singing the poetry and speaking the prose, while accompanying themselves on the *rabāb*, or spike fiddle, often with a second musician also playing the *rabāb* supporting them. Although the professional singers did not use a written text, Lane noted that a written version of the *sīra* was available in the marketplace in ten or more small quarto volumes:

> It is half prose, and half poetry; half narrative, and half dramatic. . . . The verse is not measured [i.e., in the classical Arabic poetic meters] . . . still, when read [aloud] as it always is, almost entirely in the popular (and not the literary) manner, it is pleasing in sound, as it often is in matter.[29]

In contrast, Lane estimated that some thirty more storytellers were devoted to recounting the epic of the Mamluk sultan al-Ẓāhir Baybars (1228–1277), who was one of the military commanders who defeated the Seventh Crusade led by Louis IX of France and also helped turn back the Mongol invasion by dealing them their first significant defeat in 1260, after which he became sultan.[30] These reciters also performed from memory without recourse to written texts, but they did not sing, and their performances did not involve any musical instruments:

> Much of the entertainment derived from recitations of this work depends upon the talents of the *Moḥaddit* (storyteller) [?]; who often greatly improves the stories by his action, and by witty introductions of his own invention.[31]

Search as he might, Lane could find but one single written copy of this *sīra* in six quarto volumes divided into ten parts, which he purchased. The volumes, however, were cobbled together from different copies, in different hands, the oldest of which he estimated to have been written about a century earlier.

A third group of narrators performed the *sīra* of ʿAntar. Though this work claimed widespread popularity in earlier centuries, Lane estimated that no more than six such reciters were to be found in Cairo. These reciters read directly from the book, chanting the poetry in a singsong but reading the prose in a normal voice, without any musical accompaniment. Since the poetry in this epic is older and more erudite, it was not easily understood by the masses and therefore attracted primarily listeners with some education. Lane noted that one of the other great medieval epics, that of the female warrior Dhāt al-Himma, was occasionally performed by these same reciters but that written texts of this story, always in fifty-five volumes, were almost impossible to obtain.[32] In addition, he remarked that only a few years earlier, the *sīra* of Sayf ibn Dhī Yazan had also been performed, but in the 1830s, live performances had apparently died out completely.[33]

Overall, Lane's ethnographic description portrays a very lively performance tradition of Arabic heroic narrative, with nearly one hundred professional reciters in the city of Cairo alone. More tantalizing is his description of the various modes of performance: musical sung performances with no resort to written texts, spoken recitations also with no written prompts, and public readings of written texts embellished with the storyteller's own asides and additions. Written texts were readily available for the literate classes to enjoy but not for all epics. All of these performance modes have also been documented in other Arab countries. In Marrakesh, for example, a storyteller named Sī Milūd (1936–2000) gave public readings of the various folk epics over a period of some thirty years, having taken over the practice from his predecessor.[34] Similar performances, supported by official sponsorship, also took place in the Nawfara Café in Damascus until recently.

It is clear that over many centuries, written and oral traditions of heroic chivalric epics have existed side by side and almost certainly interacted.[35] Scholarly studies of the manuscript tradition are fairly numerous, but much less research has been conducted on the fully oral epic traditions.[36] This is in part due to the fact that they are rapidly disappearing and in part due to the difficulties of recording, observing, and analyzing such vast traditions. These studies of modern oral epic traditions, however, are particularly useful as a means of understanding how the epics existed, were transmitted, and were performed from the Middle Ages onward.

3. The Village

In the village of al-Bakātūsh in northern Egypt, there were, in the early 1980s, fourteen households of hereditary professional epic singers, families in which epic singing was the sole occupation of the menfolk, though females supplemented the family income with a variety of odd jobs such as selling vegetables in the marketplace or weaving baskets from palm fronds.[37] The form of performance practiced in this region was prosimetric (alternating passages of spoken prose and sung poetry), in which the poet accompanied himself on the two-string coconut-shell *rabāb*, occasionally with a second *rabāb* player for larger performances. The epic was nearly always performed interwoven with other genres of poetry, particularly songs of praise to the Prophet Muḥammad, *madīḥ*, and a short lyric form known as *mawwāl*. The poetic form of the epic was similar to that of classical Arabic poetry (lengthy verses divided into two equal hemistichs by a medial caesura with mono-end rhyme), but the language used was the local colloquial dialect.

Until the 1980s, epic singers from the village performed regularly in a variety of different venues, including cafés, weddings, saints' festivals, harvest festivals, private evening *sahras* (gatherings), and patron circuits that were passed down from father to son.[38] As electricity spread into even the smallest villages in the Egyptian countryside, television rapidly began to replace the epic poets in cafés and homes, and electrified live music performed with microphones and speakers took their place at festivals, weddings, and other occasions. Within two decades of the arrival of electricity in the village of al-Bakātūsh, the epic-singing tradition had disappeared. By the mid-1990s, all of the epic singers had passed away, and their sons had all chosen other professions, since it was clear that reciting the Hilālī epic was no longer a viable livelihood.

None of the professional epic singers of al-Bakātūsh was literate, and all of them regularly used their thumbprints as a signature since they did not know how to write their names. And yet the best of the singers could sing versions of the Hilālī epic that were between 100 and 120 hours in length. This involved not only tremendous feats of memory but also a process of "composition in performance" very similar to that described by Milman Parry and Albert Lord among epic singers in the Balkans.[39] The epic was not a fixed and frozen text but rather a remarkably complex narrative, carefully memorized and preserved, each performance of which, however, differed. On the one hand, the story was "accordion-like," in that it could be expanded or compressed by the poet at will according to the level of response from the audience. A hero could simply mount his horse and ride into battle, or the poet could describe in loving detail each piece of clothing, armor, and weaponry and then describe the harness, saddle, and other accoutrements of his steed. In talking about adding detail or summarizing, the epic singer Shaykh Ṭāhā Abū Zayd once boasted, "I can kill off the seven kings of the ʿUqayla tribe in thirty minutes, or I can take three hours doing it!"[40] The episode in question occurs when the hero Abū Zayd is still a youth and engages seven different warriors from the enemy ʿUqayla tribe in battle, defeating them one after the other. Shaykh Ṭāhā explained that if the listeners were enjoying the battle scenes, he would stretch them out, but if they evinced little enthusiasm, he would quickly move on in the story (fig. 2).

Another element of the epic that at times changed in performance was the "tone" of different scenes. Depending upon audience reactions, scenes could be performed in a serious or even tragic tone, or they could be rendered almost comic by the poet's joking interjections; a love scene could be performed in a romantic tone acceptable for listeners at a wedding where men, women, and children were all present, or it could be performed with many erotic, even

Fig. 2. Egyptian storyteller. Photo: Dwight F. Reynolds

salacious overtones for an all-male audience. The singer Shaykh Biyelī Abū Fahmī once described a performance where he wasn't paying close enough attention and had to improvise at the spur of the moment. In the more vulgar version of the scene, one of the heroes cuts off an enemy's penis. Shaykh Biyelī, suddenly realizing that there were women listening in the next room, substituted the villain's head at the last moment, but his subterfuge didn't work, because he wasn't quick enough to change the second half of the line, "and it bounced down the road like a *khiyāra* (cucumber)!" The listeners, realizing what had happened, laughed so hard that Shaykh Biyelī started laughing as well and could not continue singing. He had to pause to smoke a cigarette and drink a cup of tea before returning to the performance.

The ability to react to an audience's mood and to deftly change aspects of the performance while remaining loyal to the story line itself is based in the poets' remarkable ability to improvise poetry while maintaining the rhyme scheme and melody (or switching to another melody when necessary).[41] This ability is in part due to the fact that they never learned a completely fixed version of the "text." Rather, in their youth, they learned the techniques of epic singing by hearing hundreds of hours of performances by different singers, which, along with the tutoring they received from their male relatives, resulted in the ability to compose poetry extemporaneously. The epic for them consisted of a traditional story line, replete with the names of hundreds of characters, not a fixed text that could and should be reproduced verbatim in each performance. One stable structural element, however, was the overall rhyme scheme of the *sīra*; the poets of al-Bakātūsh all shared a common rhyme scheme that was linked to elements in the narrative. For example, the opening episode of the epic, "The Birth of Abū Zayd," began on the rhyme *-āXiḥ*, with X representing any consonant (i.e., *rāyiḥ, wāḍiḥ, fāliḥ*, etc.) and continued on that rhyme until Khaḍra al-Sharīfa, who would eventually give birth to Abū Zayd, sang her song of complaint against fate, at which point the rhyme would change.[42]

Professional musical performances of the Banū Hilāl epic lasting dozens of hours have now disappeared, although a handful of Egyptian *rabāb* players have memorized short sections from the *sīra* (often no more than ten to fifteen minutes in length) and perform these at nightclubs, hotels, and other touristic venues. As late as the 1980s, a fascinating form of performance could still occasionally be seen, the *ṣandūq al-dunyā* (Box of the World) or *ṣandūq al-ʿajāʾib* (Box of Wonders). Itinerant performers carried large boxes around with them, set them up, and charged a few pennies for a performance. Viewers would watch through eyeholes cut into the front of the box, as a scroll painting depicting scenes from the folk epics (and other tales) was slowly turned while the performer recited and/or sang the story.[43] From the 1970s to the 1990s, cassette tapes of performances by professional epic singers were still being made, and in bookstalls and on city sidewalks, vendors still sold cheap reproductions of nineteenth-century lithograph printings of the epic, perhaps based on the manuscript versions that Lane saw in the 1830s. Sections from the *sīra* have been adapted for film, television serials, and theatrical productions, and so, although the extraordinary performances of professional epic singers have all but disappeared, tales of the Hilālī epic are still familiar to many.

4. Conclusion

Documentary evidence from earlier centuries points to the emergence of a body of very lengthy heroic chivalric narratives in Arabic beginning in the eleventh century; descriptions of how these folk epics were performed in the Middle Ages, however, are frustratingly sparse. Nevertheless, there appears to have been a constant interaction between oral performances and written manuscript traditions. Linguistic features of some written texts seem to indicate that they were taken down from oral performances, while others seem to have been the product of copyists who freely recomposed these heroic tales in a more literary style, closer to the level of Classical Arabic. Entirely oral strands of the tradition were transmitted and performed by specialized epic singers and reciters, while other more literate performers relied on written texts that they embellished with their own asides, insertions, and commentaries.

There are a vast number of times and places where Europeans might have come into contact with these traditions. Although there is no evidence that any of the specific heroic *sīra* tales mentioned above were translated in their entirety into written texts in European languages, a number of similar texts did cross over linguistic borders from the Middle East into Europe, including the *Alexander Romance*, *Kalīla wa-Dimna*, the *Tale of Barlaam and Josephat*, *Sendebar/The Seven Viziers*, and others.[44] On the other hand, it seems highly likely that performances and/or texts of Arabic *sīra* tales were encountered by Western travelers, merchants, crusaders, and captives, who may have been given rough oral translations of the gist of the stories. And of course, oral versions of these heroic adventures also circulated in a variety of ways, not least of which was the transmission effected by the many different bi- and multilingual individuals and communities around the Mediterranean.[45] The chivalric ethos reflected in *Orland furioso* and later dreamily recollected in Borges's "Ariosto and the Arabs" was one that was found in many regions of the Mediterranean, performed and remembered in many tongues.

Notes

1. These festivals celebrate and honor Sufi "saints", though the Christian sense of the term does not reflect the Arabic concept of "one who is close to God." The word *mūlid* comes from the idea of a "birth celebration," but such a translation also leads to misinterpretations, because the festivals are not actually tied to the birthdays of these figures (some argue that the *mūlids* are linked to the date of the revered figure's death, which is considered a "birth" into the afterlife, but that is debatable). The festivals are in practice bound to the solar agricultural calendar, not the Islamic lunar calendar, and the exact date of a particular *mūlid* is often not chosen until just a few days or weeks beforehand.

2. An extensive body of scholarship explores various aspects of these different traditions, but a useful survey is found in Allen and Richards 2008, pp. 243–344.

3. Dorpmüller and Kruk 2012.

4. For trickster figures, see Lyons 2012; for female warriors, see Kruk 2014.

5. "Ariosto y los Árabes," pp. 122-123.

6. See Heath 1996; Hamilton 1820; Richmond 1978.

7. The Arabic genre of *sīra* has no exact equivalent in Western literary traditions and has variously been translated as "epic," "geste," "romance," "saga," and other terms. For simplicity's sake, it will be referred to in this essay as "epic."

8. See Mittwoch 1960; the most thorough study of this body of tales and poems is Caskel 1930; see also Lichtenstädter 1935.

9. See Harris and Reichl 1997.

10. For a discussion of the early Arabic borrowing of the Persian term *diwān*, see Heinrichs 1997; the earliest appearance of this phrase seems to have been recorded by Ibn Sallām al-Jumaḥī (d. 845); see Heinrichs 1997, p. 249n1.

11. Adapted from Heinrichs 1997, p. 252; although Ibn Qutayba wrote about many diverse fields, including philosophy, law, and the physical sciences, he is best known for his contributions in philology, literature, and grammar.

12. Heinrichs 1997, pp. 259–260.

13. Heinrichs 1997, p. 260.

14. Heinrichs 1997, p. 260.

15. Shryock 1997, p. 258.

16. Sowayan 1985, p. 52.

17. The remarkable tenth-century "booklist" of the Baghdadi bookseller known as Ibn al-Nadīm makes no mention of this genre (Ibn al-Nadīm 2014), so the emergence of the written genre can be reliably dated to sometime after the eleventh century CE.

18. A useful introduction to the Arabic folk epic tradition and summaries of the most famous examples of the genre can be found in Lyons 1996.

19. Samaw'al al-Maghribī 1990, pp. 51–52; English translation in Samaw'al al-Maghribī 1964.

20. The term *sīra* was in common use for the biography of a prominent or exemplary figure, having first been applied to the biography of the Prophet Muḥammad himself and later to major political and religious figures. See Reynolds 2001, pp. 38–40.

21. Cited in Reynolds 1995, p. 7 (emphasis added).

22. Cited in Reynolds 2008, p. 260 (emphasis added).

23. Cited in Reynolds 2008, p. 266 (emphasis added).

24. Lord 1960.

25. Ibn Khaldūn 1958; see also Ibn Khaldūn 1847–1851.

26. For a discussion of these passages in the writings of Ibn Khaldūn and their relationship to the Bani Hilal epic poem, see Reynolds 2010.

27. For a summary of the evidence for the distribution of stories about the Banū Hilāl, see Reynolds 1995, pp. 2–4.

28. Lane 2003, p. 391.

29. Lane 2003, p. 392.

30. Herzog 2007.

31. Lane 2003, p. 413.

32. For more information about this female heroine, see Kruk 2014, pp. 37–109.

33. Blatherwick 2016.

34. Kruk 2006, p. 302; see also Kruk and Ott 1999.

35. See Ott 2003.

36. See Reynolds 1995; Slyomovics 1987.

37. My research in the village of al-Bakātūsh in 1982–1983, 1986–1987, 1988, 1993, and 1995 was funded with support from the Center for Arabic Studies Abroad, a Fulbright-Hays dissertation research grant, the Harvard Society of Fellows, and the Institute for Advanced Studies, Princeton.

38. These circuits consisted of annual or biannual visits to well-off families, many of them formerly large landowners before the great agricultural reforms of the 1950s and 1960s, who would ask the poets to sing for one or more evenings and then pay them with money or, more often, in kind (sacks of wheat, rice, ducks or chickens, cigarettes, etc.).

39. Lord 1960.

40. Personal communication, June 22, 1987.

41. For a more detailed analysis of the techniques used by the poets, see Reynolds 2018.

42. For a more detailed explanation of this feature, see Reynolds 2018.

43. As late as 1982, an example of one of these scroll paintings (without the box itself) was on display in the Egyptian Agricultural Museum in Cairo.

44. Vernet 1999, pp. 454–457.

45. One example of this *El libro de las batallas*, which includes accounts of battles fought by the Prophet Muhammad and other Islamic and pre-Islamic figures, translated into *aljamiado* (Castilian written in Arabic letters) in the sixteenth century. See Galmès de Fuentes 1975.

Bibliography

Allen and Richards 2008

Allen, Roger, and D. S. Richards, eds. *The Cambridge History of Arabic Literature: Arabic Literature in the Post-Classical Period.* Cambridge: Cambridge University Press, 2008.

Blatherwick 2016

Blatherwick, Helen. *Prophets, Gods and Kings in Sīrat Sayf ibn Dhī Yazan: An Intertextual Reading of an Egyptian Popular Epic.* Leiden: Brill, 2016.

Borges 1999

Borges, Jorge Luis. "Ariosto y los Árabes," in *Selected poems*, pp. 122-127, translated by Eric McHenry, edited by Alexander Coleman. New York: Viking, 1999.

Caskel 1930

Caskel, Werner. "*Aijām al-ʿarab:* Studien zur altarabischen Epik." *Islamica* 3, fasc. 5, supp. (1930): 1–99.

Dorpmüller and Kruk 2012

Dorpmüller, Sabine, and Remke Kruk, eds. *Fictionalizing the Past: Historical Characters in Arabic Popular Epic, Workshop Held at the Netherlands-Flemish Institute in Cairo, 28th–29th of November 2007, in Honor of Remke Kruk.* Leuven: Peeters, 2012.

Galmès de Fuentes 1975

El libro de las batallas: Narraciones épico-callaballeresas, edited by Alvaro Galmès de Fuentes. Madrid: Gredos, 1975.

Hamilton 1820

Hamilton, Terrick. *Antar: A Bedoueen Romance.* 4 vols. London: John Murray, 1820.

Harris and Reichl 1997

Harris, Joseph, and Karl Reichl, eds. *Prosimetrum: Cross-Cultural Perspectives on Narrative in Prose and Verse.* Cambridge: D. S. Brewer, 1997.

Heath 1996

Heath, Peter. *The Thirsty Sword:* Sīrat ʿAntar *and the Arabic Popular Epic.* Salt Lake City: University of Utah Press, 1996.

Heinrichs 1997

Heinrichs, Wolfhart. "Prosimetrical Genres in Classical Arabic Literature." In *Prosimetrum: Cross-Cul-*

tural Perspectives on Narrative in Prose and Verse, edited by Joseph Harris and Karl Reichl, pp. 249–275. Cambridge: D. S. Brewer, 1997.

Herzog 2007

Herzog, Thomas. *Geschichte und Imaginaire: Entstehung, Überlieferung und Bedeutung der* Sirat Baibars *in ihrem sozio-politischen Kontext.* Wiesbaden: Harrassowitz, 2007.

Ibn Khaldūn 1847–1851

Ibn Khaldūn. *Histoire des Berbères*, translated by Baron William MacGuckin de Slane. 2 vols. Algiers: Impr. du Gouvernement, 1847–1851.

Ibn Khaldūn 1958

Ibn Khaldūn. *The Muqaddimah*, translated by Franz Rosenthal. 3 vols. New York: Pantheon, 1958.

Ibn al-Nadīm 2014

Ibn al-Nadīm. *Kitāb al-Fihrist.* 4 vols, edited by Ayman Fu'ād Sayyid. London: al-Furqan Islamic Heritage Foundation, 2014.

Kruk 2006

Kruk, Remke. "Sīrat 'Antar ibn Shaddād." In *The Cambridge History of Arabic Literature: Arabic Literatjre in the Post-Classical Period*, edited by Roger Allen and D. S. Richards. Cambridge: Cambridge University Press, 2006.

Kruk 2014

Kruk, Remke. *The Warrior Women of Islam: Female Empowerment in Arabic Popular Literature.* London: I.B. Tauris, 2014.

Kruk and Ott 1999

Kruk, Remke, and Claudia Ott. "In the Popular Manner: Sīra Recitation in Marrakesh Anno 1997." *Edebiyat* 10 (1999): pp. 183–198.

Lane 2003

Lane, Edward. *An Account of the Manners and Customs of the Modern Egyptians* (1860). Cairo: American University in Cairo Press, 2003.

Lichtenstädter 1935

Lichtenstädter, Ilse. *Women in the Aiyam al-Arab.* London: Royal Asiatic Society, 1935.

Lord 1960

Lord, Albert B. *The Singer of Tales.* Cambridge, MA: Harvard University Press, 1960.

Lyons 1996

Lyons, M. C. *The Arabian Epic.* 3 vols. Cambridge: Cambridge University Press, 1996.

Lyons 2012

Lyons, M. C. *The Man of Wiles in Arabic Popular Literature: A Study of a Medieval Arab Hero.* Edinburgh: Edinburgh University Press, 2012.

Mittwoch 1960

Mittwoch, E. "Ayyām al-'Arab." In *Encyclopedia of Islam, Second Edition*, edited by P. Bearman, Th. Bianquis, C. E. Bosworth, E. van Donzel, and W. P. Heinrichs., Vol. 1, pp. 793–794. Leiden; Boston: Brill, 1960–2007.

Ott 2003

Ott, Claudia. *Metamophosen des Epos: Sīrat al-Muǧāhidīn (Sīrat al-Amīra Ḏāt al-Himma) zwischen Mümdlichkeit un Schriftlichkeit.* Leiden: University of Leiden CNWS Publications, 2003.

Reynolds 1995

Reynolds, Dwight F. *Heroic Poets, Poetic Heroes: The Ethnography of Performance in an Arabic Oral Epic Tradition.* Ithaca, NY: Cornell University Press, 1995.

Reynolds 2001

Reynolds, Dwight F., ed. *Interpreting the Self: Autobiography in the Arabic Literary Tradition.* Berkeley: University of California Press, 2001.

Reynolds 2008

Reynolds, Dwight F. "Popular Prose in the Post-Classical Period." In *The Cambridge History of Arabic Literature: Arabic Literature in the Post-Classical Period*, edited by Roger Allen and D. S. Richards, pp. 245–269. Cambridge: Cambridge University Press, 2008.

Reynolds 2010

Reynolds, Dwight F. "Epic and History in the Arabic Tradition." In *Epic and History*, edited by David

Konstan and Kurt A. Raaflaub, pp. 392–410. Chichester, UK: Wiley-Blackwell, 2010.
Reynolds 2018
Reynolds, Dwight F. "Composition in Performance Arab Style." *Classics@* 14 (2018). https://chs.harvard.edu/CHS/article/display/6703.
Richmond 1978
Richmond, Diana. *'Antar and 'Abla: A Bedouin Romance.* London: Quartet, 1978.
Samaw'al al-Maghribī 1964
Samaw'al al-Maghribī. *Samau'al al-Maghribi: Ifḥām al-yahūd "Silencing the Jews,"* edited and translated by Moshe Perlmann. In *Proceedings of the American Academy for Jewish Research,* Vol. 32, pp. 5–136. New York: American Academy for Jewish Research, 1964.
Samaw'al al-Maghribī 1990
Samaw'al al-Maghribī. *Ifḥām al-yahūd wa-qiṣṣat islām al- Samaw'al wa-ru'yāhu al-nabī* [*Silencing the Jews and the Story of al-Samaw'al's Conversion to Islam and His Vision of the Prophet*], edited by Muḥammad 'Abd Allāh al-Sharqawī. Beirut: Dār al-Yīl, 1990.
Shryock 1997
Shryock, Andrew. *Nationalism and the Genealogical Imagination: Oral History and Textual Authority in Tribal Jordan.* Berkeley: University of California Press, 1997.
Slyomovics 1987
Slyomovics, Susan E. *The Merchant of Art: An Egyptian Hilali Oral Epic Poet in Performance.* Berkeley: University of California Press, 1987.
Sowayan 1985
Sowayan, Saad. *Nabati Poetry: The Oral Poetry of Arabia.* Berkeley: University of California Press, 1985.
Vernet 1999
Vernet, Juan. *Lo que Europa debe al Islam de España.* Barcelona: El Acantidalo, 1999.

Performing the Medieval Greek Romance from *Digenis Akritis* to the *Erotokritos*

Adam J. Goldwyn and Przemysław T. Marciniak

Byzantine Greeks had no good words to identify the genres that most easily describe the *Orlando furioso*. They had the word for "epic," of course, *epos*, which they used to describe the works of Homer,[1] but they did not use this word to refer to any work produced during the Byzantine period. Nor did they have a word for the other genre most likely to be applied to the *Orlando furioso*: "romance" had no adequate cognate in medieval Greek, either, and even in modern Greek, the word for either a romance or a novel is *mythistorima*, a portmanteau combining "myth" and "history" coined by Adamantios Koraes (1748–1833), a folklorist and humanist who lived during the Greek revolution and wanted to organize a new modern Greek literature for the new Greek nation. The term "romance," therefore, is a kind of Western import used by Byzantine scholars in two ways: first, among themselves to organize a corpus of loosely affiliated texts that bear some generic, thematic, and structural similarities and, second, to provide an analogous frame of reference for those familiar with the Western romance tradition out of which *Orlando furioso* arose; they tell of the sexual awakenings of aristocratic young lovers and the (often chivalric-themed) trials and tribulations they must face and overcome to secure their love and eventual marriage.[2]

The Byzantine Greeks themselves used a number of related words to describe this genre. Sometimes they used simply *ta kata* (things about/concerning) followed by the names of the lovers at the center of the story, as in the case of the second-century CE ancient novel *Leukippe and Kleitophon* by Achilles Tatius. More often, however, they used words such as *ē aphēgēsis* or *diēgēsis*, words that might more suggest a tale or telling, a story, or a narrative. An example of the former is the anonymous mid-thirteenth-century romance *Tale of Livistros and Rhodamne*, while the late-fourteenth- or early-fifteenth-century romance conventionally referred to as either the *Tale of Troy* or the *Byzantine Iliad* carries the heading "The narrative of what happened in Troy, the complete destruction that happened there."[3] Interestingly enough, in his ninth-century *Bibliotheca*,

Photios calls Heliodorus's novel *drama/dramata* (codices 73 and 87). While this term would be normally used in reference to "a narrative or description of any sort that told about happenings, adventures, whether those happenings were within the bounds of possibility and probability or not,"[4] it still carries a notion of performativity. This etymological survey is important for demonstrating the ways in which scholars have understood the evolution of the genre, where performance context plays a surprisingly important role. As Margaret Mullett has remarked, the performative environment had profound implications for literature in Byzantium,[5] although we are still "at the stage of spotting performance indicators" in available sources.[6] It requires a fundamental change of perspective to imagine that much Byzantine literature, including but certainly not limited to novels and romances, was originally composed not for reading but for oral recitation, though the venues and the social, political, and literary contexts in which such performances occurred changed between the twelfth and fifteenth centuries, the golden age of the medieval Greek romance.[7]

Roderick Beaton's 1989 *The Medieval Greek Romance* established the corpus and taxonomy of some twelve to twenty works, the production of which can be broken down into two main subgenres: the twelfth-century Komnenian novels and the thirteenth-to-fifteenth-century Palaiologan romances, named after the dynasties under whose patronage they were produced.[8] Beyond their difference in time, what separates them are a variety of structural, linguistic, and prosodic/metrical concerns, in addition to what might be called the imaginary worlds in which they take place. The Komnenian novels are often considered to have a greater realism, to take place in a recognizably Byzantine world governed by rules, political structures, and cultural norms that their original audience would have recognized as mirroring their own. What is more, they are modeled on their ancient predecessors, are written in classical (i.e., Attic) Greek, and employ a whole array of rhetorical devices such as *ekphrasis* (description) and *ethopoiia* (character drawing). The Palaiologan romances, by contrast, take place in a more fairy-tale-like world; there are dragons, sorcerers, and other marvels familiar from the chivalric world of the Western romance. An important reason for the distinction between the novels and the romances is the influence of romances from the western European tradition. While the Komnenian novels draw primarily from the ancient Greek novels of the first and second century CE, the Palaiologan period featured translations and adaptations of Western romances such as Benoît de Sainte-Maure's *Roman de Troie* of the 1180s, translated into Greek as *O Polemos tēs Trōados* (The war of Troy) in the second half of the thirteenth century, Rustichello da Pisa's *Branor le Brun* (written in the late thirteenth century, translated into Greek as *O Presvis Ippotis* (The Old Knight) in the first half of the fifteenth century, and even Boccaccio's *Teseida*, which was published in Renaissance Venice and most likely catered to the Greek community there.[9] Their language is no longer the high or elevated Attic Greek of their predecessors; these novels are written in the vernacular or low register, which indicates a desire for a broader readership than that of the highly learned Komnenian novels. The anonymous author of the *Byzantine Iliad/Tale of Troy* twice mentions his choice to write in a simple or "childish" style (887 and 1061). This may be a concession to the differing audiences for such works, since, while all the Komnenian novels were produced by and for the intellectual elite in the imperial environment of Constantinople, the same cannot be said for the later Palaiologan romances, of which several were likely written either under Latin rule or in other regional Greek capitals during the Latin occupation of Constantinople.[10] On either side of these two subgenres lie the so-called proto-romance of *Digenis Akritis* and the only post-medieval Greek romance, the *Erotokritos*.[11]

The tradition of Byzantine romance writing (broadly construed here to mean the entirety of this tradition), moreover, is valuable not just for considering the trajectory of writing in Greek but also for understanding the development of romance writing/performance in the broader Mediterranean. Whereas Beaton's work largely considered the diachronic nature of the Greek romance tradition with some accounting of the translation of Western sources, recent work in the field has put these works in their broader Mediterranean context.[12] While the Western (e.g., French and Italian) influences on the Byzantine romance have long been recognized, this Mediterranean turn has increasingly suggested the importance of Byzantium's Eastern neighbors. This is the case not only for the literary influence of Eastern sources on their Byzantine counterparts[13] but also for the romances as a kind of "multiethnic" literature, to borrow a term, which features, in addition to the Greeks who are at the center of the romances, Armenians and Egyptians (in *Livistros and Rhodamne*), residents of Tarsos (*Velthandros and Chrysandza*), Arabs (*Drosilla and Charikles*), and Syrians (*Digenis Akritis*), not to mention Westerners (such as the Frankish knight in *The Tale of Achilles*) and people from places entirely fictional. Given that the Byzantine Empire warred, intermarried, traded, and looted with both its Eastern and Western neighbors and that the period of novel-romance writing stretched from just before the fall of Constantinople to the allied force of western Europeans in 1204 to just after the fall of Constantinople to the Ottomans in the East in 1453, it makes sense that this geopolitical consciousness should be reflected in the novel-romance tradition. In a context yet broader still, this period saw a flourishing of trade across the Silk Road, with Byzantine trade and diplomatic missions reaching as far as China, both preceding and following more famous travelers, such as Marco Polo, who traveled the width of Byzantium, including a stay in Constantinople, on his way to the court of Qūbilāy Khān. It is in this context that, for instance, the "Graeco-Arabic translation movement" of the centuries preceding the Komnenian literary revival can be understood as one example of the kind of East-West cultural transmission that defines the place of the medieval Greek romance tradition in the Mediterranean;[14] though perhaps less clearly understood or less clearly linear than translation, similar veins of cultural interaction define the Byzantine Empire as a central node in the diffusion of cultural production across the medieval Mediterranean. As with all such cultural interaction, war, trade, and diplomacy bring with them the exchange of stories as well, and thus, the multiethnic presence in the novel-romance tradition is a literary manifestation of real-world literary exchange.

The medieval Greek romance, therefore, can also serve as a point of comparison with the *Orlando furioso*, similarly understood as a work of multiethnic literature; like its Greek counterparts, it is a work inseparable from the context in which it was composed: interfaith love set against a backdrop of interfaith war spanning not just the length of the Mediterranean—from the siege of Paris to Orlando and Agramante's duel in Lampedusa—but also to faraway locales such as Cathay and even entirely fantastical locations: Dragon Castle in *Kallimachos and Chrysorroi* and the moon in *Orlando*.[15]

1. The Performance Context of the "Proto-Romance" Digenis Akritis

In *The Medieval Greek Romance*, Beaton calls *Digenis Akritis* the "proto-romance" because, as he understands it, the poem is "the oldest piece of writing of any length to be written in a form of modern Greek, and so stands at the head of the literary tradition in the modern Greek language."[16] As we shall see, this statement is a useful way of framing the origins and development of the genre and its performance context. Before we speak of its utility, however, it might also be useful to speak of the ways in which it is misleading, since the two are linked. The problem with this argument lies with the seemingly simple words "oldest piece of writing." To call it a "piece" is a contested proposition, insofar as there are six extant manuscripts in Greek (in addition to a Slavic version whose relation to the others is currently a matter of some scholarly dispute) of roughly the same narrative but varying in significant enough ways to perhaps indicate multiple different traditions.[17] Indeed, the search for the hypothetical "ur-*Digenis*" or **Digenis* has so far proven fruitless enough to call into question the possibility of a single source rather than multiple intersecting traditions.[18] So to speak of the *Digenis* as a single piece is itself a fraught paradigm.

Equally problematic is any claim of the *Digenis* being the "oldest." Though the setting seems to locate the story in the eleventh-century world of the Greek-Arab wars in the Anatolian borderlands (which is the reason Beaton refers to it as the oldest, since the world it constructs is older than those of the novels/romances),[19] the oldest surviving manuscript, called Grottaferrata (**G**) after the library where it is held, is actually from the fourteenth century,[20] which is several centuries after the novels/romances of which it is supposed to be the prototype. Beaton's claim that "the original early twelfth-century poem is lost beyond recall" is thus rightfully challenged by Charis Messis, who points out, "While the dating of the Urtext to the twelfth century is a conjecture, based on scattered references and the 'common sense' of modern scholars, the dating of the **G** version to the early fourteenth century is a textual reality that we need to take into serious consideration."[21] Though certainly the oldest extant manuscript does not necessarily correspond to the date of production, it is nearly certain that some form of *Digenis Akritis* was circulating in Constantinople during the period of the composition of other Palaiologan romances, and for our purposes here, it is enough to note that to speak of **G** as the oldest medieval Greek romance requires a belief in either the existence of the hypothetical ur-*Digenis* or a secure early dating for the manuscript, and no evidence for either belief has yet been found.

Related to this is the problem of "writing": the consideration of the *Digenis* at the head of the tradition of the medieval Greek romance stems in large part from the notion that behind **G**, the hypothetical ur-*Digenis*, and the other versions lies an oral tradition of folk songs. Beaton, following the romantic line of reasoning first laid out by Koraes, argues that *Digenis Akritis* has its origins in the folk tradition drawn from a corpus of "akritic songs" (*akritiká*) that circulated in the border region:

> narrative songs in which the name Diyenis [*sic*] appears, or which seem to be related to other songs in which it is found, are known as *akritiká*, after the eponymous hero of the Byzantine epic *Diyenis Akritis* [*sic*]. Narrative songs in which this name is not found, but whose subject matter otherwise belongs to a similar vaguely historical or mythical past, are known as *paraloyés*, a word of uncertain derivation, rarely appearing in the songs themselves, but which has come into its own in the realm of scholarly taxonomy.[22]

The performance context of these songs is ultimately unknown and possibly unknowable, since folk singing is inherently an ephemeral form of artistic transmission, and there has thus been little to no scholarship on how these songs were performed, where, or by whom (that is, for instance, whether there was a professional class of singers or a more amateur model). Thus, though Elizabeth Jeffreys posed the question of "the priority between the epic and folk-songs" as a central concern in 1998, any definitive answer remains elusive. Her suggestion later in the introduction to her translation of the *Digenis* remains the most viable supposition:

> stories about the legendary past, almost certainly in verse, circulated in the frontier areas of Cappadocia and on the banks of the Euphrates. . . . They coalesced around a lone hero of Arab-Byzantine parentage. . . . At some point these stories, perhaps in dialect, were brought to Constantinople, perhaps by refugees in the aftermath of the Byzantine defeat at Manizkert in 1071. . . . When in the 1140s and 1150s it became briefly fashionable in Constantinopolitan literary circles to write narratives in the manner of the novelists of late antiquity, an attempt was made to string the material about the hero Digenis into a biographical sequence and trim it with appropriate romantic elements.[23]

Thus, the manuscripts of the *Digenis* most likely represent some hybrid tradition of literary and folk singing; indeed, it is likely that whatever the origins of this narrative, eventually it split into two parallel tracks: a written version perhaps based on **Digenis* that produced the six extant manuscripts in Greek and a continuous folk tradition that existed only orally, traces of which endured far into the post-Byzantine period.

In one sense, however, the *Digenis* is a "proto-romance," since the origins of the novel/romance tradition may indeed lie in the oral folk songs from which the *Digenis* also had its origins. Though we can say with great certainty that the subsequent tradition was originally composed in written form, the novels still carry with them the marks of the oral tradition. Kostas Yiavis has noted the ways in which in the later novels, "The fiction was often made, usually through interpolated phrases (such as *akou* [listen], *legō* [I say], *dokō* [it seems to me], etc.), that the romances were orally delivered, although they were very clearly designed to be read."[24] It is, however, equally possible that such interjections are not simply ornamental but are indeed "performative residues." Such cues of orality suggest, in Beaton's words, "a written text in which techniques derived from oral poetry are used quite consciously but fulfill an entirely different function from that which they served in oral poetry. [They are] no longer 'mechanical' but 'referential.'"[25] That is to say, they enact the vestiges of the oral origins of the folk singing tradition of the hinterlands, even as it developed into a written form produced in regional capitals or at the heart of imperial power in Constantinople.

Panagiotis Roilos takes a more skeptical view of this "vocality," arguing that "even the recurrent presence of an author's self-referential allusions to his authorial voice or of his extra-referential hints at a possible oral/aural performance and reception of his work by no means constitutes a decisive factor for determining the extent to which a specific text was composed with the expectation to be (also) orally acted out."[26] For him, they are only one manifestation of what he calls the "performability" of a text, which also includes such markers as "language, metre, themes, contextual and intertextual allusions/evidence."[27] While these indicators are not necessarily proof of oral composition (though some authors claimed that they improvised their works; see below), they still suggest that the work was performed orally or at least that it was meant to create such an impression.

This last insight, moreover, can perhaps point to the performance context in which works like the *Digenis* and the oral folk tradition on which it relied were produced. In a series of articles, Mullett points to what she calls the "ephemeral performance" space of the Byzantine tent.[28] In a minimalist sense, Mullett speaks of the tent as a literal gathering space, often large enough to hold the entire court on the move. As Byzantine emperors often spent more time on campaign than in their palaces at Constantinople, and as the tent was the largest enclosed space and the imperial seat during such campaigns, the tent itself could be seen as one location for oral performance.

From a more maximalist or metaphorical perspective, the tent can serve as a stand-in for all the other ways in which travelers, soldiers on campaign, and others can exchange stories in passing ways. This ephemeral, oral transmission is, in fact, represented in ways in which stories are told in the *Digenis* itself. Book 5 of the Grottaferrata version of the story, for instance, begins with a shift into the first person, as Digenis tells the events to a fellow Cappadocian. As Digenis spends his whole life in the frontier, and as he is telling the story to another man from the frontier, we could imagine the meeting of these two people and their storytelling to have occurred in just the kind of ephemeral way Mullett suggests. In the story itself, moreover, Digenis describes an adventure he had while wandering "the waterless plains of Arabia / and making my way along the road alone."[29] He meets a young Arab woman in this barren place, and she tells him her own life story: another ephemeral tale, told by strangers in passing. (And it is significant to note, too, in this context, that the young woman provides one of several forms of female narrators in the text; she is a storyteller, but her story is only reported by a man. Similarly, the emir's mother is a narrator, penning an angry letter to her son which he reads in his tent.) In Book 6, Digenis and his wife build a tent in a beautiful meadow as their primary residence, and the tent is attacked by a group of border marauders. During breaks in their combat, the opponents exchange yet more stories: their ancestry, the reasons for the attack, their accomplishments. These, too, can be understood as tent narratives, as can the subsequent meeting of the defeated invaders once they leave Digenis. In short, the tales of border warriors would have circulated widely among border warriors and would have been told by them in the physical contexts in which they gathered; the tent, the campfire, and the road would be the physical performance contexts of the oral folk tradition.

2. The Komnenian Novels: The Performance Context

The relationship between text and performance is much clearer in the four novels produced during the Komnenian period: Theodore Prodromos's *Rhodanthe and Dosikles*; Eumathios Makrembolites's *Hysmine and Hysminias*; Niketas Eugenianos's *Drosilla and Charikles*, and Constantine Manasses's *Drosilla and Charikles* (which survives now only in fragments).[30] The performance of the Komnenian novels of the twelfth century must be considered as one part of what Roilos refers to when he designates the Byzantine Empire as "a theatre state"—at least in Constantinople and other elite urban centers.[31] The extent of spectacle, of the importance of visual symbol and sign, of ritual and pomp, was operative throughout the empire and especially in Constantinople.[32] Four urban "stages for Byzantine performance" have been identified, with the word "stage" being used here broadly for any performance space: the church, where sacred ritual was carried out; the hippodrome, where events from chariot races to public executions were staged; the street, where performers such as jugglers, singers, acrobats, dancers, and jesters plied their trade alongside grander public processions and violent political protests;[33] and, last and, for our purposes, most important, the so-called Byzantine *theatron*, which Emanuel Bourbouhakis calls "the Komnenian era's signature cultural institution."[34] Spectacles of various nature were not only omnipresent in Byzantine society, but they also performed important social functions enabling young aspiring men to attract the attention of potential patrons and secure jobs and administrative positions. In this sense, Byzantium, especially from the eleventh century onward, was indeed "a performative society."[35] It has to be noted, however, that private reading was not uncommon in Byzantium, and this could also apply to novels.[36]

Despite its name, the *theatron* should not be thought of as a theater in the ancient or modern sense of a specialized building meant for performance[37] but rather as a more abstract notion: "From the eleventh century at the latest, *theatron* described a circle of learned men who gathered around a patron, patroness or host either to listen to letters or texts that the latter had received, selected, or written, or to perform their own contributions."[38] The theater—or, perhaps better, the theatrical space—consisted of the reading rooms and studies, salons, and great halls of the imperial palace and the constellation of aristocratic households in its orbit.[39] In such spaces, "the audience gathered, either at a pre-arranged time or in a more *ad hoc* fashion; the performer stepped 'into the middle'; he read, or improvised, a rhetorical (philosophical, theological) text, which may have required multiple sittings; the audience was expected to pass judgment, usually applause (clapping and stamping the feet); the *theatron* dissolved."[40] The *theatron* in this context, then, would consist of an orator presenting to a select group of patrons an occasional work or a work on commission in one of the grander spaces of their homes. What united these *Literaturgemeinschaften* (communities of literature) was the willingness of audiences to participate in the rhetorical experience and to guess literary allusions, *similia*, and quotations and possibly to judge the manner of delivery. While what we know of the inner workings and experience of *theatra* is limited, it is tempting to think that the audiences' judgment of the performance was also a kind of performance that allowed them to display their knowledge about literature, history, and mythology by showing familiarity with the texts, events, and characters mentioned.

Such performances could be lively affairs, whose subject matter and nature might be light, bordering even on comedy. Theodore Prodromos, the author of the novel *Rhodanthe and Dosikles*, penned a short satirical speech detailing his encounter with a merciless dentist ("The Executioner of the Doctor").[41] Interestingly, this text ends with an apostrophe to Nicholas Kallikles, who was both a doctor and an accomplished poet. This might suggest that Kallikles himself was present during the first reading of the piece, making the performance even more amusing. Perhaps shorter forms, such as epigrams, could have been improvised, though certainly longer texts could not have been.

It is highly possible, for instance, that works like the twelfth-century *Synopsis Chronike* by Constantine Manasses were performed in episodes, perhaps over the course of years; as Ingela Nilsson notes:

> It seems plausible to assume that this large work was written in portions, perhaps starting as early as the late 1130s or the early 1140s, and that the references to Manuel were inserted after 1143. The episodic structure of the work indicates that it was performed in portions, but in view of its length it seems unlikely that all episodes were ever performed. One could easily imagine the performance of certain narrative highlights, such as the programmatic opening, offering an elaborate ekphrasis of the Creation, or the episodes describing particularly important or intriguing emperors of the past, such as Constantine the Great (306–337), Justinian I (527–565) or Leo the Iconoclast (717–741).[42]

Similarly, Jeffreys has remarked that each book of *Rhodanthe and Dosikles* would be "of a manageable performance length, and regular recapitulations would aid the listener."[43]

John Tzetzes's *Theogony* (another twelfth-century work), usually called "An impromptu and improvised poem by John Tzetzes, the grammarian" in the manuscripts, was, as the title suggests, composed in the moment. However, the *Theogony* is such a long and fairly complicated text that it seems almost impossible to think about it in terms of an impromptu performance, if not beyond the capacity of the author to remember (though Tzetzes once bragged that "my library happens to be in my head"), then certainly for the sake of the audience.[44] Similarly, Michael Italikos (also twelfth century) says that he improvised his monody on the partridge.[45] Improvisation was, however, perceived as one of the defining features of a rhetor from the Second Sophistic period onward.[46] Yet it remains unknown to what extent Byzantine writers used such descriptors as topoi and if they used some prearranged material to improvise. But perhaps most important, it is impossible to ascertain how much, if at all, the text performed differed from the written version.[47] Italikos confirms that he performed his text himself. But this was not always the case; for instance, letters must have been read aloud by recipients. A system built upon an ability to improvise texts diminishes the role of the intermediaries/actors/performers. Perhaps such intermediaries were required only when reciting older works (perhaps such performance is meant by Theodore Balsamon when he lists the *Achilleus* among the dignified royal games) or when the rhetor was incapable of delivering the text himself.[48]

As Paul Magdalino has rightly observed, "The rhetorical texts as we read them are the dry bones of an experience from which all sense of drama and occasion have gone now . . . in such a context, verbal recitation was only part of a total orchestration, in which architecture, decor, dress, music and choreography also played a part."[49] Though these performances can never be fully recuperated, certain texts nevertheless allow us a glimpse into what was important for a Byzantine audience. In his recent analysis of the text conventionally called the *Dramation* (Little Drama), Pablo Cavallero draws attention to the richness of the rhetorical figures that were used for sound effects and whose full potential could only be appreciated during an oral recitation in a *theatron* or similar performance space.[50]

3. The Komnenian Novels: The Social Context of the Performance Context

As elsewhere in the medieval world, both aspiring and established writers relied on aristocratic patronage by elite men and women to support themselves.[51] The Byzantine *theatron*, then, as noted earlier, must also be seen as a highly competitive setting wherein both aspiring and well-established writers sought to impress and earn the favor (and, by proxy, the employment) of a sophisticated and discerning audience that was as wealthy as it was stingy; according to Magdalino, "'Theatre' thus combined the functions of examination, interview, lecturing, entertainment, literary publication, and much more besides, for it was essentially the ritual by which the man of learning paraded his credentials and aspirations."[52] Given these stakes, it is no surprise, then, that men who were trained in the rhetorical arts would offer tour de force theatrics in performance of their own work, lavish praise of the patrons on whom they relied, and engage in aggressive disputation and slander against the men against whom they were competing. Success or failure might mean economic sustenance and artistic freedom through increased patronage; access to imperial favors such as promotions to high office within the lucrative, opaque, and hierarchical Byzantine bureaucracy; even marriage into the imperial family. Indeed, issues of power and prestige hovered in the background of every performance (and its reception) within the *theatron* as a social and political institution; as Niels Gaul notes, "Every performance, for reasons justified or fabricated, had the potential of altering an actor's social standing."[53] This applied not just to the social status of the performer (the higher the social status, the more applause) or to the audience (the higher the social status, the more weight given to their opinion) but even to the location itself: "different *theatra* were assigned different levels of prestige: those convened in a gentleman scholar's *oikos* ranked lowest, those in the imperial palace the highest; and fully public ones higher than more private occasions.[54] Take, for instance, the eleventh-century writer John Mauropous's poem "Against the man who criticized the verse 'sold for gold,' because the preposition is not rightly construed." In the poem, Mauropous defends himself against an unnamed critic who, as Floris Bernard describes it, "had found fault with a grammatical issue in poem 32. He remarked that the verb *piprasko* (sell) should govern a plain genitive case, and should not be followed by the preposition *anti* (in return for; for)."[55]As Bernard points out, "This man was a colleague (and rival) of Mauropous: a professional reader, one might say."[56] In identifying an infelicitous grammatical structure in the poem, Mauropous's critic reveals that the audience for such work was highly educated, sensitive to style and aesthetics, and also sensitive to grammatical infelicities.

Perhaps it is in the same agonistic context that we should read a series of Prodromos's texts, written in prose, such as "The Self-Proclaimed Grammarian" or "The Lover of Plato or the Leather-Tanner," and a poem, "Against an Old Man with a Long Beard." They all target unnamed persons who pretend to be *grammatikoi* (teachers) and philosophers;[57] whether or not (and probably not) Prodromos directed his text against identifiable individuals is unclear. They seem rather to be a form of "imaginary agon," where it is not the opponent who is important but the opportunity to display the speaker's (i.e., Prodromos's) knowledge and to underscore the attractiveness of his teaching program.

Both Mauropous's defense and Prodromos's satires thus explicitly confirm perhaps the most important aspect of performance in the *theatron*: the surplus of aspiring literati and the scarcity of wealthy patrons that resulted in fierce competition for patronage, whether in the traditional model of aristocrats willing to pay for entertainment or, in the case of prospective teachers, competition for students.[58]

Woven into the fabric of discourse in this *theatron*, then, is praise for patrons for their generosity, such as from John Tzetzes, who writes in the introduction to his *Allegories of the Odyssey*:

> I speak at the request
> of my queen, who was an ornament among women,
> as a result of her august command, and her worthy gifts,
> and, moreover, due to the persistence and gifts of other friends.[59]

Tzetzes praises his patron, the empress Eirene, as "an ornament among women" and also identifies his gratitude for her generosity—"her worthy gifts"—thus opening the commissioned work both by honoring her and by making explicit reference to the remuneration he received from her. It is also important to remind ourselves that writer-teachers such as Prodromos and Tzetzes could not or did not dedicate themselves to a single genre or even what we, in modern terms, might call a single artistic vision; rather, they worked for pay, fulfilling whatever commissions they were able to get. Thus, alongside his beggar poetry, Prodromos wrote satirical dialogues and epigrams, astrological and theological treatises, a grammar, and works for specific occasions such as speeches and imperial praise poetry. Some of his texts were explorations of unknown or, perhaps more accurately, unused literary forms and genres. The twelfth-century rhetor Nikoloas Kataphloron, a twelfth-century *maistor ton rhetoron* and teacher of Eustathios of Thessaloniki, wrote an introduction to a speech in which he accused the rhetors of Constantinople of being grave robbers who shamelessly stole ideas from ancient authors:

> And these blessed rhetors bring into the light and dig up the dead ones and despoil them and take from the tombs the clothes of the rhetoric and all remaining embellishments, spending whole days near tombs like the old ghosts from comedies. Like vultures and ravens with full crooked beaks they tear and snatch away the things of the dead ones and, as it seems, they claw away at each other, fighting over the corpses. This is not at all a new thing, this is an old disease of ours. . . . What surprises me about those people is the fact that they pride themselves on the things of the dead ones and they extol themselves as thieves and robbers and they perform in the *theatra* the fruits of their nightly thefts.[60]

The Constantinopolitan rhetors, constantly competing with one another for the attention of potential patrons, needed ideas from their ancient predecessors. This is perhaps why Prodromos "rebooted" (if he was the first to do so) the novelistic genre—to offer something new, something hitherto unused and unheard of. The social and peer pressure that ensued from such fierce competition might force certain people to opt out of the system altogether (with possibly severe financial and social implications). Such a decision seems to lie behind the composition of the text called "A reply to those who accuse him of spurning exhibition" written by Michael Choniates, bishop of Athens,[61] in which he explains why he refuses to exhibit his rhetorical skills. Whether this was just an isolated exception, an expression of more general opinion, or perhaps a sophisticated display of rhetorical skills in a form of *anaskeue* (refutation) is difficult to say. The four novels that emerge from twelfth-century Byzantium, then, must be understood in the socioeconomic-cultural context of the *theatron* as a competitive elite environment but also in a literary context: the authors of these novels were skilled rhetors in a variety of genres, and the novels make up a unique contribution in the sense that each of the authors only wrote one, each of which constituted a small portion in a career of much larger and more varied literary output.

4. The Palaiologan Romance: Performance Context

By the time Byzantium's last dynasty, the Palaiologans, came to power, the empire had been torn apart by a century of losing military campaigns. Constantinople itself had fallen under the rule of the Latins in 1204, and the Byzantine Empire had been fragmented into a variety of successor states, with ever more obscure members of the exiled imperial family ruling various pieces of the Aegean basin, each with its own capital. Even as successive Palaiologoi attempted to consolidate central control over the Empire and reestablish the newly liberated Constantinople as the imperial capital, the capital cities of the numerous principalities—both Greek- and Latin-occupied—vied as centers of political and cultural significance: the Despotate of Epirus, the Principality of Achaea, the Duchy of Athens, the Empire of Nicaea, and so on. Several of the translated Palaiologan romances were produced in this context, and we can perhaps assume a similar performance context to those found in the Komnenian novels, though based not always in Constantinople but also in these regional capitals. Goldwyn and Nilsson identify fifteen works that make up this corpus with some, such as the *Teseida* and *The War of Troy*, composed outside of the Byzantine Empire. Among the most important characteristics that separate the Komnenian novels from the Palaiologan romances are the latter's more fairy-tale setting and the adoption of Western ideals of chivalry. These features reflect increased cultural contact, going beyond what occurred through trade and diplomacy, to include the occupation and colonization of Greek-speaking lands by western Europeans. The increased frequency of loan words, particularly in the vocabulary of chivalry, and the infusion of syntactic structures from Old French and other Romance languages reflect the cultural mixing of such environments.[62]

Moreover, with new, imported forms came the possibility of imported performance contexts that differed from Byzantine ones. In 1223, the Ibelins, who at that time ruled Cyprus, held jousting tournaments—until then unknown in Greek-speaking lands—possibly even while dressed as Arthurian characters, and Peter Edbury suggests that "it is not entirely clear from the description [in contemporary accounts] whether this was a stage-play, in which case it appears to be the earliest known instance anywhere of the performance of an Arthurian story, or whether it was the participants in the jousts who dressed as characters out of the Arthurian cycle, in which case that too is a first."[63] Gilles Grivaud even suggests that the introduction of hastiludes in Latin-occupied Cyprus might be a reflection of this world and of its imported heroes.[64] Indeed, the Palaiologan romances themselves are replete with scenes of jousting and melee-style tournament fighting.[65]

As with the Komnenian novels, there is no direct evidence for performative readings of the Palaiologan romances, though the *theatron* (or something like it) must have remained a central locus for reading and performance. Several passages from elsewhere in Byzantine literature can give us a picture of what such performances might have looked like. In one much-discussed passage of a performance from the 1320s, Theodore Metochites inveighs against a performance of Nikephoros Choumnos:

> Sitting in the middle and reading aloud your compositions you do it as if acting in a solemn performance: you applaud, taking various obscene poses, now jumping out of bed, now falling on it again and shivering you wave your both hands, turn your head and neck, bend down and straighten up, irritating those who listen to you and look at you.[66]

It is hard to know exactly how to understand this passage. Since Metochites is mocking Choumnos, it is entirely possible that such readings were meant to emphasize only the auditory component of the spoken word and that Choumnos violated these conventions with an overly gestural performance. Such gestural and performative aspects were always part of the *theatron*,[67] but perhaps Choumnos took it to extremes, as when a modern actor is accused of overacting.[68] Certainly, gesture, movement, and other performative aspects were meant to accompany such readings, but, as with modern examples, some audiences simply did not like a particular actor's performance in a particular role.

As there is little evidence of how the performers themselves behaved, there is also little evidence of how the audience behaved. Two such passages, one real, one literary, could be underscored. The emperor Manuel II Palaiologos wrote to Theodore Kaukadenos, "I, too, found everything to be excellent even though I sat in silence while the others stamped their feet and shouted with joy";[69] while the author of the *Mazaris' Journey to Hades*, in his fictional autobiographical account of his trip to the underworld, notes that among his audience of dead philosophers and orators, "some of the audience jump with glee, others laugh sardonically, and still others fill the air with applause."[70] It is impossible to say whether these two passages recorded what might be a usual situation or whether they recorded something unusual and unprecedented. Certainly, the Palaiologan romances (similarly to the Komnenian ones) must have been performed either episodically (over several consecutive gatherings) or partially; among the original (as opposed to translated) romances, *Kallimachos and Chryssorhoe* contains a total of 2,607 verses, *Livistros and Rhodamne* has nearly 4,500 verses, and the differing manuscripts of *Velthandros and Chrysantza* contain between 1,343 and 1,820 verses. The latter could have been read in one session, which would take approximately three hours, though, of course, a given recitation could be longer or shorter depending on the performer. As the longest version of the *Tale of Achilles* has 1,615 verses and *The Tale of Troy* has 1,166, this range may reflect the length of a single session's reading, whereas longer works would require a few consecutive meetings. At 14,401 lines, *The War of Troy* is by far the longest work in the category and would certainly be impossible to sit through in a single session.

Furthermore, Nicolette Trahoulia has recently argued that the Venice copy of the fourteenth-century *Alexander Romance* was meant to provide its viewers with a kind of "multimedia" experience.[71] The illustrations of the manuscript are "structured for performance, so that the images are most effective if viewed while listening to an oral recitation of the narrative."[72] Jeffreys's recent study of the *War of Troy* points to a similar possibility, since "there are spaces left in four of the seven surviving manuscripts of the *War of Troy*, all with captions, some with numbered captions. These can only have been intended for illustrations, and arguably were part of the initial translation process."[73] There is no comparable case for any of the Komnenian novels, but Trahoulia's suggestion proves that performances of texts, at least in the Palaiologan period, were more than just about reading the text aloud or adding theatrical gestures or vocalizations.

Though the empire's fortunes rose and fell between the first conquest of Constantinople in 1204 by the Latins and the as-yet-final conquest of Constantinople by the Ottomans in 1453, the overall trajectory of the empire's decline was clear. After the fall of Constantinople, many Greek intellectuals found refuge in the Republic of Venice, and Venetian-occupied Crete saw the flourishing of the so-called Cretan Renaissance, which produced two monumental figures in the history of art and letters: the painter Dominikos Theotokopoulos, better known in the West as El Greco, and the playwright Giorgios Chortatzis, the father of modern Greek drama. According to Rosemary Bancroft-Marcus, Chortatzis's play *Erophile* marked the playwright as the first writer of secular Greek drama since Menander some eighteen hundred years before.[74] No less gifted than his two more famous contemporaries is Vitsentzos Kornaros, yet where Chortatzis and El Greco pointed toward the future of modern Greek and European art, Kornaros has been seen more as a capstone to the medieval tradition; indeed,

Beaton lists his masterpiece, the *Erotokritos*, as the only post-medieval Greek romance. Though Holton is correct that "since 1935 we have known with complete certainty that [the plot of the *Erotokritos*] derives from the French romance of chivalry *Paris et Vienne*," the work draws from a variety of romances, including the *Orlando furioso* (though the exact nature of the debt at both the socio-cultural and philological levels remains unexamined).[75] In any case, El Greco, Chortatzis, and Kornaros mastered the combination of Greek/Byzantine and Western discourses, though drama and painting would assume in subsequent centuries a primacy that the long, romantic works in verse would lose. From the perspective of performativity, the *Erotokritos* is interesting for having a radically different performance context from all the preceding works in the tradition of the medieval Greek romance; it circulated most widely in its own time as a printed book, and thus, though it often contains nods to orality, as with the author's repeated insistence on auditory words—*akousete* (listen), *groikesete* (pay attention)—and to staged drama (Holton notes "several theatrical touches"),[76] the work was primarily meant for silent individual reading rather than communal recitation, thus marking its performance context as distinct from its Komnenian and Palaiologan predecessors and inaugurating a new tradition that gave the printed word primacy over the spoken.

The legacy of the work, however, demonstrates a number of problems in defining the performance contexts of the folk song/novel/romance tradition we have been discussing. Though the *Erotokritos* was written, Roilos draws on a series of post-Renaissance sources and his own fieldwork in Crete at the end of the twentieth and the beginning of the twenty-first centuries to describe how the written text has been transformed into an oral genre, with folk singers now performing pieces of the text. If anything, the centuries-long reception history of the *Erotokritos* demonstrates the porousness of the seemingly rigid boundary separating the oral from the written and the fluidity of performance contexts across time. This fluidity, moreover, is not the sole province of the *Erotokritos*, for this movement also occurs in the other direction. If the *Erotokritos* has changed from a unified work of literature to fragmented pieces of oral performance, then the reception history of the "proto-romance" *Digenis Akritis* marks the opposite trajectory: it may have been composed orally, but the most common way of encountering the poem now is in written form, read silently on the printed page. As in the cases of the printed *Erotokritos* becoming short folk songs, recordings of modern versions of the *Digenis Akritis*, or *'opera dei pupi'* versions of the *Orlando furioso*, the evolving performance contexts of a work will always shape and reshape its interpretation.

Notes

Przemysław Marciniak acknowledges the financial support of the research project funded by the Polish National Agency for Academic Exchange (NAWA, Bekker fellowship). Adam Goldwyn completed his work on this chapter during his term as a recipient of the Alexander von Humboldt Fellowship at the Westfälische Wilhelms-Universität Münster.

1. E.g., Tzetzes 2015, pp. 309, 319, 505; and Eustathios 2016, p. 14.

2. Holton 1991, p. 205, argues that they "have as their basic plot the separation of a pair of lovers by various acts of violence and misfortune, which culminate in their eventual reunion."

3. For dating and background on these romances, see Goldwyn and Nilsson 2019, pp. xiii, xvi–xviii.

4. Walden 1894, p. 22.

5. Mullett 2010, p. 229.

6. Mullett 2017, p. 122.

7. It should be noted that Byzantine performativity and, more broadly, Byzantine theater have been studied not only by Byzantinists but also by non-Byzantinists; historians of theater who examined Byzantine performance culture from a diachronic perspective include, e.g., Puchner 2017 and, from a comparative perspective, Savarese 2009, pp. 18–23, 56–63.

8. The distinction is somewhat obscured in Beaton 1996 but has become more widely accepted since the works of Cupane 1986, Cupane 1999, and Agapitos 2004; for a recent summary of the arguments for such a distinction, see Goldwyn and Nilsson 2019, pp. 2–4. Beaton's work can be productively read in conjunction with the book-length chapter-by-chapter response by Agapitos and Smith 1992.

9. For the problematic distinction between originals, adaptations, and translations, see Yiavis 2019. For the background, dating, and editions of the romances, see Goldwyn and Nilsson 2019, pp. xiv, xvii. For a translation and study of the debt of the *Old Knight* to Homeric and Western models, see Goldwyn 2012a.

10. See, e.g., Gilles Grivaud's suggestion that *The Old Knight* was composed in Cyprus; Grivaud 2005, p. 279.

11. Holton 1991 outlines the generic continuity from the ancient Greek novels through to those of the Byzantine period and ultimately the *Erotokritos*; though he demonstrates their shared literary history, he does not detail the debt of the *Erotokritos* to its Byzantine antecedents. Holton's discussion of these also erroneously (in our view) attributes a teleology to this literary history, arguing that "the *Erotokritos* can be viewed as the culmination of the medieval Greek romance" (p. 209), when it may perhaps be better to speak of the different ways in which each work was suited to its own political, cultural, and literary context rather than a history leading up to a particular work.

12. See, e.g., Cupane and Krönung 2016; Goldwyn and Nilsson 2019.

13. See, e.g., Agapitos 2010; Agapitos 2012.

14. See Gustas 1998.

15. For the medieval romance in the context of interfaith war and marriage, see Goldwyn 2012b, which examines the children of interfaith marriages: Parzival in Wolfram von Eschenbach's version of the story, Aucassin in *Aucassin and Nicolette*, and *Digenis Akritis*, whose name (Digenis) means "of double descent," that is, from his Christian mother and converted Muslim father.

16. Beaton 1996, p. 32.

17. As Goldwyn has argued elsewhere: "convoluted and widely variant textual tradition . . . presents challenges that are impossible to reconcile in a work not specifically devoted to the study of manuscripts, oral history, and scribal practice" (Goldwyn 2018, p. 39). For the stemma and the relationship among the various versions, see the introduction by Elizabeth Jeffreys to *Digenis Akritis* 1998, pp. xviii–xxx.

18. The names "ur-*Digenis*" and "**Digenis*" refer to an assumed original (but no longer extant) text from which all subsequent extant texts derive; see *Digenis Akritis* 1998, p. xxv. For a history of the discovery and early classification of the *Digenis*, see *Digenis Akritis* 1998, p. xv; for an analysis of the priority of the folk song versus the written epics and the nineteenth-century political questions that influenced that scholarly history, see *Digenis Akritis* 1998, p. xvi. Jeffreys (2011, p. 465) has speculated about the nature of **Digenis*: "it was episodic and abrupt, made up of discrete events loosely strung together to make a biography of the hero . . . its language combined both vernacular and high-level features; and names and incidents involving its characters arguably reflect scattered incidents in the wars of the ninth and tenth centuries against Arab invaders and heretic Christians."

19. For Jeffreys's summary of the historicity of the narrative, see *Digenis Akritis* 1998, pp. xxx–xli; she concludes (p. xli): "The world-view of both **G** and **E**, and thus **Digenis* predates the arrival of the Turks in the mid-eleventh century, despite **G**'s awareness of the Turkish occupation of Ikonion and demands for tribute, while the non-hostile interaction shown between Byzantines and Arabs has been taken as a mark of historical distance from the almost constant warfare of the ninth and tenth centuries").

20. *Digenis Akritis* 1998, p. xviii: "The paper is of eastern manufacture and thus dated by current palaeographical criteria to the late thirteenth or early fourteenth centuries."

21. Beaton 1996, p. 43; more recently, Beaton 2004, pp. 17–19; Messis 2019, p. 230n1. Jeffreys writes: "There are many layers to the text that survives in Digenis **G** and **E**, demonstrated by standard philological processes: these cannot be swept aside. What is more **G** was written in South Italy, in the Terra d'Otranto. This has been known since Legrand first examined it in the 1880s. The palaeographical markers in its scribal hand are indubitable, notably the wide omegas filled in with blobs of yellow and green ink/paint. An argument could be made that **G** is the product of the secular poetic activity of the South Italian monasteries that flourished from the 11th–/12th centuries onwards, though this remains to be attempted" (private correspondence, April 2, 2019).

22. Beaton 1980, p. 2; for a history of the publication of collections of Greek folk songs, see pp. 9–11. There is also a tradition of post-medieval folk songs, mostly centering on the resistance to the Ottomans during the post-Byzantine period, as well as a separate genre of love songs and other verse.

23. *Digenis Akritis* 1988, pp. xvi, lvi.

24. Yiavis 2019, pp. 29–30.

25. Beaton 1996, p. 37.

26. Roilos 2011, p. 234

27. Roilos 2011, p. 234

28. See, e.g., Mullett 2013 and Mullett 2017, esp p. 131 for brief comments about *Digenis*.

29. *Digenis Akritis* 1998, **G** 5.25–26, p. 137.

30. For the English translations, see Jeffreys 2012.

31. Roilos 2004, p. 213.

32. Marciniak (2014, p. 425) notes that "modern students of Byzantine 'theatre' have ceased to argue whether there *was* any Byzantine theatre and have commenced studying the concept of performativity in Byzantine culture instead."

33. Marciniak 2014, pp. 428–430. See also Gaul 2018, p. 225.

34. Bourbouhakis 2014, p. 209. For performative spaces in Byzantium, see also Magdalino 1993, p. 336: "But the court was not the only venue, and imperial events were not the only occasions, when recitations were delivered. Churches and private houses, sermons, family rites of passage, and even impromptu gatherings, all provided a context for what was known as 'theatre': the *performance* of a text to an audience" (italics in the original). For a history of the word *theatron* and a discussion of the development of the Byzantine *theatron*, see Marciniak 2007, pp. 277–280. For the cultural and linguistic background and function, see Kaldellis 2007, pp. 235–238.

35. For the term "performative society," see Kershaw 2001.

36. Górecki 1984, pp. 120–125

37. See Puchner 2006, pp. 81–82.

38. Gaul 2018, p. 215. Bourbouhakis (2014, p. 209n18) notes that "the term is too widely invoked in the literature to support any single definition," though his own definition more or less agrees with Gaul and others: the *theatron* "referred to any occasion, usually informal and non-ceremonial, at which texts might be read aloud or, in keeping with the dramatic label of the venue, performed by a select and usually appreciative audience, which could include peers and potential patrons." See also Mullett 1984, p. 174: "The word *theatron* . . . was used during the Byzantine centuries for meetings of groups of friends to read aloud and comment on literary texts written, perhaps from a distance, by absent members of the circle." As we shall see, however, the word "friends" here must be used loosely, if we are to account for the frequent rivalries between participants and the sometimes barely disguised careerism of others.

39. For the *theatron* as site of imperial encomia, see Toth 2007.

40. Gaul 2018, p. 218.

41. Romano 1999.

42. Nilsson 2020.

43. Jeffreys 2012, p. 14n61. In the twelfth-century satire *Timarion*, the protagonist summarizes his adventures. Perhaps this was meant as a recapitulation for the listener.

44. Tzetzes 2015, 15.87.

45. On this text, see Agapitos 1989.

46. Cassin 2017, pp. 144–147.

47. Pliny gives a testimony to the fact that Cicero substantially reworked his speeches after delivering them; see *Letters* I, 20.

48. Theodore Prodromos claimed that his career was hindered by the fact that he stuttered: *Patrologia Graeca* 133, cols. 1297–1298.

49. Magdalino 1993, pp. 352–353.

50. Cavallero 2017, p. 120. While much has been written on orality, that is, texts composed for spoken performance, less has been written on the subject of aurality, that is, how the speech acts actually sounded as, for instance, the specific phonemes, cadences, voice pitch and timbre, and other aspects of the speaking itself were conducted. For one example of such a study, see Stone 2007.

51. See, e.g., Mullett 1984.

52. Magdalino 1993, p. 339.

53. Gaul 2018, p. 230.

54. Gaul 2018, p. 230.

55. The works of John Mauropous were edited and numbered in John Mauropus, *Iohannis Euchaitorum metropolitae Quae in codice vaticano graeco 676* (Gottingen: Dieterchianis, 1882). Poem 32 is on p. 17; poem 33 is on p. 18.

56. Bernard 2014, p. 88.

57. "Philosopher" and "teacher" could be used interchangeably; see Dölger 1953.

58. Bourbouhakis, following Magdalino, notes how the "wholesale take-over of government and consequently of élite structures by the ruling Komnenian clan . . . narrowed the avenues for advancement and recognition . . . the distribution of benefits could not be but uneven, triggering a concomitant resentment by those who felt their talents were being overlooked or, worse yet, crowded out by lesser rivals." See Bourbouhakis 2014, pp. 213–214.

59. Tzetzes 2019 pp. 15–18.

60. Loukaki 2001, p. 154.

61. Bourbouhakis 2014.

62. See, e.g., Markopoulos 2019.

63. Edbury 2005, p. 82.

64. Grivaud 2005, 271–272.

65. See, e.g., Smith 1999, p. 19; Nørgaard and Smith 1975, p. 44.

66. As cited in Marciniak 2007, p. 281 (Metochites *Or.* 14.27.1–11).

67. See, e.g., Gaul 2018, p. 222.

68. This seems to be the position that Ihor Ševčenko takes in his reading of the scene; see Ševčenko 1962, p. 253; see also Polemis 2009.

69. Dennis 1977, p. 70.

70. *Mazaris's Journey* 1975, p. 49.

71. Trahoulia 2010, pp. 148–149.

72. Trahoulia 2010, p. 148.

73. Jeffreys 2019, p. 176.

74. For which, see Bancroft-Marcus 2013.

75. Holton 1991, p. 211. An important preliminary study in this regard that deserves further exploration is Holton 1988.

76. Holton 1991, p. 213

Bibliography

Agapitos 1989
Agapitos, Panagiotis. "Michael Italikos: Klage auf den Tod seines Rebhuhns." *Byzantinische Zeitschrift* 82 (1989): pp. 59–68.

Agapitos 2004
Agapitos, Panagiotis. "Genre, Structure and Poetics in the Byzantine Vernacular Romances of Love." *Symbolae Osloenses* 79 (2004): pp. 7–101.

Agapitos 2010
Agapitos, Panagiotis. "From Persia to the Provence: Tales of Love in Byzantium and Beyond." *Annali della Facoltà di Lettere e Filosofia* 63 (2010): pp. 153–169.

Agapitos 2012
Agapitos, Panagiotis. "In Rhomaian, Frankish and Persian Lands: Fiction and Fictionality in Byzantium and Beyond." In *Medieval Narratives between History and Fiction*, edited by Panagiotis Agapitos and Lars B. Mortensen, pp. 235–367. Copenhagen: Museum Tusculanum, 2012.

Agapitos and Smith 1992
Agapitos, Panagiotis, and Ole L. Smith. *The Study of Medieval Greek Romance: A Reassessment of Recent Work*. Copenhagen: Museum Tusculanum Press, 1992.

Bancroft-Marcus 2013
Bancroft-Marcus, Rosemary. "Introduction." In Geōrgios Chortatzēs, *Plays of the Veneto-Cretan Renaissance*. Oxford: Oxford University Press, 2013.

Beaton 1980
Beaton, Roderick. *Folk Poetry of Modern Greece*. Cambridge: Cambridge University Press, 1980.

Beaton 1996
Beaton, Roderick. *The Medieval Greek Romance*. London: Routledge, 1996.

Beaton 2004
Beaton, Roderick. "Balladry in the Medieval Greek World." In *The Singer and the Scribe: European Ballad Traditions and European Ballad Cultures*, edited by Philipp E. Bennett and Richard F. Green, pp. 13–21. Amsterdam: Rodopi, 2004.

Bernard 2014
Bernard, Floris. *Writing and Reading Byzantine Secular Poetry, 1025–1081*. Oxford: Oxford University Press, 2014.

Bourbouhakis 2014
Bourbouhakis, Emmanuel C. "The End of ἐπίδειξις: Authorial Identity and Authorial Intention in Michael Chōniatēs' Πρὸς τοὺς αἰτιωμένους τὸ ἀφιλένδεικτον." In *The Author in Middle Byzantine Literature: Modes, Functions, and Identities*, edited by Aglae Pizzone, pp. 212–224. Berlin: De Gruyter, 2014.

Cassin 2017
Cassin. Barbara. "Rhetoric and Sophistic." In *The Oxford Handbook of Rhetorical Studies*, edited by Michael John MacDonald, pp. 143–156. Oxford: Oxford University Press 2017.

Cavallero 2017
Cavallero, Pablo. "Los versos bizantinos de Miguel Haploukheír: ¿Comedia, tragedia o mimo?" *Minerva: Revista de Filología Clásica* 30 (2017): pp. 61–95.

Cupane 1986
Cupane, Carolina. "Topica romanesca in Oriente e in Occidente: 'Avanture' e 'amore.'" In *Il romanzo tra cultura latina e cultura bizantina: Testi della III settimana residenziale di studi medievali, Carini, Villa Belvedere, 17–21 ottobre 1983*, edited by Hans Georg Beck, Fabrizio Conca, and Carolina Cupane, under the direction of Cataldo Roccaro, pp. 66–72. Palermo: Officina dei Studi Medievali, 1986 .

Cupane 1999
Cupane, Carolina. "Bisanzio e la letteratura della Romania: Peregrinazioni del romanzo medieval." In *Medioevo romanzo e orientale: Il viaggio dei testi*, edited by Antonio Pioletti and Francesca Rizzo Nervo, pp. 31–49. Soveria Mannelli: Rubettino 1999.

Cupane and Krönung 2016
Cupane, Carolina, and Bettina Krönung, eds. *Fictional Storytelling in the Medieval Eastern Mediterranean and Beyond*. Leiden: Brill, 2016.

Dennis 1977
Dennis, George T. *The Letters of Manuel II Palaeologus: Text, Translation, and Notes*. Washington, DC: Dumbarton Oaks Center for Byzantine Studies, 1977.
Digenis Akritis 1998
Digenis Akritis: The Grottaferrata and Escorial Versions, edited by Elizabeth Jeffreys. Cambridge: Cambridge University Press, 1998.
Dölger 1953
Dölger, Franz. "Zur Bedeutung von φιλόσοφος und φιλοσοφία in byzantinischer Zeit." In Franz Dölger, *Byzanz und die europäische Staatenwelt: Ausgewählte Vorträge und Aufsätze*, pp. 197–208. Ettal: Ettal Buch-Kunstverlag, 1953.
Edbury 2005
Edbury, Peter. "Franks." In *Cyprus: Society and Culture 1191–1374*, edited by Nicolaou-Konnari, Angel Schabel, and Chris Schabel, pp. 63–102. Leiden: Brill, 2005.
Eustathios 2016
Eustathios of Thessalonike. *Commentary on Homer's Odyssey*, edited by Eric Cullhed. Uppsala: Studia Byzantina Upsaliensia, 2016.
Gaul 2018
Gaul, Niels. "Performative Reading in the Late Byzantine Theatron." In *Reading in the Byzantine Empire and Beyond*, edited by Teresa Shawcross and Ida Toth, pp. 215–233. Cambridge: Cambridge University Press, 2018.
Goldwyn 2012a
Goldwyn, Adam. "Arthur in the East: Cross-Cultural Translations of Arthurian Romance in Greek and Hebrew, with a New Translation of 'Ο Πρεσβύς Ἱπποτές/The Old Knight." *LATCH*: *Journal of Literary Artifacts in Theory, Culture and History* 5 (2012): pp. 75–105.
Goldwyn 2012b
Goldwyn, Adam. "Interfaith Marriage in Medieval Romance." *Diesis* 2, no. 1 (2012): pp. 66–79.
Goldwyn 2018
Goldwyn, Adam. *Byzantine Ecocriticism: Women, Nature, and Power in the Medieval Greek Romance*. New York: Palgrave-Macmillan, 2018.
Goldwyn and Nilsson 2019
Goldwyn, Adam, and Ingela Nilsson, eds. *Reading the Late Byzantine Romance: A Handbook*. Cambridge: Cambridge University Press, 2019.
Górecki 1984
Górecki, Danuta. "Books, Production of Books and Reading in Byzantium" *Libri: International Journal of Libraries and Information Studies* 34, no. 2 (1984): pp. 113–129.
Grivaud 2005
Grivaud, Gilles. "Literature." In *Cyprus: Society and Culture 1191–1374*, edited by Nicolaou-Konnari, Angel Schabel, and Chris Schabel, pp. 219–284. Leiden: Brill, 2005.
Gustas 1998
Gustas, Dimitri. *Greek Thought, Arabic Culture: The Graeco-Arabic Translation Movement in Baghdad and Early 'Abbasid Society (2nd–4th/8th–10th Centuries)*. Oxford: Routledge, 1998.
Holton 1988
Holton, David. "*Erotokritos* and the Greek Tradition." In *The Greek Novel AD 1–1985*, edited by Roderick Beaton, pp. 144–155. London: Routledge, 1988.
Holton 1991
Holton, David. "Romance." In *Literature and Society in Renaissance Crete*, edited by David Holton, pp. 205–238. Cambridge: Cambridge University Press, 1991.
Jeffreys 2011
Jeffreys, Elizabeth. "Medieval Greek Epic Poetry." In *Medieval Oral Literature*, edited by Karl Reichl, pp. 459–484. Berlin: De Gruyter, 2011.
Jeffreys 2012
Jeffreys, Elizabeth, trans. *Four Byzantine Novels*. Liverpool: Liverpool University Press, 2012.
Jeffreys 2019
Jeffreys, Elizabeth. "From Herakles to Erkoulios, or the Place of the War of Troy in the Late Byzantine

Romance Movement." In *Reading the Late Byzantine Romance: A Handbook*, edited by Adam J. Goldwyn and Ingela Nilsson, pp. 166–187. Cambridge: Cambridge University Press, 2019.

Kaldellis 2007
Kaldellis, Anthony. *Hellenism in Byzantium: The Transformation of Greek Identity and the Reception of the Classical Tradition*. Cambridge: Cambridge University Press, 2007.

Kershaw 2001
Kershaw, Baz. "Dramas of the Performative Society: Theatre at the End of Its Tether." *New Theater Quarterly* 17, no. 3 (2001): pp. 2013–2011.

Loukaki 2001
Loukaki, Marina. "Τυμβωρῦχοι καὶ σκυλευτὲς νεκρῶν: Οι απόψεις του Νικολαόυ Καταφλώρον για τη ρητορική και τους ρήτορες στην Κωνσταντινούπολη του 12ου αιώνα." *Byzantina Symmeikta* 14 (2001): pp. 143–166.

Magdalino 1993
Magdalino, Paul. *The Empire of Manuel I Komnenos (1143–1180)*. Cambridge: Cambridge University Press, 1993.

Marciniak 2007
Marciniak, Przemysław. "Theatron—a Place for Performance?" In *Theatron: Rhetorische Kultur in Spätantike und Mitelalter*, edited by Michael Grünbart, pp. 277–285. Berlin: De Gruyter, 2007.

Marciniak 2014
Marciniak, Przemysław. "The Byzantine Performative Turn." In *Within the Circle of Ancient Ideas and Virtues: Studies in Honour of Professor Maria Dzielska*, pp. 423–430. Krakow: Historia Iagiellonica, 2014.

Markopoulos 2019
Markopoulos, Theodoros. "Linguistic Contacts in the Late Byzantine Romances: Where Cultural Influence Meets Language Interference." In *Reading the Late Byzantine Romance: A Handbook*, edited by Adam J. Goldwyn and Ingela Nilsson, pp. 144–165. Cambridge: Cambridge University Press, 2019.

Mazaris' Journey 1975
Mazaris' Journey to Hades: or Interview with Dead Men about Certain Officials of the Imperial Court, edited and translated by J. N. Barry, M. J. Share, A. Smithies, and L. G. Westernik. Buffalo: State University of New York at Buffalo, 1975.

Messis 2019
Messis, Charis. "The Palaiologan Hagiographies: Saints without Romance." In *Reading the Late Byzantine Romance: A Handbook*, edited by Adam J. Goldwyn and Ingela Nilsson, pp. 230–253. Cambridge: Cambridge University Press, 2019.

Mullett 1984
Mullett, Margaret. "Aristocracy and Patronage in the Literary Circles of Comnenian Constantinople." In *The Byzantine Aristocracy, IX–XIII Centuries*, edited by Michael Angold, pp. 173–201. Oxford: Oxford University Press, 1984.

Mullett 2010
Mullett, Margaret. "No Drama, no Poetry, no Fiction, no Readership, no Literature." In *A Companion to Byzantium*, edited by Liz James, pp. 227–238. Chichester, UK: Wiley-Blackwell, 2010.

Mullett 2013
Mullett, Margaret. "Tented Ceremony: Ephemeral Performances under the Komnenoi." In *Court Ceremonies and Rituals of Power in Byzantium and the Medieval Mediterranean*, edited by Alexander Beihammer, pp. 487–513. Leiden: Brill, 2013.

Mullett 2017
Mullett, Margaret. "Performing Court Literature in Medieval Byzantium: Tales Told in Tents." In *In the Presence of Power: Court and Performance in the Pre-Modern Middle East*, edited by Maurice A. Pommerantz and Evelyn B. Vitz, pp. 121–141. New York: New York University Press, 2017.

Nilsson 2020
Nilsson, Ingela. *Konstantinos Manasses, Literary Craftsman: A Byzantine Writer at Work*. Cambridge: Cambridge University Press, 2020.

Nørgaard and Smith 1975
Nørgaard, Lars, and Ole Smith, eds. *A Byzantine Iliad: The Text of Par. Suppl. Gr. 926*. Copenhagen: Museum Tusculanum.

Polemis 2009
Polemis, Ioannes. "The Treatise on Those Who Unjustly Accuse Wise Men, of the Past and Present: A New Work by Theodore Metochites." *Byzantinische Zeitschrift* 102 (2009): pp. 203–217.
Puchner 2006
Puchner, Walter. "Zur Geschichte der antiken Theaterterminologie im nachantiken Griechisch." *Wiener Studien* 119 (2006): pp. 77–113.
Puchner 2017
Puchner, Walter. *Greek Theatre between Antiquity and Independence: A History of Reinvention from the Third Century BC to 1830.* Cambridge: Cambridge University Press, 2017.
Roilos 2004
Roilos, Panagiotis. "The Sacred and the Profane: Re-enacting Ritual in the Medieval Greek Novel." In *Greek Ritual Poetics*, edited by Dimitrios Yatromanolakis and Panagiotis Roilos, pp. 210–226. Cambridge, MA: Harvard University Press, 2004.
Roilos 2011
Roilos, Panagiotis. "Oral Literature, Ritual, and the Dialectics of Performance." In *Medieval Oral Literature*, edited by Karl Reichl, pp. 225–249. Berlin: De Gruyter, 2011.
Romano 1999
Romano, Roberto. *La satira bizantina dei secoli XI–XV*. Turin: Unione Tipografico Editrice Torinese, 1999.
Savarese 2009
Savarese, Nicola. *Teatro e spettacolo fra Oriente e Occidente*. Bari: Editori Laterza, 2009.
Ševčenko 1962
Ševčenko, Ihor. *Etudes sur la polémique entre Théodore Metochite et Nicéphore Choumnos*. Brussels: Byzantion, 1962.
Smith 1999
Smith, Ole, ed. *The Byzantine Achilleid: The Naples Version*. Vienna: Der Österreichischen Akademie der Wissenschaften, 1999.
Stone 2007
Stone, Andrew. "Aurality in the Panegyrics of Eustathios of Thessaloniki." In *Theatron: Rhetorische Kultur in Spätantike und Mitelalter*, edited by Michael Grünbart, pp. 419–428. Berlin: De Gruyter, 2007.
Toth 2007
Toth, Ida. "Rhetorical Theatron in Late Byzantium: The Example of Palaiologan Imperial Orations." In *Theatron: Rhetorische Kultur in Spätantike und Mitelalter*, edited by Michael Grünbart, pp. 429–448. Berlin: De Gruyter, 2007.
Trahoulia 2010
Trahoulia, Nicolette. "The Venice *Alexander Romance*: Pictorial Narrative and the Art of Telling Stories." In *History as Literature in Byzantium*, edited by Ruth Macrides, pp. 145–165. London: Routledge, 2010.
Tzetzes 2015
Tzetzes, John. *Allegories of the Iliad*, translated by Adam Goldwyn and Dimitra Kokkini. Cambridge, MA: Harvard University Press, 2015.
Tzetzes 2019
Tzetzes, John. *Allegories of the Odyssey*, translated by Adam Goldwyn and Dmitra Kokkini. Cambridge, MA: Harvard University Press, 2019.
Walden 1894
Walden, John W. H. "Stage-Terms in Heliodorus's Aethiopica." *Harvard Studies in Classical Philology* 5 (1894): pp. 1–43.
Yiavis 2019
Yiavis, Kostas. "The Categories of 'Originals' and 'Adaptations' in Late Byzantine Romance: A Reassessment." In *Reading the Late Byzantine Romance: A Handbook*, edited by Adam Goldwyn and Ingela Nilsson, pp. 19–39. Cambridge: Cambridge University Press, 2019.

Trobar, Cantar, Recitar: Performative Poetics across the Middle Sea—An Epilogue[1]

Michael Wyatt

From antiquity through early modernity, performance in the presence of an audience, large or small (even consisting of only one spectator or listener), was an essential dimension of literary production, issuing first from the human voice and only later codified in writing.[2] This performative praxis was integral to much of the literature that Italian narrative poets of the late fifteenth and early sixteenth centuries drew on to construct their poems. It continued to thrive in their lifetimes, providing both a context for and a sounding board against which to try out their own emerging poetics; and it has endured into our own day, evolving well beyond the specific shape of Italian Renaissance narrative poetry as it engages with new thematics and technologies. The elusive relationship of immaterial and material cultures is revealed in Ariosto's *Orlando furioso* as both *summa* and *genitor* of poetic and narrative traditions linked to the translation across disparate cultures, times, and places of words and the objects that accompany them on their travels. As Eric McPhail has noted, the *Furioso* "mimes the accidental course of history . . . it resembles a *tela Penelopes* constantly rewoven in new and unexpected patterns."[3] These metaphors of miming and spinning suggest that acting and tale-telling are not only intertwined but part and parcel of the operations of Ariosto's poem, making of it an extended performance; and as a *tela*, it is a material object charged with energy.

1. *Trobar*

One of the distinguishing features of the western European chivalric literature that reached its zenith in Italy with Boiardo and Ariosto is its generic hybridity, as the initial invocation of the *Furioso* openly announces:

> Le donne, i cavallier, l'arme, gli amori,
> le cortesie, l'audaci imprese io canto.
> —*Fur.*, I 1, 1–2
> [Of ladies and knights, of arms and love, of courtly chivalry, of courageous deeds I sing.]

There is a fusion in the two *Orlandos* of residue from the *chansons de geste* that recount the fictionalized clash of Charlemagne, his knights, and his court with Muslim forces that menace the stability of Christian Europe; the legacy of Old French and Anglo-Norman romance, concerned above all with the British *matter* of Arthur and the Round Table but also encompassing the legends around Tristan; and ancient epic, including its reiteration in Petrarch and Boccaccio.[4] But among other earlier threads that echo throughout the *Inamoramento* and the *Furioso* are texts that preserve Italian *cantarini* performances, Crusade writing, the *novella*,[5] and the poetry of the Occitan troubadours. In addition to providing lyric models refracted through the poets of the Sicilian court of Frederick II and of the *stil novo*, Dante, and Petrarch, the world of troubadour social and political relations anticipated the Ferrarese court culture to which the poems of Boiardo and Ariosto were addressed.

The origins of the troubadour culture that arose in late-eleventh-century Occitania have been the subject of scholarly debate for centuries, with one of the principal points of contention being the question of Arabic influence on the early development of this lyric tradition.[6] There is growing recognition of the extent to which, from the eleventh through the thirteenth centuries, when the troubadours were active, commercial, political, and cultural engagement was frequent among Iberian Christian territories, the *taifa* kingdoms of al-Andalus that arose from the collapse of the hegemonic Cordoban caliphate in 1031, and the French territories in which Occitan was spoken. The poetic debate has for the most part been constrained by the prosodic differences between the Arabic vernacular poetic/song form *muwashshaḥ* (plural *muwashshaḥāt*) and Occitan verse,[7] as well as by mistaken assumptions about linguistic incommensurability across borderlands.[8]

But in her study of eleventh- and early-twelfth-century al-Andalus and southern France, *In Praise of Song*, Cynthia Robinson provides a compelling alternative to the contested pedigree of troubadour verse through a comprehensive profile of a specific Andalusī court culture that she persuasively argues served as an exemplar for the medieval courts of Occitania and Provence.[9] The focus of Robinson's book is the *taifa* of Saragozza in the eastern area of the northern Ebro River valley, a territory governed from 1039 by the Banū Hūd dynasty, bordered on three of its five sides by Christian kingdoms of comparable dimensions, though in this period, "boundaries [did not really function as such], were penetrable, and amorphous."[10] Citizens of Saragozza in its later years of Muslim polity were in fact criticized for their close and sustained relations with both Christians and Jews, important allies in their fight to maintain autonomy in the face of advancing North African Almohad extremism intent on wiping out what this cultivated and culturally porous *taifa* represented as an incubator of religious heterodoxy and secularization.[11] Saragozza was the last of the *taifa* kingdoms to fall to the Almohad, in 1110, though its ruler at the time,ʿImād al-Dawla ibn Hūd, established a court in exile in nearby Rueda, formed an alliance with the Christian Alfonso I of Aragon, and in 1118 joined forces with him and William IX, Duke of Aquitaine and Count of Poitou, to defeat the last Muslim rulers of Saragozza at the battle of Cutanda, thus ending the period of Muslim sovereignty in northern Spain.[12]

Drawing on the poetry of William IX and on Gerald Bond's study of the dialectic of desire and its poetic manifestations against the struggle for power and authority in eleventh- to twelfth-century France,[13] Robinson examines a number of key troubadour preoccupations that, considered alongside the poetic *habitus*[14] of contemporary Andalusī courts, provide a series of analogous developments:

> Noble love (*fin' amor* [what later came to be called "courtly love"], in the Andalusī canon, *wadd*); extended evocations of the beloved [normatively homosocial in al-Andalus, and increasingly recognized as such also in the troubadour context, especially in its earliest phase];[15] and [the evocation] of natural surroundings (*locus amoenus*; in the Andalusī model, generally a garden with frankly paradisiac implications); lovesickness.[16]

The rapport between poet and patron in al-Andalus bore clear similarities to Occitanian practices. It was predicated upon a love that, while acknowledging, legitimizing, and also at times challenging the innate power imbalance between the giver and the subject of panegyric, was "sometimes expressed as physical, sometimes as spiritual, and at times one is uncertain where to draw the line." Andalusī poets were professionals—they also frequently worked as scribes or clerics—and the patronal relationship was thus contractual and operated within a system of exchange in which the poet performed for his patron, providing him *ṭarab*.[17] Reading William of Aquitaine's small corpus of poems in tandem with the broader palette of contemporary Andalusī verse,[18] Robinson finds intersecting junctures along the spectrum of medieval poetics mediated by the Arabic root *ṭ-r-b* that became both the noun *ṭarab* and the verb *ṭaraba*;[19] migrating beyond al-Andalus in its nominal form, transformed from signifying the content of poetic song into its performer, *trobador*, in old Occitan; and, finally, settling as *troubadour* in Catalan, Occitan, and Old French.[20]

In Andalusī relations between poet and patron, there was the expectation that reward for such devotion would take a variety of forms, and if judged to be insufficient, praise could easily be transformed into ridicule.[21] Troubadour verse similarly encompasses such apparent paradoxes, "ground[ing] literary inspiration and individual suffering in the material conditions from which they spring—the courts, patrons, and bodies that allowed for their enunciation."[22] The troubadours, however, pushed into an experimental zone the more settled poetics of the Andalusī courts, daring within the same poem to both glorify and disparage the beloved, representing wildly divergent emotional states and/or tonal registers within the space of only a few lines. The Andalusī courtly preference for Classical Arabic sets it apart from the Occitan vernacular of the troubadours, determining to a great extent what could be expressed in the respective poetic repertories; and Andalusī love poetry was strongly marked by a philosophical dimension almost entirely missing in troubadour verse.[23] But the points of convergence between the two traditions are so considerable that it becomes increasingly difficult to deny a sustained, substantive encounter between them, bearing real consequences, particularly for the poets on the north side of the Pyrenees.

Two distinctive technical elements of the poetry produced in Andalusī courts would likely have had a direct impact on the early troubadours: the use of rhyme and syllabic verse, neither of which was employed in ancient Greek or Latin prosody, or in prior extant medieval European Latin or vernacular poetry.[24] Due to their aural character, the utility of such tools of the trade would not have been hard to apprehend even without fluency in Arabic, and the troubadours did indeed employ a wide range of sonic effects previously unknown in vernacular Romance [?] poetry that also served as aids in improvisational or memory-based performance, the primary vehicle of poetic communication on both sides of the Pyrenees in this period. To observe this is not to minimize the importance of writing in either tradition, and important *dawāwīn*—anthologies of poems, commentaries on them, and biographical/historical information about poets—were created in al-Andalus by, among others, Ibn Shuhayd (992–1035) and al-Fatḥ ibn Khaqān (d. 1134?).[25] The *vidas* (biographies) of the troubadours and *razos* (glosses) of their poetry followed a similar, if slightly later, process of making a literary corpus.[26] In both contexts, performance of poetry for an intimate coterie followed first by the circulation of written texts and then by the collection of poems in anthologies marks the trajectory from the private to the collective, from "creation [of the poem to the] interpretation of [its] meaning."[27]

Maria Pavlova notes that Saracen singers and musicians figure in the earlier chivalric literature that Ariosto was well acquainted with, and she suggests that he would have been aware that there was an ongoing Arabic poetic tradition, though he would not likely have had any direct access to it.[28] But the elliptical appearance of the young Spanish Saracen poet-soldier Olimpio de la Serra in *Furioso* XVI brings us into a more than spectral proximity to the lover-poets of al-Andalus:

> . . . arrivò [Ferraù] a punto
> che vide dal destrier cadere in terra
> col capo fesso Olimpio da la Serra;
>
> un giovanetto che col dolce canto,
> concorde al suon de la cornuta cetra,
> d'intenerire un cor si dava vanto,
> ancor che fosse più duro che pietra.
> Felice lui, se contentar di tanto
> onor sapeasi, e scudo, arco e faretra
> aver in odio, e scimitarra e lancia,
> che lo fece morir in Francia!
> —*Fur.*, XVI 71, 6–8; 72
>
> [As he (Ferraù) arrived, he saw Olimpio de la Serra fall from his horse, his head split open. Olimpio was a youth who could sing so sweetly to the accompaniment of the horn-shaped lyre that he boasted of softening even the flintiest of hearts. Happy he, had he known how to rest content with eminence such as this, and hold in disgust shield, bow and quiver, lance and scimitar which had brought him to an early death in France!]

The desperation of Ferraù to reach the fallen poet in the verses just preceding these together with the immediate and equally brutal revenge he inflicts upon the boy's killer in those that follow give fleeting witness to an outsized affection that equates the *Furioso*'s Andalusī poet both with the affective experience of actual Andalusī poets and with William of Aquitaine, in whose poetic corpus

> the topos of idealized friendship between male companions [is characteristic] . . . constituting a direct link with the Andalusī phenomenon of *ikwānīya*, and it is at the center of this model that soldier and lover meet and, as it were, meld into one. The importance of this topos . . . constitutes one of the most striking

> similarities between Andalusī and Provençal models. The term *ikwānīya* is used both to designate the "loving brotherhood" of *fitna* [the years between ca. 1000 and 1031, when the Cordoban caliphate and its control were in dispute] and *taifa* poet-cleric-courtiers . . . and to refer to the genre of verse produced in celebration of it. Several of William's eleven surviving "songs," in what I suggest is a reference to this topos, open with or contain references to a company [*companho, compaigno*] of male peers before which they were performed, and to whom they are arguably directed. I submit that these references are specific echoes of the Andalusī "courtly *ikwānīya*," of which, at least for the duration of his alliance with ʿImād al-Dawla ibn Hūd, William may even have formed a part.[29]

The fundamentalist Almohad forces that deposed ʿImād al-Dawla in Saragozza anticipated by a century the equivalent Catholic assault on the Cathar "heretics" in Occitania, with similarly dire consequences for the literary culture there.[30] But the preceding permeability of the cultural spaces of medieval Iberia and southern France set the stage for subsequent French, English, and Spanish literary innovations, marked by the assimilation of lyric and narrative forms emanating from these regions which demonstrated a symbiotic relationship with oral and performative traditions in their origins and transmission right through the appearance of the Italian *trovatori* and *cantarini* in the thirteenth and fourteenth centuries.

2. *Cantar*

A defining characteristic of the disparate genres that contributed to the two *Orlandos* is their relationship to "vocality,"[31] and the various terms of *Fur.* I 1, 1–2, that encompass them are united by the poet's declaration *io canto* (I sing), an apparent affirmation of the performative orientation of the poem.[32] Yet a significant impediment to the wider acknowledgment of the role of vocality in the elaboration of complex pre-modern European texts such as the *Inamoramento* and the *Furioso* is the short shrift afforded oral culture by a literary history rooted in empiricist assumptions about traceability and verification of the "source," a category to which vocal production cannot be admitted—so the argument goes—given its impermanence.[33]

French language and literature had breached northern Italy by the thirteenth century (Occitan had arrived earlier, establishing a a particular foothold special foothold in the court of Monferrat) through both oral and textual means.[34] Mixed with Venetian dialect, it became a sociolinguistic humus that provided the environment in which French narrative poetry could naturally morph into new Italian varietals.[35] Over the last century, a number of scholars have been working to accustom the contemporary critical eye and ear to the extensive evidence of the vocal and performative in and around pre-modern texts.[36] Evelyn Birge Vitz's revisionist account of medieval French romance describes a series of practices adapted to the places and occasions of performance that would have formed part of the "baggage" that accompanied French poetry as it traveled into Italy.[37] Performance of romance narrative poems and *chansons de geste* in a variety of settings was widespread in medieval France well into the thirteenth century, and it not only encompassed narration, acting, and singing but also employed dance, gesture, and rhythm.[38]

These textual and performative practices spread rapidly in Italy beginning in the thirteenth century and led to the innovation of the *ottava rima* (eight-line stanzas, rhyming ABABABCC).[39] This verse form proved to be a remarkably adaptable structure for "home-grown" chivalric poems closely related to the new phenomenon of the *cantarini* and their *cantari*, "popular" street performers and their repertories: the anonymous Franco-Veneto *L'entrée d'Espagne*, its Tuscan adaptation, *La Spagna*, and successive rewritings; the four Italian verse adaptations of the *Chanson d'Aspremont*; Andrea da Barberino's prose *Aspramonte*; and the same author's prose compilation *I reali di Spagna* were among the most influential of a large corpus of early Italian chivalric texts inextricably tied to vocality.[40] Recycling this material, lives of saints, and ancient legends, the *cantarini* were hugely popular well into the sixteenth century among all Italian social classes, and a representative slice of the *cantari* repertory is preserved in what would have been inexpensive printed pamphlets sold at open-air performances.[41] Given their contiguity with the chivalric tradition as it had evolved in France and then moved into Italy, the *cantarini* have long posed an embarrassing problem for scholarship that has sought to marginalize their activity as nothing other than superficial entertainment with little light to shed on the sophisticated literature of the period, relevant only insofar as their orality became text. But as the work of Marco Villoresi, Luca Degl'Innocenti, and other recent scholars has established, this tradition provided a dynamic imaginative laboratory with which the major narrative poets of the period—Luigi Pulci, Boiardo, Ariosto, and Teofilo Folengo—were in constant contact in the *piazze* of Florence, Ferrara, Mantua, and elsewhere. The *cantari* were palimpsests of continuous experimentation, providing a jumbled but kinetic road map for what might still be done with the wildly diverse and at times contradictory material that constituted the chivalric landscape; they also served as a continuing conduit for romance *entrelacement* (narrative interweaving) employed so conspicuously in the two *Orlandos*. Furthermore, with regard to the hybrid nature of a chivalric text such as the *Spagna*—having seen a wide diffusion in manuscript before being taken up by the *cantarini*—it represents "a circular movement rather than [one that moves from] high [to] low . . . 'literary' and 'popular' are not, for this type of production, separable categories".[42]

In addition to its central role as incubator of Italian narrative poetry in the fifteenth and sixteenth centuries, Ferrara was a crucial hub for the renaissance of theatrical culture in the years in which Boiardo and Ariosto were active there.[43] Borso d'Este promoted court spectacle, and Boiardo prepared an Italian *terza rima* version of Lucian of Samosata's *Timon the Misanthrope* to be performed for him (more than a century before Shakespeare's *Timon of Athens*).[44] The Latin comedies of Plautus and Terence were edited and staged for Ercole I before then being translated into Italian, providing models for the subsequent development of vernacular theater in Italy and beyond. A handful of contemporary witnesses describe Boiardo and Ariosto reading at court and in more private settings from their poems in progress.[45] But as performer in court entertainments, author and director of theatrical texts (his own and those of others), and creator of what was meant to be a permanent theatrical space within Castello Estense (it was destroyed in an accidental fire at the end of 1532, after just less than two years of service), Ariosto dedicated a great deal of his busy life and career to performance. In a letter to her childhood music master Girolamo da Sestola ("Il Coglia") in response to his report about the marvels of the 1532 Ferrarese Carnival season, Isabella d'Este wrote:

> Noi anchora havemo facte due comedie ma non recitate con quel bon modo che saria convenutto né come di ragione doveno esser state le vostre per il governo che ne deve haver havuto Mx. Lodovico Ariosto, al quall non se trova hogi di pare alcuno in così fate cosse.[46]
> [we too had two comedies (in Mantua), but they were not acted in the good way that would have suited them, nor were they of the quality that yours must have been due to the direction that must have been brought to them by Messer Ludovico Ariosto, who today has no equal in such things.][47]

Circumscribing the lengthy gestation of the *Furioso*, Ariosto's performative vocation left an enduring imprint upon his poem.[48] This is perhaps most evident in the division of its narrating voice between poet-*cantore* and the "individual voices of the characters of the poem: voices that qualify and at times determine, often manifestly, the way in which a character performs within the scene that the text enacts,"[49] a strategy that reflects the detachment a playwright must necessarily concede to his or her dramatis personae when they take the stage.

When Bradamante falls into the Cave of Merlin in *Fur.* II 67–76, she does so via Ariosto's appropriation of a practically symmetrical scene in the *cantari* text, *Febus-el-forte,* an *ottava rima* adaptation of the French romance *Palamedés.*[50] Though having confidently proclaimed *io canto* at the outset of his poem, Ariosto asks at the beginning of the third canto:

> Chi mi darà la voce e le parole
> convenienti a sì nobil soggetto?
> —*Fur.*, III 1, 1–2
> [who will give me voice and word fitting for such a noble subject?]

The answer to this is the voices of the *magi* who must "instruct Bradamante with regard to her ancestors and descendants."[51] Albert Ascoli has noted that "the prophecies and artwork of Merlin reappear at regular intervals" in the *Furioso* as he—working through his agent, the ambivalently altruistic Melissa—embodies a "triple role as artist-prophet-magician."[52] The images conjured up for Bradamante by this artist-magus in *Furioso* III and XXXIII, together with the vision afforded her by Melissa in the penultimate scene of the concluding canto, XLVI, are not, however, presented by Ariosto as inert pictures on the walls of a gallery or church. They are performances, *tableaux vivants*—images that appear to be in motion, accompanied by expository words—to be viewed and absorbed by their designated spectator (joined by her husband, Ruggiero, for whom she must explain everything, in the penultimate scene of the poem).[53]

This moment, the final exploit of Melissa, is presented as a spectacle of her magical powers performed through the consent of the Byzantine prince Leone, who through Melissa's ministrations has only just renounced his marriage claim to Bradamante in favor of Ruggiero:[54]

> Melissa di consenso del Leone
> O più tosto per dargli maraviglia.
> E mostrargli de l'arte paragone,
> ch'al gran vermo infernal mette la briglia,
> e che di lui, come a lei par, dispone,
> e de la a Dio nimica empia famiglia;

> fe' da Costantinopoli a Parigi
> portare il padiglion dai messi stigi.
> —*Fur.*, XLVI 78
> [Melissa had the pavilion flown to Paris from Constantinople by demon-bearers. She did it with Leo's consent, or rather [so] as to impress him with a display of her consummate skill which could bridle the worm of hell and make him do her bidding.]

The provenance of this extraordinary object is the most fantastical recounted anywhere in the *Furioso*: created in Troy by the prophetess Cassandra for her brother Hector, its cloth was embroidered with gold thread to tell the final chapter in the illustrious history of their future Este descendants—the life and deeds of Cardinal Ippolito—initiated in the prophecies of *Furioso* III.[55] After the fall of the Trojan city, the pavilion was transported first to Egypt by Menelaus, as a gift to the (invented) King Proteus, for his custodianship of the errant Helen; it subsequently passed to the historical Cleopatra VII (the last ruler of the Ptolemaic dynasty, lover first of Julius Caesar and then, fatally, of Mark Antony); next to Octavian Augustus and ancient Rome following the battle of Actium; and, finally, from there to Constantinople when Constantine the Great relocated the seat of the Roman Empire in the East.[56] Once having accomplished its role here at the end of Ariosto's poem, it returns from whence it had come as miraculously as it first appeared.

The agency of demons in the performance of *maga* Melissa's magic—the case also of Merlin's and the Saracen Atlante's enchantments—has been little touched upon in Ariosto criticism.[57] But the supernatural continued to exercise a significant force in the world that Ariosto inhabited,[58] and it is therefore of considerable interest how the conspicuous form of enchantment employed by the *Furioso*'s magicians legitimates its high designs through demonic means. As Fabrizio Lelli shows in his chapter in this volume, the pervasive practice of magic as well as scholarly reflection upon "the arcane and occult properties . . . of speech and writing . . . the links between natural forces in the universe and the magical power of words" in early modern Ferrara, were a direct consequence of the Sephardic Jewish presence there. Ippolito d'Este, like a number of contemporary figures in Ferrarese intellectual culture, had been instructed in the *occulti sensi [delle] antiche carte* (hidden meanings [of] ancient texts; *Fur.*, XLVI 89, 3–4). Might such studies have led someone in Ariosto's circle to the Arabic terms *ruḳya*—"like [the] Latin *carmen*, magical chant, consist[ing] in the pronouncing of formulae for procuring an enchantment"—and *siḥr* (magic) "applied to any action effected through recourse to a demon . . . one of the procedures [of *ruḳya*] used by the Prophet himself and, because of this, permitted in exceptional cases," provided that its end is beneficent and harms no one?[59] These would seem to be fitting descriptions for the *Furioso*'s instrumental use of magic at a moment when it was coming under increasing pressure from the humanist culture that had played such a significant role in Ariosto's *forma mentis*, at the same time that its practices were ever more subject to the scrupulous eye of the Church.[60]

3. *Recitar*

Following the cross-cultural exchanges of *trobar* and the varied ways in which *cantar* engaged with the chivalric *gesta*, we turn here to the codification of these practices in more formalized practices of recitation: first in Sicilian *cuntastorie* (or *cunto*, spoken recitation) and the *opera dei pupi* (or *opra*, the preferred term of its practitioners, puppet theater).

There is no precise evidence marking the emergence of either *cunto* or *opra*, though both were well established in Sicily by the first third of the nineteenth century, and like other forms of "popular" entertainment from the late sixteenth century forward, they provided an important cultural space for their publics faced with the rise of professional acting companies and fixed theaters intended, in Italy at least, for more privileged classes.[61] The Palermitan doctor and ethnographer Giuseppe Pitrè (1841–1916), the unqualed authority on Sicilian popular traditions,[62] provides a classic description of what *cunto* entails:

> Howsoever the rest of the world may see it, the tale of Rinaldo must always be recited in a certain manner, with the same pauses, the same intonation, in a highly pitched, often brisk, intentionally oratorical style; slowly at times, at others suddenly transformed into rapid familiar speech. Head, arms, legs, everything must take its part in the recitation: gestures are an essential dimension of the narrator's work. Atop a bench, that serves as dais, pulpit, or tribune on which the *cuntista* adroitly maneuvers, he guides his characters with the shifting of his eyes, mouth, arms, and feet, he introduces them to his public and makes them speak as the argument would have it; he never repeats himself chapter and verse, nor does he deploy empty rhetoric. He lines up his soldiers for battle, he makes them come to blows, violently shaking his hands and stomping his feet as if it were a real brawl. In the midst of such delirium, he takes a step back, another forward, raising his clenched fists as high as he can, convulsively stretching and bending his arms. The temperature rises: the orator's eyes open

> wide, his nostrils flare in synch with his breath, his words ever more frenzied. His feet alternate in stomping the ground, which thunders in the void below. Through the backward and forward movement of his arms, and between half-uttered words and clipped stresses, the dying give up the ghost and the narration returns to an evenkeel, as if no one had died, as if two or four hundred listeners had not been left suspended, hearts beating, mercilessly uncertain of the outcome of the battle hanging from the lips of the enflamed narrator. [63]

Here are all of the salient features of this singular form of recitation: its adherence to the Carolingian repertory through strict observance of a series of vocal and gestural rubrics performed within a radically circumscribed space (the performer's "bench" was situated in piazze and on street corners as well as in warehouses, these usually located near ports), such apparent limitations actually authorizing a freedom to give expression to an expansive imaginative world. Through the three principal means at his disposition—the rhythmic beating of his feet, the brandishing of his arms (fig. 1, here outfitted with a wooden sword, the only material object employed in *cunto*), and the virtuosic modulation of his voice—the *cuntista* takes his listeners on a journey recited in partially improvised prose alternating with metrically defined episodes that distinguish recited *cunto* from the verse-based song of the *cantastorie* who had still performed in Sicily into the 1970s.[64] The voice of the *cuntista* alternates between persuasion and seduction, "now thunderous, now affectionate, now faintly dramatic, to then break into a rhythmic scansion that comes close to approaching the total abstraction of sound."[65]

These sonic dimensions of *cunto* are firmly grounded in the material that it enacts: "the figure of the *cuntista* represents a sort of gatekeeper of collective wisdom and his performances assume the guise of a ritual experience . . . the long struggle between Christians and Muslims reflects the age-old conflict between Good and Evil."[66] This element in the Sicilian popular tradition is the issue that many casual observers of both *cunto* and *opra* mistake as ignorant prejudice,[67] when it is in fact a multilayered response to the complex political and cultural history of Sicily, a geographical space dominated for millennia by colonizers from across the Middle Sea that provoked a passionate indigenous desire for autonomy but also left indelible marks of alterity that have contributed to Sicily's position identity within the modern Italian state.[68]

In the *opera* dei pupi, the word of the *cuntastorie* is made thing, and in the process, "the puppeteers eliminate the artifice, simplify the rhythms, while they deepen [the emotional impact of] their characters."[69] Puppets are, in Kenneth

Fig. 1. Mimmo Cuticchio, *cunto* performance, Durham Studio Theater, University of California, Berkeley, April 19, 2010

Gross's elegant formulation, "ambassador[s] to human beings from the world of things,"[70] the fulfillment of what Pitrè had noted—with regard to the *opra*—that the early audience for *cunto* had sought "the living voice of the *cuntista* . . . put into action."[71] A striking testimony to the power of the *opra* is given by Henry Festing Jones, an English solicitor who had visited Sicily for decades before discovering the tradition in the early years of the twentieth century and later forming a close, possibly intimate relationship with the Palermitan puparo Alessandro Greco.[72] In his *Diversions in Sicily* (1909), he tells of visiting a small theater in Trapani, and his detailed account of two of its *spettacoli* gives a good sense of how successfully the chivalric tales had been transmuted into material and physical terms. Backstage he is shown "a grove of puppets hanging up against the walls like turkeys in a poulterer's shop at Christmas—scores and scores of them . . . there were almost two hundred marionettes altogether, including Turkish and Spanish soldiers."[73]

Thus amply populated, the first *spettacolo* dramatizes the death of Medoro at the hands of Ferraù, furious that Angelica had rejected him for a simple foot soldier; but following the death of her husband, Angelica will commit suicide in order to forestall Ferraù's designs on her. This is a surprising turn of events for readers only familiar with these characters in the two *Orlandos*, but Jones explains that the cycle under way in this theater—already in its fourth month of two repeated daily episodes, it will continue for another four months[74]—is derived from a prose anthology that "does not always agree with the other versions of the same story."[75] Jones also notes that the differences between the *opra* traditions in eastern and western Sicily (based, respectively, in Catania and Palermo) are a question of pliability, how easily or not the puppets can be worked in the playing space: their size determines their range of motion and their expressive capacity.[76] Indeed, his account of the *spettacoli* that he saw in Trapani is largely taken up with their technical aspects—how to manipulate a *pupo*, the easy interchangeability of its parts (particularly the head) to create different characters, what distinguishes one *paladino* from another ("the crests of their helmets")[77]—which he was able to observe close at hand, watching from the wings. The most elaborate of Jones's explanations is of the *consiglio* (council gathering) of Charlemagne's knights that, along with the *danza con la spada* (choreographic sword fight), is one of the fixed points of every *opera dei pupi* performance of the *gesta*. The *pupi* are ritually marched into a fixed formation through a carefully organized series of criss-crossing moves by the unseen *opranti* (operators/puppeteers), a moment that appears to the spectator as a visual tour de force and a show of the solidarity of the Christian *paladini* but is, in fact, technically quite straightforward (fig. 2; here a single row of *paladini*, while Jones describes a more complex double row of twice as many knights).[78]

Jones admits to not having paid close attention to the plot of the second of the Trapani *spettacoli* he saw, "The Death of Bradamante," obsessed as he was by its mechanics, but he was captivated by the final two scenes in which Marfisa (Ruggiero's sister and also now a Christian) first goes in search of Bradamante following the rout of Charlemagne's troops at Roncesvalles, only then to find her in a grotto dying of grief, "as affecting a scene as I have ever witnessed."[79] The moment is obliquely flagged in the hermit's revelation to Ruggiero of his tragic fate in *Fur.* XLI 66, though there the two women are prophesied as seeking swift revenge, destroying the feudal seat of the Christian clan of Gano di Maganza, responsible for the deaths of Ruggiero and the other *paladini*, while here the accent is on pathos, the voice of the *puparo*—by day a cobbler in a village on nearby Monte Erice—effecting its enchantment:

> Art abounds in miracles, and not the least is this, that a man can take a few watery commonplaces and by the magic of his voice transmute them into the golden wine of romance. The audience took in the glowing drops that poured from his lips and were stilled to a silence that broke in a great sob as the curtain

Fig. 2. *Consiglio* of Charlemagne's Paladins (from the left): Orlando, Bradamante, Rinaldo, Oliviero, Ruggiero di Risa, Brandimarte, Ruggiero dall'Aquila Bianca, Cladinoro, Astolfo

> fell. What did they know of loosely jointed wooden dolls or of toy stages? They were no longer in the theatre. They had wandered the woods with Marfisa, they had sought Bradamante in the leafy glades, they had found her dying in the grotto, they had received her last breath and the world would never be the same.[80]

Though Ariosto never stages the battle at Roncesvalles in his poem, its distant clamor is an inescapable aspect of the future following upon the *Furioso*'s ambiguous finale,[81] but it is the explicit *terminus ad quem* of the narrative cycles of the *opera dei pupi* and of *cunto*, as demonstrated by the multipaneled *cartellone* (placard) painted by Nicolò Rinaldi now hanging in the *teatrino* of the Figli d'Arte Cuticchio in Palermo (fig. 3).[82]

A stark testimony to the heavy price paid by the pluri-millenial tradition of chivalry and by the opposition of "Christian" and "Muslim" in the tradition of the *gesta*, the consequences of the fictional disaster at Roncesvalles are

ROTTA DI RONCISVALLE. DAL TRADIMENTO DI GANO ALLA MORTE DI ORLANDO E DEI PALADINI

eloquently recounted by Jones from his experience in a provincial Sicilian puppet theater in the early twentieth century, a space as far removed as might be imagined from either the medieval and early modern courts that had given rise to its fictive narratives or the currents animating the great urban centers of European culture in the period immediately preceding the Great War. But Jones's account of the Sicilian *opra* is echoed in these recent reflections on the mimetic power of the seemingly "simple" art of puppetry to encompass even the most ineffable corners of human desire and the most apparent contradictions of cultural conflict in its material bringing together of the artifice of performance with the realities that it aims to enact:

> What gathers in my mind is a space for a kind of theater composed by the simplest of gestures, gestures belonging to things not quite human but yet essentially bound to gravity and time. It is a space in which you find your companions among artifacts and objects, materialized ghosts—a creature with a curled wooden hand, a gaping mouth, and sticklike limbs becomes a homely kind of spirit. They are like things excavated from the ground, with dirt and dust still clinging to them, thick with time, but light, light. It is a space where shadow becomes substance, where accidents become forms of intention.[83]

Facing page
Fig. 3. Nicolò Rinaldi, *cartellone* of the battle of Roncesvalles (from the top left): under a carab tree, the Christian Gano da Maganza (second from right) plots the betrayal of the Paladins of France with the Saracen king Marsilio and his two brothers; bearing his arms, an angel appears to the pilgrim-hermit Rinaldo, telling him that he must race to Roncesvalles together with his brother Ricciardetto (asleep in the grotto on the left); Archbishop Turpino (center left) explains to the paladins that Saracens are arriving from every angle; pitched battle between the Paladins and Saracens in the Pass of Roncesvalles; angels and demons arrive to carry away the souls of those who have died; the anguish of Charlemagne (center left), who, having arrived too late with his other troops, finds Orlando dead. (Courtesy of the Associazione Figli d'Arte Cuticchio, Palermo)

Notes

This epilogue is extracted from a longer essay that will be published elsewhere in its entirety. For their assistance with my research, I would like to thank Giorgio Alberti, Marie-Cécile Bardoz, Cecilia Gaposchkin, Stephen Orgel, Maria Pavlova, and Deanna Shemek.

1. The term "Middle Sea" is typical in pre-modern Arab descriptions and maps of the region, but it has an ancient history; see Broodbank 2013.

2. For "performance" and "performativity" as used here, see Burningham 2007, pp. 1–8; Harris and Reichl 2011; Pomerantz and Vitz 2017, pp. 8–9.

3. MacPhail 2001, 44.

4. See Everson 2001, pp. 27–126.

5. For the *cantarini,* see below. Crusade accounts—historical chronicles that the chivalric *gesta* mirror in fictional and performative terms—are addressed in the longer version of this essay. On the *novella* (with Boccaccio and after, if not before, a performative genre), in the *Inamoramento* and *Furioso,* see Bruscagli in Boiardo 1995, pp. xxiv–vi; D'Amore 2002; Bigazzi 2013.

6. See Nykl 1946; Lemay 1966; Menocal 1987; Menocal 1994; Zwartjes 1997; Dainotto 2006.

7. Robinson 2002, p. xxi: "Strophic poem[s] or song[s] characterized by verses in classical Arabic and refrains . . . [in] Arabic, Romance, and/or Hebrew dialect."

8. See Robinson 2002, pp. 22–23, and Beech 2008, pp. 210–212, on language "crossing" in borderlands. On polyglot *cavalieri,* see Gesiot in this volume. Subrahmanyam (2012, pp. 4–7, 23–24) notes that the "incommensurability" traditionally ascribed to the "overlapping cultural zones" of Eurasian states and empires in the sixteenth and seventeenth centuries is better addressed in the concept of "acculturation," arguing that direct contact between differing cultures is not ipso facto a zero-sum game but potentially constructive of "interaction." Tomasin (2021) examines the liminal languages that Italian merchants employed in their business throughout the Mediterranean and as far away as England, from the late medieval period through early modernity.

9. Robinson's book thoroughly considers the questions raised by literary exchange in this region in the eleventh and twelfth centuries from the perspective of an Arabist who works across disciplinary boundaries—architecture, philology, and literary history.

10. Robinson 2002, p. 20.

11. Robinson 2002, p. 21.

12. See Cobb 2014, pp. 146–156, on the collapse of Muslim sovereignty and the consolidation of Christian power in northern Iberia.

13. Bond 1982; Bond 1996.

14. In the classical Latin sense of the term, what we now call custom—"expression, demeanour, manner, bearing" (*Oxford Latin Dictionary,* vol. 1, p. 680)—but also Bourdieu's use of the term which encompasses the determinant and defining structures of any human enterprise.

15. See Burgwinkle 1997; Robinson (2002, pp. 268n17, 336–342) considers the correspondences between the objects of William's and Andalusī poets' desire. Kay (1995, pp. 145–172) sees the same veiled gendered dynamic in the contemporary *chansons de geste.*

16. Robinson 2002, pp. 44, 344–345.

17. "A term denoting poetic and musical emotion, evoking a broad spectrum of sentiments, from the most private to the most violent: pleasure, enjoyment, emotional trauma, exaltation . . . and even a trance capable of resulting in death"; Lambert 2012.

18. Robinson 2002, pp. 342–352.

19. Robinson (2002, p. xxi) defines the verb as signifying through its various Arabic forms "to be moved (with joy or grief), delighted, overjoyed, transported with joy; to delight, enrapture, gratify . . . to make music, sing, vocalize, chant; to play music 'for someone,' to sing 'for someone.'"

20. Robinson notes that *ṭ-r-b* is "almost absent from the corpus of *muwashshahāt*"; see Robinson 2002, pp. 342–343, and note 11 above.

21. Robinson 2002, pp. 323–328.

22. Burgwinkle 2011, pp. 21–22, 23.

23. One of the poet-philosophers most closely examined by Robinson throughout her study is Ibn al-

Sīd al-Baṭalyawsī, whose treatise *Kitāb al-Ḥadā'iq* (The book of circles), translated into Hebrew, was influential for Leone Ebreo's 1532 *Dialoghi d'amore*, a text with which Ariosto was probably familiar prior to its print publication; see Bonadeo 1968, pp. 56–57; Idel 1978; Lelli in this volume.

24. The Persian polymath Abū Naṣr al-Fārābī (ca. 870–943 CE) wrote influential works on music and poetry, discussing rhyme and syllabic verse in the latter; for a French translation of his work on poetics, see al-Fārābī 2007; a partial English translation, also including a selection from his influential treatise on music (a phenomenon that al-Fārābī considered organically linked to poetic language) is in Gelder and Hammond 2008, pp. 12–23; see Dainotto 2006 for the European debate on the origins of rhyme initiated in the mid-sixteenth century by Giammaria Barbieri.

25. Ibn Shuhayd's *dīwān* has been translated into Spanish (Ibn Shuhaid 1969) and into French (Ibn Shuhayd 2013); but Al-Fath's *Qalā'id al-'Iqyān* (Necklace of Rubies), written in rhymed prose, remains (like the vast majority of Andalusī writing) untranslated into Western languages.

26. Burgwinkle 2011, p. 24.

27. Robinson 2002, p. 348.

28. See Pavlova 2020, pp. 37–38; and Dorigatti 2013, pp. 393–394.

29. Robinson 2002, p. 336.

30. Duggan 1984, 80–81.

31. See Zumthor 2002, p. 118, on his preference for this term, better suited to describing oral culture by specifically locating it in the human voice.

32. See Villoresi 2016a, pp. 246–247. Ariosto deliberately echoes here the opening of the *Aeneid*, "Arma virumque cano" (Arms and a man I sing). The transitional relationship to orality that Virgil's text demonstrates with regard to the Homeric poems—defined by a still largely preliterate world—is a useful analogue for the *Furioso*: "Like Homer's bards, [Virgil] was prepared to [and often did] perform for an audience of [privileged] listeners; but it was because of the enabling power of writing to transmit works of literature across time that he put his efforts into negotiating a relationship that the oral epic tradition had never envisaged, a relationship with an audience of [formally] educated and experienced readers"; Minchin 2014, p. 285.

33. As Dwight Reynolds shows in his essay in this volume, the oral and the written in Arabic literary culture were, and remain, complementary aspects of literary production.

34. Occitan—the language of the troubadours and much of medieval southern and central France—and the Old French of the *chansons de geste* and romance, spoken in northern France and by English elites of the period, correspond, respectively, to the *langue d'oc* and *langue d'oïl* that Dante discusses in *De vulgari eloquentia*, Bk. 1, ix, 2, though their status in France was already being displaced by Middle French at the time of the migration of French literary models and performers into Italy. See Zink 2011 on the troubadours in Monferrat; and for their medieval Italian successors, the *trovatori*, see Di Luca and Grimaldi 2017.

35. See Rajna 1900, pp. 11–18; Babbi 2011; Morlino 2015. For the diffusion of the literature and literary models issuing from Occitan and French in the wider Italian context in the period prior to Boiardo and Ariosto, see Vitullo 2000; Praloran and Morato 2007; Giammei 2018.

36. See Zumthor 1983; 1983; Bologna 2000; Zumthor 2002; Stock 1990; Duggan 2002; Ong 2002; Reichl 2011, pp. 3–119, 141–149.

37. Vitz 1999, pp. ix–xiii, 164–227.

38. Vitz 1999, p. 181. On the *chansons*, orality, and performance, see Duggan 1984; Bennett 2006; Leverage 2010, pp. 299–313 (particularly for its focus on the performance of this material in religious contexts); Ailes 2019; and Boutet 2011. See Kay 1995 on the relationship of the *chansons* to romance narrative poetry.

39. On the imact of *ottava rima* in medieval and early modern Italian writing, see Alfano 2011; on its particular suitability for performance, see Morabito 2011, pp. 374–383.

40. See Villoresi 2016b for an introduction to the complex history of the *Spagna*—generally relevant to the early manifestations of chivalric literature in Italy; and p. 135, for what he refers to as "una tradizione testuale anarchica ... quella cantarina, costantemente innovativa ... fatalmente collaborativa e poliautoriale" (an anarchic textual tradition . . . that of the *cantarini*, constantly innovative . . . fatally collaborative and poly-authorial). On the bewildering maze of Italian chivalric texts and the *canterini*, see Degl'Innocenti 2016.

41. On the *cantari*, orality, and writing, see Morabito 2011.

42. "Un movimento circolare piuttosto che alto/basso ... letterario e populare non siano, per questa produzione, categorie scindibili." See Villoresi 2016b, pp. 126–127.

43. See Catalano 1930, Vol. 1, pp. 116–126, 579–595; Villoresi 1994; and Clubb 2005.

44. See Ponte 1964.

45. See Isabella d'Este's letter to her brother Cardinal Ippolito, thanking him for having sent Ariosto (then in his service) to her in Mantua just after the birth of her son Ferrante in January 1507 and reporting that the poet had given her tremendous pleasure in her convalescence by reading from his new work; see Isabella d'Este 2017, p. 280, "Lettera 388"; see also Dorigatti 2011, pp. 33–36; Villoresi 2016a, pp. 224, 251–252. Such "readings" are to be considered fully performative; the assumption that improvisation is an essential feature of vocality is a non sequitur in that many forms of performance depend upon scripts or scenarios (and memory); see Zumthor 2002, pp. 118–123;

46. Archivio di Stato di Mantova, AG 3000 libro 50 c. 175r; my thanks to Deanna Shemek for supplying this transcription.

47. Isabella d'Este 2017, p. 555, "Lettera 783."

48. On Ariosto and spectacle, see Catalano 1930, pp. 116–126, 491–500, 572–595; Coluccia 2001; Ferroni 2008, pp. 47–84; Martinez 2014, pp. 247–250.

49. Villoresi 2016a, p. 253.

50. See Stoppino 2018, pp. 41–45.

51. Villoresi 2016b, p. 248.

52. Ascoli 1987, p. 340n143. See Kisacky 2000, pp. 82–87, on the relationship of prophecy to magic, both fundamentally performative practices, in the two *Orlandos*; and pp. 117–120 on Melissa's use of deceit in the service of the poem's ultimate "good," the union of Bradamante and Ruggiero. Ascoli (1987, pp. 149–150, 154, 157) identifies the *maga*'s pedagogy with the wiles of Dante's Ulysses, an emblematic figure of fraud.

53. On prophecy as performance, see Barletta in this volume.

54. See Bigi's note for *Fur.* XLIV 12 (Ariosto 2012, p. 1410), on the real Byzantine figures treated here with very rapid brushstrokes. But that Bradamante was briefly betrothed to the heir to the throne of Byzantium—in the lengthy 1532 addition to *Furioso* XLVI in which Leone is introduced—calls for further attention with regard to the constant interplay of fiction and history in the poem.

55. Ascoli (1987, pp. 376–393) equates Ariosto's fear of a potentially failed poetic vocation with Cassandra's unheeded prophecies. Throughout his study, Ascoli delineates a poet in continuous conflict with the dynastic endgame of his poem, a vast subject I can only signal here. See Casadei 2018, pp. 580–583, on the episode of the pavilion.

56. In Herodotus's version of the fall of Troy, Helen and Paris had escaped together to Egypt; see Bigi's notes for *Fur.* XLVI 82–83 (Ariosto 2012, p. 1493) on the "historical" trajectory of the pavilion.

57. Kisacky (2000, pp. 27–28, 124) at least draws attention to the phenomenon in the two *Orlandos*.

58. "Religion" is to be considered here an institutionalized effort at defining, containing, and redirecting the supernatural. On the question of religion in Ariosto's poem, see Jossa 2016; and Jossa's essay in this volume.

59. Fahd 2012a and 2012b (which I have adapted here). The Sicilian Jew Guglielmo Raimondo Moncada, a convert to Christianity and scholar of Arabic, active in Romagna and at the court of Urbino in the last decades of the fifteenth century, would have been familiar with these concepts; he had taught Arabic to Giovanni Pico della Mirandola—uncle of Ariosto's friend Alberto Pio da Carpi—and worked on what would remain an incomplete new translation of the Koran for Federico da Montefeltro; see Grévin 2010; Casari 2018; and Casari's essay in this volume.

60. See Prosperi 2016.

61. There must have been, however, some degree of contiguity with preceding traditions. See Roggero 2011 on sixteenth-century performers of the *gesta* in Italy; and Cavallini 1989 on the survival into the seventeenth century of the popular artists—musician-improvisers, jesters, mimes, and so on—who had since the time of the early medieval courts of France performed alongside *troubadours/trovatori* and *trouvères/canterini*. For the blind itinerant poet-performers, the *orvi-cicatti*, who were active in Sicily (and elsewhere in Italy) from the mid-sixteenth century through the time of the earliest *cuntisti*, perhaps the most tangible link to an ongoing tradition of vocal performance, see Venturini 2017, pp. 69–73.

62. His *Biblioteca delle tradizioni populari* was published in twenty-five volumes between 1871 and 1913.

63. "Cammini quanto e come vuole il mondo, il racconto di Rinaldo dev'esser recitato sempre a un modo, con le medesime pause, con la medesima cantilena, con una declamazione spesso concitata, più spesso affannosa, intenzionalmente oratoria; talora lenta, alcuna volta mutata d'improvviso in discorso familiare e rapido. Testa, braccia, gambe, tutto deve prender parte al racconto: la mimica essendo parte essenziale del lavoro del narratore. Sopra una specie di predella, che fa da bigoncia, o pergamo, o tribuna, o palcoscenico come meglio piace, sul quale si possa muovere, il contastorie coi movimenti degli occhi, della bocca, delle braccia, de' piedi conduce i suoi personaggi, li presenta, li fa parlare come ragion vuole; ne repeté per punto e per virgola i discorsi, ne declama le aringhe; fa schierare in battaglia i soldati, li fa venire a zuffa agitando violentemente le mani e pestando coi piedi come se si trattasse di vera e reale zuffa. In tanta concitazione, egli dà un passo addietro, un altro in avanti, levando in alto, quanto più alto puó, i pugni chiusi o slungando e piegando convulsamente le braccia. Il bollore cresce: gli occhi dell'oratore si spalancano, le nari si dilatano per la frequenza del respiro che sempre più concitata fa la parola. I piedi alternativamente pestando il terreno, che pel vuoto che c'è sotto rintrona; alternansi i movimenti di va e vieni delle braccia, e tra mozze parole e tronchi accenti, muore chi ha da morire, ed il racconto, monotono sempre, ritorna calmo come se nessuno fosse morto, come se duecento, quattrocento uditori non fossero stati sospesi, palpitanti, crudelmente incerti dell'esito della pugna pendendo dalle labbra dell'infocato narratore." See Pitrè 1884, pp. 345–346.

64. See Andrich 2006, p. 31; and Venturini 2017, pp. 9, 74–79.

65. "Ora tonante, ora carezzevole, ora drammatico fioco a rompersi in una scansione ritmica che arriva a toccare l'astrazione del suono." See Andrich 2006, p. 33.

66. "La figura del cuntista rappresenta una sorta di depositario del sapere collettivo e le sue performance assumono le sembianze di una esperienza rituale . . . nella lunga lotta tra Christiani e Saraceni si riflette quella ancestrale tra il Bene e il Male." See Andrich 2006, p. 33.

67. See, e.g., Marks 2016, p. 66.

68. See Gross 2011, pp. 89–99, on the reconstitutive violence and destruction that characterize the *opra*'s material forms, and their relationship to the violence at the core of chivalric narrative. The period that encompassed Arab and then Norman control of Sicily, from 827 through 1282, is arguably the most relevant for a fuller historical contextualization of the ethical, social, and political concerns of *cunto* and the *opra*. But it is no coincidence that the first concrete documentation of these performative traditions dates from the decade prior to Giuseppe Garibaldi's Sicilian campaign in 1860 which led to Italian unification the following year, closely linked among Sicilians to resistance to Spanish Bourbon rule over the island. Gaetano Greco, patriarch of the Palermitan Greco clan of *pupari*, was among the Sicilians who joined Garibaldi's army, and the Catanese *puparo* Angelo Grasso, staged a *spettacolo* in which revolutionary *pupi* aimed their rifles and shot at their Bourbon oppressors; see Venturini 2017, pp. 46–47, 38. For the national celebration of Italy's 150th anniversary in 2011, the Figli d'Arte Cuticchio in Palermo, descendants of the Grecos according to the genealogical "tree" of the *opra* (Venturini 2017, pp. 28–32) created *O a Palermo o all'inferno* about Garibaldi in Sicily.

69. "I pupari eliminano gli artefici, semplificano i ritmi, mentre approfondiscono i personaggi." See Andrich 2006, p. 55.

70. Gross 2011, p. 33.

71. "La viva voce . . . dei c[u]ntastorie . . . movimentata." See Venturini 2017, p. 23.

72. Fragments of Jones's life and career are recounted via his long friendship with Samuel Butler in Paradis 2016.

73. Jones 1909, pp. 80–81.

74. These cycles, as was the case with those of *cuntastorie*, were often even longer elsewhere, though (as Jones observes, 1909, p. 84), indoor theaters always closed for the hottest summer months. Extended performance cycles had also been typical of the *canterini*; see Villoresi 2005, pp. 27–31.

75. Jones 1909, pp. 83–84. As with the *cantari*. The two volumes of the *Storia dei paladini di Francia da Pipino re sino alla rotta di Roncisvalle seguito la morte di Carlo Magno* by Pietro Manzanares (Palermo, 1895) that Jones refers to was one of several such collections that took their cues from the thirteen volumes of the *Storia dei paladini di Francia* of Giusto Lo Dico (or Lodico; Palermo, 1858–1860). These compilations were assembled, with quite a free hand, from a wide range of published chivalric and romance sources—Lo Dico explicitly favored written texts over the oral tradition—for use by *cuntisti* and *pupari*; see Andrich 2006, pp. 48–49.

76. Jones 1909, p. 82. A Catanese *pupo* can reach 130 centimeters (51 inches) in height and weigh up to 35 kilograms (77 pounds), while their "peers" in Palermo are normally no taller than 90 centimeters (35 inches), weighing no more than 15 kilograms (33 pounds). What a large *pupo* in Catania loses in agility, however, is compensated for by other performative values in a repertory teeming with giants and other fantastical creatures; see Scattina 2017 for the most recent study of the Catanese *opra*.

77. Jones 1909, pp. 90–94; see also Andrich 2006, pp. 90–91, on the steps in the construction of a *pupo*, with accompanying photos; and pp. 92–93, on the technique of operating one.

78. Jones 1909, p. 97.

79. Jones 1909, p. 99.

80. Jones 1909, pp. 100–101.

81. See Monteverdi 1961, who argues that the battle staged on the island of Lampedusa in *Fur.*, XLI 68–102, XLII 1–23, immediately following the scene of Ruggiero and the hermit, which results in the death of Brandimarte, is a rehearsal for Roncesvalles.

82. As with the narrative elements of *cunto* and *opra*, the various *cartelloni* of Roncesvalles do not follow rigid schemes, and apart from set pieces such as Gano di Maganza's betrayal, Orlando's failure to sound his magical horn until it is too late, and the deaths of the Christian heroes, they allow for a certain degree of artistic license; see Di Palma 2006, pp. 55–60.

83. Gross 2011, p. 159.

Bibliography

Al-Fārābī 2007

Al-Fārābī. *Philosopher à Bagdad au Xᵉ siècle*. Edited by Ali Benmakhlouf, translated by Stéphane Diebler. Paris: Éditions du Seuil, 2007.

Ailes 2019

Ailes, Marianne. "The *Chanson de geste*." In *The Cambridge Companion to the Literature of the Crusades*, pp. 25–38. Cambridge: Cambridge University Press, 2019.

Alfano 2011

Alfano, Giancarlo. "Una forma per tutti gli usi: L'ottava rima." In *Atlante della letteratura italiana*, Vol. 2: *Dalla Controriforma alla Restaurazione*, edited by Erminia Irace, Sergio Luzzatto, and Gabriele Pedullà, pp. 31–57. Turin: Einaudi, 2011.

Andrich 2006

Andrich, Chiara. *Il teatro di Mimmo Cuticchio: 1967–2007*. Palermo: Associazione "Figli d'Arte Cuticchio," 2006.

Ariosto 2012

Ariosto, Ludovico. *Orlando furioso*. Edited by Cristina Zampese, introduction and commentary by Emilio Bigi. Milan: BUR Rizzoli, 2012.

Ascoli 1987

Ascoli, Albert. *Ariosto's Bitter Harmony: Crisis and Evasion in the Italian Renaissance*. Princeton, NJ: Princeton University Press, 1987.

Babbi 2011

Babbi, Anna Maria. "Scrivere in francese in Italia nel XIII secolo." In *Écrire dans la langue de l'autre*, edited by Anna Maria Babbi, pp. 37–48. Verona: Fiorini, 2011.

Beech 2008

Beech, George T. *The Brief Eminence and Doomed Fall of Islamic Saragossa, a Great Center of Jewish and Arabic Learning in the Iberian Peninsula during the 11th Century*. Zaragoza: Instituto de Estudios Islámicos y del Oriente Próximo, 2008.

Bennett 2006

Bennett, Philip E. "Orality and Textuality: Reading and/or Hearing the *Song of Roland*." In *Approaches to Teaching the* Song of Roland, edited by William W. Kibler and Leslie Zarker Morgan, pp. 146–153. New York: Modern Language Association of America, 2006.

Bigazzi 2013
Bigazzi, Roberto. "Boccaccio, Ariosto, and the European Novel." *Mediaevalia* 34 (2013): pp. 155–168.
Boiardo 1995
Boiardo, Matteo Maria. *Orlando innamorato*. 2 vols. Edited by Riccardo Bruscagli. Turin: Einaudi, 1995.
Bologna 2000
Bologna, Corrado. *Flatus vocis: metafisica e antropologia della voce*. Bologna: Il Mulino, 2000. Bolzoni 2002
Bolzoni, Lina. "'O maledetto, o abominoso ordigno': La rappresentazione della guerra nel poema epico-cavalleresco." In *Storia d'Italia, Annali 18, Guerra e pace*, edited by Walter Barberis, pp. 201–247. Turin: Einaudi, 2002.
Bonadeo 1968
Bonadeo, Alfredo. "Olimpia." *Italica* 45, no. 1 (1968): pp. 47–58.
Bond 1982
Bond, Gerald. *The Poetry of William VII, Count of Poitiers, IX Duke of Aquitaine*. New York: Garland, 1982.
Bond 1996
Bond, Gerald. *The Loving Subject: Desire, Eloquence, and Power in Romanesque France*. Philadelphia: University of Pennsylvania Press, 1996.
Bortoletti 2014
Bortolletti, Francesca. "La fortuna dell'*Orlando furioso* nelle arti performative: Scenario italiano." In *L'Orlando furioso nello specchio delle immagini*, edited by Lina Bolzoni, pp. 689–724. Rome: Istituto della Enciclopedia Italiana, 2014.
Boutet 2011
Boutet, Dominique. "The *Chanson de Geste* and Orality." In *Medieval Oral Literature*, edited by Karl Reichl, pp. 353–369. Berlin: De Gruyter, 2011.
Broodbank 2013
Broodbank, Cyprian. *The Making of the Middle Sea: A History of the Mediterranean from the Beginning to the Emergence of the Classical World*. Oxford: Oxford University Press, 2013.
Burgwinkle 1997
Burgwinkle, William E. *Love for Sale: Materialist Readings of the Troubadour Razo Corpus*. New York: Garland, 1997.
Burgwinkle 2011
Burgwinkle, William E. "The Troubadours: The Occitan Model." In *The Cambridge History of French Literature*, edited by William E. Burgwinkle, Nicholas Hammond, and Emma Wilson, pp. 20–27. Cambridge: Cambridge University Press, 2011.
Burningham 2007
Burningham, Bruce. *Radical Theatricality: Jongleuresque Performance on the Early Spanish Stage*. West Lafayette, IN: Purdue University Press, 2007.
Burningham 2017
Burningham, Bruce R. "Communities of Production." In *A Cultural History of the Theatre in the Middle Ages*, edited by Jodie Enders, pp. 145–162. London: Bloomsbury Academic, 2017.
Casadei 2018
Casadei, Alberto. "Canto XLVI." In *Lettura dell'Orlando furioso*, Vol. 2, edited by Guido Baldassare, Marco Praloran, Gabriele Buchi, and Franco Tomasi, pp. 567–587. Florence: Edizioni del Galluzzo per la Fondazione Ezio Franceschini, 2018.
Casari 2018
Casari, Mario. "'This Language Is More Valuable Than Any Other': Values of Arabic in Early Modern Italy." In *City, Court, Academy: Language Choice in Early Modern Italy*, edited by Eva Del Soldato and Andrea Rizzi, pp. 173–198. London: Routledge, 2018.
Catalano 1930
Catalano, Michele. *Vita di Ludovico Arisoto, ricostruita su nuovi documenti*. 2 vols. Florence: Leo S. Olschki, 1930.
Cavallini 1989
Cavallini, Ivano. "Sugli improvvisatori del Cinque-Seicento: Persistenze, nuovi repertori e qualche riconoscimento." *Recercare* 1 (1989): pp. 23–40.

Cavallo 2013
Cavallo, Jo Ann. *The World beyond Europe in the Romance Epics of Boiardo and Ariosto*. Toronto: University of Toronto Press, 2013.
Clubb 2005
Clubb, Louise George. "Staging Ferrara: State Theater from Borso to Alfonso II." In *Phaethon's Children: The Este Court and Its Culture in Early Modern Ferrara*, edited by Dennis Looney and Deanna Shemek, pp. 345–362. Tempe: Arizona Center for Medieval and Renaissance Studies, 2005.
Cobb 2014
Cobb, Paul M. *The Race for Paradise: An Islamic History of the Crusades*. Oxford: Oxford University Press, 2014.
Coluccia 2001
Coluccia, Giuseppe. *L'esperienza teatrale di Ludovico Ariosto*. Lecce: Manni, 2001.
Cuticchio 2017
Cuticchio, Mimmo. *Alle armi, cavalieri! Le storie dei paladini di Francia raccontate da Mimmo Cuticchio*. Rome: Donzelli, 2017.
Dainotto 2006
Dainotto, Roberto M. "Of the Arab Origin of Modern Europe: Giammaria Barbieri, Juan Andrés, and the Origin of Rhyme." *Comparative Literature* 58, no. 4 (2006): pp. 271–292.
Dall'Aglio, Richardson, and Rospocher 2016
Dall'Aglio, Stefano, Brian Richardson, and Massimo Rospocher, eds. *Voices and Texts in Early Modern Italian Society*. New York: Routledge, 2016.
D'Amore 2002
Andrea D'Amore, "Ariosto's Rewriting of Boccaccio and the Novella Tradition in the Orlando Furioso." PhD diss., Harvard University, 2002.
Degl'Innocenti 2016
Degl'Innocenti, Luca. "Paladini e canterini: Appunti sull'oralità nella tradizione cavallaresca italiana del quattro e cinquecento." In *Carlo Magno in Italia e la fortuna dei libri di cavalleria*, edited by Johannes Bartuschat and Franca Strologo, pp. 301–323. Ravenna: Longo Editore, 2016.
Di Gesù 2020
Di Gesù, Matteo. *L'*Orlando furioso*, l'Italia (e i Turchi): Note su identità, alterità, conflitti*. Macerata: Quodlibet, 2020.
Di Luca and Grimaldi 2017
Di Luca, Paola, and Marco Grimaldi, eds. *L'Italia dei trovatori*. Rome: Viella, 2017.
Di Palma 1991
Di Palma, Guido. *La fascinazione della parola: dalla narrazione orale al teatro, i cuntastorie*. Rome: Bulzoni, 1991.
Di Palma 2006
Di Palma, Guido. "Trasformazione dei cartelloni dell'opera dei pupi di area palermitana." In *Tra le tele dell'Opra*, edited by Roberto Giambrone, pp. 51–60. Palermo: Associazione Figli d'Arte Cuticchio, 2006.
Dorigatti 2011
Dorigatti, Marco. "Il manoscritto dell'Orlando furioso (1505–1515)." In *L'uno e l'altro Ariosto: In corte e nelle delizie*, edited by Gianni Venturi, pp. 1–44. Florence: L. S. Olschki, 2011.
Dorigatti 2013
Dorigatti, Marco. "Borges, Ariosto e la vita segreta dei personaggi minori." In *Lettori e interpreti del* Furioso*: Atti della giornata di studio (Milano, 3 ottobre 2012)*, *Carte romanze* 1, no. 2 (2013): pp. 377–406.
Duggan 1984
Duggan, Joseph J. "Oral Performance, Writing, and the Textual Tradition of the Medieval Epic in the Romance Languages: The Example of the *Song of Roland*." *Parergon* 2, no. 1 (1984): pp. 79–95.
Duggan 2002
Duggan, Joseph J. "Modalità della cultura orale." In *Lo spazio letterario del Medioevo: Il Medioevo volgare*, Vol. 1, Part 1, edited by Piero Boitani, Mario Mancini, and Alberto Varvaro, pp. 147–177. Rome: Salerno, 2002.
Everson 2001
Everson, Jane. *The Italian Epic in the Age of Humanism: The Matter of Italy and the World of Rome*. Oxford:

Oxford University Press, 2001.

Fahd 2012a

Fahd, T. "Rukya." In *Encyclopaedia of Islam*, 2nd ed., edited by Peri J. Bearman et al. Leiden: Brill, 2012.https://referenceworks.brillonline.com/search?s.f.s2_parent=s.f.book.encyclopaedia-of-islam-2&search-go=&s.q=Ru%E1%B8%B3ya.

Fahd 2012b

Fahd, T. "Siḥr." In *Encyclopaedia of Islam*, 2nd ed., edited by Peri J. Bearman et al. Leiden: Brill, 2012.https://referenceworks.brillonline.com/search?s.f.s2_parent=s.f.book.encyclopaedia-of-islam-2&search-go=&s.q=sihr.

Ferroni 2008

Ferroni, Giulio. *Ariosto*. Rome: Salerno Editrice, 2008.

Gelder and Hammond 2008

Gelder, G. J. H. van, and Marlé Hammond. *Takhyīl: The Imaginary in Classical Arabic Poetics*. Cambridge: Gibb Memorial Trust, 2008.

Giambrone 2006

Giambrone, Roberto, ed. *Tra le tele dell'*Opra. Palermo: Associazione Figli d'Arte Cuticchio, 2006.

Giammei 2018

Giammei, Alessandro. "L'immaginario cavalleresco." In *Il contributo italiano alla storia del pensiero: Letteratura*, edited by Giulio Ferroni, pp. 78–83. Rome: Istituto della Enciclopedia Italiana, 2018.

Grévin 2010

Grévin, Benoît. "Connaissance et enseignement de l'arabe dans l'Italie du XVe siècle, quelques jalons." In *Maghreb-Italie: des passeurs médiévaux à l'orientalisme moderne, XIIIe–milieu XXe siècle*, edited by Benoît Grévin, pp. 103–138. Rome: École française de Rome, 2010.

Grévin 2012

Grévin, Benoît. *Le parchemin des cieux: Essai sur le Moyen Âge du langage*. Paris: Seuil, 2012.

Gross 2011

Gross, Kenneth. *Puppet: An Essay on Uncanny Life*. Chicago: University of Chicago Press, 2011.

Harris 2014

Harris, Jonathan. *Byzantium and the Crusades*. London: Bloomsbury Academic, 2014.

Harris and Reichl 2011

Harris, Joseph, and Karl Reichl. "Performance and Performers." In *Medieval Oral Literature*, edited by Karl Reichl, pp. 142–202. Berlin: De Gruyter, 2011.

Ibn Shuhaid 1969

Ibn Shuhaid al-Andalusī . The Dīwān of Ibn Shuhaid al-Andalusī. Edited by James Dickie. Cairo: Dār al-Kātib al-ʿArabī, 1969.

Ibn Shuhayd 2013

Ibn Shuhayd. *L'épître des ombres et des trombes*. Translated by Philippe Vigreux. Arles: Actes Sud, 2013.

Idel 1978

Idel, Moshe. "The Sources of the Circle Images in *Dialoghi d'Amore*." *Jerusalem Philosophical Quarterly* 28 (1978): pp. 156–166.

Isabella d'Este 2017

Isabella d'Este. *Selected Letters*. Edited and translated by Deanna Shemek. Toronto: Iter, 2017.

Jones 2014

Jones, Catherine M. *An Introduction to the "Chansons de Geste."* Gainesville: University Press of Florida, 2014.

Jones 1909

Jones, Henry Festing. *Diversions in Sicily*. London: A. Rivers, 1909.

Jossa 2016

Jossa, Stefano. "'A difesa di sua santa fede': Il poema cristiano dell'Ariosto (*Orlando furioso* XXXIV 54–67)." In *Chivalry, Academy, and Cultural Dialogues: The Italian Contribution to European Culture, Essays in Honour of Jane E. Everson*, edited by Stefano Jossa and Giuliana Pieri, pp. 32–42. Cambridge: Legenda, 2016.

Kay 1995

Kay, Sarah. *The* Chansons de geste *in the Age of Romance*. Oxford: Oxford University Press, 1995.

Kisacky 2000
Kisacky, Julia. *Magic in Boiardo and Ariosto*. New York: Peter Lang, 2000.
Lambert 2012
Lambert, J. "Ṭarab." In *Encyclopaedia of Islam*, 2nd ed., edited by Peri J. Bearman et al. Leiden: Brill, 2012. https://referenceworks.brillonline.com/entries/encyclopaedia-of-islam-2/tarab-COM_1175?s.num=0&s.f.s2_parent=s.f.book.encyclopaedia-of-islam-2&s.q=tarab.
Lemay 1966
Lemay, Richard. "À propos de l'origine de l'art des troubadours." *Annales: Économies, Sociétés, Civilisations* 21, no. 5 (1966): pp. 990–1011.
Leverage 2010
Leverage, Paula. *Reception and Memory: A Cognitive Approach to the Chansons de Geste*. Amsterdam: Rodopoi, 2010.
Maalouf 1984
Maalouf, Amin. *The Crusades through Arab Eyes*. Translated by Jon Rothschild. New York: Schocken, 1984.
MacPhail 2001
MacPhail, Eric. "Ariosto and the Prophetic Moment." *Modern Language Notes* 116, no. 1 (2001): pp. 30–53.
Marks 2016
Marks, Laura U. "Gifts, Plunder, and a Secret: Wael Shawky's Cabaret Crusades." In *Wael Shawky* [English ed.], edited by Carolyn Christov-Bakargiev and Marcella Beccaria, pp. 62–73. Milan: Skira Editore, 2016.
Martinez 2014
Martinez, Ronald. "Spectacle." In *The Cambridge Companion to the Italian Renaissance*, edited by Michael Wyatt, pp. 239–259. Cambridge: Cambridge University Press, 2014.
McCormick, Cipolla, and Napoli 2010
McCormick, John, Alfonso Cipolla, and Alessandro Napoli. *The Italian Puppet Theater: A History*. Jefferson, NC: McFarland, 2010.
Menocal 1987
Menocal, María Rosa. *The Arabic Role in Medieval Literary History: A Forgotten Heritage*. Philadelphia: University of Pennsylvania Press, 1987.
Menocal 1994
Menocal, María Rosa. *Shards of Love: Exile and the Origins of the Lyric*. Durham, NC: Duke University Press, 1994.
Minchin 2014
Minchin, Elizabeth. "Poet, Audience, Time, and Text: Reflections on Medium and Mode in Homer and Virgil." In *Between Orality and Literacy: Communication and Adaptation in Antiquity*, edited by Ruth Scodel, pp. 267–288. Leiden: Brill, 2014
Morabito 2011
Morabito, Raffaele. "The Italian *Cantari* between Orality and Writing." In *Medieval Oral Literature*, edited by Karl Reichl, pp. 371–386. Berlin: De Gruyter, 2011.
Morlino 2015
Morlino, Luca. "Spunti per un riesame della costellazione letteraria franco-italiana." *Francigena*, no. 1 (2015): pp. 5–81.
Nykl 1946
Nykl, A. R. *Hispano-Arabic Poetry and Its Relations with the Old Provençal Troubadours*. Baltimore: J. H. Furst, 1946.
Ong 2002
Ong, W. J. *Orality and Literacy: The Technologizing of the Word*. 2nd ed. London: Routledge, 2002.
Paradis 2016
Paradis, James G. *Samuel Butler, Victorian against the Grain: A Critical Overview*. Toronto: University of Toronto Press, 2016.
Pavlova 2020
Pavlova, Maria. *Saracens and Their World in Boiardo and Ariosto*. Oxford: Legenda, 2020.

Pitrè 1884
Pitrè, Giuseppe. "Le tradizioni cavalleresche popolari in Sicilia." *Romania* 13, nos. 50–51 (1884): pp. 315–398.
Pomerantz and Vitz 2017
Pomerantz, Maurice A., and Evelyn Birge Vitz, eds. *In the Presence of Power: Court and Performance in the Pre-Modern Middle East*. New York: New York University Press, 2017.
Ponte 1964
Ponte, Giovanni. "Matteo Maria Boiardo scrittore di teatro." *Rassegna della letteratura italiana* 66 (1964): pp. 286–302.
Prosperi 2016
Prosperi, Adriano. "Canto III." In *Lettura dell'Orlando furioso*, Vol. 1, edited by Guido Baldassare, Marco Praloran, Gabriele Buchi, and Franco Tomasi, pp. 159–165. Florence: Edizioni del Galluzzo per la Fondazione Ezio Franceschini, 2016.
Psaki 2006
Psaki, Regina. "Chivalry and Medieval Italian Romance." In *The Cambridge Companion to Medieval Romance*, pp. 203–217. Cambridge: Cambridge University Press, 2006.
Rajna 1900
Rajna, Pio. *Le fonti dell'Orlando furioso*. 2nd ed. Florence: Sansoni, 1900.
Reichl 2011
Reichl, Karl, ed. *Medieval Oral Literature*. Berlin: De Gruyter, 2011.
Rinoldi 2005
Rinoldi, Paolo. "La tradizione dell'*Estoire d'Eracles* in Italia: Note su un volgarizzamento fiorentino." In *Studi su volgarizzamenti due-trecenteschi*, edited by Paolo Rinoldi and Gabriela Ronchi, pp. 65–97. Rome: Viella, 2005.
Robinson 1992
Robinson, Cynthia. "Arts of the Taifa Kingdoms." In *Al-Andalus, the Art of Islamic Spain*, edited by Jerrilyn D. Dodds, pp. 49–61. New York: Metropolitan Museum of Art, 1992.
Robinson 2002
Robinson, Cynthia. *In Praise of Song: The Making of Courtly Culture in al-Andalus and Provence, 1005–1134 A.D.* Leiden: Brill, 2002.
Roggero 2011
Roggero, Marina. "Orlando cantata." In *Atlante della letteratura italiana*, Vol. 2: *Dalla Controriforma alla Restaurazione*, edited by Erminia Irace, Sergio Luzzatto, and Gabriele Pedullà, pp. 287–292. Turin: Einaudi, 2011.
Scattina 2017
Scattina, Simona. "Nella bottega della famiglia Napoli: Codici e documenti dell'Opera dei pupi di tradizione catanese." PhD diss., Università degli Studi di Catania, 2017.
Stock 1990
Stock, Brian. *Listening for the Text: On the Uses of the Past*. Philadelphia: University of Pennsylvania Press, 1990.
Stoppino 2012
Stoppino, Eleanora. *Genealogies of Fiction: Women Warriors and the Dynastic Imagination in the* Orlando furioso. New York: Fordham University Press, 2012.
Stoppino 2018
Stoppino, Eleanora. "Ariosto's Genealogies." *Modern Language Notes* 133, no. 1 (2018): pp. 32–47.
Subrahmanyam 1997
Subrahmanyam, Sanjay. "Connected Histories: Notes towards a Reconfiguration of Early Modern Eurasia." *Modern Asian Studies* 31, no. 3 (1997): pp. 735–762.
Subrahmanyam 2012
Subrahmanyam, Sanjay. *Courtly Encounters: Translating Courtliness and Violence in Early Modern Eurasia*. Cambridge, MA: Harvard University Press, 2012.
Talbot 1993
Talbot, Alice-Mary. "The Restoration of Constantinople under Michael VIII." *Dumbarton Oaks Papers* 47 (1993): pp. 243–261.

Tomasin 2021
Tomasin, Lorenzo. *Europa romanza: Sette storie linguistiche*. Turin: Einaudi, 2021.
Venturini 2017
Venturini, Valentina. *Nato e cresciuto tra i pupi*. Naples: Editoriale Scientifica, 2017.
Villoresi 1994
Villoresi, Marco. *Da Guarino a Boiardo: La cultura teatrale a Ferrara nel Quattrocento* Rome: Bulzoni, 1994.
Villoresi 2005
Villoresi, Marco. *La fabbrica dei cavalieri: Cantari, poemi, romanzi in prosa fra Medioevo e Rinascimento*. Rome: Salerno, 2005.
Villoresi 2016a
Villoresi, Marco. *La voce e le parole: Studi sulla letteratura del Medioevo e del Rinascimento*. Florence: Società Editrice Fiorentina, 2016.
Villoresi 2016b
Villoresi, Marco. "Voci e scritture per le storie di Spagna." In *Carlo Magno in Italia e la fortuna dei libri di cavalleria*, edited by Johannes Bartuschat and Franca Strologo, pp. 125–142. Ravenna: Longo Editore, 2016.
Vitullo 2000
Vitullo, Juliann. *The Chivalric Epic in Medieval Italy*. Gainesville: University Press of Florida, 2000.
Vitz 1999
Vitz, Evelyn Birge. *Orality and Performance in Early French Romance*. Woodbridge, UK: Brewer, 1999.
Vitz 2017
Vitz, Evelyn Birge. "Performance and Competition of Kingship and Court in *Le Voyage de Charlemagne à Jerusalem et à Constantinople*." In *In the Presence of Power: Court and Performance in the Pre-Modern Middle East*, edited by Maurice A. Pomerantz and Evelyn Birge Vitz, pp. 17–29. New York: New York University Press, 2017.
Vitz 2018
Vitz, Evelyn Birge. "*Le Romain de la Rose* Performed in Court." In *Shaping Courtliness in Medieval France: Essays in Honor of Matilda Tomaryn Bruckner*, edited by Laurie Shepard and Daniel E. O'Sullivan, pp. 151–161. Cambridge: D. S. Brewer, 2013.
Zink 2011
Zink, Michel. "Raimbaut de Vaquieras: La poésie comme langue de l'autre." In *Écrire dans la langue de l'autre*, edited by Anna Maria Babbi, pp. 37–48. Verona: Fiorini, 2011.
Zumthor 1983
Zumthor, Paul. *Introduction à la poésie orale*. Paris: Seuil, 1983.
Zumthor 2002
Zumthor, Paul. "Una cultura della voce." In *Lo spazio letterario del Medioevo: Il Medioevo volgare*, Vol. 1, Part 1, edited by Piero Boitani, Mario Mancini, and Alberto Varvaro, pp. 117–146. Rome: Salerno, 2002.
Zwartjes 1997
Zwartjes, Otto. 1997. *Love Songs from al-Andalus: History, Structure and Meaning of the "Kharja."* Leiden: Brill, 1997.

CONTRIBUTORS

Vincent Barletta is Associate Professor of Comparative Literature and Iberian and Latin American Cultures at Stanford University. He is the author of *Covert Gestures: Crypto-Islamic Literature as Cultural Practice in Early Modern Spain* (2005); *Death in Babylon: Alexander the Great and Iberian Empire in the Muslim Orient* (2010); and *Rhythm: Form and Dispossession* (2020).

Thomas Bauer is Professor of Arabic and Islamic Studies at the University of Münster. His principal research areas are Arabic literature, rhetoric, and cultural history, in their early expressions in *Altarabische Dichtkunst* (1992) and in the Abbasid through the Ottoman periods in *Liebe und Liebesdichtung in der arabischen Welt des 9. und 10. Jahrhunderts* (1998). Recent studies have focused on Arabic literature of the Mamluk period, especially the work of Ibn Nubāta al-Miṣrī and the popular poet al-Miʿmār. In the field of cultural anthropology of the pre-modern Arabic world, Bauer has dealt with love and sexuality, death, *Fremdheit* (strangeness), and tolerance of ambiguity in *Die Kultur der Ambiguität* (2011)—in English, *A Culture of Ambiguity* (2021). Bauer was appointed member of the North Rhine-Westphalian Academy of Sciences, Humanities and the Arts in 2012, and he was awarded the distinguished Gottfried Wilhelm Leibniz Prize in 2013.

Mario Casari is Associate Professor in Persian Language and Literature at the Italian Institute of Oriental Studies, "Sapienza" University of Rome. His expertise in Arabic and Persian underpins research in the circulation of texts and cultural contacts in the Mediterranean and Middle East from late antiquity to the early modern age. In 2011, he was awarded the Al-Farabi-UNESCO prize for his book *Alessandro e Utopia nei romanzi persiani medievali*, and in 2018, he was awarded the Premio per la Cultura Mediterranea–Fondazione Carical for his translation work from Arabic and Persian. He has coauthored the most recent Italian translation from Arabic of the *One Thousand and One Nights* (Donzelli 2016, Feltrinelli 2019), with R. Denaro. As a fellow at I Tatti–The Harvard University Center for Italian Renaissance Studies (2008–2009), he engaged in research on Arabic and Persian studies in late Renaissance Italy.

Anna Contadini is Professor of the History of Islamic Art, SOAS, University of London. Her areas of interest are Arabic and Persian illustrated manuscripts, material culture of the Islamic world, and artistic and cultural connections between the Middle East and Europe, especially Italy. She graduated in Arabic and Islamic Art at the Oriental Institute of Ca' Foscari, University of Venice, and obtained her PhD in the History of Islamic Art at SOAS; she also holds a diploma in piano from the Conservatory "Benedetto Marcello" in Venice. Prior to her position at SOAS, she was a curator at the V&A, lecturer in Islamic Art at Trinity College Dublin, and curator of the Middle Eastern collection at the Chester Beatty Library in Dublin. The recipient of many prizes and honors, Contadini serves on a number of international peer-review bodies as well as on numerous editorial, scientific, and advisory boards. Her publications span studies of illustrated manuscripts and questions of materiality, translocation, and transculturation of objects within a broader social-historical and artistic context, and they include *The Pisa Griffin and the Mari-Cha Lion: Metalwork, Art, and Technology in the Medieval Islamicate Mediterranean* (2018). For a full list of her publications, see soas.ac.uk/staff/staff30791.php.

Vincenzo Farinella is Professor of the History of Art in the Department of Civilizations and Forms of Knowledge, University of Pisa. He studied Archaeology and History of Art at the University of Pisa and the Scuola Normale Superiore. His research interests include Italian art between the fifteenth and sixteenth centuries and its relationship with both classical and European art of the late nineteenth century and the early decades of the twentieth. In recent years, he has curated a number of exhibitions, including *I volti dell'Ariosto: L'*Orlando furioso *e le arti* at Villa d'Este, Tivoli (2016), with M. Cogotti and M. Preti; and *Ardengo Soffici e le avanguardie a Firenze* at the Uffizi Gallery (2016–2017), with N. Marchioni. Among his other publications are *Alfonso I d'Este, le immagini e il potere: Da Ercole de' Roberti a Michelangelo* (2014); "Avventure e metamorfosi di un genio: Raffaello da Urbino a Roma" (2016); *The Domus Aurea Book* (2019); and the introduction to *Raffaello* (Treccani, 2020). He collaborated on the Raphael exhibition in 2020 at the Scuderie del Quirinale and contributed an essay to the catalogue on Raphael's relationship with the ancient. In 2021, he is curating an exhibition on Raphael and the history of grotesques.

Jacopo Gesiot holds a PhD in Italian Studies from the University of Udine. His research focuses on Renaissance translations from Catalan and Spanish and their literary impact on Italian literature. His work encompasses a focus on subsequent allusions to medieval texts in sixteenth-century authors from diverse Romance language traditions; the archaic background of Renaissance literature, such as pilgrims' accounts in the *Orlando furioso*; and the editing of Hispanic texts of the thirteenth and fourteenth centuries, among which is a current project dedicated to the Catalan translation of Jacobus De Voragine's *Legenda aurea*. His first book, *Romanzi tiranni: La prosa iberica di cavalleria nel primo Cinquecento padano*, was published in 2018. Among his published essays are "Notizia di un plagio romanzo: Joanot Martorell nel *Duello regolato* di Fausto da Longiano" in *Rinascimento* (2019); "Dai resoconti di pellegrinaggio basso-medievali all'*Orlando furioso*: Una nota sulle fonti" in *Italianistica* (2019); and "Ripensare la lingua del *Flos sanctorum* catalano: Un esempio di scripta libraria primitiva nel ms. 713 dell'Universitat de Barcelona" in *Zeitschrift für romanische Philologie* (2020).

Adam J. Goldwyn is Associate Professor of English at North Dakota State University. He is the author of *Byzantine Ecocriticism: Women, Nature, and Power in the Medieval Greek Romance* (2018); co-translator, of the twelfth-century Byzantine grammarian John Tzetzes's *Allegories of the Iliad* (2015) and *Allegories of the Odyssey* (2019), with D. Kokkini; and coeditor of *Reading the Medieval Greek Romance: A Handbook* (2019), with I. Nilsson.

Stefano Jossa is Reader in Italian at Royal Holloway College, University of London. He has published extensively on the literary culture of the Italian Renaissance, in *Rappresentazione e scrittura: La crisi delle forme poetiche rinascimentali* (1996); *La fondazione di un genere: Il poema eroico tra Ariosto e Tasso* (2002); and *Ariosto* (2009); and on the construction of the Italian nation as expressed through literature in *L'Italia Letteraria* (2006); *Un paese senza eroi: L'Italia da Jacopo Ortis a Montalbano* (2012); and *La più bella del mondo: Perché amare la lingua italiana* (2018). He has coauthored and coedited *Citation, Intertextuality and Memory in the Middle Ages and Renaissance*, with Y. Plumley and G. Di Bacco (2012); *Comedy, Satire, Paradox, and the Plurality of Discourses in Sixteenth-Century Italy*, with A. Moroncini (special issue of *Renaissance and Reformation*, 2017); *Ariosto, the* Orlando Furioso, *and English Culture*, with J. E. Everson and A. Hiscock (2019); and *Italian Heroines: Literature, Gender and the Construction of the Italian Nation*, with S. Alessi (special issue of *The Italianist*, 2020). He has held visiting positions at the ETH, Zurich, the University of Parma, and the Università degli Studi di Roma Tre.

Fabrizio Lelli is Associate Professor of Hebrew language and literature at the Università del Salento. He has had fellowships and visiting appointments at the Università di Torino, Università Ca' Foscari in Venice, the Hebrew University in Jerusalem, the Istituto Superiore di Scienze Religiose in Florence, the Herbert Katz Center for Advanced Judaic Studies at the University of Pennsylvania, and the University of California, Los Angeles. He has published extensively in the various fields of his research activity, focusing mainly on the philosophical and mystical literature of late medieval and early modern Italian Jewish authors, among which are the critical edition, translation, and commentary of Johanan ben Isaac Allemanno, *Ḥay ha-'olamim: L'immortale, Parte I* (1995); the critical edition and translation of Eliyyah Ḥayim ben Binyamin, *La lettera preziosa* (2002); the edited volumes *Giovanni Pico e la cabbalà* (2008); *Gli Ebrei nel Salento: Secoli IX–XVI* (2013); and *Umanesimo e cultura ebraica nel Rinascimento italiano* (2016), with S. Baldassari. In the past few years, he has been working on a project aimed at preserving the memory of Jewish refugees hosted in the United Nations transit camps operated in Southern Italy after World War II.

Przemysław T. Marciniak is Professor of Byzantine Literature at the University of Silesia, Poland. He has held fellowships at Dumbarton Oaks, Princeton, Berlin, Paris, and Uppsala. Among his interests are Byzantine performativity, humor, and satire. He has edited *The Reception of Byzantium in European Culture since 1500* (2016), with C. Smythe; and *Satire in the Middle Byzantine Period: The Golden Age of Laughter?* (2020), with I. Nilsson. His essays include "Reinventing Lucian in Byzantium" in *Dumbarton Oaks Papers* (2016); "Oriental Like Byzantium: Some Remarks on Similarities between Byzantinism and Orientalism" in *Imagining Byzantium: Perceptions, Patterns, Problems* (2018); and "Theodore Prodromos' *Katomyomachia* as a Byzantine Version of Mock-Heroic Epic," with K. Warcaba, in *Middle and Late Byzantine Poetry: Texts and Contexts* (2018). He is currently working on the Byzantine perception of animals.

Claudia Ott is Research Associate, Institute for Arabic and Islamic Studies, University of Göttingen. She studied Arabic, Oriental Languages, and Islamic Studies at the universities of Jerusalem, Tübingen, and Berlin, where she completed her PhD with a dissertation on the Arabian epic, *Metamorphosen des Epos* (2003). She is well known as the German translator of the *Arabian Nights, Tausendundeine Nacht* (2004); *Das Glückliche Ende* (2016); and *Hundertundeine Nacht* (2012). In addition to this extended project, she has also published an anthology of Arabic poetry, *Gold auf Lapislazuli* (2008); and a collection of short pieces of Arabic literature intended for language study, transliterated into Latin characters and translated into German, *Erste arabische Lesestücke* (2017). She is a member of several groups that perform Middle Eastern music, founder of the IBTAHIDSCH ensemble, and cofounder and chair of the jury of the Coburg Rückert Prize. See tausendundeine-nacht.com for her publications.

Maria Pavlova is Leverhulme Early Career Fellow at the University of Warwick. She obtained a PhD in Modern Languages from the University of Oxford, where she then became a Randall MacIver Junior Research Fellow at St Hugh's College. Her first monograph, *Saracens and Their World in Boiardo and Ariosto* (2020), explores the figure of the religious and cultural "Other" in fifteenth- and sixteenth-century Italian chivalric texts, focusing in particular on Boiardo's *Inamoramento de Orlando* and Ariosto's *Orlando furioso*. Among her other publications are *"Dreaming Again on Things Already Dreamed": 500 Years of Orlando Furioso (1516–2016)* (2019), with M. Dorigatti; as well as articles and book chapters on different aspects of Italian narrative poetry, from anonymous fifteenth-century *cantari* to Torquato Tasso's *Gerusalemme liberata*.

Monica Preti, Head of Academic Programs in the History of Art and Archaeology at the Auditorium du musée du Louvre, is also Director of the museum system "Pistoia Musei". Her research explores the relationship between art and literature in the sixteenth and seventeenth centuries, the history of taste, as well as the history of collecting and museums from the eighteenth through the twentieth century. Among her books edited or authored: *Imaginaire de l'Arioste, l'Arioste imaginé* (Gourcuff Gradenigo, 2009), with Michel Jeanneret; *L'Arioste et les arts* (2012), with M. Paoli, Officina Libraria; *I voli dell'Ariosto, L'Orlando furioso e le arti* (exh. cat., with M. Cogotti and V. Farinella, Villa d'Este, Tivoli, 2016); and, more recently, *Da Gerusalemme a Pechino da Roma a Vienna: Sul "Saggio di architettura storica" di J. B. Fischer von Erlach* (2019), with M. Folin, Panini.

Dwight F. Reynolds is professor of Arabic Language and Literature at the University of California, Santa Barbara. His interests encompass Arabic oral epic, folklore, and medieval and modern literary and musical traditions. He is author of *Heroic Poets, Poetic Heroes: The Ethnography of Performance in an Arabic Oral Epic Tradition* (1995); *Arab Folklore: A Handbook* (2007); *The Musical Heritage of al-Andalus* (2021); and *Medieval Arab Music and Musicians* (forthcoming). He is also editor and coauthor of *Interpreting the Self: Autobiography in the Arabic Literary Tradition* (2001), with K. Brustad; and *The Cambridge Companion to Modern Arab Culture* (2005); section editor for popular prose of *The Cambridge History of Arabic Literature: The Post-Classical Period*; coeditor of *The Garland Encyclopedia of World Music*, Vol. 6, *The Middle East* (2002), with V. Danielson and S. Marcus; and coeditor of *Bestsellers and Masterpieces: The Changing Medieval Canon* (forthcoming), with H. Blurton.

Giovanni Ricci is Professor Emeritus of Early Modern History, University of Ferrara. His interests are in the social and cultural history of the Renaissance and relations between Christian Europe and the Muslim world. Among his books are *Ossessione turca: In una retrovia cristiana dell'Europa moderna* (2002); *I Turchi alle porte* (2008); and *Appeal to the Turk: The Broken Boundaries of the Renaissance* (2018; also in Italian and Turkish).

Massimo Rossi is Curator of the Map Collection and Research Coordinator for Geographical Studies, Benetton Studies Research Foundation, Treviso. His PhD is in Historical Geography from the University of Genoa. He is a member of the scientific board of the Bertoliana Library, Vicenza. He coordinates the section "History of Cartography" for the Italian Center for Historical-Geographical Studies and is a member of the scientific board of its journal, *Geostorie*. He has taught geography as an adjunct professor at the universities of Padua, Ferrara, and IUAV in Venice and is a member of the cultural center Deputazione di Storia Patria per le Venezie, dedicated to the study of the history of the Venetian Republic. He is part of the Istituto Centrale per il Catalogo Unico working group for the development of the national cartographic catalogue. Among his publications are "La geografia del *Furioso*: Sul sapere geo-cartografico alla corte estense" in *Lucrezia Borgia: Storia e mito* (2006); "Riflessioni sulla riscoperta di Tolomeo e su alcune "anomalie" del canone nella cultura geografica padana tra XV e XVI secolo" in *Schifanoia* (2016); and *La geografia serve a fare la guerra?* (catalogue of the Benetton Foundation exhibition, 2016).

Michael Wyatt is Resident Scholar in the Department of French and Italian at Dartmouth College and Lecturer in Comparative Literature. His work is engaged with the premodern cultural and intellectual history of Italy, focused within a European and Mediterranean matrix, and dealing particularly with translation as both textual and socio-political practice. Among his publications are *The Italian Encounter with Tudor England, A Cultural Politics of Translation* (2005); *Writing Relations: American Scholars in Italian Archives, Essays for Franca Nardelli Petrucci and Armando Petrucci* (2008), with Deanna Shemek; and *The Cambridge Companion to the Italian Renaiossance* (2014).

PHOTO CREDITS

Alamy Stock Photo: p. 389 fig. 1

Amsterdam, Courtesy of the Rijksmuseum Museum: p. 282 fig. 11c

Berlin, Gemäldegalerie: p. 297 fig. 22

Bologna, Biblioteca Universitaria: p. 288 fig. 16; Museo Civico Medievale, with permission of Istituzione Bologna Musei. I Musei Civici d'Arte Antica (Photo: Guido Piacentini): p. 295 fig. 21

Brescia, Musei Civici di Arte e Storia: p. 325 fig. 3

Chicago, Courtesy of The Art Institute: p. 269 fig. 3

Hartford, Conn., Wadsworth Atheneum: p. 325 fig. 2

Istanbul, Topkapı Palace Museum Library: p. 267 fig. 1

Ithaca, Courtesy of Cornell University: p. 276 fig. 6

Jerusalem, The Israel Museum, The Rothschild Miscellany: p. 170 fig. 1

London, British Museum: p. 323 fig. 1, p. 342 fig. 2, p. 343 fig. 3; Victoria & Albert Museum: p. 367 fig. 13

Madrid, Thyssen-Bornemisza National Museum: p. 172 fig. 2

Milan, Biblioteca Nazionale Braidense: p. 357 fig. 8

Modena, © Archivio di Stato di Modena: p. 76 fig. 1, p. 77 fig. 2; Biblioteca Estense, with permission of *Ministero per i Beni e le Attività Culturali e per il Turismo - Gallerie Estensi, Biblioteca Estense Universitaria* (Photos: Norihito Hayashi): p. 235 fig. 1, p. 236 fig. 2, p. 246 fig. 6, p. 274 fig. 5, p. 279 fig. 8, p. 280 fig. 9, p. 281 fig. 10, p. 282 fig. 11a, p. 284 fig. 12, p. 285 fig. 13, p. 286 fig. 14, p. 287 fig. 15, p. 290 fig. 17, p. 291 fig. 18, p. 294 fig. 19, p. 295 fig. 20

München, Courtesy of Bayerische Staatsbibliothek: p. 271 fig. 4

New York, The Metropolitan Museum of Art: p. 351 fig. 5

Oxford, University of Oxford, Bodleian Library: p. 174 fig. 3

Ott, Claudia: p. 155 fig. 1

Palermo, Courtesy of the Associazione Figli d'Arte Cuticchio: p. 437 fig.1, p. 439 fig. 2, p. 440 fig. 3

Paris, Bibliothèque nationale de France: p. 240 fig. 3, p. 242 fig. 4, p. 245 fig. 5, p. 344 fig. 3, p. 363 fig. 12; © Musée du Louvre, Département des Arts graphiques (Photo M. Jeanneteau): p. 344 fig. 3

Reggio Emilia, Biblioteca Comunale "A. Panizzi": p. 353 fig. 6, p. 358 fig. 9

Reynolds, Dwight F.: p. 393 fig. 2

Rossi, Massimo: p. 250 fig. 7, p.251 fig. 8

Sassuolo, Ducal palace: p. 331 fig. 4

Toronto, Courtesy of the Aga Khan Museum: p. 165 fig. 2

Vatican City, Musei Vaticani: p. 346 fig. 4a-b

Venice, Copyright of the Marciana Library: p. 278 fig. 7

Washington, DC, Courtesy of National Gallery of Art: p. 268 fig. 2

We have made every effort to obtain permissions for all copyright-protected images. If you feel any material has been included in this publication improperly, please contact the publisher.

INDEX OF NAMES

The names of literary and mythological figures are given in italics.

I Tatti Research Series

The I Tatti Research Series is dedicated to ongoing projects at the Harvard University Center for Italian Renaissance Studies. Its volumes expand on themes explored during conferences and seminars and cover a wide spectrum of disciplines including art history, architecture, history, philosophy, literature, music, and the history of science.

The series examines all aspects of the Italian Renaissance — broadly understood to include the period from the fourteenth to the seventeenth centuries. At the same time, it investigates dialogues between Renaissance Italy and other regions around the world, in addition to the period's roots in classical antiquity and its enduring impact on modernity.

PUBLISHED AND FORTHCOMING VOLUMES

Vol. 1 ***The Renaissance in the 19th Century: Revision, Revival, and Return,*** **edited by Lina Bolzoni and Alina Payne**

Vol. 2 ***Seachanges: Music in the Mediterranean and Atlantic Worlds, 1550–1800,*** **edited by Kate van Orden**

Vol. 3 ***Sacrifice and Conversion in the Early Modern Atlantic World,*** **edited by Maria Berbara**

Vol. 4 ***Ariosto and the Arabs: Contexts for the Orlando Furioso,*** **edited by Mario Casari, Monica Preti, and Michael Wyatt**

Vol. 5 *The Mongol Empire in Global History and Art History,* edited by Anne Dunlop

Printed in the month of April 2022 on the presses of Esperia, Lavis (Trento).

FSC
www.fsc.org
MISTO
Carta | A sostegno della gestione forestale responsabile
FSC® C021437

Ex Officina Libraria Jellinek et Gallerani